DICTIONARY OF

Dogmatic Theology

DICTIONARY OF
Dogmatic Theology

PIETRO PARENTE
ANTONIO PIOLANTI · SALVATORE GAROFALO

TRANSLATED FROM THE SECOND ITALIAN EDITION BY

EMMANUEL DORONZO, O.M.I., S.T.D., PH.D.
ASSOCIATE PROFESSOR OF THEOLOGY
THE CATHOLIC UNIVERSITY OF AMERICA

FIRST ENGLISH EDITION

THE BRUCE PUBLISHING COMPANY
MILWAUKEE

Imprimi potest: Stanislaus A. Larochelle, O.M.I., Superior Provincialis
Nihil obstat: John A. Schulien, S.T.D., Censor librorum
Imprimatur: ✠ Moyses E. Kiley, Archiepiscopus Milwaukiensis
May 1, 1951

Made in the United States of America

PREFACE TO THE FIRST ITALIAN EDITION

It is not in order to follow the fashion of our hurried day with its predilection for outlines, condensations, and telegraphic style, but to fill the need of a class of Christians for whom the catechism is too little and theology too much, that we have set about compiling this brief DICTIONARY OF DOGMATIC THEOLOGY for laymen.

It should be judged according to its purpose: choice of the entries and their development, style, bibliography — all must be considered in relation to the reader, who is the cultured layman.

To achieve brevity and clarity, we have sacrificed erudition, dialectic virtuosity, technical formalism, and many other things. What we have set our hearts on doing is to enlighten the mind of the reader by presenting the substance of dogmatic doctrine in a form that is pleasing to the non-theologian and that conveys synthetically but faithfully the riches hidden in the scholastic formulas.

Both the choice of entries and their manner of treatment prove difficult in works of this kind. It has been our desire, in this first attempt, to present an all-inclusive work, but we do not presume to have successfully accomplished this end. The readers will judge and their observations and suggestions will be a guide in any future attempts.

Two able colleagues have collaborated with me, and others have been generous in their counsels: Professor Piolanti, whose name I wish to place next to my own, has treated the sacramental and ecclesiastical material.

We indulge the hope that our labor is not in vain.

PIETRO PARENTE

Rome, October 1, 1943

PREFACE TO THE SECOND ITALIAN EDITION

The flattering reception accorded to the first edition of this DICTIONARY, out of print in a few months despite the difficulties of the moment, assures us that our labor has not been in vain. Evidently the work responds, at least in substance, to the desires of many people, and so it is with pleasure that we take it in hand again with the purpose of eliminating the defects, enriching the material, and rendering it in every way possible more worthy of the readers, especially the more discerning and exacting ones.

Favorable judgments have been welcome, but even more so the critical observations, insofar as these have been more useful. Criticisms of the first edition were put to good use. We wish to avail ourselves of this opportunity to remind our readers of the criteria that have guided us in the compilation of the DICTIONARY.

1. The work is to be judged and evaluated for what it sets out to be: a clear and concise ready-reference book of dogmatic theology for cultured laymen.

2. As a consequence, the development of the entries is reduced to the necessary minimum. The scientific exactness of concept and expression is tempered in order to maintain contact with readers not accustomed to the scholastic style.

3. The choice of items is governed by the limits imposed by dogmatic theology proper; account, however, being taken of borderline material (philosophy, history, ethics and moral theology, ascetics, and law).

4. The bibliography is not and does not intend to be exhaustive. In general, works that are voluminous or too scientific or difficult of access are not cited. To cite for the sake of citing is pure ostentation, particularly in works of popularization.

In this second edition we have continued to be inspired by these criteria, but have wished to go along with the best suggestions. Speculative theology has been integrated by the addition of more than 150 entries; so-called positive theology has been amplified, considerable space being given to biblical, historical, and philosophical entries. Nor have we failed to insert the most interesting items of ascetics, mystical theology, ethics, and law that are more closely connected with dogma.

Moreover, the general and special bibliographies have been retouched and brought up to date. Finally, we have favored the request for a synthesis of all the dogmatic material: this will serve to overcome the inevitably fragmentary character of the DICTIONARY, orientating the reader in the vast field of theology.

We confidently await the public judgment on this laborious rewriting.

Beside my name I wish to place, in addition to the already known name of Prof. Piolanti, also that of Prof. Garofalo, for his long-standing extensive co-operation in biblical material.

May this humble work strike or rekindle in the minds of men that light of Christian faith, which is the best reconstructive force in this grave hour of the world.

PIETRO PARENTE

Rome, June 29, 1945

BIBLIOGRAPHY*

General

The Catholic Encyclopedia, Ch. G. Hebermann, 17 vols. (New York and London, 1907–1922).
Catholicisme Hier, Aujourd'hui, Demain, Jacquemet.
Dictionnaire Apologétique de la Foi Catholique, D'Alès.
Dictionnaire d'Archéologie chrétienne et de Liturgie, Cabrol, Leclercq.
Dictionnaire de la Bible, Vigouroux. *Supplément au Dict. de la Bible,* Pirot.
Dictionnaire d'Histoire et de Géographie Ecclésiastique, Baudrillart, Richard, Rouzies.
Dictionnaire de Spiritualité, Viller.
Dictionnaire de Théologie Catholique, Vacant, Mangenot, Amann.
Cayré, F., *Manual of Patrology and History of Theology,* trans. H. Howitt, 2 vols. (Paris, Tournai, Rome, 1936–1940).
McSorley, J., *An Outline History of the Church by Centuries* (St. Louis: Herder, 1944).
Mourret, F., *A History of the Catholic Church,* trans. N. Thompson, 6 vols. (St. Louis: Herder).
Otten, B., *A Manual of the History of Dogmas,* 2 vols. (St. Louis, 1918).
Poulet, Ch., *A History of the Catholic Church,* trans. S. A. Raemers, 2 vols. (St. Louis: Herder).
Quasten, J., *Patrology,* 4 vols. (Utrecht and Westminster, Md., 1950–).
Tixerant, J., *History of Dogmas,* trans. H. L. B., 3 vols. (St. Louis: Herder, 1910–1916).
——— *A Handbook of Patrology,* trans. S. A. Raemers (St. Louis: Herder, 1946).

Among the numerous Latin manuals of theology one may easily find and usefully consult: Tanquerey, *Synopsis theologiae dogmaticae,* 3 vols., published in numerous editions by Desclée; Hervé, *Manuale Theologiae Dogmaticae,* 4 vols. (Westminster: The Newman Bookshop, 1943); *Collectio Theologica Romana,* of Peter Parente and A. Piolanti, 6 vols., recently published by Marietti, Turin, Italy.

General works of ampler size are the 12 Latin volumes of Billot, published by the Gregorian University, Rome, Italy, and the 12 English volumes of Pohle-Preuss, *Dogmatic Theology* (St. Louis: Herder, 1945–1946).

Very useful also to the English reader will be M. J. Scheeben's work, *The Mysteries of Christianity,* trans. C. Vollert (St. Louis: Herder, 1946), and *The Teaching of the Catholic Church,* ed. G. D. Smith, 2 vols. (New York, 1949), which is a summary of the popular work *Treasury of the Faith Series,* 36 small volumes, edited by the same (London, 1928).

---

* The original bibliography, here as well as in the text, has been revised and augmented in order to make it suitable to users to whom works in English are more available. — *Trans.*

Particular

God

Arendzen, J. P., *The Holy Trinity* (New York, 1937).
Breton, V., *The Blessed Trinity,* trans. V. B. Miller (St. Louis, 1934).
Garrigou-Lagrange, R., *The One God,* trans. B. Rose (St. Louis: Herder, 1943).
——— *God: His Existence and His Nature,* trans. B. Rose (St. Louis: Herder, 1947–1948).
——— *Predestination,* trans. B. Rose (St. Louis, 1939).
——— *Providence,* trans. B. Rose (St. Louis, 1944).
Gelle, F., *Le mystère de la Sainte Trinité* (Paris, 1921).
Hall, F. J., *The Being and Attributes of God* (New York, 1909).
Heydon, J. K., *The God of Reason* (New York, 1942).
Hugon, E., *Le mystère de la très Sainte Trinité* (Paris, 1930).
Klein, F., *The Doctrine of the Trinity,* trans. D. J. Sullivan (New York, 1940).
Leen, E., *The Holy Ghost* (London, 1937).
Messenger, E. Ch., *Evolution and Theology. The Problem of Man's Origin* (New York, 1932).
Miller, B. V., *God the Creator* (New York, 1928).
Parente, Peter, "Il mistero della SS. Trinità," in *Il Simbolo,* I (Assisi, 1941).
Pohle-Preuss, *Dogmatic Theology,* I and III *God,* 2 vols.; II *The Divine Trinity* (St. Louis: Herder, 1946).
Reany, W., *The Creation of the Soul* (New York, 1932).
Stufler, J., *Why God Created the World, or the Purpose of the Creator and of Creatures,* trans. E. Sutcliffe (Stanbrook, 1937).
Woods, H., *The Creator Operating in the Creatures* (San Francisco, 1928).

Christ

Adam, K., *The Son of God,* trans. Ph. Hereford (New York, 1934).
Arendzen, J. P., *The Atonement* (Cambridge, 1928).
——— *Whom Do You Say? A Study in the Doctrine of the Incarnation* (New York, 1941).
Bougaud, E., *The Divinity of Christ* (Baltimore, 1926).
Boylan, P., *The Incarnation* (Cambridge, 1926).
D'Alès, A., *Le dogme de Nicée* (Paris, 1926).
——— *Le dogme d'Ephèse* (Paris, 1931).
De Grandmaison, L., *Jesus Christ,* 3 vols. (New York, 1930–1934).
Fahey, D., *The Kingship of Christ* (Dublin, 1931).
Fillion, L. C., *The Life of Christ,* trans. N. Thompson, 3 vols. (London, 1928–1930).
Garrigou-Lagrange, *Christ the Savior,* trans. B. Rose (St. Louis, 1950).
Graham, A., *The Christ of Catholicism* (New York, 1947).
Grimal, J., *The Priesthood and Sacrifice of Our Lord Jesus Christ,* trans. Keyes (Philadelphia, 1915).
Heris, Ch. V., *The Mystery of Christ,* trans. D. Fahey (Westminster, Md., 1950).
Hugon, E., *Le mystère de l'Incarnation* (Paris, 1931).
——— *Le mystère de la Rédemption* (Paris, 1927).
Lebreton, J., *The Life and Teachings of Jesus Christ,* 2 vols. (Milwaukee, 1935).
Lepin, M., *Christ and the Gospel* (Philadelphia, 1910).
Marmion, Columba, *Christ in His Mysteries* (Edinburgh, 1924).

Mersch, E., *The Whole Christ,* trans. J. R. Kelly (Milwaukee, 1938).
Parente, Peter, "Il Verbo," in *Il Simbolo,* II (Assisi, 1942).
Petrovits, J. J. C., *Devotion to the Sacred Heart* (St. Louis, 1925).
Pohle-Preuss, *Dogmatic Theology,* IV *Soteriology* (St. Louis, 1945); V *Christology* (1946).
Prat, *Jesus Christ,* trans. Heenan, 2 vols. (Milwaukee, 1950).
Ricciotti, J., *The Life of Christ,* trans. A. I. Zizzamia (Milwaukee, 1947).
Rivière, J., *The Doctrine of the Atonement,* 2 vols. (London, 1909).
Vonier, A., *Christ, the King of Glory* (London, 1932).
——— *The Personality of Christ* (London, 1916).

The Blessed Virgin Mary

Bourke, C., *Mary. A Study of the Mother of God* (Dublin, 1937).
Campana, E., *Maria nel dogma cattolico* (Turin, 1943).
Du Manoir, H., *Maria,* 3 vols. (Paris, 1949–).
Garofalo, L., *Le parole di Maria* (Rome, 1943).
Hogan, S. M., *Mother of Divine Grace* (London, 1921).
Jaggar, J. B., *The Immaculate Conception* (New York, 1925).
Le Rohellec, J., *Mary, Mother of Divine Grace,* trans. L. Rigby and D. Fahey (London, 1937).
McKenna, B. A., *The Dogma of the Immaculate Conception* (Washington, D. C., 1929).
O'Connell, R. V., *Mary's Assumption* (New York, 1930).
——— *Our Lady Mediatrix of All Graces* (Baltimore, 1926).
Pohle-Preuss, *Dogmatic Theology,* VI *Mariology* (St. Louis, 1946).
Roschini, G. M., *Mariologia,* 4 vols. (Milan, 1940–1949).
Scheeben, M. J., *Mariology,* trans. T. L. M. J. Geukers, 2 vols. (St. Louis, 1946–1947).
Smith, G. D., *Mary's Part in Our Redemption* (London, 1938).
Smith, M., *Unspotted Mirror of God* (Denver, 1943).
Ullathorne, *The Immaculate Conception of the Mother of God* (London, 1905).
Vassall, Phillips, O.R., *The Mother of Christ in Tradition, Theology, and Devotion* (London, 1922).
Vonier, A., *The Divine Motherhood* (London, 1921).

Grace. Virtues Ascetical and Mystical Theology

Bainvel, I. V., *Nature et surnaturel* (Paris, 1931).
Bastable, P. K., *Desire for God. Does Man Aspire Naturally to the Beatific Vision?* (London, 1947).
Cuthbert, Fr., *God and the Supernatural* (London, 1920).
Descoqs, P., *Le mystère de notre élévation surnaturelle* (Paris, 1938).
Divine, A., *Manual of Ascetical Theology* (London, 1902).
Froget, B., *The Indwelling of the Holy Spirit in the Souls of the Just,* trans. S. A. Raemers (New York, 1921).
Garrigou-Lagrange, R., *The Love of God and the Cross of Jesus,* trans. Sr. Jeanne Marie, Maryknoll (St. Louis, 1948).
——— *The Three Ages of the Interior Life,* trans. Sr. M. Timothea Doyle (St. Louis, 1947–1949).
——— *Christian Perfection and Contemplation,* trans. Sr. M. Timothea Doyle (St. Louis, 1937).

Goupil, A., *Les vertus théologales* (Paris, 1935).
Joyce, G. H., *The Catholic Doctrine of Grace* (London, 1930).
Lumbreras, P., *De gratia* (Rome, 1948).
Many, V., *Marvels of Grace,* trans. A. D. Talbot (Milwaukee, 1934).
Matthews, J. V., *With the Help of Thy Grace* (Westminster, Md., 1944).
McKenna, P. P., *The Theology of Faith* (Dublin, 1914).
Murray, *Tractatus De Gratia* (Dublin, 1877).
O'Connor, W., *The Eternal Quest* (New York, 1947).
Parente, Pascal, *The Mystical Life* (St. Louis, 1946).
——— *The Ascetical Life* (St. Louis, 1947).
——— *The Well of Living Waters* (St. Louis, 1948).
——— *Spiritual Direction* (St. Meinrad, Ind., 1950).
Pohle-Preuss, *Dogmatic Theology,* VII *Grace* (St. Louis, 1946).
Poulain, A., *The Grace of Interior Prayer,* trans. L. L. Yorke Smith (London, 1928).
Pourrat, P., *Christian Spirituality,* trans. W. H. Mitchell and S. P. Jacques, 3 vols. (London, 1922).
Rondet, H., *Gratia Christi, Essai d'histoire du dogme et de théologie dogmatique* (Paris, 1948).
Saudreau, A., *Les degrés de la vie spirituelle* (Paris, 1920).
Scheeben, M. J., *The Glories of Divine Grace,* trans. by a Benedictine monk (New York, 1886).
Tanquerey, A., *The Spiritual Life. A Treatise on Ascetical and Mystical Theology,* trans. H. Branderis (Philadelphia, 1938).
Wirth, E. J., *Divine Grace* (New York, 1903).

Sacraments

Brodie-Brosnam, J. B., *The Sacrifice of the New Law* (London, 1926).
Coghlan, D., *De SS. Eucharistia* (Dublin, 1913).
Connell, Fr. J., *De Sacramentis* (Brugis, 1933).
D'Alès, A., *L'Eucharistie* (Paris, 1933).
Dalgairns, J. B., *The Holy Communion,* 2 vols. (London, 1911).
De la Taille, M., *The Mystery of Faith and Human Opinion Contrasted and Defined,* trans. J. B. Schimpf (London, 1913).
——— *The Mystery of Faith,* 2 vols. (New York, 1940–1950).
Divine, A., *The Sacraments Explained* (London, 1905).
Doronzo, E., *De sacramentis in genere* (Milwaukee, 1946).
——— *De Baptismo et Confirmatione* (Milwaukee, 1947).
——— *De Eucharistia,* 2 vols. (Milwaukee, 1948).
——— *De Poenitentia,* 4 vols. (Milwaukee, 1949–).
Dowd, E. F., *A Concept of the Modern Catholic Thought on the Essence of the Eucharistic Sacrifice* (Washington, D. C., 1937).
Fortescue, A., *The Mass* (London, 1913).
Gannon, P. J., *Holy Matrimony* (London, 1928).
Gasquet, A., *Sacramentals* (London, 1928).
Girh, N., *The Holy Sacrifice of the Mass, Dogmatically, Liturgically and Ascetically Explained,* trans. from the 6th German ed. (St. Louis, 1931).
Hanley, P. J., *Extreme Unction* (New York, 1907).
Hedley, J. C., *The Holy Eucharist* (London, 1907).
Hesburgh, T. M., *The Relation of the Sacramental Characters of Baptism and*

Confirmation to the Lay Apostolate (Washington, D. C., 1946).
Janot, E., *Les sept fontaines* (Paris, 1939).
Joyce, G. H., *Christian Marriage* (London, 1948).
Kern, J., *De Extrema Unctione* (Ratisbon, 1907).
Kilker, A. J., *Extreme Unction* (St. Louis, 1927).
Kurtscheid, B., *A History of the Seal of Confession,* trans. F. A. Marks (St. Louis, 1927).
Lambing, A. A., *The Sacramentals of the Holy Church* (New York, 1892).
MacDonald, A., *The Sacrifice of the Mass in the Light of Scripture and Tradition* (London, 1924).
Mahoney, E. J., *The Secular Priesthood* (London, 1930).
Martindale, C. C., *The Sacramental System* (New York, 1928).
Masure, E., *The Christian Sacrifice,* trans. I. Trethowan (London, 1944).
——— *Le sacrifice du chef* (Paris, 1932).
O'Donnell, M. J., *Penance in the Early Church* (Dublin, 1907).
O'Dwyer, M., *Confirmation* (Dublin, 1915).
Piolanti, A., *Il corpo mistico e le sue relazioni con l'Eucaristia* (Rome, 1939).
——— *De Sacramentis,* 2 vols. (Rome, 1945).
Pohle-Preuss, *Dogmatic Theology,* VIII–XI *The Sacraments* (St. Louis, 1945–1946).
Pope, H., *The Doctrine of the Catholic Church Touching Indulgences* (London, 1915).
Pourrat, P., *The Theology of the Sacraments* (London, 1924).
Quinn, A., *Extreme Unction* (Dublin, 1920).
Rauschen, G., *Eucharist and Penance in the First Six Centuries of the Church,* trans. from the second German edition (St. Louis, 1913).
Thurston, H., *The Catholic Church and the Confessional* (London, 1928).
Tixeront, J., *Holy Orders and Ordinations,* trans. S. A. Raemers (St. Louis).
Villien, A., *Les sacrements* (Paris, 1931).
Vonier, A., *A Key to the Doctrine of the Eucharist* (Westminster, 1946).
Wirgman, A. F., *The Doctrine of Confirmation* (London, 1902).

Eschatology

Arendzen, J. P., *What Becomes of the Dead? A Study in Eschatology* (London, 1925).
Bartmann, B., *Purgatory,* trans. E. Graf (London, 1936).
Billot, *De Novissimis* (Rome, 1908).
——— *La Parousie* (Paris, 1920).
Buckley, J., *Man's Last End* (St. Louis, 1949).
Canty, *Purgatory, Dogmatic and Scholastic* (Dublin, 1886).
Coleridge, *The Prisoners of the King* (London, 1936).
Jackson, Shirley, *The Millennial Hope* (Chicago, 1918).
Jugie, M., *Purgatory and the Means to Avoid It,* trans. M. G. Carroll (Westminster, Md., 1949).
Lanslots, D. I., *The End of the World and of Man* (New York, 1925).
Morton, V., *Thoughts on Hell; A Study in Eschatology* (London, 1899).
Osterley, W. O. E., *The Doctrine of the Last Things* (London, 1908).
Oxenham, *Catholic Eschatology* (London, 1878).
Pohle-Preuss, *Dogmatic Theology,* XII *Eschatology* (St. Louis, 1946).
Raupert, J. G., *Hell and Its Problems* (Buffalo, 1917).

Rickaby, J., *Everlasting Punishment* (London, 1916).
Sadlier, *Purgatory* (New York, 1886).
Sasia, J. C., *The Future Life* (New York, 1918).
Schneider, W., *The Other Life* (New York, 1920).
Sutcliffe, E. F., *The Old Testament and the Future Life* (Westminster, 1947).
Vaughan, J. S., *Life Everlasting* (London, 1922).
Vonier, A., *The Life of the World to Come* (London, 1926).

Church

Agius, G., *Tradition and the Church* (Boston, 1928).
Anger, J., *The Doctrine of the Mystical Body of Christ,* trans. J. Burke (New York, 1931).
Arendzen, J. P., *The Church* (Cambridge, 1928).
Bainvel, J., *Is There Salvation Outside the Catholic Church,* trans. J. L. Weidenhan (St. Louis, 1917).
Baudrillart, A., *The Catholic Church, the Renaissance and Protestantism,* trans. Ph. Gibbs (London, 1908).
Berry, E. S., *The Church of Christ* (London, 1927).
Boylan, E., *The Mystical Body* (Westminster, Md., 1947).
Carrère, J., *The Pope,* trans. A. Chambers (London, 1925).
Chapman, J., *Ecclesia: The Church of Christ* (London, 1906).
Clerissac, H., *The Mystery of the Church* (New York, 1937).
D'Arcy, M. C., *Catholicism* (London, 1927).
Doyle, F. X., *The Defense of the Catholic Church,* combined with a study of the life of Christ (New York, 1927).
Duchesne, L., *The Churches Separate From Rome,* trans. A. H. Matten (London, 1907).
Fahey, D., *The Mystical Body of Christ in the Modern World* (Dublin, 1944).
Finlay, P., *The Church of Christ* (New York, 1928).
Fisher, A., *De salute infidelium* (Essen, 1886).
Fortescue, A., *The Orthodox Eastern Church* (London, 1916).
Gruden, J. C., *The Mystical Christ.* Introduction to the study of the supernatural character of the Church (St. Louis, 1936).
Huby, J., *The Church and the Gospels* (New York, 1931).
Jung, N., *Le Magistère de l'Eglise* (Paris, 1935).
Kösters, L., *The Church: Its Authority,* trans. E. Kaiser (St. Louis, 1938).
Lattey, C., *The Church* (Cambridge, 1928).
——— *The Papacy* (Cambridge, 1924).
Lippert, P., *L'Eglise du Christ* (Lyon, 1933).
Martindale, C. C., *The Faith of the Roman Church* (London, 1950).
McNabb, V., *Infallibility* (London, 1927).
Mersch, E., *The Whole Christ.* The historical development of the doctrine of the Mystical Body in scripture and tradition, trans. J. R. Kelly (Milwaukee, 1938).
Rousseau, R., *The Church of Christ* (Milwaukee, 1936).
Ryan, J. A., and Millar, J. F. X., *The State and the Church* (New York, 1924).
Sertillanges, A. D., *The Church,* trans. A. G. McDougall (London, 1922).
Sheen, F., *The Mystical Body of Christ* (New York, 1935).

Apologetics

Baierl, J. J., *The Theory of Revelation,* 2 vols. (Rochester, 1927).
Batiffol, P., *The Credibility of the Gospels* (London, 1912).
Bonniot, P. J., *Le miracle et ses contrefaçons* (Paris, 1887).
Brunsmann-Preuss, *A Handbook of Fundamental Theology,* 4 vols. (St. Louis, 1931).
Cotter, A. C., *Theologia Fundamentalis* (Weston, 1940).
Devivier, F. W., *Christian Apologetics* (London, 1924).
Falcon, J., *La credibilité du dogme catholique* (Paris, 1933).
Felder, H., *Christ and the Critics,* trans. T. L. Stoddard, 2 vols. (London, 1924).
Fenton, J. C., *The Concept of Sacred Theology* (Milwaukee, 1941).
——— *We Stand With Christ* (Milwaukee, 1942).
Finlay, P., *Divine Faith* (London, 1917).
Garrigou-Lagrange, R., *De Revelatione* (Paris, 1926).
Gibbons, J., *Faith of Our Fathers,* 69 ed. (Baltimore, 1917).
Hettinger, F., *Revealed Religion,* 2 vols. (London, 1905).
Joyce, G. H., *The Question of Miracles* (Roehampton, 1914).
McKenna, P. P., *The Theology of Faith* (Dublin, 1914).
McNabb, B., *Frontiers of Faith and Reason* (London, 1937).
O'Brien, J. A., *Truths Men Live By* (New York, 1946).
Schmidt, W., *The Origin and Growth of Religion* (New York, 1931).
Sheehan, M., *Apologetics and Christian Doctrine* (Dublin, 1929).
Sheen, F., *Religion Without God* (London, 1928).
Walshe, T. J., *The Principles of Catholic Apologetics* (New York, 1919).

St. Thomas Aquinas

Bourke, V. J., *Thomistic Bibliography 1920–1940* (St. Louis, 1945).
Chenu, M. D., *Introduction à l'étude de Saint Thomas d'Aquin* (Montreal, Paris, 1950).
Chesterton, G. K., *St. Thomas Aquinas* (London, 1933).
Collins, J. B., *The Catechetical Instructions of St. Thomas Aq.,* trans. with commentary (San Francisco-London, 1939).
D'Arcy, M. C., *Thomas Aquinas, Selected Writings* (New York, 1939).
Deferrari, R. J., and Barry, Sr. M. Inviolata, *A Lexicon of St. Thomas Aquinas,* (Washington, D. C., 1948–).
Farrell, W., *A Companion to the Summa,* 4 vols. (New York, 1941–1942).
Firminger, W. K., *The Most Devout Exposition of the Lord's Prayer of St. Thomas Aq.,* trans. with introduction and notes (London, 1927).
Garrigou-Lagrange, R., *Reality: A Synthesis of Thomistic Thought,* trans. P. Cummins (St. Louis, 1950).
Grabmann, M., *Introduction to the Theological Summa of St. Thomas* (St. Louis, 1930).
Hughes, P., *St. Thomas, Meditation for Lent,* trans. (London-New York, 1938).
Mandonnet, P., and Destrez, J., *Bibliographie Thomiste* (Le Saulchoir, Kain, Belgium, 1921).
Maritain, J., *St. Thomas Aquinas, Angel of the Schools,* trans. J. F. Scanlan (New York, 1938).
Meyer, H., *The Philosophy of St. Thomas Aquinas,* trans. F. C. Eckoff (St. Louis).

O'Neill, F., *St. Thomas Aq., The Blessed Sacrament and the Mass,* trans. with introduction and notes (London, 1935).
Pegis, A. C., *The Basic Writings of St. Thomas,* 2 vols. (New York, 1945).
St. Thomas, *The Summa Theologica,* trans. by the Dominican Fathers of the English province, 22 vols., 2nd rev. ed. (London, 1912–1936).
——— *The Summa Theologica,* trans. by the Dominican Fathers, 3 vols. (New York, 1948). First complete American edition.
——— *The Summa Contra Gentiles,* trans. by the Dominican Fathers from the Leonine ed., 5 vols. (London-New York, 1928–1929).
——— *Compendium of Theology,* trans. C. Vollert (St. Louis).
Schapcote, L., *On the Power of God.* Translation of St. Thomas' *De Potentia Dei* (New York, 1934).
Sertillanges, A. D., *St. Thomas Aquinas and His Work,* trans. G. Anstruther (London, 1933).

Aids

The Dictionary of Dogmatic Theology cannot be fully utilized without these substantial aids:

1. The Bible in the Vulgate edition with a good commentary.[1]

2. *Enchiridion Symbolorum* of H. Denzinger–C. Bannwart–J. B. Umberg, ed. Herder. It collects, in the form of an ample anthology, the principal definitions and the formulas of the faith issued by the *magisterium* of the Church (creeds, councils, acts of the Roman pontiffs).[2]

3. *Enchiridion Patristicum* of Rouet de Journel, ed. Herder. It is an anthology of the teaching of the Fathers on the principal dogmas of the Christian faith.[3]

4. St. Thomas, *Summa Theologica* and *Summa contra Gentiles* (Leonine text in small format, edited at Rome in 1948 for the first work and in 1934 for the second). A better edition of the *Summa Theologica* is that of the Dominican Fathers of the Canadian Province, 5 vols. (Ottawa, 1941–1945). There is an English translation of both works mentioned above.

Principal Theological Reviews

Angelicum, organ of the Dominican University (Pontificio Ateneo Angelico), at Rome, Italy.
Antonianum, organ of the Franciscan University (Pontificio Ateneo Antoniano), at Rome, Italy.

[1] E.g., J. E. Steinmueller, *A Companion to the Scripture Studies,* 3 vols. (New York, 1941–1943); Charles Pickar, *A Commentary on the New Testament* (Washington, D. C., 1942).

[2] The acts of the councils have been gathered in large collections by various authors. It suffices to cite J. D. Mansi, Bishop of Lucca (d. 1775), who published *Sacrorum Conciliorum Nova et Amplissima Collectio* (Florence and Venice, 1759, 1789), in 31 vols. (reprinted at Paris in 35 vols. in 1901 ff.). For the later councils there is the *Collectio Lacensis* of the Jesuit Fathers, published at Fribourg in 7 vols., 1870–1890 (Vol. 7 contains the acts of the Vatican Council).

[3] The writings of the Fathers were diligently collected by J. P. Migne in the monumental *Patrologiae Cursus Completus* (Latin series of 221 vols. and Greek series of 161 vols.). In addition there are two later collections, more critical but far from being completed: the *Corpus* of Vienna and the *Corpus* of Berlin.

There are being published at present two English translations of the main works of the Fathers: *Ancient Christian Writers,* edited by Joannes Quasten and J. C. Plumpe (Washington, D. C.: Catholic University Press, 1948–); *The Fathers of the Church* (New York, 1947–).

Divus Thomas, organ of the Vincentian Fathers' "Collegio Alberoni," at Piacenza, Italy.
Doctor Communis, organ of the Pontifical Roman Academy of St. Thomas Aquinas.
Ephemerides Theologicae Lovanienses, organ of the Catholic University of Louvain, Belgium.
Euntes Docete, organ of the Pontifical University "De Propaganda Fide," at Rome, Italy.
Gregorianum, organ of the Jesuit University (Università Gregoriana), at Rome, Italy.
Journal of Theological Studies, Oxford.
La Scuola Cattolica, organ of the Major Seminary of Milan, Italy.
Nouvelle Revue Theologique, edited by the Jesuit Fathers, at Louvain, Belgium.
Recherches de Science Religieuse, Paris.
Revue de Sciences Religieuses, organ of the Catholic University of Strasbourg, France.
Revue Thomiste, directed by the Dominican Fathers in France.
The American Ecclesiastical Review, published by the Catholic University of America Press, Washington, D. C.
Theological Studies, published by the Jesuit Fathers in the United States.
The Thomist, edited by the Dominican Fathers in the United States.
Zeitschrift fur katholische Theologie, Innsbruck.

ABBREVIATIONS

AAS	*Acta Apostolicae Sedis*
ASS	*Acta Sanctae Sedis*
CE	*The Catholic Encyclopedia*
CIC	*The Code of Canon Law*
DA	*Dictionnaire apologétique de la Foi catholique*
DACL	*Dictionnaire d'Archéologie chrétienne et de Liturgie*
DB	*Enchiridion Symbolorum* (Denzinger, Bannwart, Umberg)
DBV	*Dictionnaire de la Bible* (Vigouroux)
DBVS	*Dictionnaire de la Bible, Supplément* (Pirot)
DDC	*Dictionnaire de droit canonique*
DHGE	*Dictionnaire d'histoire et de géographie ecclésiastique*
DS	*Dictionnaire de spiritualité*
DTC	*Dictionnaire de Théologie Catholique*
EB	*Enchiridion biblicum*
EFHE	*Enchiridion fontium historiae ecclesiasticae* (Kirch)
RJ	*Enchiridion patristicum* (Rouet de Journel)
O.T. (Lat., V.T.)	Old Testament
N.T. (N.T.)	New Testament
Abd. (Abd.)	Abdias
Acts (Acts)	Acts of the Apostles
Ag. (Ag.)	Aggeus
Amos (Amos)	Amos
Apoc. (Apoc.)	Apocalypse
Bar. (Bar.)	Baruch
Cant. (Cant.)	Canticle of Canticles
Chron. (1–2 Par.)	Chronicles (1–2 Paralipomenon)
Col. (Col.)	Epistle to the Colossians
1–2 Cor. (1–2 Cor.)	1–2 Epistles to the Corinthians
Dan. (Dan.)	Daniel
Deut. (Deut.)	Deuteronomy
Eccles. (Eccl.)	Ecclesiastes
Ecclus. (Eccli.)	Ecclesiasticus
Eph. (Eph.)	Epistle to the Ephesians
Esd. (Esdr.)	Esdras
Esth. (Esth.)	Esther
Exod. (Exod.)	Exodus
Ezech. (Ez.)	Ezechiel
Gal. (Gal.)	Epistle to the Galatians
Gen. (Gen.)	Genesis
Hab. (Hab.)	Habacuc
Heb. (Hebr.)	Epistle to the Hebrews
Isa. (Isa.)	Isaias

James (Jac.)	Epistle of St. James
Jer. (Jer.)	Jeremias
Job (Job)	Job
Joel (Joel)	Joel
John (Johan.)	Gospel of St. John
1–2–3 John (1–2–3 Joh.)	1–2–3 Epistles of St. John
Jonas (Jon.)	Jonas
Jos. (Jos.)	Josue
Jude (Judas)	Epistle of St. Jude
Judges (Jud.)	Judges
Judith (Judith)	Judith
1–2 Kings (1–2 Reg.)	1–2 Kings
3–4 Kings (3–4 Reg.)	3–4 Kings
Lam. (Threni)	Lamentations
Lev. (Lev.)	Leviticus
Luke (Lc.)	Gospel of St. Luke
1–2 Mac. (1–2 Mac.)	1–2 Machabees
Mal. (Mal.)	Malachias
Mark (Mc.)	Gospel of St. Mark
Matt. (Mt.)	Gospel of St. Matthew
Mich. (Mich.)	Micheas
Nah. (Nah.)	Nahum
Neh. (Neh.)	Nehemias
Num. (Num.)	Numbers
Osee (Os.)	Osee
1–2 Pet. (1–2 Petr.)	1–2 Epistles of St. Peter
Phil. (Phil.)	Epistle to the Philippians
Philem. (Philem.)	Epistle to Philemon
Prov. (Prov.)	Proverbs
Ps. (Ps.)	Psalms
Rom. (Rom.)	Epistle to the Romans
Ruth (Ruth)	Ruth
Soph. (Soph.)	Sophonias
1–2 Thess. (1–2 Thess.)	1–2 Epistles to the Thessalonians
1–2 Tim. (1–2 Tim.)	1–2 Epistles to Timothy
Tit. (Tit.)	Epistle to Titus
Tob. (Tob.)	Tobias
Wisd. (Sap.)	Wisdom
Zach. (Zac.)	Zacharias

SYNTHESIS OF THEOLOGICAL DOCTRINE

Christian doctrine is not a fragmentary collection of truths, as a casual reader of this manual might suspect, but a compact system of truths organically elaborated, in which reason moves in the light of faith and divine revelation. It is also science, but science that transcends the subject matter and the method of common human sciences, because its principles consist in a datum or known fact which rests on the authority of God, the infallible Truth. The datum or premise is divine revelation consigned in two sources: Holy Scripture and Tradition. Custodian and authentic interpreter of both these sources is the living and infallible teaching authority (*magisterium vivum et infallibile*) of the Church instituted by Jesus Christ.

The act of faith is a free adhesion of reason to truth revealed by God and as such proposed by the Church. Faith is a humble act of reverence to God the Creator, who is absolute Truth; a reasonable reverence, however, because faith, while of the supernatural order on account of its object, which is revealed truth, and on account of grace which helps the will and the intellect to adhere to the divine word, nevertheless has *presuppositions* which appertain to the sphere and domain of reason. Such are the existence of a personal God distinct from the world, the fact of divine revelation historically ascertainable, the value of the testimony of Christ and the Church He founded.

The serene study of these prerequisites prepares for faith because it demonstrates the credibility of revealed truth, but does not determine the act of faith ("I believe"), which depends negatively on the good dispositions of the subject and positively on the grace of God.

The Vatican Council (Sess. 3, Ch. 4) affirms that "right reason demonstrates the foundations of faith"; and so Catholic doctrine proclaims the rights and dignity of human reason even with respect to faith just as it defends the integrity of human freedom with respect to divine grace.

Apologetics is a scientific introduction to theology, demonstrating the possibility and the fact of divine revelation, proving in a rational way the presuppositions of faith. In the first place, apologetics takes from sound philosophy the conclusion of the objective value of human knowledge. This truth assured, it gives the proof of the existence of God, utilizing that part of philosophy known as theodicy or natural theology: subjective proof from the light of truth that shines in the intellect, or the thirst of an infinite good that burns in the heart, or the force of the moral law which dominates conscience: objective proof from the beauty, perfection, unity, and order of the world in which we live. Both orders of proof draw their demonstrative validity from the principle of causality, which, showing the characteristics of limitation and contingency of cosmic reality and of our own internal world (the effect), constrains the affirmation of an adequate Cause of both these characteristics in which is seen the *raison d'être* of ourselves and the world.

The principle of causality makes us understand not only the distinction between God and the universe, but also the determination of their mutual relationship, which is actualized in the creative act. But this metaphysical demonstration does not remain in the sphere of abstract speculation; it has a confirmation in the individual and collective consciousness, in the ethico-religious patrimony of humanity. Religion, tendency, guiding norm, and indestructible force of the spirit, is like the nervous system of human history and manifests in a thousand forms the persuasion of moral relationship between man and God, as between son and father. These relationships are generally consecrated by the concept of a divine revelation. There is not a religion that does not jealously guard a code or a tradition with the sacred title: Word of God.

Confronted with this constant and universal affirmation, not even a twentieth-century man can remain indifferent. If God has spoken, man must listen to Him and draw from the divine word a rule of life and of orientation toward his supreme destiny.

Hence the historical quest to find the true revelation.

Among the numerous religions, which claim a divine origin, Christianity presents more evident and sure guarantees of truth. It embraces and dominates the whole history of humanity; its code is the Bible, which records the pact (testament) between God and men and which is divided into two broad phases: the Old Testament which prepares the advent of Christ, the Messias, and the New Testament which accompanies and enriches the kingdom of Christ on the move. This great book, which opens with the description of the creation (Genesis) and closes with the sinister flashes of the end of the world (Apocalypse), contains sublime truths and supernatural elements (prophecies and miracles) which seal its divine character. No book has been studied so passionately as the Bible, not to mention the myriad number of souls who have absorbed light and strength of holiness from it to the point of heroism. Let it suffice to speak of the ferocity of historical and philosophical criticism that has been unleashed on the Bible for more than a century. All the resources of genius and erudition have been engaged in turn; from this crucible, the Bible (particularly the Gospels) not only emerged substantially unchanged, but even forced the respect of its most hostile critics by virtue of its historicity and its authenticity.

Now, the Bible is centered on Christ, in whom are accomplished marvelously the Messianic prophecies of the Old Testament and from whom irradiates the new light of the Gospel sealed by the miracles, especially that of Christ's own resurrection. The historicity and authenticity of the Bible being demonstrated, its contents must be accepted without reserve. Since Christ, on whom is focused the entire ancient revelation, declares Himself to be the representative of God and speaks and acts in His name, the teaching of both Testaments must be accepted as something divine; and Jesus

Christ, who seals His statements with miracles, must be recognized as the Revealer par excellence and, what is more, as true Son of God, as He claims to be. In guarantee of His truthfulness stand the ancient prophecies fulfilled in Him, His own miracles and prophecies, His wonderful psychological and moral equilibrium, the testimony, often in blood, of His followers, the sublimity and victorious strength of His doctrine.

Christ, moreover, has founded a Church in the form of a perfect society with its hierarchy, its teaching authority, its means of sanctification (the sacraments). He also declared that He will remain in this Church to the end of the world, making Himself one with it, especially with its visible head (the pope), to whom He has entrusted the task of acting for Him and taking His place, by governing, by teaching, and by sanctifying.

Recapitulating the rational procedure of Christian apologetics, we may trace it schematically as follows:

Man, with his intellect made for truth, examines himself and the universe outside of himself and discovers in it the character of creation, of effect, from which he ascends to a First Cause, to a creating and provident God. Religions deal with relationship with God, with divine revelation; in his search for truth, man encounters Christianity, which offers the greatest guarantees of truth. Here revelation has Christ as its center, a divine Representative, nay, the very Son of God, who corroborates His declaration with supernatural facts. God, therefore, has spoken in the Bible through the prophets, has spoken through the mouth of His incarnate Son, Jesus Christ.

And so man can and, what is more, should believe in Christ, in His word, His laws, His divine institutions.

But since the demonstration of apologetics is not mathematical but of a moral nature, the intellect can remain perplexed, especially in the face of transcendent and mysterious truths and of laws imposing sacrifices and renunciations. The conclusion of every good apologete, then, will be the possibility and the moral necessity of believing; but the act of faith itself, the "credo," needs the impulse of grace, and so it is free and meritorious.

Where apologetics ends, theology begins. It supposes the truth of revelation (objectively) and the assent of faith (subjectively). The object of theological science is God in Himself and the created world, man especially, in relation to God.

The source of theology is divine revelation contained in Holy Scripture and Tradition and understood through the interpretation of the living and infallible teaching of the Church. Therefore theological argumentation is based on the authority of God's revelation, and so is substantially dogmatic. A dogma is a truth revealed by God and defined as such by the Church; a truth, therefore, sacred and unchangeable in itself. Dogma both contains a truth accessible to human reason and, at times, a truth which transcends its capacity (a mystery). In the first instance, reason understands the truth and accepts it not only in homage to God who proposes it, but also motivated by its intrinsic evidence. Thus it is, for example, with the immortality of the soul, which is a truth of reason and of faith. In the case of mysteries, reason adheres only through faith and on the authority of God.

From revealed truth, theology, by a dialectic process illuminated by faith, draws "theological conclusions," which are a further explanation of the revealed truth and a more or less immediate radiation from it. These conclusions are certainly more than a merely rational truth, but do not have divine value like dogma.

It is evident that dogma, even though it surpasses the capacity of human intelligence (as, for example, the mystery of the Holy Trinity), can never be in contradiction with rational principles, because it is always God who is the one source of supernatural and natural truths. God cannot be in contradiction with Himself. Theology strives to demonstrate at least that the mystery is not repugnant or counter to reason.

In a broad sense, all the sacred sciences which constitute the sum of ecclesiastical knowledge belong to theology, because they move in the orbit of faith's light and cannot prescind from the supernatural, which dominates human life in relation to God. But theology, par excellence and in the strict sense, is dogmatic theology, with which we are dealing in this work.

Dogmatic theology includes the following treatises:

1. *Triune God.* In this treatise we study the existence, the essence, the attributes of God, especially intelligence and will with relation to the world and man. We also study the inner life of God, who is revealed as being one substance in three distinct Persons which are constituted by the *relations* between the terms of the two immanent *processions* (of intellection and volition).

2. *God as Creator.* God is the Creator of all things, including man. God not only has created these out of nothing, but conserves their being by His continual influence and determines their actions. For the angels and for man God has disposed a supernatural order, destining these privileged creatures to the immediate vision of His own essence. Both angels and men fall into sin: for the fallen angels, pure intelligences, no reparation; for man, composed of spirit and matter, God decrees redemption through the means of His incarnate Son. Original sin, transmitted in all the children of Adam (except the Immaculate Virgin Mary), wounds human nature without, however, destroying its essential properties. It creates in the life of man a vexatious sense of moral uneasiness, which gradually resolves itself in an appeal to the future Saviour.

3. *The Man-God.* The Son of God (*Verbum*—Word) takes human nature and makes it His own, partaker of His own personal subsistence. There is thus a "theandric" (divine-human) being, two distinct natures and only one person. It is Jesus Christ who goes forward to endure suffering, even the martyrlike death of torture on the cross, to free man from the slavery of evil and sin. Redemption is accomplished with the life, the passion, and the death of Jesus, followed by His glorious resurrection. Man, however, must make it his own, adhering freely to Christ by faith and grace, the

source of energies for a new life whose happy fullness lies in the future possession of God.

4. *Grace.* Grace is the fruit of the Redemption. This divine force is communicated to man through Christ the Redeemer. It is a certain participation of the very nature and the inner life of God. This force does not strangle but, on the contrary, demands the co-operation of free will for sanctification, the road that must be taken to arrive at the supreme goal: eternal life in God.

5. *The sacraments.* The sacraments are the channels of grace, a prolongation, as it were, of the sacred and holy humanity of the Saviour, the source of supernatural life. The assumed humanity is the instrument conjoined to the Word for the sanctification of souls. The sacraments are *separate* instruments, which derive supernatural efficacy from the first instrument (Christ's humanity). The Holy Eucharist is the center of sacramental vitality, containing in Itself the very source of grace. The other sacraments accompany man from the cradle to the grave in the various phases of his mortal life, providing him with specific helps for all the difficulties and struggles to be overcome in the conquest of heaven.

6. *The Church.* By an ineffable mystery Christ found a way to incorporate in Himself the men who answer His call. He instituted the Church as a Mystical Body, of which Christ is the head and the faithful the members. The Church is a social organism, with a visible hierarchic structure and a spiritual vitality, nourished by Christ through the sacraments. The life of the Church springs from Christ the Redeemer and is guarded and regulated by the bishop of Rome, successor of St. Peter, constituted by the Lord as the foundation stone of His Church and its supreme pastor. This marvelous Mystical Body, synthesis of all God's works, rich in the light of truth and inexhaustible lifeblood of supernatural life, is open to all men of good will. The soul enters it, meets with Christ, purifies itself in Him, is transformed, treads firmly with Him the return road to the heart of God whence it came into being at the moment of its creation.

These are the principal treatises that constitute the solid organism of dogmatic theology. This sacred science is like an itinerary, which scans the pace of infinite Wisdom and Love toward Its creature and the pace of the creature, who has found again the way of salvation, the way that leads to His Father's house. God, Thought and Love, who contemplates Himself in the Word, His Son, and loves Himself in His Spirit, wishes a being outside of Himself to whom to communicate His perfections, His love, His life: hence the work of creation, in which man, made to the image of God and enriched by grace and other privileges, dominates. Man falls miserably into guilt and remains under the weight of sin and of the divine malediction for centuries. Eternal Love does not tolerate so much ruin and, bending over His wayward creature, He becomes one with it by taking on his flesh; hence the Incarnation of the Word and the Redemption, which reopens the roads to heaven. And the Word inserts Itself and rests in the breast of humanity to save it; thus we have the Church with its infallible teaching body, with her graces and sacraments, sources of supernatural life. The Church is the marriage between God and man, as it were, the prolongation of the Incarnation in which Christ continues His redeeming work made up of suffering and love, living in every soul which, through the struggles and tribulations of the present life, yearns for the light and peace of life eternal.

A true romance: romance or drama made up of truth and living reality, in which man, in contact with Christ, redeems himself from guilt, liberates himself from evil, recaptures his true being, and moves on to the conquest of God, his beginning and his necessary end.

DICTIONARY OF DOGMATIC THEOLOGY

A

Abelard. See "Outline of the History of Dogmatic Theology" (p. 302).

absolution. See *penance.*

Acacians. Followers of Acacius, disciple of Eusebius and his successor as bishop of Caesarea in Palestine (340–366). Acacius followed in the steps of Eusebius in favoring and embracing Arianism (*q.v.*) in a milder form. An ambitious and incoherent man, he caused St. Cyril to be deposed as Patriarch of Jerusalem (357), became sect chief at the Synods of Seleucia and of Constantinople (359–360), and dominated the situation under the Emperor Constantius. He accepted the Nicene faith under Jovian (against Arius), but under Valens returned to heresy, and was deposed by the Lampsacan Synod (365).

Acacius and his followers are called also *Omei* from the Greek term ὅμοιος (like), which summed up their teaching. They reject the *Anomoeanism* (*q.v.*) of Aëtius and Eunomius, who taught the dissimilarity (ἀνόμοιος) between the Father and Son; they do not admit the ὁμοούσιος (consubstantial) defined at the Council of Nicaea (325) nor do they accept the ὁμοιούσιος of the Semi-Arian followers of Basil of Ancyra, who held a *substantial* similarity or likeness between Father and Son; but they stop at simple similarity (ὅμοιος) between the two divine Persons, appealing to the authority of St. Paul, who calls Christ the image of the Father. According to St. Hilary, this similarity proposed by the Acacians referred only to the concord or harmony of the will of the Son with that of the Father. In other words, these heretics were returning to full-fledged Arianism.

BIBLIOGRAPHY

CAYRÉ, *Manual of Patrology,* trans. Howitt, Vol. 1 (Paris, Tournai, Rome, 1936), p. 316. CLIFFORD, "Acacians," *CE.* GWATKIN, *Studies in Arianism* (Cambridge, 1910). LE BACHELET, "Acaciens," *DTC.* TIXERONT, *History of Dogmas,* trans. H.L.B., Vol. 2 (St. Louis, 1914), pp. 48–57.

accidents, eucharistic. See *eucharistic accidents.*

acolythate (Gr. ἀκόλουθος — he who accompanies, an attendant). The fourth minor order (see *orders, holy*). The office of the acolyte is to carry the candlestick, to light the lights of the Church, and to offer the water and the wine for the Eucharist (cf. *Roman Pontifical*). The origin of this order goes back at least to the third century, for Pope Cornelius in his letter to Fabius of Antioch (261) attests that at Rome there were 42 acolytes. Their functions, various in the beginning, were gradually determined and fixed in the current form.

BIBLIOGRAPHY

ST. THOMAS, *Summa Theol.,* III, *Suppl.,* q. 57, a. 2. DUCHESNE, *Christian Worship: Its Origin and Evolution,* trans. 2 ed. (London, 1904), pp. 344, 352, 366. KURTSCHEID, *Historia Iuris Canonici,* Vol. 1 (Rome, 1941). LECLERCQ, "Acolyte," *DACL.* MEEHAN, "Acolyte," *CE.* TIXERONT, *Holy Orders and Ordinations,* trans. S. A. Raemers (St. Louis).

action, divine. See *operation, divine.*

Act, Pure. Connected with the Aristotelian theory of *being,* divided into *act* and *potency.* Heraclitus had reduced all reality to movement or change (πάντα ῥεῖ); Parmenides, on the contrary, had conceived reality as an intelligible being, denying motion. Aristotle, in an effort to explain change or becoming, so evident in things, came to discover that the being of the world has necessarily two phases: one of indetermination, of poverty, of capacity, of development; the other of determination, of acquisition and enrichment. *Example:* the seed which becomes a plant. The first phase is called *potency;* the second, *act.* Potency, or potentiality, means limited reality, which may be reduced to the minimum, to the boundary of nothingness, like prime matter; act, on the other hand, means the richness of realization and, therefore, of being. Act paces regularly the march of being toward an always greater perfection, and so the more a thing is act, the more it is rich in perfection, i.e., in being. A being can be conceived and can exist which is all act without any potency. Such a being would be, therefore, all perfection, i.e., all being, without possibility of development, and so without possibility of change. This Being is *God,* called *Pure Act,* because He is subsisting being (see *essence, divine*), fullness of being, and, therefore, immutable.

St. Thomas, following Aristotle and understanding movement as a passage from potentiality to act, proves (in the first argument or *via*) the existence of God as *Prime Mover Immobile,* who moves all without being moved, i.e., as Pure Act, Source of all perfection, Possessor of all being, in whose fullness the world participates through creation, and to whom it tends, in its becoming, as to its proper end.

BIBLIOGRAPHY

St. Thomas, *Summa Theol.,* I, q. 2, a. 3; *Compendium Theologiae* (St. Thomas here refers all the attributes and perfections of God to the concept of Pure Act). Dubray, "Actus et Potentia," *CE;* "Actus purus," *CE.* Garrigou-Lagrange, *Le sens commun* (Paris, 1922), p. 205 ff. Sertillanges, *Saint Thomas d'Aquin,* Vol. 1 (Paris, 1925), p. 70 ff.

acts, notional. See *notions, divine.*

"ad extra, ad intra." See *operation, divine.*

adoptionism. Christological heresy which represents Christ not as the true natural Son of God, but as the adopted Son. This error is closely connected with subordinationism (see *subordinationists*) and was spread at Rome in the second century by Theodotus the Elder, excommunicated by Pope Victor in 190, and at Antioch in the third century by Paul of Samosata, who also was condemned. Adoptionism and subordinationism deny substantially the divinity of the Word, and so prepare the way for Arianism (*q.v.*).

In the eighth century in Spain, two bishops, Felix of Urgel and Elipandus of Toledo, while admitting the divinity of the Word, natural Son of the Father, thought that Christ, in His holy humanity, could be called adopted Son of God. This is mitigated adoptionism, also proscribed (cf. Council of Frankfurt and Friuli, *DB,* 311 and 3007; and the letter of Hadrian I to the Spanish Bishops, *DB,* 290). Really Christ is only natural Son of God and not adopted Son, even according to His humanity, because the terms to which filiation is referred is the person, and in Christ the person is only one, that of the Word, true Son of God (*q.v.*).

BIBLIOGRAPHY

St. Thomas, *Summa Theol.,* III, q. 23. Amann, "L'Adoptianisme espagnol du VIII siècle," *Revue de sciences religieuses,* 1936.

POHLE-PREUSS, *Dogmatic Theology,* IV *Christology* (St. Louis, 1946), pp. 196–206. SOLLIER, "Adoptionism," *CE.* See under *subordinationists.*

adoption, supernatural. Mentioned explicitly several times by St. Paul with the proper legal term of the language of the Temple: *υἱοθεσία.* Thus in his letter to the Romans 8:15: "For you have not received the spirit of bondage again in fear: but you have received the spirit of adoption of sons, whereby we cry: Abba (Father)" (cf. Eph. 1:5; Gal. 4:5). The term evokes the current concept of juridical adoption usually defined as: a gratuitous assumption of an outside person as son with the right of inheritance. This human adoption is a *moral* substitute of natural filiation, which creates a right in the adopted person without changing his physical nature or personality. The adoption spoken of in Holy Scripture transcends the natural order and therefore also the natural concept of common adoption, with which it agrees only analogously. In fact, man, who by faith answers Christ's call, according to the documents of revelation, is enriched by sanctifying grace, which establishes between the creature and God a relationship of paternity and sonship by virtue of a *spiritual regeneration* which resolves itself into an ineffable participation of the very nature of God. Cf. John (Prologue of the Gospel): "He gave them the power to be made the sons of God, to them who are born of God"; 2 Peter 1:4: "He hath given us most great and precious promises: that by these you may be made partakers of the divine nature."

Supernatural adoption therefore means an intrinsic transformation of the soul, a vital divine communication, which makes man *domesticus Dei,* i.e., a member of the divine family (Eph. 2:19), like to God in being and action. In the ancient liturgy and in the writings of the Fathers divine adoption is a dominant motif: the Greeks especially (St. Athanasius, St. Basil, St. Cyril of Alexandria) illustrate the relationship between our adoptive filiation and the natural filiation of Jesus Christ with respect to the Father, and prove that the one is the effect of the other. The Scholastics go deeper into this truth (cf. St. Thomas), and after the Council of Trent the theologians fix the expression of this truth in these terms: adoption is a formal effect of sanctifying grace by which the faithful become sons of God, and so brothers of Jesus Christ, their Coheir of eternal life.

BIBLIOGRAPHY

ST. THOMAS, *Summa Theol.,* III, q. 23. BELLAMY, "Adoption," *DTC.* FROGET, *The Indwelling of the Holy Spirit,* trans. S. A. Raemers (New York, 1921). GALTIER, *L'habitation en nous des trois Personnes* (Paris, 1928). SOLLIER, "Adoption," *CE.* TERRIEN, *La grâce et la gloire* (Paris, 1897).

Adventists. A Protestant sect founded by W. Miller, an American, at the beginning of the nineteenth century. They were called Adventists because of their belief in a proximate advent or return of Christ on earth. Miller, interpreting Daniel and the Apocalypse in his own way, believed he could determine the date of the advent of Jesus, first as March 22, then as October 22, 1844.

The prophecy unfulfilled, Miller's numerous followers split into different groups, among which the *Seventh Day Adventists* became the most numerous and prominent. (They are so called because they are defenders of the Sabbath, i.e., rest from work on Saturday instead of Sunday.) Their first leader was R. Creston. Afterward they were headed at Washington by J. White and his wife, Ellen, who claimed to be a prophetess. From America this sect was propagated to England and Germany.

The Adventists' doctrine is a hybrid mixture of Catholicism, Judaism, and Protestantism: they hold the Bible as the one rule of faith with preference for the eschatological books; they attribute a body to God, and venerate Christ as Son of God, all love for man, for whom He has given His blood. Faith is not sufficient for salvation, but man's co-operation with divine grace is necessary. There is no hell, but at the end of the world the reprobate will be annihilated; after the final judgment, the millenary reign of Christ, flanked by 144,000 Seventh Day Adventists, will take place. They are vegetarians and teetotalers.

BIBLIOGRAPHY

HAVEY, "Adventists," *CE.* TANQUEREY, "Adventistes," *DTC.*

aeons. See *Gnosticism.*

Affairs, Extraordinary Ecclesiastical (Congregation of). See *Holy See.*

Agnoetism (from the Gr. ἄγνοια — ignorance). Christological error of Themistius, Alexandrian deacon of the sixth century. According to the more probable opinion, Themistius was a Severian Monophysite (see *Monophysitism*). While the Aphthardocetes (see *Docetism*), disciples of Julian of Halicarnassus, maintained the incorruptibility of the human nature of Christ, the Severians attributed to it common infirmities and passibility (i.e., subjectivity to suffering). Themistius goes farther and attributes ignorance to Christ-Man. The question had come up, from the first centuries, about the text of Mark 13:32, in which Christ says that He is ignorant of the day of judgment. During the Arian controversy the followers of Arius used that text to deny the divinity of Christ: the Fathers responded that ignorance, if indeed there were any, was in the humanity, not in the divinity of the Word. The Latins, however, are in agreement in denying any ignorance in Christ.

St. Cyril of Alexandria defends the perfect knowledge of Christ-God against the Nestorians, who attributed all our defects to Christ-Man, including ignorance. However, he concedes that in His humanity there was a merely *apparent* ignorance. Better and more definitively, St. Augustine: Christ-Man knew the day of judgment but His mission of Master did not demand His revealing it to us. The error of Themistius was condemned by the Patriarch of Alexandria, Timotheus. St. Gregory the Great expounds clearly the Catholic doctrine in a "Letter to Eulogius," another patriarch of Alexandria, eliminating every true and proper ignorance from the humanity of Christ.

The Scholastics express this doctrine with the formula: Christ was ignorant of the day of judgment in the sense that He did not know it with knowledge communicable to men.

Some Protestants do not hesitate to attribute a certain ignorance to Christ (see *kenosis*); the rationalists and modernists go even further (see *science of Christ*).

BIBLIOGRAPHY

HUGON, *Le mystère de l'Incarnation* (Paris, 1931), p. 243. LEBRETON, *Histoire du dogme de la Trinité,* Vol. 1 (Paris, 1927), p. 581. MARIC, *De Agnoëtarum doctrina* (Zagreb, 1914).

agnosticism (from the Gr. ἀ [privative] γιγνώσκω — I do not know). The word was coined and used by Huxley in the *Spectator* in 1869, in England. Agnosticism is a system based on skepticism, which denies our capacity of knowing any truth.

In theology, agnosticism is applied to the existence of God or to His nature. A classical example of agnosticism is the doctrine of Moses Maimonides, a Jewish philosopher († 1204), who held that the attributes which we refer to God have no objective value and maintained that reason can know nothing about the divine essence. St. Thomas confutes him, demonstrating the value of our knowledge of God which, although inadequate, is however true analogically (see *analogy*). At an age closer to ours, agnosticism has been systematically affirmed in two broad philosophical currents: positivism and Kantianism (*q.v.*).

a) *Positivistic agnosticism* (Comte, Littré, Spencer): Starting from empiricism and sensism, it restricts the limits of human knowledge to the phenomenon and the experimental fact. It is not, therefore, so much concerned with the essence as with the existence of natural things. This is the only knowledge which has the character of evidence. On the contrary, the intimate nature of things and their first cause, namely God, is mysterious. Here is the zone of the *Unknowable,* object of religion. God and His marvels do not concern us and, therefore, it is better not to bother about these things (Littré) or we may admit them temporarily for a practical, moral, social motive (Spencer), pending scientific progress, which will be able to eliminate religion altogether.

b) *Kantian agnosticism:* The one objective reality for us is the phenomenon which makes an impression on our senses; the thing in itself (the noumenon) escapes us and reason replaces it by its forms or *a priori* categories, which are subjective. Much less can we arrive at God with reason, who transcends all Nature. I have the idea of God, but I cannot demonstrate His reality outside of myself (*Critique of Pure Reason*). But God can and should be affirmed by the will, as a necessary postulate (*Critique of Practical Reason*).

Modernism, adopting Kantian immanentism, adopts also its agnosticism.

BIBLIOGRAPHY

St. Thomas, *Summa Contra Gentiles,* l. 1, cc. 1–36. Chossat, "Agnosticisme," *DA.* Flint, *Agnosticism* (London, 1903). Garrigou-Lagrange, *The One God,* trans. Rose (St. Louis, 1943), pp. 306–381. Ladd, *Philosophy of Knowledge* (New York, 1897). Lucas, *Agnosticism and Religion* (Baltimore, 1895). Michelet, *Dieu et l'Agnosticisme contemporain* (Paris, 1920). Shanahan, "Agnosticism," *CE.* Ward, *Naturalism and Agnosticism* (London, 1903).

Albert the Great. See "Outline of the History of Dogmatic Theology" (p. 302).

Albigenses. Heretics, followers of the ancient Manichaeans (*q.v.*), who expanded considerably toward the end of the twelfth century (Languedoc) with their headquarters in *Albi,* whence they took their name. Actually they called themselves *Cathars* (Gr. *καθαρός* — pure) and were known in other countries of Europe also under other names: *Catharins, Patharins, Publicans, Bulgars,* etc. The Albigensian Cathars succeeded in gaining popularity and in organizing themselves in a way that threatened the Church and Catholic civilization.

Doctrine: They professed Manichaean *dualism* in order to explain evil. There are two principles: one good, creator of spirit and light; the other bad, creator of matter and darkness. The bad principle is the God of the Old Testament; the good principle is the God of the New Testament. The good God had created the angels, many of which sinned and were constrained to descend into bodies, becoming men. God (one, not triune), sends Jesus, one of His angels, to free spirit from matter (redemption of men). Jesus had an apparent body (Docetism), and neither suffered nor died nor rose again, but simply taught. The primitive Church has degenerated, beginning with Constantine; God dwells in the hearts of the faithful rather than in the Church. The spirits pass from one body to the other (metempsychosis) to purify themselves until complete expiation.

The Cathars, starting from the principle that matter is evil in itself, abhorred matrimony, riches, food, and sense pleasures. The faithful were placed in one of two categories: either that of the *perfect,* who obligated themselves, even by vow, to the rigorous practice of Cathar ethics and ascetics; or that of the *believers,* to whom much liberty was granted. The perfect was constituted in his high grade by means of the *consolamentum,* a kind of baptism consisting in the imposition of hands, and so assumed the mission of going and preaching the new religion. The faithful received the consolamentum in danger of death to insure salvation. There was also a kind of public confession, a blessing and breaking of bread, and a hierarchy of bishops and deacons. The more dangerous element of this heresy was the category of believers, the great mass whose only requirement was faith and the desire of the consolamentum in case of danger of death: for the rest they were granted complete freedom, which degenerated easily in unbridled license.

This heresy was not only a danger for the Church, but also for civil society. Innocent III, greatly worried about it, published the famous crusade against the Albigenses, which is justified fully from a moral and social standpoint, even if in some cases it shows dark spots and exaggerations. St. Dominic, mild and luminous soul, contributed by his preaching and his example to the conversion of the Albigenses to the Catholic faith, not to their destruction. About that time the *Inquisition* (*q.v.*) was inaugurated as a doctrinal proceeding against heretics. The sectarian spirit has falsified in many points the history of these events: but now many calumnies have been exposed by the calm study of the documents.

The Albigenses were condemned in their false doctrines by the IV Lateran Council (1215). Cf. *DB,* 428 ff.

BIBLIOGRAPHY

Dondaine, *Un traité néo-manichéen du XII siècle* (Rome, 1939), an interesting document, recently discovered. Mandonnet, *St. Dominic and His Work,* trans. Sr. M. B. Larkin (St. Louis). Schmidt, *Histoire et doctrine de la secte des Cathares ou Albigeois* (Paris, 1849). Tocco, *L'eresia nel medio evo* (Florence, 1884). Twigge, "Albi and the Albigensians," *Dublin Review,* 1894. Weber, "Albigenses," *CE.*

allegorism. A method of exegesis of Holy Scripture championed among the Hebrews by Philo of Alexandria († 42) and introduced into the Christian world by the teachers of the famous theological school of Alexandria in Egypt, founded in the second century. The greatest luminary of this school, Origen (186–254), codified the principles of allegorism. In conformity with the constitution of man, as conceived by the Platonic philosophy (body-soul-spirit), he distinguished in the texts of the Bible three senses: (1) *corporal* or *literal,* for the beginners; (2) *psychic* or *moral,* for the proficient; (3) *pneumatic* or *spiritual,* for the perfect. Not all the sacred texts, however, have all three senses; some lack the first.

Allegorism was justified with the following reasons: if the literal sense of the Bible were always held, absurdities or immoral actions would have to be admitted; Paul used the allegorical method for some texts of the Old Testament; material things — according to the Platonic theory — are figures of supersense realities. It was the need of apologetics that made Origen adopt allegorism, although he was outstanding in works of textual criticism. The Chiliadists, insisting on the literal sense of the Bible, maintained the reality of a millennial kingdom of all pleasures (see *millenarianism*); the Gnostics interpreted literally the texts which attributed to God a human aspect and quality; the *Jews* denied that Christ was the Messias, because He had not founded a kingdom of material and political prosperity according to the letter of the ancient prophecies. Exaggeration in the application of Origen's method led, however, to the pulverization of the Bible, to metaphysical fantasies which seriously endangered the value and solidarity of the texts.

The Antiochian school, founded at the end of the third century, fought against the Alexandrian school — represented by St. Athanasius († 373), Didymus the Blind († 398), and St. Cyril of Alexandria († 444). It insisted on the intelligently literal interpretation of the holy texts and developed the doctrine of the typical sense (see *senses of Scripture*) and the theory according to which the literal sense is at the base of a more profound and deeper penetration especially of the Messianic prophecies. The most celebrated representative of this current, which triumphed over allegorism, was St. John Chrysostom († 407). Recently the ancient allegorism has been favorably restored by P. Claudel, *Introduction au livre de Ruth,* Paris, 1938.

BIBLIOGRAPHY

Cadiou, *La jeunesse d'Origène* (Paris, 1936). Cayré, *Manual of Patrology,* trans. Howitt, Vol. 1 (Paris, Tournai, Rome, 1936), pp. 173, 185–188, 201–204. Höpfl-Gut, *Introductio generalis in S. Scripturam* (Rome, 1940), pp. 531–536. *Institutiones Biblicae,* Vol. 1 (Rome, 1937), pp. 469–476.

Americanism. Term popularized at the end of the past century in the movement and controversy arising from the ideas and methods of Father P. Hecker, founder of the American Society of Paulist Missionaries. Rather than a system, Americanism is a tendency based on certain principles of a practical nature which lack coherence. Leo XIII, aware of the danger, sent the apostolic letter "Testem Benevolentiae" to Cardinal Gibbons (1889) and through him to the episcopacy of the United States. In this pontifical document the principal errors of Americanism are brought out: necessity of the adaptation of the Church to the exigencies of modern civilization, through abrogation of some old canons, mitigation of ancient severity, orientation toward a more democratic method; more latitude for individual freedom of thought and action, since the Holy Spirit acts on the conscience of the individual more directly than the hierarchical organization (influence of Protestantism); abandonment or subduing of the *passive virtues* (mortification, penance, obedience, contemplation), and concentration on the *active virtues* (action, apostolate, organization); favoring the religious congregations of active life. The Pope, after this calm examination, concludes with these grave words: "We cannot approve these opinions which constitute the so-called Americanism."

Prescinding from the intentions of the "Americanists," certainly their doctrinal and practical position cannot be made to agree easily with the doctrine and traditional spirit of the Church. Rather, to put it mildly, it opens the way to theoretical and practical errors among which the preference attributed to activism calls for special mention, while Jesus Christ and His saints all gave more importance to prayer and the interior life, on which depends the success of every Christian apostolate.

BIBLIOGRAPHY

Coppinger, *La polémique française sur la vie du Père Hecker* (Paris, 1898). Delattre, *Un Catholicisme Américain* (Namur, 1898). Deshaves, "Américanisme," *DTC*. Elliott, *Life of Hecker* (New York, 1891). Hecker, *The Church and the Age* (New York, 1887). Holden, "A Mith in L'Américanisme," *Catholic Historical Review*, 31 (July, 1945), pp. 154–170. Lambertini, *L'Américanisme* (Paris, 1899). Leo XIII, Encyclical "Testem Benevolentiae," official English text, *The Catholic World*, 69 (April, 1899), pp. 133–139. Mc Avoy, "Americanism and Frontier Catholicism," *Review of Politics*, 5 (July, 1945), pp. 275–301; "Americanism, Fact and Fiction," *Catholic Historical Review*, 31 (July, 1945), pp. 133–153; "The Formation of the Catholic Minority in the United States," *Review of Politics*, 10 (Jan., 1948), pp. 13–34. Maignen, *Etudes sur l'Américanisme, Le Père Hecker est-il un saint?* (Rome-Paris, 1898). O'Connell, *A New Idea in the Life of Father Hecker* (Fribourg, 1897). Pallen, "Testem Benevolentiae," *CE*.

Anabaptists (or Rebaptizers). Followers of a fanatic sect who rebaptized adults in the belief that baptism conferred on infants was invalid. This was the logical consequence of the Lutheran principle, according to which *faith alone justifies:* infants are not capable of an act of faith, and consequently their baptism is invalid. The movement, begun at Zwikau, in Saxony, in 1521–1522 by Nicholas Storch and Thomas Münzer, spread rapidly in southern Germany, and acquired adherents especially among the lower classes (artisans and peasants). Two currents quickly formed within the movement, the one pacific and the other revolutionary; this last got the upper hand and involved the sect in an iconoclastic struggle which brought destruction and desolation to many provinces (churches destroyed, priests killed, goods confiscated, etc.), and which provoked a fierce repression (the peasants' war).

The inspiring idea of the sect was the establishment of God's kingdom in individual souls by direct divine influence. The individual joins the Communion of Saints independently of any external form (and so, abrogation of ecclesiastical and civil authority, of the priesthood, the sacraments, the Bible, and so forth), by mere collaboration of the individual with the impulses of the Holy Spirit (they admitted, therefore, the efficacy of good works).

The Anabaptist system, therefore, has nothing in common with Lutheranism except the starting point (only faith justifies), which was applied rigidly to the baptism of infants, but was at once softened by admitting the value of good works. After its political reverses, Anabaptism lost its revolutionary character and became organized on purely religious principles (Mennonites of Frisia). Since the most vital part of their doctrine has been absorbed by the Baptists, the Anabaptists today consist of small, scattered groups in Germany, England, and the United States.

BIBLIOGRAPHY

Bax, *Rise and Fall of the Anabaptists* (London, 1903). Bernard, "Anabaptistes," *DHGE*. Newman, *A History of Anti-Pedobaptism from the Rise of Pedobaptism to A.D. 1609* (Philadelphia, 1897); *A History of the Baptist Churches in the United States* (New York, 1894) (in *Amer. Church Hist.*, Series II, 1–56). Weber, "Anabaptists," *CE*.

analogy (Gr. ἀνάλογος — similar, proportionate, relative to another). A relationship between two things, either because of likeness or causal dependence. Analogy is the basis and soul of all human language: man always reasons and knows by way of comparison, because the natural tendency of the intellect to unity inclines it to discover the connections and relations among different things in order to conquer their multiplicity.

Aristotle perceived the importance of analogy and fixed its fundamental laws (cf. *VII Physic.*, c. IV; *Poster. Anal. II*, cc. XIII and XIV; *Ethic. ad Nic.*, I, c. 6; *Metaphysic.*, b. IV, c. 1; b. X, c. 1; b. XII, c. 4). St. Thomas devoted much study to analogy in order to defend the value of our knowledge of divine things against the agnostic current of Jewish medieval philosophy (Rabbi Moses Maimonides). According to St. Thomas, the supposition made that God is the cause of the world, there must be a relation of *likeness* between one and the other, which swings between a minimum and a maximum of similarity, in such a way, however, that the creature is not so similar to God as to attain formal identity (*univocity*) nor so dissimilar as to be altogether extraneous (*equivocity*). This relationship of likeness between Creator and creature is called analogy of *attribution* when it consists in the simple relationship of effect to its proper cause (e.g., Matter and God), without any intrinsic reason of likeness. If, on the other hand, that relationship, in addition to causal subordination, includes also a formal likeness between the creature and God, then it is called analogy of *proportionality*.

On the basis of this latter kind of analogy, a created perfection, e.g., goodness, can be attributed to God and to man under the same *formal concept,* not in the same way, because man participates in the divine goodness imperfectly, while God is goodness itself. In every case, created perfections must be purged of every imperfection before being attributed to God. In this way we form the many concepts of God according to the perfections of His creatures. These concepts, although not expressing the divinity adequately, are not false, because just as only one perfect principle responds to the multiple created perfections which represent it imperfectly, so to the diverse concepts, which we get from things, there responds only one supreme idea imperfectly expressed.

The analogical process is realized in three phases: (1) affirmation — God is good (because creatures are good); (2) negation — God is not good (in the way creatures are good); (3) eminence — God is goodness itself (in a transcendent way). Analogy works even in the field of revelation, where incomprehensible mysteries are expressed in analogical formulas taken from common language (*natural analogy*); in addition, there is *supernatural analogy* or the *analogy of faith,* consisting in comparing the mysteries among themselves to understand them better, as the Vatican Council states, Sess. III, Ch. 4 (*DB,* 1796).

BIBLIOGRAPHY

St. Thomas, *Summa Theol.*, I, q. 13. Peter Parente, "Quid re valeat humana de Deo cognitio secundum S. Thomam," *Acta Pont. Acad. Romanae S. Thomae Aq.* (1935). Penido, *Le rôle de l'analogie en théologie dogmatique* (Paris, 1931).

Anaphora. See *Canon of the Mass.*

anathema (Gr. ἀνάθεμα). In the proper sense it meant something vowed to God, votive offerings (*ex-voto*) hung in the temples, from ἀνατίθημι — I put on, I hang (cf. Jud. 16:19; 2 Mac. 9:16; Luke 21:5). But in the Septuagint the word *anathema* generally translates the Hebrew חרם, meaning a thing or person destined to destruction by God. In the New Testament it conserves the Hebrew meaning with a slightly distinct nuance: thing or person struck by God's malediction and intended for ruin (cf. 1 Cor. 12:3; 16:22; Rom. 9:3; Gal. 1:8–9).

In ecclesiastical language, it appears for the first time in the Council of Helvira (305) with a not-well-defined meaning. Later in the canons of Laodicea and of Chalcedon, anathema adds to excommunication the idea of a special curse which aggravates the penalty of separation from the Church. In the *Decretales* anathema corresponds to major excommunication, fulminated in the most solemn manner. In current discipline, it is no more than excommunication inflicted with those external solemnities contained in the Pontificale Romanum (cf. *CIC,* can. 2257). Anathema, in actual Church discipline, is the term also used for *ipso facto* excommunication incurred by those denying a solemnly defined truth, as is concluded principally from the dogmatic canons of the Council of Trent and the Vatican Council: "If anyone denies [this truth] . . . let him be anathema," i.e., excommunicated.

BIBLIOGRAPHY

AMANIEU, "Anathème," *DDC.* GIGNAC, "Anathema," *CE.* VACANT, "Anathème," *DTC.* VIGOUROUX, "Anathème," *DBV.*

angel (Gr. ἄγγελος — messenger; Hebr. מַלְאָךְ — mal' âk). In Holy Scripture it signifies *messenger* or *minister of God.* St. Gregory the Great notes that nearly every page of written revelation attests to the existence of the angels: suffice it to recall in the Old Testament the Cherubim placed to guard the earthly paradise after the fall of Adam and Eve, the three angels who appeared to Abraham, the Seraphim of which Isaias speaks, the Angel Raphael who helped Tobias, Michael and Gabriel recalled by Daniel, and reappearing in the New Testament, in which testimonies are more numerous (cf. the Apocalypse, the Gospels in the story of the birth of Jesus, and the Resurrection; St. Paul enumerates various classes of angels).

The IV Lateran Council speaks explicitly of the creation of the angels (*DB,* 428), which is therefore a truth of faith. Creation *ab aeterno* is excluded (IV Lat. Council and Vatican Council say *ab initio temporis*); it is not known precisely when the angels were created. Scripture and Tradition speak of a boundless number. The angels are *pure spirits;* such, in fact, Holy Scripture calls them constantly, although a few Fathers have attributed some kind of corporal nature to them. As spirits the angels do not need a material place to exist, but may be present in a material place by way of *action* (St. Thomas).

From the Scripture it is known that the angels are distributed in nine groups: Thrones, Dominations, Principalities, Powers, Virtues, Archangels, Angels, Cherubim, and Seraphim (names corresponding to various functions).

According to the more probable opinion (St. Thomas), the angels are not individuals of the same species, as man is, but every individual angel constitutes a species (because of the absence of matter which individualizes and multiplies forms numerically). The angels were all created in the state of sanctifying grace (they are, in fact, called saints, friends of God); but not all persevered in grace. Many of them committed, immediately after creation, a sin of pride, abusing their freedom (Lateran Council, *DB,* 428). Revelation speaks several times of the sin of the angels: "God spared not the Angels that sinned" (2 Pet. 2:4; cf. 1 John 3:8). They were punished immediately and cast into hell: Christ attests He saw Satan being hurled down like a lightning bolt (Luke 10:18).

St. Thomas comments that the angel, understanding as by intuition, adheres unchangeably, once free choice is made, to good or to evil: therefore, the angels did not have and will not have any way to repent, differently from men, who understand by reasoning progressively.

As the good angels assist and help men for their good and salvation, so the demons (*q.v.*) entice to evil with temptation and can invade the body by *obsession,* by which the body becomes a sort of instrument of the evil spirit.

BIBLIOGRAPHY

St. Thomas, *Summa Theol.,* I, qq. 50–64. Arrighini, *Gli Angeli* (Turin, 1937). Bareille, "Le culte des Anges à l'époque des Pères de l'Eglise," *Revue Thomiste* (March, 1900). Boyer, *De Deo creante et elevante* (Rome, 1940), p. 457 ff. Pope, "Angel," *CE. The Teaching of the Catholic Church,* ed. Smith, 2 vols. (New York, 1949), pp. 248–285.

Anglicanism. Predominant form of English Protestantism which, because of its conservative character, has kept itself closer to Catholicism and more resistant to the dissolving currents of modern thought. The Anglican Church had a painful origin. King Henry VIII (1509–1547), once greeted by the pope as *Defensor Fidei* because of his love for religion and a theological writing against Luther, allowed himself to be carried away by license and the thirst for gold to the consummation of his own apostasy and that of his kingdom. Lawfully married to Catherine of Aragon, he became infatuated with the courtesan Anne Boleyn. With the connivance of Thomas Cranmer (a supporter of Lutheranism), appointed Archbishop of Canterbury, Henry determined to marry Anne at any cost. Pope Clement VII threatened the sovereign with excommunication. Henry took revenge by severing from Rome and having himself proclaimed the religious head of the Church of England. The life of Henry VIII is sullied with immorality and dark crimes: he put Anne Boleyn to death and married successively four women, killing each in turn. He persecuted the Catholics in the realm and confiscated their churches and monasteries. But, notwithstanding the pleas of Cranmer and others, Henry refused openly to embrace Protestantism; rather, with his famous *6 articles,* he maintained the chief tenets of Catholic doctrine and cult, except dependence on the Holy See.

Protestantism, however, spread in England in the six years of the reign of Edward VI, still a child († 1553). Mary, a Catholic who succeeded Edward VI, tried to counter this great evil with perhaps too violent a repression. Elizabeth, daughter of Anne Boleyn, succeeded Mary and rekindled her father's persecution against the Catholics, favoring the Protestant current by adopting 39 of the 42 articles of Cranmer and making the hierarchy a docile instrument of the royalty. Pius V excommunicated her (1570). Elizabeth may be called the real foundress of the *Anglican Church* which, however, soon began to undergo crises and schisms (*Puritans,* supporters of pure Calvinism; *Presbyterians,* priests adverse to the episcopacy; *Congregationalists,* democrats who wanted independence and autonomy for every religious community or congregation; *Baptists,* etc.).

Deism and Illuminism (*qq.v.*) dried up in great part the supernatural life of the Anglican Church which, under the action of internal ferment and the external influences of the various Protestant sects, developed into three different tendencies, which are called the three churches: (1) *High Church,* conservative with its episcopal hierarchy and sacramental-liturgical organism; (2) *Broad Church,* liberal, open to the currents of independent lay thought; (3) *Low*

Church, left wing, more anti-Roman, dedicated especially to the evangelical movement. In the High Church there developed during the past century the so-called Tractarianism (Tracts), soul of the Oxford Movement, headed by Pusey, Keble, and Newman. The last became a convert to Catholicism, and a cardinal. This movement contributed to clarify the position of Anglicanism, orientating it progressively more and more toward Catholicism. In 1896, however, Anglicanism was struck in its episcopal hierarchy by Leo XIII, who declared their ordinations invalid by reason of the interruption in the succession of its bishops. However, among the Protestant Churches the Anglican seems most suitable to serve as a bridge for a return to Rome (see *Protestantism*).

BIBLIOGRAPHY

D'ALÈS, "Réforme (IX. Anglicanisme moderne)," *DA,* cols. 702–733. BISHOP, *Edward VI and the Book of Common Prayer* (London, 1891). CHURCH, *The Oxford Movement* (London-New York, 1891). COOLEN, *L'Anglicanisme d'aujourd'hui* (Paris, 1932). JOHNSON, *Anglicanism in Transition* (London, 1938). MARCHAL, "Puséyisme," *DTC.* MOYES, "Anglicanism," *CE.* RUST, *The First of the Puritans and the Book of Common Prayer* (Milwaukee, 1949). TRÉSAL, "Réforme (VI. La Réforme en Angleterre)," *DA,* cols. 647–675; *Les origines du schisme Anglican* (Paris, 1908).

Anglican orders. The title of the ordinations performed in the schismatic Anglican Church according to the Edwardian rite, or the *Ordinal* promulgated by Edward VI in 1550, at Cranmer's instigation. The imposition of hands being retained, the form of ordination is reduced to these words: Receive the Holy Spirit. The sins that you will remit, shall be remitted, those that you will retain, shall be retained. Be a faithful dispenser of the word of God and of His holy sacraments.

After mature historical and theological investigation, Leo XIII in the bull, *Apostolicae Curae,* solemnly declared these ordinations to be invalid (*irritae prorsus omninoque nullae, DB,* 1866). The reasons on which the Pontiff bases his statement are both the lack of due form and of intention on the part of the minister, and the preceding declaration of Paul IV.

In fact, the form studiously omits any word that might indicate power of offering the sacrifice, which is the chief power conferred by the sacrament of orders (see *orders, holy; matter and form*). From this *illegitimate* change of the form one may logically conclude the lack of intention on the part of the minister, since whoever changes voluntarily a rite established by Christ in the conferring of a sacrament, shows that he does not wish to do what Christ instituted and what the Church faithfully repeats (see *intention*).

Besides, it is historically certain that the authors of the Edwardian rite wanted to exclude absolutely all reference to the Mass; therefore, their intention was diametrically opposed to that of Christ who instituted holy orders for the principal purpose of renewing the Eucharistic sacrifice.

Already in 1555, Paul IV, in the bull, *Praeclara carissimi,* and the brief, *Regimini universalis,* had declared null the orders conferred according to Edward's *Ordinal* — a declaration which traced the guidelines constantly followed by his successors.

Thus, since the entire Anglican hierarchy descends from Matthew Parker, who was consecrated bishop according to the Edwardian rite, it is absolutely devoid of holy orders and of the character annexed thereto.

BIBLIOGRAPHY

BARNES, *The Pope and the Ordinal* (1898). BRANDI, *Le ordinazioni anglicane* (Rome, 1908). GASPARRI, *De la valeur des Ordinations Anglicanes* (Paris, 1895). MARCHAL, "Ordinations Anglicanes," *DTC.* SMITH, *Anglican Orders* (London, 1896). SYDNEY, "Ordination," *DA.*

animism. A theory formulated by Ed. B. Tylor in the past century to explain the origin of religion. Like Spencer, Tylor starts from the premise of *evolutionism* (*q.v.*) then in vogue and maintains that man evolved from the animals. Through consideration of the phenomena of sleep and dreams, sickness and death, Tylor comes to discover in himself a vital principle distinct from the body, that is the soul, to which he attributed a kind of survival. Hence, the cult of ancestors (*manism*), whose spirits are said often to become incarnate in other bodies (*metempsychosis*). Primitive man, once in possession of the concept of soul, by an anthropomorphic tendency projected his own image on Nature, and saw in everything a body animated by the spirit. Thus began animism, which led to the cult of the forces of Nature and consequently to polytheism. By means of animism Tylor explains also the origin of fetishism and idolatry (*qq.v.*); the fetish is any object chosen by a spirit for its habitation; reduced to the figure or representation of a superior spirit, the fetish becomes an idol, by identification of the symbol with the symbolized being. Idolatry, thus, is said to derive also from animism. Later on, by selection and by giving prominence to one of the gods (idols), it is claimed that monotheism gained acceptance.

Tylor's theory, in the beginning, was hailed enthusiastically but quickly met with failure. Eminent scholars have pointed out the flaws and inconsistencies of the animistic structure. Its foundation especially, evolutionism, is anything but solid. Moreover, it is not true that religion follows on animism; in many primitive peoples it precedes animism. Nor is it true, as Tylor would have it, that animism was universal and uniform: it is but one of the phenomena found here and there in the history of human culture. But what checkmates the whole theory is the proved fact that monotheism, as cult of the *Great Being,* is found in primitive peoples before animism and polytheism, which seem rather religious degenerations.

BIBLIOGRAPHY

ALGER, *Critical History of the Doctrine of a Future Life* (Philadelphia, 1864). BRINTON, *Religions of Primitive Peoples* (New York, 1897). BUGUICOURT, "Animisme," *DA.* DRISCOLL, "Animism," *CE.* HEINZELMANN, *Animismus und Religion* (Gütersloh, 1913). MÜLLER, *Lectures on the Origin of Religion* (London, 1878). PASCHER, *Der Seelenbegriff des Animismus E. B. Tylor* (Würzburg, 1929). TYLOR, *Primitive Culture* (London, 1891).

Anomoeanism (Gr. ἀνόμοιος — dissimilar). A sect founded by Aëtius and Eunomius (*Eunomians*) in the second half of the fourth century. They adhered to Arianism (*q.v.*), maintaining that the Word is dissimilar to the Father, in so far as it is *generated,* and therefore is not God like the Father, since the true divinity is without beginning and so not generated (ἀγέννητος). Anomoeanism, especially as presented by Eunomius, has interesting aspects also as regards other sectors of theology, beside the Trinitarian.

Eunomius, speaking of the attributes of God, denies their value, reducing them all to mere anthropomorphic names (*nominalism*); only one attribute has real value, namely the attribute of ἀγεννησία (ingenerability), which reveals to our mind the divine essence in an adequate manner, as by intuition (a prelude of *ontologism*).

St. Basil and St. Gregory of Nyssa confuted the errors of the Eunomians both in the theological and in the philosophical fields.

BIBLIOGRAPHY

LE BACHELET, "Aëtius," *DTC;* "Eunomius," *DTC.* PETER PARENTE, *De Deo Uno* (Rome, 1938), p. 78. TIXERONT, *History of Dogmas,* trans. H.L.B., Vol. 2 (St. Louis, 1910), p. 49 f.

Anselm. See "Outline of the History of Dogmatic Theology" (p. 302); *innocence; satisfaction of Christ.*

anthropomorphism (Gr. ἄνθρωπος— man and μορφή — form). The tendency of man to consider external things as if they were an imitation of himself. In *philosophy* anthropomorphism leads to extravagant conceptions, like the panpsychism of Thomas Campanella with its soul for all created things, or the cosmic sensism of Bernardine Telesio with its universal sensation, which recalls the hylozoism (living matter) of the pre-Socratics. In *religion,* we find an anthropomorphistic expression in animism (*q.v.*), kindred to these philosophical aberrations, and which is held by some authors as the origin of religion. Anthropomorphism is even more manifest in the concept of a divinity, formed to man's likeness with his vices and virtues. The religious mythologies are generally anthropomorphic; suffice it to mention the Greco-Roman mythology. In Christian revelation anthropomorphism is found in the language and in certain episodes of the Old Testament, which attribute to God human members and at times human ways of acting (as when it speaks of God repenting, suffering, etc.). Evidently here it is a matter of metaphorical speech and style, as is proved from the context of the holy books and the sublime concepts they suggest about the nature of God (see *essence, divine*). The so-called *theophanies* (apparitions of God) in the Old Testament have special theological interest, as the one made to Moses from the burning bush. Some Fathers think they were personal manifestations of the *Word* (*q.v.;* see *Logos*); more correctly, the theophanies were sensible *signs* of the divine presence, by which the Word appeared as a man in the midst of men.

In the history of Christian thought there is mention of the gross error of the so-called *anthropomorphites* who, following in the steps of a certain *Audius,* in the fourth century, spread the opinion in Syria and Egypt that the biblical metaphors about God are to be understood in the literal and proper sense. St. Augustine and other Fathers speak of this error as childish and unworthy of refutation.

BIBLIOGRAPHY

Bareille, "Anthropomorphites," *DTC.* Chollet, "Anthropomorphisme," *DTC.* Flint, *Theism* (New York, 1903). Fox, "Anthropomorphism," *CE.* Vigouroux, "Anthropomorphisme," *DBV.*

Antichrist (Gr. ἀντί — χριστός — adversary of Christ). The term is John's but the concept is common also to other biblical authors (cf. Ezech.. Chs. 28–29; Dan., Chs. 7–8; Matt. 24:5, 24; Mark 13:6, 22; Luke 21:8; 2 Thess. 2:3–12; 1 John 2:18–22; 4:3; 2 John 7; Apoc. 11:7 ff.; Chs. 13–14).

The Antichrist is, in general, a force hostile to the person and work of Christ. The common interpretation of the Christian writers sees in the Antichrist a person distinct from Satan but sustained by him, who will manifest himself in the last days, before the end of the world, to attempt a decisive attack on and triumph over Jesus and His Church. Paul describes him as "the man of sin . . . the son of perdition, who opposeth and is lifted up above all that is called God, or that is worshipped, so that he sitteth in the temple of God, shewing himself as if he were God. . . . Whose coming is according to the working of Satan, in all power, and signs, and lying wonders, and in all seduction of iniquity to them that perish; because they receive not the love of the truth, that they might be saved" (2 Thess. 2:3–4, 9–10).

What thwarts the unleashing of this formidable power is a mysterious obstacle which is at the same time considered in the abstract as a force, or in the concrete as a person. The precise identification is difficult and varies among scholars. Among modern exegetes the opinion according to which the Antichrist is not a person, but a collectivity, is gaining ground: the Antichrist signifies the agents of anti-Christianity in all times. St. John speaks of "many Antichrists" who recognized neither Jesus nor the Father. St. Paul says that the mystery of iniquity is already at work; only now someone is holding him back, until he is removed (2 Thess. 2:7). If the obstacle is always in action and is already fighting the Antichrist, this means the Antichrist too must be in existence continually. But it may be noted that the obstacle impedes the *manifestation* of the Antichrist, not his *personal* work. The Antichrist will reveal himself in the last phase of the anti-Christian struggle which rages in all times and is slowly preparing the apparition of the "son of perdition" at the end of time.

BIBLIOGRAPHY

ALLO, *L'Apocalypse* (Paris, 1933). BUZY, "Antéchrist," *DBVS*, cols. 297–305. JOWETT, *Excursus on the Man of Sin, in Epistles of St. Paul* (London, 1859). MAAS, "Antichrist," *CE*. NEWMAN, "The Patristic Idea of Antichrist," No. 83 of *Tracts for the Times*, republished in *Discussions and Arguments on Various Subjects* (London, New York, Bombay, 1897); *The Protestant Idea of Antichrist, in Essays Critical and Historical* (*ibid.*, 1897). PRAT, *The Theology of St. Paul*, trans. Stoddard, Vol. 1 (Westminster, 1926). RATTON, *Antichrist: An Historical Review* (London, 1917). RIGAUX, *L'Antéchrist et l'opposition au royaume messianique dans l'A. et le N.T.* (Gembloux, 1932). TONDELLI, *Gesù Cristo* (Turin, 1936), pp. 388–402. WORDSWORTH, *On the Apocalypse* (London, 1849).

Antidicomarians (Gr. ἀντίδικος — litigator, and Mary). A religious sect sprung up in Arabia in the fourth century, which denied Mary's virginity, abusing certain texts of Holy Scripture (see *virginity of Mary*). St. Epiphanius wrote them a letter confuting their doctrine point by point. Later on all adversaries of the virginity of Mary came to be called Antidicomarians or simply Antimarians.

BIBLIOGRAPHY

QUILLIET, "Antidicomarianites," *DTC*. See under *virginity of Mary*.

antitype. See *senses of Scripture*.

Aphthartodocetism. See *Docetism*.

Apocrypha (Gr. ἀπόκρυφον — hidden thing, from the verb ἀποκρύπτω — I hide). For the ancients, *apocryph* was a book containing religious doctrines reserved for the initiated; in Church language, on the contrary, it was a book not admitted to public reading in the community, notwithstanding the similarity it presented with the inspired books of the Bible by reason of the name of its presumed author and of its contents. An apocryph, therefore, is a book to be excluded in so far as it is noncanonical (see *Canon of the Bible*). Such books were of suspect origin and circulated by sects endeavoring to give an authoritative foundation to their teachings. Certain of them, however, are the results of the pious curiosity of readers who failed to find in the sacred books enough minute details on the persons and episodes of sacred history, wishing to complete them with material which very rarely was from a good source but usually was the product of sheer fantasy. Some of these books written in good faith found credence among the faithful and the ecclesiastical writers.

In the current official Latin edition of the Bible the *III and IV Books of Esdras* and the *Prayer of King Manasses*, based on canonical texts, are inserted as an appendix. Certain liturgical texts, e.g., the *Requiem* (4 Esd. 2:34 f.) were derived from the afore-mentioned two books. Modern scholars give particular attention to this considerable literary production which is of interest for the knowledge of the religious and moral ideas current in the times of Christ.

The vast apocryphal literature, of difficult access to ordinary readers, follows the major and minor divisions of both Testaments.

The Old Testament Apocrypha, nearly always by Jewish authors, have a Messianic theme and have at times undergone Christian interpolations.

Some, like *Solomon's Odes,* seem entirely Christian in origin. They may be distinguished, although inadequately, in *historical* (dedicated to the great Old Testament figures), *didactic* (of ethical content), and *prophetic* or *apocalyptic* (containing presumed revelations about the angels, the mysteries of nature, the future sort of Israel, and the person and reign of the Messias). *The Book of Jubilees* or Little Genesis is noteworthy among the Apocrypha of the first kind; written by a moderate Pharisee toward the end of the second century B.C., it narrates the story of the world from creation to the exodus from Egypt, distributing it in jubilary periods of 49 years. Others are: *III Esdras, III Machabees, Ascension of Isaias,* and *Testament of Solomon.* Among the didactic books are to be noted: the *Testament of the Patriarchs,* in which Jacob's sons prophesy the coming of the Twelve Tribes descending from them; the *Psalms of Solomon and of David;* the *Odes of Solomon;* the *IV Book of the Machabees.* Among the prophetic books, the *Book of Henoch,* to which the Apostle Jude probably refers in his Letter (5:14 f.), is well known. It is made up of various Jewish writings of the first and second centuries B.C., and is important for the knowledge of the first religious ideas of the Jewish contemporaries of Jesus. In it the Messias is called "Son of Man." Other books of this same class are: the *Assumption of Moses, IV Esdras,* the *Apocalypse of Baruch,* and the *Sibylline Oracles* (a book of Jewish propaganda among the pagans).

The New Testament Apocrypha go back to the second and third centuries A.D., and are divided into *Gospels, Acts, Epistles,* and *Apocalypses.* The *Protoevangelium of James* is the most diffused of the gospels; it relates the life of Mary and Joseph and the childhood of Jesus; it influenced Christian art very extensively, and liturgy drew from it the Feast of the Presentation of Mary in the Temple. Other gospels are: *According to the Hebrews; of the Ebionites; According to the Egyptians; of Peter; of Thomas; of Nicodemus.* Among the *Acts* of the Apostles we may recall those *of Peter; of Paul; of John; of Andrew; of Thomas.* The apocryphal *epistolary* is also very rich, and includes the *Letter of Abgarus, King of Edessa* to Jesus and the reply of the Redeemer; the *Epistle of the Apostles;* the *Epistle of St. Paul to the Laodiceans;* his *III Letter to the Corinthians;* the letters exchanged between St. Paul and Seneca, the philosopher. Among the *apocalypses* we may cite the *Apocalypse of Paul; of Peter; of Thomas.* In general, the apocryphal literature is mediocre and jumbled. It betrays imitation of its inspired models without catching, however, their spontaneity and balanced moderation.

BIBLIOGRAPHY

Amann, "Apocryphes du Nouveau Testament," *DBVS,* cols. 460–533. Cayré, *Manual of Patrology,* trans. Howitt, Vol. 1 (Paris, Tournai, Rome, 1936), pp. 156–165. Frey, "Apocryphes de l'Ancient Testament," *DBVS,* cols. 354–460. Reid, "Apocrypha," *CE.*

Apollinarianism. Christological error of Apollinaris, Bishop of Laodicea (*c.* 350), which opens the way to Monophysitism (*q.v.*). Apollinaris started out in the struggle against Arianism by maintaining that Christ was really God incarnate (θεὸς ἔνσαρκος), i.e., the Word, Son of God, united to the human nature. But the better to defend the union between the divine and the human elements, he suggests the concept of a human nature consisting only of flesh and a sensitive soul with the Word performing in that nature the function of the intellective soul (νοῦς). This is the best-known and most diffused form of Apollinarianism which, however, was expressed in other fashions by various of its followers. Apollinaris spread his error even under the name of St. Athanasius — who had always been very kind to him — by fraudulent writings in one of which he placed the famous expression: μία φύσις τοῦ Λόγου σεσαρκωμένη (the incarnate nature of the Word is one). This formula was afterward adopted by St. Cyril as if it were really of Athanasius, and was used as a weapon by the Monophysites, who appealed to St. Cyril's authority (see *Eutychianism*).

Apollinaris was deposed and his error condemned in 377 and 382 by Pope St. Damasus (cf. *DB,* 65).

BIBLIOGRAPHY

D'Alès, *Le dogme d'Ephèse* (Paris, 1931), pp. 25–62. Rainy, *The Ancient Catholic Church* (New York, 1902). Sollier, "Apollinarianism," *CE.* Voisin, *L'Apollinarisme* (Louvain, 1901).

apologetics (Gr. ἀπολογητική — defense). The rational demonstration and defense of the truth of the Christian faith. By reason of its universality, it is distinct from *apologia* (apology), which is the defense of a particular truth. More closely, the proper object of apologetics is the *rational credibility* of the true religion, and hence the demonstration of the *fact of divine revelation* through Jesus Christ, God's Legate, who entrusted that revelation to His Church.

Apologetics thus has a *philosophical* part (the existence of a personal God, the ideas of religion and revelation, the necessity of revelation, and its discernibility by means of the miracle); and a *historical* part (Jesus Christ, divine Legate, historical value of the Gospels, foundation of the Church). Apologetics treats all this in the light of reason in order to dispose the mind for the divine gift of faith through the rational demonstration of the motives of credibility. According to the expression of the Vatican Council (Sess. 3, Ch. 4, *DB,* 1799), "right reason demonstrates the foundations of faith." Apologetics, therefore, is distinct from theology (*q.v.*), which proceeds in the realm and the light of faith.

Its *method* is twofold, one rather *extrinsic,* or the *philosophico-historical* approach, and the other rather *intrinsic,* the *psychological* approach. The former is the traditional method which was developed systematically in Scholasticism from the philosophical viewpoint, and in modern theology (from the seventeenth century) from the critico-historical viewpoint. In the past century, however, the psychological method was developed under the influence of the French Oratorian Fathers (Ollé-Laprune and Fonsegrive). It acquired a new form in the works of Blondel, who introduced the method of *immanence* (consideration of man in his intimate tendency to act, to accomplish, and to achieve, and in his inability to attain his ideal end; facts that necessarily involve an *appeal* or call for a superior help, and a real need, which only Christianity is able to satisfy). The two methods are not self-exclusive but, on the contrary, mutually integrative and complementary.

BIBLIOGRAPHY

Aiken, "Apologetics," *CE.* Devivier-Sasia, *Christian Apologetics* (San José, Calif., 1903). De Tonquedec, "Méthode d'immanence," *DA.* Fenton, *We Stand With Christ* (Milwaukee, 1942), pp. 1–9. Gardeil, *La crédibilité et l'apologétique* (Paris, 1908). Le Bachelet, "Apologétique," *DA.* Monti, *Apologetica scientifica* (Turin, 1923).

apologists. See "Outline of the History of Dogmatic Theology" (p. 301), *subordinationists.*

apostasy. See *infidels.*

Apostles. See *members of the Church.*

apostolicity (mark of the Church). The fourth and last characterizing mark or property which the Nicene-Constantinople Creed attributes to the true Church of Christ. Like the other three marks of the Church, it issues from the intimate nature of the Church itself. Since the Church is humanity organized socially in Christ, that is, hierarchically in Peter and the "college" of the Twelve, apostolicity is the backbone of its constitution, the guarantee of its continuity, and the condition of its fruitfulness.

Holy Scripture attests that Christ established His Church on the rock of Peter and the foundation of the Apostles (Matt. 16:18–19; Eph. 2:20; Apoc. 21:14), and the history of the nascent Church, narrated in the Acts, shows us the Apostles at work, preaching a doctrine transmitted by the Master, applying the means of salvation instituted by Him, and exercising the authority derived from Him. They then appoint successors for themselves with the same aims and purposes of teaching, sanctifying, and governing. Apostolicity implies, therefore, a *legitimate* continuity of succession to the chair occupied by Peter and the apostolic "college," with the keeping of the same doctrine, of the same sacraments, and the same authority. We may imagine it as the uninterrupted relay of the popes (successors of Peter) and of the bishops (successors of the Apostles), transmitting each to the next one, throughout the ages, the torch of the same faith, the chalice of the same blood of Christ, the pastoral rod of the same authority. "Like the first branches of a tree do not die, but renew themselves and extend themselves, spreading their vital force into the new part, so it is in the Church through the succession of the pastors (bishops). In it, the episcopacy renews itself from time to time, but only by diffusion and prolongation of the apostolic life. The apostolicity of the Church is not for us, therefore, a remote or a passing fact, but something ever present, because today too the life of the Church comes from Christ into the Apostles, from the Apostles into their legitimate successors, and from them into us" (*Card. Capecelatro*).

A distinction is made between *formal* apostolicity, described above, and *material* apostolicity. This last means apostolic origin but with a lack of legitimate continuity, in so far as it is separated from Peter living in the Roman pontiff, to whom the bishops are subject just as the Apostles in their time were to Peter. The schismatic Oriental Church, styled the "orthodox" church, has only material apostolicity.

BIBLIOGRAPHY

St. Thomas, *In Symbolum Apostolorum expositio,* a. 7–8. Journet, *L'Eglise du Verbe Incarné:* I. "La hiérachie apostolique" (Paris, 1943). MacLaughlin, *The Divine Plan of the Church* (London, 1901). Milner, *The End of Religious Controversy* (London, 1818). Moore, *Travels of an Irish Gentleman in Search of a Religion* (London, 1833). O'Reilly, "Apostolicity," *CE.* Smarius, *Points of Controversy* (New York, 1865). Vellico, *De Ecclesia* (Rome, 1940), p. 512 ff.

appropriation. The attribution which we make of a thing or action to one or another of the three divine Persons, according to our way of thinking, but not without foundation in reality. The foundation is a certain *affinity* between the thing or action attributed and the Person to whom it is attributed. Absolutely and strictly speaking, however, every action or effect *ad extra* (see *operation, divine*) is common to all three Persons. The *ad intra* actions, indeed, are proper and individual (see *notions, divine*), like "generating," "saying the Word," etc. In general, all that is connected with *beginning* is customarily attributed to the Father, like creation and omnipotence; what is related to *intellect,* to the Son, like wisdom and light; to the Holy Spirit, all that refers to *love,* like goodness and holiness (see *indwelling of the Holy Trinity*).

BIBLIOGRAPHY

St. Thomas, *Summa Theol.,* I, q. 39, a. 7–8. De Regnon, *Etudes de théologie positive sur la Sainte Trinité* (Paris, 1898). Sauvage, "Appropriation," *CE.* Scheeben, *The Mysteries of Christianity,* trans. Vollert (St. Louis, 1946), pp. 132–136, 190–197. Vacant, "Appropriation aux Personnes," *DTC.*

"a priori," "a posteriori." These two classical expressions of Scholastic philosophy are generally used to qualify rational knowledge in its syllogistic or demonstrative form. For the Scholastics these expressions have a determined, fundamental meaning: *a priori* means a *deductive* process of reasoning, in which one goes from the cause (*prius* — before) to the effect (*posterius* — after); *a posteriori* indicates the contrary procedure, i.e., from the effect to the cause (*induction*).

The argumentative process usually called *propter quid* (on account of which) and that called *a simultaneo* (from a simultaneous notion) are usually classed as *a priori.* The first of these proceeds from the proximate adequate cause to the effect, e.g., from the spirituality of the soul to its immortality, from divine infinity to immutability, while the second starts from the analysis of the terms or from the intimate connection between properties of one same subject, e.g., from the idea of God as necessary being to His existence (Leibnitz). The process called *quia* is classed as *a posteriori.* Examples of such reasoning are: from the operations of the soul (knowledge and free will) to its spirituality, or from the created world to God the Creator.

In modern philosophy, especially in that of Kant, *a priori* and *a posteriori* have taken on the particular meaning, respectively, of element which precedes *experience* and element which derives from experience (see *apriorism; Kantianism*).

BIBLIOGRAPHY

Boyer, *Cursus Philosophiae,* Vol. 1 (Paris, 1935), p. 240 ff. Viglino, *Logica* (Rome, 1941), p. 331 f.

apriorism (Lat. *a priori*). A theory which posits in the human mind ideas which precede experience or are independent of it. Distinction must be made between: (*a*) *a priori knowledge,* which is no more than either an intellective intuition or an innate idea which precedes all sense experience; and (*b*) *a priori demonstration,* which is a process of knowledge going from cause to effect and is also called demonstration *propter quid* (to distinguish it from *a posteriori* demonstration, called *quia*).

Apriorism applied to our knowledge of God manifests itself: (1) as *ontologism* (Malebranche, Gioberti) — at the base of all our knowledge there is an immediate intuition of God (*primum logicum* and *primum ontologicum* — first in the mind and first in reality); (2) as *innatism* (Descartes) — the idea of God is innate, i.e., infused by God Himself in our soul; (3) as *transcendental subjectivism* (Kant) — there is in us an idea of God, which, however, does not imply His objective reality; instead, God is a postulate of practical reason. These three forms of apriorism conflict with the Catholic doctrine, especially as defined by the Vatican Council (see *God*). The so-called *ontological* argument of St. Anselm, sometimes styled *a simultaneo,* is close to apriorism. It attempts to demonstrate the existence of God from analysis of the concept that we have of God: God is the Being than whom we can think none greater or more: as such, He must have all perfections, including that of existence: therefore, God exists. Descartes, Leibnitz, and some modern theologians have reworked this argument in various forms; but many reject it, as did St. Thomas, because it hides an illegitimate passage from the logical (mental) to the ontological (real) order.

BIBLIOGRAPHY

BOYER, *Cursus Philosophiae,* Vol. 2 (Romae, 1936), p. 297 ff. GARRIGOU-LAGRANGE, *God,* trans. Rose, Vol. 1 (St. Louis, 1947), Ch. 2. SERTILLANGES, *St. Thomas d'Aquin,* Vol. 1 (Paris, 1925).

Aquarians. Heretics who, in imitation of the Ebionites, Marcionites, Encratites, abstained from the use of wine not only at meals but also in the Eucharistic celebration, consecrating in bread and water. Wine for them, as for all the Manichaean sects, was a work of the principle of evil and a dangerous vehicle of impurity. Their presence is noted in Roman Africa in the middle of the third century, as appears from a letter of St. Cyprian to Cecilius (the first *De Sacrificio Missae* treatise), written to confute the usage of consecrating without wine. In this same letter the holy Bishop of Carthage explains the symbolic significance of the few drops of water infused in the chalice of wine: water (people) is united to the wine (Jesus Christ) in order that one sole sacrifice be made of head and members.

BIBLIOGRAPHY

BAREILLE, "Aquariens," *DTC.* BATIFFOL, "Aquariens," *DACL.*

Arianism. Trinitarian heresy started at Alexandria about the beginning of the fourth century. Arius, a priest of Alexandria trained, however, at the Antioch school under Lucian, was its author. Chief points of this heresy are: (*a*) The one true God is *not generated* (ἀγέννητος) and is not communicable to creatures. (*b*) In order to create the world God generated the *Word,* who, since He had a beginning, is not God, but an *intermediary* being, between God and the world. (*c*) The substance of the Word, therefore, is *different* from the substance of God (the Father). He is called *Son* of the Father, not in the proper and natural sense, but in the sense of *adopted* Son.

Arius evidently draws the elements of his heresy a bit from Gnosticism (transcendence of God and the intermediate Being between God and the world: *subordinationism*), and a bit from the erroneous theory of adoptionism (*q.v.*), professed by Paul of Samosata at Antioch in the third century. Warned by the Patriarch of Alexandria, Arius did not abandon his false opinions. Instead he left his diocese and took refuge with his friend Eusebius of Nicomedia, in Asia Minor, where he continued to spread his errors among the people chiefly through a literary composition, a mixture of prose and poetry, called *Thalia.* In 325 the Council of Nicaea, assembled in Bithynia with the Emperor Constantine and over 300 bishops in attendance, defined the Word to be of the same substance of the Father, ὁμοούσιος (consubstantial), and hence true God equal to the Father. St. Athanasius, as deacon, later patriarch, of Alexandria, was the soul of the Council and of the whole struggle against the great heresy which, nonetheless, continued to circulate craftily under insidious forms (see *Semi-Arians*).

BIBLIOGRAPHY

D'ALÈS, *Le dogme de Nicée* (Paris, 1926).

BARRY, "Arianism," *CE*. CAYRÉ, *Manual of Patrology*, trans. Howitt, Vol. 1 (Paris, Tournai, Rome, 1936), pp. 309–322. DE REGNON, *Etudes de théologie positive sur la Sainte Trinité* (Paris, 1898). GWATKIN, *Studies on Arianism* (London, 1900). LE BACHELET, "Arianisme," *DTC*. NEWMAN, "Causes of the Rise and Successes of Arianism," *Tracts Theological and Ecclesiastical* (London, 1902).

Aristides. See "Outline of the History of Dogmatic Theology" (p. 301).

articles, fundamental. The subject of a religious controversy that arose with Lutheranism in the sixteenth century. From its beginnings, the Lutheran reform saw itself threatened by fragmentarism and by that instinctive and fatal tendency to schism, which is inherent in the doctrine of *liberty of thought* (see *free thought*) and which was to produce the dizzy whirl of the innumerable sects of which Protestantism today is composed.

Having eliminated the infallible *magisterium* of the Church, the Lutherans were quickly forced to seek another way in order to form at least an embryonic unity in the midst of such a great confusion of ideas. Accordingly, the device of *fundamental articles* was invented which, in the intention of several theologians of the Reformation, were to constitute a minimum creed or doctrine of faith, acceptable to all the sects. Introduced by Calixtus in Germany, by Turretin in Switzerland, and by Cranmer in England, the system of fundamental articles was zealously elaborated in France by Jurieu, who was refuted effectively by Bossuet with arguments which retain their force today.

Actually, the system of fundamental articles, as a substitute for the living *magisterium* of the Church, does not hold up. Evidently there is a gradation among the mysteries and the other revealed truths so that one is more important than another; but both Scripture and Tradition do not permit the faithful to accept certain revealed truths and reject others, even when these are of less importance. The Christian is called to adhere to Christ and His teaching *integrally;* the unity of faith is the dominant motif of divine revelation on which St. Paul insists energetically, as, e.g.: "I beseech you, brethren, by the name of our Lord Jesus Christ, that you all speak the same thing, and that there be no schisms among you: but that you be perfect in the same mind, and in the same judgment" (1 Cor. 1:10). There is, then, no place for selection in the truths proposed to the faith of the believers, as the Protestants would have it. Even were there the possibility of selection in order to effect the unity desired, it would still have to be proved that there is someone or something having the right to establish what the fundamental articles indispensable of belief are; and so, willy-nilly, the Protestants return to the concept of a *regula fidei* (rule of faith) imposed by a teaching authority, which is what they denied.

BIBLIOGRAPHY

MÜLLER, *Die Bekenntnischriften der reformierten Kirchen* (1903). NIEMEYER, *Collectio Confessionum in ecclesiis reformatis publicatarum* (1840).

articles of faith. An expression which gained popularity in the Scholastic epoch (eleventh century) to indicate especially the propositions or statements contained in the *Apostolic Symbol* (see *Symbol*), i.e., the Apostles' Creed, which was first called *sententiae* (sentences). All theologians agree in calling the revealed truths of the *Symbol* articles of faith, but differ in the specific determination to be given to the concept *article.*

The best and most precise description of *article* is found in St. Thomas (*Summa Theol.,* II–II, q. 1, a. 6), who says that the term derives from the Gr.

ἄρθρον, an organic part or element of an organism. Therefore, not any truth of revelation is called an article, but only those truths in which the formal reason of faith (to believe *on the authority* of God) is present and which is bound up organically with the principal body of revealed doctrine. Thus understood, the articles of faith in theological science have the function of *fundamental principles,* which the theologian accepts without discussion as being certain and sure by virtue of the authority of God, absolute truth. Analogously in human sciences subordinated among themselves one takes, without discussion, its basic principles from another, e.g., physics from mathematics, architecture from geometry.

BIBLIOGRAPHY

St. Thomas, *Summa Theol.,* II–II, q. 1, a. 6; *Opusc. De articulis fidei.* MacDonald, *The Symbol* (New York, 1903). Suarez, *De fide theologica,* disp. 2, *Opera omnia,* Vol. 12 (Paris, 1858).

Artotyrites (Gr. ἄρτος — bread and τυρός — cheese). Heretics of the third century who celebrated the Eucharist with bread and cheese, under the pretext that the patriarchs of old nourished themselves with such food, and that Jesus Christ would not have departed from their eating habits at the Last Supper.

BIBLIOGRAPHY

Bareille, "Artotyrites," *DTC.*

ascetics, asceticism (Gr. ἀσκέω — I practice). Ascetics or ascetical theology is the science of Christian perfection. It is based on dogma, from which it draws light and vitality; it presupposes moral theology and goes beyond it, leading man from the observance of the law to that of the evangelical counsels (poverty, chastity, obedience). It is distinguished from mystics or mystical theology (see *mystics*), for which it is a preparation.

Asceticism consists in the practice of the Christian virtues in order to effect the union of the soul with God, in so far as possible, on this earth. The Greeks had a physical *ascesis* (athletics) and an intellectual and moral ascesis, as that, e.g., of the Stoics and the Neo-Platonists, intended to free the spirit from the chains of the passions and of material things.

Christian asceticism is defined by Christ Himself, who invites to renunciation, abnegation, and the struggle for the conquest of heaven. The Apostles and the saints of all times have understood the lesson and carried it out in full, imitating the example of Jesus Christ. St. Thomas (*Summa Theol.,* II–II, q. 24, a. 9) has outlined, in a schema that has been classical since his time, the whole of Christian asceticism. Asceticism, according to the Angelic Doctor, tends to render man perfect in his relationships with God; this perfection ripens through *love* in three consecutive phases: (1) *beginners'* phase, consisting in withdrawal from sin by repression of the passions, especially concupiscence (the practice of mortification of the body and its senses comes in here); (2) phase of the *progressives* (positive phase), i.e., of those who progress in good by the practice of all the virtues under the impulse and dominion of charity; (3) phase of the *perfect,* proper to those who, having triumphed over sin, are masters of themselves through subjection of their passions, and, therefore, adhere to God through charity and in Him foretaste the happiness of heaven. These three grades are also called the three ways: *purgative, illuminative, unitive.*

The *Spiritual Exercises* of St. Ignatius of Loyola are a marvelous treatise on asceticism. It has been lightly said that Christian asceticism deadens and depresses the spirit, debases man, and alienates him from life; the best answer is the simple list of great ascetics who, touching the highest spheres of Christian perfection, have impressed new orientations on the life of peoples: St. Benedict, St. Bernard, St. Francis of Assisi, St. Dominic, St. Catherine of Siena, St. Ignatius, St. Theresa.

BIBLIOGRAPHY

DIVINE, *Manual of Ascetical Theology* (London, 1902). DOYLE, *Principles of Religious Life* (London, 1906). DUBLANCHY, "Ascétisme," *DTC;* "Ascétique," *DTC*. Fox, *Religion and Morality* (New York, 1899). HAMON, "Ascétisme," *DA*. MUTZ, "Theology (Ascetical)," *CE*. PASCAL PARENTE, *The Ascetical Life* (St. Louis, 1947), pp. 3–17, 181–188, 231–236. SAUDREAU, *Les degrés de la vie spirituelle* (Paris, 1920). SCHLAGER, "Ascetism," *CE*.

aseity. See *essence, divine*.

aspersion. See *baptism*.

Assumption of the Blessed Virgin. The passage of the Blessed Virgin in soul and body from earth to life in heaven. Being immune from *original* sin (see *Immaculate Conception*), she was not subject to death, which is a penalty of that sin. For that reason some writers (e.g., Epiphanius in the fourth century) doubted, and others (Palestinian tradition) denied, the death of the Blessed Virgin. But Tradition, in prevalent part, teaches that Mary died *in fact,* although she did not incur the *debt* of death. Thus, St. Augustine, St. Modestus of Jerusalem, St. John Damascene, and others were of that opinion; thus also the liturgy (*Gregorian Sacramentary, Mass of the Assumption*) which introduced the feast under the titles: *"Dormitio"* (Sleeping), *"Depositio"* (Depositing or Burial), and *"Pausatio"* (or Pausation) — all terms relating to death. It was fitting that Mary should die, when even the Son of God had died. But Mary's death, if it took place, was a death without corruption, an ineffable passing.

Many legends on the death of the Virgin flourished (*Historia Euthymii,* recorded by St. John Damascene, *Homily II, PG,* 86, col. 748 ff.; *Liber Transitus Sanctae Mariae, PG,* 5, col. 1233). But abundant liturgical documentation, dating at least from the sixth century, attests the explicit faith of the Church in the corporeal assumption of the Virgin Mary into heaven by God's power: Emperor Maurice (582–602) fixed the feast (which already existed) on August 15; there are five testimonies in the *Mozarabic Missal* (sixth century), *Gothic-Gallican Missal* (seventh century), and in the *Sacramentarium Gregorianum*. As regards the doctrine of the Assumption we have the writings of St. Gregory of Tours (sixth century), St. Modestus of Jerusalem (seventh century), St. Andrew of Crete, St. Germain of Constantinople, and St. John Damascene (eighth century); nor are traces and indications lacking in the earlier Fathers (Timothy of Jerusalem and Gregory of Nyssa). In the Scholastic epoch, the theologians (e.g., St. Thomas) treat the Assumption as an indisputable truth.

After the Vatican Council the definability of this truth, as a dogma of faith, has been increasingly emphasized by the theologians and very recently the opportuneness of the definition has been widely debated. Pope Pius XII on November 1, 1950, authoritatively settled the question by defining this dogma *ex cathedra,* in strikingly similar circumstances to those in which, nearly a century ago (December 8, 1854) his predecessor Pius IX defined the twin dogma of the Immaculate Conception, likewise implicitly contained in the same fundamental truth of the divine maternity.

BIBLIOGRAPHY

St. Thomas, *Summa Theol.*, III, q. 27, a. 1; q. 83, a. 5, ad 8; *Expositio in Salutationem Angelicam*. Campana, *Maria nel dogma cattolico* (Turin, 1936). Holweck, "Assumption of the B.V.M.," *CE*. Jugie, *La mort et l'Assomption de la Sainte Vierge* (Vatican City, 1944). Mattiussi, *L'Assunzione corporea della Virgine Madre di Dio* (Milan, 1924). O'Neill, "The Assumption of the Blessed Virgin according to the teaching of Pius IX and St. Thomas," *Irish Ecclesiastical Record*, 44th year, n. 524, pp. 113–136. Pohle-Preuss, *Dogmatic Theology*, VI *Mariology* (St. Louis, 1946), pp. 105–119.

As regards the question of the definability of the Assumption and the recent development of theological literature on this dogma, see various articles published during 1948–1950 in the principal theological reviews (*Gregorianum, Divus Thomas, Marianum*, etc.), particularly: Filograssi, "Theologia catholica et Assumptio B.M.V.," *Gregorianum*, Vol. 31 (1950), n. 3, pp. 323–360. Carol, "The Definability of Mary's Assumption," *The American Ecclesiastical Review*, Vol. 118 (1948), pp. 161–177; "Recent literature on Mary's Assumption," *ibid.*, Vol. 120 (1949), pp. 376–387. The theological and dogmatic content of the Apostolic Constitution of Nov. 1, 1950, defining this dogma, is amply explained by Filograssi in his recent article "Constitutio Apostolica 'Munificentissimus, Deus' de Assumptione B.M.V.," *Gregorianum*, Vol. 3 (1950), n. 4, pp. 483–525.

ataraxia. See *suffering*.

Athanasius. See "Outline of the History of Dogmatic Theology" (p. 301 f.); *Arianism*.

atheism (Gr. ἀ θεός — without God). The attitude of those who ignore or deny God. Atheism is: (*a*) *theoretical*, if it is founded on judgments of the mind; (*b*) *practical*, if it prescinds from reasoning and shows itself in the manner of living. Theoretical atheism can be either *negative* or *positive*, according as it implies ignorance of God or denial of God with motivation. The question which apologists and theologians pose is twofold:

1. *Are there or can there be negative atheists?* Many answer negatively; others admit the fact and, consequently, the possibility with various limitations (for some time; not for one's whole life; relative and not absolute ignorance; etc.). The more correct answer: absolute and invincible ignorance of the existence of God, in principle, cannot be conceded because it is impossible for human reason not to ascend from experience of the external world and the internal world of man to the cause of them, as well as it is impossible for man not to feel at all the force of the moral law (see *God*). The Vatican Council speaks to this effect. But it is also true that relative ignorance of God is possible on account of abnormality, or some period of psychological darkness; likewise, it is also possible that a *clear idea* of the existence of God be lacking.

2. *Does positive atheism exist or is it possible?* Here also there is a divergence of opinion, which, however, is not substantial. The more probable answer: Since the existence of God is not *immediately evident*, man can fail to see the force of the arguments advanced to prove it and can, consequently, accept some contrary argument, forming thus a false conviction. But a positive atheist is always guilty, at least *initially*, for lack of prudence, of careful consideration, and of more accurate and dispassionate investigation. An atheist really convinced and in perfect good faith is a hypothesis bordering on the absurd.

BIBLIOGRAPHY

Aveling, "Atheism," *CE*. Boedder, *Natural Theology* (New York, 1891). Flint, *Antitheistic Theories* (New York, 1894). Lilly, *The Great Enigma* (New York, 1892). Sertillanges, *Les sources de la croyance en Dieu* (Paris, 1928). Shea, "Steps to Atheism," *The Amer. Cath. Quart. Rev.* (1879). Toussaint, "Athéisme," *DTC*.

Athenagoras. See "Outline of the History of Dogmatic Theology" (p. 301).

attention. The application of the mind to what one is doing at the moment. It is an act of the intellect and is formally distinct from intention, which is an act of the will (see *intention*). Attention, in opposition to distraction, is termed *internal* when it excludes all wandering of the mind on things extraneous to the act being done; it is called *external* when it excludes all those external actions which are incompatible with internal attention; e.g., one who draws, reads, talks, etc., during prayer, does not have the external attention of prayer.

Now, as regards *meditation,* all are in agreement in requiring internal attention; as regards satisfaction of the obligation of reciting the *Breviary,* some say that external attention is enough (Durand, Lugo, Tamburini, Noldin), but many say that internal attention is required as well (Cajetan, D. Soto, Suarez, Billuart). This last opinion is considered more probable and more common by St. Alphonsus. In the *administration* of the sacraments, external attention is enough for validity, but internal attention is required for liceity. In *reception* of the sacraments, on the other hand, no attention is necessary in the subject for *validity,* while for *liceity,* not only external but also internal attention is required.

BIBLIOGRAPHY

St. Thomas, *Summa Theol.,* II–II, q. 83, a. 13. Oblet, "Attention," *DTC.* Prümmer, *Manuale Theologiae Moralis,* Vol. 2, n. 354–359; Vol. 3, n. 61, 87. Thamiry, "Attention," *DDC.* Vernay, "Attention," *DS.*

attributes of God. The human mind, considering the various perfections of creatures, forms different concepts and attributes them to God analogically (see *analogy*), e.g., good, just, omnipotent. Again, revelation gives many names of God (Creator, Holy, Eternal, etc.). The attributes are properties predicated of God as being (*static* attributes) or as acting (*dynamic* attributes). At first sight these multiple and diverse attributes would seem to be in conflict with the divine *simplicity* (*q.v.*). Hence the dilemma: either the attributes have a real and ontological value, and then God is no longer simple; or they do not have a real value, and then nearly all revelation and theology are a vain play on words.

The problem consists in determining the distinction between the essence and the attributes, as well as the mutual distinction among the attributes themselves. Distinction is opposed to identity and can be *real* or *logical,* according as two or more things are distinct in themselves, *ontologically* (e.g., the soul and body, the body and one of its parts, the person and the qualities of the person), or are distinct only in our mind *as concepts* (e.g., the same person considered as a doctor, an artist, a citizen, is really only one subject, which is distinct logically in three). Logical or conceptual distinction (*distinctio rationis*) may be purely such, as when I designate the same person by two names: Tullius, Cicero; and then it is called *distinctio rationis ratiocinantis* (rational of the "rationalizer"). But, while it remains a logical or conceptual distinction, it can have a foundation in ontological reality; it is then termed *distinctio rationis ratiocinatae* (rational of the thing rationalized on), e.g., between the living body and its life.

In God, while every kind of real distinction is excluded (see *simplicity*), a logical distinction with real foundation is commonly admitted. The real attributes are logically distinct among themselves and from the essence because they involve formally different *concepts,* like justice and mercy; but they are not pure *concepts,* because there corresponds to them a true reality, i.e., the infinite essence of

God, which in its simple actuality transcends our finite intellect and contains in an eminent manner all the perfections signified by those attributes. On account of the purest simplicity of God, every attribute includes the others. The properties of the divine Persons are something else; they necessitate a real distinction, which is, however, only relative, not absolute (see *Trinity; relation, divine; notions, divine*).

BIBLIOGRAPHY

St. Thomas, *Summa Theol.*, I, q. 13. Flint, *Theism* (Edinburgh, 1879). Fox, "Attributes (Divine)," *CE*. Garrigou-Lagrange, *God*, trans. Rose, 2 vols. (St. Louis, 1947–1948); *The One God*, trans. Rose (St. Louis, 1943), p. 163 ff. Peter Parente, *De Deo Uno* (Rome, 1938), p. 183 ff. Pohle-Preuss, *Dogmatic Theology*, I *God: Knowability, Essence, Attributes* (St. Louis, 1946), p. 177 ff. *The Teaching of the Catholic Church*, ed. Smith, 2 vols. (New York, 1949), pp. 79–110.

attrition. See *contrition*.

audients (auditors). See *catechumen*.

Augustine. See "Outline of the History of Dogmatic Theology" (p. 302); *Augustinianism; grace; Pelagianism; predestination; Semi-Pelagianism; sin, original*.

Augustinianism. Term of broad historical and doctrinal signification, used in philosophy and theology to indicate the tendency, the spirit, and the doctrine of St. Augustine, according to the development obtained in the interpretations of the various schools. *Philosophically,* Augustinianism, which in various points is connected with *Neoplatonism,* dominates the Middle Ages up to the advent of *Aristotelianism,* introduced in the schools by St. Thomas and his teacher, St. Albert the Great. The principal philosophical theories of Augustinianism were: fusion of theology with philosophy and so of the natural with the supernatural, the primacy of Good over Truth and of the will over the intellect, divine illumination of the intelligence, sharp division of the soul from the body, plurality of substantial forms in one composed being and, therefore, also in man, *rationes seminales* in matter (see *cosmogony*), hylomorphic composition (matter and form) applied also to spiritual creatures. This current prevailed in the school of St. Victor and in the Franciscan Order (St. Bonaventure, Scotus), and developed a sharp hostility against St. Thomas and his doctrine based on Aristotle.

Theologically, Augustinianism triumphs as a vigorous affirmation of the supernatural against Pelagianism (*q.v.*) at the Councils of Ephesus and of Orange (2nd), but degenerates in the erroneous interpretations of *predestinarianism* (*q.v.*), and later, through the medium of nominalism, passes after being deformed into the heresy of Luther, Calvin, Baius, and Jansenius (see *Lutheranism; Calvinism; Baianism; Jansenism*), all of whom appeal to St. Augustine in their aberrations. In the sixteenth century, the *Bannesians* claim for themselves St. Augustine's concept on grace and predestination, having recourse to the sound interpretation given by St. Thomas; however, the *Molinists,* especially the congruists, believe they too can adopt the principles of St. Augustine to their system. Finally in the seventeenth and eighteenth centuries the Augustinians, Noris, Berti, and Belelli, returning rigidly to the doctrine of St. Augustine, attempted to demonstrate its difference, notwithstanding apparent similarity, from Jansenism. Benedict XIV approved the work of Cardinal Norisio. A new, very mitigated interpretation of Augustinianism reappears in the system of the *Sorbonnians,* as it is called, to which adhere Thomassinus and St. Alphonsus; these theologians distinguish an *ordinary* and an *extraordinary* or special grace, of which only the second *morally* determines the will to the salutary act (moral predetermination).

BIBLIOGRAPHY

EHRLE, "L'Agostinismo et l'Aristotelismo nella Scolastica del sec. XIII," *Xenia Thomistica* (1925), Vol. 3, pp. 517–588. GAILLARD, *Etudes sur l'histoire de la doctrine de la grâce depuis saint Augustin* (Lyon, Paris, 1897). PORTALIÉ, "Augustinianisme," *DTC;* "Augustinisme," *DTC.*

authenticity (Gr. *αὐθεντία,* in the later meaning of authority or author of a book). It means, in the *juridical sense,* that a book is authoritative, has an indisputable and definitive value. Tertullian (*De prascr. haer.,* 16) seems to have been the first to apply this word to the sacred books.

In opposition to the apocrypha (see *Canon of the Bible*), written on human initiative, the sacred Scriptures are authentic in the juridical sense in so far as they enjoy infallible authority, being inspired by God, essential Truth. They are, therefore, authentic documents of divine revelation.

The originals or autographs of the inspired writings are authentic in the full sense of the word; in absence of the originals, the copies are authentic inasmuch as they reproduce the originals faithfully. The Hebrew text of the Old Testament and the Greek text of the New Testament are, therefore, authentic. A translation can be called authentic when it is declared such by the competent authority, i.e., by the Church. The Council of Trent (*EB,* 41) declared authentic the Latin version called *Vulgata* (Vulgate) because it was used for many centuries by the Church. Inasmuch as it is authoritative, it has probative value in matters of faith and morals (see *Vulgate*). Intensification of the scientific method in biblical studies popularized the term *authenticity* in a sense that may be called *critical;* namely, a book is said to be authentic when it is really of the author or of the time to which it is attributed, or when its origin is legitimate, not vitiated by fraud. It is a question, therefore, of the human origin of Holy Scripture and of research on the human authors of the sacred books, a research which — except for cases where there exists explicit affirmation of the Scripture itself or of the *magisterium* of the Church — is conducted with rational methods of investigation.

BIBLIOGRAPHY

HOEPFL, "Authenticité," *DBVS,* cols. 666–676. MAINAGE, "Canonicité et authenticité," *Rev. Sc. Phil. et Théol.,* 2 (1908), pp. 96–98. MANGENOT, "Authenticité," *DTC,* cols. 2584–2593.

B

babies deceased without baptism. On the fate of these little ones, some doctors expressed themselves too rigorously, others with too great indulgence.

St. Augustine (followed by St. Gregory the Great, St. Anselm, Gregory of Rimini, the torturer of infants, Bossuet, Berti) taught that they are damned, although punished with very light suffering. Many theologians, on the contrary, considered the most benign hypotheses. Cajetan taught that they could be saved by an act of faith made by their parents in their name. Klee thought that in the first instant of separation of the soul from the body they might be illumined in such a way as to be able to choose between good and evil. Schell believed to discern in their death a kind of martyrdom, since they die on account of Adam's sin. These opinions, despite the laudable intentions of their proponents, are not in agreement with the sound principles of Catholic theology.

The more common teaching constantly favored by the Church is that these babies are not only exempt from any suffering, but enjoy a natural happiness not very different from what man would have possessed had he not been elevated to the supernatural order. They are, however, subject to the pain of loss (*poena damni*), which consists in the privation of the possession of God (see *penalty; sin, original*).

BIBLIOGRAPHY

ST. THOMAS, *Comment. in II Sent.*, dist. 33, q. 2, a. 2; *Quaest. Disp. De Malo*, q. 5, a. 2. D'ALÈS, *De Baptismo et Confirmatione* (Paris, 1927), pp. 152–158. PIOLANTI, *De Sacramentis*, Vol. I (Rome, 1945), pp. 190–192. POHLE-PREUSS, *Dogmatic Theology*, III *God: Author of Nature and the Supernatural* (St. Louis, 1945), pp. 300–307.

Baianism. An erroneous system of Michel de Bay (*Baius* in Latin), professor at Louvain in the second half of the sixteenth century. The root of this error lies in the confusion (begun by Luther) between the natural and the supernatural order (see *supernatural*). It may be said that Bay is a *Pelagian* (see *Pelagianism*), in the earthly paradise, and in principle is a *Lutheran* after original sin. He had a heretical mentality, but fortunately sincere faith saved him by inducing him to submit to the judgment of the ecclesiastical authority.

The chief points of Baianism are: (*a*) original justice (grace, supernatural and preternatural gifts; see *justice*) was in reality a property of man as an *integral part* of his nature and so was *due* to that nature and not gratuitous; (*b*) original sin corrupted human nature intrinsically, weakening its freedom which has become a slave to concupiscence, making it a sin in itself; (*c*) fallen man, therefore, is incapable of any good, unless grace, integrant force of his nature, is restored to him and confers on him the capacity of doing acts *naturally* good, which through the will of God are meritorious of eternal life; (*d*) grace is not a *habit* (see *Lutheranism*), but is the good *activity* itself, under the impulse of the Holy Spirit, corresponding to a need of nature itself; (*e*) man is either under the dominion of grace and of right love, excited by the Holy Spirit, which make his actions good and worthy of heaven; or under the power of concupiscence and earthly love, which make all his actions sins (the works of the pagans, deprived of grace, are "vices in the garb of virtues"); (*f*) *efficacious* and irresistible grace is necessary for every good work; it determines the will intrinsically without destroying or hampering freedom, since only *extrinsic* coaction is contrary to freedom, not intrinsic necessity.

Bay, proceeding thus in the direction of *pessimism*, prepared the way for *Jansenism* (*q.v.*). In 1567 Pius V condemned 79 propositions extracted from the writings of Bay, who submitted. However, he remained attached to his principles and discussed pontifical infallibility in an unfavorable tone (cf. *DB*, 1001–1080). The currents of modern religious *immanentism* (*q.v.*) are connected with Baianism in many respects.

BIBLIOGRAPHY

JANSEN, *Baius et le Baianisme* (Louvain, 1927). KROLL, "The Causes of the Jansenist Heresy," *Am. Cath. Quart.* (1885). LE BACHELET, "Baius," *DTC*. SOLLIER, "Baius," *CE*.

Bañez. See "Outline of the History of Dogmatic Theology" (p. 303); *Bannesianism*.

Bannesianism. The development of the teaching of St. Thomas on the *divine concourse*, on *grace*, and on *predestination* (*qq.v.*), elaborated by the Dominican, Dominic Bañez (1528–1604), professor at the University of Salamanca and author of acute commentaries on the *Summa Theologica* of Aquinas.

Bannesianism is the antithesis of Molinism (*q.v.*). Toward the end of the sixteenth century, in order to combat Lutheranism and Calvinism (*qq.v.*) more effectively, the Jesuit theologians, in the delicate questions on the relationship of free will with grace and predestination, took as a starting point human freedom, proceeding from that to the influx of God. On the other hand, the Augustinian and Thomistic tradition proceeded in the opposite direction. Louis Molina in 1588 published his famous work *Concordia,* in which he defended the *simultaneous* divine concourse, i.e., divine action parallel to human action, and the *middle knowledge* (*scientia media*) of God (see *science, divine*). He hoped thereby to eliminate the difficulties of reconciling human freedom with the divine influence in every human action. Bañez, having been requested to pass judgment on the matter, pointed out certain erroneous propositions in the *Concordia.* Thus a sharp controversy was kindled between the Jesuits and the Dominicans which, referred to the pope at Rome, was hotly discussed in many sessions (*Congregatio de Auxiliis*), without arriving at a conciliation of the two tendencies. Discussion continues even today on these matters in theological schools.

Bañez interprets St. Thomas so as to solve the problem with the following principles: (*a*) God moves the human will in the natural order: the divine motion moves the will previously (*prevenit*) and determines it to choose this or that thing (*premotion* or rather physical predetermination); (*b*) in the supernatural order, efficacious grace is a predetermination to the salutary act; (*c*) notwithstanding this predetermination in the two orders, the will remains free because it does not lose the capacity of resisting the divine influence, although in fact it does not resist (freedom in the *divided sense,* not in the *composite sense*); (*d*) God foresees the free future acts in the *decrees of His will,* by which He decides to give the predetermination to the will of those persons whom He wishes to induce infallibly to good; (*e*) predestination, bound with efficacious grace freely distributed, does not depend on the prevision of our merits (*ante praevisa merita*).

Bañez goes further than St. Thomas, although he remains substantially faithful to the Angelic Doctor's principles.

BIBLIOGRAPHY

Del Prado, *De Gratia et Libero Arbitrio* (Freiburg, 1907). De Regnon, *Bannésianisme et Molinisme* (Paris, 1890); *Bagnez et Molina* (Paris, 1883). Gayraud, *Thomisme et Molinisme* (Toulouse, 1889). Mandonnet, "Bañez," *DTC.* Volz, "Bañez," *CE.*

baptism (Gr. βαπτισμός — washing). The sacrament of spiritual purification and regeneration.

Variously *prefigured* in the creation, the flood, the passage of the Red Sea, the rock struck by Moses, *predicted* on several occasions by the prophets (Isa. 44:3–4; Ezech. 36:25–26; Zach. 13:1), and immediately *prepared* by the baptism of the Precursor, this sacrament was directly instituted by Jesus Christ with a progressive determination of the elements which constitute it. He indicated vaguely the exterior rite in His baptism in the Jordan, where on the water (matter) there appeared mysteriously the Holy Trinity ("The Father in the voice, the Son in the flesh, the Holy Spirit in the dove"), in whose name it must be conferred (form); He inculcated its necessity in His colloquy with Nicodemus (John 3:5); He established particular use of baptism before His passion (John 9:1–6, collate John 4:1–2); He imposed it as a universal law on the day of His Ascension: "Going therefore, teach ye all nations; baptizing them in the name of the Father, and of the Son, and of the Holy Ghost" (Matt. 28:19).

The *ministers,* from the last cited text, are the Apostles and their successors, the bishops, who soon were to be helped in their ministry by the priests and in particular cases by the deacons (Acts 8:12–16). From the earliest times baptism conferred (in case of necessity) by the simple faithful was recognized as valid. In the third century baptism conferred by heretics, and later baptism conferred by infidels, was also recognized as valid; the IV Lateran Council (1215) defined that this sacrament is always valid, by whoever it may be administered (*DB,* 696).

In the exact words of Matt. 28:19, *water* is indicated implicitly (however it had been explicitly designated in John 3:5) and the *Trinitarian formula* clearly as constitutive elements of the *external* rite of baptism. The water, moreover, can be applied in three ways: by immersion (ancient usage, cf. Rom. 6:3–11), or infusion (common use in the Latin Church), or aspersion (in case of necessity).

The *effects* of baptism are the character and the grace of regeneration. The *character* (see *character, sacramental*) of baptism is a true participation, although only initial, of the Priesthood of Christ, in so far as it confers the three prerogatives of all priesthood: (1) *sacerdotal being,* because the character is an ontological consecration; (2) *sacerdotal power,* because, although it is principally a receptive faculty, it is also secondarily an active faculty both in the line of ascending mediation, in so far as it renders all the faithful capable of offering *mediately* (through a priest) the Eucharistic sacrifice, and in the line of descending mediation, as it renders simple Christians suitable to administer the sacrament of matrimony; (3) the *congruous exercise* of the priestly power, because it demands, amplifies, and defends *grace.* With respect to the Church, the character is the first and fundamental *distinctive* sign, which differentiates the faithful from the infidels, and the *insertive* sign of incorporation into the mystical body of Christ (cf. *CIC,* can. 87).

The *grace* of baptism is regeneration (John 3:5), which implies (Rom. 6:3–11), on the one hand, death to sin (original and actual, mortal and venial, with all its penal consequences), i.e., total separation from the old Adam; and, on the other, resurrection to a new life accomplished through insertion in Christ, the new Adam, by means of sanctifying grace. Inasmuch as Christ exerts His action by the infusion of grace, He functions as *Head,* constituting the faithful His own *members.* Inasmuch as the effect of Christ's influence is grace, He configures them to His nature, making them His brothers through likeness to Him (Rom. 8:29). Now, since Christ is our Head and our older Brother, natural Son of God, in and through Him we become adoptive sons of the Father, who sends into us His Spirit ("in whom we call: Abba, Father." Rom. 8:15). Sons of God, we have a right to the helps (actual grace), to the food (Eucharist), to the inheritance of the Father (beatific vision) (cf. Rom. 8:17). Finally, being brothers of the First-born of the Father, sons of the same Father, we all form one family, the Church, vivified by the circulation of the same spiritual goods, the "Communion of Saints."

This second effect (the grace of regeneration) may be obtained by way of exception, so to speak (*quasi per baptismi supplementa,* i.e., through quasi-substitutes for baptism), either by an act of charity (*baptismus flam-*

inis, of flame) or by martyrdom (*baptismus sanguinis,* of blood). But all, babies (see *babies deceased without baptism*) and adults, must in one way or another participate in the Church to be able to enter God's kingdom (John 3:5; Mark 16:15).

BIBLIOGRAPHY

St. Thomas, *Summa Theol.,* II, qq. 66–71. D'Alès, *Baptême et Confirmation* (Paris, 1928). Bellamy, Bareille, Bour, Ermoni, Ruch, Mangenot, "Baptême," *DTC.* Connell, *De Sacramentis* (Brugis, 1933), pp. 105–144. Cuttaz, *Les effets du Baptême* (Paris, 1934). Doronzo, *De Baptismo et Confirmatione* (Milwaukee, 1947). Duchesne, *Christian Worship, Its Origin and Evolution,* trans. McClure (London, 1903). Fanning, "Baptism," *CE.* Gasquet, "The Early History of Baptism and Confirmation," *Dublin Review* (1895), p. 116 ff. Jacono, *Il battesimo nel pensiero di S. Paolo* (Rome, 1935). Lemonnyer, *Notre Baptême d'après Saint Paul* (Paris, 1930). Pohle-Preuss, *Dogmatic Theology,* VIII *The Sacraments,* Vol. I, *The Sacraments in General, Baptism, Confirmation* (St. Louis, 1945), p. 204 ff. *The Teaching of the Catholic Church,* ed. Smith, 2 vols. (New York, 1949), pp. 767–802. Vacant, "Baptême," *DTC.*

Barnabas. See "Outline of the History of Dogmatic Theology" (p. 301).

Basil. See "Outline of the History of Dogmatic Theology" (p. 301 f.).

beatification. The recognition and declaration of the sanctity of a servant of God, made by the competent authority (in the current discipline, by the Holy See). Such declaration is *formal* when the Roman pontiff — after juridical proof that public cult has not been given to the servant of God, demonstration of the heroic quality of his virtues or the fact of his martyrdom, authentic recognition of miracles worked through his intercession — permits public cult of the servant of God under determined conditions and limitations. The declaration is *equivalent,* on the other hand, when the Holy See confirms the public cult paid to a servant of God *ab immemorabili,* after juridical discussion on the fame of sanctity or on his martyrdom.

In the first centuries the authority of the bishop was sufficient to approve the cult of martyrs. Likewise, in the early Middle Ages the bishops confirmed or at least permitted the cult spontaneously offered by the faithful. Only in the twelfth century did Alexander III reserve to the Holy See the causes of beatification — a reservation that was not entirely effective until the constitution, *Coelestis Jerusalem,* of Urban VIII (1634), forbade severely the paying of public cult to any servant of God who was not regularly beatified. This constitution permitted, however, that those "blessed" should continue to be so honored to whom public cult had been paid *ab immemorabili* or at least for 100 years, even though they had not been beatified officially. In the eighteenth century Benedict XIV, with that juridical acumen with which he was distinguished, codified into a system the procedure for beatification, now substantially incorporated in the Code of Canon Law.

None, even the uninitiated in juridical studies, can fail to recognize the supreme prudence, evident in every procedural step of the beatification process. The Church really proceeds, as the saying goes, "with feet of lead."

BIBLIOGRAPHY

Beccari, "Beatification and Canonization," *CE.* Benedict XIV, *De Servorum Dei beatificatione et Beatorum canonizatione.* Indelicato, *I fondamenti giuridici del processo di beatificazione* (Rome, 1944). Ortolan, "Beatification," *DTC.*

beatific vision. See *vision, beatific.*

beatitude. The ultimate perfection of the intellectual being. Boethius defines it: "A state perfect by the cumulation of all goods" (*De Consolat. Philos.,* III, 2).

Beatitude may be considered *objectively* and *subjectively* (*formally*): in the first sense it is the *supreme good,* capable of rendering the intellectual being perfectly happy; in the second sense it is the perfect happiness of the intellectual subject who enjoys that good. Scotus and, in part, St. Bonaventure, place beatitude preferentially in an act of the will (*love*); St. Thomas makes it consist principally in the intellect (*knowledge*), on which the will follows.

For man, in the actual state of things, beatitude is the beatific vision (see *vision, beatific*), i.e., God seen intuitively (immediately, directly, "face to face") in His essence (supreme, *supernatural* end). But beatitude in the *highest grade* belongs to God alone: objectively, He is the *summum bonum* (supreme good), and *subjectively,* He knows Himself and loves Himself in an infinite way, and so is infinitely blessed or happy. This divine happiness may neither be diminished or increased by creatures: when revelation speaks of God's sorrow or increase in joy it speaks in figures so as to be intelligible to men. By the Incarnation God put Himself in a condition to taste our joys and sorrows with a human heart.

The word *beatitude* is also used to signify the eight rules promulgated by Jesus in the Gospel (Matt. 5:3–11): "Blessed are the poor . . . Blessed are the meek . . . " etc. They go under the name of *Sermon on the Mount,* and are the synthesis of the gospel message.

BIBLIOGRAPHY

St. Thomas, *Summa Theol.,* I, q. 26. Gardeil, "Béatitude," *DTC.* Sertillanges, *Saint Thomas d'Aquin,* Vol. 1 (Paris, 1925), p. 273.

Beghards (old German *beggam* — to beg; to pray). One of the numerous religious sects which seethed, as it were, between the twelfth and thirteenth centuries in Europe. Actually the Beghards are a derivation of the Beguines, women consecrated to a life of chastity and, often, of poverty. Both societies were orthodox in the beginning, but soon began to deviate, especially the Beghards, who tried to imitate the extravagances of other sects, as that of the Fraticelli (Little Friars).

It is interesting from a theological viewpoint to know the doctrine they professed and spread. We have an authentic summary of it in the propositions condemned by the Council of Vienne (1311–1312). Man may attain in this life so great spiritual perfection as to become impeccable. Arrived at this height, man can do without fasts, prayers, obedience to authority, and, besides, should no longer worry about his body, to which he may give anything it wishes without sinning. Moreover, the perfect spiritual man can, even in this life, rise to the vision of God without the *light of glory* (*"lumen gloriae"*). What we are naturally inclined to is not sinful; the contemplative mystic should not lower himself to the cult of the Eucharist and of the humanity of Christ (*DB,* 471, 478).

Aversion to the Roman Church is another characteristic of Beghardism. The features of the later *quietism* (*q.v.;* see *Molinosism*) are easily discernible in this heresy.

BIBLIOGRAPHY

Gilliat, Smith, "Beguines"; "Beghards," *CE.* Mosheim, *De beghardis et beguinabus commentarius* (Leipzig, 1790). Vernet, "Béghardes, Béguines hétérodoxes," *DTC.*

Bellarmine. See "Outline of the History of Dogmatic Theology" (p. 303).

Berengarian heresy. Berengarius of Tours, archdeacon of Angers (1000–1088), was educated in the School of Chartres under the direction of Fulbert, but quickly departed from the example and teaching of his pious master. Indulging in his rationalistic proclivities, he denied the truth of transubstantiation (*q.v.*), giving the following reasons: (1) the accidents are inseparable from their substance, and, therefore, since they remain unchanged after consecration, we must conclude that their substance also remains without any change; (2) it is impossible for a substance to be transformed into another preexisting substance. Having rejected transubstantiation, it was logical he should deny the Real Presence. He did, advancing these arguments: (*a*) were Christ present in the Eucharist, He would have to be multiplied and to be distant from heaven; (*b*) the Eucharist, moreover, is a sacrament, i.e., a *signum rei sacrae* (sign of a sacred thing), according to the definition of St. Augustine; therefore, the eucharistic bread and wine do not contain, but merely signify the body and blood of Christ. Such dialectic shows not only heretical daring, but also philosophical poverty and lack of theological judgment.

The audacious statements of the archdeacon provoked a heated polemic in which the best minds of the age united (Lanfranc of Bec, Guitmund of Aversa, Adelmann of Brescia, Durandus of Troarn, etc.). Several condemnations of the Church followed: seven councils assembled in order to bend the crafty scholastic, who finally in the Roman Synod (1079) accepted a Eucharistic formula, worked out by Alberic of Monte Cassino, in which transubstantiation and the Real Presence were clearly enunciated. But his was a feigned submission, for as soon as he returned home he began to defend his error again; overcome finally by grace, he performed ten years of penance, and died reconciled with the Church. Although a contemporary writer reports that even common people took an interest in the Berengarian heresy, the polemic was confined within the walls of the theological schools, with the effect rather of occasioning more profound study of the doctrine (the word *transubstantiation* was then coined), and with it an increase in Eucharistic piety.

BIBLIOGRAPHY

Cappuyns, "Bérenger de Tours," *DHGE*. Doronzo, *De Eucharistia,* Vol. 1 (Milwaukee, 1948), Index Analyticus, "Berengarius." Macdonald, *Berengarius and the Reform Sacramental Doctrine* (London, 1930). Matronola, *Un testo inedito di Berengario di Tours e il Concilio Romano del 1079* (Milan, 1936). Sauvage, "Berengarius of Tours," *CE*. Vernet, "Bérenger de Tours," *DTC*.

Berengarius. See *Berengarian heresy*.

Bernard. See "Outline of the History of Dogmatic Theology" (p. 302).

Bible. The noun *bible* reproduces the Greek neuter plural τὰ βιβλία (the books), which passed into medieval Latin and into the modern languages in the singular form with the meaning of the collection of all the books inspired by God, commonly called Holy Scripture. While the Greek word brings out the composite character of the divine book, i.e., the multiplicity of books contained therein, the derived word (*Biblia,* Bible) stresses its one author and one spirit.

The 74 books of the Bible are divided into two large sections: the Old and the New Testaments (*qq.v.*). The word *Testament,* according to the meaning of the original Hebrew noun (*berith*) and of the Greek term which translated it from the beginning (διαθήκη), can mean either that those books contain the dispositions with which God promised (Old Testament) and granted (New Testament) to His faithful, the goods culminating in the possession of eternal happiness, or that they contain the series of *pacts* and alliances by which, in the course of the centuries, God bound man to Himself in view of His Redemption.

The Old Testament, initially the sacred patrimony of the Hebrew people elected by God as depositary of His promises of Redemption, passed subsequently, completed by the New, by legitimate inheritance to the Church, which is the real *Israel,* the authentic chosen people, in favor of whom the divine promises of old were fulfilled.

Actual Church legislation (*CIC,* cans. 1391, 1399, 1400) forbids the faithful to read vernacular translations of the Bible which do not have the approbation of the Holy See and are not published under the vigilance of the bishops, furnished with annotations extracted from the Fathers and Catholic interpreters. The editions of the original texts and of the ancient versions, as well as translations by Catholic authors, are permitted to scholars.

BIBLIOGRAPHY

Darlow, Moule, *Hist. Catalogue of the Printed Editions of Holy Scripture* (London, 1903–1904). Graham, *Where We Got the Bible* (St. Louis). Höpfl, Gut, *Introductio generalis in S. Scripturam* (Rome, 1940). *Institutiones Biblicae,* ed. Pontifical Biblical Institute, Vol. 2 (Rome, 1937). Maas, "Scripture," *CE.* Messmer, *Outlines of Bible Knowledge* (London–St. Louis, 1910). Pickar, *A Commentary on the New Testament* (Washington, D. C., 1942). Pope, *Catholic Student's Aids to the Bible,* 3 vols. (London, 1913); *The Laymen's New Testament* (New York, 1938). Rooney, *Preface to the Bible* (Milwaukee, 1949). Schumaker, *A Handbook of Scripture Study,* 3 vols. (St. Louis, 1923). Seisenberger, *Practical Handbook for the Study of the Bible* (New York, 1933). Steinmueller, *A Companion to Scripture Studies,* 3 vols. (New York, 1941–1943). Vaughan, *Concerning the Holy Bible, Its Use and Abuse* (London, 1904).

Billot. See "Outline of the History of Dogmatic Theology" (p. 303).

bishops (Gr. ἐπίσκοπος — inspector, superintendent). The successors of the Apostles, from whom they have inherited by divine right the triple power of instructing, sanctifying, and governing a portion of the flock of Christ (cf. Matt. 28:19).

The Apostles, having had the mandate of constituting by conquest the kingdom of God in the world, had no territorial limitations. But the function of conquest, being directed to the organization of the ecclesiastical society, was of its nature transient (personal prerogative). In fact, from the beginning the Apostles, put in charge of the individual communities, founded in the various regions of their apostolate persons that might represent them during their lifetime and be their replacements after death (cf. 1 Tim. 6:1–2; 2 Tim. 2:25; 4:2; Titus 1:13; 2:1).

It is true that in the inspired documents bishops and priests (presbyters) are named promiscuously, but at the end of the first century and at the beginning of the second we learn from the letters of St. Ignatius of Antioch († 107) that every Church was ruled by its bishop (*monarchical episcopate*).

The bishops, through consecration, which is the most suggestive ceremony of Catholic liturgy, are elevated to the apex of the Christian priesthood, the episcopal character being impressed on their souls by virtue of which they are vested with the *power of orders,* which implies the power of confirming and ordaining (cf. Council of Trent, sess. 23, cans. 6 and 7; *DB,* 966, 967). The *power of jurisdiction,* on the other hand, which includes the twofold faculty of teaching and governing, is transmitted to them by the *missio canonica,* which is a juridical act directly or indirectly emanating from the pope, the head of the bishops as Peter was the prince of the Apostles. The power of jurisdiction of the bishops is *ordinary* and *immediate* in their own dioceses, notwithstanding the primacy of the Roman pontiff (Vatican Council, *DB*, 1828).

The priests are subalternately united to the bishop like "chords to the zither" (Ignatius Martyr, Ephes. 3–4), as are the deacons and the inferior ministers who help him in the performance of his divers functions and ecclesiastical offices.

BIBLIOGRAPHY

St. Thomas, *Summa Theol.*, II–II, q. 108, a. 4, ad 2; q. 184, a. 6, ad 1; *Summa Contra Gentiles*, l. 4, c. 76. Ermoni, *Les origines de l'Episcopat* (Paris, 1905). Michiels, "Évêques," *DA*. Pohle-Preuss, *Dogmatic Theology*, XI *The Sacraments*, Vol. 4, *Extreme Unction, Holy Orders, Matrimony* (St. Louis, 1946), pp. 80–93. Prat, Valton, "Évêques," *DTC*. Ruffini, *La gerarchia della Chiesa negli Atti degli Apostoli e nelle lettere di S. Paolo* (Rome, 1921). Taunton, *The Law of the Church* (London, 1906). Van Hove, "Bishops," *CE*.

See under *orders, holy*.

body, human. The material constitutive element of man. Holy Scripture maintains that the body of the first man was formed by God Himself, by special action, from the earth (Gen. 2:7; cf. Tob. 8:8; Ecclus. 33:10; Wisd. 7:1, etc.).

The integral evolutionists extend evolution of the lower species up to man (soul and body); according to them, the human body is the result of the development of the animals nearest to man (the apes). Reasons: (*a*) the discovery of skeletons which are halfway between man and ape (e.g., the *Pithecanthropus erectus* of Java); (*b*) the great anatomic affinity of the human body and those of lower animals. The *Biblical Commission* (Response of 1909; see *cosmogony*) forbids the calling in doubt of the historicity of the biblical account of the special creation of man. The reasons adopted by the evolutionists are uncertain and equivocal; anatomic affinity proves only the harmonic unity of nature. While natural reason has no opposition to make to the biblical account, it recognizes, on the other hand, the absurdity of a body generated by animals and then informed by a soul (see *soul*): a substantial form cannot inform a matter which is organized and which belongs to a level below its perfection. Moreover, evolutionism has yet to prove why apes do not continue to produce human bodies or, what is more, men.

The body of Eve, according to the sacred text, was formed from a rib taken from Adam by God. The divine action has a deep meaning, both proper and figurative, according to the Fathers: (1) the profound unity of the two sexes and the subordination of woman to man; (2) Eve symbolizes the Church, issued from the wounded side of Christ.

Catholic doctrine energetically defends also the unity of the human race derived from one couple, Adam-Eve (*monogenesis*). Paleontology, ethnology, racialism cannot advance against this truth any difficulties worthy of consideration (see *evolutionism*).

BIBLIOGRAPHY

St. Thomas, *Summa Theol.*, I, qq. 91–92. Boyer, *De Deo creante et elevante* (Rome, 1940), pp. 178 ff. De Sinéty, "Transformisme," *DA*. Marcozzi, *Le origini dell-uomo* (Rome, 1942). Sertillanges, *Dieu ou rien*, Vol. 1 (Paris, 1933).

Body, Mystical. See *Mystical Body*.

Bogomile (Bulgar. *bog-mile*, equivalent of the Gr. θεόφιλος — friend of God). A sect with a basic dualistic cast (see *Manichaeism*), which spread from the tenth to the fourteenth centuries particularly in Bulgaria, with some ramifications in Bosnia-Herzegovina, Greece, and Hungary. It was attacked and condemned by Popes Honorius III, Gregory IX, Boniface VIII, and Benedict XII. A Bogomilian strain still subsists in Bulgaria.

Like every sect infected by Manichaeism, it rejects: (*a*) all specifically Christian truths; (*b*) the hierarchical form of the Church; (*c*) sacramental organism and external cult. It retains only the recital of the *Pater Noster* and is characterized by its claim of establishing direct relations with God through a purely interior cult, including attainment of the beatific vision on earth with bodily eyes.

BIBLIOGRAPHY

Bardy, "Bogomiles," *DHGE*. Gagov, *Theologia antibogomilistica Cosmae Presbyteri Bulgari saec. X* (Rome, 1942). De Guibert, *Documenta ecclesiastica christianae perfectionis studium spectantia* (Rome, 1931), nn. 126–138. Jugie, "Bogomiles," *DS*. Weber, "Bogomili," *CE*.

Bonaventure. See "Outline of the History of Dogmatic Theology" (p. 302).

Breviary. See *liturgy*.

Buddhism. See *suffering*.

bull (Lat. *bulla* — imprint of a seal made to authenticate public documents). One of the most solemn documents emanating from the Roman pontiff, having a determined external form and varying in content according to the intention of the pope.

Its external form distinguishes it from all other documents of the Roman Curia: it bears, not on the front but on the first line, the name of the reigning pontiff, e.g., *"Pius Episcopus Servus Servorum Dei."* In the date, the years are computed from the coronation of the pontiff, but, in case the bull antedates coronation, the phrase *"A die suscepti Apostolatus"* is used. It has a lead seal (*bulla*) attached to it, on one side of which is impressed the name of the holy pontiff, and, on the other, the names of SS. Peter and Paul. If the bull is one of grace, the cords from which the seal hangs are of red or yellow silk; if it is one of justice, the cords are of hemp.

Its content may be dogmatic or disciplinary. Very famous dogmatic bulls are: *Unam Sanctam,* published in 1302 by Boniface VIII, defining that subjection to the Roman pontiff is a necessity for salvation for every human creature (*DB,* 469); *Auctorem Fidei,* with which Pius VI, in 1794, condemned the Synod of Pistoia; *Ineffabilis Deus,* with which, in 1854, Pius IX defined the dogma of the Immaculate Conception.

BIBLIOGRAPHY

Ortolan, "Bulle," *DTC*. Pitra, "Etudes sur les lettres des papes, in *Analecta Novissima* (Frascati, 1885). Thurston, "Bulls and Briefs," *CE*.

C

Cajetan. See "Outline of the History of Dogmatic Theology" (p. 303).

Calvinism. The heretical system of Calvin (John Chauvin), who was born at Noyon, France (1509) but who lived most of his life at Geneva, Switzerland, where he exercised the most powerful influence on the populace. Switzerland was already disturbed by the religious ideas of Zwingli, a contemporary of Luther, with whom Calvin agreed on various fundamental points of the Reformation although he was generally more moderate. Calvin borrowed from one and the other, adding his own personal principles.

He adopted the *Lutheran concepts* on liberty of thought (individual interpretation of the Holy Scripture), on original sin and its consequences, on extrinsic justification, and on the sufficiency of faith without works (see *Lutheranism*). Proper to Calvin himself are the following: (*a*) the "inadmissibility" of grace (grace or justification being conceived as an imputation made to us of the holiness and merits of Christ): whoever by faith is justified can no longer lose such a favor and is certain to be saved (Luther spoke only of the certainty of justification, not of eternal salvation); (*b*) absolute *predestination* decreed by God for some people independently of any merit or demerit. God destines, according to His choice, to hell or to paradise; hence the works of those predestined to beatitude, even if evil, are considered as good by God, while the works of the future damned are evil without qualification. Moreover, he departs from Luther in that he wants a strongly organized Church: one that dictates even to the State. Calvin's Church is that of those predestined to eternal life, i.e., of the faithful adhering to Christ by faith; it is invisible in itself, but visible in the ministry of the pastors.

Calvin admitted only two sacraments: *baptism* and *the Supper,* and as regards the nature of these he sided rather with Zwingli than with Luther. The sacraments for Calvin were *external signs* which attested the grace of God in us and the honor with which we compensate God. His eucharistic doctrine was rather obscure; it has been interpreted later by the Calvinists in the sense that the faithful receiving consecrated bread and wine receive from Jesus, who is in heaven, a divine force (denial of *transubstantiation,* of the *Real Presence,* and even of the *symbolism* which is characteristic of the sacramentary teaching of Zwingli).

The principal work of Calvin is *Institutiones religionis Christianae* (4 vols.). He followed the principles of Luther, systemized them logically, but did not name his comrade. Calvinism was condemned together with Lutheranism by the Council of Trent.

BIBLIOGRAPHY

Audin, *Histoire de la vie, des ouvrages et des doctrines de Calvin* (Paris, 1841). Barry, "Calvinism," *CE.* Baudrillat, "Calvin et Calvinisme," *DTC.* Freschi, *Giovanni Calvino* (Milan, 1934). Maimbourg, *Histoire du Calvinisme* (Paris, 1682).

Cano, Melchior. See "Outline of the History of Dogmatic Theology" (p. 303).

canonization. The solemn pronouncement by which the pope declares that a blessed actually enjoys the beatific vision and imposes worship of the saint on the whole Church. The Roman pontiff is infallible in this judgment, according to the more common doctrine. Whereas beatification (*q.v.*) is a preliminary judgment, not infallible but only permissive of worship, canonization is a definitive and infallible judgment which orders worship. In virtue of this pontifical act: (1) worship of veneration (*cultus duliae*) is due to the saints; (2) their image must be surrounded with a halo; (3) their relics may be exposed and venerated; (4) the Mass and Holy Office may be celebrated in their honor; (5) feast days may be dedicated to their memory, and so on.

Although the Church intervened from the beginning to regulate the cult of the martyrs and confessors and laid down rules, which were later slowly developed and codified (see *beatification*), it was only under Urban VIII, however, that a clean-cut distinction was made between beatification and canonization, and both were absolutely reserved to the Holy See.

BIBLIOGRAPHY
BECCARI, "Beatification and Canonization," *CE*. BENEDICT XIV, *De Servorum Dei beatificatione et Beatorum canonizatione*. CAGNA, *De processu Canonizationis a primis Ecclesiae saeculis usque ad Codicem J. C.* (Rome, 1940). ORTOLAN, "Canonisation," *DTC*. VON HERTLING, "Canonisation," *DS*.

Canon of the Bible (Gr. κανών — rule). Designates the collection or catalogue of those books which, since they are inspired by God, are the rule of truth and light. A book is, therefore, canonical which is found in the Canon, inasmuch as it is inspired by God and as such has been recognized by the Church.

From the sixteenth century it has been the custom to call *protocanonical* the books on whose divine origin there has been unanimous consent of the whole Church *from the beginning,* and *deuterocanonical* those books whose inspiration was challenged prior to about the fifth century. The term *deuterocanonical* does not have an absolute value in so far as it does not indicate a book which at a *second* (δεύτερος), i.e., later time, was introduced into the Canon; even the books of a doubtful authenticity had been received into the Canon of the Church from the beginning.

The Hebrews, followed by the Protestants who have also influenced schismatic Churches, repudiate the following deuterocanonical books of the Old Testament: Tobias, Judith, Wisdom, Ecclesiasticus, Baruch, 1 and 2 Machabees, passages of Esther and Daniel — books and passages all written and preserved in Greek. The deuterocanonical books of the New Testament are: the Epistles to the Hebrews, of James, 2 of Peter, 2 and 3 of John, of Jude, and the Apocalypse.

Books with titles and content similar to those of the Old or New Testament, but not recognized by the Church as inspired, and excluded from the Canon, are called Apocrypha (*q.v.*).

The Protestants call the deuterocanonical books *apocryphal,* reserving the term *pseudepigrapha* (with false title) for the books which we call apocryphal.

BIBLIOGRAPHY
MANGENOT, "Canon des livres saints," *DTC*. REID, "Canon of the Holy Scripture," *CE*. SEISENBERGER, *Practical Handbook for the Study of the Bible* (New York, 1933), pp. 195–207. STEINMUELLER, *A Companion to Scripture Studies,* Vol. 1 (New York, 1941), pp. 44–103. ZARB, *De historia canonis utriusque Testamenti* (Rome, 1934).

Canon of the Mass (Gr. κανών — rule). That body of prayers of the Mass which begins after the *Sanctus* and ends with the *Amen* before the *Pater Noster*. The Canon has been designated by different names. In ancient times it was called the prayer (εὐχή) *par excellence,* because the supreme Gift, namely, Jesus Christ, was asked in it; it was called also *Action,* from the Latin expression *agere causam* (to defend a case at law): in fact, the priest, in the person of Christ, defends the cause of the whole Church before God the Father. The Greeks call it *anaphora* (ἀναφορά), i.e., offering. In the Middle Ages it was called *canon consecrationis,* because in those prayers the bread and wine are consecrated, to distinguish it from the communion (*canon communionis*) which follows. The Latins preferred the term *canon,* as expressing the fixed and regular part of the Mass.

The present-day Canon in the Roman Missal is that of St. Gregory the Great and goes back, therefore, to the end of the sixth century. There are elements in it which warrant the assertion that at the end of the fourth century it was substantially the same as today. The central nucleus of the Canon takes its inspiration from the words and actions of Jesus at the Last Supper. If, in fact, the passages which were added later are left out of consideration (*memento* of the living and dead, in connection with the reading of the *diptychs* or tables with the names of the living and the dead to be prayed for), the fundamental theme of the Canon is thanksgiving to God for the work of Redemption (Christ *"gratias egit"*), which is renewed in the sacrificial consecration (Christ consecrated bread and wine) and again offered to the Father in union with the Son and the Holy Spirit. The priest, faithful to the command of Christ "Do this for a commemoration of Me," commemorates His passion, death, resurrection, and ascension and, together with all the Church, renews the offering which He made of Himself.

At first the Canon was recited aloud, but later it became the custom to pronounce it in a low voice and with the most profound recollection, perhaps to surround such sacred words with a halo of mystery. This does not mean that the people should not know the rich content of this prayer. Rather it is the desire of the Church that the faithful be impregnated in its spirit and follow the priest, repeating the same formula "which is penetrated with faith and perfumed with piety, full of power and action. Its simple language has a vital character and an imprint of antiquity, which moves the pronouncer with the same impression produced by the mysterious shadows of the basilicas of the Eternal City" (*Gihr*). It is noteworthy that the Council of Trent has declared the Canon of the Mass to be immune from all error (*DB*, 742).

BIBLIOGRAPHY

Botte, *Le canon de la Messe Romaine,* édition critique, introduction et notes (Louvain, 1935). Cagin, *L'Anaphore apostolique* (Paris, 1919). Doronzo, *De Eucharistia,* Vol. 2 (Milwaukee, 1948), p. 1194 ff. Fortescue, "Canon of the Mass," *CE.* Molien, *La prière de l'Eglise,* Vol. 1, *Messe et Heures de Jour* (Paris, 1923). Moureau, "Canon de la Messe," *DTC.* De Puniet, *La Liturgie de la Messe* (Avignon, 1928). Vigourel, *Le canon romain de la Messe* (Paris, 1915).

Capreolus. See "Outline of the History of Dogmatic Theology" (p. 303).

Carlostadius (Carlstadt). See *Presence, Real, Eucharistic (fact).*

catechesis (Gr. κατήχησις from ἠχή — sound, noise; therefore κατηχέω — I resound, echo, make heard, teach). At the dawn of Christianity it meant the oral teaching of the evangelical doctrine. The term is found in St. Paul and in St. Luke, especially as a verb (cf. 1 Cor. 14:19; Acts 18:25).

It is customary to distinguish between an apostolic catechesis — the preaching of the gospel heralds, sober and plain exposition, but lively and replete with the teaching of Jesus Christ — and a catechesis of the Fathers of the Church, which is the first development of the teaching as adapted to the common intelligence of the neophytes, especially under the simple form of the homily. But in a stricter sense, catechesis is the careful instruction which, from the first centuries, accompanies and is a part of the catechumenate (see *catechumen*) in its various steps. There was an *introductory* catechesis, which was given to the candidates before admission to the real catechumenate; we have an interesting example of this in St. Augustine's *De catechizandis rudibus,* which treats not only about the subject matter, but also of the *method* of teaching religious truths.

After this initial preparation the aspirant was admitted to the catechumenate, at first as an *audient* (auditor), then as a *competent;* and the catechesis became progressively more extensive and more profound, up to the teaching of the great mysteries and the sacraments. In this connection, the most complete and precious document is the 24 catecheses of St. Cyril of Jerusalem, in which are distinguished: an introduction (*protocatechesis*); 18 catecheses for those to be baptized (φωτιζόμενοι — to be illumined), which treat of sin, penance, baptism, and faith, and develop the articles of the Creed in a popular style; and, finally, the 5 mystagogical or sacramental catecheses for the newly baptized (νεοφώτιστοι — neo-illumined). The old catechesis gave birth to the *Catechism,* a compendium of Christian doctrine adapted to children and adults.

BIBLIOGRAPHY

HÉGAR, *Histoire du catéchisme depuis la naissance de l'Eglise jusqu'à nos jours* (Paris, 1900). DUCHESNE, *Christian Worship, Its Origin and Evolution,* trans. McClure (London, 1903).

catechumen (κατηχούμενος from κατηχέω — I re-echo, inform, teach). The official name of the aspirant to baptism who was being carefully prepared for the Christian initiation. The catechumenate, embryonic in the apostolic age, was gradually and progressively organized to accommodate the influx of converts to the new faith (from the end of the second century, under Emperor Commodus). It consisted in the instruction of the mind (catechesis, *q.v.*), which gave rise to existent schools (cf. the Alexandrian *Didascaleion*), and in the formation of the heart by means of rites, prayers, and ascetic practices (fasting, penances). Its organization varied according to the different churches, but generally included *two classes* of candidates: *audient* and *competent* catechumens, corresponding to the two periods of preparation: remote, which lasted up to three years, and *proximate,* which coincided wholly or partially with Lent and closed with the conferring of baptism on the night before Easter Sunday, when the *competents* became *faithful* or *neophytes* (regenerated).

Admission to the catechumenate, especially after defections occurred in time of persecutions (*lapsi* — fallen from the faith into the sin of denial), was strictly controlled. A well-known Christian introduced the *novice,* who underwent certain ritual ceremonies (insufflation, imposition of hands, etc.). After a more or less extended period of prayers, instruction, and probation, the catechumen, properly examined, was promoted to the class of the *competents,* who were the object of a more intense intellectual and moral formation. They prepared for the coming baptism with fasts, penances, a kind of secret confession, which, however, was not sacramental; they attended a part of the Mass, learned the *Credo* and the *Pater Noster* (which was consigned to them and carefully explained: *traditio*), and finally they were admitted to the secret knowledge of the sacraments. Having received baptism, they remained in their white garbs until the first Sunday after Easter (hence the name of week *in Albis,* and Sunday *in Albis*). The catechumenate gradually disappeared with the introduction of the practice of baptizing babies.

BIBLIOGRAPHY

BAREILLE, "Catéchuménat," *DTC.* DUCHESNE, *Christian Worship, Its Origin and Evolution,* trans. McClure (London, 1903). SCANNELL, "Catechumen," *CE.*

catholicity (mark of the Church). Catholicity (Gr. καθολική — general, universal) is the third note or property which the Nicene-Constantinople Creed attributes to the Church. Like unity and sanctity, this prerogative descends as a natural corollary from the essence of the Church itself. If, in fact, the Church is humanity socially and supernaturally organized in Christ, of its very nature it embraces all individuals of the human race; it is, in other words, universal.

The whole of the gospel teaching, as well as the sympathy manifested by Christ for the Gentiles, were a prelude to the universal message which He entrusted to His Apostles on the moment of leaving the earth: "Going therefore, teach ye all nations" (Matt. 28:19). He had said, during His ministry, that the kingdom of God is comparable to a mustard grain, grown into a full and leafy tree and stretching its branches over all the earth. He had compared it to a handful of leven which made the whole mass of flour rise, and to a net cast into the sea and gathering all kinds of fishes in its mesh. The Church is catholic *de jure,* because it is like a seed destined to ferment the whole human mass, permeating its various intellectual and moral, civil and religious aspects. It is catholic *de facto* because, with the special assistance of God, from the beginning it waxed strong among all peoples, breaking all barriers, overcoming all persecutions, and making its enemies bow in defeat.

BIBLIOGRAPHY

St. Thomas, *In Symbolum Apostolorum Expositio,* a. 7–8. "Catholicité": various articles by Batiffol, Labrune, Delos, Allo, Schmidlin, Sertillanges, in a special issue of *Revue des Sciences Philosophiques et Théologiques* (October, 1928). Moureau, "Catholicité," *DTC.* Ricciotti, *Il cattolicesimo* (Florence, 1939). Thurston, "Catholic," *CE.*

causality of the sacraments (fact). Revelation states, on the one hand, that the sacraments produce grace, and determines, on the other hand, the limits and conditions of this causality. The sacraments both in Scripture and in Tradition are represented:

1. *As instruments in the hands of God,* ordained to infuse grace, just like the brush in the hands of Leonardo da Vinci was the means of painting the Last Supper. God the Father, according to the words of St. Paul, has saved us through means of the laver of regeneration (Tit. 3:5); the Holy Spirit, according to the teaching of St. Ephrem († 373), penetrates the waters of the sacred font to *elevate* and purify souls (*Adv. scrutatores,* sermo 40).

2. *As instruments which produce their effects immediately,* i.e., by the simple performance of the rite, independently of the merits of minister or subject. St. Luke attests that the faithful received the Holy Spirit by the simple imposition of hands by the Apostles (Acts 8:17; 19:6), while St. Paul exhorts Timothy (2 Tim. 1:6) to revive the grace which had been communicated to him by the same rite. The Fathers of the fourth and fifth centuries compare baptism to a mother's breast: "That saving wave [water] has become for you both a sepulchre and a mother" (Cyril of Jerusalem, *Catech. Mystag.* 2, 4); from which we rightly conclude that in their doctrine the sacraments are endowed with a real and immediate efficacy, as the causality of the mother in the generation of her offspring is real and immediate. Parallel to these testimonies, which enunciate the objective effectiveness of the external rite, are many others excluding dependency of such efficacy on the merits of the minister or the recipient; suffice it to cite the classic words of St. Augustine which, pronounced on the occasion of the Donatist controversy (see *Donatism*), represent the synthesis of Tradition: "Baptism does not have its value from the merits of the one who administers it or even of the one who

receives it, but by reason of its own holiness and efficacy, communicated to it by Him who instituted it" (*Contra Cresconium,* 4, 19). In addition, we have the constant practice of recognizing as valid even baptism administered by heretics, and the custom of apostolic origin of baptizing children prior to their use of reason.

3. *As instruments demanding moral dispositions in the subject,* as prerequisites absolutely necessary for the production of their effect in the soul. Similar to the craftsman who cannot form iron into an artistic form with his instrument unless the iron is first made malleable by heat, so the heavenly Artist cannot introduce grace in man through the sacraments, unless the soul has first been made flexible to the intention of the divine art by the fire of penitence and love. The sources of revelation inculcate the necessity of faith and penance (cf. the exhortations addressed in Acts 2:38–41, to the first converts: "Do penance, and be baptized . . . for the remission of your sins" and the fervent solicitations to virtue addressed to the catechumens and penitents by the Fathers) and point out the *dispositive* or preparatory function of faith and penance with respect to the justification produced by the sacramental rites.

Basing herself on these sure testimonies, the Church defined (*against the Protestants*) that the sacraments are real instruments in the hands of God, and that through the objective application of the rite (*ex opere operato, q.v.*) they produce the effect of grace in every subject who does not put an obstacle to it (*non ponentibus obicem;* see *obex*) (*DB,* 799, 849, 951).

BIBLIOGRAPHY

St. Thomas, *Summa Theol.,* III, q. 62 (with the commentaries of Cajetan, Gonet, Billuart, Gotti, etc.). Bucceroni, *Commentarius de sacramentorum causalitate* (Paris, 1884). Diekamp, Hoffmann, *Theologiae Dogmaticae Manuale,* Vol. 4 (Rome, 1934), pp. 34–41. Doronzo, *De sacramentis in genere* (Milwaukee, 1946), pp. 137–159. Hugon, *La causalité instrumentale dans l'ordre surnaturel* (Paris, 1924). Mattiussi, *De Sacramentis* (Rome, 1925). Pohle-Preuss, *Dogmatic Theology,* VIII *The Sacraments,* Vol. I, *The Sacraments in General, Baptism, Confirmation* (St. Louis, 1945), pp. 122–152.

causality of the sacraments (mode). If faith teaches us that the sacraments are true instrumental causes that produce grace *ex opere operato,* it nevertheless leaves us free to discuss the intimate nature of this causality. In the course of seven centuries theologians have proposed many opinions which run the gamut, with an indefinite variety of nuances, from nominalistic minimism to the realism of St. Thomas.

William of Auxerre, followed by Ockham and his disciples, maintained that the sacraments are causes of grace, in as much as by a kind of pre-established harmony the intimate action of God, which infuses grace, always corresponds to the sacramental rite externally performed by the minister. This is a sort of sacramental occasionalism, which robs the sacraments of the dignity of true efficient causes; for this reason it was totally abandoned after the Council of Trent.

Cardinal Lugo, with many Jesuits and Scotists, maintained that the sacraments, dignified by the blood of Christ, morally move God to communicate grace. This is the famous *moral* causality, so brilliantly defended in the past century by Cardinal Franzelin, which leaves the majority of theologians indifferent today because, even prescinding from the difficulty of conceiving dignification of a rite by Christ without an objective and real influence, it seems to displace the sacraments from the order of efficient causality into that of final causality. It also seems not to preserve perfectly the nature and definition of instrumental causality.

Billot with some of his disciples (Van Noort, Manzoni) believes that the sacraments are *intentional* efficient causes. But according to the principles of that philosophy, which the eminent theologian held so dear, intentional causality, which is the causality proper to the *sign,* is of the *formal* kind; how, then, can it be asserted that the sacraments are *efficient and formal* causes of grace?

Capreolus, together with some old interpreters of St. Thomas, believed the sacraments to be real efficient instruments, which, under the influx of God, produce in the soul not grace itself (which he held to be *created* and as such producible by God only) but a kind of *ornatus,* i.e., adornment or disposition calling for the infusion of grace. Apart from its many incongruences, this system seems to clash with the data of revelation which affirm that the sacraments are productive of grace itself, not only of a disposition for grace.

St. Thomas, finally, teaches that the sacraments are instrumental causes which, under the motion of God, the Principal Cause, by a real and mysterious influence are able to produce sanctifying grace itself (*physico-perfective* causality). This teaching, which merely puts into philosophical language the vivid expressions of Holy Scripture and the Fathers, harmonizes perfectly with many other parts of the theological system constructed by the Angelic Doctor, and has always obtained an extensive following among the most famous theologians.

BIBLIOGRAPHY

ST. THOMAS, *Summa Theol.,* III, q. 62. BILLOT, *De sacramentis,* Vol. 1 (Rome, 1931), pp. 102–141. DORONZO, *De sacramentis in genere* (Milwaukee, 1946), pp. 159–197. FRANZELIN, *De sacramentis* (Rome, 1911), pp. 106–125. MALTA, "De causalitate intentionali sacr. animadversiones quaedam," *Angelicum* (1938), pp. 337–366. MARQUART, "De la causalité du signe," *Revue Thomiste* (1937), p. 40 ff. POHLE-PREUSS, *Dogmatic Theology,* VIII *The Sacraments,* Vol. 1, *The Sacraments in General, Baptism, Confirmation* (St. Louis, 1945), pp. 152–160. VAN HOVE, "Doctrina G. Altissiodorensis de caus. sacr.," *Divus Thomas* (Piacenza, 1930), pp. 305–324.

cause, causality. In Aristotelian-Thomistic philosophy, *cause* is defined: "Principle which properly and directly has an influence into the being of another." It is, therefore, a *realizing* (reality making) force.

We distinguish: (1) *efficient* cause, in which the above definition is fully verified; (2) *final* cause (*id propter quod,* or that on account of which), which is the motive of the efficient cause; (3) *formal* cause (*id per quod,* or that by which), which unites with matter in order to determine it specifically, either in the substantial order (e.g., the soul, substantial form of the body), or in the accidental order (e.g., the figure, form of a statue); (4) *material* cause (*id ex quo,* or that of which), which, together with the form, concurs intrinsically in the constitution of a determined being. The *exemplary* cause (*id secundum quod*) is reductively a *formal extrinsic* cause.

The interplay of causality is evident in the world: but the English phenomenalist, David Hume, denied causality, and Kant reduced its value to that of a subjective category of man's mind. For Christian philosophy, the principle of causality ("every effect has its cause"): (1) has ontological (real, objective) value, i.e., really is in things; (2) is so evident as to resolve itself proximately in the first principles of the human mind (principles of identity and contradiction). In fact, given a being which has the characteristics of "effect" (i.e., which is participated and contingent), the intellect sees in it, as implicit, the exigency of a cause. All our theodicy or natural theology is based on the principle of causality.

Other divisions are: (*a*) *principal* cause, which produces or otherwise actuates the effect, of and by itself; (*b*) *instrumental* cause, which acts in dependence on the principal cause; (*c*) *univocal* cause, which produces an effect equal to itself (horse begets horse); (*d*) *equivocal* cause, which produces an effect diverse from itself (the sun, as cause of the plant); (*e*) *analogical* cause, which produces an effect in some way similar to itself (see *analogy*).

BIBLIOGRAPHY

AVELING, "Cause," *CE*. FABRO, "La difesa critica del principio di causalitá," *Rivista di Filosofia Neoscolastica* (1936). GARRIGOU-LAGRANGE, *The One God,* trans. Rose (St. Louis, 1943), pp. 112–123. PETER PARENTE, "Rapporto tra partecipazione e causalitá in S. Tommaso," *Acta Pont. Acad. Romanae S. Thomae Aquinatis* (Rome, 1941).

celibacy of the clergy (Lat. *caelibatus* — status of one who is not joined in matrimony). The example and the teaching of Jesus Christ, Son of a Virgin and Mirror of unstained purity, as well as the example of the Apostles, who, following Jesus, abandoned their families, exercised a powerful attraction on the first Christian generations. Hence, the high esteem which the nascent Church had for virginity; an esteem which exercised a great influence on the choice of persons appointed for the cult.

Actually at the beginning of the third century, Tertullian and Origen tell us of the great number of continent clerics, and at the beginning of the fourth century, Eusebius of Caesarea gives us the intimate reason for this: "It is fitting that whoever is dedicated to the divine ministry abstain from the use of matrimony, so that free from all earthly care he may be better able to attend to preaching" (*Dem. Evang.,* l. 1, c. 9; *PG.,* 22, 81). These testimonies assure us of the widespread custom of clerical celibacy, but no document of the first centuries tells of an established law. Rather the Nicene Council tolerates, for the Oriental Church, the use of legitimate matrimony for priests and deacons. This is still the constant rule in the Oriental Church up to the present day.

In the West, however, a very much more rigorous tendency must have developed very early, since the Council of Elvira, Spain (in 306), was able to promulgate a canon of the following tenor: *Placuit in totum prohibere episcopis, presbyteris et diaconibus vel omnibus clericis positis in ministerio abstinere se a coniugibus suis et non generare filios; quicumque vero fecerit ab honore clericatus exterminabitur* ("It is the will of the council that bishops, priests, deacons, and all clerics engaged in the ministry abstain from wives and the generation of children under the penalty of expulsion from the honor of the clerical state"; *EFHE,* 399). This is the first law on celibacy, and pointed the way which was afterward to be followed rigidly by the Latin Church. The aptness of this law is set forth in magistral fashion by J. de Maistre in his classical work *Le Pape,* l. 3, c. 3, and especially by Pius XI, in the encyclical *Ad Catholici Sacerdotii* (1935), which exalts sacerdotal chastity as the most beautiful gem of the Catholic clergy.

BIBLIOGRAPHY

CARACCIOLO DI TORCHIAROLO, *Il celibato ecclesiastico, studio storico teologico* (Rome, 1912). KURTSCHEID, *Historia Iuris Canonici,* Vol. 1 (Rome, 1941). POHLE-PREUSS, *Dogmatic Theology,* XI *The Sacraments,* Vol. 4, *Extreme Unction, Holy Orders, Matrimony* (St. Louis, 1946), pp. 130–137. THURSTON, "Celibacy of the Clergy," *CE*. VACANDARD, "Célibat," *DTC*. ZACCARIA, *Storia polemica del celibato* (Rome, 1774). Clerical celibacy was particularly attacked by H. Ch. Lea, *Historical Sketch of Sacerdotal Celibacy,* 2 vols. (Philadelphia, 1907).

censures, ecclesiastical. See *penalty.*

censure, theological (Lat. *censere* — estimate, evaluate, decree). A judgment unfavorably qualifying a theological expression, opinion, or entire doctrine. This judgment can be *private,* if given by one or more theologians on their own authority, or *public* and *official,* when promulgated by the ecclesiastical authority. The Church has the right, in theological matters, to judge and reprove, in virtue of its teaching mission and its infallibility in matters of faith and morals, which obliges her to safeguard and protect from all contamination, direct or indirect, the sacred deposit of divine revelation. The exercise of this right by the Church is very old (cf. the definitions of the councils, the *Index of Prohibited Books,* the propositions of various authors condemned throughout the centuries).

The formulas of censure are multiple, with a gradation from slightest to greatest rigor. They may be classified in three categories:

1. With respect to *doctrinal content,* a proposition can be censured as: (*a*) *heretical,* when openly opposed to a truth of faith, defined as such by the Church — according to its greater or lesser opposition, the proposition may be termed *proximate to heresy* (*proxima haeresi*) or *of heretical savor* (*sapiens haeresim*); (*b*) *erroneous in faith* (*erronea*), when opposed to a grave theological conclusion, which derives from a revealed truth and a premise of reason; if it is opposed to a simple opinion among the theologians, the proposition is censured as *temerarious* (*temeraria*).

2. With respect to its defective *form,* a proposition is judged *equivocal, doubtful, captious, suspect, bad sounding,* etc., although not in contradiction with any truth of faith from a doctrinal viewpoint.

3. With respect to the *effects* which it can produce, considering the particular circumstances of time and place, although it is not erroneous in content or form. In this case the proposition is censured as *perverse, vicious, scandalous, dangerous, seductive of the simple,* etc.

Ecclesiastical censures are to be carefully distinguished from these theological censures. The former are medicinal penalties (e.g., excommunication).

BIBLIOGRAPHY

Newman, *A Letter to the Duke of Norfolk in Certain Difficulties of Anglicans* (London, 1892). Quilliet, "Censures Doctrinales," *DTC.* Sessa, *Scrutinium doctrinarum . . .* (Rome, 1709). Sollier, "Censures (Theological)," *CE.* Tanquerey, *Synopsis Theol. Dogmaticae,* Vol. 2 (Paris, 1926), p. 116 ff. Viva, *Damnatarum thesium theologica trutina* (Padova, 1737).

character, sacramental (Gr. χαρακτήρ — impressed mark, die, seal, sign). An indelible sign impressed on the soul by baptism, confirmation, and holy orders, in consequence of which these sacraments cannot be administered twice to the same person.

This doctrine, vaguely referred to in Holy Scripture (2 Cor. 1:21–22; Eph. 1:13–14; 4:30) and extensively developed by the Fathers, especially by St. Augustine who was the first — on the occasion of the Donatist controversy (see *Donatism*) — to bring out clearly the separability of the character from grace, exalting its Christological and ecclesiological function, reached perfect systemization with the Scholastics, who explained its intimate nature from both the philosophical and the theological aspect.

Philosophically it is a spiritual reality (a real or ontological consecration), to be classified in the predicament of quality, as a physical, instrumental faculty, which is indelible both in this life and in the next.

Theologically it is: (1) *in relation*

to Christ, a participation of His priesthood, in so far as it confers on the faithful a power (initial in baptism, more developed in confirmation, perfect in orders) of offering the sacrifice of the New Testament and of imparting grace through the administration of the sacraments. This power is a reflection, as is evident, of the functions of reconciler of men with God through means of the sacrifice of Calvary (ascendant mediation) and of sanctifier or dispenser of the divine gifts to men through means of the sacraments (descendant mediation) which belong to the humanity of Jesus Christ in virtue of the hypostatic union. (2) *With reference to grace* it is an exigent cause, a defense, and, in certain cases, an effective cause. It is an exigent cause of grace because in its quality of supernatural consecration it is like a precious stone, which must be placed in its proper setting in order to shine in all its splendor; that setting is grace. It is also a safeguard of grace because, as the Fathers say, while it frightens away the demons, it attracts the custody of the good angels as well as the special benevolence and attention of the heavenly Father, who sees in the "seal" a participation of the divine light which shines on the human brow of the only-begotten Son. Finally, in the case of reviviscence, the character is taken and used by God as an instrumental cause to produce that grace whose infusion had been impeded by moral indisposition (*obex*) of the subject. (3) *With respect to the Church* the character is a *distinctive* sign marking the faithful from the infidels, and a *constitutive* sign of the hierarchy, in so far as it distributes in different grades the members of the kingdom of Christ: simple citizens (baptism), soldiers (confirmation), leaders (orders).

This doctrine was rejected by the Protestants, who considered the character as a creation of the Roman pontiff (Luther) and more precisely of Innocent III (Chemnitz), or as an escape found by St. Augustine to conciliate the antinomies of his sacramental theory (Harnack). The Council of Trent defined the central nucleus of the doctrine exposed above (*DB,* 852).

BIBLIOGRAPHY

St. Thomas, *Summa Theol.,* III, q. 63 (with the commentaries of Cajetan, John of St. Thomas, Billuart, Paquet). Brommer, "Die Lehre vom sakramentalen Charakter," *Der Scholastik* (Paderborn, 1908). Connell, *De sacramentis* (Brugis, 1933), pp. 90–97. Doronzo, *De sacramentis in genere* (Milwaukee, 1946), pp. 264–338. Durst, "De characteribus sacramentalibus," *Xenia Thomistica,* Vol. 3 (Rome, 1924). Farine, *Der sakramentale Charakter* (Freiburg i.-Br., 1904). Pierce, "The Origin of the Doctrine of the Sacramental Character," *The Irish Theological Quarterly,* Vol. 6 (1911), n. 2, pp. 196–211. Moureau, "Caractère sacramentel," *DTC.* Piolanti, *De Sacramentis,* Vol. 2 (Rome), pp. 96–114. Pohle-Preuss, *Dogmatic Theology,* VIII *The Sacraments,* Vol. 1, *The Sacraments in General, Baptism, Confirmation* (St. Louis, 1945), pp. 76–96. Ryan, "Character," *CE.* Scheeben, *The Mysteries of Christianity,* trans. Vollert (St. Louis, 1946), pp. 582–592.

charism (Gr. χάρισμα — gift). In general, any gift that the benevolence of God grants man; in particular, a gratuitous and transitory supernatural gift conferred on the individual in view of the general good, for the building of the Church, Mystical Body of Christ.

The prophet Joel (2:28; cf. Acts 2:16 ff.) had predicted for the Messianic epoch an abundant effusion of the Holy Spirit, and Jesus, before ascending into heaven, promised to the disciples that singular marvels would accompany and confirm their preaching (Mark 16:17–18).

St. Paul gives four lists of gifts bestowed on the nascent Church, but they are neither alike nor complete (1 Cor. 12:8–10, 28–30; Rom. 12:6–8; Eph. 4:11; cf. 1 Cor. 14:26).

Lack of sufficient elements makes identification of the individual gifts difficult. He speaks of the gifts of *apostolate, prophecy, discernment of spirits, teaching, exhortation, canticles, tongues, interpretation;* and of a gift of *evangelist.* In virtue of these gifts, which could invest any of the faithful, the Christian communities were instructed and edified with discourses of various kinds. Other gifts were intended for the spiritual direction and charitable assistance of the faithful: gifts of *government,* of *ministry,* of *alms,* gifts of *patronate* (of orphans and widows), of *hospitality,* of *faith* (effective of miracles), gifts of *healing,* of *power* (e.g., the resurrection of the dead).

The gifts were very important in the life and constitution of the primitive Church, contributing efficaciously to the growth and propagation of the faith.

BIBLIOGRAPHY

LEMONNYER, "Charisme," *DBVS.* MARÉCHAUX, *Les charismes du St. Esprit* (Paris, 1921). PASCAL PARENTE, *The Mystical Life* (St. Louis, 1946), pp. 210–220. PRAT, *The Theology of St. Paul,* trans. Stoddard, Vol. 1 (Westminster, 1927), pp. 127–129, 423–426. WILHELM, "Charismata," *CE.*

charity. A theological virtue infused together with grace, which inclines the will to love God for Himself. The three theological virtues (faith, hope, and charity) have God as their object, but while faith refers to God *as not seen* and hope *as not yet attained,* charity makes one tend to God and adhere to Him *as already possessed.* Therefore charity is the most important not only of the theological virtues, but also of all the other virtues. The primacy of charity is clearly affirmed by St. Paul in a beautiful page of 1 Cor. 13:13: "Now there remain faith, hope, and charity, these three: but the greatest of these is charity." The Apostle adds that in this life nothing avails, not even martyrdom, without charity, and that in the other life faith and hope will cease, but charity never. Not less enlightening is the testimony of St. John on the excellence of charity: to him belongs the well-known expression which defines God as charity and reveals the efficacy of this virtue in determining a mutual indwelling between God and man: "God is charity: and he that abideth in charity, abideth in God, and God in him" (1 John 4:16). Furthermore, the entire Gospel is the happy message of love. This fundamental motif of revelation is largely developed by the Fathers, especially St. Augustine.

As regards theology, it is enough to recall the teaching of St. Thomas who, notwithstanding his intellectualistic tendency, admits the primacy of charity and deeply studies the reasons for this primacy. According to him, the excellence of charity is shown principally from its *object* or *formal motive,* which is the goodness of God considered absolutely in itself; therefore, charity is not *interested love* (*amor concupiscentiae*), but love of pure friendship (*amor benevolentiae*), which seeks and reposes not in one's own good, but in the good of the Beloved. Even when charity makes one love creatures, its motive is always the goodness of God which shines in them. Moreover, St. Thomas demonstrates that charity is the root, the mover, and the form of all the other virtues, because it has as its object the last end, God in Himself, to which charity directs all supernatural activity of the spirit with a continual influence, either latent or manifest.

Charity is so intimately connected with sanctifying grace (Scotus and others identified them) that through sin they are both lost together, while the other virtues can remain, although in a condition of sterility (*inform virtues*). Charity can be more or less perfect, but on its grade of intensity and purity depends the whole moral life of man and his eternal destiny: "Inchoate charity, therefore, is inchoate justice; advanced charity is advanced justice" (St. Augustine, *De Natura et Gratia,* 70). The theologians distinguish various grades in the love of God, from distinct viewpoints; the distinction of St. Thomas is sober and effective (*Summa Theol.,* II–II, q. 24, a. 9): first grade, of the *beginners* (detachment from sin, liberation from slavery to the passions); second grade, of the *proficient* (tenacious struggle for the stable conquest of good); third grade, of the *perfect* (adhesion to God, prelude of the blessed life).

BIBLIOGRAPHY

St. Thomas, *Summa Theol.,* II–II, q. 23 ff. Noble, *L'amitié avec Dieu, Essais sur la vie spirituelle d'après Saint Thomas d'Aquin* (Paris, 1927). Schultes, "De caritate ut forma virtutum," *Divus Thomas* (Piacenza, 1928), pp. 1–28.

chiliasm. See *millenarianism.*

chirotony. See *imposition of hands.*

Chrysostom. See "Outline of the History of Dogmatic Theology" (p. 302).

Church (Lat. *Ecclesia.* Gr. ἐκκλησία — assembly, meeting, convocation). The kingdom of God on earth governed by the apostolic authority (D. Palmieri).

Institution. Jesus Christ, as is strikingly evident on every page of the Gospel, represented Himself to the world as the founder of "the kingdom of God," which in its earthly phase is ordained to gather together all men (cf. the parables of the kingdom): the people.

As rulers of the kingdom He appointed the Apostles (cf. Luke 6:13; Matt. 18:15–18; John 20:21; Matt. 28:18–19, etc.): the clergy in the people (see *bishops*).

As head of the Apostles He constituted St. Peter (cf. Matt. 16:18–19; John 21:17): the primacy in the clergy (see *primacy of St. Peter*).

With these elements our Lord instituted a real society, hierarchically constituted (with subjects and superiors), visible to the eyes of all, but with a nonpolitical and religious end (cf. Matt. 4:3–10; 5:3–12; 6:33; 16:26–27, etc.), assigning it the function of applying, through the centuries, the fruits of the Redemption.

Essence. From this we clearly understand that the Church is the continuation and the prolongation of the *Incarnate Word,* His Mystical Body (Rom. 12:4–6; 1 Cor. 12:12–27; Eph. 4:4), which actualizes in each individual as in all humanity the work of the Redemption, through the offering of the sacrifice of the Mass and the exercise of the triple ecclesiastical power (*magisterium, ministerium, jurisdictio* — teaching, ministry, jurisdiction).

As its Founder is a Person subsisting both in the human and in the divine nature, so the Church is at the same time a human and divine society; the human element, visible, perceptible to the senses, consists of the multitude of men socially organized; the spiritual, invisible, divine element is furnished by the supernatural gifts which put the human aggregate under the influence of Christ and of the Holy Spirit, Soul and unitive Principle of the whole organism (theandric constitution of the Church). The Church is, therefore, the union of man with Christ in a social form, "the social synthesis of the human and the divine" (*Sertillanges*).

Properties. If the Church is the union of humanity with Christ in a social, hierarchically organized form, it has to be necessarily *one,* since

Christ is one and the human race is one; it has to be *holy,* because contact with Christ is sanctifying; it must be *catholic,* i.e., universal, since the union of humanity in Christ embraces (in tendency) all the individuals of the human species; it must be *apostolic,* because, since it is a union in hierarchical form, it is necessarily based on Peter and the Apostles and their successors, who constitute the hierarchy (see *unity; sanctity; catholicity; apostolicity*).

One, holy, catholic, apostolic: These are the four properties of the Spouse of Christ: its individual characteristics which become also marks of identification; when considered in historical reality they appear to the eyes of all as distinctive signs of the true institution of Jesus Christ (see *marks of the Church*).

Power and operations. Operatio sequitur esse (operation or action follows being). Being human-divine, visible and invisible, the Church operates in a way corresponding to its nature: through a teaching body (*magisterium*) which transmits the divine thought in the clothing of human words; through a *ministry* which, by means of sensible rites, the sacraments, infuses supernatural life; through a *government* which makes known the laws of the spirit in a form perceptible to the experience of the senses (see *hierarchy*).

Errors about the Church. Since the Church is the prolongation of Christ in time and space, there is a very striking analogy between the Christological and the ecclesiological errors. Just as some erred with respect to Christ by denying His divinity (*Jews, Gentiles, rationalists*), His humanity (*Docetae, Phantasiasts*), or others by separating the two natures (*Nestorians*), or by absorbing one nature in the other (*Monophysites*); so also with respect to the Church, some deny her divinity or divine mission in the world (*Jews, pagans, rationalists*), her humanity or visibility (*Wycliffe, Huss, Protestants*), her social, external perfection hinged on the Roman pontiff (*Eastern Schismatics, Gallicans, Febronians,* etc.); others separate her from the civil society (*liberals*), and, finally, there are those who would have her absorbed in the State (*regalists*).

The many *documents of the magisterium* concerning the Church are collected in *DB* under the heading *"Ecclesia."*

BIBLIOGRAPHY

St. Thomas, *Summa Theol.,* III, q. 8. Braun, *Aspects nouveaux du problème de l'Eglise* (Fribourg en Suisse, 1944). Dublanchy, "Eglise," *DTC.* Joyce, "Church," *CE.* Madebielle, "Eglise," *DBVS.* Scheeben, *The Mysteries of Christianity,* trans. Vollert (St. Louis, 1946), pp. 539–557. Sertillanges, *L'Eglise* (Paris, 1931), 2 vols. Stolz, *De Ecclesia* (Freiburg i.-Br., 1940). *The Teaching of the Catholic Church,* ed. Smith, 2 vols. (New York, 1949), pp. 70–75, 691–732. Wiseman, *Lectures on the Church.* See the classical treatises "De Ecclesia" by Bellarmine, Passaglia, Wilmers, Franzelin, Mazzella, Billot, D'Herbigny, Diekmann, Van Noort, Bainvel, Schultes, Vellico, Zapelena, etc.

See under *kingdom of God.*

circumcision (Lat. *circumcidere* — to cut around). The Hebraic rite which consists in cutting the membrane of the foreskin (*praeputium*) of males. Many ancient peoples also practiced it (e.g., the Egyptians), but when God in the Old Testament prescribed this practice to Abraham and his descendants He made it a sign or symbol of the religious pact which bound that patriarch and the heirs of His promise to Himself.

The solemnity and precision of the holy narrative (Gen. 17) show the importance of the ceremony. God appeared to the ninety-year-old Abraham and revealed His name to him, "the Omnipotent," and changed the patriarch's name from Abram to Abraham, and his wife's from Sarai to Sara, to indicate that a new era was about to begin for them. After having required the patriarch to pledge a perfect life and complete adherence to Him, God established a covenant with Abraham and his descendants, in which Abraham obligated himself to offer exclusive cult to God, to be faithful in His service, and to bear the symbol of this covenant in his flesh: circumcision. On His part, God pledged to protect the patriarch, to give him a numerous offspring, to reserve to him the Messianic blessing (see *Messias*) and to give him the land of Canaan (Palestine) as his possession. Thus Abraham became "the friend" of God. This friendship aimed at re-establishing communion of man with God, broken by Adam's guilt, and at a return to grace, which involves the remission of original sin. Circumcision in the Old Testament had an effect analogous to baptism in the organization established by Christ.

The efficacy of circumcision did not lie in the rite considered as a material action, but in its symbolism; and so, even in the ancient law, insistence was placed on the "circumcision of the heart," i.e., on purity of intention and docility to the will of God (Deut. 10:16; 30:6). Circumcision was practiced on the infant after birth — eight days after, according to the custom — and the infant received its name on that occasion (Luke 2:21).

Circumcision with its relative moral obligations was necessary to be able to share in the blessing and promises made to Abraham. Carnal descent from the patriarch was not sufficient.

BIBLIOGRAPHY

ASHER, *The Jewish Rite of Circumcision* (London, 1873). DORONZO, *De sacramentis in genere* (Milwaukee, 1946), Index Analyticus: "Circumcisio"; *De Baptismo et Confirmatione* (Milwaukee, 1947), pp. 248–254. ERMONI, "Circoncision," *DTC*. LESÊTRE, "Circoncision," *DBV*. REMONDINO, *History of Circumcision* (London, 1891). TIERNEY, "Circumcision," *CE*. VACCARI, "De vi circumcisionis in V. Foedere," *Verbum Domini*, 2 (1922), pp. 14–18.

circumincession (Gr. περιχώρησις). The mutual immanence of the three divine Persons, none of whom may stand without the others: the Father is in the Son, and vice versa; the Son and the Father are in the Holy Ghost, and vice versa. The reason of such circumincession lies in the numerical unity of the divine essence common to the three Persons. It is a truth of faith (cf. Council of Florence, *DB*, 704). In the Gospel, Christ Himself reveals (John 10:38; 17:21) that the Father is in Him and He in the Father. Tradition speaks of it constantly, but with a difference in concept between East and West. The Occidentals think of the Trinity rather in a *static* sense (each Person resides in the other, according to the term *sessio*); the Greeks, on the other hand, conceive circumincession in a *dynamic* sense (like a vital cycle in which the divine life flows and reflows from one to the other of the Persons: χώρησις — motion, advance).

The Trinitarian diagram of the Latins is:

$$\begin{matrix}\text{Father}\\ \text{Son}\end{matrix} > \text{Holy Spirit}$$

That of the Greeks is:

$$\text{Father} \rightarrow \text{Son} \rightarrow \text{Holy Spirit.}$$

The two concepts do not differ substantially.

BIBLIOGRAPHY

ST. THOMAS, *Summa Theol.*, I, q. 42, a. 5. CHOLLET, "Circumincession," *DTC*. HUGON, *Le mystere de la très sainte Trinité* (Paris, 1930), p. 354. JUGIE, "De Processione Spiritus Sancti," *Lateranum* (1936). KLEIN, *The Doctrine of the Trinity*, trans. Sullivan (New York, 1940), pp. 242–249. POHLE-PREUSS, *Dogmatic Theology*, II *The Divine Trinity* (St. Louis, 1946), pp. 281–289.

Clement Alex. See "Outline of the History of Dogmatic Theology" (p. 301).

Clement Rom. See "Outline of the History of Dogmatic Theology" (p. 301).

clergy (Gr. κλῆρος — lot, part; according to the dictum: *quasi in sortem Domini vocati* — "called to the lot of the Lord, so to speak"). The body of all the persons dedicated to the divine cult, from the lowest cleric to the Holy Father. Entrance into the clergy is effected through a sacred ceremony called *tonsure* (*q.v.*). The members of the clergy (divided into *major clerics,* if they have been marked with the orders of subdiaconate or higher, and *minor clerics,* if they have received only tonsure or minor orders) have the right of exercising the power of order and jurisdiction inherent in the grade occupied in the twofold *hierarchy* (*q.v.*), the right of receiving benefices, offices, and ecclesiastical pensions, and the right to reverence from the laity. In addition, the clergy enjoy four privileges: of *canon,* of *forum,* of *personal immunity,* and of *competence* (see *tonsure*).

The clergy, on the other hand, are bound by grave obligations. These obligations are: (*a*) *positive:* greater sanctity than that of the laity, many practices of piety, and, above all, the recitation of the *canonical hours* (the Breviary or divine office), cult of the sacred sciences, canonical obedience to their respective bishops, chastity (see *celibacy*), the wearing of ecclesiastical dress, and visible tonsure; (*b*) *negative:* abstention from everything unbecoming to their dignity and to their character, such as military service of a combatant kind, clamorous lawsuits, the medical profession, the legal profession, frequenting markets or exchanges, etc. Such are the rules sanctioned by the Church in the Code of Canon Law (Can. 108–144), drawn from her two thousand years' experience.

If it is true, alas, that certain members of the clergy, by violating their sacred bonds imposed on them by the Church, have not done honor to the class to which they belong, it is also admitted by all serious historians that the priestly class, as a whole, has been the spiritual ferment which has raised in all epochs the mass of the Christian people. Moreover, the clergy have given very real and illustrious contributions to every branch of human knowledge and activity.

BIBLIOGRAPHY

FANNING, "Cleric," *CE.* GOYENECHE, *Iuris Canonici Summa Principia,* Vol. 1 (Rome, 1935), pp. 147–170. KURTSCHEID, *Historia Iuris Canonici,* Vol. 1 (Rome, 1941). ROMANI, *Institutiones Juris Canonici* (Rome, 1941).

cleric. See *clergy; hierarchy.*

"communicatio idiomatum" (communication of idioms) (Gr. ἰδίωμα — property). The mutual attribution of the properties of the divine and of the human nature in Christ. It is legitimate on account of the hypostatic union, through which Christ is but one Person and so only one subject of attribution, which possesses both natures with their respective properties. The Nestorians (see *Nestorianism*), who placed in Christ two distinct subjects (persons), the Man and the Word, denied such mutual exchange of attributions between the two natures. The Monophysites, on the contrary, who fused into one the two natures, exaggerated the exchange of attributes to the point of eliminating the line of distinction between the divine and the human in Christ.

The Church has condemned one and the other error, and declared such communication legitimate on the basis of the *personal unity* of Jesus Christ (Council of Ephesus), while at the same time it maintained firmly the distinction of the two natures with their respective properties (Council of Chalcedon). In the light of these two definitions, the correct sense of the "communication of idioms" amounts to this: the mutual attribution of the properties of the two natures is not made directly to the natures themselves, taken as natures and *in abstracto,* but through the Person and in force of the unity of Person, the incarnate Word, real God and real Man. And so we may say of Christ: God is Man, the Christ-Man is God, the Immortal is mortal (because it is always the Person of the Word to whom we attribute that which is proper to one or to the other nature). But we may not say that the divinity is the humanity (because here attribution would be made between the two natures directly, without any reference to the Person).

On account of this communication, the Church sings in the Creed that the Only-Begotten of the Father has become man, suffered, died for us, and was buried.

BIBLIOGRAPHY

St. Thomas, *Summa Theol.,* III, q. 16. Maas, "Communicatio idiomatum," *CE.* Michel, "Idiomes (Communication des)," *DTC.* Peter Parente, *De Verbo Incarnato* (Rome, 1939), p. 129. Pohle-Preuss, *Dogmatic Theology,* IV *Christology* (St. Louis, 1946), pp. 184–196.

Communion, eucharistic (Lat. *cum* — with, and *unio* — union: i.e., union with another). The participation in the sacrificial banquet in which the faithful feed on the body and blood of Christ.

The effects of this participation are the individual and social union of the faithful with Christ, ordained to the glorification of the soul and the body.

The individual union (*incorporatio*) is taught in a sublime way by Jesus Christ in the discourse of the eucharistic promise: the two mysteries of the trinitary life, mutual immanence of the Father in the Son and the procession of the Son from the Father, are repeated, in a way, in the relationship of Christ with the faithful: "He that eateth my flesh, and drinketh my blood, abideth in me, and I in him. As the living Father hath sent me, and I live by the Father; so he that eateth me, the same also shall live by me" (John 6:57–58).

The social union (*concorporatio*) revealed in a classical Pauline text: "For we, being many, are one bread, one body, all that partake of one bread" (1 Cor. 10:17), is re-echoed by St. Augustine: *"O Sacramentum pietatis, o signum unitatis, o vinculum caritatis"* (*In Johannem,* tr. XXVI, 13).

The glorious resurrection (*ius ad gloriam* — right to glory) is promised by the Lord in the sermon at Capharnaum: "He that eateth my flesh, and drinketh my blood, hath everlasting life: and I will raise him up in the last day" (John 6:55), whence St. Ignatius Martyr († 107) exalts the Eucharist as the "drug of immortality and the antidote for death" (Eph. 20:2).

The *intimate nature* of these effects cannot be understood except in consideration of the general economy of the sacraments, of which they are the crown. Tradition represents the Eucharist as the perfection and summit (*consummatio*) of the whole supernatural order. As such it should complete the whole spiritual organism in its being (habitual grace), in its faculties (the virtues), in its activity (actual grace), and in its fruits (good works). In fact, as is drawn from a number of theological documents, the Eucharist produces more abundant habitual grace, increases charity, queen of all the virtues, to the highest grade, excites, with frequent *stimuli* of actual grace, that fervor from which shoot up luxuriantly, as a natural consequence, in greater number and perfection the good works that merit life eternal. Now, as is easily understood, effects of this kind constitute full incorporation in Christ, the most perfect union among the faithful, the highest right to glorification of soul and body, through which the individual faithful as well as the whole Church reach the acme of spiritual perfection, i.e., maturity for the beatific vision. After the Eucharist only one thing remains to be attained, i.e., glory.

BIBLIOGRAPHY

St. Thomas, *Summa Theol.*, III, q. 79. Cuttaz, *Pain vivant* (Paris, 1937). Dalgairns, *Holy Communion* (Dublin, 1892) Doronzo, *De Eucharistia,* Vols. 1 and 2 (Milwaukee, 1948), Index Analyticus: "Communio." Gasquet, *L'Eucharistie et le Corps Mystique* (1925). Hedley, *The Holy Eucharist* (London, 1907). Petroccia, *Universae fraternitatis causa* (Montiscasini, 1926). Piolanti, *Il corpo mistico e le sue relazioni con l'Eucaristia in S. Alberto Magno* (Rome, 1939). Pohle-Preuss, *Dogmatic Theology,* IX *The Sacraments,* Vol. 2, *The Holy Eucharist* (St. Louis, 1946), pp. 236–254. Smith, *Communion Under One Kind* (London, 1911). De la Taille, *Mysterium Fidei* (Parisiis, 1941), Elucidationes 36–49. Vonier, *A Key to the Doctrine of the Eucharist* (Westminster, 1946), pp. 250–257.

Communion of Saints. A truth of faith, which constitutes one of the articles of the Creed.

It consists in an intimate *union* and in a mutual *influence* among the members of the Church Militant, Church Suffering, and Church Triumphant (the Church on earth, in purgatory, and in heaven). This union and participation of the proper goods of the Church is founded chiefly on the truth of the Mystical Body (*q.v.*), through which all men in the *large sense* belong to Christ in virtue of the Incarnation and the Redemption; in the *strict sense* they are but one thing in Christ, as members of one sole organism, by force of baptism and, therefore, of faith and charity. In this mystical organism, which is the Church, Christ the Head injects the supernatural life of grace by means of the Holy Spirit, who is like the soul. United to Christ, the faithful are united among themselves; and this union is reinforced by the *sacraments,* channels of that grace which is the participation of the divine nature and the cause of the indwelling of the Holy Trinity in each sanctified soul. The gospel image of the vine (Christ) and the tendrils (Christians), the doctrine developed by St. Paul (1 Cor., Col., Eph., Rom.) about the Mystical Body and the Church, are a living expression of the dogma of the Communion of Saints, i.e., of all Christian souls for whom Christ prayed at the Last Supper: "That they all may be one, as thou, Father, in me, and I in thee" (John 17:21).

The Eastern Fathers of the Church illustrate this dogma in the light of the Holy Spirit, who diffuses supernatural life in all Christians. The Western Fathers prefer to explain it from the focal point of the Church, Mystical Body of Christ, temporal and eternal society of the redeemed. Both considerations lead to the concept of a common life, of a vital and mystical communion, in reason of which Christians fighting for good on earth, the souls in purgatory, and the blessed in heaven, communicate mutually one to the other the fruits of the Redemption, kept in the treasury of the Church, by *prayer* and by *charity.*

BIBLIOGRAPHY

St. Thomas, *Summa Theol.*, III, q. 8. Bernard, "Communion des Saints," *DTC.* Mura, *Le corps mystique du Christ,* Vol. 1 (Paris, 1936). Sollier, "Communion of Saints," *CE.* Tyrrell, "The Mystical Body," *Hard Sayings* (New York, 1902).

companation. See *transubstantiation.*

competents. See *catechumen.*

comprehensors. The blessed who enjoy the beatific vision (*q.v.*), i.e., the immediate intuition of the divine essence. The term *comprehensor* is used to indicate one who has arrived in the celestial country and who has reached God, the Supreme End, in opposition to one who is still a pilgrim on earth (*viator*). But we are *not* to understand comprehensor in the sense that the blessed *comprehend* God, exhausting God's intelligibility. Only God comprehends Himself; the blessed see Him through the light of glory, more or less intensively, but not with exhaustive knowledge — *totum* but not *totaliter,* as the theologians say. However, each blessed, subjectively considered, is fully happy, since he sees as much as he is able to see.

BIBLIOGRAPHY

See under *vision, beatific.*

conclave (Lat. *conclave* — locked room; from *cum* — with, and *clavis* — key). A closed place (ordinarily in the Vatican) where the cardinals assemble to elect the pope, or the assembly itself.

According to current discipline, as last amended by Pius XI, a conclave must assemble between 15 to 18 days after the death of the pope. The purpose is to give even the most distant cardinals a chance of attending the assembly.

On the day set, toward evening, the cardinals, each accompanied by a secretary and an attendant (*cameriere*) enter the conclave. All the doors are closed, and the only means of communication are the *ruote,* sort of revolving dumb-waiters, which are constantly guarded. Outside are posted the "maggiordomo" of the Sacred Palaces, representing the clergy, and the marshal of the holy Roman Church, representing the laity.

The next morning, in the Sistine Chapel, the election procedure begins. Election may be in one of three ways: *per quasi inspirationem* (by quasi inspiration), when all acclaim as pope a member of the sacred college of cardinals or an outsider; *per compromissum* (by compromise), when all agree to refer to certain of the electors the assignment of choosing the new pope; *per scrutinium,* or direct voting. When a candidate receives a majority vote of two thirds plus one he is regularly elected, and upon acceptance becomes *ipso facto* Roman pontiff, successor of Peter and Vicar of Christ. Immediately all the baldachini (canopylike structures) are lowered in the Sistine Chapel, except that of the newly elected pope. The Cardinal Protodeacon announces thereupon the result of the election from the balcony of St. Peter's, and the new pontiff imparts from there his apostolic blessing *urbi et orbi,* i.e., to the Eternal City and the world.

The history of the election of the pope and of the changes undergone by the conclave may be read in any manual of Church history.

BIBLIOGRAPHY

CHELODI, *Ius de personis,* ed. Ciprotti (Vicenza, 1942). DOWLING, "Conclave," *CE.* HESTON, *The Holy See at Work* (Milwaukee, 1950). LECTOR (MGR. GUTHLIN), *Le Conclave* (Paris, 1894). NEGRO, *L'Ordinamento della Chiesa Cattolica* (Milan, 1940).

concourse, divine. The influence of the first Cause on creature activity. The finite being, dependent on God in its being (see *creation; conservation*), must, consequently, depend on Him also in its operations, according to the Scholastic adage: *Operatio sequitur esse.* Very few theologians, among whom Durand, reduced this operational dependence only to the creative and conservative action of God, who would concur *remotely* (*concursus mediatus*) in the operation of creatures, inasmuch as He has given being and the power of action to them. On the other extreme, others stressed divine intervention in such a way as to eliminate creature action (e.g., the occasionalism of Malebranche). Sound theology is unanimous in admitting the necessity of a positive action of God on the creature in order to explain creature activity (*concursus immediatus*). This truth, although not one of defined faith, has its foundation in revelation: "Lord . . . thou hast wrought all our works for us" (Isa. 26:12); "In him we live, and move, and are" (Acts 17:28).

Reasons: (*a*) Only God *is* His Being, and so is essentially His operation (see *operation, divine*); the creature, on the contrary, receives its being and, therefore, must receive the impulse to operation, since a potency cannot pass to act of and by itself (see *Act, Pure*). (*b*) God, as first efficient and final Cause of the universe, has absolute dominion over all things, and so it is absurd to exempt the activity of creatures from divine influence. (*c*) All creature activity is *realizing,* i.e., it produces in some way and touches the *being* or reality of things; but *being,* the most universal effect, must go back, in last analysis, to God as its proper and *principal* Cause, to whom the creature is subordinate as an instrumental or secondary cause. St. Thomas, in his *De Potentia,* q. 3, a. 7, fixes the divine concourse in four points. God is cause of the action of every creature (including man): (1) inasmuch as He creates it; (2) inasmuch as He conserves it; (3) inasmuch as He moves it to act; (4) and uses it as an instrument (*concursus immediatus*).

On these points is based the theory of *physical premotion,* developed by the rigid Thomist Bañez (sixteenth century), to the point of affirming a *predeterminatio ad unum* (predetermination to one thing), by which God would not only start man to act, but push him to do *this* rather than *that* (taking from man *active indifference*). Such interpretation (see *Bannesianism*) was attacked by the Jesuit Molina, who proposed immediate divine concourse, not exercised *on* the creature but *with* the creature in relation to the same effect: a kind of parallelism between God and the creature co-operating together (*concursus simultaneus*). This opinion, while safeguarding human freedom, is certainly foreign to the thought of St. Thomas (see *Molinism*).

A divine motion is admissible which makes the creature pass to the exercise of the act, providing the creature itself contributes to the specification of the act (see *Thomism*).

BIBLIOGRAPHY

St. Thomas, *Summa Theol.,* I, q. 105; *Quaest. Disp. De Potentia,* q. 1, a. 7. On the interpretation of the doctrine of St. Thomas see the controversy between Garrigou-Lagrange, *Dieu,* Appendix (Paris, 1928) and D'Alès, *Providence et libre arbitre* (Paris, 1927). Pohle-Preuss, *Dogmatic Theology,* III *God: Author of Nature and the Supernatural* (St. Louis, 1945), pp. 61–78.

concupiscence (Lat. *concupere* — to long for). Psychologically, it is generally understood as a function of the sense appetite which is divided into *irascible* (with respect to good or bad, difficult to attain) and *concupiscible* (with respect to good or bad, easy to attain). In this sense, like all passions, concupiscence is a natural property good in itself, but which may be used for good or for bad.

Morally, the word *concupiscence* is a disordered inclination to sense pleasures, against the direction of reason; accepted still more strictly, it is sensuality. Concupiscence, understood in a moral sense, is also called *fomes peccati* (that which *foments,* incites to sin). Luther (see *Lutheran-*

ism) held this concupiscence (of which St. Paul speaks, Rom. 7:18), as sinful in itself and invincible. The Church, however, teaches that concupiscence, though a consequence of original sin (see *integrity*), is not a sin in itself. Concupiscence only inclines to sin, and that not irresistibly, since with good will and God's grace man can conquer it and in so doing can acquire merit for the struggle (cf. Council of Trent, *DB,* 792).

A small number of theologians, under the influence of certain misinterpreted expressions of St. Augustine, believed that original sin consists in concupiscence. St. Thomas put it clearly for all: concupiscence enters into the constitution of original sin, not indeed as a *formal* element, but only as a *material* element. It remains even after baptism *ad agonem* (to make us fight for heaven; Council of Trent).

BIBLIOGRAPHY

St. Thomas, *Summa Theol.,* I–II, q. 82, a. 2. Beraza, *De Deo elevante* (Bilbao, 1924), p. 133 ff. Ming, "Concupiscence," *CE.* Murray, *Tractatus De Gratia* (Dublin, 1877).

confession, sacramental (Lat. *confiteor* — I manifest). The integral, sincere, and clear avowal of the sins committed after baptism, made to a priest who has jurisdiction in order to obtain absolution.

Its *necessity* stems from the judicial nature of the sacramental power given by Christ to His Church (John 20:21–23). Unless the judge knows the inner condition of the soul he cannot give a sure judgment on its dispositions, and so does not have the necessary elements to use his power favorably or unfavorably. To reinforce this easy deduction it would not be difficult to adduce a great number of testimonies proving that from the first centuries the Church has maintained: *Quod iudex non novit non iudicat, sicut medicus quod ignorat non curat* ("What the judge does not know, he does not judge, just as the doctor does not cure what he does not know").

But confession does not appear less necessary if it is considered from the side of sin, which is a profanation of the whole human being. To raise oneself, therefore, from sin, it is not sufficient for the soul to purify itself in the crucible of repentance, but it is also required that the lips open themselves to confession. By manifesting what is going on in the human conscience, external confession harmonizes the heart and the tongue, re-establishing order in the whole human person. Such order and harmony is a good which can only come from an act of virtue, of the most difficult virtue, humility. This external humiliation of declaring oneself a sinner before one's fellow man strengthens and renders more efficacious the internal disposition which fortifies the penitent in waging unlimited warfare on sin and its consequences; therefore, the Catechism of the Council of Trent exalts auricular confession as the rock of Christian virtue.

The reformers of the sixteenth century haughtily rejected confession, designating it as "the slaughterhouse of consciences," but today there is a faint re-echoing which bears a tinge of homesickness for the practices of the old paternal home and of regret for the work of Protestantism which has broken the bond that attached the people to the ear of their spiritual director (see *penance*).

BIBLIOGRAPHY

St. Thomas, *Summa Theol.,* III, *Suppl.,* qq. 6–10. Doronzo, *De Poenitentia,* Vol. 2 (Milwaukee, 1951). Galtier, "Confession," *DA* and *DTC.* Geddes, Thurston, *The Catholic Church and Confession* (New York, 1928). Hanna, "Penance (Confession)," *CE.* Jenkins, *The Doctrine and Practice of Auricular Confession* (London, 1783). Kurtscheid, *A His-*

tory of the Seal of Confession, trans. Marks (St. Louis, 1927). MELIA, *A Treatise on Auricular Confession* (Dublin). PETAZZI, *La Confessione* (Gorizia, 1934). POHLE-PREUSS, *Dogmatic Theology,* X *The Sacraments,* Vol. 3, *Penance* (St. Louis, 1946), pp. 181–216. WISEMAN, *Lectures on the Principal Doctrines and Practices of the Catholic Church* (London, 1844). The sacrament of penance and confession was particularly attacked by H. Ch. Lea, *A History of Auricular Confession and Indulgences in the Latin Church,* 3 vols. (Philadelphia, 1896).

confessions of faith. See *Symbol.*

confirmation (Lat. *confirmo* — I confirm, make stable, etc.). The sacrament of the Christian youth and of the soldiers of Christ. The frequent predictions of the prophets concerning an abundant effusion of the Spirit of God in the Messianic times (Isa. 58:11; Ezech. 47:1; Joel 2:28; etc.), and the reiterated announcement of Christ about the descent of the Holy Spirit with the mission of completing the supernatural education of the Apostles (John 14:16; 15:26; 17:1; etc.), pointed to an institution complementary to baptism. In harmony with these precedents, the Saviour must have established that sacred rite during the forty days between Easter and the Ascension, for immediately after Pentecost we see it used by the Apostles, i.e., by those Twelve who introduced themselves to the world as executors of the Master's will, and never as the inventors of new religious rites (cf. 1 Cor. 4:1). "When the apostles, who were in Jerusalem, had heard that Samaria had received the word of God, they sent unto them Peter and John. Who, when they were come, prayed for them that they might receive the Holy Ghost. For he was not yet come upon any of them: but they were only baptized in the name of the Lord Jesus. Then they laid their hands upon them, and they received the Holy Ghost" (Acts 8:14–17; cf. 19:1–6).

The bishop, from the very beginning, has been the *minister* of this sacrament. It was the Apostles, and not the deacon Philip, who administered the first confirmation. It is fitting that a sacramental act, which implies completion and perfection, come within the ordinary powers of one who enjoys the fullness of priesthood. But this episcopal prerogative is not absolutely reserved to the bishops, because priests of the Oriental rite, by a sort of general delegation of the Church — while still remaining extraordinary ministers of confirmation — commonly confer this sacrament. Priests of the Latin rite can be authorized by the Roman pontiff to confer confirmation in cases provided for in the Code of Canon Law.

The *matter* is twofold: the imposition of hands (Acts 8:14–17) and the anointing (resulting from Tradition). The *form* is constituted by the words: "I sign thee with the sign of the cross, and I confirm thee with the chrism of salvation, in the name of the Father, and of the Son, and of the Holy Ghost. Amen."

Effects. The Fathers, liturgy, and the theologians are unanimous in exalting the effects of confirmation as a "complement," "perfection," "crown" of baptism.

The *character* of confirmation perfects that of baptism, especially because: (*a*) It enlarges the sphere of baptismal activity, especially in descendant mediation. In fact, while baptism confers the limited power of administering the sacrament of matrimony, confirmation renders the faithful a participant in a certain way of the ecclesiastical teaching authority (*magisterium*), by deputizing to profess, diffuse, and safeguard *ex officio* the patrimony of the faith, under the direction of the legitimate pastors. (*b*) It augments the exigencies of grace because, being a more precious gem than the baptismal character, it requires a more brilliant setting (sanctifying grace) in which to be mounted. Moreover, since it is a more active power, intended for more difficult actions, such as the intrepid defense of religion, it requires greater abundance of divine aids. (*c*) It assigns a special place in the Mystical Body, introducing the Christian officially into the public life of the Church with the honor of bearing all the sacrifices that are inherent in the defense of the Christian name.

The *grace* of confirmation perfects that of baptism: (1) because this sacrament of fullness makes the faithful "similar to Christ inasmuch as from the first instant of His conception He was full of grace" (St. Thomas, III, q. 72, a. 1. ad 4); (2) because it brings to virile maturity the supernatural organism "which from imperfect becomes immediately perfect" (*ibid.,* III, q. 72, a. 8. ad 4); (3) because by extending the circulation of the supernatural life, it develops the whole Mystical Body. On the one hand, abundant meritorious works are produced by the spiritual organism directed toward new conquests, works that enrich *ad intra* the treasury of the Church; on the other hand, in virtue of the simultaneous and compact advance of the soldiers of Christ, the breast of the Church is extended *ad extra* to receive and regenerate new souls for Christ.

The Protestants of the sixteenth century saw in confirmation nothing more than a *superfluous* ceremony, whose origin must be traced back to some ancient catechesis in which the adolescents gave an account of their faith to the Church. They were condemned by the Council of Trent, Sess. VII (*DB,* 871–873).

BIBLIOGRAPHY

St. Thomas, *Summa Theol.,* III, q. 72. Connell, *De sacramentis* (Brugis, 1933), pp. 147–170. Coppens, *L'imposition des mains et les rites connexes dans le N.T. et dans l'église ancienne* (Paris, 1925). Cuttaz, *Notre Pentecôte, la grâce du Chrétien militant* (Paris, 1925). Doronzo, *De Baptismo et Confirmatione* (Milwaukee, 1947). Gasquet, "The Early History of Baptism and Confirmation," *Dublin Review* (1895), p. 116 ff. O'Dwyer, *Confirmation* (Dublin, 1915). Piolanti, *De Sacramentis,* Vol. I (Rome, 1944), pp. 97–212. Pohle-Preuss, *Dogmatic Theology,* VIII *The Sacraments,* Vol. 1, *The Sacraments in General, Baptism, Confirmation* (St. Louis, 1945), p. 276 ff. Ruch, Bareille, Bernard, Ermoni, Marchal, Mangenot, Ortolan, "Confirmation," *DTC.* Scannell, "Confirmation," *CE. The Teaching of the Catholic Church,* ed. Smith, 2 vols. (New York, 1949), pp. 803–838. Wirgman, *The Doctrine of Confirmation* (London, 1902).

congregations, Roman. See *Holy See.*

congruism. A system derived from *Molinism* (*q.v.*) of which it keeps the fundamental principles. Congruism is connected especially with the name of Suarez, but is linked also to others, particularly to Bellarmine. The doctrinal point on which this system pivots is the nature of the efficacy of grace with respect to human freedom. The Thomists see generally a sharp difference between Molinism and congruism; the Molinists, on the contrary, maintain that the two systems coincide in thought, their mutual difference being only verbal.

Briefly: Molina terms efficacious that grace which attains its effect not by itself, but through the free consent of the man who receives it; God foresees that effect through the means of the so-called *middle knowledge* (*scientia media*). There is no entitative difference between sufficient grace and efficacious grace: the same grace can turn out inefficacious through lack of consent of the free will in a given subject, but can be efficacious in another subject who consents. Suarez develops and integrates this teaching of the Master, saying that the efficacy of grace depends on its adaptation to the psychological *conditions* of the individual, to the *circumstances* of time and place: this adaptation renders the grace *congruous,* proportioned to the subject in such a way that the effect follows infallibly, without violating the freedom of choice of the subject himself. Bellarmine even grants that congruous grace has an intrinsic efficacy of its own, which is not *physical* (St. Thomas) but *moral* (St. Augustine), in so far as it attracts and persuades to action.

All the congruists agree with Molina in maintaining that grace, in order to be efficacious, is conditioned by the free consent of man. Suarez, however, departs from Molina and approaches Thomism when he speaks of an *absolute predestination,* in the intentional order, independently of any human merit foreseen by God (*ante previsa merita*). For the predestined, God is said to prepare the most congruous graces.

In 1613 the General of the Jesuits, Claude Aquaviva, ordered that the theologians of the company should follow congruism.

BIBLIOGRAPHY

De Regnon, *Bañez et Molina* (Paris, 1883). Lang, *De Gratia* (Freiburg i.-Br., 1929), p. 499. McDonald, "Congruism," *CE.* Pesch, *De Gratia* (Freiburg i.-Br., 1926), prop. 22, p. 176 ff. Quilliet, "Congruisme," *DTC.*

conscience (Lat. *cum* — with, and *scire* — to know). In the proper sense, conscience is not a faculty, but an *act* of reflex knowledge, directed on what one has done or ought to do (St. Thomas). When the cognitive act has, as its object, actions already done, it is called *psychological conscience* (real *reflexion* of the acting subject on his own activity); and it is *sensitive* if it regards only the senses and their sensations (the Scholastics call it *sensus intimus,* inner sense, i.e., the point of confluence and of control of all sense life). But psychological conscience, more properly so called, is an act of the *intelligence,* with which the subject reflects on his inner activity and knows himself as acting person or acting *ego* (*conscientia sui*).

Modern philosophy attaches great importance to this psychological conscience to the point of making it a constitutive element of the *person* (*q.v.*). If the cognitive act considers the action to be done with regard to its end, it is called *moral conscience,* which is distinguished into *habitual* and *actual.* The former is a disposition of the intellect to know promptly the supreme principles of human activity with reference to the end (*moral principles*), e.g., that one must do good and avoid evil. This disposition of the intellect is called also synteresis. *Actual* conscience consists in a practical judgment of the reason on the morality of an action to be done; it is, therefore, an application of the universal principles of synteresis to particular practical cases. This conscience may be *certain,* if there is no fear of erring, or *doubtful,* if there militate motives in favor of, or against, the action; moreover, moral conscience may be *true* or *erroneous,* according as it discerns right or is mistaken. The error is *invincible* or without guilt if it cannot be avoided, or vincible and therefore guilty if it can be overcome. It is not licit to act in doubt, but the doubt must be removed by reflexion, advice, and prayer, and we must arrive at a *moral* certitude on the honesty of the action. Man is always obliged to follow the dictate of a conscience which is certain, even if that same conscience happens to be erroneous (invincibly). It can happen that one be unable to remove all doubt; then he may follow a *probable* opinion founded on serious motives (*probabilism*), nor is he obliged to follow the *safer* opinion, as the tutiorists would have it.

The question of freedom and *responsibility* is closely connected with conscience: conscience which obliges, commands, prohibits, reproves, and causes remorse is an evident sign of free will; and if man is free he is also *responsible* for his actions before the tribunal of humanity, and still more before that of his conscience, which would be an enigma if it were not subject to a supreme law, to a supreme Legislator, and to a supreme Judge. Such is the Christian doctrine which condemns all forms of *determinism* and the absolute autonomy of moral conscience, as professed by Kant.

BIBLIOGRAPHY

St. Thomas, *Summa Theol.*, I, q. 79, a. 13. Humphrey, *Conscience and Law* (London, 1896). Moisant, "Conscience," *DA*. Newman, *Grammar of Assent* (London, 1903). Noldin-Schmitt, *Summa Theologiae Moralis*, Vol. 1, *De principiis* (Oeniponte, 1927), p. 205 ff. Rickaby, "Conscience," *CE*.

conservation. The continuation of the creative act, with which God sustains the being of creatures either by positive influence in it or by removing the causes that tend to destroy it (negative conservation).

This truth is implicit in the definitions with which the *magisterium* of the Church affirms divine providence and government (*qq.v.*). Expressive texts are found in Holy Scripture: "But if thou turnest away thy face, they shall be troubled: thou shalt take away their breath, and they shall fall, and shall return to their dust. Thou shalt send forth thy spirit, and they shall be created: and thou shalt renew the face of the earth" (Ps. 103:29–30). St. Paul expresses energetically the concept of the conservation of things: "All things were created by him and in him . . . and by him all things consist" (Col. 1:16–17).

Reason: A marble statue lasts even after the death of its sculptor, because it *existed* as marble independently of him, and only afterward it has received its form or figure. But the world was created from nothing, i.e., received from God *all its being,* which is an actuality derived and participated from God. Now, every creature, as participated and contingent being, for the same reason that it cannot *begin* to be by itself, cannot *continue* to be independently of the source of being, which is God, the Creator. If for one instant a creature could exist without the divine action, for that instant at least the contingent creature would exist by itself, that is to say, it would have the reason of its being in itself — an evident absurdity. By withdrawing His conservative action, God could destroy in whole or in part what He has created (*absolute power*); but in His wisdom and goodness He preserves all things (*ordered power*).

BIBLIOGRAPHY

St. Thomas, *Summa Theol.*, I, q. 104; *Quaest. Disp. De Potentia*, q. 5. Sertillanges, *St. Thomas d'Aquin*, Vol. 1 (Paris, 1925), n. 296.

Consistorial Congregation. See *Holy See.*

"consortium," divine. A communication or participation of the divine nature to the human soul by means of sanctifying grace. The Apostle (2 Pet. 1:14) speaks of the great gifts which the divine power of Christ has made to us according to the promises of old, in order that we may become sharers (Gr. κοινωνοί; Lat. *consortes*) of the divine nature. This participation is identified by the best exegetes with that supernatural life, kindled and sustained by the Holy Spirit in the Christian, which St. Paul calls χάρις (grace) and πνεῦμα (spirit, rule of the spirit in opposition to the flesh).

Tradition sees in the expression of St. Peter sanctifying grace. St. Thomas

(*In 2 Sent.*, d. 26, q. 1, a. 3) translates the teaching of Holy Scripture and Tradition into this philosophical language: operation is proportionate to the nature from which it proceeds and to its faculties; since the meritorious acts of eternal life surpass the conditions of human nature, God through means of grace elevates man to a participation of the divine nature in order that he may be capable of a deiform activity, proportionate to his supernatural end, which is the beatific vision. This participation is mysterious, like all divine things; hence the explanations attempted by the theologians vary. Certainly divine *consortium* is not to be understood as a substantial communication of the divine nature to man (this smacks of pantheism) or as a likeness of a purely *moral* order (this is too little). The divine *consortium* is of a *physical, real* order; if sanctified man is capable of obtaining really the same *object* of the activity of God, which is the divine essence contemplated and loved, he must also, as *subject* or principle of operation, have been really elevated to a divine level.

A modern theologian very aptly compares grace and divine *consortium* with the beatific vision and the Incarnation. In these three mysteries, the uncreated Act (God) actuates terminally a finite potency in different ways:

Incarnation — in the line of subsistence

Beatific vision — in the intentional line

Divine *consortium* — in the accidental physical line

But the mystery still remains (see *indwelling of the Holy Trinity; Incarnation; vision, beatific*).

BIBLIOGRAPHY

St. Thomas, *Comment. in 2 Sent.*, dist. 26. Gardeil, *La structure de l'âme et l'expérience mystique* (Paris, 1927), p. 370 ff. De la Taille, "Actuation créée par acte incréé," *Revue de sciences religieuses* (1928), p. 260 ff.

consubstantial (**Homoousian**) (Gr. ὁμοούσιος — of the same nature). The term, consecrated by the Nicene Council (325) and incorporated in the Symbol (Creed), to express the substantial unity of the Son and the Father. Distinct by way of relationship (*Paternity–Filiation*), they have the same nature, or essence, or substance (οὐσία), not only *specifically* but also *numerically;* the essence of the Father and the Son is one, sole essence. This was the answer given by the solemn *magisterium* of the Church to the heresy of Arius, who taught that the Word was *created* by God and, therefore, could not be homogeneous, i.e., of the same nature as God, so much so that God, as *First Principle,* cannot be called *generated* as the Holy Scripture calls the Word. God is absolutely ἀγέννητος (not generated). The Arians rejected the Homoousian because they were not able to conceive a spiritual generation, eternal, without a shadow of change, and free of any causal process, as is precisely the generation of the Son of God.

The term *homoousian* was not new, being found in pre-Nicene Tradition, e.g., in Origen; moreover, in 269 it had been prohibited in a Synod at Antioch in the false *Sabellian* sense which the heretic Paul of Samosata abusively attributed to it, namely, in the sense not only of unity of essence, but of personal unity between Father and Son. The Council of Nicaea evidently reconsecrated the term according to genuine Tradition (*essential unity*).

The consubstantiality of Son and Father involves absolute equality of both (see *Arianism*).

BIBLIOGRAPHY

Tixeront, *History of Dogmas,* trans. H.L.B., Vol. 2 (St. Louis, 1914), pp. 19–36, 259–

271. D'ALÈS, *Le dogme de Nicée* (Paris, 1926); *De Deo Trino* (Paris, 1934), p. 70 ff.

contemplation. In a generic sense, it means attentive (visual or intellectual) observation of an attractive thing, which strikes the senses or the intelligence. In a religious sense, contemplation belongs to mystics (*q.v.*) and can be defined with St. Thomas (*Summa Theol.,* II–II, q. 180): a simple "intuition" of truth, of which love is the motive and the term. Likewise St. Bonaventure defines it as a savory knowledge of truth. The object of contemplation is God, with His mysteries and His works, especially with respect to man. Contemplation admits of *grades,* in such a way that it can ascend from a fleeting, intuitive glimpse illumining the soul in a moment of grace, up to a foretaste of the beatific vision of the divine essence, as was the happy lot of St. Paul.

Certain authors (Lejeune, Poulain) distinguish between an *acquired* contemplation (human activity in cooperation with grace) and an *infused* or properly so-called mystical contemplation (exclusively divine gift), which has as its characteristic mark an *experimental perception* of God, accompanied by extraordinary, psychological phenomena (ecstasies, stigmata, etc.). Other more recent authors (Gardeil, Garrigou-Lagrange) prefer to reduce all contemplative life to but one kind of species, broken down into various grades. Thus they identify it with the mystical life, as a progressive development in the supernatural life lived by the Christian, through grace and the supernatural gifts, in Christ and through Christ. This contemplation does not necessarily involve the extraordinary, psychic phenomena, which are not essential to it, but certainly does imply an altogether special knowledge of God and divine things, a *delightful* knowledge which anticipates, in a measure, the beatific vision, to which the entire supernatural life is ordained.

The mystics call it *experimental* knowledge, by analogy with sensation, which is immediate and alive. In fact, the mystic-contemplative person not only knows God but, in a certain way, *feels* Him present in himself; rather than a clear vision he has an obscure perception of the divine *Friend* near him in the mysterious shadows. *Ontologically* speaking, the sanctified man is the temple of God who dwells in him; *psychologically,* by way of mystic contemplation, he comes to experience the divine presence. All Christians can and should aspire through a healthy asceticism to this mystical-spiritual perfection, in which intuition and love of God are the prelude of eternal life. The extraordinary phenomena, which sometimes accompany this elevation of the spirit, may result in dangerous aberrations when man pursues them without cultivating the supernatural life of the spirit, which is a gift of God and, at the same time, a daily conquest. Prayer (*q.v.*) is the very web of mystical contemplation.

St. Gregory the Great, from whom St. Thomas takes his inspiration, is the master of contemplative life in the West; in the East the pseudo-Dionysius the Areopagite is the outstanding doctor. In times closer to ours Spain gave two great mystics; St. John of the Cross and St. Teresa, glories of the Carmelite Order, have left us wonderful descriptions of their supernatural experience. For Italy it suffices to recall St. Francis of Assisi and St. Catherine of Siena with their priceless writings.

BIBLIOGRAPHY

DEVINE, *A Manual of Mystical Theology* (London, 1903). FONCK, "Mystique," *DTC.* GARDEIL, *La structure de l'âme et l'expérience mystique* (Paris, 1927). GARRIGOU-LAGRANGE, *Christian Perfection and Contempla-*

tion, trans. Doyle (St. Louis, 1937). GURDON, "Contemplative Life," *CE.* LEJEUNE, "Contemplation," *DTC.* PASCAL PARENTE, *The Mystical Life* (St. Louis, 1946), pp. 53–94. POULAIN, *The Graces of Interior Prayer,* trans. Smith (London, 1928); "Contemplation," *CE.*

contrition (Lat. *conterere* — reduce to little bits). The Council of Trent defines contrition: "Sorrow of the soul and detestation of sin committed, with the resolve to sin no more" (Sess. 14, Ch. 4; *DB,* 897). It is, therefore, not a vague sentiment but a decisive act of the will which, in knowledge of all the deformity of sin, flees and detests it, and nourishes the firm resolve not to fall back into it.

Contrition can be either perfect or imperfect. *Perfect* contrition arises in the heart of the sinner, who grieves for his sin in so far as it is an offense against God, in whom he considers the paternal goodness which has been ungratefully scorned. Moved, therefore, by a pure love, called *benevolence* or *charity,* the penitent, as it were, breaks his heart to bits under the blows of sorrow, whence the name of contrition, a quasi crushing into bits of the penitent heart. With such repentance, all permeated with the flames of charity, there always goes hand in hand (given the intention of confession) justification, or the remission of guilt, because *ubi caritas, ibi Deus est.*

To make the sacrament of penance efficacious, *imperfect* contrition (attrition — breaking into larger parts) is sufficient. It rises in the soul of him who seriously renounces sin, for a supernatural motive indeed (like the fear of hell or the ugliness of sin), but inferior to perfect charity. Instead of seeing in God the image of the Father the penitent sees the image of the Judge, who threatens severe punishments to the transgressors of His laws.

When attrition (namely *internal, supernatural,* and *universal* sorrow for sins committed) is "informed" by absolution, the penitent from attrite becomes contrite, that is, he becomes justified, because then there is a valid sacrament which, *ex opere operato,* infuses grace infallibly connected with charity. So the faithful who approach the tribunal of penance still shaking with a fear which the theologians call *servile,* in virtue of the Passion of Christ which works through the sacramental rite, go away reinvigorated with a feeling of filial love and serene confidence in the goodness of the heavenly Father (see *penance*).

BIBLIOGRAPHY

ST. THOMAS, *Summa Theol.,* III, *Suppl.,* qq. 1–5. BENAGLIO, *Dell'Attrizione quasi materia e parte del sacramento della Penitenza secondo la dottrina del Concilio di Trento* (Milan, 1846). BERNARD, ORTOLAN, "Contrition," *DTC.* BEUGNET, "Attrition," *DTC.* DORONZO, *De Poenitentia,* Vol. 1 (Milwaukee, 1949), Index Analyticus: "Contritio"; Vol. 2 (Milwaukee, 1951). GALTIER, "Amour de Dieu et attrition," *Gregorianum* (1928), pp. 373–416. HANNA, "Contrition," *CE.* PERINELLE, *L'attrition d'après le Concile de Trente et d'après St. Thomas* (Caen, 1927). POHLE-PREUSS, *Dogmatic Theology,* X *The Sacraments,* Vol. 3, *Penance* (St. Louis, 1946), pp. 132–180. *The Teaching of the Catholic Church,* ed. Smith, 2 vols. (New York, 1949), pp. 934–954.

Co-Redemptrix. A title in recent use to express the co-operation of the Blessed Virgin in the work of Redemption performed by Christ. The idea of Mary's co-operation in our salvation is as old as Christianity and has its dogmatic foundation in the divine maternity, through which both Christ and His work belong, in a certain sense, to Mary, who conceived, bore, and nourished the Redeemer, and in addition offered Him in the Temple and suffered with Him, shared with Him spiritually His martyrlike death on the cross. Such is the classic, indisputable doctrine. Very recently, however, under the special impulse of the theological faculty of Louvain, with Bittremieux at its head, a great controversy has flared up as to the value and the extension of that co-operation of Mary, and, therefore, as to the legitimacy and the nature of the titles: *Mediatrix* and *Co-Redemptrix* (see *mediation*).

Certain doctrinal points: (1) Mary, as Mother of Christ, is a partaker of His life and His works and so, in a broad sense, may be called Mediatrix and Co-Redemptrix; (2) in the designs of God, Mary is associated with Christ in the triumph over sin, as Eve joined with Adam in the ruin of the human race; (3) Mary consented to the passion and death of Christ, adding to them her own maternal anguish, thus meriting (*de congruo;* see *merit*) the prerogative of treasurer and distributor of the fruits of the Redemption. This doctrine is founded on Holy Scripture and is extensively developed by the Fathers. The *magisterium* of the Church has always taught it.

Controversial points: (1) May Mary be called Mediatrix between God and men, like Jesus Christ and subordinately to Him? (2) May Mary be called truly Co-Redemptrix together with Christ, in the sense that she has added efficaciously, on her own part, works of her own to the work of the Redeemer? (3) Given that Redemption consists in the *condign* satisfaction and merit of Christ (see *Redemption*), can it be said that Mary, together with Christ, has satisfied the divine justice with her sufferings and has merited for us grace and salvation?

Some theologians, adhering closely to Tradition, answer *negatively,* fearing to take from the dignity of the *one Mediator* and true Redeemer, and out of reverence for the classical thesis of the *necessity of the Incarnation* (*q.v.*). Others follow the *affirmative* position, utilizing also recent pontifical documents (Pius X, Benedict XV, Pius XI), which seem to favor this second opinion.

It is still a moot question with no clear and sure solution in sight. But surely the association of the Blessed Virgin Mary with the Redeemer, her Son, involves a participation that is even direct and immediate, although mysterious, in the redemptive work of Jesus Christ. And so the title *Co-Redemptrix* is justified.

BIBLIOGRAPHY

MERKELBACH, *Mariologia* (Paris, 1939), Bibliography, p. 309. O'CONNELL, *Our Lady Mediatrix of All Graces* (Baltimore, 1926), pp. 23–32. ROSCHINI, *Mariologia,* Vol. 2 (Milan, 1942), p. 297 ff.

cosmogony (Gr. κόσμος — world, and γόνος — generation, origin). Signifies the origin of the world, which in ancient times has been the subject of mythological poems and philosophical inquiries. What interests us theologically is the *Mosaic* cosmogony, or biblical account of creation contained in the book of Genesis. This account, called also *hexaemeron* (the work of six days) arranges the creation of all things in six days progressively, from matter to the vegetable world, to the animal world, and to man. The Scholastics reduced creation to three phases: (*a*) *opus creationis:* creation of the heaven and the earth in an "inform" stage; (*b*) *opus distinctionis:* division of light from darkness, of the earth from the waters; (*c*) *opus ornatus:* the creation of living beings. But from the beginning of Christianity the Mosaic account has had different interpretations according to two main currents, the one *allegorical* and the other *literal.*

1. *Allegorism:* Introduced in the Alexandrian School, it was adopted soberly by St. Augustine, who maintains that Moses does not have the intention of narrating the exact his-

tory of creation, but of affirming the truth that all has been created by God, and that human work and rest on the Sabbath are an imitation of the work and repose of God; therefore, Moses arranges creation according to the days of the week. Moreover, St. Augustine holds that all was created in an instant and afterward developed gradually according to the *rationes seminales* (seminal reasons or causes) put in matter by God. This opinion has nothing to do with the evolutionism of our times (Darwin), which admits the evolution of one species into another, foreign to the Augustinian conception. Allegorism, contained by St. Augustine within the limits of orthodoxy, has degenerated in later times to the point of *mythologism*. Therefore, it is to be considered with caution. Modern Catholic exegetes steer clear of it.

2. *Literalism:* The Mosaic account is understood according to the letter (many Fathers and theologians). Some modern Catholics, interpreting the Hebrew word *yôm* (day) as an indeterminate period (*periodism*), push the literal sense so far that they attempt to maintain perfect agreement between the Bible and geological discoveries (*concordism*), notwithstanding grave difficulties.

The Church, as far back as the IV Lateran Council (*DB,* 428), attributed to God not only global creation, but also the distinct creation of the spiritual and material creatures. As regards the Mosaic account, we have the answer of the *Pontifical Biblical Commission* (1909), which establishes firmly these points: (*a*) the account is substantially historical and literal and, therefore, exaggerated allegorism and mythologism are false; (*b*) certain facts, with regard to the foundations of Christian doctrine, are certainly historical and literal (e.g., the creation of man and woman, original sin, etc.); (*c*) it is unnecessary, however, to interpret literally the individual expressions, and so, for example, the word *day* can be taken in its literal sense or in the sense of a period of time; (*d*) Moses did not intend to teach the creation with scientific exactness, but in a *popular* manner, according to the language of the day; the account is, therefore, a true, popular story without scientific pretensions.

BIBLIOGRAPHY

St. Thomas, *Summa Theol.,* I, qq. 66–74. Boyer, *De Deo creante et elevante* (Rome, 1940), p. 90 ff. Janssens, *De Deo Creatore* (Freiburg i.-Br.). Mangenot, "Hexaméron," *DTC.*

council. The assembly of the bishops convoked to define questions of faith, morals, and discipline. The council is *general* (*ecumenical*) when it represents the whole Church, and *particular* when it represents a part of the Church — a nation (*national* council), or several provinces (*plenary*), or only one province (*provincial*).

An *ecumenical* council (Gr. οἰκουμενικός), representing the whole Church, requires the presence of the head (either the pope or his legate), and representation of the bishops of the majority of the ecclesiastical provinces. Since the Roman pontiff enjoys primacy over the whole Church (see *Roman pontiff*), there can be no ecumenical council which is not convoked through his authority, presided over by him (or his legate), and confirmed by his infallible assent (see *infallibility of the pope*). In the ecumenical council, the episcopate and the pope are the twofold subjects of jurisdiction, really but not adequately distinct, like the head is really but not adequately distinct from the body; hence the ecumenical council is not above the pope, but the pope is superior to the council, for which reason there is no appeal from pope to council. This follows naturally from the Vatican Council definitions on the pontifical primacy (cf. *DB,* 1831).

Since dogmatic definitions of an ecumenical council are infallible, they are irreformable, but its disciplinary measures are subject to modification by one superior to the council itself, i.e., by the Roman pontiff.

BIBLIOGRAPHY

St. Thomas, *Summa Theol.,* I, q. 36, a. 2, ad 2; I–II, q. 1, a. 10. Bellarmine, *De Conciliis et Ecclesia,* l. 1–2. Forget, *Les conciles eucuméniques* (Paris-Rome). Mazzella, *De Ecclesia* (Rome, 1892), n. 1016 ff. Palmieri, *De Romano Pontifice* (Rome, 1931), thes. 28. Romani, *Institutiones Iuris Canonici,* Vol. 1 (Rome, 1941), nn. 359–363. Wilhelm, "Councils," *CE.*

creation. According to Catholic doctrine, the act by which God *made from nothing* all things. To create means to realize a being (i.e., to bring it into actual existence) in all its concreteness, to produce a thing which in no wise previously existed, either in itself or in the potentiality of a subject, *ex nihilo sui et subjecti,* as the Scholastics put it. The sculptor carves a statue: the statue as such did not exist, but it did exist as marble. On the contrary, God by His creative act realized the world, when there existed nothing outside of Himself. Pagan philosophy, even that of Plato and Aristotle, never reached a true concept of creation, which, however, is naturally knowable to human reason. This concept is a *datum* of Christian revelation.

It is a matter of faith that God has created the universe from nothing (cf. Apostles' Creed, IV Lateran Council, Vatican Council: *DB,* 428, 1783, 1801 ff.). In Holy Scripture we read: "In the beginning God created heaven, and earth" (Gen. 1:1). The Hebrew verb *barah* of itself does not necessarily include the sense of creating from nothing, but the context demands it, and such is the understanding of the text in Jewish tradition (2 Mac. 7:28). In the New Testament revelation is clearer and peremptory; the Prologue of St. John's Gospel is sufficient: "All things were made by him: and without him was made nothing that was made" (1:3; cf. Col. 1:15 f.).

The Fathers, from the first centuries, develop and defend the concept of universal creation, even of matter, against the Neoplatonists, the Gnostics, and the Manichaeans. Reason proves that, outside of divine creation, there is no other way to explain the existence of the world. The proofs of the existence of God are based on creative divine causality. The world has actually all the characteristics of an effect, that is, of a being *ab alio* (from another), because it is finite, mutable, contingent, multiple. Moreover, the other systems excogitated to solve the problem are absurd (materialism, pantheism, absolute dualism, with two eternal independent principles, God and the world, and idealistic monism).

The creative act is exclusively of God, formally immanent (identical with His essence) and virtually transient (see *operation, divine*). According to St. Thomas it is also in the creature as a *relation* (transcendental and predicamental), which implies order to and dependency on God. Together with the universe, God created *space,* and *time* which is the measure of motion of mutable things (see *eternity*).

BIBLIOGRAPHY

St. Thomas, *Summa Theol.,* I, qq. 44–45. Boyer, *De Deo creante et elevante* (Rome, 1940). Miller, *God the Creator* (New York, 1928). Mivart, *Lessons from Nature* (New York, 1876); *Genesis of Species* (New York, 1871). Peter Parente, *De creatione universali* (Rome, 1943). Pinard, "Création," *DTC* and *DA.* Pohle-Preuss, *Dogmatic Theology,* III *God: Author of Nature and Supernatural* (St.

Louis, 1945), pp. 3–60. SERTILLANGES, *Saint Thomas d'Aquin,* Vol. 1 (Paris, 1925), p. 279 ff. SIEGFRIED, "Creation," *CE. The Teaching of the Catholic Church,* ed. Smith, 2 vols. (New York, 1949), pp. 180–213. VAUGHN, *Faith and Folly* (London, 1901).

creationism. The doctrine of the Church about the origin of the individual soul. Holy Scripture clearly states the divine origin of the *soul* (*q.v.*) by way of creation, as well as its spirituality and immortality. But in the very bosom of the Church, from the first centuries, there arose the question of the origin of the individual souls of men.

Origen, under the influence of Platonism, was of the opinion that God had created *ab aeterno* a great number of spirits (angels and souls) and then had condemned the human souls to "inform" material bodies in expiation of an incurred guilt. This extravagant opinion, flavored by the excessive spiritualism of Plato and of the Gnostics, was rejected by the *magisterium* of the Church together with other errors of Origen (see *Origenism*). Opposed to this opinion is that of Tertullian, a realist, lover of the concrete, who, although the author of *De anima,* the first treatise of Christian psychology that was substantially orthodox, fell into the vulgar error of *traducianism* (*q.v.*), according to which the souls of the children would derive from the corporeal seed of the parents. This opinion also was explicitly condemned by the Church (*DB,* 170: Letter of Anastasius II to the Bishops of Gaul, 498).

Tradition, especially in the East, stands for creationism, according to which the individual souls are created by God, one by one, and infused into the embryonic bodies in the maternal womb. But the Pelagian heresy (see *Pelagianism*), which denied the transmission of original sin to the sons of Adam, threw some confusion on the doctrine of creationism in connection with the difficulty of explaining the transmission of that sin into a soul created instantly and directly by God. Even St. Augustine felt the irksomeness in confronting this difficulty. He rejected the traducianism of Tertullian, appreciated creationism and would have liked to embrace it, but in order better to expound the transmission of original sin against Pelagius he leaned toward a *spiritual traducianism,* according to which the soul of the offspring derives from the souls of the parents, like light from light. But the Church continued to teach creationism more or less explicitly (cf. the Letter of Anastasius II, *loc. cit.;* also a document of Leo IX, *DB,* 348; and of Alexander VII, *DB,* 1100).

Human reason itself does not see any way, outside of creationism, of explaining the origin of the soul, as St. Thomas demonstrates (*Summa Theol.,* I, q. 90, a. 2). A spiritual substance cannot, in fact, derive from matter, as is evident, nor can it emanate from another spirit, as spiritual traducianism asserts, because spiritual substances do not divide or split or change one into the other; they must, therefore, derive from God through creation.

BIBLIOGRAPHY

ST. THOMAS, *Summa Theol.,* I, q. 90. DRISCOLL, *The Soul* (New York, 1898). MERCIER, *Psychologie,* Vol. 2 (Paris, 1923), p. 331 ff. MIVART, *Origin of Human Reason* (London, 1889). PETER PARENTE, *De creatione universali* (Rome, 1943), p. 92 ff. POHLE-PREUSS, *Dogmatic Theology,* III *God: Author of Nature and the Supernatural* (St. Louis, 1945), pp. 171–178. SIEGFRIED, "Creationism," *CE.* ZACCHI, *L'uomo* (Rome, 1921).

credibility. See *apologetics.*

Creed. See *Symbol.*

cross (Lat. *crux* — torment, from the verb *cruciare*). The implement upon which was accomplished the ignominious and cruel torture of crucifixion. Crucifixion, in Roman law, was the severest of capital punishments. It was particularly applied to slaves, for the expiation even of the slightest faults. It was used first by the Persians and then introduced into Greece by Alexander the Great. The Romans took it from Carthage.

Cicero (*C. Verrem,* II, 5, 62–67) upheld the thesis that no Roman citizen should, for any reason, be crucified. In the time of the Empire, in the provinces — like Judea — the cross was intended for rebels, brigands, and poor wretches.

Pilate, under the pressure of the Sanhedrin and of the mob, condemned Jesus to crucifixion. None of the Evangelists describes the crucifixion, which was performed according to Roman custom. The condemned went to the place of execution, carrying on his shoulders the transverse bar of the cross called *patibulum.* The vertical bar was permanently set in the place of crucifixion.

The cross of Jesus was a *crux immissa* whose two bars crossed at right angles at a great distance from the base (it is also called the Latin cross). On the small segment above the transverse bar was nailed the tablet with the motivation of the sentence on it. The cross of Jesus measured about 13 feet or more in height, for the soldier needed a cane to extend the sponge, steeped in water and vinegar, to the crucified Christ.

Toward the middle of the crossbar there was a support on which the condemned could rest, so as not to have the entire weight of the body bear on the nails with which the hands were fastened. It is probable that the Romans took into consideration the delicate sense of modesty of the Hebrews and consented, against the Roman custom, to let Jesus wear a loin cloth.

BIBLIOGRAPHY

ALGER, *History of the Cross* (Boston, 1858). HOLZMEISTER, *Crux Domini atque crucifixio quomodo ex archaeologia romana illustrentur* (Rome, 1934). MARUCCHI, "Cross" and "Crucifix," *CE.* RICCIOTTI, *The Life of Christ,* trans. Zizzamia (Milwaukee, 1947).

cult (Lat. *cultus,* from *colere* — to honor). Basically, cult denotes a kind of honor, which in turn is a sign of esteem given to a person for his excellence. But cult adds to honor or esteem the feeling of one's own *inferiority* and subjection with respect to the person honored. Thus, in the proper sense, cult is the external manifestation of honor paid to a superior person in recognition of his excellence and our own submission. Since God is the supreme Being and the absolute Lord of the universe, to Him is due worship in its highest grade. This worship coincides with the essential characteristic of religion which, precisely, consists in honoring God for His excellence and in serving Him as Lord. Worship, in the sense of religion, is due exclusively to God (whence we understand the gravity of the offense of idolatry); an inferior form of religious worship may be licit with respect to creatures only insomuch as these have reference to God and manifest His perfections.

Distinctions: Cult of its nature is not only internal but also external: *external* cult is either *private* (individual) or *public* (official — authorized by the Church). The singular worship reserved to God alone is called *latria* (Gr. λατρεύειν — to serve) or *adoration;* that given to the saints is called *dulia* (Gr. δουλεύειν — to serve) or *veneration.* The worship of the Blessed Virgin is called *hyperdulia.* A *relative* cult is given to images and to relics; it is called relative because it is referred to the person which the image represents and to which the relic belonged by reason of contact.

The humanity of Christ is the object of latreutic worship with this difference, that God is adored in Himself and on account of Himself, while the humanity of Christ is adored in itself, not on account of itself, but on account of the Word, to which it is hypostatically united. *Errors:* iconoclasts, Protestants (*qq.v.;* see *Heart of Jesus*).

BIBLIOGRAPHY

St. Thomas, *Summa Theol.,* II–II, q. 81. Cabrol, "Worship," *CE.* Chollet, "Culte," *DTC.* Duchesne, *Christian Worship, Its Origin and Evolution,* trans. McClure (London, 1903). Peter Parente, *De Verbo Incarnato* (Rome, 1939), pp. 143, 382 ff. Pohle-Preuss, *Dogmatic Theology,* VI *Mariology* (St. Louis, 1946), pp. 139–180.

Cyril Alex. See "Outline of the History of Dogmatic Theology" (p. 301).

D

Damascene. See "Outline of the History of Dogmatic Theology" (p. 302).

damned. The creatures (angels or humans) who are in hell (*q.v.*) and, therefore, are condemned to eternal punishment, i.e., subjected to the separation from God (*poena damni*) and to the various positive sufferings which afflict the soul and, after the resurrection of the flesh, the body as well (*poena sensus*). The determining cause of damnation for human beings is the state of personal mortal sin at the moment of death, which has not been eliminated by an act of contrition, or of attrition united with a sacrament (penance or, if impossible, extreme unction). The doctrine of the Church, drawn from divine revelation, is explicitly stated in the Constitution of *Benedict XII* (*DB,* 530): "We define that according to the common order of God, the souls of those dying in actual mortal sin, immediately after their death descend into hell, where they are tormented with the pains of hell."

Babies who die without baptism are not numbered among the damned, because they are subject only to the penalty of loss (*poena damni*), and will not suffer any pain of sense (see *babies deceased without baptism; limbo; penalty*). Adults who die without baptism would go to limbo if they had no other sin except original sin. The theologians, however (*Summa Theol.,* I–II, q. 89, a. 1, ad 6), find it morally, or at least psychologically impossible, that a man reach the use of reason and adult age without choosing between good and evil, i.e., without determining himself to good or to evil (in the choice of the ultimate end), and, therefore, without justifying himself, with the help of grace, or without committing a grave sin, by rejecting grace and acting against right reason.

Since it is the certain teaching of the Church that hell is not only a state or condition but also a *place,* it follows that the damned are confined to the infernal place and are there in the manner spiritual substances are locally present (according to the better opinion, by way of *action*). It is evident that, after the resurrection of the flesh, the bodies of damned men will be locally present in hell. We have it from Holy Scripture that the demons (*q.v.*) can be outside hell, among men, bringing with them their infernal suffering; but it is held that *ordinarily* damned men cannot wander outside of the place of their torment. It is not impossible, however, to conceive that God permit a damned soul to appear in some form to the living for a worthy and adequate motive, as we read in certain serious documents of Tradition. So, likewise, God can suspend the application of the decree of damnation immediately after the death of a person, in view of the prayers of a saint, and grant the return to life of that person in order that he may be converted and die in the state of grace (cf. the miracle of St. Philip Neri on the son of Prince Massimo).

BIBLIOGRAPHY

St. Thomas, *Summa Theol.,* III, *Suppl.,* qq. 97–99. Billot, *De Novissimis* (Rome, 1921), p. 52 ff.

See under *hell.*

death. The separation of the soul, which continues to live, from the body, which is dissolved into its elements. Of its very nature the soul is immortal, being pure spirit, and, therefore, simple and not subject to decomposition. The body, like all material things, is subject to corruption, according to nature's law. But God had provided by a special privilege for the integrity and immortality of the human body: *Deus creavit hominem inexterminabilem* ("God created man incorruptible," Wisd. 2:23). Corporeal death is the consequence of sin, according to the divine threat: "In what day soever thou shalt eat of it, thou shalt die the death" (Gen. 2:17). "By one man sin entered into this world, and by sin death" (Rom. 5:12). Death is the universal law to which even Jesus Christ wished to subject Himself. Death is not only the terminus of earthly life, but also the deadline for *meriting.* Christ calls death "the night . . . when no man can work" (John 9:4), and St. Paul: "It is appointed unto men once to die, and after this the judgment" (Heb. 9:27). Now the judgment decides inexorably man's destiny. This truth is amply developed by Tradition, and, while not defined, it is taught by the ordinary *magisterium* of the Church (*DB,* 530 ff., and 693; cf. also 203 ff. where Origen's opinion on the possibility of a final redemption after death is condemned).

Physiologically, the moment of real death does not coincide with but follows that of apparent death. A recent theory, called *"Illumination of the Agonizing,"* holds that the soul between these two moments can undergo a beneficial crisis of conversion under a special divine influence. This theory would indeed broaden the salvation path, but it has not found wide acceptance.

BIBLIOGRAPHY

St. Thomas, *Summa Contra Gentiles,* l. 4, c. 95. Michel, "Mort," *DTC. The Teaching of the Catholic Church,* ed. Smith, 2 vols. (New York, 1949), pp. 1101–1114.

See under *eschatology.*

Decalogue (Gr. δεκάλογος — ten words, i.e., commandments). The name is taken from the Bible itself (Exod. 34:28; Deut. 4:13; 10:14) and designates the commands of a religious and moral nature that constituted the foundation of the pact, concluded by God on Sinai with Israel, which made them chosen people. With the exception of the precept of the Sabbath (i.e., the day of rest from work), the Decalogue contains natural laws which have a universal value, and, therefore, remain in force, with the improvements added to them by Christ in the Christian Church (Matt. 5:17–47). The pact contained also a contingent series of dispositions of civil character (Exod. 21:1–23) for the regulation of the life of the Israelitic nation.

Since the Decalogue was consigned by God Himself to Moses, written on two tablets of stone which were afterward preserved in the Ark (Exod. 40:20) in testimony of the covenant concluded, it is probable that its original form was in brief sentences, as is the case in the majority of the present precepts. In later literary editing, a few explanations were added here and there (Exod. 20:1–17; Deut. 5:6–21). The order of certain commandments is not constant in the text tradition.

The extension of the form of the first commandment, Exodus 20:2–6, has been the subject of discussion:

"2. I am the Lord thy God. . . . 3. Thou shalt not have strange gods before me. 4. Thou shalt not take to thyself a graven thing, nor the likeness of any thing that is in heaven above, or in the earth beneath, nor of those things that are in the waters under the earth. 5. Thou shalt not adore them, nor serve them. I am the Lord thy God, mighty, jealous, visiting the iniquity of the fathers upon the children, unto the third and fourth generation of them that hate me: 6. And shewing mercy unto thousands to them that love me, and keep my commandments."

Verses 4–6 are, obviously, an explanation of the commandment true and proper, as contained in Verses 2–3. Therefore, Catholics (together with the ancient Jews of Palestine and the Lutherans) do not consider them a commandment distinct from the preceding. They simply prohibit any figuration of the divinity, because the cult of images among the peoples that came into contact with Israel was, without exception, a cult in the service of polytheism and of idolatry. The Hellenist Jews, the Fathers of the Greek Church, the Calvinists, and certain modern Catholics consider Verses 4–6 as a new (i.e., the second) commandment, and so they join in one the last two commandments (coveting both the possessions of one's neighbor as well as his wife) which are more logically considered as separate by the other exegetes just mentioned, who see in Verses 2–6 only one commandment with its attached explanation. Indeed, the passion which inclines man to desire his neighbor's property is different from that which prompts him to covet his neighbor's wife.

Certain Protestants wrongly blame the Catholic Church for having suppressed in the Decalogue the precept relative to images. The real extension of the text of the commandment is not a theological question, but a problem of exegetics, which is of free discussion among students of various faiths and different Christian professions.

BIBLIOGRAPHY

EBERHARTER, "Décalogue," *DBVS,* cols. 341–351. STAPLETON, "Commandments of God," *CE.* VACCARI, "De praeceptorum Decalogi distinctione et ordine," *Verbum Domini,* 17 (1937), pp. 317–320, 329–334.

"de condigno." See *merit.*

"de congruo." See *merit.*

definition, dogmatic. The solemn declaration of the Church on a truth contained in the sources of divine revelation (Holy Scripture and Tradition) and proposed to the faithful, who, therefore, are obliged to believe it on the authority of God, who has revealed it. Written and oral revelation contain a complexus of truths more or less clearly enunciated. First of all, a distinction must be made between what is *formally,* i.e., essentially revealed, and what is deducible, by way of reasoning, from a revealed principle or premise (*virtual* revelation). The formally revealed truth is obviously divine and bears with it the whole weight of the authority of God, supreme and infallible Truth. The virtually revealed truth, on the contrary, is the result of a divine element and a human element, and cannot impose itself on the conscience of the believer in the name of God. The

Church is the custodian of the deposit of divine revelation and, therefore, has the duty not of creating divine truth, but of seeking it in the sources of revelation, bringing it into light, should it not be *explicit,* and of proposing it as such for belief.

The declaration of the Church can be made by way of the *ordinary magisterium* (unanimous consent of the Fathers and the theologians, unanimous preaching of the bishops, consent of the faithful, liturgical usage), or by way of the *extraordinary magisterium* (solemn declaration of the pope, through a bull or other document; declaration of an *ecumenical council* [see *council*] or of a particular council approved by the pope; symbols and professions of faith emanating from or approved by the Church). A dogmatic definition is a truth proposed in the second way; it constitutes in the strictest sense a *formal dogma* (see *dogma*), which is also called a truth of *divine-Catholic faith,* to which the faithful cannot refuse their assent without falling into heresy (*q.v.*). It should be noted, however, that, generally, to constitute a dogma or a truth of divine-Catholic faith, the function of the *ordinary magisterium* is in itself sufficient, as the Vatican Council declares, Sess. III, Ch. 3 (*DB,* 1792): *Fide divina et Catholica ea omnia credenda sunt, quae in verbo Dei scripto vel tradito continentur et ab Ecclesia sive solemni judicio sive ordinario et universali magisterio tamquam divinitus revelata credenda proponuntur* ("All those things are to be believed on the basis of divine and Catholic faith which are contained in God's word, either written or handed down by Tradition and are proposed for belief as being divinely revealed by the Church, whether by solemn judgment or by the ordinary and universal *magisterium*").

BIBLIOGRAPHY

De Grandmaison, *Le dogme chrétien, sa nature, ses formules, son développement* (Paris, 1928). Garrigou-Lagrange, *De Revelatione per Ecclesiam catholicam proposita* (Paris, 1925). Harty, "Definition (Theological)," *CE.*

deism. Etymologically it should mean a system in which God is affirmed; a meaning coincident with that of theism. Usage, however, not only distinguishes but even opposes the one to the other. *Theism* is an orthodox system, which Christian theodicy (natural theology) admits integrally (in opposition to atheism and pantheism). *Deism,* on the other hand, is a rationalistic conception of the Divinity, based on human reason with the systematic exclusion of divine revelation. The deistic affirmation presents a God mutilated in His nature and attributes; according to the scope of this mutilation, deism has various gradations. In the beginning (sixteenth century) the word *deists* was applied to identify the *Socinians* (see *Unitarianism*); in the seventeenth century deism gained ground in England as *Rational Christianity* (Cherbury, Collins, Bolingbroke, and others); in the eighteenth century it became the insignia of the *Encyclopedists* (Voltaire and Rousseau especially). By minimizing the divinity, deism approaches closer and closer to atheism or pantheism.

BIBLIOGRAPHY

Aveling, "Deism," *CE.* Forget, "Déisme," *DTC.* Leland, *A View of the Principal Deistical Writers* (London, 1754). Savons, *Les déistes anglais et le christianisme* (Paris, 1882).

demon, devil. Two words of Greek origin: δαίμων, of uncertain root, and διάβολος (from διαβάλλω — I accuse, calumniate) — accuser, both used to indicate the angels rebellious to God and for that reason cast into hell.

In the Greek classics (Homer, Hesiod, Herodotus, Plato, Plutarch) the use of δαίμων is frequent (much more than that of διάβολος), but with a varying meaning: *numen* (deity), doing good or evil to man, *genius* or protecting spirit (cf. the demon of Socrates), intermediary between the divinity and man, and at times also *fate, destiny*.

The concept of good or bad spirits, intermediary between God and the world, is met also in other religions and systems of mythological philosophy (Gnosticism); but Christian revelation presents so characteristic a teaching on the subject of the demons that derivation from outside sources cannot be sustained. In the Old Testament the figure of Satan (from שָׂטַן — ensnare, persecute) flashes sinister, as the adversary of man who, under the figure of a serpent, determines the fall of Eve and Adam, requests and obtains God's consent to torment Job, excites Saul and incites David to evil. Mention is made of the devil in the book of Tobias, and in the book of Wisdom, which attributes to him the introduction of death in the world (Wisd. 2:24). The name of Satan, demon, devil, occurs more frequently in the New Testament. Satan tempts Jesus in the desert (Matt. 4:1); the Pharisees attribute the miracles of Jesus to Satan, but the Saviour proves their accusation to be stupid by showing His power in chasing out the devils and their head from the obsessed (cf. especially Mark's Gospel); Jesus says He saw Satan hurled down from heaven like a lightning bolt (Luke 10:18); He forewarns the Apostles against His assaults (Luke 22:31); on the vigil of His passion and death, He declares that Satan is already judged and overcome (John 16:11).

The Fathers develop these data and furnish the material to the Scholastics for a definitive doctrinal systemization, to which the *magisterium* of the Church has contributed certain details (cf. IV Lateran Council, *DB*, 428).

The chief points of the Catholic doctrine on the devil are: (*a*) God created the angels (*q.v.*) who are good by nature, but some sinned and deliberately became bad; (*b*) it is not the devil who created matter and bodies; (*c*) Satan and his followers were punished by God by being cast into hell, whence they insidiously ensnare and persecute men, but only in so far as God permits (see *temptation*); (*d*) the devils, like all the angels, are pure spirits endowed with intellect and will; (*e*) these pure spirits were adorned with grace from the first instant of their creation: many fell into a sin of pride and were lost irremediably because, due to their spiritual nature, once they have made their free choice between good and evil they are immutable in their will and so without possibility of repentance; (*f*) the devil by sinning lost his supernatural gifts, but he retains his spiritual nature, rich in intelligence and in will tenaciously bent on evil; (*g*) the devils hate men who are destined to replace them in heaven.

BIBLIOGRAPHY

St. Thomas, *Summa Theol.*, I, q. 63 ff. Kent, "Demon," *CE;* "Demonology," *CE;* "Devil," *CE.* Mangenot, Ortolan, "Démon," *DTC.* Pascal Parente, *The Mystical Life* (St. Louis, 1946), pp. 237–244. Peter Parente, *De creatione universali* (Rome, 1943), p. 64 ff. *The Teaching of the Catholic Church*, ed. Smith, 2 vols. (New York, 1949), pp. 276–282.

deposit of faith. The expression occurs in the two letters of St. Paul (1 Tim. 6:20; 2 Tim. 1:14), in connection with the idea of doctrines of the faith. The "deposit" which St. Paul transmits to his faithful collaborator is the whole of divine revelation (1 Tim. 6:1; 4:6) made up of the dogmas of faith, Christian morals, the sacraments, Holy Scripture, the hierarchical constitution of the Church. The juridical concept of *deposit* requires that it be not the property of the guardian but of the consignor who has handed it over to him to keep it in a safe state. The "deposit of faith" has come from God and is entrusted to those to whom a special assistance of the Holy Ghost is assured (2 Tim. 1:14), i.e., to those who succeed the Apostles in their *magisterium* and in their ministry.

Christ has transmitted the deposit whose content cannot be subjected to alterations. The privilege of infallibility in the safeguarding of the deposit belongs to the Church "pillar and ground of the truth" (1 Tim. 3:15): personal infallibility is the exclusive prerogative of Peter, foundation of the Church (Matt. 16:18), and of his successors in the apostolic primacy. To keep the deposit does not mean, however, to bury it, as the servant blamed in the parable did with the talents of his master (Matt. 25:14–30; Luke 19:11–27). The Church finds in the "deposit of faith" the riches that she communicates to her children, the arms with which she fights her adversaries, adapting herself with wonderful wisdom to the needs of men and of the times. Her living faith determines the content and the extension of the deposit which could not be and never was intended to be a complete inventory of Christian beliefs and institutions.

BIBLIOGRAPHY

MEDÉBIELLE, "Dépot de la Foi," *DBVS*, cols. 374–395. SPICQ, "St. Paul et la loi des dépots," *Revue Biblique*, 40 (1931), pp. 481–502.

descent of Christ into hell. Clearly affirmed in the New Testament (Acts 2:24, 27–31; 1 Pet. 3:19 f.; 4:6), this truth is found explicitly formulated since the fourth century in the Symbol (Creed), into which it was introduced without opposition and without any polemic end whatever. Since the Word through His Incarnation accepted all the conditions inherent in human nature — sin excepted — the soul of Christ in the interval between His death and resurrection went to the sojourn of the dead (*descendit ad inferos*). *Inferi* means "lower regions." It indicates the place where the dead were in a state of natural happiness, waiting for the Redemption which would open for them the gates of heaven. It is to be noted that during those three days the body of Christ remained in the tomb, while the soul left the body, the divinity was never separated either from the soul or from the body. Consequently, Christ descended into hell in His soul and in His divinity.

In the regions beyond the grave, Jesus announced the accomplishment of the Redemption to the just of the Old Testament. The biblical texts mentioned above present various difficulties of interpretation, and patristic tradition is not always unanimous in determining their meaning. The detailed accounts of the Apocrypha (*q.v.*) about Christ's activity in the limbo of the Fathers are disputable. However, the dogma itself is clear in its essential lines.

BIBLIOGRAPHY

ST. THOMAS, *Summa Theol.*, III, q. 52, a. 1–8. CHAINE, "Descente du Christ aux enfers," *DBVS*. HOLZMEISTER, *Comment. in ep. 1 Petri* (Paris, 1937), pp. 295–354. POHLE-PREUSS, *Dogmatic Theology*, V *Soteriology* (St. Louis, 1945), pp. 91–101. QUILLIET, "Descente de Jésus aux enfers," *DTC*. TONER, "Limbo," *CE*. TRICOT, "Pierre (Saint)," *DTC*, cols. 1766–1771. VITTI, various articles in *Verbum Domini*, 7 (1927), pp. 111–118, 138–144, 171–181. VOSTÉ, *De mysteriis vitae Christi* (Rome, 1940), pp. 423–444.

See under *limbo*.

desire of God. Properly speaking, desire is an inclination of the sense appetite or of the will toward an absent good. Improperly speaking the inclination of the intellect toward truth is also called desire. That creatures, man especially, tend to God consciously or unconsciously is a truth of faith and of reason since God is the efficient and final Cause of all things. In man, fashioned after the image of God, that tendency is more accentuated and, since the fall of man, this desire has become more dramatic, a real homesickness. But there is a longstanding theological question with respect to the desire of the beatific vision: Can man without revelation and grace desire to see the essence of God in an "intuitive" way, i.e., face to face?

Scotus and his school answer affirmatively, adding that such desire is *innate;* i.e., quasi instinctive, independent of the explicit knowledge of its object. This opinion binds man more intimately to God and presents the supernatural order as the object of a natural inclination; not clearly understood at the time of the condemnation of Baianism (*q.v.*), it has been revived lately by several theologians of various schools.

The *Thomists,* on the contrary, starting from a standpoint of rigid distinction between the natural and supernatural orders, maintain that there cannot arise in man a desire of the beatific vision without revelation, and that such desire can in no way be efficacious without grace. St. Thomas (*Summa Theol.,* I, q. 12, a. 1, and in other works) speaks of a "natural desire" which arises in man at the sight of created effects, namely the desire of seeing also their first Cause, God in Himself.

Commentary on this statement of St. Thomas has led to an abundance of literature with the most varied solutions. Following the current of thought headed by Ferrariensis (Sylvester of Ferrara), we may hold, as more probable, the following interpretation: the desire of which St. Thomas speaks is really natural, not, however, innate (instinctive) but *elicited,* i.e., dependent on the knowledge of created things (effect), from which arises the desire to know their Cause (God). But God cannot be known fully except through the beatific vision; therefore, without knowing it, man with such natural desire tends *materially* to the beatific vision. In that desire is rooted the possibility of the elevation of man to the supernatural order (*obediential potency*), but it would remain a mere inefficacious tendency without the help of grace.

BIBLIOGRAPHY

St. Thomas, *Summa Theol.,* I, q. 12, a. 1. Bainvel, *Nature et Surnaturel* (Paris, 1920). De Lubac, *Surnaturel* (Paris, 1946), pp. 431–438, 481–494. Donnelly, "The Gratuity of the Beatific Vision and the Possibility of a Natural Destiny," *Theological Studies,* Vol. II (1950), pp. 374–404. Fernandez, various articles in *Divus Thomas* (Piacenza, 1930). Finili, "Natural Desire," *Dominican Studies,* Vol. 1 (1948), pp. 311–359; Vol. 2 (1949), pp. 1–15. Sestili, *De naturali intelligentis animae capacitate atque appetitu intuendi divinam essentiam* (Naples, Rome, 1896). Vallaro, various articles in *Angelicum* (1934–1935).

destiny. In popular language it signifies an obscure and inescapable law which determines an event, a series of events, or the whole course of the life of a man, of a people, of an institution. In this sense destiny has fate as a synonym. It is quite common today, especially in those professing no faith, to find an uncontrolled consciousness of this obscure law, which slips into a banal superstition.

The concept of destiny is predominant in pagan religions and is not extraneous to philosophical systems. The Greeks personified destiny, making it a capricious ruler not only of poor mortals, but even of the gods themselves. Destiny is the omnipotent and inexorable *Moira* (Μοῖρα), which predetermines everything in its immutable decrees; it is the *Fatum* (spoken, decreed) of the Latins. The *Parcae, Fortune,* are plastic representations of the same concept, particularly with respect to human life.

Stoicism is the most fatalistic of the philosophical systems. It has a whole theory on destiny as an unescapable law of the universe, which is conceived as a Whole destined to run its ascendant and descendant parabola, whirling in its rigid fatality all its parts, man not excluded. Marcus Aurelius gathers in his *Memories* the sad echo of this Stoic determinism which compromises human freedom. Cicero had already reacted against this inhuman conception in his work *De fato,* and, given the alternative between divine fate and human freedom, he decisively takes his stand for freedom up to the point of denying the influence of divine providence on man.

Christianity eliminates the mythology of destiny and corrects the pagan philosophical deviations attached thereto. St. Augustine (cf. *De Civitate Dei*) reduces destiny simply to divine providence, in which shine the wisdom and love of God and to which all creatures are subordinate in being and in action.

St. Thomas develops the traditional thought of the Fathers when, speaking of the influence of God on creatures, on man especially, he demonstrates that such influence does not perturb but perfects creature activity and is harmoniously compatible with human freedom (see *concourse, divine*). There is a causal connection between the knowledge, will, and omnipotence of God, on the one hand, and creature activity, on the other: but this connection, however mysterious, does not do violence to, but helps both the necessary and the free causes in unfolding their activity according to their proper nature, necessarily or freely (see *prescience*).

St. Thomas treats explicitly of *Fatum* and defines it: *Ordinatio secundarum causarum ad effectus divinitus provisos* ("the ordering of second causes to effects divinely provided for"). So *fate* is nothing more than the law impressed in second causes by the thought and will of God. The Christian, therefore, will say *providence* instead of *destiny* or *fate.*

BIBLIOGRAPHY

St. Thomas, *Summa Theol.,* I, q. 116. (Refer to this question St. Augustine, *De civitate Dei,* V, and Boethius, *De consolatione philosophiae,* IV.) Chollet, "Destin," *DTC.*

deuterocanonical. See *Canon of the Bible.*

devotion (Lat. *devovere* — to vow, to offer, to consecrate, especially to the Divinity). In the strict sense it is an internal act of religion, which St. Thomas defines (*Summa Theol.,* II–II, q. 82, a. 1): *Voluntas prompte faciendi quod ad Dei servitutem pertinet* ("The will of doing promptly what pertains to the service of God").

Devotion consists, therefore, essentially in the promptness of the will to serve God, namely, to subordinate our whole life to His glory and desires. In this sense devotion is a part of cult or worship; in fact, it is its very soul. Worship actually is a manifestation of honor rendered to a superior person in recognition of his excellence and of our own submission. Worship, therefore, includes an *internal* action (of the intellect and the will) and an *external* action (the manifestation of esteem and subjection). If by *devotion* we understand, in addition to the intimate disposition of the will, also an external manifestation, then it coincides with worship, as often happens in common language.

Devotion in this second sense can, like worship, be *private* or *public;* the distinction between one and the other depends on a single element: the intervention or approbation of ecclesiastical authority (bishop or Holy See). A devotion can be external, even spread among the faithful in some place, without being public, through lack of explicit ecclesiastical approbation (*CIC,* Cans. 1257, 1261, 1259). The Church proceeds slowly in approving new devotions or forms of cult because of the danger of superstition and of theological errors, which can be mingled in them.

With respect to devotion in the *strict sense,* which is of special interest to us here, it is noteworthy that: (1) it has, as essential elements, an illuminated *faith* and an ardent *charity.* Faith always yields a more congruous knowledge of God, charity always makes the soul adhere more strongly to Him, detaching it from creatures and from itself by the elimination of self-love. The devout soul, therefore, seeks nothing but God. (2) It has, as extrinsic cause, God, from whom it must be sought by prayer; as intrinsic cause, meditation of the eternal truths (*Summa Theol.,* II–II, q. 82, a. 3). (3) It has, as immediate effect, progress in perfection and spiritual joy. Opposed to devotion, which is prompt eagerness, alacrity, and lively adherence to God, is sloth of spirit and its consequent tepidity.

BIBLIOGRAPHY

St. Thomas, *Summa Theol.,* II–II, q. 82; *Opusculum De perfectione vitae spiritualis.* Dublanchy, "Dévotion," *DTC.* Faber, *Growth in Holiness* (London, 1855), p. 396 ff. Meynard, *Traité de la vie intérieure,* Vol. 1 (Paris, 1899), pp. 85 f., 207 f., 403 f., 530 f.

diaconate (Gr. διάκονος — servant). The second in the ascendant line of major orders (see *orders, holy*). It is of divine institution, as appears from Holy Scripture (Acts 6:1 ff.; Phil. 1:1; 1 Tim. 3:8, 13), and still more explicitly from Tradition.

Many functions, even of an administrative and jurisdictional order, being reserved to the deacons in antiquity, their position was very highly honored and in some instances gave occasion to pride and to irreverent behavior toward the bishop.

At Rome, the dying pope would entrust the goods of the Church to the archdeacon (first deacon) for transmission to his successor in the papacy. Gradually, the power of the archdeacons became so exorbitant that it seriously interfered with ecclesiastical life. After ample and full praise of their good services rendered in the past, the Council of Trent reduced the archdeacons to mere capitular dignitaries.

Of the numerous offices of the deacon, the *Roman Pontifical* has conserved three: to serve the priest or the bishop at the altar, to baptize, and to preach.

BIBLIOGRAPHY

St. Thomas, *Summa Theol.,* III, *Suppl.,* q. 37, a. 2. Forget, "Diaconesses," *DTC;* "Diacres," *DTC.* Kurtscheid, *Historia Iuris Canonici,* Vol. 1 (Rome, 1931). Lamothe-Tenet, *Le Diaconat* (Paris, 1900). Leclercq, "Diacre," *DACL.* Pohle-Preuss, *Dogmatic Theology,* XI *The Sacraments,* Vol. 4, *Extreme Unction, Holy Orders, Matrimony* (St. Louis, 1946), pp. 99–105. Ruffini, *La gerarchia della Chiesa negli Atti degli Apostoli e nelle lettere di S. Paolo* (Rome, 1921). Thurston, "Deacons," *CE.* Tixeront, *Holy Orders and Ordinations,* trans. Raemers (St. Louis).

See under *hierarchy; orders, holy.*

Diaspora (Gr. διασπορά — dispersion). Refers to the community of Hebrews living outside the boundaries of Palestine.

The earliest dispersions or "displacements" of the Hebrews date from the fall of the Kingdom of Israel in 722 B.C. and from the fall of the Kingdom of Juda in 598 B.C., when the Assyrians and Babylonians, in order to cut off any idea of revolt, transferred the majority of that people to distant regions. Later the Hebrews spread throughout the world for commercial reasons, their nomad instinct being favored by the marvelous highway network of antiquity.

Points of departure of the Diaspora were Jerusalem, Babylonia, and Alexandria of Egypt for the Mediterranean countries, and Antioch of Syria for Asia Minor. From the first century B.C., Rome was the principal center from which the Jews moved into the West.

The communities of the Diaspora were solidly organized and afforded excellent bases for the penetration of Christianity into the Greco-Roman world.

BIBLIOGRAPHY

Ricciotti, *Storia d'Israele,* Vol. 2 (Turin, 1934), pp. 203–230. Van den Biesen, "Diaspora," *CE.* Vandervorst, "Dispersion," *DBVS,* cols. 432–445.

diocese (διοίκησις — administration). The territory over which a bishop or other prelate extends his jurisdiction. It is an established fact that the division of ecclesiastical dioceses and provinces was originally modeled on the division and territorial extension of the provinces of the Roman Empire. Later, however, changes in historical, political, and social conditions brought about a radical modification of the primitive boundaries.

The *Pontifical Yearbook* gives the exact listing of all dioceses of the Catholic world, with the names of their bishops.

BIBLIOGRAPHY

Claeys Bouuaert, "Diocèse," *DDC.* Kurtscheid, *Historia Iuris Canonici,* Vol. 1 (Rome, 1941). Romani, *Institutiones Iuris Canonici,* Vol. 1 (Rome, 1941), nn. 344–349. Van Hove, "Diocese," *CE.*

diptych. See *Canon of the Mass.*

"discens Ecclesia." See *"Ecclesia discens."*

divination. See *superstition.*

divinity of Jesus Christ. A fundamental dogma of Christianity.

The divinity of Christ is foreshadowed in the Old Testament:

1. *Messianic texts* (Gen. 3:14 ff.; 12:1–3; 49:14; Num. 24:17; Ps. 2, 44, 71, 88, 109; Isa. 7:14; 9:6; Mich. 5:2; Jer. 23:6; Dan. 7:13; Mal. 3:1). These texts have their full strength when considered in the light of the New Testament; taken in themselves they are not all indisputable, but at least suggest a vague idea of the *transcendent* nature of the future Messias. A particular value must be attributed to Isa. 9:6, where the Messias is prophesied as אֵל גִּבּוֹר — *'el gibbôr* (strong God), a title given elsewhere to Jahweh. Not less valid is the prophecy of Malachias 3, which announces the Precursor and the Messias who will enter the temple as Dominator (Hebr. *ha' adôn* — name of Jahweh).

2. *Sapiential texts,* which represent the divine Wisdom as personified in such a way as to suggest a distinction of terms or subjects in the Divinity (Prov. 8:12 ff.; Ecclus. 24:5 ff.; Wisd. 7:21 ff.; 18:4).

In the New Testament the divinity of Christ is evident:

1. The predicted Messias is Christ (in the whole Gospel).

2. In the *Synoptics* (Matt., Mark, Luke) Christ is the unique Son of God (Gr. ἀγαπητός — most beloved, unique): Matt. 3:17; 17:5; Mark 1:11; 9:7; He is confessed as such by St. Peter (Matt. 16:16 ff.), whom Jesus approves and praises. Moreover, Jesus distinguishes His relationship to the Father in the expressions "My Father," "Your Father," never associating Himself with mere men by saying "Our Father." Before the Sanhedrin He declares Himself to be the Son of God and is condemned for it. He affirms Himself superior to Solomon (Matt. 12:41); He completes the divine law (Matt.

5:21), remits the sins of Mary Magdalen, of the paralytic, and promises eternal life to those who love Him above all things and follow Him. He rises from the dead and ascends into heaven.

3. *St. John's Gospel.* Christ is the eternal Word, truly God; He is the One-Born of the Father, who exists before Abraham, who is but one sole thing with the Father, and who sends the Holy Spirit.

4. *St. Paul* declares energetically the divinity of Christ, especially in Rom. 9:5; Col. 1:15; 2:9; Phil. 2:6 ff.; Heb. 1:11; Tit. 2:13.

Tradition is a unanimous chorus, a testimony in words, in art, in life, in blood, sealed by the Council of Nicaea (325).

BIBLIOGRAPHY

BOUGAUD, *The Divinity of Christ* (Baltimore, 1926). FABRI, *Il Cristianesimo rivelazione divina* (Assisi, 1942), p. 273 ff. LEPIN, *Le Christ Jésus* (Paris, 1929). POHLE-PREUSS, *Dogmatic Theology,* IV *Christology* (St. Louis, 1946), pp. 9–38. Various treatises *De Verbo Incarnato.*

See under *Jesus Christ.*

divorce. In a strict sense, the solution of the marriage bond, by which the husband and wife can contract new nuptials; in a broader sense it is separation (as regards home, living, etc.) of the parties, the matrimonial bond remaining firm. Divorce, in the strict sense, was permitted to the Jews by God *ob duritiam cordis eorum* ("on account of their hardheartedness"). It so permeated Roman and barbarian custom as to make it particularly difficult for the Church to get the faithful and the legislators to accept the principle of the indissolubility of the conjugal bond, which the Church had taken from the natural law, and especially from revelation.

Although divorce is not directly contrary to the primary end of marriage, i.e., procreation and education of the offspring (and that is why God could dispense temporarily from the primitive law of the indissolubility of marriage), it is, however, diametrically opposed to the secondary end of matrimony, which is the mutual help and the reciprocal harmony of the husband and wife, as is quite evident to whoever reflects on the many disorders following in the wake of and occasioned by divorce (hatred, rancor, vengeance, abandonment of the offspring, discord among families, degradation of the woman). These and similar reasons moved the divine Restorer of the family and of human society to revoke the concession made in the Old Testament and restore the institution of marriage to its original indissolubility. In an incisive sentence Jesus declared: "Every one that putteth away his wife, and marrieth another, committeth adultery: and he that marrieth her that is put away from her husband, committeth adultery" (Luke 16:18; cf. 1 Cor. 7:10–11; Rom. 7:2–3).

The thought of the Master was illustrated by the Fathers and applied constantly by the Roman Church, which had to undergo gigantic struggles with libertine emperors and princes, as in the case of Henry VIII who, on the occasion of Rome's prohibition of his divorce, caused a whole people to be separated from the true faith. The divine truth was permanently and precisely defined in the Council of Trent (*DB,* 975, 977). The Oriental Schismatics and the Protestants, great champions of divorce, bring up in objection a phrase of the Lord: "Whosoever shall put away his wife, excepting for the cause of fornication, maketh her to commit adultery: and he that shall marry her that is put away, committeth adultery" (Matt. 5:32; cf. 19:9). We reply immediately that the incidental phrase, even if separated from the rest of the text of the gospel teaching and from Tradition, does not necessarily imply that Christ *permits* divorce in the case of adultery of one of the parties. In fact, if we stick close to the force of the words used, and to the content, we see that Christ, expounding the law of indissolubility, wants to prescind from the very thorny question (for His audience) of adultery; and so, what He intends to say is: whoever sends away his wife (prescinding, for the purpose at hand now, from the case of adultery), makes her commit sin.

Recently, *Allgeier,* a lucid German exegete, endeavored to reconstruct the Aramaic sentence employed by Jesus Christ, and has come to the conclusion that the incidental phrase is merely an exclamation interposed by the divine Master to give greater strength to His words: "Whoever will have sent away his wife — and you must not do that — makes her commit adultery." If this is so, the whole difficulty disappears. In conclusion: even if, exegetically, there may remain a bit of obscurity, it is fully dissipated by Tradition.

BIBLIOGRAPHY

St. Thomas, *Summa Theol.,* III, *Suppl.,* q. 67, a. 1, ad 4; *Summa Contra Gentiles,* l. 3, c. 123. Leo XIII, *Encyclical Arcanum* (1880). Perrone, *De matrimonio,* Vol. 3, pp. 243–389. Pohle-Preuss, *Dogmatic Theology,* XI *The Sacraments,* Vol. 4, *Extreme Unction, Holy Orders, Matrimony* (St. Louis, 1946), pp. 183–216. Romani, *Institutiones Iuris Canonici,* Vol. 2, p. 55. Smith, "Divorce," *CE.* Villien, "Divorce," *DTC.*

"docens Ecclesia." See *"Ecclesia discens."*

Docetism (Gr. δοκέω — I seem; δόκησις — appearance). An obscure heresy of the first centuries, which reduced Christ's humanity to an appearance, compromising the veracity of the Gospel in its account of the human life, passion, and death of the Saviour, and with it the value of the whole work of Redemption. Traces of confutation of this error are found in St. Paul and St. John (cf. Col. 1:20; 1 Tim. 2:5; 1 John 4:2). A little later, St. Ignatius Martyr defends the reality of the flesh assumed by the Son of God against the *Docetae;* St. Irenaeus (*Adv. haereses,* l. 3) does likewise. Tertullian (*De carne Christi*) and St. Augustine (*Contra Faustum*) attack various forms of Docetism current among the Gnostics (Simon, Saturninus, Marcion) and the Manichaeans. In the fifth century, Docetism was welcomed by the Monophysites (see *Eutychianism*), who admitted an absorption of the human nature in the divine, reducing the humanity of Christ, of which the Gospel speaks, to a mere phantasm (whence the name *Phantasiasts*), impassible, incorruptible (whence the name *Aphthartodocetism* of Julian of Halicarnassus; from the Gr. α [privative] and φθείρω — I corrupt). Other Monophysitist leaders, like Severus of Antioch, admitted the passibility of Christ's humanity and, therefore, were called *Phthartolatrae.*

As the Docetae compromised the reality of Christ's passion, and thereby the value of the Redemption, so they were constrained to deny or pervert the truth of the *Eucharistic mystery.*

BIBLIOGRAPHY

Arendzen, "Docetae," *CE.* Bareille, "Docètes et Docétisme," *DTC.* Cayré, *Manual of Patrology,* trans. Howitt, Vol. 1 (Paris, Tournai, Rome, 1936), pp. 34, 70, 104, 162, 190, 237, 263. Tixeront, *La théologie anténicéenne* (Paris, 1905).

Doctors of the Church. Those ecclesiastical writers who, not only by reason of the holiness of their lives and the orthodoxy of their doctrine but especially by the eminence of their knowledge, have been honored by the Church with this title.

The Doctors differ from the Fathers

of the Church (*q.v.*) for three reasons: (1) it is not necessary for them to have lived in ancient times; (2) it is required that their learning be really extraordinary so as to merit the liturgical praise of *Doctor Optime, Ecclesiae sanctae lumen* ("Excellent Doctor, light of the holy Church"); (3) it is required that this title be conferred on them in a sufficiently explicit way (actually a solemn act of the pope is needed).

Following is the list arranged in chronological order of the Doctors of the Church: SS. Athanasius, Basil, Gregory of Nazianzus, John Chrysostom (the four great doctors of the East), Ambrose, Jerome, Augustine, Gregory the Great (the four great doctors of the West), Ephraem, Hilary of Poitiers, Gregory of Nyssa, Cyril of Jerusalem, Cyril of Alexandria, Peter Chrysologus, Leo the Great, John Damascene, Isidore of Seville, Bede the Venerable, Peter Damian, Anselm, Bernard, Bonaventure, Thomas Aquinas, Albert the Great, John of the Cross, Peter Canisius, Robert Bellarmine, Francis de Sales, Alphonsus Liguori, Anthony.

BIBLIOGRAPHY

FRANZELIN, *De Traditione* (Rome, 1882), pp. 172–215. PACE, "Doctor," *CE*. VALTON, "Docteur de l'Eglise," *DTC*. VAN LAAK, *De Patrum et theologorum magisterio* (Rome, 1933).

dogma (Gr. δοκεῖν — seem, opine, maintain opinion). Originally, it meant *opinion*. The classics use it with the meaning of *criterion*, rule, law; in this last sense, it is found in the New Testament (Luke 2:1; Acts 16:4). The earliest Fathers use it to indicate a principle of moral doctrine (rather than a principle of faith in general). From the fourth century, the meaning of dogma as *truth of faith* begins to prevail (Cyril of Jerusalem, Gregory of Nyssa). The Scholastics preferred *article* or *sentence* in the last sense. From the seventeenth century, the theoretical doctrine of faith is separated from the moral doctrine, and called dogmatic theology — a division which has remained to the present time.

A dogma, in the technical use of the word, is a truth revealed by God, and proposed as such by the *magisterium* of the Church to the faithful, with the obligation of believing it. Thus understood, a dogma is a divine truth and, therefore, immutable (Vatican Council, *DB*, 1800). The modernists, having reduced dogma to a *symbolic* expression of religious sentiment in continual development (see *symbolism*) or to a practical rule or norm of religious consciousness (see *pragmatism*), have admitted an *intrinsic evolution* of dogma which must correspond to the indefinite phases of that sentiment and of that consciousness. These errors were condemned by Pius X (encyclical *Pascendi* and decree *Lamentabili, DB*, 2026 and 2079 ff.).

According to Catholic doctrine, a dogma cannot undergo intrinsic and substantial changes; there is an evolution, however, on the part of the faithful as to understanding and expressing a dogma (extrinsic and subjective evolution). This legitimate progress appears in the history of the dogmatic formulas defined by the Church, as gradually the meaning of the truths, contained in the sources of divine revelation, came to be more profoundly and clearly understood.

BIBLIOGRAPHY

COGHLAN, "Dogma," *CE*. DE GRANDMAISON, *Le dogme chrétien* (Paris, 1928). DUBLANCHY, "Dogme," *DTC*. GARDEIL, *Le donné révélé et la théologie* (Juvisy, 1932). GARRIGOU-LAGRANGE, *Le sens commun — La philosophie de l'être et les formules dogmatiques* (Paris, 1922). LÉPICIER, *De stabilitate et progressu dogmatis* (Rome, 1910). NEWMAN, *Idea of a University* (London, 1899). PINARD, "Dogme," *DA*.

Donatism. Draws its name from Donatus the Great, its chief proponent.

Ideologically it is linked up with the error of the rebaptizers, due to these facts: Tertullian, having first denied the validity of baptism by heretics (based on the false reason that heretics, being deprived of grace, are incapable of transmitting it to others), found in St. Cyprian († 258) an ardent and intelligent champion of his thesis. St. Cyprian requested Pope Stephen I to confirm it, but the Pope, founded in the Roman Tradition, replied with the famous rescript: *Nihil innovetur, nisi quod traditum est*" ("No innovation in traditional practices"). The Donatists, following the trajectory of the ideas of these two African scholars, pushed their position to its extreme but logical consequences: If the heretics cannot baptize validly, being devoid of the Holy Spirit and His grace, neither can sinners do so, for the same reason; sinners, therefore, cannot communicate grace through administration of the sacraments.

The *historical occasion* for such development of the erroneous principle of Tertullian and Cyprian presented itself at the beginning of the fourth century when the Emperor Diocletian ordered the Christians to hand in their sacred books to be burned. Those who complied were called *traditores* (traitors, or handers-over) and were considered public sinners. Felix of Apthonga, who consecrated Cecilian Bishop of Carthage, was accused of this crime. Certain priests of Carthage, backed by the bishops of Numidia, took advantage of the principle of the rebaptizers and deduced with ease from it that Cecilian was invalidly ordained bishop. This last appealed to Rome and won. But the rebels set up Majorinus as bishop and, in 315, upon his death, Donatus the Great, who organized the schism in a solid hierarchical way and so gave his name to it.

Donatism was founded on two principles readily understandable to the people: (1) the Church is a society of saints; (2) the sacraments administered by sinners and heretics are invalid. Bolstered by the fanatical zeal of the Circumcellions and propagandized by sharp writers (Parmenianus, Ticonius, Petilianus, etc.), the new sect spread and consolidated so deeply that it endangered the existence of Catholicism in Roman Africa. Neither the repeated intervention of the emperors nor the brilliant polemics by St. Optatus of Milevis were able to break the spirit of the rebels. Only at the beginning of the fifth century, with imperial support, did the serried logic and winning charity of St. Augustine succeed in weakening definitively the century-old schism and bringing into clear light the Catholic principle, according to which: (1) the Church Militant is not a society of saints but a *corpus permixtum* (mixed body) of good and bad; (2) the sacraments draw their efficacy from Christ and not from their ministers, and hence they are *sancta per se et non per homines* ("holy of themselves and not by virtue of men").

BIBLIOGRAPHY

Chapman, "Donatists," *CE.* Doronzo, *De sacramentis in genere* (Milwaukee, 1946), Index Analyticus: "Donatistae." Leclercq, *L'Afrique chrétienne* (Paris, 1904). Monceaux, *Histoire litéraire de l'Afrique chrétienne* (Paris, 1905). O'Dowd, "Donatism and Anglicanism," *Irish Eccles. Record,* 4th series, Vol. 18 (August, 1905). Tixeront, *History of Dogmas,* trans. H.L.B., Vol. 2 (St. Louis, 1914), pp. 200–228.

E

Easter. See *Pasch.*

Ebionites (Hebr. *ebion* — poor). A *Jewish-Christian* sect of the Apostolic

Age, living in Palestine. Their doctrine can be reconstructed from the testimonies of Irenaeus, Origen, Tertullian, and Epiphanius: There is only one God, the Creator. Jesus is a pure man, born of Mary and Joseph, who becomes the Christ of God through His fidelity in the observance of the law. Every Christian can become like Him and be saved through the Jewish observances. The only authentic Gospel is that of St. Matthew; St. Paul and his epistles are to be rejected.

Toward A.D. 100 the Ebionites came into contact with the Essenes, another Jewish sect that had separated from official and ritual Judaism for a purer and more perfect life. From this contact stemmed the so-called *Esseno-Ebionism,* whose teachings are set forth particularly in the form of biographical novels in the pseudo-Clementine documents (*homilies, contestation, epitome*): God is one; He has a face and members; He created all things in antithetic pairs (Cain and Abel, light and darkness, etc.); only one Prophet exists, who manifested himself in Adam, Moses, and, finally, in Christ, who is son of God, but not God, because God is not, like Christ, generated (a prelude to Arianism, *q.v.*); the soul is free and immortal and will be recompensed by God according to its merits. Circumcision is admitted as well as baptism (renewed, in a certain way, by a daily bath); vegetarianism and early marriage are recommended; bloody sacrifices are forbidden. Briefly, Ebionism is a hybrid merger of Essene, Jewish, and Christian elements, and has in itself the germs of future heresies.

BIBLIOGRAPHY

Arendzen, "Ebionites," *CE.* Bareille, "Ebionites," *DTC.* Epiphanius, "Haereses (Panarion)," 30, *PG,* 41, 400 ff. Mansel, *The Gnostic Heresies of the First and Second Centuries* (London, 1875). Tixeront, *History of Dogmas,* trans. H.L.B., Vol. 1 (St. Louis, 1910), pp. 163–170.

"Ecclesia discens" (learning **Church**) (Lat. *discere* — to learn). That part of the members of the Church which consists of subjects. The Church is a society of unequals, in which by divine right some are superiors (the pope and the bishops) and have the authority of teaching, while the others are subjects (all the other faithful) and have the obligation of accepting the teaching of faith and morals imparted by the legitimate pastors. Hence the theological distinction of *Ecclesia docens* (teaching Church — pope and bishops) and *Ecclesia discens* (learning Church — the other faithful).

Even the priests, while they do indeed have care of souls, like parish priests, belong to the *Ecclesia discens,* although the bishops ordinarily use their priests in the service of teaching the divine word; the bishops are teachers by virtue of their function, while the priests are such only by participation and delegation.

Moreover, the bishops, united with the pope in their teaching, enjoy active infallibility (infallibility in teaching). The faithful, in so far as they are the recipients of this teaching and assimilate the doctrines without error, enjoy a sort of reflex infallibility, called by the theologians *passive* infallibility (infallibility in believing).

BIBLIOGRAPHY

Carretti, *Propedeutica alla Sacra Teologia* (Bologna, 1927), lez. 18. De Guibert, *De Christi Ecclesia* (Rome, 1928), pp. 266–268. Various treatises *De Ecclesia.*

"Ecclesia docens." See *"Ecclesia discens."*

ecstasy (Gr. ἔκστασις from ἐκ — from, outside of, and ἵστημι — I put). An extraordinary state in which a person is, as it were, outside of himself. There is a whole gamut of ecstatic phenomena, running from simple *deliquium,* quasi-absolute insensibility, levitation, bilocation, bleeding stigmata, to clairvoyance bordering prophecy. Ecstasy may be induced by *extrinsic agents* (alcoholic beverages, anesthetics, solitude, fixation of the senses or of the mind on determined objects, etc.); or it may spring from a *subjective impression* in contemplation of the beauty of nature or art; or it may be determined without motives, unexpectedly, even in babies. Unprejudiced physiologists often reduce all forms of ecstasy to pathological phenomena of hysterical catalepsy, of neurosis, or of hypnotism as in the *medium* of spiritism (*q.v.*). According to Catholic teaching, a distinction is to be made between: (*a*) *natural ecstasy,* of spontaneous origin, artificial or pathological, with phenomena explicable by the laws of physical or psychic nature; (*b*) *preternatural ecstasy,* with phenomena requiring the intervention of a superior force (devil); (*c*) *supernatural ecstasy,* due to a special action of God on the rational creature.

The first lies in the field of medical science, but the last two require the judgment of the theologian. Diabolic ecstasy is marked with phenomena and actions contrary to faith and morals. Supernatural ecstasy is proper to holy and privileged souls, and consists chiefly in that superior knowledge of God, made up of love and experience, which constitutes the apex of contemplation (*q.v.*). The somatic phenomena, e.g., stigmata, may accompany supernatural ecstasy, but are not in themselves the proof of it. As the highest grade of contemplation, ecstasy consists primarily in *cognition,* an intellectual *experience* of God, which is analogous to sensation (the mystics speak of *spiritual senses*), through which a quasi contact is made with *Him.* The ecstatic, in this phase, though not seeing the divine essence, has clear knowledge of supernatural truths and mysteries: this is explained by direct infusion of intelligible species by God. An ardent *love* accompanies this knowledge, and incites the will to accept any sacrifice for God. A more elevated form of ecstasy is *rapture* or *flight* of the spirit, in which the soul is transported and seemingly absorbed in God with flashing rapidity. Ecstasy is prevalently *passivity* of the soul: but this fact does not eliminate personality (as in the nirvana of Buddha), or liberty, or merit.

The foregoing is all gathered from actual descriptions left by the great mystics, outstanding among whom are SS. Catherine of Siena, John of the Cross, Teresa, and Catherine of Genoa.

BIBLIOGRAPHY

Hamon, "Extase," *DTC.* Pacheu, *Introduction a la psychologie des mystiques* (1901). Pascal Parente, *The Mystical Life* (St. Louis, 1946), Index: "Ecstasy." Poulain, *Les graces d'oraison* (1909). Pourrat, *La spiritualité chrétienne,* 4 vols. (1921–1928).

See under *mystery; contemplation.*

efficacy of the sacraments. See *causality of the sacraments* (*fact*).

elect. Those predestined by God to eternal life. Several questions are connected with this entry (see *predestination*), but only two are examined here: (1) the character of divine election and its relationship to divine knowledge, love, and predestination; (2) the number of the elect.

1. *Character of divine election.* St. Thomas frequently reminds us of the difference between God's love and ours. We love a creature attracted by the perfection that we find in it and that can be helpful to us; while God, unable to undergo any external influence, loves the creature by infusing into it the good it did not have.

Our love, then, is the effect of the perfection of the thing loved; God's love, on the contrary, is the cause of that perfection: *Amor Dei est infundens et creans bonitatem in rebus* ("The love of God is infusing and creating goodness in things," *Summa Theol.,* I, q. 20, a. 2). Therefore, while we are moved by the perfection of a creature, prefer that creature to others and love it, God first loves a creature and then prefers it on account of the perfection He has bestowed on it by loving it. Hence, the Thomists find this succession (logical, and not chronological — *rationis et non temporis*) in the divine acts: *love, election, predestination.* Thus, election as fruit of God's love is absolutely *gratuitous,* as is also predestination to eternal life. But in order to love a creature with preference (predilection), God must first know the elect, and so a certain foreknowledge must precede the "fore-love" or election. If we ask what is the cause of this choice, the Thomists reply that it depends *exclusively* on the Goodness of God who communicates Himself to whom He wishes; the Molinists insist generally that prevision (foresight) of the elect's merits must, in addition to the divine goodness, be a contributory factor in God's choice. In any system, the distinction between elect and nonelect remains enveloped in deep mystery, as St. Augustine recognized long ago. If, indeed, in the abstract and intentional order election is independent of the consideration of human merit, practically, in the order of execution, it is certain that merits (in the adult) are a condition of salvation that cannot be prescinded from, just as demerits are a requisite condition for damnation.

2. *Number of the elect.* The question has been discussed from the earliest centuries, there being two opposite tendencies: one optimistic, opening heaven's portals wide to the majority of men, the other more *rigorous,* reducing the elect to a few. In ancient times the rigoristic tendency predominated, while today even the theologians are somewhat more liberal, although they reject the exaggerated optimism of certain authors (e.g., the *Humanists*). The truth is that God alone knows, with certainty and *ab aeterno,* the exact number of the elect; in the liturgy, the Church says this expressly: *Deus cui soli cognitus est numerus electorum in superna felicitate locandus* ("God to whom alone is known the number of the elect who are to be put in the place of happiness above"). We can — harmoniously with God's wisdom and the redeeming work of Jesus Christ — think that the elect are more numerous than the reprobate, but each faithful, as far as he is concerned, must pray, fight, and even fear for his salvation, according to the warning of the Apostle: "With fear and trembling work out your salvation" (Phil. 2:12).

BIBLIOGRAPHY

St. Thomas, *Summa Theol.,* I, q. 23, a. 4 and 7. Garrigou-Lagrange, "Prédestination," *DTC.* Maas, "Elect," *CE.* Michel, "Elus (nombre des)," *DTC.* Peter Parente, *De Deo Uno* (1938), p. 307 ff.

elevation (to supernatural order). A truth of faith that God not only created man with his natural perfections of soul and body (*qq.v.*), but also enriched him with *supernatural* and *preternatural* gifts (*qq.v.*), in view of the end which He had appointed for him and which transcends human nature, namely, the beatific vision (see *vision, beatific*). The Council of Trent speaks of the "sanctity and justice in which [Adam] was constituted" (*DB,* 788). Pius V condemned Bay (see *Baianism*) who denied this elevation to the supernatural order.

1. Adam was enriched with *sanctifying grace* and the *virtues* and *gifts* deriving therefrom. The entire New Testament speaks of the work of the Redemption, as a return to the original state (rehabilitation). But the Redemption consists chiefly in the restoration of the reign of grace in the human soul (cf. St. Paul); therefore, in the primitive state of Adam there must have been grace with the virtues and the supernatural gifts. St. Augustine, re-echoing the other Fathers, writes (*De Genesi ad litt.*, 6, 24, 35): "We will renew ourselves in our spirit according to the image of Him who created us, an image which Adam lost by sinning."

2. Adam had also the preternatural gift of *integrity* (*q.v.*), which includes immunity from *concupiscence* (*q.v.*), from *corporal death* and from *ignorance*. This supernatural and preternatural endowment constituted Adam in the *state of innocence* or *original justice,* which in Adam God had bequeathed, as it were, to all human nature after the fashion of an *accidens speciei* (St. Thomas), i.e., a property added gratuitously to all mankind, which was virtually in Adam as in its origin and source (see *innocence*).

BIBLIOGRAPHY

St. Thomas, *Summa Theol.,* I, q. 94 ff. Beraza, *De Deo elevante* (Bilbao, 1924). Boyer, *De Deo creante et elevante* (Rome, 1940). Peter Parente, *De creatione universali* (Rome, 1943), p. 159 ff. *The Teaching of the Catholic Church,* ed. Smith, 2 vols. (New York, 1949), pp. 311–319.

empiricism (Gr. ἐμπειρία — experience). A philosophical system which reduces all reality to the data of experience, whether internal (data of consciousness) or external (data of sense perception). Empiricism is a *method* rather than a system, which makes sensation the only means of knowledge, and the sensible phenomenon the only reality. Therefore, it is principally found in positivism and materialism (*qq.v.*), and from the gnosiological standpoint it is also known as sensism.

Empiricism is traced back to the *atomism* of the Abdera's School (Leucippus, Democritus, etc.); to *Stoicism,* which reduced everything to corporal substance, and to *Epicureanism.* In more modern times empiricism, favored by the scientific methodology of Francis Bacon, was developed in England by the materialism of Hobbes († 1679), which found favor also with the French Encyclopedists, the sensism of G. Locke († 1704), and more decisively in France the sensism of Condillac († 1780) and Comte († 1857). Likewise pragmatism (*q.v.*) is characterized psychologically by empiricism, and so is the intuitionalist philosophy of Bergson. Obviously, empiricism makes the construction of any metaphysics impossible by denying objective value to any reality that transcends sensation or psychological experience. It is, therefore, opposed to sound philosophy and to religion.

BIBLIOGRAPHY

De Broglie, *Le Positivisme et la science expérimentale* (Paris, 1880). Ladd, *Philosophy of Knowledge* (New York, 1897). Maréchal, *Le point de départ de la métaphysique* (Paris, 1923). Mercier, *Critériologie* (Louvain, 1906). Siegfried, "Empiricism," *CE.* Sortais, *La philosophie moderne jusqu'à Leibniz* (Paris, 1922). Tonnard, *Précis d'histoire de la philosophie* (Paris, 1937), p. 779.

Encratites (Gr. ἐγκράτεια — mastery of self, continence). Heretics who observed a rigorous temperance (abstinence from wine, meat, conjugal relations) for fundamentally Manichaean motives (see *Manichaeism*). The Encratite movement developed in the second century under the direction of Tatian, called by St. Jerome *princeps encratistarum,* of Dositeus of Cilicia and of a certain Severus, through whose work an Encratite sector broke up into small groups with individual names: *Apotactici* (abstinents), *Hydroparastatae* (aquarians), *Saccophors* (because they dressed in sacks). A strong propaganda, favored by the rigoristic tendencies of certain primitive ascetics, stimulated the widespread influence of the sect. St. Epiphanius, in the middle of the fourth century, points out their existence on the borders of the Church. They were effectively attacked by Clement of Alexandria and Origen, and severe juridical measures were taken against them.

BIBLIOGRAPHY

ARENDZEN, "Encratites," *CE*. BAREILLE, "Encratistes," *DTC*. CRUTTWELL, *A Literary History of Early Christianity* (1893).

encyclical (Gr. ἐγκύκλιος — circular, revolving in a circle, periodical). A letter that the pope sends to all the bishops in communion with the Apostolic See in order to make known to the whole Church his mind and will on some point of dogma, morals, or Church discipline. The popes of modern times especially have made great use of such circular letters, enriching them with a large and intense doctrinal content.

The encyclicals of Leo XIII are famous. They deal with the most vital problems concerning ecclesiastical constitution or social and political life: *Aeterni Patris* (1879) on Thomistic philosophy; *Arcanum divinae sapientiae* (1880) on Christian marriage; *Diuturnum illud* (1881) on the State; *Immortale Dei* (1885) on the Christian constitution of governments; *Libertas* (1888) on freedom and civil activities; *Rerum Novarum* (1891) on social and labor problems; *Providentissimus* (1893) on biblical studies; *Satis cognitus* (1896) on the unity of the Church; *Mirae caritatis* on the Eucharist.

Well known is the encyclical, *Pascendi* (1907), with which Pius X condemned modernism.

The encyclicals of Pius XI are numerous and profound, and a very good match for those of Leo XIII.

Pius XII gave us, in 1939, his first encyclical *Summi Pontificatus*, an outstanding document of juridical wisdom and Christian charity, followed by the others on the Mystical Body, Holy Scripture, St. Cyril of Alexandria (defender of Church unity), which develop themes vibrating with current interest and importance.

BIBLIOGRAPHY

CHAUPIN, *Valeur des décisions doctrinales et disciplinaires du Saint-Siège* (Paris, 1929), pp. 50–55. EYRE, *The Pope and the People* (London, 1897). MANGENOT, "Encyclique," *DTC*. THURSTON, "Encyclical," *CE*. WYNNE, *The Great Encyclical Letters of Leo XIII* (New York, 1903).

end, ultimate. The supreme term to which is ordained the action of the efficient cause. The end is the *final cause;* hence whatever is said of the final cause applies to the end (see *final cause*). The *ultimate* and *primary* end of creation is the divine goodness communicated to creatures (*extrinsic glory of God*). Now this effusion of goodness and glory of God may be considered *objectively,* in so far as it shines by itself in the life of the universe, and *formally,* in so far as it is known and loved by the one who is capable, namely: by the rational creature. This is the *absolute* ultimate end, to which divine providence orders all things. Nothing escapes this end, not even rebellious man, since the sinner leaves the order of divine love only to enter inexorably that of divine justice.

Here, however, we wish to speak of the *relative* last end of man. The lower beings have a proper finality too, which for all of them consists in the attainment of their perfection and which is realized in their subordination to the higher beings, and definitively, to man (*anthropocentric relative finality*). Man, made to God's image and likeness, is not ordered to any other created being, because his spirit, naturally extended toward an infinite Good and an infinite Truth, cannot find its specific perfection and satisfaction in finite things, i.e., in any creature whatsoever. Therefore, his ultimate end will be a supreme Good, capable of satisfying his unlimited aspiration, and so of actuating in full his specific perfection of rational creature. This Good can be but God, who is, therefore, man's proper final end.

God, however, may be considered *objectively* as the highest Good in Himself, and *subjectively* with respect to man, as the object of man's happiness (see *beatitude*). Formally, then, the ultimate end of man is the possession of God, effected through knowledge and love. This end could be limited within the *natural* order; but we know from revelation that God has elevated man to the *supernatural* order (grace — beatific vision) from the first instant of creation (see *elevation*), and that this order, disturbed by original sin, has been restored by the Redemption. God, ultimate end of man in the natural order, determines the ethical world based on morality (relationship between human action and human end, expressed in the law). God, ultimate end of man in the supernatural order, determines *meritorious* activity which, under the impulse of *charity* (*q.v.*), tends dynamically to the beatific vision, supreme goal in which will be actuated fully the perfectibility of man, who in the intuitive knowledge and love of God will achieve his end and implicitly also the end of the universe, of which he is the apex and synthesis.

BIBLIOGRAPHY

St. Thomas, *Summa Theol.*, I–II, qq. 1–15. Aveling, "Man," *CE.* Janvier, "La béatitude," Conférences de N.D. (1903). Richard, "Fin dernière," *DTC.*

energumeni (Gr. ἐνεργούμενος — furious). In ecclesiastical language energumen is one who is under the evil influence of the devil as manifested by phenomena beyond the power of nature (vision of the future, introspection of consciences, overpowering strength, etc.) or by morbid effects (epilepsy, paralysis, melancholy, deafness). Energumeni, rare in the Old Testament (cf. 1 Kings 16:23; 19:9; Tob. 6:8, 19; 8:3), appear frequently around Christ in the hope of obtaining cure. In the Church, their number has progressively decreased, but they have never completely disappeared. A very old liturgical practice, called *exorcism* (*q.v.*), for the purpose of expelling the devil, still exists in the Church. The possession of energumeni by the devil is called *obsession* (Lat. *obsidere* — occupy, besiege), and consists in the use the evil spirit makes of the body of his victim as an instrument. The devil can influence the soul only *indirectly,* through sensations (see *demon, devil*).

BIBLIOGRAPHY

Kent, "Demoniacs," *CE.* Leclercq, "Démoniaque," *DACL.* Ortolan, "Démoniaques," *DTC.* Smit, *De daemoniacis in historia evangelica* (Rome, 1913).

epiklesis (Gr. ἐπίκλησις — invocation). The name used to designate the prayer that is read in many eastern liturgies after the consecration. The epiklesis, taken literally, asks God to effect the transubstantiation, as if the words of consecration already pronounced had not had their full effect.

For this reason, from the fourteenth century certain Greeks, like Nicholas Cabasilas, Simeon of Thessalonica, Marcus Eugenicus, maintained that the epiklesis is absolutely necessary for transubstantiation. Later they were followed also by two Latin theologians, the Dominican Ambrose Catarino and the Franciscan Christopher Cheffontaines, who maintained that transubstantiation is the effect of the words *Quam oblationem,* which in the Roman canon precede the consecration.

But the most ancient patristic tradition, represented by St. Justin, St. Irenaeus, Tertullian, St. Ambrose, St. John Chrysostom, St. Augustine, etc., has constantly attributed to the words of institution the power of changing the elements into the body and blood of Christ.

The Church, therefore, in its ordinary *magisterium,* has on more than one occasion inculcated the ancient doctrine; not long ago Pius X has explicitly declared: "The Catholic doctrine on the sacrament of the Eucharist is not safe if the Greek doctrine is held acceptable, according to which the words of consecration do not have their effect until after the epiklesis" (Letter to the apostolic delegates of the Orient, Dec. 26, 1910).

As regards the apparently singular fact that the epiklesis requests transubstantiation anew, after it has happened, there are two convenient explanations: (1) St. Thomas says that the epiklesis is asking for the spiritual transmutation of the mystical body; (2) Bossuet holds that it is characteristic of the liturgy to go back over what occurred solely at one instant, in order to make the whole effect of that single occurrence better understood.

BIBLIOGRAPHY

St. Thomas, *Summa Theol.,* III, q. 8, a. 4, ad 9. Brinktrine, *De Epiclesis Eucharisticae origine et explicatione* (Rome, 1923). Doronzo, *De Eucharistia,* Vol. 1 (Milwaukee, 1948), Index Analyticus: "Epiclesis." Fortescue, "Epiklesis," *CE.* Jugie, *Theologia Dogmatica Christianorum Orientalium,* Vol. 3 (Paris, 1930), pp. 256–301; *De forma Eucharistiae* (Rome, 1943). Pohle-Preuss, *Dogmatic Theology,* IX *The Sacraments,* Vol. 2, *The Holy Eucharist* (St. Louis, 1946), pp. 210–216. Salaville, "Epiclèse," *DTC;* "Eucharistique (Epiclèse)," *DA.* Tyrer (non-Catholic), *The Eucharistic Epiklesis* (London, 1918).

episcopate. See *bishops; hierarchy; orders, holy.*

eschatology (Gr. ἔσχατα — last things; λόγος — discourse). That part of theology which treats of the end of life and of man's future after death (*the last things:* death, judgment, heaven, hell, purgatory, the end of the world, and the resurrection of the body).

The eschatological doctrine, revealed substantially in Holy Scripture, is developed in Tradition gradually and occasionally in connection with erroneous opinions on one or other of its various elements. Thus in the second and third centuries, millenarianism (*q.v.*) was much discussed, with writings pro and con. The fourth and fifth centuries were characterized by great polemics against *Origenism* (an aggregate of errors drawn from the writings of Origen, often badly interpreted), which cast doubt on the eternity of the pains of hell and suggested the idea of a final catharsis or purification for all, the demons included. Orthodox eschatology finds its first schematic organization in St. Augustine, and its definitive and complete systemization in the development of the Scholastic teaching, synthesized by St. Thomas. As regards the recent eschatological theories on the kingdom of God announced in the Gospel, see *Parousia.*

BIBLIOGRAPHY

St. Thomas, *Summa Theol.,* III, *Suppl.,* qq. 69–81; *Summa Contra Gentiles,* l. 4, c. 79–97. Arendzen, *What Becomes of the Dead? A Study in Eschatology* (London, 1925). Batiffol, "Apocatastasis," *CE.* Billot, *De Novissimis* (Rome, 1908). Braun, *Aspects nouveaux du problème de l'Eglise* (Fribourg en Suisse, 1942), p. 113 ff. Lanslots, *The*

End of the World and of Man (New York, 1925). OESTERLY, *The Doctrine of the Last Things* (London, 1908). OTTEN, *Manual of History of Dogmas,* Vol. 2 (St. Louis, 1915), pp. 418–437. OXENHAM, *Catholic Eschatology* (London, 1878). POHLE-PREUSS, *Dogmatic Theology,* XII *Eschatology* (St. Louis, 1946), pp. 103–120. SALMOND, *Christian Doctrine of Immortality* (Edinburgh, 1903). SASIA, *The Future Life* (New York, 1918). SUTCLIFFE, *The Old Testament and the Future Life* (Westminster, 1947). TANQUEREY, *Synopsis theologiae dogmaticae,* Vol. 3 (Paris, Rome, 1930), p. 587 ff. *The Teaching of the Catholic Church,* ed. Smith, 2 vols. (New York, 1949), pp. 1101–1282. TONER, "Eschatology," *CE.*

essence, divine. Essence, in general, is the formal element, constitutive and distinctive of a being. A being is specifically what it is, precisely on account of its essence. Man is man on account of *animality and reason* (essence). What is God essentially?

Old and New Testament revelation answers: God is spirit, wisdom, goodness, omnipotence, holiness; God is eternal, immutable, the synthesis of all perfections, infinite, unique. But these are so many concepts formed from our knowledge of creatures and attributed to God *analogically* (see *analogy*); they are only an attempt of the human intellect to express the divine essence. Ecclesiasticus declares: "We shall say much [about God], and yet shall want words: but the sum of our words is, He is all" (43:29). But even this concept is very vague. There is, however, a passage in Exodus 3:13 ff., in which God reveals Himself to Moses, saying: "I am who am," more properly: "I am who is"; nay, the Hebrew text has: "I am the Is" (Is — *Jahweh*). And this is the most sublime revelation: God is Being of Himself, or Being Itself. From this stems the theological teaching on the divine essence.

The theologians distinguish: *physical* essence, which in God is the aggregate of all the perfections; and *metaphysical* essence, i.e., that most formal reason without which God cannot be conceived and which is the source of all His perfections. For some, the metaphysical essence of God is *infinity,* for others *intellectuality,* and for others *aseity* (being from oneself). But the opinion most consonant with revelation is the one which places the metaphysical essence of God in *being*. While in creatures the existence is participated and thus is distinct from their essence, in God essence and existence are identical. Being subsisting by itself (*ens per se,* or *esse subsistens*), accounts for the infinity of God and for all the other attributes, while it places an abyss between Him and the created world (see *Tetragrammaton*).

BIBLIOGRAPHY

ST. THOMAS, *Summa Theol.,* I, q. 3, a. 4. BITTREMIEUX, "Deus est suum esse, creaturae non sunt suum esse," *Divus Thomas* (Piacenza, 1930). GARRIGOU-LAGRANGE, *The One God,* trans. Rose (St. Louis, 1943), pp. 156–162. MICHEL, "Essence," *DTC.* POHLE-PREUSS, *Dogmatic Theology,* I *God: Knowability, Essence, Attributes* (St. Louis, 1946), pp. 144–176.

eternity. Eternity is made up of two essential characteristics: the absence of a beginning and of an end, and the absence of all succession and change.

The Scholastics distinguish: (*a*) *time* (defined by Aristotle: measure of movement according to a "before" and an "after"), which involves change, even *substantial,* in things; (*b*) *aevum,* proper to spiritual beings (duration of souls and angels), which involves a beginning but not an end, and admits of only an *accidental* change; (*c*) *eternity,* which excludes all limitation, all change, all succession. It is a truth of faith that God alone is properly and simply eternal (see *immutability*). There are immortal creatures, like human souls and the angels (*qq.v.*), which have a beginning, but on account of the simplicity of their nature do not tend to perish. According to St. Thomas, the hypothesis is not absurd of an eternal world (i.e., which never began), created so and conserved by God. In the absolute sense, however, no creature can be eternal, i.e., in such a sense as to exclude not only beginning and end, but also change and succession, and to possess in act (i.e., actually and together) its entire perfection. Absolute eternity belongs to God alone, as defined by Boethius: *Interminabilis vitae tota simul et perfecta possessio* ("Perfect and simultaneous possession of a life without terms — beginning and end").

Eternity excludes and transcends time, and so in God there is no past or future, but only a changeless present. The problem of "before" and "after" makes no sense in God, to whom all of time in its succession is always present, like all the successive points of a circumference are simultaneously present to its center. This is the divine *presentiality,* one of the most important elements in the solution of the problem of the so-called prescience or foreknowledge of God.

BIBLIOGRAPHY

St. Thomas, *Summa Theol.,* I, q. 10. Garrigou-Lagrange, *The One God,* trans. Rose (St. Louis, 1943), pp. 276–292. McDonald, "Eternity," *CE.* Pohle-Preuss, *Dogmatic Theology,* I *God: Knowability, Essence, Attributes* (St. Louis, 1946), pp. 306–314. Sertillanges, *St. Thomas d'Aquin,* Vol. 1 (Paris, 1925), p. 203 ff. *The Teaching of the Catholic Church,* ed. Smith, 2 vols. (New York, 1949), pp. 98–101.

Eucharist (Gr. εὐχαριστεῖν — to thank). The sacrament which, under the species or appearances of bread and wine, contains truly, really, and substantially the body and blood of Jesus Christ, which is offered in sacrifice and distributed as spiritual food of souls.

In other words, the Eucharist is the prolongation of the Incarnation (Leo XIII): as the Word of God became present in human form to *procure* salvation for us by rendering due homage to God and condign satisfaction for sin, so Christ renders Himself present under the eucharistic veils to *apply* to us the work of the Redemption, in its ascendant phase, by renewing the sacrifice of the cross, and in its descendant motion by distributing grace through the sacramental rite of Holy Communion.

The eucharistic Mystery embraces, therefore, the Real Presence (see *Presence, Real*), the sacrifice of the Mass (*q.v.*), and the sacrament of Communion (see *Communion, eucharistic*). On account of the multiplicity of the mysteries it includes, the Eucharist is the compendium of faith, the center of gravitation of Christian piety, and the polar star that directs all the activity of the Catholic Church. The numerous names given to the Eucharist reflect, as in a prism of many facets, the variety of its aspects: Most Holy Sacrament, Body of Christ, Body of the Lord, the Holy Sacrifice of the Altar, Mass, Synaxis, Viaticum, Communion, Divine Table, etc.

BIBLIOGRAPHY

St. Thomas, *Summa Theol.,* III, qq. 73–83 (with the classical commentaries of Cajetan, Gonet, Contenson, Billot, etc.). D'Alès, *Eucharistie* (Paris, 1933). Coghlan, *De SS. Eucharistia* (Dublin, 1913). Connell, *De Sacramentis* (Brugis, 1933), pp. 173–287. Doronzo, *De Eucharistia,* 2 vols. (Milwaukee, 1948). Filograssi, *De SS. Eucharistia* (Rome, 1940). Garrigou-Lagrange, *De Eucharistia* (Turin, 1943). Goossens, *Les origines de l'Eucharistie* (Gembloux, 1931). Hedley, *The Holy Eucharist* (London, 1907). Hugon, *La Sainte Eucharistie* (Paris, 1924). Labauche, *Lettres à um etudiant sur la Sainte Eucharistie* (Paris, 1911). Lebreton, "Eucharistie," *DA.* Mattiussi, *De SS. Eucharistia* (Rome, 1925). Pohle, "Eucharist," *CE.* Pohle-Preuss, *Dogmatic Theology,* IX *The Sacraments,* Vol. 2, *The Holy Eucharist* (St. Louis, 1946). Rauschen, *Eucharist and Penance in the First Six Centuries of the Church,* trans. from the second German edition (St. Louis, 1913). Ruch, Bareille, Bour, Vernet, De Ghellinck, Mangenot, Godefroy, "Eucharistie," *DTC*. Scheeben, *The Mysteries of Christianity*, trans. Vollert (St. Louis, 1946), pp. 469–535. Tissot, *The Real Presence* (New York, 1873). Vonier, *A Key to the Doctrine of the Eucharist* (Westminster, 1946), pp. 53–85. Wiseman, *Lectures on the Real Presence* (London, 1842).

eucharistic accidents. The species of bread and wine (quantity, color, taste, and smell) which remain unvaried. They are an absolute, necessary condition for the body and blood of Christ to be present in a sacramental manner (see *Presence, Real, Eucharistic* [*fact*]). In fact, if the accidents did not remain, the presence of the body of Jesus could only be *in specie propria,* that is, by adaption of the single parts of the glorious body to the corresponding parts of surrounding space, so that remaining enclosed in place *A* it could not simultaneously be in place *B,* just as a quart of water cannot be in its entirety simultaneously contained in two bottles of one quart each. The accidents remain unchanged, and the body of Christ, which is contained *locally,* one time only, in heaven, can be made present "after the manner of substance" as many times as there are eucharistic consecrations. In this manner the claim of absurdity cannot be made, the absurdity of a body many times distant from itself. Distance is the interval between two bodies locally present in space, and so it does not occur in the case of Christ's body in heaven and the same body in the Eucharist, seeing that in the host it is not present locally (i.e., *after the manner of quantity*), but only sacramentally (i.e., *after the manner of substance*).

There has been much discussion among philosophers and theologians on the *nature* of the accidents, but the data of Tradition as well as the declarations of the Church, made at Constance (*DB,* 582) and at Trent (*DB,* 884), lead us to accept the classic doctrine of the Scholastics. The Scholastics constantly maintained that the sacramental species are not subjective modifications of the senses (against Descartes) or effects produced divinely in the place of the bread and wine (against the atomists and dynamists), but that they are the same numerical realities which had the substances of bread and wine as their subject of inhesion before transubstantiation. After transubstantiation these realities remain without any natural subject, sustained in their first being by that same divine omnipotence which, having been able to form in the Virgin's womb the body of Christ without human seed, can also in an eminent manner supply the effect of substance with relation to the accidents.

On corruption of the eucharistic species, the Real Presence ceases immediately because their relationship of container with respect to the body of Christ vanishes, without the body of Christ being subject to any change.

BIBLIOGRAPHY

St. Thomas, *Summa Theol.,* III, q. 77. D'Alès, *De Eucharistia* (Paris, 1929), pp. 94–98. Billot, *De sacramentis,* Vol. 1, pp. 436–440. Doronzo, *De Eucharistia,* Vol. 1 (Milwaukee, 1948), pp. 315–384. Jansen, "Eucharistiques (Accidents)," *DTC*. Pohle-Preuss, *Dogmatic Theology,* IX *The Sacraments,* Vol. 2, *The Holy Eucharist* (St. Louis, 1946), pp. 143–158. Van Hove, *De SS. Eucharistia* (Mechliniae, 1941).

Eutychianism. Christological heresy of Eutyches, Archimandrite of Constantinople, also called *Monophysitism* because, in opposition to *Nestorianism,* it defends the substantial unity of Christ up to the point of positing in Him not only *one* Person, but also one theandric nature (Monophysitism: Gr. *μόνη* — one, and *φύσις* — nature). The genesis of this heresy lies entirely in an attempt to exaggerate the position of St. Cyril of Alexandria against Nestorianism; in his polemic fervor the holy Doctor had advanced some extreme expressions on the profound unity of the Man-God (unity not of nature but only of person) and had adopted a famous Apollinarianistic phrase (see *Apollinarianism*): *μία φύσις τοῦ Λόγου σεσαρκωμένη* (the incarnate nature of the Word is one) which he attributed to St. Athanasius. But the concept of a fusion of the divine and human natures of Christ is foreign to the mentality of St. Cyril. The Eutychians appeal abusively to his authority. Besides, Eutyches, a man of no great ability, maintained stubbornly and without reasons that before the union there were two natures, but after the union there was one sole nature in Christ. His disciples advanced various explanations, often fantastic, of that statement of their master: they speak of *mixture* of the two natures, of *absorption* of one in the other, of *formal union* similar to that of the soul with the body. All these formulas compromise inexorably the integrity of one or of both natures.

The Council of Chalcedon (451) condemned the new heresy, vindicating precisely the *integrity* of the two natures and their real distinction, notwithstanding the personal unity: Christ is one, sole subject (Person), the Word, who incarnating Himself remains perfect God and becomes perfect man. Distinction and not division, union and not confusion or transformation: the two natures, subsisting in the Person of the Word, remain integral with their respective properties. The Council follows and repeats in its definitions the doctrine expounded by Pope St. Leo the Great in his famous letter to Flavian, Bishop of Constantinople (449).

Monophysitism spread widely on account of its definite *mystic* character, giving rise to various churches and sects, among which is noteworthy that of the Jacobites (from Jacob Baradai, Bishop of Odessa, † 578) which still remains in the East with its hierarchy (see *Theopaschism; Docetism*).

BIBLIOGRAPHY

Cayré, *Manual of Patrology,* trans. Howitt, Vol. 2 (Paris, Tournai, Rome, 1940), pp. 52–71. Chapman, "Eutychianism," *CE;* "Monophysites and Monophysitism," *CE.* Jugie, "Monophysisme," *DTC.* Lebon, *Le monophysisme sévérien* (Louvain, 1909).

evil. The subject of a problem that has always harassed philosophers and theologians. The first who attempted an integral solution of the old question was St. Augustine — constrained to study it in his struggle against *Manichaeism* (*q.v.*), which by the side of the Principle of good put the Principle of evil, according to the *Mazdaistic* conception of the Persians. St. Augustine refuted this extravagant dualism by bringing to service the neoplatonic (cf. Plotinus) concept of *evil* as *non-being,* i.e., as privation of being and, therefore, of goodness. The Pseudo-Dionysius speaks along the same line (*De Divinis Nominibus,* Ch. IV). From these sources St. Thomas drew his principles in developing on repeated occasions the important doctrine of evil in relation to creation, divine providence (*q.v.*) and knowledge (see *science, divine*) and divine motion in creatures (see *concourse, divine*).

The chief heads of the Thomistic teaching are: (1) metaphysically, evil is a partial *privation* of good, and, therefore, it is rather a non-being (*non ens*); e.g., blindness means absence, lack of the good of sight in a man who ought to have it. (2) Where there is fullness of being, pure act (God), evil is not possible; but evil blends with good where there is *po-*

tency, and, therefore, defectibility. From the viewpoint of being, evil has its roots in the *limitation* and in the *multiplicity* of created beings. From the viewpoint of operation, evil is inserted between potency and act, inasmuch as the former may not attain the latter; e.g., the seed that does not develop. (3) Evil, inasmuch as it is non-being, cannot cause (realize, give being), nor can it be caused unless *per accidens* by good itself. Thus God in creating the world (good) is the indirect cause also of evil which has its subject in created good, necessarily limited and multiple. (4) Evil is not in the intention or in the idea of God, who knows it through good, of which it is the privation. Evil, both *physical* and *moral* (sin) is entirely on the part of creatures, which are deficient in acting because limited in being. (5) Evil is not contrary to providence, because God provides, in an orderly way, rather for the universal good, which demands often the sacrifice of the particular good. Moreover, He who does not will but permits evil is able to draw good from evil. For example, original sin, which has aggravated physical and moral evil in the world, was permitted by God, who, however, grafted, as it were, onto it the wondrous work of the Redemption.

BIBLIOGRAPHY

St. Thomas, *Quaest. Disp. De Malo.* Clarke, *The Existence of God: A Dialogue* (London, 1887). Jolivet, *Le problème du mal d'après St. Augustin* (Paris, 1936). Peter Parente, "Il male secondo la dottrina di S. Tommaso," *Acta Acad. Pont. Romanae S. Thomae Aq.* (1940). Rickaby, "Evil and Necessity," *Month* (Nov., 1898). Sertillanges, *St. Thomas d'Aquin,* Vol. 1 (Paris, 1925), p. 61 ff. Sharpe, "Evil," *CE.* Smith, *The Problem of Evil* (London, 1906). *The Teaching of the Catholic Church,* ed. Smith, 2 vols. (New York, 1949), pp. 228–241.

evolutionism. The scientific theory, according to which all present living beings are the result of a progressive transformation from one or more primordial elements. It is also called *transformism.* This theory arose at the beginning of the past century from the work of the French botanist John de Lamarck and, more proximately, from the work of Charles Darwin, from whom the theory took the name of *Darwinism.*

Lamarck assigned, as the cause of the evolution of species, adaptation to environment and natural finalistic tendency of the organisms (*internal factors*); Darwin attributed the evolution of species to natural selection and the struggle for existence (*external factors*). The Dutchman, H. de Vries, also made an important contribution to the evolutionistic theory, admitting real natural mutations in plants (*mutationism*). The new theory aroused great enthusiasm: the materialist Haeckel used it as a weapon of propaganda for his atheistic monism, even using fraud in scientific experiments. But quickly, after the enthusiasm boiled down, doubts and delusions set in, once scientists began to examine the facts more accurately.

This is not the place for a scientific exposition and an adequate refutation of this complex system; a cursory evaluation of it from a philosophico-theological standpoint will be appropriate and sufficient. Atheistic *materialistic evolutionism,* philosophically and theologically speaking, is just as absurd as materialism and atheism (*qq.v.*). But there is a *theistic evolutionism,* which desires to be linked with Christianity; it is *integral* or *partial.* The former maintains the evolution of all living beings from one or a few primordial organisms up to the human body inclusively (the soul is excluded, being an effect of creation). The latter, partial evolutionism, admits an evolution of various primitive organisms, restricted, however, within the limits of principal groups or genera. Theistic evolutionism, whatever its form, always supposes an influence of God, immediate or mediate, on the progressive development of the organisms. Its adherents mistakenly appeal to St. Augustine (see *cosmogony*). *Scientifically* speaking, evolutionism lacks solid foundations; serious difficulties militate against it from systematics, geology, paleontology, and embryology, which at one time seemed to favor it. The *stability* of the *species* is the reef of destruction of the whole system.

Philosophically, if we prescind from a direct divine intervention, evolutionism clashes with the principle of causality, which does not admit derivation of a higher effect from a lower cause (the more from the less). Theologically speaking, it is possible to admit hypothetically a kind of partial evolutionism, provided it is subordinated to the influence of the First Cause. Such evolutionism could embrace the vegetable and the animal kingdom, but could not be inclusive of man, for, according to divine revelation, man's soul was created by God and placed in a body which He fashioned. But such a concession would have to be backed up by probative scientific evidence which, up to now, is lacking.

BIBLIOGRAPHY

Baule, *Le transformisme au regard de la science et de la foi* (Paris, 1936). De Sinéty, "Transformisme," *DA*. Dorlodot, *Darwinism and Catholic Thought*, trans. Messenger (London, 1922). Gaia, *L'evoluzione e la scienza* (Rome, 1921). Muckermann, "Evolution," *CE*. Wasmann, *The Problem of Evolution* (London, 1912).

"ex cathedra." See *infallibility*.

exegesis (Gr. ἐξήγησις, from the verb ἐξηγεῖσθαι — to explain). The art of finding and proposing the true sense of a text, and, in the theological field, of a text of Holy Scripture. It is an art insomuch as it applies the rules and principles of both the rational and the theological orders, which the science of hermeneutics (*q.v.*) establishes.

The process of interpretation of a biblical text starts with the determination of the text itself through the principles of *textual criticism*. Through the means of the rules of hermeneutics the exact exegesis of the text is given, recourse being had, whenever necessary, to *literary criticism* to determine the literary style of the book in which the text under examination is contained, and to *historical criticism* to locate it in its time relations. The supreme purpose of exegesis is to illuminate through human words the fullness of the light and thought of God.

BIBLIOGRAPHY

See under *hermeneutics*.

exemplary cause. That according to which something is made (see *cause*). It is proper to intelligent being to act according to ideas conceived in the mind, which are, therefore, exemplary causes of the effects produced. *Plato* placed *ideas* in a supersense world, subsisting in themselves outside the mind of God; according to such ideas the Demiurge molded and arranged the material world (*exemplarism*).

Catholic doctrine, based on divine revelation, teaches that God, as He is the efficient cause, so He is also the exemplary cause of the created universe. In Holy Scripture, divine wisdom is called the craftsman of the universe and God Himself is compared to an architect who creates and forms things according to his mind's plans and designs. That is why theologians distinguish in the mind of God the so-called *architype ideas,* exemplary causes of creation;

these ideas are the divine essence itself, as known by God as imitable outside of Himself. Absolutely speaking, the divine Idea is but one, the Word (*q.v.*), but the architype ideas are said to be many, inasmuch as in the Word the divine essence is viewed as imitable in various ways. By virtue of exemplary causality there is in all things an imprint of God, which in irrational creatures is a simple mark, while in men, who have thought and will to the likeness of God, it reaches the intensity and perfection of an image.

BIBLIOGRAPHY

St. Thomas, *Summa Theol.,* I, q. 44, a. 3; q. 45, a. 7. Peter Parente, "Rapporto tra partecipazione e causalitá in S. Tommaso," *Acta Pont. Acad. Romanae S. Thomae Aq.* (1941).

existentialism. A philosophical current started in the past century by the Dane, Sören Kierkegaard († 1855), and developed by recent scholars (Heidegger, Jaspers, Marcel, Abbagnano) in a variety of interpretations and connotations. Existentialism originated as a reaction to Hegelian idealism, but today is generally presented as an antithesis to abstractism or transcendentalism and as adhesion to the *concrete existence* of the individual man.

Existence is the basic problem of existentialism. There is in man a collective, public, and superficial existence, enslaved to the tyrannical exigencies of the mass, of society; but there is in him a more deep, more proper and subjective, more free existence: the *authentic existence,* which *is* not, but *is being made,* which is not static but dynamic, and constitutes our own proper unmistakable personality. Descending into the depths of his own personality, man discovers that his own real, authentic existence is in tragic conflict with his superficial existence, and feels himself seized by *anguish.* This anguish or distress is determined by consciousness of our own *finiteness,* by the sense of *guilt,* by the desire of emancipating ourselves from the crowd, and of being truly ourselves. To discover oneself in this authentic existence is to find out one's own possibilities and stretch forward to a future of conquest: but on the horizon of these aspirations the specter of *death* looms as an inexorable barrier, and increases the distress of the spirit. In this way, living authentically is living with the thought of death. For Kierkegaard (a Protestant) the tragic discovery of this real existence resolves itself in an appeal to the supernatural and, what is more, to an appeal without further ado to Christianity; but the other existentialists have eliminated this religious motive in order to stand aside in the *problematicity* of life and thought, and be free from the worries of definitive solutions.

From a philosophical standpoint, existentialism tries to be *realistic* and claims to be so, even with a Thomistic penchant, in Marcel; but in the others it remains caught in a Kantian position, halfway between realism and idealism. Its pessimistic tinge, its tendency to affirm the irrationality of life, its agnostic attitude toward God and the supernatural world, make existentialism unacceptable, without important reservations, to the Christian. But is must be recognized that existentialism, with its realistic motives, has broken the spell of the haughty dreams of idealism and revived the problem of individual life by spurring consciences to find an adequate solution.

BIBLIOGRAPHY

Fabro, *Introduzione all'esistenzialismo* (Milan, 1943). Jolivet, *Les doctrines existentialistes* (Abbaye Saint-Wandrille, 1948). Kniper, "Aspetti dell'esistenzialismo," *Acta Pont. Acad. Rom. S. Thomae Aq.,* Vol. 9 (1944), pp. 99–123.

"ex opere operato." The Council of Trent, sess. VII, can. 8, defined: "If anyone shall say that the sacraments of the New Law do not confer grace *ex opere operato,* let him be excommunicated" (*DB,* 851).

The expression *ex opere operato* and its contrary *ex opere operantis* were used for the first time by Peter of Poitiers († 1205), and long before the Council of Trent had a precise and fixed meaning in Scholastic usage; in fact, in theological speech *opus operatum* means the objective act considered in itself independently of the moral value that may derive from the one who does the act. *Opus operantis,* instead, means the act subjectively considered, in so far as it has a moral value deriving to it from the person acting.

Applied to sacramental theology, the *opus operatum* is nothing more than the sensible sign validly performed, i.e., the external rite consisting of matter and form (*q.v.*) administered according to the institution of Christ; the *opus operantis,* on the contrary, is the act of either the minister or the subject inasmuch as it has a moral or meritorious value. Now since causality *ex opere operato* is opposed to that *ex opere operantis,* to affirm the first is the same as to deny the second. Therefore, the Tridentine Fathers, by saying that the sacraments produce grace *ex opere operato,* teach that the grace of the sacrament is caused by the sacramental rite validly placed and not by the merits of the minister or the subject. Thus with a brief formula they disposed of the Lutheran principle, according to which confidence or fiducial faith (*opus operantis*) is the cause of grace and not the sacrament itself, and they consecrated the Catholic doctrine already formulated by St. Augustine: "Baptism has its value, not through the merits of the minister, or through those of the receiver, but on account of its own proper holiness, communicated to it by Him who instituted it" (*Contra Cresconium,* l. IV, c. 19).

(See *causality of the sacraments.*)

BIBLIOGRAPHY

DORONZO, *De sacramentis in genere* (Milwaukee, 1946), Index Analyticus: "Opus Operatum." FRANZELIN, *De sacramentis* (Rome, 1911), thes. 7. MICHEL, "Opus operatum," *DTC; Les décrets du Concile de Trente* (Paris, 1938), p. 206 f. VAN NOORT, *De sacramentis,* Vol. 1 (Hilversum, 1927), n. 44.

exorcism (Gr. ἐξορκισμός — the act of conjuring up). A rite administered by a person legitimately deputized for the purpose of expelling devils, especially from *energumeni* (*q.v.*). Authority over the devil was directly conferred by Christ on the Apostles and disciples; in the primitive Church we find numerous references to the practice of exorcisms. In the middle of the third century the office of exorcist (see *exorcistate*) was established. In the actual discipline, only a priest is permitted to exorcise according to the formulas of the *Roman Ritual* and after explicit authorization from his bishop. In the liturgy, exorcism is very frequent (e.g., in the baptismal ceremonies, the blessing of holy water, etc.). Exorcism supposes that persons and elements may be infested with malign spirits who seek to impede the fruitful use of holy things.

BIBLIOGRAPHY

ST. THOMAS, *Summa Theol.,* III, q. 71, a. 2–4. ARENDT, *De sacramentalibus* (Rome, 1900), pp. 329–385. FORGET, "Exorcisme," *DTC.* TONER, "Exorcism," *CE.*

See under *exorcistate.*

exorcistate (Gr. ἐξορκιστής — he who conjures out). The third of the four minor orders (see *orders, holy*).

The functions proper to this order is to impose the hands on the obsessed, whether baptized or catechumens, and to recite prayers in order to expel the devil from the body. In the first period of the Church this office did not constitute an ecclesiastical dignity but was a gratuitous gift (charism) granted by the Holy Spirit even to laymen; only in the third century did it rise to the dignity of a minor order.

In the present Church discipline, exorcisms are reserved to priests practicing them with prudence and authorized to do so by their bishops (see *exorcism*).

BIBLIOGRAPHY

St. Thomas, *Summa Theol.,* III, *Suppl.,* q. 37, a. 2. Kurtscheid, *Historia Iuris Canonici,* Vol. 1 (Rome, 1941). Leclercq, "Exorciste," *DACL.* Tixeront, *Holy Orders and Ordinations,* trans. Raemers (St. Louis). Toner, "Exorcist," *CE.*

See under *exorcism.*

experience, religious. In the generic sense it can be defined as the aggregate of psychological impressions relative to the origin and development of religion in the consciousness and life of man. Thus understood, religious experience is no more than religion intimately lived and felt in the various phases of its development in each religious subject, and has nothing heterodox about it. Christian consciousness day by day lives the drama of its faith, of its relationship with God, believed and loved, and through ascetic exercise can attain, with the help of grace and of the heavenly gifts, the sphere of mystical life (see *mystics; contemplation*), in which religious experience manifests itself intensely in the phenomena that accompany union and contact with God (see *ecstasy*).

The term "religious experience" in later times has taken on a specific meaning in certain currents of religious philosophy, like pragmatism and modernism (*qq.v.*), in open conflict with Catholic doctrine. The American, W. James, is the author and principal proponent of a whole complicated theory on religious experience (cf. his work, *Varieties of Religious Experience,* 1902). He studies the religious fact chiefly as an individual psychological phenomenon, in which *sentiment,* breaking through from *subconsciousness* (*q.v.*), holds sway over the functions of intelligence. This psychological experience has, as its proper object, not a God personally distinct from man, but "the divine," vaguely felt as something that transcends man and at the same time is immanent in him, and toward which the soul has sentiments of love or fear, of filial confidence or desperation, of joy or sadness.

All religions, according to James, are in their essence reduced to this kind of experience and, therefore, it cannot be said that one is more true than another, all religions being expressions of that experience. This theory has its roots in Lutheranism (*q.v.*), which denied reason and faith, as intellective acts, affirming in their stead a kind of *fiducial faith* and *sentiment;* a tendency which found later justification in Kantianism (*q.v.*) with the playing down of reason (agnosticism) and recourse to the will and to faith for religious certitude. Contributory to James's theory was the sentimental theology of Schleiermacher († 1834), a disciple of Kant, who was in turn followed by Ritschl († 1889), who, while admitting the historical fact of the Christian religion documented by Holy Scripture, subjected all Christian truths, including the divinity of Christ, to the control (*value judgment*) of sentiment or religious experience. A. Sabatier († 1901) made himself a popularizer of these ideas; and Le Roy added to them the attractiveness of Bergson's philosophy. Modernism has adopted without reserve this current of psychological immanentism, thus compromising the substance of Catholic doctrine.

Indeed, religious experience, upheld systematically as a criterion of knowledge and of ethico-religious life, opens the way to all aberrations of which sentiment — blind, individual, undisciplined by the light and strength of reason — is capable. It reduces religion to the status of a psychological caprice, denying, together with the dignity of the intellect, the personality of God, the historical fact of revelation, and all external religious facts, which impose themselves upon our conscience instead of stemming from it.

The Church has condemned this tendency by rejecting Lutheranism (Counc. of Trent), Molinosism, and modernism (*qq.v.; encycl., Pascendi*).

BIBLIOGRAPHY

Leclère, *Pragmatisme, Modernisme, Protestantisme* (Paris, 1909). Michelet, "Religion," *DA*, col. 899 ff. Pacheu, *L'expérience mystique et l'activité subconsciente* (Paris, 1911). Pinard, "Expérience religieuse," *DTC*.

expiation (Lat. *expiatio* from *piare* — to placate by a sacrifice the divine wrath; hence *piaculum* — a means for placating the divinity). The act by which man seeks to placate the divine wrath caused by a sin or an offense, and to regain heavenly favor by subjecting himself to a penalty. The feeling of guilt accompanied by the fear of punishment and, therefore, the desire of expiation are found in nearly all peoples and religions. Generally sacrifice has also an expiatory character: the bloody immolation of animals (of man at times) was to serve to placate God, divert His punishment, and purify the people from the crime committed. This concept is also found in the Hebrew religion, especially in the feast of *Kippurim,* in which a goat was killed and its blood sprinkled on people and things in sign of purification and reconciliation with God (Lev. 16:16; cf. Heb. 9:19–28).

In the Catholic religion the concept of expiation integrates the doctrine of Redemption (*q.v.*), especially in relation to the passion of Jesus and His bloody sacrifice on the cross. Isaias of old (Ch. 53) had predicted that the future *Messias* would be the expiatory Victim for the sins of men; the Gospels re-echo this sublime thought when they say that Christ will give His life in redemption (*λύτρον*) and His blood to remission of sins (Matt. 20:28; 26:28). Still more emphatic is the insistence of St. Paul on the expiatory value of the death and the blood of the Saviour, using the technical term *ἱλαστήριον* (instrument of expiation) to specify the sacrifice of Christ (Rom. 3:25). Tradition, too, is rich in testimonies emphasizing this truth.

Hence we understand why the Church has condemned the following proposition of modernism: "The teaching on the expiatory death of Christ has its origin not in the Gospel but in Paul" (decree, *Lamentabili, DB,* 2038). According to the teaching of the Church, therefore, the expiatory character of the death of Jesus is simply a revealed truth. However, not all the doctrine of Redemption lies in this truth. Luther and his followers deformed the concept of the Redemption by restricting their view to the external aspect of the passion and death of Christ, in which they saw only a punishment of God for our sins (*penal substitution*). Christ thus would be a passive Victim of the vindictive justice of God. Expiation corrects this ultra-severe concept with the idea of the spontaneity with which Christ accepted death to pay off the punishment due for our sins. Catholic doctrine rejects the Lutheran theory, accepts the theory of expiation, and goes beyond it to a more adequate concept of *vicarious satisfaction* (see *satisfaction of Christ*), which brings out the *moral* content of Redemption (love, humility, obedience of Christ). Expiation and satisfaction are mutually integrative: in the former, the passion of Christ is the *principal means* of reparation, in the latter, the passion is *concomitant.*

BIBLIOGRAPHY

KENT, "Atonement," *CE.* MADEBIELLE, "Expiation," *DBVS.* OXENHAM, *The Catholic Doctrine of the Atonement* (London, 1865). RIVIÈRE, *The Doctrine of the Atonement,* trans. from the French, 2 vols. (London, 1909). *The Teaching of the Catholic Church,* ed. Smith, 2 vols. (New York, 1949), pp. 952–954.

extreme unction (Lat. *extrema* — last; *unctio* — anointing, unction). The sacrament of the dying. The Apostle St. James, in his Catholic Letter, writes: "Is any man sick among you? Let him bring in the priests of the church, and let them pray over him, anointing him with oil in the name of the Lord. And the prayer of faith shall save the sick man: and the Lord shall raise him up: and if he be in sins, they shall be forgiven him" (5:14–15). In this inspired text are found all the elements constitutive of the sacrament of the sick.

Its *institution* is indicated in the incidental phrase *in nomine Domini,* which in the Greek original means "by virtue of the command and on the authority of the Lord," i.e., of Christ, because in the style of the New Testament the term *Kyrios* (*Dominus,* Lord) is the proper epithet of Jesus Christ.

The *ministers* are the "presbyteri," by which we are to understand not the old men or ancients of the people but the duly ordained bishops and priests, as the Church has always understood in theory and in practice.

The *elements of the rite* are expressly indicated in the *oil* (the matter) and the prayer (the form). Olive oil blessed by the bishop is used to anoint various parts of the body, which are the most likely instruments of sin — eyes, ears, nostrils, mouth, hands, feet — and at the same time the sacramental formula is recited. The Latin form is: "Through this holy unction and His most pious mercy, may the Lord pardon you all evil you have committed with the eyes, with the ears," etc.

The *effects* are summarized by the Council of Trent when, synthesizing the data of Tradition, it calls this sacrament *consummativum paenitentiae* (sess. 14, exord., *DB,* 909), i.e., completing and perfecting the sacrament of penance. It completes the effects of the sacrament of forgiveness because it completes the incorporation in Christ restored by penance; strengthens the soul for the last struggle against the devil; removes the remnants (*reliquiae*) of sin, flinging down the last obstacles to perfect adhesion to Christ; disposes the sick to suffer and die in Christ and for Christ, associating him with the sufferings and death of Christ the Head.

Particularly, this sacrament makes the supernatural organism robust and fit to overcome the supreme weaknesses of the spirit, aggravated by the exhaustion of the flesh. In fact, the wounds of original sin cured by baptism, and of personal sins healed by penance, weaken the spiritual organism of the soul, which, at the point where the body is about to break down and the devil makes his final assault, finds itself exposed to the grave danger of succumbing in the supreme struggle. To obviate such a danger, the sacramental grace of extreme unction increases the virtue of hope, by which the sick gives himself with confidence into the hands of the divine mercy and multiplies the helps of actual grace, effecting for the sick a strong shield against the darts of the enemy. This is the *alleviatio* (the relief), of which the Apostle speaks. To all this are added the maternal attentions of the Church, who increases her efficacious assistance for this child whom she is rebearing unto eternal life: She invokes all the saints of heaven, calls on the souls in purgatory, assembles the just on earth who pray unseen around the bed of the dying, while the priest, official representative of the Church, performs the sacred rite, in which "the devotion of the recipient, the personal merit of the ministers, and the general merit of the whole Church are of very great help" (St. Thomas, *Suppl.*, q. 32, a. 3). In the case where the sick man is unable to confess his sins, this sacrament supplies for the effects of the sacrament of penance, and, should the Lord judge it expedient, it procures also bodily health.

The *subject* is the *adult and sick* Christian; therefore, extreme unction cannot be administered to one in good health, even if he is very close to death, like the soldier entering combat, or even the condemned going up to the gallows.

The definitions of the Council of Trent against the Protestants, who call extreme unction "a hypocritical farce" (Calvin), are found in sess. 14, right after the canons on penance (*DB*, 926–929).

BIBLIOGRAPHY

ST. THOMAS, *Summa Theol.*, III, *Suppl.*, qq. 29–33. BORD, *L'Extrème Onction* (Louvain, 1923). CAPPELLO, *De Extrema Unctione* (Turin, 1942). HANLEY, *Extreme Unction* (New York, 1907). KERN, *De sacramento Extremae Unctionis* (Freiburg i.-Br., 1907). KILKER, *Extreme Unction* (St. Louis, 1927). MCDONALD, "The Sacrament of Extreme Unction," *The Irish Theological Quarterly*, Vol. 2 (1907), n. 7, pp. 330–345. POHLE-PREUSS, *Dogmatic Theology*, XI *The Sacraments*, Vol. 4, *Extreme Unction, Holy Orders, Matrimony* (St. Louis, 1946), pp. 1–51. QUINN, *Extreme Unction* (Dublin, 1920). RUCH, GODEFROY, "Extrème Onction," *DTC*. SCHMITZ, *De effectibus Extremae Unctionis* (Freiburg, 1893). TONER, "Extreme Unction," *CE*. *The Teaching of the Catholic Church*, ed. Smith, 2 vols. (New York, 1949), pp. 990–1021.

extrinsicism. See *justification; Redemption.*

F

faith. In general faith consists in believing the word of another. In a technical and supernatural sense, faith is adhesion of the intellect, under the influence of grace, to a truth revealed by God, not on account of its intrinsic evidence but on account of the authority of Him who has revealed it. St. Paul defines faith: "The substance of things to be hoped for, the evidence of things that appear not" (Heb. 11:1).

Faith is formally in the intellect as a *habit* (one of the three theological virtues infused by God together with sanctifying grace) and as an *act*. But in the act of faith the will also concurs, because the divine truths, often surpassing the rational capacity of man, lack that evidence which usually determines the assent of the intellect. Therefore, the intervention of the will is necessary in order to move the intellect to adhere to the revealed truth, although incomprehensible, out of homage to God. Hence, faith is a *rationabile obsequium,* a free submission of human reason to the eternal Truth who unveils Himself, and as such is *meritorious.* The formal motive of faith is exclusively the *authority of God,* which constitutes an *extrinsic evidence,* while science requires intrinsic evidence; consequently, faith is *obscure,* but possesses a *firmness* and *certainty* superior to those of any purely human knowledge.

Faith, both in its beginning and its successive development, is always the effect of the grace of God (cf. the II Council of Orange against the Semi-Pelagians). It is indispensable for sanctification and salvation (Council of Trent), but is not sufficient without good works: *Fides sine operibus mortua est* (St. James).

Luther reduces faith to a blind *trust* or *confidence* in the divine mercy, the modernists to a *sentiment erupting* from the subconscious (see *subconsciousness; Lutheranism; modernism*). Cf. Council of Trent, sess. VI, cc. 6–7 (*DB,* 2074); Vatican Council, sess. III, cc. 3–4 (*DB,* 1789–1800); encyclical, *Pascendi* (*DB,* 2074).

BIBLIOGRAPHY

St. Thomas, *Summa Theol.,* II–II, qq. 1–16. Aveling, "Faith and Science," *Westminster Lectures* (London, 1906). Bainvel, *La foi et l'acte de foi* (Paris, 1908). Harent, "Foi," *DTC.* Manning, *The Grounds of Faith* (1852); "Faith and Reason," *Dublin Review* (July, 1889). McNabb, *Oxford Conferences on Faith* (London, 1905). Newman, "The Introduction of Rationalistic Principles into Revealed Religion," *Tracts for the Times* (1835). Petazzi, *Analisi psicologica dell'atto di fede* (Vicenza, 1927). Pope, "Faith," *CE.* Scheeben, *The Mysteries of Christianity,* trans. Vollert (St. Louis, 1946), pp. 762–796. *The Teaching of the Catholic Church,* ed. Smith, 2 vols. (New York, 1949), pp. 10–35. Ward, "The Agnosticism of Faith," *Dublin Review* (July, 1903).

faith, articles of. See *articles of faith.*

fatalism. See *destiny; freedom.*

Father. The proper name of the First Person of the Holy Trinity, which has its foundation in the intellective generation (see *procession, divine*) from which originates the Son — Word. This paternity with respect to the Son is to be taken in the *proper* and natural sense. Besides, God is called in a figurative or analogous sense Father of the universe, the effect of His omnipotence, and, in a sense more connected with His true paternity He is called the Father of men, especially by virtue of sanctifying grace (see *grace, habitual*) which makes the rational creature *the adopted son* of God, and sharer, in a way, of the natural filiation of the incarnate Word. Two other proper titles belong to the Father: Principle and Unbegotten (Ingenerate, Unborn). He is called *Principle,* because He is the first term and the first source, as it were, whence derive the processions of the Son and of the Holy Spirit. But in the Holy Trinity we must exclude all concepts of chronological *priority* and of productive *causality,* because the three Persons are perfectly equal and hence coeternal. The Father is called *Unbegotten* (*Ingenitus; Innascibilis;* ἀγέννητος) not only in the sense that, unlike the Son, He is not generated, but also because, unlike both the Son and the Holy Spirit, He is not proceeding from any principle.

BIBLIOGRAPHY

St. Thomas, *Summa Theol.,* I, q. 33. Hugon, *Le mystère de la très Sainte Trinité* (Paris, 1930), p. 172 ff. Joyce, "Trinity," *CE.* Klein, *The Doctrine of the Trinity,* trans. Sullivan (New York, 1940), pp. 108–130. Lebreton, *Histoire du dogme de la Trinité,* Vol. 2 (Paris, 1928), p. 635.

Fathers, Apostolic. See "Outline of the History of Dogmatic Theology" (p. 301).

Fathers of the Church. The ecclesiastical authors who, according to the classical definition of Mabillon, *"doctrina eminent, sanctitate florent, antiquitate vigent, qui expressa vel tacita Ecclesiae designatione gaudent"* (*Praef. ad opera S. Bernardi,* § 2, No. 23). This means that, to be honored with the title of Father of the Church, an ecclesiastical author must possess four qualifications; eminent doctrine, holiness of life, antiquity, recognition (explicit or tacit) by the Church. Such are, for example, SS. Ignatius of

Antioch, Justin, Irenaeus, Cyprian, etc. Others who stand out only with respect to doctrine or antiquity are called simply *ecclesiastical writers,* like Tertullian, Origen, Lactantius, Eusebius, etc.

The morally unanimous consent of the Fathers in matters of faith or morals is an irrefragable testimony of divine Tradition (*q.v.*). This consent may be established either directly (from explicit testimonies) or indirectly: (*a*) from the agreement, e.g., of all the Western Fathers, (*b*) from the testimonies of many Fathers outstanding in doctrine and authority, living in different times and places, when their statements have gone uncontradicted, (*c*) or even from the testimonies of a few, provided they have been given in such circumstances that it may be argued they reflect the common faith of the Church.

BIBLIOGRAPHY

Bright, *The Age of the Fathers* (London, 1903). Chapman, "Fathers of the Church," *CE.* Cruttwell, *A Literary History of Early Christianity* (London, 1893). Hurter, *Theologiae Dogmaticae Compendium,* Vol. 1 (Oeniponte, 1900), nn. 183–195. Mazzella, *De Ecclesia* (Rome, 1892), n. 342 ff. Newman, *The Church of the Fathers* (London, 1840).

fear. See *gifts of the Holy Ghost.*

Ferrariensis. See "Outline of the History of Dogmatic Theology" (p. 303).

fetishism (Portuguese *feitico,* derived from Lat. *factitius* — thing done, constructed). A lower form of religion which, according to evolutionistic ethnologists, is the first rung (A. Comte), or the second, after animism (*q.v.*) or after atheism (Tylor, Lubbock), of the ladder in the development of human civilization. But these opinions are not based on the direct study of documents: they have lost all value today, due to discoveries made through strictly methodical studies. Fetishism, in reality, consists in the use of magical objects, amulets, etc., which are considered as symbols or as receptacles of the Divinity, but not as the Divinity Itself. Certain primitive peoples believe that divine spirits or ancestor souls are hidden in the fetishes. Fetishism is usually practiced by peoples of secondary *cultures* (not primitive) and, therefore, is rather a degeneration of religion, which passed from the cult of a supreme being (monotheism) to polytheism. Fetishism had its greatest development in West Africa (see *animism; idolatry*).

BIBLIOGRAPHY

Brinton, *The Religions of Primitive Peoples* (New York, 1897). Driscoll, "Fetishism," *CE.* Haddon, *Magic and Fetichism in Religions, Ancient and Modern* (London, 1906). Glyn Leonard, *The Lower Niger and Its Tribes* (London, 1906). Norris, *Fetishism in W. Africa* (New York, 1904).

fideism. A system which exaggerates the function of faith in the knowledge of truth. There is a fideism which has shown itself openly in the very bosom of the Church under different forms more or less pronounced. The *Neoplatonic-Augustinian* current at the time of Scholasticism reacted, on the basis of sentiment and of faith, against the rationalistic tendencies. This reaction affirmed itself without moderation in nominalism, but became heterodox in Luther. Mistrust of reason lurks in the works of Pascal, finds a systematic exposition in Daniel Huet, Bishop of Avranches († 1721), if indeed he is the author of *Tractatus de debilitate intellectus humani* (Muratori doubts it), and becomes organized into a system in *traditionalism* (*q.v.*).

But a worse fideism (because it is *naturalistic*) is that derived from *Kantianism* (*q.v.*), based on *The*

Critique of Practical Reason; its most outstanding representative is the German, Jacoby, who places above reason an intuitive faculty (*vernunft*) which reaches God. The positivists (Mill, Spencer) and the pragmatists (James) often appeal to faith to affirm the Divinity, which they are not able to demonstrate by way of reason (see *positivism; pragmatism*). The modernists, with their theory of religious sense and experience (*q.v.;* also *modernism*) draw close to fideism.

As the Church defends the dignity of human freedom while affirming the efficacious power of grace, so it does not fail to defend reason's dignity in its affirmation of the rights of faith (cf. Vatican Council, sess. III, *DB,* 1781 ff.).

BIBLIOGRAPHY

BAINVEL, *La foi et l'acte de foi* (Paris, 1908); "Foi-Fidéisme," *DA.* HONTHEIM, *Institutiones theodiceae* (Freiburg, 1926), p. 44 ff. SAUVAGE, "Fideism," *CE.*

"Filioque." The term which the Catholic Church uses in the Creed: *Qui [Spiritus] ex Patre Filioque procedit* ("Who proceeds from the Father and the Son") to signify that the Holy Spirit has His origin from both the Father and the Son.

The "Filioque" was not in the Nicene-Constantinople Symbol originally, but was inserted into it in Spain in the sixth century; later in France in Charlemagne's time, then in Germany, in Italy, and finally also at Rome (eleventh century).

One of the oldest and main points of accusation of the *Greek schismatic Church* against the Roman Church is the insertion of the "Filioque" in the Symbol and the consequent corruption of the traditional doctrine. To this we can respond: (1) The *magisterium* of the Church cannot *change* the Creed, but can add to it an expression, or, what is more, a truth of faith, e.g., that of the Eucharist, in order to integrate it. (2) The addition of the "Filioque" is legitimate because Holy Scripture affirms that the Holy Spirit is *sent* by the Son (John 15:26), *will receive* from the Son (John 16:14), and is the Spirit of Christ (Rom. 8:9) — expressions which cannot be understood unless we admit the procession of the Holy Spirit not only from the Father, but also from the Son.

As regards Tradition, it is to be noted that the Greek Fathers agree (at times even verbally) with the Latins in saying that the Holy Spirit proceeds from the Father and from the Son (Ephraem, Epiphanius, and others). But it is also true that while the Latins use more often the formula *a Patre et a Filio,* the Greeks generally prefer the other formula *a Patre per Filium.* It is, however, evident that the two formulas say substantially the same thing.

Consequently, the schismatic Greeks wrongfully reprove the Roman Church, which is perfectly in the right.

BIBLIOGRAPHY

ST. THOMAS, *Summa Theol.,* I, q. 36, a. 2–4. HUGON, *Le mystère de la très Sainte Trinité* (Paris, 1930), p. 213 ff. JUGIE, "De processione Spiritus Sancti," *Lateranum* (Rome, 1936). MAAS, "Filioque," *CE.* POHLE-PREUSS, *Dogmatic Theology,* II *The Divine Trinity* (St. Louis, 1946), pp. 168–190.

final cause. The end for which one acts; it is the mover of the efficient cause and consequently of the other causes.

Divisions: (*a*) *finis qui* (i.e., to which one tends) and *finis cui* (the subject to which one directs the good he wishes to do); (*b*) *finis operis* (derives objectively from the action itself) and *finis operantis* (intended explicitly by the agent); (*c*) *finis remotus,* to which *finis proximus* is ordered. The end is always a good (at least something perceived as good): the agent, however, can tend either to communicate its own good (love of benevolence) or to acquire a good which it does not have (love of concupiscence).

Against materialism, fatalism, and rationalism, the Catholic teaching affirms that God is the final cause, i.e., the supreme end of creatures. The Vatican Council (sess. III, cans. 1 and 5; *DB,* 1783, 1805), states precisely that God has created everything for His glory; namely, not to increase His happiness, but to manifest freely His perfections, by communicating His goods to creatures. It is a question of the extrinsic glory of God which adds nothing to His intimate happiness.

Holy Scripture: Ps. 18: "The heavens shew forth the glory of God"; Prov. 16:4: "The Lord hath made all things for himself." The *Fathers:* St. Gregory of Nyssa summarizes their thought in a fine image: God uses the creation of the world to fete His glory as in an open book. *Reason* sees clearly that God, supreme Intelligence, has created the world for an end and that this end can only be God Himself. If God would act for an end outside of Himself, He would be subordinated to it, and this is counter to His nature of *First Being.* In this *primary* end, however (glory of God), is implicit the *secondary* end, which is the good of the creatures themselves, of man especially. Thus the apparent egoism of God resolves itself into sublime love of benevolence, since in God alone, to whom he tends as to his end, man finds his supreme perfection, God being infinite Truth and Goodness, capable of satisfying the infinite thirst of our minds and hearts.

BIBLIOGRAPHY

St. Thomas, *Summa Theol.,* I, q. 44, a. 4 (see also q. 20 on divine love). Aveling, "Cause," *CE.* Garrigou-Lagrange, *God: His Existence and His Nature,* trans. Rose (St. Louis, 1947–1948).

"fomes peccati." See *concupiscence; Immaculate Conception.*

foreknowledge. See *prescience.*

form (Gr. μορφή). In philosophy and theology form is used in the *proper sense* to indicate the formal, intrinsic cause, which constitutes the nature of things. It is applied to the angelic world (separate forms), to the human composite (soul, form of the body), to material things which are composed of matter (passive and determinable element) and form (active and determining element, the ἐντελέχεια of Aristotle).

In an *analogical sense,* form is said of all that implies actuation, perfection. Thus it is applied to grace (supernatural, accidental form), to charity which informs faith (i.e., perfects it: *fides formata*), to the words as the determining element of the sacramental sign (see *matter and form of the sacraments*).

BIBLIOGRAPHY

Aveling, "Form," *CE.* Michel, "Forme," *DTC.*

fortitude. See *gifts of the Holy Ghost; virtue.*

"forum internum"—"forum externum." See *hierarchy.*

Franzelin. See "Outline of the History of Dogmatic Theology" (p. 303).

Fraticelli. A sect of vagabond religious of the thirteenth and fourteenth centuries, deriving probably from the rigoristic tendency represented in the Franciscan Order by the so-called *Spirituals* opposed by the *Conventuals* of more moderate views. The story of the Fraticelli is very obscure and complicated; into it enter popes, with different attitudes, and princes, as well as theological, ascetical, political, and juridical controversies. Suffice it to recall here that the Fraticelli, sprung up already in the time of Nicholas III, consolidated and gained strength with the blessing and protection of Celestine V, and fell into disgrace with his successor, Boniface VIII; through struggles and troubles they managed to get by up to the pontificate of John XXII (1316), who tried to put an end to their activities by disbanding the sect and condemning its errors.

From this condemnation (Constitution *Gloriosam Ecclesiam, DB,* 484 ff.) we can deduce the principal errors of the Fraticelli which had their repercussions on the heresies of the following centuries. Foremost of all, the Fraticelli are independent spirits, rebellious to the authority of the Church; to justify themselves, they invented the *theory of the two Churches:* one carnal, rich, corrupt, with the pope at its head; the other spiritual, poor, pure, and holy, to which belong the Fraticelli and their followers. Priests and bishops stained with sin lose their power of jurisdiction and of administering the sacraments. The Gospel and Christ's promises are fulfilled only in the family of the Fraticelli. The sacrament of matrimony is detestable, and the end of the world is near (*DB,* 484–490).

It seems that the Fraticelli were influenced by other sects, indulging somewhat in sensuality. In the social field this sect contributed more or less directly to weakening the principle of the right of *private property,* by criticizing the luxury and riches of the official Church. Condemned, they did not disband; as late as the fifteenth century we find them going around spreading errors and stirring up strife, in Italy especially. Two saints in that century, John Capistrano and James della Marca, worked efficaciously to convert them.

BIBLIOGRAPHY

Bihl, "Fraticelli," *CE.* Callaey, *L'idéalisme franciscain au XIV siècle* (Louvain, 1911). De Nantes, *Histoire des spirituels dans l'ordre de Saint François* (Paris, 1909). Vernet, "Fraticelles," *DTC.*

freedom. An essential property of the will which consists radically in the *dominium* over one's own actions, by which the will can *will* or *not will,* and will *this* rather than *that.* The will is an appetitive faculty proper to every intelligent being. It has for its object, "good," which coincides with *being,* and has therefore no limits, like "true," object of the intelligence. Thus the will has a quasi-infinite potentiality with reference to pure and absolute good. Should the will be confronted with the absolute good, its adequate object and end, it could not fail to adhere to it, but would adhere to it *necessarily* (not, however, with *blind* necessity). But since the human will operates in the midst of creatures, limited beings and limited goods, it cannot be determined necessarily by any of them. On the contrary, it dominates them with an *active indifference,* according to which it can choose one or the other or none, consequent on the judgment of reason, which considers the relationship of those particular goods as means, more or less useful, to the end.

Freedom may be: of *exercise* or *contradiction* (to will or not will), of *specification* (to will this rather than that), and of *contrariety* (to will good or, its contrary, evil). To be able to do evil is a defect of the human will, which *per se* tends to good. The true freedom lies in the choice of good. This is *physical freedom* or *free will,* which is proved by the testimony of the individual and of the social conscience: man feels he is free before, during, and after the action; and on the basis of this certainty, humanity punishes or rewards, respectively, the one doing evil or the one doing good. Without freedom there would be no responsibility, and, therefore, no moral world.

In addition to physical freedom, also called psychological freedom, there is a *moral freedom,* which consists in immunity from obligation (law): this liberty, absolutely speaking, exists only in God, who is the Author of Law. In man, there is immunity from this or that law, but not from all law. Hence, human freedom is limited; *physically* man has freedom of will, but *morally* his will is subordinated to the exigencies of the law and of the supreme end of life.

Errors: fatalism, which subordinates the world and man to an ironclad and blind will, called also destiny (*q.v.*). Still more insidious is *determinism,* according to which man believes himself to be free, whereas his action is the result of psychological and external coefficients, which necessarily determine it.

The Church has always defended human freedom, even with respect to the divine knowledge and will, and to the action of grace; she has condemned every attack on freedom (see *Lutheranism; Jansenism; predestination*). Cf. *DB,* 317, 615, 1904. As to the freedom of God, and of Jesus Christ as Man, see *will, divine; will of Christ.*

BIBLIOGRAPHY

St. Thomas, *Summa Theol.,* I, q. 83; *Quaest. Disp. De Malo,* q. 6, a. 1; *De Veritate,* q. 22. Alexander, *Theories of the Will* (New York, 1884). Fonsegrive, *Essai sur le libre arbitre* (Paris, 1896). Maher, "Free Will," *CE.* Mercier, *Psychologie* (Paris, 1923), p. 96 ff.

freedom of Christ. See *will of Christ.*

free thought (free inquiry). The basic principle of Lutheranism (*q.v.*). Having eliminated the authority of the Church and its infallible *magisterium,* Luther gave the believer the Bible, telling him that this is the sole source and the only rule of his faith. There is no intermediary between God and man; the believer goes to the sacred books, reads them, *examines them freely,* and draws from them the truth to be believed and the law to be observed. Very quickly, however, Luther became aware of the implicit danger in such a principle. When he saw opinions and tendencies multiply according to the individual choice of the faithful, he raised his voice to impose his creed, paying no heed to the incoherence of his action; what is more, he had recourse to the secular arm of the princes. But liberty of thought, i.e., freedom of examination of the Scriptures, had taken over consciences and was producing its bitter fruits: the disregard for the ecclesiastical authority was followed by scorn of all authority, rebellion against all law and everything imposed from without.

Free thought *ad absurdum* and the whole demagogic tide, that infests the eighteenth and nineteenth centuries, have their first root in the doctrine of free inquiry introduced by Luther. In religion, this harmful principle has produced the innumerable Protestant sects in a process of gradual decay and disintegration that nothing succeeds in arresting. "Liberty of thought," as explained above, has no foundation in Holy Scripture: rather it is excluded by the institution of the *teaching authority of the Church* (see *magisterium of the Church*).

BIBLIOGRAPHY

Bouvier, "Réforme" (XV. "Principe et essence du Protestantisme," iii. "Le libre

examen et la libre conscience"), *DA,* cols. 801–804.
See under *Lutheranism; Protestantism.*

fruits of the Mass. The eucharistic sacrifice has a fourfold efficacy (cf. Council of Trent, *DB,* 950): *latreutic* (it adores and praises God), *eucharistic* (thanks Him for benefits bestowed), *impetrative* (obtains new graces), and *propitiatory* (moves the divine mercy to the pardon of sins). The first two effects regard God, the last two, men.

The offerers of the Mass are three: the Principal (Jesus Christ), the ministerial (the priest), and the general (the faithful). Inasmuch as the Mass is the work of Christ it produces its effects *ex opere operato* (*q.v.*), i.e., independently of the merits and dispositions of the priest and the faithful; in this sense the Mass is an ever pure sacrifice (*oblatio munda*) which cannot be stained by any iniquity of its secondary ministers (cf. Council of Trent, *DB,* 939). Inasmuch as it is the work of the priest and the faithful, it obtains the four effects *ex opere operantis,* i.e., in the measure of the holiness and fervor of the minister and the assistants, and in this sense it is said that the Mass of a holy priest is better than that of a sinner. The effects that derive to men (the impetrative and the propitiatory) are commonly called fruits of the Mass, of which we distinguish: (1) the *general fruit,* in favor of the whole Church; (2) the *special fruit,* in favor of the person for whom the Mass is celebrated; (3) the *most special fruit,* which is inalienably reserved to the celebrant.

BIBLIOGRAPHY

BILLOT, *De sacramentis,* Vol. 1 (Rome, 1931), pp. 640–658. DE LA TAILLE, *L'oecuménicité du fruit de la Messe* (Rome, 1926); *Mysterium Fidei* (Paris, 1931), Elucidatio 31. DORONZO, *De Eucharistia,* Vol. 2 (Milwaukee, 1948), pp. 1064–1158. MÜLLER, *The Holy Mass, The Sacrifice for the Living and the Dead* (New York, 1879). POHLE-PREUSS, *Dogmatic Theology,* IX *The Sacraments,* Vol. 2, *The Holy Eucharist* (St. Louis, 1946), pp. 371–397. VAN HOVE, *De Eucharistia* (Mechliniae, 1941), pp. 295–311.

future, futurible. See *prescience.*

G

Gallicanism. A complexus of theories developed in France, especially in the seventeenth century, which tended to restrict the authority of the Church regarding the State (*Political Gallicanism*) or the authority of the pope regarding councils, bishops, and clergy (*Ecclesiastico-Theological Gallicanism*).

The remote roots of Gallicanism go back to the polemic literature occasioned by the struggle between Pope Boniface VIII and Philippe le Bel, King of France, and then to the turbid period of the *Western Schism,* which exposed to contempt the pontifical dignity contested by various antipopes. Peter d'Ailly, who played an important role in the Council of Constance (1414–1418), collected and developed principles of other writers who preceded him, and formulated a whole doctrine on the superiority of councils over the pope and on the derivation of the jurisdiction of the episcopacy and the clergy directly from God, and not through the pope.

Four famous articles were approved in the Council of Constance, under the tumultuous chairmanship of d'Ailly (a cardinal now), which reflect his antipapal teaching. The Gallicans of the seventeenth century cited these articles as articles of defined faith, while Martin V and Eugene IV refused to recognize them as legitimate. Another precedent of Gallicanism is the *Pragmatic Sanction* of Bourges (1438), compiled by the clergy and signed by Charles VII of France, in which are repeated the principles about the superiority of the council, defined by a faction of the Council of Basel, opposed to the orders of Eugene IV.

In the seventeenth century, under Louis XIV, an absolutist in politics and religion, Gallicanism set itself up officially as a system. The French atmosphere, even in universities like La Sorbonne, was by this time impregnated with teachings adverse to papal jurisdiction: Peter Pithou († 1596) and Peter Dupuy († 1651) had already compiled, with commentary heightened by much erudition, the list of *Libertés de l'Église Gallicane;* Dupuy was encouraged by the astute Richelieu. The question of the *regalia* (right of the king to receive the incomes of vacant bishoprics), moved Louis XIV to call a general assembly of the clergy (1681), from which came forth the *Déclaration du clergé gallican* in 4 articles, formulated by Bossuet, which was immediately approved and promulgated by the King (1682):

ART. 1. Absolute independence of the king and the princes, in temporal matters, from the ecclesiastical authority.

ART. 2. The pope is subordinate to general councils.

ART. 3. The pontifical authority is moderated by the sacred canons, and, in any case, cannot touch the rules and customs of the Gallican Church.

ART. 4. The papal judgment lacks value, unless the consent of the Church concurs in it.

These four articles, which were immediately condemned by the Church (*DB,* 1322 and 1598), reappear in the seventy-seven organic articles which Napoleon I added abusively to the concordat stipulated with Pius VII (1802).

BIBLIOGRAPHY

DEGERT, "Gallicanism," *CE.* DUBRUEL, "Gallicanisme," *DTC.* DUBRUEL, ARQUILLIÈRE, "Gallicanisme," *DA.* FAUCHET, *Traité des libertés de l'Eglise gallicane* (1590). HOTMAN, *Traité des droits ecclésiastiques, franchises et libertés de l'Eglise gallicane* (1594). LE VAYER DE BOUTIGNY, *Traité de l'autorité des rois touchant l'administration de l'Eglise* (London, 1753); this book is a fundamental and complete source on the Gallican system. De Boutigny was one of the prominent counselors of King Louis XIV.

genealogy of Christ. Is recorded by two Evangelists: by Matthew, at the beginning of his narrative (1:17) and by Luke after the story of the infancy of Jesus (3:23–38). No serious difficulty can be advanced as to the origin and preservation of this genealogy, because it is a characteristic of the Orientals, and of the Hebrews especially, to preserve with accuracy the memory of their ancestors. Official documents also facilitated this work, because important rights depended on descendancy. The specific difficulty in the genealogy of Jesus is that from David to Joseph only two of the ancestral names are the same in Matthew and Luke. Matthew follows the descending line from Abraham to Joseph, and Luke the ascending line from Joseph to Adam; both go through David of whom the Messias was to be the "son." Both are obviously sketchy and incomplete.

But how are we to explain that while in Matthew the father of Joseph is called Jacob, in Luke he is called Heli, and so the ancestors of Jesus in Matthew are not those recorded by Luke?

Various solutions of this singular problem have been attempted from the first Christian centuries. The oldest and most common has recourse to the Hebraic law of the *levirate* (*levir* — brother-in-law), according to which the widow of a man dead without sons had to be married by her brother-in-law, and the first-born son received the name of the deceased in order to give him a descendant. Joseph, therefore, is said to be the natural son of Jacob but the legal son of Heli, brother of Jacob who had died without sons. Matthew, then, gives the natural genealogy and Luke the legal.

A readier and more recent solution sees in Matthew the genealogy of Joseph and in Luke, Mary's. So that Luke 3:23 should be understood thus: "Although Jesus was held the son of Joseph, he was really only the son of Mary, whose father was Heli, etc."

Some modern authors have recourse to a particular form of adoption in use among the Hebrews: Joseph's case was that of the husband of an only daughter and heiress, who entered his father-in-law's family with the full rights of a son and shared in the genealogy of that family. Thus Luke gives the *adoptive* genealogy of Joseph, which corresponds to the list of Mary's ancestors. The quality of daughter-heiress in Mary has not, however, been definitively proved.

BIBLIOGRAPHY

HOLZMEISTER, in *Verbum Domini,* 23 (1943), pp. 9–18. MAAS, "Genealogy of Christ," *CE.* PRAT, *Jesus Christ; His Life, His Teaching, and His Work,* trans, Heenan, 2 vols. (Milwaukee, 1950). RICCIOTTI, *The Life of Christ,* trans. Zizzamia (Milwaukee, 1947). VOSTÉ, *De conceptione virginali Jesu Christi* (Rome, 1933), pp. 83–110.

generation. See *Only-Begotten; procession, divine; Son.*

gift. See *charism.*

gifts of the Holy Ghost. The gifts of the Holy Ghost are dispositions infused by God, by which the sanctified soul is made docile to and ready for the impulses of the Holy Spirit for the purpose of salutary activity.

There is an explicit text of Isaias (11:1, 2) that enumerates seven gifts: intellect, counsel, wisdom, knowledge, fortitude, piety, and fear. This text is inserted in the liturgy of the sacrament of confirmation. Leo XIII, in his encyclical *Divinum illud,* develops the doctrine of the gifts according to the principles of St. Thomas (*ASS,* 29, 654).

There is a scholastic question on the nature of these gifts; namely, whether they are an *actual* movement or a *habitual* disposition. St. Thomas and the majority of the theologians are for the second opinion. The gifts are infused habits distinct from virtues. The difference is that while the virtues are *intrinsic* principles of activity, the gifts are dispositions of the faculties of the soul to receive the external impulse of the Holy Spirit. Billot appropriately compares the virtues to the motors of a ship and the gifts to sails unfurled and ready to receive the impulsion of the wind.

The gifts are distributed as follows:

in the reason	1. intellect	theoretical	simple apprehension
	2. counsel	practical	
	3. wisdom	theoretical	judgment
	4. knowledge	practical	
in the will	5. fortitude (with respect to oneself)		
	6. piety (with respect to others)		
in the irascible and concupiscible appetites	7. fear of the Lord (moderating the sense appetites — concupiscible and irascible)		

The gifts of the Holy Ghost, together with the virtues and sanctifying grace, which is the root of both the gifts and the virtues, constitute the so-called *supernatural organism,* which may be represented graphically as follows:

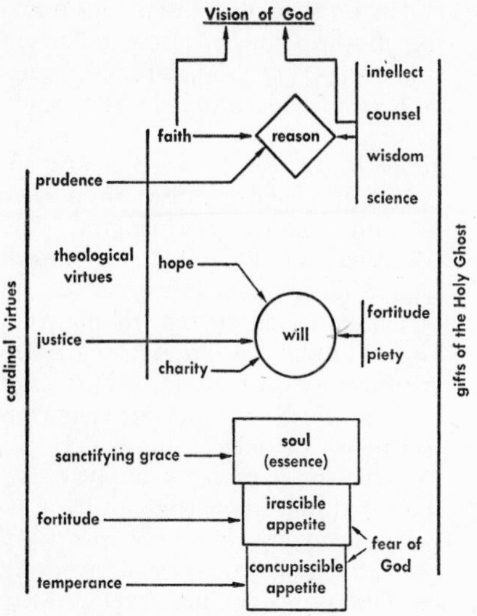

BIBLIOGRAPHY

St. Thomas, *Summa Theol.,* I–II, q. 68. Billot, *De Virtutibus* (Rome, 1928). Forget, "Holy Ghost," *CE.* Gardeil, "Dons du Saint-Esprit," *DTC.* Pascal Parente, *The Ascetical Life* (St. Louis, 1947), pp. 152–162. *The Teaching of the Catholic Church,* ed. Smith, 2 vols. (New York, 1949), pp. 634–658.

gnosis. See *Gnosticism.*

Gnosticism (Gr. γνῶσις — knowledge). A very complex system of religious doctrines and practices, philosophical, theurgical, and mystagogical in character, which began in the Alexandrian period in Judeo-pagan circles and developed in the first centuries of Christianity.

The basic principle of the "gnosis" is: In religion there is a common faith, which may be sufficient for the ordinary people, but there is also a higher knowledge, reserved to the learned, which offers a philosophical explanation of the common faith. Christian Gnosticism draws various elements from Plato, from Persian Mazdaism, from the pagan mysteries, and applies them to the Christian religion by using and abusing the *allegorical exegesis* of Holy Scripture. The Christian "gnosis" may be defined as a theosophic philosophism, tending to absorb divine revelation in order to make a religious philosophy of it. It developed in Syria with Simon Magus, Menander, and Saturninus, and in Egypt (Alexandrian gnosis) with Basilides, Valentine, and their respective disciples. Despite differences, the "gnosis" is reducible, more or less, to this outline: (*a*) God is the inaccessible Being (Platonic transcendence), who can have no contact outside of Himself; opposed to God but coeternal with Him is matter (Platonico-Persian dualism), bad in its nature (pessimism); (*b*) between God and matter is the *pleroma* or *ogdoad,* an intermediate, supersense world (the hyperuranium of Plato) inhabited by beings called aeons, emanating one from the other or disposed in pairs (*syzygies*); (*c*) one of the aeons, the *Demiurge* (God of the Old Testament) worked matter into the actual form of this world; (*d*) a divine spark from that superior world fell one day on the matter of this world of ours and remained there to suffer as in a prison (soul in the body); (*e*) another of the aeons (Christ) descended into this world, took the appearance of a body (see *Docetism*) and lived and died to free spirit from matter (Redemption); (*f*) side by side with these theories there was a moral teaching, often lax, and a superstitious cult, in which the sacraments appear deformed. Marcion developed some Gnostic elements along lines of a very predominant and austere asceticism.

Gnosticism constituted one of the gravest dangers for the newborn Christianity; Judaism was the other. Fortunately, Gnosticism was anti-Jewish. The Fathers spotted the menace immediately and endeavored to eliminate it. St. Irenaeus refutes Gnosticism in the 5 books of his *Adversus Haereses*. His position, like that of Tertullian, is conservative, with uncompromising reaction; but in Alexandria, Clement and Origen used the false gnosis to build up a *Christian gnosis* (science in service of the faith): hence theology was born.

BIBLIOGRAPHY

ARENDZEN, "Gnosticism," *CE*. BAREILLE, "Gnosticisme," *DTC*. MANSEL, *The Gnostic Heresies of the First and Second Centuries* (London, 1875). TIXERONT, *History of Dogmas,* trans. H.L.B., Vol. 1 (St. Louis, 1910), pp. 153–183.

God. In all peoples, in all times and places, the idea of, and the faith in, a *supreme being,* creator and lord of the universe, and of man especially, has always been existent and lively. According to the best historians of comparative religion, polytheism is a degeneration of primitive monotheism (*q.v.*). The idea of God does not stem exclusively from the revelation made to the first parents, as traditionalism (*q.v.*) would have it, but it is also the result of spontaneous reflection of human reason on the world. St. Paul (Rom. 1:18 ff.) affirms that the Gentiles, outside of the sphere of the Hebrew religion, knew God through creatures, but did not adore Him duly, and through their own malice fell into idolatry. Against all forms of agnosticism (*q.v.*) the Church has defined in the Vatican Council, sess. III, c. 2, that man with the sole light of reason can arrive at the sure and certain knowledge of God, by considering created things, which are a reflection and a manifestation of the perfections of God the Creator. Moreover, the Church has always rejected the opinion, diametrically opposed to agnosticism, which holds that God is the object of a direct and immediate intuition (ontologism).

The theologians translate this teaching of the Church in the following statements: (1) God, supreme being, who transcends infinitely all created nature, cannot be known intuitively either by an *innate* idea or sentiment (ontologism and innatism are outside of and against psychological consciousness). (2) God can be known and, what is more, His existence can be demonstrated, by starting not from God Himself (*a priori*), but from creatures (*a posteriori*), which even at first blush present the characteristics of an effect, in which the exigency of a cause is implicit. (3) This natural knowledge of God is never adequate, but only *analogical* (see *analogy*). St. Thomas, working on these principles, has developed five *arguments* or ways of demonstrating the existence of God:

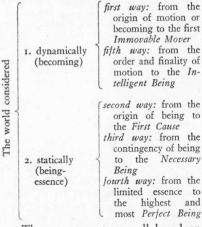

The world considered	1. dynamically (becoming)	*first way:* from the origin of motion or becoming to the first *Immovable Mover*
		fifth way: from the order and finality of motion to the *Intelligent Being*
	2. statically (being-essence)	*second way:* from the origin of being to the *First Cause*
		third way: from the contingency of being to the *Necessary Being*
		fourth way: from the limited essence to the highest and most *Perfect Being*

These arguments are all based on the *principle of causality,* and to them are to be reduced all the other arguments, which take as a point of departure either the universal truths of our intellect, our desire of a supreme Good, or the moral law engraved in our hearts.

As to the argument of St. Anselm, see *apriorism*. As regards the knowledge of God in the other life, see *vision, beatific.*

BIBLIOGRAPHY

St. Thomas, *Summa Theol.*, I, q. 2. Chossat, Mangenot, Le Bachelet, Moisant, "Dieu," *DTC*. Driscoll, *Christian Philosophy, God* (New York, 1900). Flint (non-Catholic), *Theism* (Edinburgh, 1877). Garrigou-Lagrange, *The One God,* trans. Rose (St. Louis, 1943); *God: His Existence and His Nature,* trans. Rose (St. Louis, 1947–1948); "Dieu," *DA*. Hall, *The Being and Attributes of God* (New York, 1909). Heydon, *The God of Reason* (New York, 1942). Rickaby, *Of God and His Creatures* (St. Louis, 1898). Sertillanges, *Les sources de la croyance en Dieu* (Paris, 1928); *Dieu ou rien* (Paris, 1933). *The Teaching of the Catholic Church,* ed. Smith, 2 vols. (New York, 1949), pp. 41–46, 79–109. Toner, "God," *CE*. Zacchi, *Dio,* 2 vols. (Rome, 1925).

goodness. See *perfection.*

Gospels (Gr. εὐαγγέλιον, from εὐ-αγγέλλω — good news, happy message). In the time of Christ and the Apostles, the *gospel* is the good news of universal Redemption contained in the preaching of Christ. Very soon, however, already in the first generation of Christians, the term indicated the four books of Matthew, Mark, Luke, and John, which contain the story of that announcement.

Matthew, called to the Apostolate from the Capharnaum customs, wrote his Gospel with the intention of demonstrating to the Jews of Palestine that Jesus, in whom all the ancient prophecies were fulfilled, was the awaited Messias. Mark, disciple of Peter, preserved in his book the memory of the living preaching of the Apostle to the Romans, in which the figure of Jesus Man-God is presented with enchanting freshness of details. Luke, Antioch physician and disciple of Paul, gathered together with scrupulous care the materials, covering the words and actions of the Lord's life, most suited to the instruction and edification of the Christian communities converted from paganism. These first three Gospels resemble one another substantially in the general narrative plan of Jesus' life and also in their mode of treating the material. This property, which makes it possible to arrange the three stories in three parallel columns so as to allow the eyes to take them in at a glance, has given rise to their name of *Synoptics,* i.e., "visible together" in the same glance. The Gospel of John, beloved disciple of Christ, departs sensibly from the plan and mode of presentation common to the three Synoptics. John gives greatest development to the Jerusalem ministry of Jesus, not high-lighted by the other three, during which Jesus spoke more often and more clearly of His divinity.

The *authenticity* (*q.v.*) of the four Gospels is assured by an uninterrupted series of detailed and precise historical testimonies, beginning with Papias, bishop of Hierapolis in Phrygia and disciple of the Apostles (first decades of the second century), and continuing from century to century consistently and without contradiction. In addition to statements of particularly authoritative writers, like St. Irenaeus (*c.* 140–202), bishop of Lyons and spiritual bridge between East and West, there are also official documents, like the list of the books of the New Testament, called by the name of its discoverer, the *Canon of Muratori,* written at Rome around A.D. 185. Both the authors and the documents are echoes of a tradition that goes back evidently to the first years of the Church and that has been weighed and sifted in the course of disputes with the heretics. In the second- and third-century writers, there is so great a number of quotations of the text of the four Gospels that these could be nearly reconstructed integrally therefrom. An implacable adversary of primitive Christianity, the Epicurean philosopher Celsus, writing about A.D. 178, recognizes in the four Gospels a work of

Jesus' disciples, and mentions the fact that the heretics had tried to bend them in support of their teachings, in order to avail themselves of such authoritative writings.

The internal examination of the Gospels — their language, the mentality they reflect, the customs they mention, their historical and geographical references, when confronted with the most recent and most certain discoveries — confirms the authenticity of these four books as unanimously affirmed by Christian Tradition.

As regards the *date* of the Gospels, it is an established fact that they were circulated widely and recognized in the second century in all the Christian communities of the East and West; they must, therefore, have been written in the first century. The historical testimonies, convalidated by internal textual examination, permit the conclusion that Matthew, Mark, and Luke wrote before the destruction of Jerusalem (A.D. 70). More precisely, Matthew and Mark published their books before the death of Peter and Paul (A.D. 64 or 67); Luke concludes abruptly the narrative of the Acts in the year 62, and declares that his Gospel has preceded this second of his books (Acts 1:1). Because the ancient testimonies are nearly unanimous on the priority of Matthew and Mark over Luke, the first two Gospels must have been published before A.D. 60. Matthew, according to some scholars, goes back to A.D. 42–50.

That the work of the four biographers of Jesus has been transmitted *integrally* down to us is shown by the exceptional condition of privilege the text enjoyed. There are fully 1500 manuscript codices of the Greek text of the Gospels; two of them were copied in the fourth century, while some papyrus fragments go back to the third and second centuries. Many ancient versions in western and eastern languages afford an effective check on the Greek text as contained in its actual codices. Many thousands of text variants (different readings), none of which compromises the sense of the text in matters of faith and morals, allow us to state that the Greek gospel text read today is substantially identical with the original. In this connection, it is noteworthy that there is no manuscript of the Greek or Latin classics which goes back beyond the ninth century A.D., and even those prior to the twelfth century are extremely rare.

The *historicity* of the Gospels, i.e., their objectivity, is declared by the authors themselves (Luke 1:1–4; John 20:30 f.; 21:24) and was a necessary postulate for their acceptance by the Church. Besides, no one would have dared to narrate things that were false, or to alter the facts, when there existed, on the one hand, jealous witnesses of these facts like the Apostles and, on the other, fierce enemies of Christianity, like the Jews, who had played leading roles in the life of Jesus and who would have found an easy matter in their polemics, had they been able to find the historians of the Nazarene in error. But the best the Hebrew literary tradition can do is to observe silence on the life and teaching of the Master of Galilee.

Non-Catholic criticism contests the historical value of a considerable part of the Gospels only because it contains supernatural facts. The efforts of this criticism which, from the eighteenth century, commits itself to the absurd task of explaining the life of Jesus to the exclusion of every supernatural element, have resulted in a "tower of Babel" (Loisy) of opinions that pulverize the texts without succeeding in drawing from them any possible organic meaning.

BIBLIOGRAPHY

FORTESCUE, "Gospels," *CE*. DE GRANDMAIson, *Jesus Christ,* 3 vols. (New York, 1930–1934). Höpfl-Gut, *Introductio specialis in N.T.* (Rome, 1938). Lagrange, *Preface to his commentaries on the four Gospels.* Lepin, "Evangiles canoniques," *DA.* Ricciotti, *The Life of Christ,* trans. Zizzamia (Milwaukee, 1947). Rose, *Studies on the Gospels,* trans. Fraser (London, 1903).

government of God. God, efficient and final cause of the world, has a design in His mind, according to which He leads created things to their end. Such design or plan is called providence (*q.v.*). But a plan must be actuated; the actuation or realization of providence is called *government.* Government has to do with the *being* and the *operation* of creatures, and, therefore, includes *conservation* (of being) and *motion* or *concourse* (in operation). Schematically:

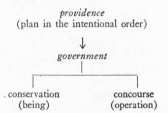

providence
(plan in the intentional order)

↓

government

conservation (being) | concourse (operation)

The Vatican Council (sess. III, c. 1.), teaches that God guards and *governs* by His providence all the things He has created. The texts of Holy Scripture that speak of providence apply as well to divine government. In Wisdom 14:3 it is said explicitly: "Thy providence, O Father, governeth it." The Fathers of the Church exalt the wisdom of divine government in all creatures (cf. *RJ* under the word "Gubernatio").

The attainment of their end is the supreme perfection of created things; it is reasonable to attribute this attainment to God, to whom their first perfection, that of being, belongs (creation). The divine government is not exercised directly in everything, but God also uses second causes, either necessary or contingent, according to the effects He wishes to realize, without doing violence to nature or disturbing it. God in His wisdom acts *fortiter, suaviter* (strongly, sweetly) and reaches His ends infallibly, despite apparent creature reluctances or defections. Nothing escapes the control and the power of His wisdom and of His omnipotent will.

BIBLIOGRAPHY

St. Thomas, *Summa Theol.,* I, q. 103.
See under *providence, divine.*

grace (Gr. χάρις; root χαρ — concept of pleasure, of joy; Lat. *gra-tus,* whence *gratia*). Both in the classic and modern usage it has various meanings, reducible to two aspects: (1) *subjective* (beauty, benevolence, favor, gratitude); (2) *objective* (gift, benefit). In the Hellenistic religious language χάρις had already come to mean an interior strength infused by the gods. In the Old Testament is found the word "grace" (Hebr. חֵן *chèn,* whence the name Anna) in the sense of benevolence (cf. Gen. 18:3). In the New Testament it is most frequent in Paul (110 times), and quite often used by Luke, John, and Peter, prevalently in the sense of a gratuitous gift of God to men (*gratia Dei*).

The doctrine of grace was extensively developed by St. Augustine against the Pelagians (see *Pelagianism*) who denied it, thus compromising the whole supernatural order. The Church *magisterium* on repeated occasions took up the matter of grace, especially in the Council of Carthage (418, *DB,* 101 ff.); II Council of Orange (529, *DB,* 174 ff.); Council of Trent (sess. VI, *DB,* 793–843); in the condemnation of Baianism by Innocent X (*DB,* 1902 ff.). From these documents we draw the definition of grace: "A gratuitous gift infused by God into the rational creature with reference to the end of eternal life."

Divisions: (1) grace *gratis data,* given to a person for the good of others (e.g., gift of prophecy), and grace *gratum faciens,* given for the good of the receiver himself.

2)

actual grace (transient divine movement)	operant — co-operant antecedent — subsequent exciting — helping sufficient — efficacious
habitual grace (permanent habitlike gift)	sanctifying grace (in the essence of the soul) infused virtues (in the faculties) gifts of the Holy Ghost

Grace, in general, confers on man the capacity or power to act supernaturally, in a way proportionate to life eternal. It transcends the natural order.

BIBLIOGRAPHY

St. Thomas, *Summa Theol.*, qq. 110–111. Joyce, *The Catholic Doctrine of Grace* (New York, 1920). Nieremberg, *The Marvel of Divine Grace,* trans. Lovat (London, 1917). Peter Parente, *Anthropologia supernaturalis* (Rome, 1943). Pohle, "Grace," *CE.* Pohle-Preuss, *Dogmatic Theology,* VIII *Grace* (*Actual and Habitual*) (St. Louis, 1946). Van der Meersch, *De divina gratia* (Brugis, 1924); "Grâce," *DTC.* Wirth, *Divine Grace* (New York, 1903).

grace, actual. The transient supernatural influence of God in the soul, moving it to the salutary act, i.e., to an act ordained to sanctification and eternal life. The existence of this grace, as distinct from habitual grace, is attested to by Holy Scripture, which speaks of illumination (Ps. 12:4), of attraction (Cant. 1:3; John 6:34), of impulse (Acts 9:5). Thus also Tradition: St. Augustine, who had to deal most with grace, speaks rather rarely about sanctifying grace, but continually about actual grace — or perhaps about both without distinction. The Council of Trent (sess. VI, c. 6, *DB,* 798) describes actual grace as disposing man to justification.

A great part of the systematic doctrine about actual grace, however, was developed immediately after the Council of Trent, on the occasion of *Baianism* and *Jansenism* (*qq.v.*), which adulterated the concept of the supernatural influence of God with respect to human activity. A violent controversy flared up between Dominicans and Jesuits (see *Bannesianism* and *Molinism*) about the essence of actual grace.

Molinists: actual grace is essentially the same as the supernatural vital act (e.g., salutary thought or deed), which comes at once from God insomuch as it is supernatural, and from our faculties insomuch as it is vital. Some Molinists, however, following Bellarmine, admitted that actual grace is a divine motion, at least for *indeliberate acts. Thomists:* actual grace is a *supernatural physical premotion,* by which God moves the soul (in potency) to a salutary act. It is reduced to a *fluent quality,* preceding the act and moving to it (according to Bañez and his followers, to the point of determining free will specifically to this, rather than to that object). See *concourse, divine; grace.*

BIBLIOGRAPHY

St. Thomas, *Summa Theol.*, I–II, q. 109; q. 110, a. 2. Del Prado, *De Gratia et libero arbitrio,* Vol. 1 (Freiburg, Helv., 1906). Peter Parente, *Anthropologia supernaturalis* (Rome, 1943). Pohle-Preuss, *Dogmatic Theology,* VII *Grace* (*Actual and Habitual*) (St. Louis 1946), pp. 3–270. *The Teaching of the Catholic Church,* ed. Smith, 2 vols. (New York, 1949), pp. 584–621. Van der Meersch, *De divina gratia* (Brugis, 1924), p. 222 ff.; "Grace," *DTC.*

grace, efficacious. A supernatural, divine influence, on account of which the human will is determined, infallibly but freely, to act with respect to eternal life.

The characteristic note of this grace is the infallibility of the effect. Testimonies of Holy Scripture are not lacking and they are all to the effect that God's dominion and power is absolute, and that no creature, even man endowed with free will, can resist it: "As the divisions of waters, so the heart of the king is in the hand of the Lord: whithersoever he will he shall turn it" (Prov. 21:1); "I will cause you to walk in my commandments, and to keep my judgments, and do them" (Ezech. 36:27). An example of most efficacious grace is the conversion of Paul on the Damascus road.

St. Augustine, more than the other Fathers, develops amply the doctrine of efficacious grace, to which he attributes all the supernatural good of man, man's free will remaining intact: "Man through mysterious ways is drawn to will by Him who knows how to work in the innermost recesses of the human heart, not that men believe without willing — which is impossible — but that from not willing they become willing" (*Enchir.*, 98). And again: "We do not defend grace in such a way as to seem to destroy free will" (*De peccatorum meritis et remissione*, 2, 18). Cf. Council of Trent, sess. VI, can. 4 (*de iustificatione*), *DB*, 814.

But the controversy lingers on between Molinists and Thomists on the essence of efficacious grace. The *Thomists* defend *intrinsic* and absolute efficacy: efficacious grace is the supernatural *physical predetermination* to which the human will is subordinate and which *de facto* it does not resist (although *being able to resist*, as the Council of Trent says). But for the *Molinists* grace is efficacious, not by itself, but dependently on the consent of our free will, which can always resist and leave the grace without fruitful effect. Between these two extremes there is, nowadays especially, a tendency toward a reasonable *syncretism*, which rejects *physical predetermination* on the one hand, for it does not seem to fit even in the framework of St. Thomas' thought and in a certain sense compromises free will, and, on the other hand, abhors also the Molinistic concept of a divine grace that must go begging the consent of man. Such syncretism proposes an intrinsic, divine *motion* in the human will (of the natural or supernatural order, as the case may be) which moves physically and immediately to the act as regards the *exercise* of the act, but leaves the will free to determine itself with respect to the *specification* of the same act, through choice of the object made by the reason, on which, however, God exercises His influence by way of *illumination*.

But no system will ever be able to eliminate the mystery that lies in conciliating the internal and efficacious motion of God with the freedom of the will that is moved.

BIBLIOGRAPHY

DEL PRADO, *De gratia et libero arbitrio*, 3 vols. (Freiburg, Helv., 1906). DE REGNON, *Bañez et Molina* (Paris, 1883). POHLE, "Grace (Controversies on)," *CE*. POHLE-PREUSS, *Dogmatic Theology*, VII *Grace* (*Actual and Habitual*) (St. Louis, 1946), pp. 231–248. *The Teaching of the Catholic Church*, ed. Smith, 2 vols. (New York, 1949), pp. 617–621. VAN DER MEERSCH, *De divina gratia* (Brugis, 1924), p. 258 ff.

See under *grace, sufficient; Molinism; Thomism.*

grace, habitual. A divine gift infused by God into the soul, as something *permanent* by its nature. In the strict sense, habitual grace is that infused into the very essence of the soul, and is called also *sanctifying* and *justifying* grace, inasmuch as it confers holiness and makes righteous one who had been a sinner. In a broader sense, habitual grace includes, in addition to sanctifying grace, also the *virtues* and the *gifts* of the Holy Ghost, which are like a ramification of sanctifying grace and are received in the faculties of the soul (see *gifts of the Holy Ghost; virtue*).

The Scholastics, starting from the data of revelation, developed an abundant doctrine on habitual grace with the help of the Aristotelian theory about *habits*. But Luther, opposing this theory on account of his nominalistic mentality, rejected the entire traditional doctrine and reduced sanctifying grace to an extrinsic, divine *favor* or to an extrinsic *imputation* of Christ's sanctity to the sinner, who remains in himself intrinsically corrupted and incurable (see *Lutheranism*). The Protestants have followed in their master's footsteps up to our times, with however a few exceptions (Liddon, Sanday). Bay (see *Baianism*) conceives grace *dynamically,* i.e., only as *actual,* and identifies it with morally good and salutary action, namely: with the *observance* of the divine precepts which, according to him, is possible only with grace, *integrative* element of the creature.

The Church has condemned both of these errors (Council of Trent, session VI, canon 11, *DB,* 821; Prop. 42 of Bay, *DB,* 1042), appealing to revelation (especially St. Paul and St. John), which manifests to us grace as a *regeneration,* a *new life,* a *divine energy,* diffused by the Holy Spirit and *inherent* in the soul. Hence the true theology of sanctifying grace is that grace is a *divine quality* (Catechism of the Council of Trent) or entitative habit inherent in the soul, upon which it confers a mode of divine being, a participation of the divine nature, according to St. Peter (see *consortium, divine*), adoptive divine filiation (Rom. 8:15; Gal. 4:5; John 3:1), and the right of inheritance to eternal life (Rom. 8:17). Tradition, in the East especially, is rich in concepts and developments with respect to sanctifying grace, boldly termed *"divinization of man"* (Irenaeus, Origen, Cyril of Alexandria).

Sanctifying grace is lost through mortal sin (Council of Trent, *DB,* 808), is conserved and increased through good works, done under the influence of God, and by means of the sacraments duly received (Council of Trent, *DB,* 834 and 849). See *indwelling of the Holy Trinity; justification.*

BIBLIOGRAPHY

St. Thomas, *Summa Theol.,* I–II, q. 110. Bouillard, *Conversion et grace chez S. Thomas d'Aquin* (Paris, 1944). Boyer, *Tractatus de gratia divina* (Rome, 1938). Lemonnyer, *Théologie du N. Testament* (Paris, 1928). Pascal Parente, *The Ascetical Life* (St. Louis, 1947), pp. 18–27. Pohle-Preuss, *Dogmatic Theology,* VII *Grace (Actual and Habitual)* (St. Louis, 1946). Rondet, *Gratia Christi* (Paris, 1948). *The Teaching of the Catholic Church,* ed. Smith, 2 vols. (New York, 1949), pp. 549–583.

grace, necessity of. Necessary is equivalent to inevitable, indispensable. There is a twofold necessity: *physical* necessity, in connection with the laws of nature in its being and operation; *moral* necessity, with reference to human conditions and customs. The first is more rigorous.

Grace, divine gift for the conquest of eternal life, is inserted in man as a new principle of activity, which strengthens, purifies, and elevates man's faculties to the supernatural order. Since intellect and will are the faculties specific to man, the necessity of grace is considered with reference to their objects, i.e., truth and goodness.

A. *Grace is necessary:*

1. *physically* (as an internal gift):
   - *a)* to know truths that are objectively supernatural, e.g., mysteries
   - *b)* for supernatural faith (adherence of intellect and will to the revealed word of God; see *faith*)

2. *morally* (as an external gift; revelation): to know the moral-religious truths easily, certainly, and without admixture of error. Although proportionate to human reason, these truths still present difficulties due to the condition of mankind after the original sin

Cf. Vat. Council, sess. III, DB, 1786.

The reason of both necessities lies in the disproportion (absolute in the first case, relative in the second) between the natural capacity of the intellect and the objects just mentioned.

B. *Internal grace is necessary:*

1. *morally*
   - (cf. C. Carthag., *DB,* 104, 105, 106, 107):
     - *a*) to do *all* good according to *all* the precepts of the *natural* law
     - *b*) to love God above all things, not only *affectively* but also *effectively* (in every action)
     - *c*) to avoid for a long time *all* mortal sins
   - (cf. C. Trent, sess. VI, can. 22, 23, *DB,* 832–833):
     - *d*) to persevere for a long time in sanctifying grace
     - *e*) to avoid *all* venial sins in the state of sanctification (the privilege of Mary)
2. *physically:*
   - *a*) for any *salutary* act whatsoever, i.e., for any act meritorious of eternal life (C. Carthag.; II C. Orange; C. Trent, *DB,* 105, 179, 180, 811, 812, 813)
   - *b*) for *preparing* for grace (cf. II Counc. Orange, *DB,* 176, 179; C. Trent, *DB,* 798, 813)
   - *c*) for *final perseverance* (C. Trent, *DB,* 826).

In this second diagram, the *moral* necessity of grace is founded on human infirmity as a result of original sin (which infirmity, however, does not take from man the capacity to do *some* good with his solely natural faculties; cf. the condemnation of *Lutheranism, Baianism,* etc.); the physical necessity, on the contrary, is founded on the transcendency of the supernatural order with respect to man.

BIBLIOGRAPHY

St. Thomas, *Summa Theol.,* I–II, q. 109. Billot, *De gratia Christi* (Rome, 1923), p. 59 ff. Peter Parente, *Anthropologia supernaturalis* (Rome, 1943), p. 54 ff. Pohle, "Grace," *CE.*

grace, sacramental. A supernatural gift added by the action of the individual sacraments to sanctifying grace (see *grace, habitual*). The theologians discuss the intimate nature of this addition to common sanctifying grace. Certain older theologians (Paludanus, Capreolus) believed it to be a supernatural habit, really distinct from sanctifying grace; many others (Cajetan, Soto, Suarez, Lugo) opined, on the other hand, that it consists in a simple right to special helps or actual graces, to be obtained at the opportune moment; but the majority hold with John of St. Thomas and the Salmanticenses (Salamanca University doctors) that it is an accidental modification and a reinvigoration of sanctifying grace.

Without going into a detailed discussion, we may observe that the three opinions referred to, although not intrinsically false, seem, however, to be one-sided because, while each illustrates a true aspect of the problem, none of them embraces it in its entirety. Accepting, therefore, the true substance of the various opinions and integrating it with other views — within the framework of St. Thomas' rapid sketch (*Summa Theol.,* III, q. 62, a. 2) — we hold that sacramental grace is a *new orientation* of the whole supernatural organism toward the end to which the individual sacraments tend. The supernatural organism is constituted by grace (which is like the soul in the natural organism), by the virtues and gifts of the Holy Spirit (which correspond to the soul's faculties) and by the impulses of actual grace (which correspond to the natural motions). Sacramental grace invests all these parts of the organism and *adapts* them to the particular end of each sacrament, and in this way *modifies* and reinforces sanctifying grace, augments and perfects those virtues and gifts which correspond to the particular end of the sacrament (like faith in baptism and charity in the Eucharist), casts finally the roots of a permanent right to have at the opportune moment all those helps of actual grace that excite, accompany, and bring to completion the supernatural acts, through the repetition of which the faithful attain the proximate end of the sacrament and the final end of salvation.

Thus, in particular, the sacramental grace of baptism gives to the faithful the orientation of son of God; that of confirmation disposes the adolescent to fight for the defense of the faith; the grace of penance and of extreme unction impresses in the soul of the Christian a penitential attitude; orders and matrimony perfect the souls of God's ministers and of the married couples, respectively, by directing and strengthening them to perform their different duties of ruling, instructing, and sanctifying the faithful (orders), and of generating in chastity and rearing in mutual harmony the new members of God's family (matrimony).

The Eucharist, finally, perfects all these orientations and unifies them, directing them under the impulse of charity toward the final goal of the whole supernatural order which is union with God in Christ, here on earth in a veiled manner, then face to face in the beatific vision (see *Communion, eucharistic*).

BIBLIOGRAPHY

St. Thomas, *Summa Theol.*, III, q. 62, a. 2. Billuart, *De sacramentis*, diss. 3, a. 5. Brazzarola, *La natura della grazia sacramentale nella dottrina di San Tommaso* (Grottaferrata, 1941). Connell, *De sacramentis* (Brugis, 1933), pp. 79–85. Doronzo, *De sacramentis in genere* (Milwaukee, 1946), pp. 212–233. Hugon, *Tractatus dogmatici*, Vol. 3 (Paris, 1948), pp. 93–104. Michel, "Sacrements," *DTC*, Cols. 629–631. Piolanti, *De sacramentis*, Vol. 1 (Rome, 1945). Salmanticenses, *Cursus Theologicus*, tract. 22.

grace, sufficient. A supernatural gift which confers on man the power to act, if he so wills, in a salutary way (i.e., with reference to eternal life).

Luther and Calvin (see *Lutheranism*), having denied human free will after original sin, conceive only a *most efficacious* grace, which determines necessarily the will of the man who is predestined to eternal life. Bay and Jansenius (see *Baianism* and *Jansenism*) reject sufficient grace, which they hold harmful, and admit only efficacious grace, which integrates nature and impels it infallibly along the road of salvation. The Church has condemned these and similar errors (*DB*, 1092 ff., 1226, 1363, 1521).

Holy Scripture speaks of graces granted by God, which did not have their effect, and the Lord reproves man, who, though being able to, has refused to profit by them: "I called, and you refused" (Prov. 1:24); "Jerusalem, Jerusalem . . . how often would I have gathered together thy children, as the hen doth gather her chickens under her wings, and thou wouldst not?" (Matt. 23:37.) The Fathers repeat the same thought: St. Augustine (*Enchir.*, 95): "Nor was God certainly unjust in not willing their salvation, because they could save themselves if they had willed to do so." The Council of Trent (sess. VI, cap. 11, *DB*, 804) repeats the words of St. Augustine: "God does not command impossible things, but commanding He tells you to do what you can and to ask for what you cannot do, and He helps you that you may be able to do."

There is a divergency between Thomists and Molinists on the nature of sufficient grace in its relation to efficacious grace (*q.v.*). The *Thomists* hold a sharp difference and distinction between the two graces, because efficacious grace (*premotion,* or *supernatural physical predetermination*) always and infallibly obtains its effect; sufficient grace, instead, confers only the potency or power to *act,* which power, however, never passes to act. The *Molinists* think that one same numerical grace is only sufficient, if man resists and frustrates the effect, and is efficacious if man consents to it by his free will and profits by it, passing on to the salutary action.

It is more correct to say that sufficient grace is also a motion to the act, like efficacious grace, but it is *impedible;* i.e., it is not of such kind as to overcome all internal and external impediments (passions, temptations, etc.), which exercise sinister activity on the will and render it more stubborn.

BIBLIOGRAPHY

St. Thomas, *Summa Theol.,* I–II, q. 109, a. 10, ad 3; q. 112, a. 2, ad. 2. Billot, *De gratia Christi* (Rome, 1923), p. 180. Del Prado, *De gratia et libero arbitrio,* Vol. 2 (Freiburg, Helv., 1907). Peter Parente, *Anthropologia supernaturalis* (Rome, 1943). Pohle-Preuss, *Dogmatic Theology,* VII *Grace* (*Actual and Habitual*) (St. Louis, 1946), pp. 42–47, 167–186, 231–248.

See under *grace, efficacious; Molinism; Thomism.*

Gregory Nazianzus. See "Outline of the History of Dogmatic Theology" (p. 301).

Gregory of Nyssa. See "Outline of the History of Dogmatic Theology" (p. 301); *Anomoeanism.*

Gregory the Great. See "Outline of the History of Dogmatic Theology" (p. 302); *agnosticism.*

H

hagiographer (Gr. ἅγιος — holy, and γράφω — I write). Designates the author of a book numbered in the official canon of the Bible (see *inspiration; Canon of the Bible*).

Heart of Jesus. Being only a subject of *pious attention* with SS. Anselm, Bernard, Matilda, and Gertrude, the *devotion* to the Sacred Heart begins with the Ven. Landsperge, Peter Canisius (16th century), and later with St. John Eudes. But the spark of the true and *proper cult,* which suddenly flamed in the world, were Christ's apparitions to St. Margaret Mary Alacoque († 1690), which created quite a sensation and gave rise to different opinions. Nearly a century passed before the Church decided to permit the Feast of the Sacred Heart with its liturgy, under Clement XIII (1765). From Pius IX on, the popes have vied with each other in promoting this cult so fruitful since its beginning.

Theological particulars: (1) The approved worship of the Sacred Heart has its foundation and justification in the sources of revelation and not in the apparitions and private revelations made to St. Margaret, which were only an *occasion* for its introduction. (2) This cult is part of the adoration which is to be paid to the humanity of the Saviour, on account of its hypostatic union with the Word. (3) The material object of this worship is the physical Heart of Jesus, in so far as it belongs to the Word; the formal object is the love, of which the Heart is the organ (at least *manifestative*) and the symbol, according to the common usage of men. More profoundly the worship of the Sacred Heart has as its object the Man-God, as living Love, which manifests itself in all the divine works, from the Creation to the Redemption to the Eucharist (the great gift for life on earth), and to the beatific vision (the supreme gift for life in heaven).

BIBLIOGRAPHY

BAINVEL, "Coeur (sacré de Jésus)," *DTC;* "Heart of Jesus," *CE; Devotion to the Sacred Heart,* trans. Leahy (London, 1924). NILLES, *The Devotion to the Sacred Heart,* trans. Kent (London, 1905). PETROVITS, *Devotion to the Sacred Heart* (St. Louis, 1925). TERRIEN, *La dévotion au Sacré-Coeur de Jésus, d'après les documents authentiques et la théologie* (Paris, 1893).

heaven. See *paradise.*

hell. In the proper sense, it is the *state* and the *place* of the damned, i.e., of those who, having died in mortal sin, undergo an eternal punishment. At times, in Scripture and the Fathers, the meaning of hell is extended to limbo and purgatory (like the Hades of the pagans and the Sheol of the Hebrews). The gospel revelation, completing and developing the scattered elements of the Old Testament, throws a full light on this mystery. The description of the judgment made by Jesus Himself (Matt. 25) and His final sentence to the reprobate: "Depart from me, you cursed, into everlasting fire," would suffice to establish the existence of hell. Repeatedly the Saviour recalls the thought of hell under effective images (*Gehenna of fire, exterior darkness, weeping and gnashing of teeth, burning furnace*). Expressive too is the parable of the rich man and Lazarus. The context of these and other passages precludes doubt on the proper sense of the word *eternal* (Gr. αἰώνιος).

Tradition is unanimous on the existence and the eternity of hell, if we except a few discordant voices between the third and the fifth centuries, influenced by the *personal* opinions of Origen, who thought that probably after long expiation all creatures would be purified and united forever with God. A few Fathers underwent his influence, but St. Augustine, re-echoing the protests of others, refuted these strange opinions in the name of Tradition and Holy Scripture. *Origenism* was condemned by Pope Victor (Synod of Constantinople, 543, and II Council of Constantinople, 553, *DB,* 230 ff.). Moreover, the Church's doctrine is clear and constant: *Symbolum Athanasianum,* IV Lat. Council, II Council of Lyons, Council of Florence, and Council of Trent (*DB,* 40, 429, 464, 693, 835).

Nature of hell: (*a*) pain of loss (*poena damni*), which is the gravest punishment and consists in the privation of God, supreme supernatural end of man; (*b*) pain of sense (*poena sensus*), namely: that which comes from external things which God uses to afflict the devils and the souls of the damned (as well as their bodies after the resurrection). The chief pain of sense is *fire,* not figurative but *real,* which torments the spirit *per modum alligationis,* says St. Thomas, i.e., through a bond or link put by God between fire and soul. The pain of hell is substantially immutable; certain theologians admit an accidental mitigation, which is difficult, however, to prove. Nothing certain can be said about the place of hell (see *damned; demon; penalty*).

BIBLIOGRAPHY

ST. THOMAS, *Summa Theol.,* III, *Suppl.,* q. 97 ff.; *Summa Contra Gentiles,* l. 4, c. 90. BERNARD, "Enfer," *DA.* BRÉMOND, *La Conception catholique de l'enfer* (Paris, 1907). HEWIT, "Ignis Aeternus," *The Catholic World,* 67 (1893). HONTHEIM, "Hell," *CE.* MEW, *Traditional Aspects of Hell* (London, 1903). MORTON, *Thoughts on Hell, A Study in Eschatology* (London, 1899). POHLE-PREUSS, *Dogmatic Theology,* XII *Eschatology* (St.

Louis, 1946), pp. 45–74. PORTER, "Eternal Punishment," *The Month* (July, 1878). RAUPERT, *Hell and Its Problems* (Buffalo, 1917). RICHARD, "Enfer," *DTC*. RICKABY, *Everlasting Punishment* (London, 1916). SUTCLIFFE, *The Old Testament and the Future Life* (Westminster, 1947). *The Teaching of the Catholic Church*, ed. Smith, 2 vols (New York, 1949), pp. 1176–1210.

See under *eschatology*.

heresy (Gr. αἵρεσις — choice). Originally it meant a doctrine or doctrinal attitude contrary to the common doctrine of faith. It gave, thus, the concept of an elite, adjusting doctrine to its own will. In the New Testament the word is used several times; St. Peter aptly determines the sense of heresy, saying that through it the path of truth is desecrated, men are perverted and the Lord denied (cf. 2 Pet. 2:1).

Tertullian (*De praescript.*, c. 6) explains heresy as an arbitrary choice of doctrines, without taking account of the common *regula fidei* (rule of faith) of the Church. St. Thomas reduces heresy to a type of positive *infidelity*, by which some have a certain faith in Christ without accepting integrally all the dogmas (*Summa Theol.*, II–II, q. 11, a. 1).

Limiting our consideration to the *objective* aspect (the subjective aspect belongs to moral theology), we define heresy: "A teaching which is directly contradictory to a truth revealed by God and proposed to the faithful as such by the Church." In this definition two essential characteristics of heresy are brought out: (*a*) opposition to a revealed truth; (*b*) opposition to the definition of the Church *magisterium*. If a truth is contained in the deposit of revelation, but has not been proposed to the faithful by the Church, it is called a *truth of divine faith;* if the revealed truth is also defined and proposed for belief by the ordinary or the extraordinary *magisterium* of the Church, it is called a truth of *divine-Catholic faith*. Heresy in the full sense of the word is opposed to a truth of divine-Catholic faith. If the denial concerns a revealed truth which is clear and commonly admitted as such, but has not been defined by the Church, the one who denies such a truth is called *proximus haeresi* (very close to heresy).

As regards the relationship of the heretic to the Church, see *members of the Church*.

BIBLIOGRAPHY

ST. THOMAS, *Summa Theol.*, II–II, q. 11. MICHEL, "Hérésie," *DTC*. VAN NOORT, *De fontibus revelationis* (Amsterdam, 1911), n. 259 ff. WILHELM, "Heresy," *CE*.

hermeneutics (Gr. ἑρμηνεύειν — to interpret). The art of interpreting texts, particularly the sacred texts of the Bible. Hermeneutics is to exegesis (*q.v.*) what logic is to philosophy, in so far as the art of hermeneutics establishes the laws which exegetical science applies in order to find the true sense of the texts, like logic establishes the laws of correct reasoning.

The norms in use for the interpretation of ancient profane writings are not entirely adequate for the biblical texts, which present particular difficulties inherent in their divine origin and their religious-dogmatic character. Indeed, their human aspect subjects them to the common rules of interpretation, but at the same time their character of inspired writings demands also a code of particular norms (see *inspiration*). The objective of hermeneutics is threefold: (1) To determine the nature and the different species of the biblical sense, i.e., of the truth which God, principal Author of the Bible, intends to express through the words written by the hagiographer (*q.v.*), who is only the secondary author of the biblical text. (2) To establish the principles which regulate the interpretation of the

Bible. (3) To find the most convenient way of proposing, according to the various aptitudes of the readers, the true sense of the texts. Each of these three parts has its proper name, i.e., *noematics* (from νόημα — sense), *heuristics* (from εὑρίσκω — I find), *prophoristics* (from προφέρω — I propose).

Recent ecclesiastical documents, particularly the encyclical *Divino afflante Spiritu* of Pius XII (Sept. 30, 1943), have given the sacred hermeneutics a development equal to the progress of the profane sciences, safeguarding the perfect harmony between the rights of reason and the demands of faith.

BIBLIOGRAPHY

Chase, *Chrysostom, A Study in the History of Biblical Interpretation* (London, 1887). Cruveilhier, "Herméneutique sacrée," *DBVS*. Kortleitner, *Hermeneutica biblica* (Oeniponte, 1923). Maas, "Hermeneutics," *CE;* "Exegesis," *CE*. Steinmueller, *A Companion to Scripture Studies,* Vol. 1 (New York, 1941), pp. 225–249.

See under *Bible*.

heterodox. See *orthodox*.

hierarchy (Gr. ἱερὰ ἀρχή — sacred authority). The body of persons participating in ecclesiastical power, which is divided into power of orders and power of jurisdiction.

The power of *orders* is immediately directed to the sanctification of souls through the offering of the sacrifice of the Mass and the administration of the sacraments. The power of *jurisdiction,* on the other hand, is immediately directed to ruling the faithful with reference to the attainment of life eternal, and is actuated through the authoritative teaching of revealed truths (*sacred magisterium*), and through the promulgation of laws (*legislative power*), together with the authoritative decision of legal actions involving its subjects (*judicial power*), and the application of penal sanctions against transgressors of the law (*coactive* or *coercive power*). These last three powers are functions of the same sacred jurisdictional authority with which the Church is endowed as a perfect society.

The power of jurisdiction is divided into: (1) power of *forum externum,* when directed principally to the common good, in so far as it regulates the social relations of the members and produces public juridical effects; and power of *forum internum,* when directed principally to private good, in so far as it regulates the relations of consciences with God and is exercised *per se* secretly and with prevalently moral effects; (2) *ordinary* power, when *ipso jure* (by law) it is connected with an office, and *delegated* power, when it is granted to a person by commission or delegation. Ordinary power is further divided into proper, i.e., annexed to an office and exercised in one's own name (*nomine proprio*), and *vicarious,* i.e., annexed to an office but exercised in another's name.

Since sacred power is twofold, hierarchy is likewise twofold, and therefore we have in the Church the *hierarchy of orders,* constituted by the body of persons having the power of orders in its different grades (see *orders, holy*), and the *hierarchy of jurisdiction,* consisting in the series of those persons who have the power of teaching and governing.

In both hierarchies there are grades, i.e., the *fundamental* grades, which have their source in divine right (episcopate, priesthood, and diaconate in the hierarchy of orders; papacy and episcopate in the hierarchy of jurisdiction) and the *secondary* grades, which have been instituted by the Church.

The two hierarchies, although very closely related, are really distinct. They are distinct in their mode of *origin* (orders are conferred by the appropriate sacrament, while jurisdiction originates through canonical mission) and in their *properties* (the valid use of orders, in most cases, cannot be prevented, while jurisdiction is revocable). They are, however, *mutually related,* because jurisdiction supposes orders and, vice versa, the exercise of orders is moderated by jurisdiction; and also because both come from God and directly or indirectly lead to God.

Those members of the Church who belong to the twofold hierarchy are called *clerics* (Gr. κλῆρος — lot, portion, sort, i.e., *in sortem Domini vocati* — "called to the lot of the Lord"), while all the others are called laics, laymen, laity (Gr. λαός — the people). Since in its bosom the Church carries superiors and subjects, really distinct by divine right, it is an *unequal* society, i.e., a society in which the members do not have equal rights and duties.

BIBLIOGRAPHY

St. Thomas, *Summa Theol.,* II–II, q. 39, a. 3. Billot, *De Ecclesia,* Vol 1 (Rome), theses 15–24. De Dunin Borkowski, "Hierarchy of the Early Church," *CE.* Romani, *Institutiones Iuris Canonici,* Vol. 1 (Rome, 1941), n. 312 ff. Ruffini, *La gerarchia della chiesa negli Atti degli Apostoli e nelle lettere di S. Paolo* (Rome, 1921). *The Teaching of the Catholic Church,* ed. Smith, 2 vols. (New York, 1949), pp. 1031–1053. Van Hove, "Hierarchy," *CE.*

holiness (mark of the Church). See *sanctity (mark of the Church).*

holiness of Christ. See *sanctity of Christ.*

Holy Ghost. The proper name of the Third Person of the Holy Trinity. The choice of this name is suggested by the idea of *impulse* proper to love, according to which the Holy Spirit proceeds. In the sense of "immaterial being" the term *spirit* is attributed also to the other Persons of the Holy Trinity. The Holy Spirit is called also *Love.* In fact, Love is a motion or tendency of the will to good: but it is predicated of the Holy Spirit in a *terminal* and concrete sense, inasmuch as He is the term of divine volition.

Since the epoch of the Fathers (St. Augustine) there has been discussion on the nature of the second procession, psychologically more obscure than the first. The Scholastics in particular have studied the question of the formal *principle* of the two processions. With reference to the Holy Ghost there are two opinions: (*a*) He proceeds from *mutual love* of the Father and the Son, as from His formal principle *quo* (School of St. Victor); (*b*) He proceeds from essential divine love (common to the three Persons). St. Thomas acutely explains: The formal, *remote* principle *quo* is the essential love, while the proximate *principium quo* is the mutual love of Father and Son; the formal principle *quod* are the two *Persons,* from which the Holy Spirit proceeds.

Finally the Holy Spirit is called *Gift,* according to the nature of love which consists in giving itself. The liturgy (cf. the *Veni, Creator Spiritus*) calls the Holy Ghost by several other names: Finger of the Right Hand of the Father, Living Source, Fire, Charity, Unction, Paraclete, etc.

BIBLIOGRAPHY

St. Thomas, *Summa Theol.,* I, qq. 36–38. Barry, *God the Holy Ghost* (Boston, 1901). Froget, "Holy Ghost," *CE.* Hugon, *Le mystère de la très Sainte Trinité* (Paris, 1930), p. 213 ff. Joyce, "Trinity," *CE.* Klein, *The Doctrine of the Trinity,* trans. Sullivan (New York, 1940), pp. 184–210. Palmieri, "Esprit-Saint," *DTC.* Pohle-Preuss, *Dogmatic Theology,* II *The Divine Trinity* (St. Louis, 1946), pp. 92–112, 205–218. Scheeben, *The Mysteries of Christianity,* trans. Vollert (St. Louis, 1946), pp. 95–114, 181–197. Slipyi, *De principio spirationis in Sanctissima Trinitate* (Leopoli, 1926). *The Teaching of the Catholic Church,* ed. Smith, 2 vols. (New York, 1949), pp. 143–179.

Holy See. By this name is designated not only the person of the Roman pontiff (see *Roman pontiff; pope*), but also the whole system of departments, tribunals, and offices through which the pope governs the universal Church (cf. *CIC,* Can. 7). With the expansion of Christianity and the progressive actuation of the supreme rights inherent in the *prima sedes* (primate see), the Bishop of Rome found himself quickly besieged with so enormous a work load of administrative and juridical matters that he could not take care of it personally. He was therefore constrained to entrust a part of it to certain members of his clergy (especially the deacons); hence the establishment of organized offices which were later called the "Roman curia." After the Council of Trent, when centralization had reached its fastest pace, Sixtus V reorganized the Curia in a form responding to the new needs of the Church, by creating the *Roman congregations.* The Sixtine organization remained with little variation up to Pius X, who by the constitution *Sapienti Consilio* of 1908 introduced radical changes, which were systemized definitely in the Code of Canon Law (Cans. 242–244). According to this reorganization the Roman Curia is now composed of eleven congregations, three tribunals, and five offices.

The *congregations* are made up of groups of cardinals set up permanently with the function of handling certain definite types of ecclesiastical matters. Their power is disciplinary and administrative. Here is the list of them according to the order established by the Code, together with a brief indication of their respective duties: *The Supreme Congregation of the Holy Office* is charged with the defense of Christian faith and morals. The *Consistorial Congregation* is so called because its duty is to prepare whatever concerns the holding of consistories, but its sphere of competency is much broader and includes the creation, conservation, and suppression of dioceses, the naming of bishops, etc. The *Congregation of the Sacraments* has charge of the administration of the sacraments and the celebration of the Mass. The *Congregation of the Council* is in charge of the discipline of the diocesan clergy and of the faithful throughout the world. The *Congregation of the Religious* supervises the regular functioning and discipline of the religious societies. The *Congregation of the Propagation of the Faith* presides over all the missionary activity of the Catholic Church. The *Congregation of Rites* occupies itself with matters of holy liturgy and the beatification and canonization of saints. The *Ceremonial Congregation* is in charge of the pontifical ceremonial and settles certain questions of precedence. The *Congregation of Extraordinary Ecclesiastical Affairs* deals with many questions, particularly matters in connection with civil laws and concordats negotiated by the Holy See with national governments. The *Congregation of Seminaries and Universities* supervises all that concerns the regime, the discipline, temporal administration, and the studies of seminaries, and directs the functioning of universities dependent on the Holy See. The *Oriental Congregation* is the most recent, having been constituted by Benedict XV in 1917, but it is a very important one in that it deals with the persons, discipline, and rites of all the Eastern Churches in communion with the Holy See.

The *tribunals* or courts of the Roman Curia are the *Holy Penitentiary,* for the internal forum (of conscience), and the *Holy Roman Rota* and the *Apostolic Signature,* for the external forum. Their respective duties are indicated in Canons 258–259.

The *offices* are the *Apostolic Chancery,* the *Dataria,* the *Apostolic Chamber,* the *Secretariat of State,* and the *Secretariat of Briefs to Princes and Latin Letters.* As regards their respective duties, cf. Canons 260–264.

BIBLIOGRAPHY

BAUMGARTEN, "Holy See," *CE.* FORGET, CHOUPIN, "Curie Romaine," *DA.* GOYENECHE, *Iuris Canonici Summa Principia,* Vol. 1 (Rome, 1935), pp. 241–258. HESTON, *The Holy See at Work* (Milwaukee, 1950). KURTSCHEID, *Historia Iuris Canonici,* Vol. 1 (Rome, 1941), pp. 246–251. MARTIN, *The Roman Curia as It Now Exists* (London, 1913). OJETTI, *De romana curia* (Rome, 1910).

Homoousian. See *consubstantial.*

hope. See *virtue.*

Hugh of St. Victor. See "Outline of the History of Dogmatic Theology" (p. 302).

hylomorphism, sacramental. See *matter and form (of the sacraments).*

hyperdulia. See *cult.*

hypostatic union (Gr. ὑπόστασις — *substance* — *suppositum* or subsisting subject, hence person). At the time of Nestorianism (fifth century), St. Cyril of Alexandria, in his effort to defend the truth and *reality* of the union of the human and the divine natures in Christ, repeatedly used the expression: ἕνωσις καθ' ὑπόστασιν—union according to *hypostasis* or hypostatic union (as against the ἕνωσις σχετική κατὰ θέλησιν — accidental, moral union, of Nestorius). The Cyrilian expression was incorporated in the acts of the Council of Ephesus (431) and of the following councils, always with the meaning of substantial, real union, with a leaning toward the signification of *personal* union, which was *explicitly* consecrated in the III Council of Constantinople (680), defining that the two natures converge in one sole *person* and in one hypostasis (*DB,* 290).

Starting from these positive data, the precise concept of hypostatic union is determined as a *personal* union, in which is effected the Incarnation of the Word in a singular way, completely different from the case of a mere man. The union in us between body and soul is that of two incomplete substances and terminates in *one nature* and *one person.* The union proper to Christ is that of *two complete and distinct natures* (Council of Chalcedon) and terminates in one sole Person, that of the Word, already pre-existing at the act of Incarnation (Council of Ephesus).

The hypostatic union is a *mystery* of faith, which the theologians try to illustrate on the basis of the concept of *personality* (see *person*); but, unfortunately, this concept is not the same in the various schools. If we hold with some theologians that personality is constituted formally by subsistence, understanding subsistence as the proper existence of a substance, the hypostatic union is effectively illustrated by saying that the human nature of Christ, substantially complete and determined, did not have its personality because it did not have its own proper existence, but was elevated to participate in the divine existence of the Word, and, thus, in His divine Personality. There is in Christ, then, only one Person (the Word), because there is only one existence, only one subsistence, the Word's — a real, profound union, as the Council of Ephesus states; but, at once, a permanent distinction of the two integral and perfect natures, as the Council of Chalcedon defines (see *Incarnation; person; Nestorianism; Monophysitism*).

BIBLIOGRAPHY

ST. THOMAS, *Summa Theol.,* III, q. 2. JUGIE, *Nestorius et la controverse nestorienne*

(Paris, 1912). MICHEL, "Hypostase," *DTC;* "Hypostatique (Union)," *DTC.* OTTEN, *A Manual of History of Dogmas,* Vol. 2 (St. Louis, 1915), pp. 171–197. POHLE-PREUSS, *Dogmatic Theology,* II *The Divine Trinity* (St. Louis, 1946), pp. 220–228; IV *Christology* (1946), pp. 89–146. SARTORI, *Il concetto di ipostasi e l'enosi dogmatica ai concilii di Efeso e di Calcedonia* (Turin, 1927). TERRIEN, *S. Thomae Aq. doctrina sincera de unione hypostatica* (Paris, 1894).

I

iconoclasts (Gr. εἰκών — image, and κλάω — I break). Adversaries of images who in the eighth century, under the leadership of the Eastern Emperor Leo III, waged pitiless war on sacred images, forbidding their *use* and their *cult.* Some were adverse only to the cult of images (Iconomachi).

Politically speaking, it is not clear for what motive Leo III took on this struggle which, in addition to disturbing the conscience of the faithful, destroyed treasures of art; some think that the Emperor by so doing wished to please the Jews and Moslems who fought in great numbers in his army; others think that he was convinced personally of the orthodoxy of that aversion. *Theologically,* iconoclasm is a consequence of *Monophysitism* (*q.v.*). In fact, the Monophysites, admitting the transformation of Christ's humanity into the Divinity, logically had to disapprove of the iconographic representation of the Saviour in merely human forms. Pope Gregory II energetically resisted the imperial persecution; his successor, Gregory III, condemned the new heresy in a council held at Rome (731), defending the use and worship of images in the name of Tradition. Leo armed a fleet, which was sent against Ravenna, faithful to the Pope, but the fleet was destroyed in a storm. Constantine V Copronymus, successor of Leo III, intensified the persecution, making many martyrs; he assembled a Council at Hieria (753), which condemned the defenders of the worship of images, among whom was St. John Damascene. But in 787, under the auspices of Empress Irene, an ecumenical council was celebrated, the second of Nicaea, which solemnly condemned the heresy and defined the orthodoxy of the use and worship of sacred images.

BIBLIOGRAPHY

BRÉHIER, *La querelle des images* (Paris, 1904). EMEREAU, "Iconoclasme," *DTC.* FORTESCUE, "Iconoclasm," *CE;* "Images," *CE.* HEURTEBIZE, "Images (Culte des)," *DTC.* TIXERONT, *History of Dogmas,* trans. H.L.B., Vol. 3 (St. Louis, 1916), pp. 421–467.

idealism. According to the most authoritative of modern idealists, it may be defined: "A conception which reduces the world to a spiritual act, namely, the act of thinking, by unifying the infinite variety of Nature and man in one absolute unity, in which the human is the divine and the divine is the human" (G. Gentile, *Teoria generale dello spirito*). This is modern idealism carried out to its extreme consequences (*Gentilian actualism*); but the historical genesis of idealism goes back to Parmenides, who is said to have been the first to have looked on the true reality as pure thought. Certainly idealism, as exaltation of the spirit or thinking subject, has its root in the philosophy of Descartes († 1650). Subordinating reality to human thought, he inaugurated that subjectivism (*q.v.*) which, across the English school (Locke, Berkeley, Hume), reaches Kant and goes as far as to substitute the *a priori* categories of thought for *noumenal* reality, which is said to be unknowable in itself (see *Kantianism*). This is the starting point of German idealism, which gradually reduced all reality, even *phenomenal,* to the transcendental ego (panegoism of Fichte), or to the absolute (Schelling), or to the *idea* in continual flux of becoming (panlogism of Hegel). German idealism entered Italy through B. Spaventa († 1873), took strong root through Benedetto Croce, and triumphed with Giovanni Gentile. Italian idealism, the most radical, may be represented schematically as follows:

1. All reality resolves itself entirely and solely in the spirit as pure thinking act or thought (actualism).

2. Outside of this thought nothing is real, nothing transcendent; everything is immanent in it (immanentism-monism).

3. The spirit or thinking act is in continual becoming, i.e., produces itself through an immanent creative process (*autocthesis*), by which it puts itself into reality and at the same time surpasses itself, under different aspects (dialectical dynamism).

4. The Spirit runs a tri-phase cycle, thesis–antithesis–synthesis, in which the genesis of all reality lies. Croce distinguishes four grades or phases of the immanent activity of the spirit—two of the theoretical order (aesthetics, logic), and two of the practical order (economics, ethics). Gentile distinguishes three phases: (*a*) pure subjectivity (art); (*b*) objectivation (religion); (*c*) synthesis of the subject-object (philosophy).

5. Individual men are so many *empiric egos,* unified in a *transcendental ego,* the thinking act, in which all that is real (God and the world) exists in the flux of becoming.

Apart from other difficulties, idealism is absurd for the following reasons: (1) because it affirms that the spirit or thinking act creates itself, admitting thus the inconceivable principle of a thing cause of itself; (2) because it identifies finite with infinite, contingent with absolute, and admits the possibility of an evolution of the transcendental ego, given as an infinite, eternal, and, hence, most perfect being; (3) because it fails to explain the distinction, the variety, and the contrariety of the individual consciences, coefficient elements and actors in the drama of human life; (4) because it removes the distinction between error and truth, bad and good, and proclaims that the spirit in the act of thinking is always truth and goodness, and that evil and error are the past of the spirit itself.

Idealism, both as a *pantheistic* system and as a *relativism* in the field of morals, is irreconcilable with Christianity.

BIBLIOGRAPHY

Bradley, *Appearance and Reality* (London, 1897). Carson, "The Reality of the External World," *Dublin Review,* 125 (1899). Cordovani, *Cattolicismo e Idealismo* (Milan, 1928). Dehove, "Idéalisme," *DA.* Eucken, *Christianity and the New Idealism* (New York, 1909). Lyon, *Idéalisme en Angleterre au XVIII siècle* (Paris, 1888). Willmann, "Idealism," *CE.* Zacchi, *Il nuovo idealismo italiano di B. Croce e di G. Gentile* (Rome, 1925).

idolatry (Gr. εἰδώλων λατρεῖα—worship of idols). Consists in paying to false divinities the worship due only to God. Some Fathers call idolatry the gravest offense to God, as it robs Him of His honor by putting the Creator after creatures.

In its most vulgar form, it identifies the divinity (whatever this is) with the idol (material image); in this sense it is akin to fetishism (*q.v.*), which, however, rather than a religion is an ignoble sorcery of an individual and utilitarian character.

In a more elevated form, according to the opinion and teaching of the idol-worshiping priests and scholars, idolatry is said to represent the idol as an image of the divinity, to which the worship is properly directed. But it is historically proved that the idol-worshiping peoples hold that the divinity informs the idol with its spirit, which remains ever present in the idol and bound to the idol. Against the rationalists, the Catholics demonstrate, by an objective criticism of the documents, that idolatry is not the first stage of religion, but is rather a degeneration: religion went from monotheism to polytheism, not vice versa. Man fell into idolatry, under the pressure of his passions, as he gradually lost sight of the supreme and true God (Rom., Ch. 1). The sense of the divine, basic to all religion, is also at the root of idolatry: but it undergoes a deviation from the celestial spheres down toward earthly things, very likely under the influence of animism (*q.v.*), an ancient belief that everything is animated and moved by a spirit. The Church was always very rigorous, during the persecutions, with Christians who fell into idolatry (see *animism; fetishism*).

BIBLIOGRAPHY

Bugnicourt, "Animisme," *DA*. Chantepie de la Saussaye, *Manuel d'histoire des religions* (1904). Hull, *Studies on Idolatry* (Bombay, 1906). Michel, "Idolatrie," *DTC*. Ring, *Religions of the Far East* (Milwaukee, 1950). Tixeront, *History of Dogmas*, trans. H.L.B., Vol. 1 (St. Louis, 1910), pp. 346–354. Wilhelm, "Idolatry," *CE*.

idolothyte (thing offered to an idol, from Gr. εἰδώλῳ θύω — I sacrifice to the idol). One of the most delicate cases of conscience for the first Christians was the lawfulness of eating meats offered to the gods by the pagans in their temples. At that time, Greco-Roman society was permeated with a religious consciousness, and every occasion of life, happy or sad, was marked with sacrificial offerings to the gods. The flesh of the immolated victims was eaten in places adjoining the temple, or in family banquets, or distributed to friends, or sold to butchers and entered into public use.

At the Apostolic Council of Jerusalem it was decided that Christians converted from paganism should abstain from meats of pagan sacrificial origin (Acts 15:20, 29) out of respect for their Jewish brothers, who felt an instinctive repugnance for the use of idolothytes. In A.D. 56, six years later, the faithful of Corinth put the question to St. Paul in all its practical aspects: (1) May Christians buy meat from butchers who purchase their meat from the temples or who, in butchering it, practice religious rites? (2) May they accept invitations to banquets at which they suspect idolothytes will be served? (3) May they participate in a sacred banquet of pagans for reasons of social obligation or convenience?

In his answer to these three questions (1 Cor., Chs. 8–10) St. Paul is guided by two principles: (1) an idol is nothing, and so it cannot make holy or unholy the meat offered to it; (2) animals were given by God for man's food. Accordingly, his answer to the first query is affirmative; such is also the answer to the second, except there be someone at the table who might be scandalized. The answer to the third query, however, is negative, because the grave scandal here implied cannot be permitted for any reason, since it is a question of direct participation in an act of idolatrous worship: one cannot drink from the "demon's cup" after having sipped the "Lord's chalice."

BIBLIOGRAPHY

Allo, *Première épître aux Corinthiens* (Paris, 1934), pp. 195–252. Mangenot, "Idolothytes," *DTC*. Prat, *The Theology of St. Paul*, trans. Stoddard, Vol. 1 (Westminster, 1926), pp. 115–119.

Ignatius Martyr. See "Outline of the History of Dogmatic Theology" (p. 301); *Roman pontiff*.

illumination of the agonizing. See *death; infidels*.

Illuminism (or Enlightenment). A philosophico-religious current which spread in the eighteenth century from England into France, Germany, and Italy. Illuminism took up the spirit of Humanism and of the Lutheran Reformation and affirmed the autonomy of reason released and emancipated from all civil and religious authority, openly hostile to all tradition, and destined to enlighten with its light the mysteries of the world and of life. The leader of this current was the Englishman Herbert of Cherbury († 1648), who professed a naturalistic religion reduced to a few fundamental truths in which all religions agree. There is a close connection between this theory and the deism (*q.v.*) of Tindal, Toland, Collins, and Bolingbroke. Illuminism also proclaimed the autonomy of the will in the moral field: neither religion nor civil laws can be sources of morality, but only the individual conscience by a kind of instinct (ethico-aesthetic sense). Individual ethics become social ethics by moderating egoism with altruism through sympathy (A. Smith).

English Illuminism passed into France, where it degenerated into materialistic and atheistic Encyclopedism (De la Mettrie, Holbach, Diderot, Voltaire). J. J. Rousseau, with his romantic naturalism, was influenced by French Illuminism. In Germany, Illuminism identified itself with Samuel Reimarus († 1768), who rejected all Christian revelation as an imposture, and still more with Ephraem Lessing, aesthete, littérateur, and dramatist, who drew all his inspiration from the principle that truth is a perennial, personal conquest, and not a gift or immutable possession. In Italy, Illuminism had its influence on the Revival of the second half of the eighteenth century in the field of social and economic sciences (A. Genovesi, G. Filangieri, G. R. Carli, etc.). However, in this country, where Christian tradition was more tenacious, Illuminism did not in general undergo the ethico-religious degenerations it knew beyond the Alps.

BIBLIOGRAPHY

Gentile, *Dal Genovesi ad Galluppi* (Naples, 1903). Hibben, *The Philosophy of Enlightenment* (London, 1910). Rostan, *Les philosophes et la société française au XVII siècle* (Paris, 1911).

image. Usually means the drawn or sculptured reproduction of a person in his bodily likeness, e.g., a photograph. Philosophically, an image is a reproduction of a knowable object in the sensitive or in the intellective faculty (sensible or intelligible species). In theology, image is of special interest in the question of worship (see *cult*). The Church from remote centuries adopted and defended the worship of the saints and their images: in the II Nicene Council (A.D. 787) the iconoclasts (*q.v.*) were condemned for opposing the custom of venerating images of our Lord, of the Blessed Virgin, and of the saints.

According to Holy Scripture, God created man to His *image and likeness* (Gen. 1:26 ff.). Though the two words are synonymous in the Hebrew text, some Fathers make a distinction, referring image to the natural properties of man and likeness to the supernatural gifts with which Adam was enriched. Rigorously speaking, Holy Scripture affirms no more than a relationship of resemblance between God the Creator and man. This resemblance evidently does not refer to the body of man but to his soul, which really reflects in itself analogically certain divine perfections, like immateriality, intellect, and will with their respective operations. St. Thomas sees also in the human spirit an *image of the Trinity,* inasmuch as in God the Word is generated by the Father and from them both proceeds the Holy Spirit, who is Love, and likewise in us there is a mental word or concept of the thing known, followed by a movement of love or inclination toward that thing. Trinitarian theology waxes eloquent on this relationship of resemblance between human psychology and the intimate life of God (see *Trinity*).

In a stricter and theologically more interesting sense, the term *image* is attributed to the Word according to St. Paul: *"Who is the image of the invisible God"* (Col. 1:15). In fact, the Word (*q.v.*) is the term of the divine intellection, proceeding from the Father by way of spiritual generation: the son is born to the image of his father. The concept of image is even more profound in the Word, because He is not only like the Father, but also of the identical substance of the Father (see *consubstantial*). Less correctly can the Holy Spirit be called image of the Son (as some Eastern Fathers do), because the Holy Spirit proceeds through love, and love does not produce, but supposes resemblance.

BIBLIOGRAPHY

St. Thomas, *Summa Theol.*, I, q. 45, a. 7; q. 35. Hetzenauer, *Theologia Biblica* (Freiburg i.-Br., 1908), pp. 537–539.

See under *iconoclasts; Trinity; consubstantial.*

Immaculate Conception. Solemnly defined in the bull, *Ineffabilis,* by Pius IX, December 8, 1854. It is, therefore, a truth of Catholic faith that the Virgin Mary from the first instant of her conception was preserved immune from original sin, in view of the future merits of Christ.

This singular privilege was not ignored by the *magisterium* of the Church before its definition; suffice it to mention that a liturgical feast of the Conception of Mary existed at least since the seventh century in the East and the ninth century in the West (first at Naples, then in England and Ireland and in the rest of Europe). In the Western Church this truth was obscured and made progress slowly against contradictions and difficulties, because from the fifth century onward the ecclesiastical writers were forced to defend against Pelagianism (*q.v.*) the universal transmission of original sin, and hence the universality of the Redemption. But its champions were never lacking. Characteristic of this fact is the controversy that arose in the thirteenth century between Dominicans and Franciscans: the former, led by St. Thomas, denied that Mary was exempt from original sin, but admitted her sanctification in her mother's womb immediately after conception. The Franciscans, led by Scotus, maintained first the possibility and then the fact of Mary's privilege. However, St. Bonaventure, the great Franciscan, agreed with St. Thomas and St. Bernard. Apart from the anti-Pelagian preoccupations, imperfect knowledge of the theologians on the physiology of fecundation and conception sharpened and confused the issue. From Sixtus IV, who approved the Feast of the Immaculate Conception, down to Gregory XVI, who had the beautiful title of "Immaculate" inserted in the preface of the Mass and the litanies, the Church smoothed the way for the solemn definition of Pius IX.

The privilege of Mary is implicit in the text of Genesis 3:15, where the triumph of the Woman and of her Offspring (Christ) over Satan is prophesied. Moreover, Mary, before the Incarnation, is greeted by the angel as "full of grace" (κεχαριτωμένη — permanently full of divine grace), an expression in which the Fathers recognize perfect sanctity, without limit of time. The parallelism *Adam-Eve* (slaves of Satan and ruin of mankind) and *Christ-Mary* (victors over Satan and salvation of men) is familiar to the Fathers (Justin, Irenaeus, Tertullian, etc.). Ephraem has vivid expressions on the incontaminated purity of Mary. St. Augustine, notwithstanding his fight against the Pelagians, does not dare to mention Mary when it is question of sin (*De natura et gratia,* 36, 42; *RJ,* 179).

Theological reason: It is repugnant that the Mother of Christ, victor of Satan and of sin, should have been subject to one and the other, even for one instant.

BIBLIOGRAPHY

Harper, *The Immaculate Conception,* re-edited by Rickaby (1919). Holweck, "Immaculate Conception," *CE.* Jaggar, *The Immaculate Conception* (New York, 1925). Le Bachelet, Jugie, "Immaculée Conception," *DTC.* Livius, *The Blessed Virgin Mary in the Fathers of the First Six Centuries* (London, 1893). Lumbreras, *S. Thomas and the Immaculate Conception* (Notre Dame, Ind., 1923). McKenna, *The Dogma of the Immaculate Conception* (Washington, D. C., 1929). Merkelbach, *Mariologia* (Paris, 1939). Pius IX, bull, *Ineffabilis.* Pohle-Preuss, *Dogmatic Theology,* VI *Mariology* (St. Louis, 1946), pp. 39–71. Scheeben, *Mariology,* trans. Geukers, Vol. 2 (St. Louis, 1947), pp. 32–111. Storff, *The Immaculate Conception* (San Francisco, 1925). Ullathorne, *The Immaculate Conception of the Mother of God* (Westminster, 1905).

immanence (method of). See *apologetics; immanentism.*

immanentism. A philosophico-religious system which, in its most rigid form, reduces all reality to the subject, which is said to be the source, the beginning, and the end of all its creative activity. It is basically that same *subjectivism* (*q.v.*) which began with Descartes as a tendency to start from the subject and progressively to absorb in it the whole object. This absorption is already accomplished in the substantialistic monism of Spinoza with its definitely *pantheistic* character; in Kant it undergoes a slight limitation in so far as the *phenomenon* is admitted as objective reality, at least fundamentally. But with German *idealism* (Fichte, Schelling, Hegel), immanentism becomes resurgent and reaches its apex in the Italian idealism of Croce and Gentile, according to whom all reality is immanent in the act of thought.

Besides this intellectualistic development, immanentism receives a *sentimentalistic* one in the works of Schleiermacher. This current, closer to the religious problem, became so strong all through the nineteenth century as to threaten to eclipse the first. In the *pragmatism* (*q.v.*) of James, sentiment and action, no longer the idea, are the essence of religion. Finally, *modernism* (*q.v.*) steps in, making the divine gush forth from sentiment and *religious experience* (*q.v.*). The historical fact of revelation is in function of religious consciousness, in which God continues to reveal Himself in fact, and all religion becomes an individual, subjective, and personal matter. Consequences of this absolute immanentism are: (*a*) God is no longer personally distinct from man and the world; (*b*) revelation and religion are not tied down to fixed truths and immutable dogmas, but they develop and are transformed according to the phases of sentiment and of religious consciousness. In view of these grave consequences, the Church has condemned immanentism (cf. encyclical, *Pascendi,* against modernism).

But the *method of immanence,* adopted by Blondel and other Catholics in *apologetics,* is another thing altogether: it consists in starting from the subject in the defense of religion, i.e., in making man feel the discomfort and unrest of his mind, the need of God and of the supernatural which lies dormant in every heart, and thus orienting men to the true, revealed religion, to Christ's Church.

This method of immanence is not heterodox in itself; used cautiously, it can be an effective preparation for the *historical* method.

BIBLIOGRAPHY

ILLINWORTH, *Divine Immanence* (London, 1898). MICHELET, *Dieu et l'agnosticisme contemporain* (Paris, 1920). STEFANINI, *L'Azione* (Milan, 1915). THAMIRY, "Immanence," *CE*. DE TONQUÉDEC, *Immanence* (Paris, 1913); "Immanence (Méthode d')," *DA*. VALENSIN, "Immanence (Doctrine de l')," *DA*.

immensity. See *infinity*.

immolation. See *Mass; sacrifice of Christ*.

immortality. Immunity from death. As regards the immortality of the body, together with other gifts to Adam and Eve, see *integrity*.

Here we shall consider only the immortality of the soul, which is at once a truth of faith and reason. Divine revelation is wholly ordered to eternal life, the supernatural destiny of man. In Holy Scripture, life on earth is termed a *pilgrimage* to a country above (Gen. 47:9; Heb. 11:13–16). Ecclesiastes states the same explicitly: "before . . . the dust return into its earth from whence it was, and the Spirit return to God, who gave it" (12:7): the allusion is to the creation of man, whom God made of body formed from the earth and soul infused directly by Himself into the body (Gen. 2:7).

In the Gospel Jesus refutes the Sadducees by reminding them that God is the God of Abraham and of the other Patriarchs, who cannot be altogether dead, because God is the God of the living, not of the dead (Matt. 22:31 ff.); and in another place He admonishes: "Fear ye not them that kill the body, and are not able to kill the soul: but rather fear him that can destroy both soul and body in hell" (Matt. 10:28). Tradition is unanimous on this doctrine, and that is why the *magisterium* of the Church has never felt the need of defining a truth which has always been apparent in the conscience of the faithful: only the V Lateran Council spoke up against the audacious denials of certain *neo-Aristotelians* (*DB*, 738).

Thus the immortality of the soul is a truth of faith. But it is also a truth of reason. The best of the old philosophers admitted and proved it: a famous dialogue of Plato, perhaps the most beautiful he wrote, the *Phaedon*, is also a celebrated demonstration of the immortality of the soul. The soul of its very nature is immortal; Christian philosophy and theology prove it with the following arguments:

1. The human soul is *spiritual*, as is demonstrated from the fact that its specific *operation*, intellection and volition and consequently its *being*, is independent of matter. Now, *spirit* is of its nature simple, i.e., not composed of parts, and so, not corruptible, not subject to decomposition, like matter.

2. Man naturally aspires to *immortality;* witness history and human institutions. Now, this aspiration which is rooted in the conscience of mankind cannot be a mere idle aspiration.

3. Man conceives *truth*, which is eternal, timeless, and spaceless. But he could not conceive it unless he too were of the same make-up, for there must be proportion between conceiver and conceived, between subject and object.

4. No adequate *sanction* is had in this life for man's goodness or malice. God's wisdom and justice demand such a sanction; hence, there must be another life.

BIBLIOGRAPHY

ST. THOMAS, *Summa Theol.*, I, q. 75; *Summa Contra Gentiles*, l. 2, c. 65 and 80.

Alger, *The Destiny of the Soul, A Critical History of the Doctrine of a Future Life* (New York, 1889). Coconnier, "Ame," *DA*. Maher, "Immortality," *CE*. Mercier, *Psychologie*, Vol. 2 (Louvain, 1928), p. 347 ff. Plat, *Destinée de l'homme* (Paris, 1898).

immutability. Excludes all passage or motion of being from one to another terminus; hence it is the opposite of any development or evolution. *Immanentism* and *idealism,* since they identify the world and God by reduction of both to the act of thinking, of necessity conceive God as being in continual evolution. On the contrary, divine revelation declares the absolute immutability of God in contrast to the ever becoming of the universe: "With whom there is no change, nor shadow of alteration" (James 1:17). St. Paul (Heb. 1:10) repeats the words of Psalm 101: "They [the heavens] shall perish but thou remainest: and all of them shall grow old like a garment: And as a vesture thou shalt change them, and they shall be changed. But thou art always the selfsame, and thy years shall not fail" (27–28). The IV Lateran and the Vatican Councils comment with the expression, *Deus incommutabilis* (*DB*, 428, 1782).

Reason confirms and illustrates this truth: the being that changes and develops, and thus passes from "the less" to "the more," has to be imperfect, has to be potency that becomes act, that acquires something it did not have before, something new. Now all this is opposed to the concept of being *per essentiam* (whose essence is to be) and to the concept of act, pure, simple, perfect, infinite (see *Act, Pure; simplicity of God; perfection; infinity*). Therefore, evolutionism of God is anthropomorphism, and advances the absurdity of an Infinite-Finite.

BIBLIOGRAPHY

St. Thomas, *Summa Theol.*, I, q. 9. Garrigou-Lagrange, *God: His Existence and His Nature,* trans. Rose (St. Louis, 1947–1948); *The One God,* trans. Rose (St. Louis, 1943), pp. 268–275. Pohle-Preuss, *Dogmatic Theology,* I *God: Knowability, Essence, Attributes* (St. Louis, 1946), pp. 298–305.

impanation. See *transubstantiation.*

impeccability. Impossibility, physical or moral, of sinning.

It is a doctrine of faith that Jesus Christ not only had immunity from all sin (i.e., *impeccantia* — absence of sin, *de facto*), but also impeccability in the real and true sense of the word. Jesus Christ Himself challenges His enemies with these solemn words: "Which of you shall convince me of sin?" (John 8:46.) St. Paul had proclaimed Christ: "High priest, holy, innocent, undefiled, separated from sinners" (Heb. 7:26). 1 St. Peter and 1 St. John attest categorically that in Christ there is no shadow of guilt. So, too, the Fathers, whose thought is summed up energetically by St. Cyril of Alexandria: "They are altogether stupid who say that Christ could have sinned."

The reason for Christ's impeccability is in the *hypostatic union;* the Person in Christ being only one (i.e., the Word of God), only one also is the subject to which the divine and the human actions are attributed. If, therefore, there should be even the slightest sin in Christ, it would have to be attributed to and predicated of the Word of God, which is absurd. Secondary causes of this impeccability were also the beatific vision, the fullness of grace and the supernatural gifts which enriched the soul of Jesus Christ. All things considered, the impeccability of Christ, though belonging to the moral order, has a metaphysical foundation.

Impeccability is predicated also of Mary on account of her superhuman dignity as the Mother of God, on account of her exemption from original sin and, consequently, from the foment of concupiscence, and on account of the fullness of grace with which her soul was adorned. But Mary's impeccability was not intrinsic like Jesus', but *extrinsic* rather, i.e., due to a special assistance of God. In fact, there was no sin in Mary, not even venial (Council of Trent).

BIBLIOGRAPHY

Hugon, *Le mystère de l'Incarnation* (Paris, 1931), p. 292 ff. Richard, "Impeccabilité," *DTC*. Various treatises, *De Verbo Incarnato*.

impenitence. The opposite of penance, which is a virtue inclining the free will to be sorry for the sin committed and to form the intention of never again offending God. Essentially the virtue of penance tends, as St. Thomas says (*Summa Theol.*, III, q. 85, a. 2), to the destruction of sin inasmuch as it is an offense against God. Such destruction is not physical but of the moral order, consisting in a reversal of the mind which repudiates evil by detaching itself from it and directing itself to good. In the Gospel this salutary disavowal is efficaciously expressed by the word μετάνοια — change of mind (cf. Matt. 4:17). Impenitence, on the other hand, is persistence in the state of sin and, therefore, of separation from God. This persistence may be merely a state of fact (e.g., if the sinner does not repent out of negligence), or it may be a bad disposition of the will which refuses to repent and make reparation for the offense against God.

Impenitence is distinguished into *temporary* and *final,* just as *perseverance* (*q.v.*): temporary impenitence is the persistence in sin for a certain period of one's life. If it is voluntary and malicious it constitutes a specific sin by itself, it is even a sin against the Holy Spirit (*Summa Theol.*, II–II, q. 14, a. 2). It is, therefore, of interest to the sinner and his duty to raise himself up after the fall, returning contrite and humiliated to the heart of God. Not to do so out of malicious intention constitutes an additional guilt, as has been said; to fail to do so out of neglect does not constitute a new sin, unless particular circumstances demand such repentance. Christian perfection requires that penance follow immediately after sin, but perfection is not commanded. The Church obliges all faithful to receive the sacrament of penance once a year; however, independently of such law, there is a moral obligation of repenting at least in danger of death and before receiving a sacrament of the living (as Communion, confirmation, matrimony).

Final impenitence refers to the last moment of life; it is equivalent to death in the state of sin. It can be a mere condition of fact, as in the case of a man who died in the state of sin because he had no means or time to do penance. But it is also possible that a man refuses obstinately to repent while he is living and, moreover, that he resolves not to repent even at the moment of death, refusing in advance any religious help. This would be a case of final impenitence, as a direct sin, which aggravates, before God's tribunal, the condition of the sinner hardened in his guilt.

Obduration in sin and blindness to sin, which are obstinacy in evil (removable, however, with God's grace and good will), dispose the sinner to final impenitence.

BIBLIOGRAPHY

St. Thomas, *Summa Theol.*, III, q. 85; I–II, q. 79; *Summa Contra Gentiles,* l. 3, c. 157, 160, 162. Doronzo, *De Poenitentia,* Vol. 1 (Milwaukee, 1949), Index Analyticus: "Impoenitentia." Richard, "Impénitence," *DTC*.

imposition of hands. This expression, which the Greeks translate by χειροτονία or χειροθεσία, signifies the simple and spontaneous gesture of placing the hands on the head or any other noble part (e.g., the eyes, the forehead) of a person or even of an animal (as in the Jewish ceremony of the scapegoat) for the purpose of producing an effect (e.g., a blessing, a healing), or of conferring a power. It may be said that the use of this rite is threefold: biblical, liturgical, sacramental.

In Holy Scripture, particularly in the New Testament, we find the imposition of hands often practiced by Christ, the Apostles, and the first evangelic missionaries, in order to produce a healing. In the various liturgies it is used quite frequently during the ceremonies that precede or follow the administration of certain sacraments, e.g., of baptism. In Christian antiquity it took on singular importance in the reconciliation of penitents and heretics. Probably in the sacrament of confirmation and certainly in holy orders (*qq.v.*), the χειροτονία is a constitutive and, therefore, indispensable part of the sacramental sign (*matter* of the sacrament; see *matter and form of the sacraments*).

BIBLIOGRAPHY

Coppens, *L'imposition des mains et les rites connexes dans le N.T. et dans l'Eglise ancienne* (Wetteren-Paris, 1925). De Puniet, "Confirmation," *DACL*. Doronzo, *De Baptismo et Confirmatione* (Milwaukee, 1947), Index Analyticus: "Impositio manuum"; *De Poenitentia*, Vol. 3 (Milwaukee). Galtier, "Imposition des mains," *DTC*. Morrisroe, "Imposition of hands," *CE*. Van Rossum, *De essentia sacramenti Ordinis* (Rome, 1931).

Incarnation (Gr. σάρκωσις). The word had its origin in the Prologue of St. John: *Et verbum caro factum est* — "The Word became *flesh,*" i.e., *man* (a substitution characteristic of the Semitic languages, and one used in the Bible, e.g., Gen. 6:12).

The equivalence of the two terms, *flesh* and *man,* is consecrated officially in the Nicene-Constantinopolitan Creed, which says that the Word was σαρκωθείς (incarnate) and ἐνανθρωπήσας (made man). The Incarnation is also called in Holy Scripture: *manifestation* (of God) in the flesh, *epiphany* (manifestation), *annihilation, economy.* The Incarnation is understood in two different meanings: (*a*) As a divine *action,* forming in the womb of the Virgin Mary a human nature and uniting it to and making it subsist in the Person of the Word. This *action* is common to the three divine Persons, since it is an action *ad extra.* (*b*) As the *term* of that divine action; it is the mysterious union of the divine nature and of the human nature in the Person of the Word. The incarnate Word is Jesus Christ.

Necessity: The Incarnation was not *absolutely* necessary, because God could have repaired in various other ways the ruin caused by Adam's sin. But it was *hypothetically* necessary, i.e., the supposition granted that God demanded a reparation according to the requirements of justice. That God actually did so demand is implicit in the sources of revelation. Therefore, since no creature could repair an offense against God, being morally *infinite,* a Man-God was necessary, who is capable of dying and of offering an infinite reparation.

Purpose: The theological schools are not in agreement. The Scotists hold that God willed the Incarnation for itself and independently of Adam's sin, and that the Word would therefore have become incarnate even if Adam had not sinned. The Thomists, on the contrary, teach that the Incarnation was ordered or directed to the Redemption as to its principal end; if, therefore, original sin had not been committed, the Word would not have become incarnate, in the present order of the world established by divine providence.

The first opinion seems attractive in a way, but only the second is based on the documents of revelation, which are decisive when it comes to events depending on God's free choice. The sense of these documents is summarized in the following words of the Creed, frequently repeated by the Church in the liturgy of the Mass: *Qui [Verbum] propter nos homines et propter nostram salutem descendit de coelis et incarnatus est* ("on account of us and for our salvation, came down from heaven and became incarnate").

BIBLIOGRAPHY

St. Thomas, *Summa Theol.,* III, q. 1. Arendzen, *Whom Do You Say? A Study in the Doctrine of the Incarnation* (London, 1927). Drum, "Incarnation," *CE.* Freddi, Sullivan, *Jesus Christ the Word Incarnate* (St. Louis, 1904). Hugon, *Le mystère de l'Incarnation* (Paris, 1913). Michel, "Incarnation," *DTC.* Scheeben, *The Mysteries of Christianity,* trans. Vollert (St. Louis, 1946), pp. 313–404. Various treatises *De Verbo Incarnato,* e.g., Billot, Van Noort, D'Alès, Peter Parente.

incorporation, mystical. See *Mystical Body.*

indefectibility (of the Church). That prerogative of the Church in virtue of which it will endure to the end of time, keeping inviolate the deposit transmitted to it by its divine Spouse (therefore, it implies also infallibility). This prerogative, too, flows from the very nature and purpose of the Church; since, in fact, the Church is to take over and continue Christ's work, it must last as long as there is a soul to be saved on earth. Moreover, the Saviour has explicitly promised: "Behold I am with you all days, even to the consummation of the world . . . and the gates of hell shall not prevail against it [the Church]" (Matt. 28:20; 16:18). St. Ambrose, echoing Christ's words, compares the Church to a ship "which is continually buffeted by high seas and storms, but which can never be sunk because its main mast is Christ's cross, its skipper is the Father, its prow keeper is the Holy Spirit, its rowers are the Apostles" (*Liber de Salomone,* Ch. 4).

History has fulfilled the divine promise. Each age has put to the test the stability of the Church: the persecutions of the first centuries, the Trinitarian and Christological heresies from the fourth to the eighth centuries, schism in the East and Nicholaism in the West, the pope-emperor struggle of the Middle Ages, the Reformation, and the French Revolution — all these storms have buffeted the temple of God, which has remained immovable in the midst of crumbling empires, institutions and civilizations, that had seemed to defy the ravages of time. *Stat crux dum volvitur orbis.*

The Vatican Council affirmed, therefore, that "the unconquered stability of the Church is a great and perennial motive of credibility and an irrefutable testimony of its divine mission, whereby like a sign lifted among the peoples (Isa. 11:12), it invites the infidels to itself and assures its sons that the faith they profess is based on the most solid foundation" (*DB,* 1794).

BIBLIOGRAPHY

Mazzella, *De Ecclesia,* n. 738 ff. Tanquerey, *De Ecclesia,* n. 105. Other treatises *De Ecclesia.*

"Index" (of prohibited books). An official list of books prohibited by the Church as erroneous or dangerous in matters of faith or morals. From the first centuries the Church has always been on the alert against the circulation of writings that might endanger in any way the salvation of souls. Suffice it to recall, e.g., the *Gelasian Decree* (496), by which certain books of a religious content were denounced and prohibited. But the discovery of printing compelled the Church to even stricter vigilance. Paul IV is the author of the *first official Index* (1557 and 1559), to which the Council of Trent added a preface of guiding principles and rules, sanctioned by Pius IV (1564). Gradually the *Index* was amended, extended, and brought up to date by Popes Clement VIII, Alexander VII, and Benedict XIV. It underwent an integral and quasidefinitive systemization in the *Index of Leo XIII,* with the Constitution *Officiorum ac munerum* (1896), and the annexed *Decreta Generalia.* In 1910 the official *Index* appeared in an edition brought up to date, which was re-edited in 1929 and 1938.

Paul IV had instituted also a *Congregatio Indicis* (Congregation of the Index) with the function of watching over the press; under Benedict XV, this congregation was completely absorbed by the Holy Office (1917), which has a Section for the Censorship of Books, to which matters regarding the *Index* are entrusted. A book may be placed on the *Index* either by virtue of an apostolic letter or of a simple decree of the Holy Office. This insertion prohibits to all the faithful: publication or reprinting (without authorization) of the book, reading of it, possession, sale, translation, communication to others of its contents. Those who read or keep with them books expressly prohibited by apostolic letter incur excommunication reserved in *a special way* to the Holy See (*CIC,* Can. 2318).

The Church has the right and the duty to prohibit those books which can do harm to souls, as is obvious from her divine mission. Nor is this prohibition injurious to freedom, but is rather a valid help of this most noble human faculty, directing it to good, which is its natural object, and preserving it from evil, its ruin. Even civil governments adopt at times press censorship.

As regards books prohibited even independently of the *Index,* see *CIC,* Canons 1385–1405. The faithful who must read prohibited books for reasons of research can obtain permission from the Holy Office.

BIBLIOGRAPHY

Forget, "Index," *DA.* Leo XIII, Constit. Apost., *Officiorum ac munerum* (Feb., 1896). Ojetti, "Roman Congregations (VII)," *CE.* Périès, *L'Index* (Paris, 1898). Teouvenin, "Index," *DTC.*

indifferentism. Systematic attitude toward the various forms of religion, for which no interest is shown (*negative indifferentism*) or which are held to have all the same value (*positive indifferentism*). The position that all religions are false is called *irreligious indifferentism;* the belief that all religions are good and useful for this life and the next is termed *religious indifferentism.* A particular form of this tendency is known as social-political indifferentism, characteristic of liberalism (*q.v.*), which leaves the religious question to the individual conscience and holds that society and the State should be nonconfessional (nondenominational, nonsectarian), i.e., without any religion, and grant full liberty and equality of treatment to all kinds of cult.

In the eighteenth century, Illuminism (*q.v.*), putting aside divine revelation and reducing religious doctrine and practice to a few rational principles, inaugurated *naturalistic religious indifferentism* (akin to deism), which spread extensively in the past century with the help of the autonomous moralism of Kant. From the breakdown of Protestantism into hundreds of different sects there arose, on the other hand, a sort of *supernaturalistic indifferentism,* which judges equally useful for eternal salvation all the Christian religious forms that lay claim to divine revelation. Recently the Protestants attempted to unite all their sects in a common religious entity of minimum content, and invited even the Catholic Church into this hybrid union!

Negative indifferentism is detestable because it denies the supreme end of life to which religion is directed.

Positive indifferentism is irreligious and impious; socio-political indifferentism is illogical and unjust, because without examination of the value of the various religions it relegates them all to the same treatment, and because it offends the consciences of the citizens by taking no interest in the religious factor.

Supernaturalistic indifferentism is absurd, because by giving the same value to conflicting religions it puts God, who would be the Revealer of them, in contradiction with Himself.

The conclusion is that the religious problem is of great individual and social interest, hence, it must be attentively examined psychologically and historically in order to come to a selection of what is true from what is false, and to adhere to that one religion which offers the soundest guarantees of truth and supernaturality.

The Church has condemned the various forms of indifferentism (cf. especially the *Syllabus,* Nos. 15–18, *DB,* 1715 ff.).

BIBLIOGRAPHY

Balfour, *The Foundation of Belief* (London, 1895). Calvet, *Le problème catholique de l'union des Eglises* (Paris, 1921). Fox, "Indifferentism," *CE.* Hoffman, *Origins and Development of Secularism* (New York, 1940). Michelet, *Dieu et l'agnosticisme contemporain* (Paris, 1909). McLaughlin, *Is One Religion As Good As Another?* (London, 1891). Newman, "The Difficulties of Latitudinarism," *Tracts for the Times,* Vol. 5, n. 85. Richard, "Indifférence religieuse," *DTC.* Schanz, *A Christian Apology* (New York, 1891).

See under *liberalism.*

indissolubility. See *divorce.*

indulgences. In Imperial documents of the Christian epoch (cf. Codices of Theodosius and of Justinian) indulgence meant *amnesty* or condonation of penalty. Since the IV Lateran Council (1215), the Church has used indulgence in the sense of the remission of penalty due for sin after the guilt of sin has been remitted.

The precise concept of indulgence has been fixed by the *Code of Canon Law* in these terms (Can. 911): "A remission, before God, of the *temporal punishment* due for sins already remitted with respect to their *guilt,* which the ecclesiastical authority, drawing from the *treasure* of the Church, grants to the living after the manner of *absolution,* and to the dead after the manner of *suffrage.*" An indulgence is, therefore, a payment for the penal obligations of sinners made before God out of what may be likened to a public treasury, namely: the Church treasury (infinite merits of Christ, merits of the Blessed Virgin and of the saints).

The indulgence is an *extrasacramental* act and, as such, belongs exclusively to the *jurisdictional* power (pope and bishops), which, for a *just cause,* may grant to the faithful, on determined *conditions,* the benefits of the treasury of the Church, by way of a *partial* or *total* condonation of the *temporal* punishment due for sins already remitted (as to guilt), a punishment for which the Christian would have to give satisfaction either in this life with good works or in purgatory for a determined time. The Church customarily attaches indulgences to various good works (prayers, pilgrimages, almsgiving), which are not *causes,* but mere *conditions* of the fruit of the indulgence. For the souls in purgatory, indulgence works *per modum suffragii,* in the sense that, since the Church does not have jurisdiction outside of this world, it presents to God the merits of Christ in order that in view of them God may condone their penalty. The exercise of the Church's power is *direct* in the case of the living, *indirect* in behalf of the dead. Such power is based on these dogmatic foundations: (*a*) the Communion of Saints (*q.v.*), which makes possible the interchange of spiritual merits and goods among the members of the Mystical Body of Christ; (*b*) The "power of the keys" granted to Peter and his successors, through which the Roman pontiff, and, subordinately, the bishops, can draw from the infinite treasury of the Church, and apply its goods to souls, efficaciously in the sight of God.

In the course of the centuries, many were the abuses and misunderstandings in the matter of indulgences, but the Church has always deplored and condemned them.

BIBLIOGRAPHY

St. Thomas, *Summa Theol.,* III, *Suppl.,* qq. 25–27. Donelan, *Treasury of Indulgences* (London, 1921). Galtier, "Indulgences," *DA.* Hedley, *The Catholic Doctrine of Indulgences* (San Francisco). Kent, "Indulgences," *CE.* Lépicier, *Indulgences, Their Origin, Nature and Development* (London, 1895). Magnin, "Indulgences," *DTC.* Nicolaus Paulus, a specialist in the field, wrote several important articles in German reviews (1898 ff.), particularly in *Zeitschrift für katholische Theologie.* Pohle-Preuss, *Dogmatic Theology,* X *The Sacraments,* Vol. 3, *Penance* (St. Louis, 1946), pp. 232–264. Pope, *The Doctrine of the Catholic Church Touching Indulgences* (London, 1915). *The Teaching of the Catholic Church,* ed. Smith, 2 vols. (New York, 1949), pp. 976–980. The Catholic doctrine on indulgences was particularly attacked by H. Ch. Lea, *A History of Auricular Confession and Indulgences,* 3 vols. (Philadelphia, 1896). The third volume deals with indulgences.

indwelling of the Holy Trinity. By virtue of sanctifying grace all the Trinity comes to dwell in the soul of the just. This indwelling, attested to by the Gospel, is connected with an invisible divine mission (see *mission, divine*) and does not present difficulties, but is rather in full harmony with that theological principle according to which God is present where He acts and more intimately present where He acts more intensely (see *presence of God*). But in the seventeenth century a controversy was kindled on account of an opinion of Petavius, followed by Thomassin. These theologians thought that sanctifying indwelling should be attributed to the Holy Ghost, as something proper to the third divine Person which, in a manner analogous to the hypostatic union of the Word, unites itself ineffably and personally to the soul of the just. Not a few modern theologians have adopted this opinion. However, it involves serious difficulties. Indeed, grace which constitutes the title of indwelling is the effect of an *ad extra* operation (see *operation, divine*), and therefore it belongs equally to the three Persons. Hence, one cannot see how indwelling can be proper to the Holy Spirit. Moreover, the traditional doctrine does not recognize any hypostatic union except that of the Word.

However, it must be recognized that the work of sanctification (and, therefore, inhabitation or indwelling), being a work of love, *refers* more remarkably to the Holy Spirit (at least in the line of *exemplary causality*) than to the Father and the Son. But this reference may well be reduced to a simple *appropriation* (*q.v.*), without going so far as to call indwelling a *personal property* of the Holy Spirit. It is to be noted that Petavius and those who follow him say that the union of the sanctified soul is with the Person and not in the Person of the Holy Spirit.

Recently, profound studies have been made on the manner or mode in which God dwells in the soul, with the result that a *subjective* presence of God (God as agent) is distinguished from an *objective* presence of God (God as known and loved) which a few theologians understand to be no less than a mystical experience of the Divinity.

BIBLIOGRAPHY

St. Thomas, *Summa Theol.*, I, q. 43, a. 3 and 6. Froget, *The Indwelling of the Holy Spirit,* trans. Raemers (New York, 1921). Galtier, *L'habitation en nous des trois personnes* (Paris, 1950). Michel, "Trinité (Missions et Habitation des Personnes de la Trinité)," *DTC,* cols. 1830–1855. Retailleau, *La Sainte Trinité dans les justes* (Angers, 1932).

inerrancy of the Bible. The immunity from all possibility of error and from all error *de facto,* which belongs to the Holy Scriptures by virtue of their divine inspiration. St. John affirms: "The Scripture cannot be broken [contradict itself]" (10:35), and Christian antiquity, despite its various exegetical tendencies, has always unanimously maintained the inerrancy of the sacred texts.

Leo XIII, in his encyclical *Providentissimus Deus,* affirmed: "So true is it that no error may lurk under inspiration, that inspiration not only excludes every error, but it is necessary that it exclude and repel every error, as it is necessary that God, the Supreme Truth, be not the Author of any error" (*EB,* 109).

Inerrancy of the Holy Scripture is a dogma of faith (cf. *EB,* 433).

BIBLIOGRAPHY

Bea, *De S. Scripturae Inspiratione* (Rome, 1925), nn. 73–98. Durand, "Inerrance biblique," *DA.* Florit, *Ispirazione e inerranza biblica* (Rome, 1943). Mangenot, "Inspiration de l'Ecriture," *DTC,* cols. 2207–2266. Pesch, *De Inspiratione S. Scripturae* (Freiburg i.-Br., 1906), nn. 346–372; Suppl., nn. 13–68.

infallibility of the pope. That dogma "which teaches as divinely revealed truth that the Roman pontiff when speaking *ex cathedra* — namely: when, as pastor and teacher of all Christians, by virtue of his supreme, apostolic authority, defines that a teaching regarding faith and morals must be held true by the universal Church — enjoys, through the divine assistance promised to him in the Blessed Peter, that same infallibility with which the divine Redeemer has willed His Church to be endowed. . . . Therefore, the definitions of the Roman pontiff are of themselves [*ex sese*] and not through the consent of the Church, irreformable" (*DB,* 1839).

This definition of the Vatican Council clearly determines the nature, the conditions, the object, and the subject of that high pontifical prerogative. Infallibility implies neither inspiration nor revelation (*qq.v.*), but a *divine assistance* which preserves the pope from error in his *ex cathedra* definitions. Although enjoying such a privilege, the holy pontiff is not thereby dispensed from preparatory studies, research, and prayer, which dispose him for the prudent exercise of his office of universal teacher of the Church.

In the phrase *ex cathedra* the *conditions* of infallibility are determined, namely: (1) that the pope speak as pastor and teacher of the whole Church — excluding therefore from the sphere of infallibility what he may propose as a private teacher, even were he to act as a teacher of theology or to write religious books; (2) that he manifest in some way, especially by the tenor of his words and the circumstances chosen for their pronouncement (as happened in 1854 in the definition of the dogma of the Immaculate Conception) his *intention* of proposing, as a dogma, to all the Church (even if materially he should address someone in particular) some truth *contained* in the deposit of revelation; the discourses and exhortations, which he addresses to the faithful and to pilgrims are not, therefore, within the scope of infallibility.

The *objects* of infallibility are exclusively, therefore, doctrines which concern faith and morals, or which are intimately connected therewith.

These requisites verified, the pope enjoys that same infallibility which Christ conferred on His Church. Are there perhaps two infallibilities? No! Only one is the infallibility given by Christ to His Church, i.e., that same infallibility conferred on Peter and his successors, which is said to be given to the Church because it was bestowed for the good of the Church and is exercised by its head. As man's life is one but derives from the soul and is diffused through all the body, so infallibility is diffused and circulates in the whole Church, both in the teaching Church (active infallibility) and in the learning Church (passive infallibility), but dependently on the head, who can exercise it by himself (*ex sese*) in such a way that his definitions are irreformable, i.e., not subject to correction, even without the consent of the Church (against the Gallicans). Often, however, the pope exercises his infallibility through those great assemblies of bishops, called the ecumenical councils (*q.v.*). Such prerogative of the pope is based on the most explicit promise of the Lord (Luke 22:31–32) and on the clearest testimonies of Tradition from St. Irenaeus of Lyons to St. Augustine, from St. Innocent I to St. Leo the Great. All the Vatican Council did was to recapitulate 18 centuries of lived history.

BIBLIOGRAPHY

St. Thomas, *Quodlibetum 9,* q. 7, a. 16. Dublanchy, "Infaillibilité du Pape," *DTC.* Gibbons, *Faith of Our Fathers* (Baltimore, 1890). Rivington, *The See of Peter* (London, 1894). Toner, "Infallibility," *CE.* Various treatises *De Ecclesia* and *De Romano Pontifice,* mentioned under *Church* and *Roman pontiff.*

infants. See *babies deceased without baptism.*

infidels. According to the obvious meaning of the word, *infidel* is one who has not faith (morally speaking, is one who does not stand by his promises, his obligations, his duties). Faith (*q.v.*), understood theologically as adherence of the intellect to the truths revealed by God, may be lacking through the fault or without the fault of the individual. We distinguish, therefore: (*a*) the *positive* infidel, who refuses assent to revealed truth proposed as such with sufficient evidence; (*b*) *negative* infidel, who does not have any knowledge at all of divine revelation, and so has not the means of exercising an act of faith. The infidel properly so called, either positive or negative, is the *nonbaptized* person. But the name is at times extended to include the baptized fallen into heresy (*q.v.*), which is the denial of some truth of faith defined by the Church, or the baptized fallen into *apostasy,* which is the abandonment of the whole doctrine of faith. The positive infidel, the heretic, and the apostate, being in *bad faith,* voluntarily shut off from themselves the way of salvation. But those who are born in heresy and are in good faith (*material,* not *formal* heretics) may be saved by the action of divine grace, although they are not incorporated in the Catholic Church.

The gravest problem is the salvation of the infidels who, without guilt, are ignorant of divine revelation, and thus of Jesus Christ and His Church. Without revelation faith is impossible, and without faith salvation is impossible (St. Paul and the Council of Trent). And the traditional adage still aggravates the situation: *Extra Ecclesiam nulla salus* ("Outside the Church, no salvation"). The theologians try to solve the problem in various ways: (1) God wants all to be saved (1 Tim. 2:4 ff.) and so gives to all the means and the grace sufficient for them to be saved, even outside the Church, when they are ignorant of its existence. (2) God can bring to the infidel some trace or spark of revelation to make it possible for them, under the impulse of grace, to make an act of faith, as a starting point in their salvation. (3) Whoever, under the divine influence, makes an act of faith and then attains sanctification by adhering to God and His will, does already belong in some way to the Church. Since he has an *implicit* desire of baptism, he belongs to the Church *in voto*. (4) The infidel who would die with only original sin, and without any personal sins, would go to limbo and not to hell.

At any rate, salvation is more difficult for an infidel than for a Christian. Hence the importance and the necessity of the missions.

BIBLIOGRAPHY

BAINVEL, *Is There Salvation Outside the Catholic Church?*, trans. Weidenhan (St. Louis, 1917). BOUDINHON, "Infidels," *CE*. CAPERAN, *Le problème du salut des infidèles* (Toulouse, 1934). FISCHER, *De salute infidelium* (Essen, 1886). HUGON, *Hors de l'Eglise, point de salut* (Paris, 1927). LOMBARDI, *La salvezza di chi non ha la fede* (Rome, 1943). MARTINDALE, "Paganism," *CE*.

infinity. The absence of limits or terms. Such indetermination may be taken in two senses: (*a*) as the *privation* of a determination that a thing should have naturally; e.g., prime matter, devoid of any form; (*b*) as the *negation* of a determination which a thing neither has nor requires, e.g., a form without matter. Evidently, the privative infinite implies imperfection, while the negative infinite involves real and true perfection, on which account it may also be called *positive:* it excludes limits because it implies fullness. Act and form, negatively and positively infinite of themselves, are limited by potency and matter in which they are received, and so their infinity is only *relative,* because circumscribed by a genus or a species; if, however, an act transcends all genera and species, as *being* does, then it is the *absolute* infinite. Only God is such, because only God is essentially *Being,* subsisting Being Itself (see *essence, divine*). This positive and absolute infinity of God does not exclude, however, His *determinateness* or concreteness, which implies personal distinction, not limitation.

From the divine infinity there derive two other attributes: *immensity* and *ubiquity*. God is immense because infinity excludes all limits and measurements; hence God is everywhere and no creature can escape His presence. The formal reason of this ubiquity (omnipresence) is the action that God exercises on the universe to maintain it in being and move it to its multifarious operation. Thus is solved the question of the relationship between the finite and the Infinite without falling into pantheism: In a certain sense God is immanent in the world, and the world in God, but without confusion, the distinction between one and the other remaining, as between cause and effect.

BIBLIOGRAPHY

ST. THOMAS, *Summa Theol.,* I, qq. 7–8. FULLERTON, *The Conception of the Infinite* (Philadelphia, 1887). GARRIGOU-LAGRANGE, *God: His Existence and His Nature,* trans. Rose (St. Louis, 1947–1948); *The One God,* trans. Rose (St. Louis, 1943), pp. 236–252. Sertillanges, *St. Thomas d'Aquin,* Vol. I (Paris, 1935), p. 193 ff. *The Teaching of the Catholic Church,* ed. Smith, 2 vols. (New York, 1949), pp. 88–91. Zimmerman, "Infinity," *CE.*

influence, divine. See *concourse, divine.*

infusion. See *baptism.*

"Ingenitus" (Ingenerate, Unborn). See *Father.*

innocence (state of). The condition in which God placed Adam and Eve as soon as He created them. This state, called also *original justice,* implies sanctifying grace with the respective infused virtues and gifts (*supernatural* order), as well as certain privileges integrative of human nature (*preternatural* order). The state of innocence is entirely a gratuitous gift of God, to which man had no right and no active capacity (see *obediential potency*). God could have left man in the state of *pure nature,* i.e., of nature in its own proper order and condition, with its final destination to a natural end. In the state of innocence, the body and the sensitive life (passions) were subject to reason through means of the gift of *integrity* (*q.v.*); the soul was subject and united to God, by the supernatural gift of *grace,* which made man fully holy and just. Sin, therefore, in our first parents was difficult, but not impossible, because they were not confirmed in grace nor did they, like the blessed in heaven, see God directly in His essence. Our first parents sinned in fact, and their sin was proportionally as great as the light and the grace they enjoyed.

Admitting, as revelation demands, the fact of primitive innocence or original justice, the theologians discuss the essence of this justice; some think it adequately distinct from grace and reducible, as St. Anselm says, to a *natural rectitude* of the will. But the best opinion is that of St. Thomas, who rightly maintains that: (*a*) original justice is a gratuitous gift added to human nature by the divine liberality; (*b*) this justice implies perfect subjection of the soul to God through sanctifying *grace,* which is the *formal* element of the justice itself; in addition, it implies subjection of the passions, especially of concupiscence, by means of the gift of *integrity,* which is its *material* element; (*c*) grace is the cause and root of both subjections.

BIBLIOGRAPHY

St. Thomas, *Summa Theol.,* I, q. 95, a. 1; *Comment. In 2 Sent.,* dist. 32, q. 1, a. 1, ad 1. Kors, *La justice primitive et le péché originel d'après St. Thomas* (Paris, 1930). Michel, "Justice originelle," *DTC.* Peter Parente, *De creatione universali* (Rome, 1943), p. 190. Scheeben, *The Mysteries of Christianity,* trans. Vollert (St. Louis, 1946), pp. 201–239.

Inquisition (Latin *inquisitio* — inquiry, search, investigation). *Juridically,* it refers to a new procedure introduced in the beginning of the thirteenth century. According to Roman law, all the acts of a criminal trial were completely public; the Church held to this principle throughout the twelfth century. It was Innocent III († 1216) who, observing that public prosecutions had become weak and gave an easy opening to cruel vengeances, established that some acts of the canonical procedure should be carried out in secret. To these procedural acts the name "inquisition" was given.

Historically, it indicates the famous tribunal instituted by Gregory IX, about 1231, in which a special judge called *inquisitor haereticae pravitatis* (inquisitor of heretical crime) functioned, distinguished from ordinary judges by the following characteristics: (*a*) he enjoyed a jurisdiction which was variable as to territory, and limited, as regards matter, to cases of obstinate heresy only; (*b*) he had a permanent pontifical delegation; (*c*) such delegation, however, did not annul the ordinary jurisdiction of the bishops over the same matter. The inquisitor and the bishop were two parallel judges in questions concerning heresy.

The *specific character* of the inquisitorial trial was not constituted by the crime, or the procedure, or the torture, or the penalty (death by burning at the stake) — elements all more or less common to all civil and ecclesiastical trials of the time, but by the fact that the inquisitor was an exceptional judge, although having a permanent delegation.

The *motive* that induced the Pope to create this exceptional court was the religious policy of Frederick II who, before Philip the Fair, attempted to usurp the rights of the Church, making himself an arbitrary judge of heretics. Gregory IX, with the new tribunal, determined the limits of imperial competency in religious matters and introduced a sharp division between the responsibilities of Church and State.

The *procedure* of the Inquisition manifests its intimate nature: as soon as the inquisitor had assumed his office he published a *time of grace,* consisting in a preaching period that lasted one month. The guilty who confessed were, in exchange for their promise and guarantee to renounce heresy, free from all further prosecution.

The *charges* against heretics were briefed and then communicated to the accused, without the names of the witnesses — to avoid reprisal. The accused was invited to *defend himself personally,* but could not use an attorney (in deference to the preceding law which prohibited attorneys to defend the causes of heretics); but he had the right of *appeal to the pope,* which was a real escape valve!

The *penalties* were most varied. The gravest was excommunication (separation from the body of the Church) and consequent handing over to the secular arm, which nearly always meant death by burning at the stake; the secular power condemned the heretic on its own authority, considering him as a criminal who, by the profession of false theories, was trying to sever the religious unity of the State and so disturb the public order. The Inquisition functioned as described up to 1542, when Paul III, with the spread of Protestantism, reorganized the ancient institution and centralized everything in Rome (*Roman Inquisition*) establishing new inquisitors who had the right to decide *in propria instantia* all appeals against the procedure of the delegates.

Altogether different was the *Spanish Inquisition* instituted at the request of Ferdinand and Isabel by Sixtus IV (1478) to proceed juridically against apostates (Hebrews, baptized and recidivist). It quickly became a political instrument in the hands of the Spanish kings. There have been enormous exaggerations in the attribution to this tribunal of crimes and misdeeds for which, even were they true, the Church could not be blamed. Too easily forgotten is the fact that, thanks to the Spanish Inquisition, Spain was first freed from internal enemies of her faith and then preserved from the invasion of Protestantism. Moreover, as Landrieux rightly remarks, however grave the excesses of the Spanish Inquisition are painted, they are nothing in comparison to the ferocious persecutions and the orgies of cruelty which Luther unleashed in Germany, and, after him and because of him, Calvin at Geneva, Henry VIII and Elizabeth in England, Christian II in Denmark, Gustaf Wasa in Sweden, Jeanne d'Albret in Navarre, and the Huguenots and Jacobins in France. On this point the incomparable apologist, Joseph de Maistre, has cleverly ridiculed Voltaire, in his fourth letter on the Inquisition.

BIBLIOGRAPHY

Blötzer, "Inquisition," *CE*. Douais, *L'Inquisition* (Paris, 1906). Giraud, *Histoire de l'Inquisition,* 2 vols. (Paris, 1940–1941). Guraud, "Inquisition," *DA*. Maycock, *The Inquisition* (London, 1928). Rodrigo, *Historia verdadera de la Inquisición,* 3 vols. (Madrid, 1876–1877). Vacandard, *L'Inquisition. Etude historique et critique sur le pouvoir coercitif de l'Eglise* (Paris, 1907); "Inquisition," *DTC*. The Inquisition as an institution of the Catholic Church was particularly attacked by H. Ch. Lea, *A History of the Inquisition in the Middle Ages,* 3 vols. (New York, 1888); *History of the Inquisition in Spain,* 4 vols. (London, New York, 1906–1907).

inspiration (Latin *inspirare*—breathe into; infuse, in a figurative sense, said especially of sentiment). In the ecclesiastical sense inspiration is, in general, an influence or motion of God in the soul, and, more strictly, in the will. But the theologians usually indicate by this term a charismatic impulse that moves men to communicate to others what God wishes them to communicate. When the communication is oral, we have prophetic inspiration; when it is written, hagiographic or biblical inspiration. St. Paul (2 Tim. 3:16–17) affirms that "All the Scripture [is] inspired by God," and St. Peter (2 Pet. 1:21) points out the nature of such inspiration: "The holy men of God spoke, inspired by the Holy Ghost."

Leo XIII, in his great encyclical on biblical studies, *Providentissimus Deus* (Nov. 18, 1893), defined inspiration: "A supernatural action through means of which God excited and moved the Sacred Writers to write, and assisted them in writing, in such a way that they would conceive rightly in their thought, they would want to write faithfully, and they would express appropriately and with infallible truth all that He wanted them to express" (*EB,* 110).

According to the constant and explicit declaration of the sources of revelation, God is the Author of the Holy Scriptures. He is not, however, the only and direct author, as if He had produced the holy books as they are, but He is the *principal Author,* on whom goes back all the responsibility for the books; however, for their compilation and editing God used men, who are the *secondary and instrumental authors*. But since man is not a blind, but a conscious and free instrument, he puts in his own proper action, which is manifested in the external form of the writing of the book. In this way we speak of the style of Isaias, Jeremias, Matthew, Paul, etc.

The inspirative action of God in man includes: (*a*) an *enlightening of the mind,* by which the sacred author perceives correctly what he is to write and judges infallibly its truth or falsity; (*b*) a *movement of the will,* by which God influences the hagiographer to decide to write what he has conceived and judged; (*c*) *assistance of the executive faculties* in order that, in the choice of words and expressions, the hagiographers be protected against errors or deviations that could compromise the manifestation of the divine thought.

It should be noted that God's action on the hagiographer's mind is not a revelation proper, because the hagiographer can have information of his own, deriving, e.g., from direct participation in the events he narrates, or acquired in advance through divine intervention. Revelation, however, is necessary when man must communicate for God truths of the supernatural order, of which the knowledge surpasses his human intellectual possibilities.

God's inspirative influence is not necessarily perceived by the inspired author, since God acts in rational creatures without doing any violence to their nature.

The solemn Church *magisterium* in the Councils of Florence, Trent, and Vatican has defined the inspiration of the Bible as a dogma of faith.

BIBLIOGRAPHY

Bea, *De Inspiratione S. Scripturae* (Rome, 1935). Cotter, *Theologia Fundamentalis* (Weston, 1940), pp. 581–634. Durand, "Inspiration de la Bible," *DA;* "Inspiration," *CE.* Florit, *Ispirazione e inerranza biblica* (Rome, 1943). Lusseau, *Essai sur la nature de l'inspiration scripturaire* (Paris, 1930). Mangenot, "Inspiration de l'Ecriture," *DTC.* Pesch, *De Inspiratione Scripturae* (Freiburg i.-Br., 1906); with the Supplementum (1926). Steinmueller, *A Companion to the Scripture Studies,* Vol. 1 (New York, 1941), pp. 6–43.

integrity (gift and state). A property of every being inasmuch as it has all that its specific nature requires. From this *natural* integrity is distinguished a *preternatural* integrity that God added to the natural perfection of Adam. In this sense integrity is a gratuitous gift of God, and establishes man in the *state of integrity* by which nature, in addition to its properties, is enriched with privileges that complete and elevate its perfection. These privileges are reduced to three: (1) immunity from *concupiscence* (*q.v.*), i.e., from the disorderly inclinations of the sense appetite; (2) *immortality* of the body as well as immunity from sickness and other sufferings; (3) *infused knowledge,* proportionate to the ordinary life of man.

The first privilege is attested to by Holy Scripture, which tells us that our first parents were both naked and did not blush, but as soon as they sinned they realized they were nude and tried to hide and cover themselves. Psychologically speaking, blushing on account of nudity is provoked by the insolence of the senses, which man is no longer capable of controlling and dominating. The second privilege is implicitly contained in the divine threat: "In what day soever thou shalt eat of it, thou shalt die the death" (Gen. 2:17). Actually Adam did not die when he sinned; the sense, then, of the divine words are: "You will become mortal," as, moreover, St. Paul explains: "By one man sin entered into this world, and by sin death" (Rom. 5:12). Death is a natural law for all bodies, but God had established exemption from death for the human body: with sin the natural law comes back into play, with the addition of a penal or punitive character. The third privilege is dimly alluded to when Holy Scripture says that Adam, hardly issued from God's hands, was able to give appropriate names to all the animals and to determine the intimate nature of matrimony (Gen. 2:19). This could not be an acquired knowledge, and, therefore, it was infused by God (cf. Ecclus. 17:5).

The first two privileges belong to the defined doctrine of faith (Council of Trent, *DB,* 792 and 788).

BIBLIOGRAPHY

St. Thomas, *Summa Theol.,* I, qq. 94, 95, 97. Boyer, *De Deo creante et elevante* (Rome, 1940), p. 275 ff. Peter Parente, *De creatione universali* (Rome, 1943), p. 185 ff.

intellect. See *gifts of the Holy Ghost.*

intellectualism. Holding to the obvious sense of the word, we would understand it as a system in which the intellect predominates, just as in *voluntarism* (*q.v.*) the value and function of the will are stressed. But the vicissitudes of history have rendered the meaning of the word *intellectualism* equivocal. Subtleties aside, we can say that there is a heterodox and an orthodox intellectualism from a philosophico-theological viewpoint. Thomistic-Aristotelian philosophy is the orthodox intellectualism, affirming the primacy of the intellect and defending the capacity of human reason — however subordinate to faith — both in the field of natural truth and also in the supernatural order as regards the intelligibility and illustration of dogma and hence the value of the dogmatic formulas by which revealed truths are expressed. All the scientific elaboration of theology (*q.v.*) around the data of revelation is the proof that justifies that intellectualism which has been accepted into the bosom of the Church.

There is, however, an exaggerated and heterodox intellectualism that subordinates everything to human reason of which it proclaims the full sufficiency and absolute domain, even with respect to supernatural facts and truths. Intellectualism so understood coincides with rationalism (*q.v.*), and the Church rightly condemns it, assigning certain limits to the capacity of reason, as when the Vatican Council defines the moral necessity of divine revelation for the knowledge of the sum total of ethico-religious truths (of the natural order) capable of decisively orienting human life toward the supreme end. Likewise the Church has condemned (Encycl., *Pascendi, DB,* 2071 ff.) the modernists (*q.v.*), who, adhering to anti-intellectualistic and agnostic systems, undervalue reason and its argumentations, and adopt in its stead the sentimental movements of subconscious *religious experience* (see *experience, religious*).

Between the two extremes, absolute rationalism and agnosticism, there is a gradation of systems oscillating between the primacy of the *intellect* and the primacy of the *will.* The Church leaves this middle zone to free discussion (*Thomism-Scotism*), so long as neither faculty is excluded, but merely stressed at the expense of the other. It is undeniable, however, that Thomistic intellectualism is the Church's favorite, as is clearly shown in official documents (cf. Leo XIII, Encycl., *Aeterni Patris;* Pius X, *Motu proprio, Doctoris Angelici; CIC,* Cans. 589, 1366; Pius XI, Encycl., *Studiorum ducem,* etc.).

BIBLIOGRAPHY

GARRIGOU-LAGRANGE, *Le sens commun* (Paris, 1922). ROUSSELOT, *L'intellectualisme de Saint Thomas* (Paris, 1908); "Intellectualisme," *DA.*

intention (of the minister of the sacraments). In general, an act of the will by which one determines to do something: in the case of the minister, the will to administer the sacrament.

The minister, being human, is a *free instrument,* and that is the real reason why his *intention,* at least *virtual,* to act as the representative of Christ in the administration of the sacrament, is absolutely necessary — whereas the moral dispositions (faith and the state of grace) are not required — in order that the sacrament produce the grace. It depends, in fact, on the free act of will of the animated agent, as man is, that in each and all cases he commit himself as an instrument in the hands of Christ. Besides, only the intention of acting ministerially can determine *ad unum* the sacramental meaning of the external rite, susceptible *per se* of multiple significations.

The Council of Trent in defining against Luther and Calvin the necessity of intention in the minister (*DB,* 854) determines also its object: *faciendi quod facit Ecclesia* ("The minister must intend to do what the Church does"). In this expression, which sums up and sanctions a century-old theological formula, is indicated the relationship of dependency of the minister on the Church. The harmony of the plan of salvation chosen by Christ, the manifestation of the spiritual in the corporeal (Tertullian: *caro salutis cardo,* i.e., "the flesh is the hinge of salvation"), demanded that the activity of the minister be in a direct relationship of dependency on the visible society, the Church, which is the perennial manifestation of Christ. In fact, only in dependence on the ministerial power of the Church, indefectibly faithful to the mandate of its Founder, do men of all times and places find the guarantee of the continuity of the means of salvation established by the Redeemer.

The Church, moreover, is a well-organized body, in which every vital movement, linked to an external rite, must depend in some way on the visible head. It is necessary, therefore, that every infusion of new vital energies, caused by the sacraments, be *in some way dependent* on the visible head of the Church and on her hierarchy, which is the pope's coadjutor "in ministering the blood of the Lamb for the universal body of the Christian Religion" (St. Catherine of Siena).

We purposely say: "it must depend in some way," because this dependency can be various and from a maximum can descend to a minimum necessary to preserve the bond of reference. In fact, it can be *explicit,* as in the Catholic priest who absolves the penitent, and *implicit* as in the infidel who, ignorant of the Church and her rites, is induced to administer baptism *ad intentionem petentis* (according to the intention of the one asking); it can, moreover, be *direct,* as in all ministers having communication with the Apostolic See, or *indirect,* as may be found in heretics and schismatics, who by the very fact that their respective sects or churches keep and repeat what Rome did when they separated from her, indirectly put themselves in a position of dependency on, and connection with, the Catholic Church.

BIBLIOGRAPHY

St. Thomas, *Summa Theol.,* III, q. 64, a. 8–10. Billot, *De sacramentis,* Vol. 1 (Rome, 1932), p. 187 ff. Billuart, *De sacramentis,* diss. 5, a. 7. Delany, "Intention," *CE.* Doronzo, *De sacramentis in genere* (Milwaukee, 1946), Index Analyticus: "Intentio." Franzelin, *De sacramentis* (Rome, 1911), pp. 200–259. Pohle-Preuss, *Dogmatic Theology,* VIII *The Sacraments,* Vol. 1, *The Sacraments in General, Baptism, Confirmation* (St. Louis, 1945), pp. 175–187. Rambaldi, *L'oggetto dell'intenzione sacramentale nei teologi dei secoli XVI e XVII* (Rome, 1944). Thouvenin, "Intention," *DTC.* Van Noort, *De sacramentis,* Vol. 1 (Hilversum, 1927), nn. 110–112.

intercession (of the saints). An ancient custom of the Catholic Church, invoking the saints and commending oneself to their intercession with God. The Cathars, the Waldensians, Wicliffe, Luther, and more recently the modernists attacked the legitimacy of that usage, rejecting it as idolatrous, as derogatory to the worship due to Christ (the one Mediator, according to St. Paul, between man and God), and as a sign of little confidence in God's mercy.

The Council of Trent (sess. 25, *DB,* 984), outlining the reasons of the ancient custom, defends its legitimacy and utility and reproves the contrary teaching as impious: "The Holy Synod orders all the bishops, and all the others having the duty and charge of teaching, that — according to the usage of the Catholic and Apostolic Church, in force since the first times of the Christian religion, and according to the consensus of the holy Fathers of the Church and the decrees of the Councils — they instruct accurately the faithful especially about the intercession and invocation of the saints . . . teaching them that the saints, ruling together with Christ, offer their prayers for men to God, and that it is good and useful to invoke them supplicantly and to have recourse to their prayers and to their powerful help in obtaining benefits from God through Jesus Christ, His Son our Lord, who is our only Redeemer and Saviour. Those who do not admit that the saints, blessed in heaven, should be invoked, or who say that the saints do not pray for men, or that . . . their invocation is idolatry, or . . . is contrary to the dignity of the one Mediator between God and men, Jesus Christ, or that it is stupid to supplicate with voice or thought those who reign in heaven: all these do think impiously." In this decree, is found the solution of all aspects of the question.

1. The saints can intercede for us in imitation of Jesus Christ, who (as Man) is always alive to intercede for us with the Father (Heb. 7:25).

2. The prayer we address to God is an act of *latreutic cult* (see *cult*) because we believe that the omnipotent God can fulfill all our desires. The prayer made to the saints, on the other hand, is an act of mere *dulia*, because we expect the fulfillment of our desires not from their power, but from their *intercession* with God, who can grant us a grace directly in view of their prayers and their merits, or can also work a miracle through means of them.

3. The saints see in the beatific vision our conditions and our supplications.

4. The intercession of the saints is directed to Christ the Mediator, through whom all heavenly favors descend upon us.

5. God sees our needs and could provide directly, but it pleases the divine Wisdom to communicate His gifts through intermediaries. After Jesus, Mediator between God and men, Mary, the Mediatrix of all graces, excels over the angels and the saints, and so the Church addresses supplications to her in a special way.

BIBLIOGRAPHY

St. Thomas, *Summa Theol.*, II–II, q. 83, a. 4. D'Alès, "Prière," *DA*. Fonck, "Prière," *DTC*. Gibbons, *Faith of Our Fathers* (Baltimore, 1890). Scannell, "Intercession," *CE*.

interdict. A censure or medicinal penalty, by which the faithful (lay and clerics), though remaining in the communion of the Church, are deprived of certain sacraments and other sacred things. It differs from *excommunication,* which severs from communion with the other faithful, and from *suspension,* which is inflicted only on clerics. The interdict is distinguished as follows:

- As regards the subject:
  - *personal,* if it strikes a determined person
  - *local,* if it strikes directly a territory and indirectly all the persons in it: it then can be
    - *general,* if it includes all the territory
    - *particular,* if it includes only a part of the territory, e.g., a church, a monastery
- As regards the effects:
  - *total,* if it prohibits the use of all the sacred things
  - *partial,* if it forbids the use of certain sacred things

By force of a *general, local* interdict — limiting our consideration to the most common form of interdict — are prohibited, in a certain territory, the celebration of any rite and the solemn administration (*in forma solemni*) of any sacrament (except on Christmas, Easter, Pentecost, Corpus Christi, and the Assumption). The following ceremonies are permitted, only in the cathedrals and parish churches: (1) celebration of one daily Mass; (2) administration of baptism, Communion, penance; (3) keeping of the Blessed Sacrament; (4) assistance at the celebration of matrimony, but without the nuptial blessing; (5) obsequies for the dead, without solemnity; (6) blessing of the oils and of the baptismal font; (7) sacred preaching; (8) administration of Viaticum in private form. In all these ceremonies bells are never rung, nor is the organ played, and all external pomp is avoided.

This penalty is traced to the first centuries of the Church, but acquired its greatest development and its proper characteristic marks in the Middle Ages, when it was applied with full rigor, occasionally striking whole kingdoms, like France and England. Later the pope mitigated its consequences, permitting the administration of some sacraments in private form. In recent times it seemed to have come into disuse, when suddenly it was applied, with happy effectiveness, by Pope Pius X, on Adria (1909) and Galatina (1913).

The current discipline is established in the *Code of Canon Law* (Cans. 2268–2277).

BIBLIOGRAPHY

Boudinhon, "Interdict," *CE*. Chelodi, *Jus poenale,* ed. Dalpiaz (Trent, 1935), pp. 52–57. Prümmer, *Manuale theologiae moralis,* Vol. 3, nn. 527–530. Richter, *De origine et evolutione interdicti* (Rome, 1934), 2 volumes in the collection, *Textus et Documenta* of the Gregorian University. Smith, *Elements of Ecclesiastical Law* (New York, 1884). Taunton, *The Law of the Church* (London, 1906).

investiture. A ceremony having a juridical effect. Three elements are distinguished in the conferring of an ecclesiastical benefice: (1) *Designation of the person* — this gives the right *to* the thing (*ius ad rem*). It can be performed by the parishioners and the patron with respect to the parish priest, by the cathedral chapter with respect to the bishop. (2) *Canonical institution* (*institutio canonica*) performed by the legitimate superior — this confers the right *in* the thing (*ius in re*), namely, the real right over the benefice and the actual spiritual jurisdiction. (3) *Investiture,* namely, the installation, by which the beneficiary takes actual possession of the benefice either personally or by proxy.

These clear-cut ideas emanated from the bitter *fight on investitures,* which took place in the Middle Ages. In the eleventh century the emperor, because of a complexity of historical circumstances, arrogated to himself the right not only of presenting the person of the bishop or the abbot, but also of conferring on him — at the moment he invested him with the feuds annexed to the bishopric or the monastery — the spiritual power as well, by the consignment of the ring and crosier. Moreover, the sovereign's great care and interest was to choose, as his candidates, persons with good managerial and vassal qualifications, rather than good priests. In this way the Church was threatened with becoming a large, imperial fief. Hence the firm opposition of the popes, especially of St. Gregory VII. The long struggle, after many vicissitudes, was finally ended by the Concordat of Worms (1122), in which a clear distinction was made between the spiritual jurisdiction and the temporal power, and between the *designatio personae* and the *institutio canonica.*

If we consider the many difficulties surrounding this struggle, as well as its tenacious bitterness due to the material interests at stake, the victory of the Church, splitting the leaden lid that weighed down on it, is for us one of the proofs of its indefectibility.

BIBLIOGRAPHY

Kurtscheid, *Historia Iuris Canonici,* Vol. 1 (Rome, 1941), pp. 225–234. Löffler, "Investitures," *CE*. Van Hove, "Investiture," *CE*.

Irenaeus. See "Outline of the History of Dogmatic Theology" (p. 301); *Roman pontiff.*

J

Jahweh. See *Tetragrammaton.*

Jansenism. The heresy of Jansenius (Janssens, † 1638), a Dutchman who lived a long time at Louvain, where the memory and teaching of Baius (Bay) was still prevalent. Jansenism is a development of *Baianism* (*q.v.*). It gained strength and was disseminated through politico-religious maneuvers and intrigues, in which Duvergier, Abbé de St. Cyran, and later the turbulent Arnauld played particularly important roles. Quesnel followed in their footsteps. From its inception the heresy took on a polemic tone, not always dignified, mainly against the Jesuits who, by affirming their *Molinism* (*q.v.*) at Louvain, had attacked Baius, and covertly against the Roman Curia and the Holy See by contesting their right to intervene in theological questions.

From the doctrinal viewpoint, which alone is of interest here, Jansenism may be synthesized as follows: (*a*) It holds in their entirety the fundamental principles of Baianism on original justice, on the sin of Adam and the consequent intrinsic corruption of human nature, etc. (*b*) In particular, Jansenius develops the relationship of grace with free will, by following, as he says, the footsteps of St. Augustine: Adam, before sin, was free and could sin because he had only sufficient grace, which St. Augustine called *auxilium sine quo non;* after sin, with freedom lost, man needs for *every good act an efficacious grace* (*auxilium quo*) which determines the will infallibly; this intrinsic determination is not opposed to freedom. (*c*) The twofold love of Baius is reduced in Jansenius' thought to the twofold *conquering delectation* (*delectatio victrix*): one earthly, which determines to sin, the other heavenly (efficacious grace), which determines to good and therefore to eternal life. Man is a slave of one or the other of these delights. (*d*) In the actual state of man, sufficient grace is no longer granted, but only efficacious grace exists, and man cannot resist it. (*e*) God predestines to hell or to heaven prior to any consideration of merit; Christ died only for the predestined, who alone receive efficacious grace (see *Calvinism*).

Conclusion: Such doctrine contains a dark and gloomy pessimism, which the Jansenists have tried to mitigate with the idea of resignation, without being able, however, to overcome terror and desperation. Jansenism had great influence on Christian thought, art, and life. It is a credit to the Society of Jesus to have fought Jansenism with *Molinism* in dogmatic theology and with *probabilism* in moral theology.

Jansenius, who had become a bishop before he died, left his chief work, the *Augustinus,* the teaching of which was condemned after the death of its author. See the Propositions condemned by Innocent X, *DB,* 1092 ff.

BIBLIOGRAPHY

De Becdelièvre, "Jansénisme," *DA.* Carreyre, "Jansénisme," *DTC.* Forget, "Jansenius" and "Jansenism," *CE.*

Jehovah. See *Tetragrammaton.*

Jerome. See "Outline of the History of Dogmatic Theology" (p. 302); *Vulgate.*

Jesus Christ (Jesus: Hebr. *Ieshua'* — Saviour; Christ: Gr. Χριστός — Anointed, i.e., Messias). The Son of God made Man.

The Gospels enable us to reconstruct the picture of Christ's life and understand His teaching with perfect adherence to the framework of historical reality that preceded and accompanied them. The period of the infancy of Jesus constitutes a complete and well-defined cycle. Polarized about the two small villages of Bethlehem in Judea and Nazareth in Galilee, the events of those early years had few spectators. A silence of thirty years followed the sudden light of the birth of Christ and the episodes of His recognition in the Temple of Jerusalem by Simeon and Anna. But whoever attentively meditates these facts will be convinced that in them are found all the premises and signs of His future public manifestation. At the age of about thirty years Jesus appeared suddenly on the banks of the Jordan. For some preceding months John, having come from the desert, had been urging the crowds of Judea to moral renovation in expectation of the imminent appearance of the Messias whose Precursor he declared himself to be. Jesus, too, wished to receive the baptism of penance, and a voice from heaven identified in the "carpenter's son" the only-begotten Son of God. After a forty days' retreat in the desert, Jesus began in earnest His public ministry, and John retired humbly into the background, directing the crowd and six of his best disciples to join the new Master. During His life, Christ limited His teaching and work to the children of Israel, of that chosen people who awaited the fulfillment of the Messianic promises made by God to their Fathers. After His death, when Israel had shown a complete ignorance of the fulfillment of its own time as the chosen people, the opportunity was extended to all peoples.

After a brief sojourn in Galilee, Jesus moved — *about the beginning of the year 28* — toward Jerusalem, the heart of the Jewish nation. An act of authority in the Temple — expulsion of the profaners — drew the attention of the leaders and of the crowd upon Him. The leaders immediately showed themselves hostile to one who declared Himself Master and attributed to Himself an authority which put Him above all human measurement and set Him against the whole tradition of thought and piety zealously guarded by the Doctors of Jerusalem and by the members of the Sanhedrin, the supreme tribunal of the nation.

The crowd was enthused by the new preaching and the miracles accompanying it, but was inconstant and unable to believe with conviction. Jesus made some isolated conquests even among the personalities of the Sanhedrin. On the way back to Galilee, Samaria recognized Him as Messias and Saviour of the world, but this episode, because of its restricted circumstances, did not have any general repercussions. During His first year of ministry Christ labored in Galilee, making Capharnaum His headquarters; He called definitively in His service twelve disciples, among whom were eleven Galileans, and began His teaching by tracing the broad lines of the new moral law. The crowd was bewildered and the Pharisees scandalized because Jesus claimed for Himself the authority of perfecting and of interpreting definitively the Law of God. Numerous miracles confirmed His words and provoked a vast popular movement in the region. Toward the end of the year, Jesus began to speak of the kingdom of God (*q.v.*) veiling His teaching in parables, in order to avoid the misunderstanding of His doctrine of a spiritual kingdom by a nationalistic crowd which dreamed of the reconstruction of the earthly kingdom of Israel. The first year ended with a brief excursion to the eastern territories of the Lake of Tiberias where the pagan population predominated. The Pharisees of Jerusalem followed Jesus into Galilee and made several attempts to stir up controversies with the secret hope of putting Jesus outside the law.

The second year of ministry — A.D. 29 — opened with the sending of the disciples on a brief mission which gave them their first experiences in the apostolate. The crowd made concrete efforts to revolt for the purpose of investing Jesus with regal dignity. The Master insisted, however, that their attention and efforts be turned to the kingdom of God, but He was constrained to withdraw from the crowds and take refuge in the near-by pagan territories. He devoted intense care to the formation of the disciples and, when at Caesarea, Peter declared the faith of the apostolic college in His Messianic dignity and in His divinity, He revealed His intention of founding on the Apostles His Church. From this moment, His detachment from the Synagogue became more evident. The old religion began to crumble on itself, while on its ruins the new house of God began to rise, which would be open to all peoples. Jesus began to speak of His Passion and devoted Himself to a more careful formation of the disciples in preparation for their hours of darkness. The Transfiguration preceded the death on the cross to signify that such death will not be the fall of Christ to His enemies, but the spontaneous acceptation and execution of a planned design.

Jesus resolutely marched to Jerusalem. The Feast of the Tabernacles (September-October) and that of the Dedication (November-December) of A.D. 29 found Him in the capital, in the Temple, winning over enemies and friends with the marvel of His teaching and miracles. The Master spoke more openly of His Divinity, fighting the Pharisees and Sadducees on their own ground and unmasking their voluntary blindness and hypocrisy, the cause of the moral failure of the whole people. The Sanhedrin did not forgive Him and convinced itself of the necessity of suppressing Him, but they feared the crowd.

The beginning of *the third year of ministry* — A.D. 30 — found Jesus in Trans-Jordan, and later in Galilee. Toward February of the same year Jesus returned to Jerusalem for the last time, knowing that He was going to suffer His violent death.

The miracle of the resurrection of Lazarus, in the immediate vicinity of the capital, precipitated events. The Sanhedrin awaited a propitious occasion to have Him put to death. For the third time Jesus spoke in a detailed way about His Passion. The Sunday preceding the last Easter (March-April), He did not prevent, as on former occasions, the crowd from acclaiming Him Messias and accompanying Him into the Temple, filling it with their enthusiastic shouts. Tuesday was spent in polemics and threats directed against the Pharisees, traitors of God; that same day Jesus pronounced the great discourse in which He announced the end of that city which soon would become the murderess of God, and spoke of the end of the world which will see Him as inescapable Judge and uncontested Ruler. Wednesday Judas arranged the price of betrayal. Thursday evening, during the traditional Paschal banquet, Jesus instituted the Eucharist and abandoned Himself to intimate confidences. Well into the night He was arrested at Gethsemani, after His human nature in a painful agony felt the huge weight of a redemption that demanded bloody immolation. At dawn the Sanhedrin condemned Christ as a blasphemer, because He called Himself Son of God. In an effort to obtain the Roman procurator's consent, to whom the death sentence was reserved, they attempted to put the trial on a political basis, but feeling Pilate's resistance, who was convinced of Jesus' innocence, the Sanhedrin finally disclosed its real charge: self-attribution of divine sonship, a charge not within the judicial power of Pilate. The death sentence was pronounced, the penalty being that of wretches and rebels: the cross.

At three in the afternoon of Friday, the crime was consummated, but Jesus' death was accompanied by prodigies which shook to the depths the conscience of many. Sunday at dawn the sepulcher of Joseph of Arimathea, in which Jesus was placed in burial, was found empty, but the Crucified returned that same day in the midst of His own, offering many proofs of the reality of His resurrection. During forty days He completed the work of instruction and formation of the disciples; then, disappearing from their sight, He ascended into heaven, having given them the command of dispersing into the world and preaching to all the Gentiles, communicating to all the benefits of the Redemption, and of awaiting in Jerusalem the coming of the Holy Spirit.

The teaching of Jesus is both ancient and new; it presupposes the knowledge of the ideal and historical premises which constitute its base. The ancient, divine revelation had been made and entrusted to the people of Israel which was, in the fullness of time, to transmit it to the whole world. Christ came to justify and confirm the revelation of the Old Testament and to complete it definitively. For this reason, during His earthly life, He did not step outside the borders of Israel, though He preached and died for all men. Jesus has revealed the mysteries of the intimate nature and life of God: That same God who had revealed Himself to the Fathers of old as the "One God" essentially, is also "Triune" personally. He has an only-begotten Son who became incarnate — the Christ — in order to fulfill the will of the Father who wished to be reconciled forever with man in the blood of His Son which would cancel efficaciously Adam's offense. The third person is the *Holy Spirit,* whom the Father and Son will send after the death of the Redeemer to complete His work by the bountiful distribution of supernatural gifts.

Jesus proved that in Him were realized the ancient prophecies, by declaring Himself the Messias and the Son of God, heir of the "eternal" throne of David for the foundation of a kingdom "not of this world" in which all men would be admitted with equal rights. That kingdom is the Church, and its "glory" consists of the supernatural riches with which Christ has endowed it. The sacraments are the channels of grace which redeems and renovates man by conferring on him a participation of the divine nature which makes him "Son of the Lord," intimately united to Him. A mysterious bond holds all the believers among themselves together with Jesus who is "but one thing" with His faithful in the unity of a vital organism: the Mystical Body. The Eucharist is the supreme gift which perpetuates for each and all the offering that Christ made of Himself, because the marvels of the Redemption are the fruit of His bloody immolation. The law of the kingdom is summed up in the precept of love, and the true religion consists in actuating truth in love; it does not play itself out in the external observance of precepts, but it is a living of love and, therefore, of sacrifice; it is an imitation of the Son; it is being Christlike.

The enemy of the kingdom is God's own enemy — Satan, whom Jesus defeated forever by rescuing man from slavery to evil.

The divinity of the Messias, His

sorrowful passion, the supernatural character of His kingdom, the union of all men without distinction in a new organism wherein circulates the vital fluid of grace, a religion of freedom and of the spirit, i.e., of love — these were the rocks on which Israel ran afoul. Misled by heads and by religious sects incapable of rising above the fictitious framework of thought and action, created by a substantial misunderstanding of the authentic revelation of God; incapable of breaking from the concept of a Messianic kingdom confined to the borders of their own nation and limited to material prosperity; obsessed with an external religious practice weighed down and vitiated by a parasitical excrescence of human precepts, the people of Israel showed themselves incompetent to the task and failed to attain the goal set for them by God. The millennial divine plan, however, did not fail, nor were the ancient promises frustrated. The Apostles are the authentic Israel through which the message of the Redemption and its gifts are given to the world.

The story of divine revelation and of human redemption, patiently prepared by God during thousands of years of waiting, culminates in the teaching and the work of Christ which is of all times. The new Adam repairs the sin of the first Adam and reconciles all men with God. Thus there is a return to primitive unity and happiness; in the poverty of time it is possible for us to garner eternal riches, and in the suffering and melancholy of the world we prepare our happiness in the eternal possession of God.

BIBLIOGRAPHY

Braun, *Où en est le problème de Jésus* (Bruxelles-Paris, 1932). De Grandmaison, *Jesus Christ,* 3 vols. (New York, 1930–1934); "Jésus Christ," *DA.* Farrar, *Life of Christ* (London, 1864). Felder-Stoddard, *Christ and the Critics,* 2 vols. (London, 1924–1925). Fillion, *The Life of Christ,* trans. Thompson, 3 vols. (London, 1928–1930). Geikie, *The Life and the Word of Christ* (London, 1877). Lebreton, *The Life and Teaching of Jesus Christ,* 2 vols. (Milwaukee, 1935). Maas, *The Life of Jesus Christ* (St. Louis); "Jesus Christ," *CE.* Michel, "Jésus-Christ," *DTC.* Pohle-Preuss, *Dogmatic Theology,* IV "Christology" (St. Louis, 1946). Ricciotti, *The Life of Christ,* trans. Zizzamia (Milwaukee, 1947). *The Teaching of the Catholic Church,* ed. Smith, 2 vols. (New York, 1949), pp. 360–512. Thibaut, *Le sens de l'Homme-Dieu* (Paris, 1942).

John of St. Thomas. See "Outline of the History of Dogmatic Theology" (p. 303).

judgment, divine. The accounting for one's own life, which every man must render after death to God, Lord and supreme Judge, to receive reward or punishment according to his merits. Judgment is twofold: particular and universal.

1. *Particular judgment* will take place immediately after death, as is proved (*a*) from Holy Scripture: the parable of the rich man and Lazarus, of whom the first dies and goes to hell, the other to Abraham's bosom (paradise), two places eternally separated by an impassable abyss; St. Paul, close to death, yearned for the "crown of justice," which Christ the Judge will give him and those who will have lived like him (2 Tim. 4:6); elsewhere he says explicitly: "It is appointed unto men once to die, and after this the judgment" (Heb. 9:27). (*b*) Tradition, after some wavering as to details, declares itself clearly and explicitly from the fourth century: St. Hilary: "The day of judgment is the eternal retribution either of felicity or of punishment." St. Augustine distinguishes the judgment that follows death immediately when the souls have gone out of their bodies (*de corporibus exierint*), and the universal judgment which will take place after the resurrection of the bodies.

(*c*) The Church *magisterium* confirms this truth especially in the II Council of Lyons (1274), in a bull of Benedict XII (1336), and in the Council of Florence (*DB,* 464, 530, and 693). (*d*) Reason recognizes the necessity of a divine sanction and, therefore, of a divine judgment on the use made of the gift of life and its powers (cf. the history of all religions).

The discussion and the proclamation of the verdict in this judgment take place by way of internal *mental illumination.*

2. *Universal judgment* is a truth of faith (cf. the Creed: "[Christ] will come to judge the living and the dead"). In Matthew, Chapter 25, we find a lifelike description of it. St. Paul, on several occasions (2 Cor. 10; Rom. 14:10; 2 Thess. 1–2, etc.), refers to it. St. Augustine expounds systematically the traditional doctrine (*De Civitate Dei,* XX, 30): The Judge will be the Man-God, who will appear on the clouds of heaven, accompanied by the angels, and will manifest, confirming them, the verdicts of the particular judgments — in this case too, most likely, by way of internal illumination.

BIBLIOGRAPHY

St. Thomas, *Summa Theol.,* III, *Suppl.,* q. 88; *Summa Contra Gentiles,* l. 4, c. 91. McHugh, "Judgment (Divine)," *CE.* Pohle-Preuss, *Dogmatic Theology,* XII *Eschatology* (St. Louis, 1946), pp. 18–27, 103–120, 149–160. Rivière, "Jugement," *DTC. The Teaching of the Catholic Church,* ed. Smith, 2 vols. (New York, 1949), pp. 1132–1140.

jurisdiction. See *hierarchy.*

justice. (Lat. *justitia* from *ius* — right). It includes essentially the concept of right which, *subjectively,* is the inviolable moral power of having or doing something in one's own utility, and, *objectively,* is that which is due to another. It is evident that "right" implies a relationship of *alterity* (i.e., distinction) between two persons, so that to the right of the one there corresponds the duty of the other. Justice, as an *act,* consists in giving each his own, i.e., what is due to him; as a virtuous *habit,* it is defined as the constant and perpetual will to give to each what is his, i.e., what by right belongs to him. Applying this concept to the relationship of man not only toward his fellow men, but also toward God, we have justice in the broad sense, which is equivalent to holiness, as we see in the language of the Bible, in which the holy man is the *just* man. But in the strict sense justice is a relationship between men and can be distinguished in: (*a*) *commutative,* in so far as it regulates the relations between single individuals; (*b*) *distributive,* between superiors and subjects; (*c*) *legal,* between the individual and society. The first two are included under the name of *particular* justice, because they regard the private good; the third is called *general* justice, because its object is the common good. Strictly speaking, the true justice is the *commutative* justice, in which is verified the concept of perfect correspondence (the right–duty equation), which is the basic element of justice.

So-called *social* justice, which, strictly speaking, refers to the relations between the individual and the social organism, is generally reduced to general-legal justice. Among the moral virtues (*prudence, justice, fortitude, temperance*), justice holds the primacy, because the other virtues have regard to the good of the individual in himself, while justice looks to the good of one's fellow men; namely, to the common good, which transcends the individual good. Cicero (*De Officiis,* I) correctly writes that man's goodness is measured principally by his justice. In the *natural order* this virtue is a habit acquired through exercise of the will in respecting the rights of others. But, according to Catholic doctrine, with sanctifying grace God infuses into the soul and its faculties the theological virtues, the gifts of the Holy Spirit and with them the cardinal virtues, among which is justice. In the supernatural order, therefore, justice is a habit infused by God in the soul, which inclines the will to give to each his own, according to the various relationships examined above.

Justice, like every other virtue, enters into the Christian categorical imperative: *declina a malo et fac bonum* ("decline from evil and do good"); and, therefore, it implies not only the obligation to do good to others, but also that of not impeding or injuring the rights of others.

BIBLIOGRAPHY

St. Thomas, *Summa Theol.,* II–II, qq. 57–58. Baucher, "Justice (Vertu de)," *DTC.* Ming, *The Data of Modern Ethics Examined* (New York, 1896). Pesch, *De virtutibus moralibus* (Freiburg i.-Br., 1923), p. 104 ff. Slater, "Justice," *CE.*

justice, original. See *innocence (state of).*

justification. The passing, under the action of divine grace, from the state of injustice or aversion from God to the state of justice (in the biblical sense, holiness).

This divine work is likened by Jesus Christ to a *regeneration* (John 1 and 3); St. Paul calls it a "new creation in Christ" (καινὴ κτίσις; 2 Cor. 5:17). It is precisely St. Paul who develops more copiously the doctrine of justification with an abundance of motifs that all converge on the same concept of an interior transformation, whose term is the *homo novus.* The Lutheran interpretation does St. Paul an evident injury by claiming to reduce this thought to the theory of an *extrinsic* justification (imputation of Christ's holiness to incurable man). Some modern Protestants have abandoned this extravagant exegesis and have approached the traditional Catholic interpretation (Sanday, Jülicher, Zahn, and others).

The Council of Trent, sess. VI, assembles and determines in clear and concise expressions the traditional doctrine (cf. especially chapters 7, 8, 9, and corresponding canons). Justification in newborn babies is effected through baptism instantaneously, but in adults (ordinarily at least) is effected in two phases: (1) *Preparation:* under the influence of actual (*exciting*) grace, the sinner begins to turn toward God by acts of faith, sorrow, and love (Council of Trent, sess. VI, can. 6). (2) *Information:* in the subject, so prepared, God works the supernatural renovation, which consists in a single act, having two aspects, one *negative* (the *remission* or real destruction of sin), and the other *positive* (the infusion of sanctifying grace with the virtues and the gifts that accompany it) (cf. Council of Trent, sess. VI, cans. 7, 8). This is the *divinization* of man of which the Eastern Fathers often speak (cf. Cyril of Alexandria).

BIBLIOGRAPHY

St. Thomas, *Summa Theol.,* I–II, q. 113. Lemonnyer, *Théologie du N. Testament* (Paris, 1928). pp. 77 ff., 115 ff. Newman, *Lectures on the Doctrine of Justification* (London, 1900). Peter Parente, *Anthropologia supernaturalis* (Rome, 1943), p. 228 ff. Pohle, "Justification," *CE.* Scheeben, *The Mysteries of Christianity,* trans. Vollert (St. Louis, 1946), pp. 613–648.

K

Kantianism. The philosophical system of Emmanuel Kant (born at Koenigsberg in 1724, † 1804), which dominates modern thought in all sectors, not excluding the religious.

Kant's starting point is the critical problem, namely: the value of knowledge. He rejects *empiricism,* which claims that all knowledge comes from sense experience only, and criticizes *rationalism,* which holds that knowledge is built with universal concepts. For these two systems, the natural order is a sure presupposition (*dogmatism*), while for Kant it exists in function of the act of knowledge, i.e., it is formed by our knowing faculty under the stimulus of sensations. Therefore, according to Kant, knowledge is not only a *synthesis* (deriving from experience), or only an *analysis* (deriving from the knowing subject), but is a *synthesis a priori* (deriving from experience and at once from principles or *a priori* and subjective forms, which organize and give value to the experimental data). We must distinguish the phenomenon (the external thing as it appears to us) from the noumenon (thinkable, namely the thing in itself). Only the phenomenon is known through means of the impressions the external thing makes on our senses; but it is not possible to grasp the thing in itself, in its ontological reality, namely the *noumenon;* however, we fill this lacuna by attributing to the thing our *a priori* concept (Kantian category), which renders it thinkable but does not assure us that it really is the way we think it (critical agnosticism).

There are three knowledge phases or functions:

1. *Sensibility* (*transcendental aesthetics*), in which the *material* elements are the impressions of the external world, and the *formal* elements are the two pure intuitions *"space-time"* under which are disposed and classified the data of sensations.

2. *Intelligence* (*transcendental analytics*), of which the material element is the fruit of the first phase (*perceptions*), and the formal element are twelve *a priori* forms or *categories,* reducible to four fundamental ones: *quantity, quality, relation,* and *modality.*

3. *Reason* (*transcendental dialectics*), of which the material elements are the judgments formulated in the antecedent phase, and the formal elements are three ideas: ego (soul), world, God.

Thus Kant in his *Critique of Pure Reason* saves only the phenomenal aspect of objective reality, substituting *a priori* forms and principles for the substantial reality of the things in themselves. God, therefore, is thinkable, but not demonstrable. But in his *Critique of Practical Reason* he attempts to redintegrate the reality of God, of the world, and of man by way of *will* and *faith.* Consequently what we have here is a playing down of the value of reason, incapable of getting to external things in themselves. Science and metaphysics are based on *a priori* synthetic judgments, in which the formal element is subjective. Reason, shut up in itself, is declared *autochthonous,* creative, as it were, of reality, and *autonomous* inasmuch as everything is immanent in it and nothing can be imposed on it from outside. Whence the *autonomous ethics* with its *categorical imperative* erupting from and immanent in the rational subject; whence the abolition of revealed religion, of worship with rites and prayers, God being a subjective postulate of reason. If Kantianism, from a philosophical standpoint, encounters many difficulties, theologically considered it compromises the very bases of Catholic doctrine, as appears from *modernism,* which has adopted *Kantian immanentism* (*qq.v.*).

BIBLIOGRAPHY

Caird, *Critical Philosophy of Kant* (London, 1889). Franchi, *Ultima Critica* (1888). Turner, "Kant," *CE.* Valensin, "Criticisme kantien," *DA.* Watson, *Kant and His English Critics* (London, 1888); *The Philosophy of Kant Explained* (Glasgow, 1908).

kenosis (Gr. κένωσις, from κενόω — I empty, void). A term derived from the text of St. Paul's letter to the Philippians (2:7), where it is said that the Word ἑαυτὸν ἐκένωσεν (*exinanivit semetipsum,* according to the Vulgate version — emptied himself). This passage has given rise to the *kenotic* theory, started by Luther in the sixteenth century and developed in the past century by certain German Protestants (Thomasius and Gess) and by many Anglicans (Sanday, Gore, Mackintosh, etc.). According to Luther, the Word is said to have transmitted His divine properties to the assumed humanity (*omniscience, omnipotence, ubiquity,* etc.), but Christ the Man, except for one or another circumstance of a rather private character (like the Transfiguration), did not use them openly. According to some contemporary Protestants, the Word in His Incarnation stripped Himself of certain divine attributes by a sort of *self-limitation.*

This whole theory: (*a*) is absurd in itself, since it is based on the erroneous thesis of the possibility of a mutation or a real limitation in the divine nature; (*b*) it does not follow from the text of St. Paul, which Catholic exegetes explain adequately in this sense: The Word seemed to strip Himself of His divine glory when He lowered Himself to the point of taking on human nature (*formam servi accipiens* — "taking the form, i.e., the nature of a servant") and of mingling as Man among men, and, furthermore, of living a life of privations and undergoing the humiliations of an opprobrious passion and death.

This sound interpretation is the general one of the Fathers of the Church.

BIBLIOGRAPHY

Gaudel, "Kénose," *DTC.* Hall (non-Catholic), *The Kenotic Theory* (New York, 1898). Harty, "The Modern Kenotic Theory," *Irish Theol. Quarterly,* Vol. 1 (1906), nn. 1 and 2. Maas, "Kenosis," *CE.* Prat, *The Theology of St. Paul,* trans. Stoddard, Vol. 1 (Westminster, 1927), pp. 456–465.

kingdom of God. A central concept for the understanding of the economy of salvation, constituting the primary object of Christ's preaching.

In the Old Testament God, as Creator, is the King of the universe and, in a particular way, of Israel, "His" people. The kingdom of God is extended into the future with the foundation of the Messianic kingdom — universal, spiritual, and eternal.

A "kingdom of God" is frequently mentioned in the Gospel; St. Matthew calls it also "kingdom of heaven" — by obvious substitution of the name of "God," according to the Hebrew fashion. The notion of the kingdom of God is complex. It expresses a present and a future reality; present and in continual becoming and progress, pending the future kingdom which will be in the total and perfect possession of beatitude in heaven. It is both *internal-invisible,* i.e., the kingdom of grace in the souls, and *social-visible,* inasmuch as it coincides with the Church founded by Jesus Christ on earth.

BIBLIOGRAPHY

De Grandmaison, *Jesus Christ,* 3 vols. (New York, 1930–1934), Index. Frey, "Royaume de Dieu," *DBV,* cols. 1237–1257. Madebielle, "Eglise," *DBVS.* Maurice, *The Gospels of the Kingdom of Heaven* (London, 1888). Pope, "Kingdom of God," *CE.* Vitti, "La recente interpretazione del Regno di Dio nel sistema escatologico," *Scuola Cattolica,* 60 (1932).

Kingship of Christ. With the encyclical of Pius XI *Quas primas* (1925), the Kingship of Christ was incorporated in the universal liturgy (Feast of Christ the King) and into the category of truths declared revealed by the solemn *magisterium* of the Church. This truth, however, goes back to Old Testament times, in which the future Messias was prophesied as King (Psalms 2, 44, 71; Isa. 9:6 ff.; Dan. 2:44; 7:13 ff.). In the New Testament, the Archangel Gabriel says to Mary: "And of his kingdom there shall be no end" (Luke 1:33; cf. John 18:37). St. Paul says: "For he hath put all things under his feet" (2 Cor. 15:26); St. John: "And he hath on his garment and on his thigh written: King of kings and Lord of lords" (Apoc. 19:16). St. Augustine synthesizes patristic tradition (*De Consensu Evangeliorum*): "Christ as man has been constituted King and Priest."

Reasons: (*a*) Christ is King by *birthright,* because He is Son of God, even according to His humanity which subsists in the Person of the Word; (*b*) by *acquired right,* because He has ransomed with His blood mankind from the slavery of sin, which weighed on all creatures, as St. Paul (Rom. 18:19) says; (*c*) Christ is King because He has the threefold power — *legislative, judicial,* and *executive,* as the Gospel attests (Matt. 5:21; 28:18; Mark 16:16; Acts 10:42, etc.). The kingdom of Christ is of a spiritual nature, but does not exclude extension, at least *indirect,* to temporal things; it is also *social,* not only individual.

The royal powers of Christ have been communicated to the Church and to the Roman pontiff, who is her visible head: "As the Father hath sent me, I also send you" (John 20:21).

BIBLIOGRAPHY

ST. THOMAS, *Summa Theol.*, III, qq. 58–59. CHAMBLAT, *La Royauté du Christ selon la doctrine catholique* (Paris, 1931). MICHEL, "Jésus Christ," *DTC,* cols. 1355–1359.

knowledge, divine. See *science, divine.*

knowledge of Christ. See *science of Christ.*

L

latria. See *cult.*

law. St. Thomas defines it: "An order of reason regarding the common good and promulgated by the one who is in charge of the community." The essential concept of law is its moral *obligatory* force with respect to *human* action.

Law is *divine* or *human.* The divine law is threefold: *eternal, natural,* and *positive.* The eternal law is in God's essence and coincides with His wisdom and will, from which derives and on which depends the life of the universe (physical and moral world). The natural divine law is that impressed in creatures to direct them to their proper end; it is *physical* in irrational creatures, and *moral* in man, to whom it is promulgated through his own conscience (*q.v.*). The *positive* divine law is that *revealed* in Holy Scripture (Old and New Testaments) or oral Tradition.

Human law is divided into *ecclesiastical* (emanating from the pope, the bishops, the councils) and *civil* (emanating from the competent authorities of the governments of nations).

Human *legislative* power supposes jurisdiction or power of government. The *object* of law must be *honest, just,* and physically and morally *possible.* The *subject* of law is man, constituted under the power of the legislator and having the use of reason.

For a law to be effective it must be *promulgated,* i.e., formally proposed and communicated to the collectivity of the subjects. Obviously the *divine* law is sacred, because through conscience it obliges all rational creatures under penalty of sanctions which transcend the limits of this life. The *ecclesiastical* law is sacred, intimately connected as it is with the divine law; sacred also is *civil* law, based on a power that derives from God: *Non est potestas nisi a Deo* ("There is no power but from God"; Rom. 13:1).

Civil law is binding in conscience, according to the best opinions, provided it is not in conflict with divine or ecclesiastical law. Neither divine nor human law is violable deliberately without guilt, which is measured according to the matter or content of the law itself and the will to oblige on the part of the legislator. However, if a law is *merely penal,* transgression involves penalty but not guilt. The subject may be dispensed from the observance of the positive law by the superior who has power of jurisdiction over him. A *privilege* is a special favor granted against or outside the common law.

Law, the *remote* rule of morality, must become the *proximate* rule of moral action, through the medium of conscience.

BIBLIOGRAPHY

ST. THOMAS, *Summa Theol.,* I–II, qq. 90–108. D'ALÈS, "Loi divine," *DA.* BOUDINHON, "Law (Canon)," *CE.* CATHREIN, "Law," *CE.* FARGES, *La liberté et le devoir, fondements de la morale et critique des systèmes de morale contemporaine* (Paris, 1902). NOLDIN-SCHMITT, *Summa theologiae moralis,* Vol. 1 (Oeniponte, 1927), p. 112 ff. SLATER, "Law (Divine)," *CE.*

learning Church. See *"Ecclesia discens."*

lectorate (Lat. *lector* — reader). The second of the four minor orders (see *orders, holy*), by which is conferred the power of reading the Holy Scripture aloud in Church, before the priest or bishop explains its content.

From earliest antiquity mention is made of the lector or reader: St. Justin refers to him and Tertullian speaks explicitly of him. In the fourth century admission to the lectorate was the ordinary way of initiating young men into the ecclesiastical life.

The lectorate is the only minor order of the Latin rite now in use in the Greek Church.

BIBLIOGRAPHY

FORTESCUE, "Lector," *CE.*

Leontius Byzantinus. See "Outline of the History of Dogmatic Theology" (p. 302).

Leo the Great. See "Outline of the History of Dogmatic Theology" (p. 302); *Eutychianism.*

liberalism. A doctrinal current, quite complex and changeable, which has had various interpretations and practical applications, not easily definable. The basic concept of liberalism is liberty, taken as emancipation and independence of man, society, and State, from God and His Church.

Born of Encyclopedism, liberalism finds a philosophical justification in Kantianism (*q.v.*), and gains strength with naturalism and rationalism (*qq.v.*); with the French Revolution it enters the sociopolitical field and manifests itself as exaggerated *democracy* (sovereign people), as separatism with respect to the relations between Church and State ("A free church in a free State"), as indifferentism in matters of religion and worship, and as *abstentionism* (noninterference) of the State in economics ("Leave everything to private initiative").

In the first half of the past century this dangerous and erroneous current made great inroads among Catholic ranks, assuming a more moderate form and insisting especially on the separation of Church from State and on broad-mindedness with regard to a liberal spirit. Characteristic in this connection was the Catholic-Liberal movement in France, led by Félicité de Lamennais, and followed enthusiastically by Lacordaire, a Dominican, Montalembert, and others. These sought, with the best of intentions but to no avail, to Christianize liberalism, fundamentally adverse to revealed religion. The Church was forced to intervene, first warning, then condemning.

The principal documents of the Church *magisterium* are: (1) The encyclical, *Mirari vos,* of Gregory XVI (1832). (2) The encyclical, *Quanta cura,* with the attached *Syllabus,* of Pius IX (1864). (3) The encyclicals, *Immortale Dei* and *Libertas,* of Leo XIII (1885 and 1888).

In the *Syllabus* (*q.v.*) is found the explicit and detailed condemnation of liberalism, whether philosophical, theological, religious, or sociopolitical. Certain modern tendencies with a more attenuated liberal tinge are to be distinguished from this classic liberalism.

Leo XIII, in his two famous encyclicals, confirms the condemnation given by Pius IX in the *Syllabus,* maintaining vigorously the rights of God and of the Church with regard to the individual and the State, which cannot divest itself of interest in the religious problem or put the Catholic Church on a par with other cults. But, in consideration of contingent difficulties, he does not condemn the government which, for reasons of freedom of conscience, permits in its territory — even where the majority of citizens is Catholic — the free exercise of other religious forms. This is a tolerance, therefore, of practical necessity, similar to that with which God tolerates evil by the side of good in the world; but the principle remains intact, namely: the truth and the right of the Catholic religion and Church in its relations with the individual, with society, and with the State.

BIBLIOGRAPHY

Billot, *De Ecclesia Christi,* Vol. 2 (Rome, 1922), pp. 15–58. Constantin, "Libéralisme," *DTC.* De Pascal, "Libéralisme," *DA.* Gibbons, *Faith of Our Fathers* (Baltimore, 1890). Gruber, "Liberalism," *CE.* Manning, "Liberty of the Press," *Essays,* third series (London, 1892). Ming, *Data of Modern Ethics Examined* (New York, 1897). Weill, *Histoire du catholicisme libéral en France 1828–1908* (Paris, 1909).

liberty. See *freedom.*

liberty of Christ. See *will, divine; will of Christ.*

liberty of thought and inquiry. See *free thought* (*free inquiry*).

Liebermann. See "Outline of the History of Dogmatic Theology" (p. 303).

limbo (Lat. *limbus* — border, hem of a garment). According to the present teaching of the Church, it is a place adjoining hell, where the just who died in the grace of God before Christianity dwelled until they were liberated by Christ, and where babies who die without baptism dwell and remain forever.

Holy Scripture speaks of *Abraham's bosom* as sojourn of the just (Luke 16:22), but not of a place for babies who died without baptism. Tradition begins, especially with the Greek Fathers, to differentiate between adults who die in personal sin and infants who die with only original sin, who cannot enter the heaven of the blessed and yet cannot share the fate of the damned in hell. In reacting against Pelagianism, which denied the transmission of original sin and its consequences, St. Augustine, endeavoring to defend this truth, held that babies who die without baptism will be subjected to the pain of fire, albeit very slight, on account of original sin. This opinion later on influenced some theologians, but did not hinder the course of the other more correct and more benign opinion, according to which babies who die without baptism will suffer only privation of the *beatific vision*. This opinion was defended and developed by St. Thomas, and from then on prevailed in the schools. We find it in a letter of Innocent III to the archbishop of Arles, and in the Constitution *Auctorem fidei* with which Pius VI condemned the Synod of Pistoia (*DB*, 1526).

The babies in limbo will not enjoy the vision of God, but will not be unhappy on this score, since the beatific vision is a *supernatural good* of which they have no knowledge. Some theologians (Billot) think that limbo is the eternal residence not only of babies and abnormal adults who did not have the use of reason, but also of certain classes of men of low-grade civilization, who are comparable to babies in the lack of development of moral consciousness.

A strange opinion has recently gained favor in the theologies of Protestants and Orthodox Schismatics who, by abusive interpretation of some gospel expressions (Matt. 12:32; 1 Pet. 3:18; 4:6), hold that all pagans are evangelized in limbo after their death and given the possibility of conversion and salvation. This opinion is critically untenable.

BIBLIOGRAPHY

St. Thomas, *Summa Theol.*, III, *Suppl.*, q. 69, a. 4–7; *Quaest. Disp. De Malo*, q. 5. Billot, several articles published in *Etudes* (1920–1922). Caperan, *Le problème du salut des infidèles* (Toulouse, 1934). Gaudel, "Limbes," *DTC*. Toner, "Limbo," *CE*.
See under *descent of Christ into hell*.

liturgy (Gr. λειτουργία, from λεῖτον ἔργον — public office or ministry). The official worship the Church renders to God, or, to describe it more extensively, the complexus of the acts by which the Church, in union with Christ, her Head, and externally represented by His ministers, offers to God the homage of adoration and of praise (ascendant mediation) and communicates to souls the divine gifts of grace (descendant mediation).

According to this concept, the liturgy includes essentially the celebration of the Eucharistic Sacrifice with the attached official prayer (recitation of the Breviary) and the administration of the sacraments with the annexed use of the sacramentals (*qq.v.*).

Since the homage paid to God and the infusion of grace into souls must be perennial, in application of the merits acquired by Christ by the acts of religion emanating from Him from the first instant of the Incarnation, the liturgy, on the one hand, renews daily the offering of the Mass and repeats the administration of the sacraments, and, on the other hand, establishes an annual cycle in which are repeated the mysteries of the birth, death, and glorious life of Jesus Christ, from which Christian worship draws all its value. "The Church renews each year her youth, like an eagle, because in the liturgical cycle she is visited by her Spouse in proportion to her necessities. Each year she receives Him, as a baby in the crib (Advent and Christmas period), as fasting on the mountain (Lent), as immolating Himself on the cross and as risen from the sepulcher (Paschal cycle), as founding the Church, instituting the sacraments, sitting at the right hand of the Father in the act of sending the Holy Spirit (period of Pentecost). The whole cycle is studded with saints; by contemplating them we know the way that leads to Christ. Above all shines Mary, offering herself as a mirror of justice wherein is reflected all holiness possible in a simple creature" (Guéranger, *L'Année liturgique,* Préface Générale).

For twenty centuries the Church, like an industrious bee, has been working on her liturgical books, which may be divided into two classes: (1) The *Missal* and the *Breviary,* containing the formulas and the rites necessary for the celebration of the Mass and the recital of the Psalmody, the *"sacrificium laudis"* (books referring to ascendant mediation). (2) The *Pontifical* and the *Ritual,* containing the formulas and rites for the administration of the sacraments and the sacramentals (books referring to descendant mediation).

The study of the origin, development, and content of these books constitutes *liturgical science,* while the learning of the ceremonies accompanying the use of them is called *liturgical practice.*

BIBLIOGRAPHY

Callevaert, *De sacra liturgia universim* (Brugis, 1933). Caronti, *The Spirit of the Liturgy,* trans. Michel (Collegeville, 1926). *Cours et conférences des Semaines Liturgiques* (published at Louvain, Abbaye de Mont César). Fortescue, "Liturgy," *CE.* Lefebvre, *Catholic Liturgy,* trans. by a nun of Stanbrook (Edinburgh, 1923). Oppenheim, *Institutiones liturgicae* (Turin-Rome), 1937 ff. Schuster, *Liber Sacramentorum* (Turin-Rome, 1941).

"loci theologici" (theological sources). The expression has become classic, following the work of Melchior Cano, O.P. († 1560), entitled *De locis theologicis,* which, on the road of theology is likened to a milestone: the end of a long stretch and the beginning of a new journey faithfully traveled by posterity. According to Cano's definition, which re-echoes ideas familiar to Aristotle (*τόποι*), to Cicero (*sedes et domicilia*), and to Rudolphus Agricola, skillfully adapted, however, to the altogether particular nature of theology, the theological sources or *loci* are: *tamquam domicilia omnium argumentorum theologicorum, quibus, theologi omnes suas argumentationes sive ad confirmandum sive ad refellendum inveniunt"* ("the building or arsenal, as it were, of all theological arguments, in which theologians find all their argumentations either to prove or to refute"; M. Cano, *De locis theologicis,* l. 1, c. 3). Since theology is founded on revealed truths contained in Holy Scripture and Tradition, the interpretation of which is entrusted to the living *magisterium* of the Church (*q.v.*) manifested through the definitions of the councils, the decisions of the popes, the common teaching of the Fathers and the theologians, Cano distinguished seven *loci theologici,* in the strict

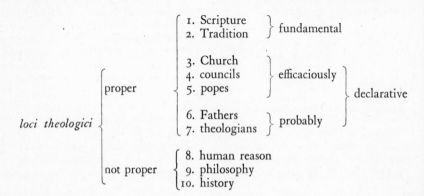

loci theologici
- proper
  - 1. Scripture, 2. Tradition — fundamental
  - 3. Church, 4. councils, 5. popes — efficaciously } declarative
  - 6. Fathers, 7. theologians — probably } declarative
- not proper
  - 8. human reason
  - 9. philosophy
  - 10. history

sense of the word: Holy Scripture, Tradition, the *magisterium* of the Church, the councils, the decisions of the popes, the holy Fathers, and the theologians. He added three more, as *not proper,* or annexed, namely: human reason, philosophy, and history.

BIBLIOGRAPHY

CANO, *De locis theologicis,* ed. Cucchi (Rome, 1900). GARDEIL, "Lieux théologiques," *DTC.* LANG, *Die Loci Theologici des Melchior Cano und die Methode des dogmatischen Beweises* (München, 1925). STOLZ, *Introductio in S. Theologiam* (Freiburg i.-Br., 1941), pp. 99–101. WILHELM, "Loci Theologici," *CE.*

Logos (Gr. Λόγος — thought, word; Lat. *verbum*). The term with which St. John designates the Son of God, the Second Person of the Holy Trinity (Gospel, Prologue; Apoc. 19:13). In all the New Testament only St. John uses this designation in a personal sense. For this reason many rationalist critics have maintained, and some still maintain, the thesis of the derivation of the Prologue of St. John from Hellenistic philosophical teachings, flourishing in Alexandria at that time, and more precisely from the Jewish philosopher Philo, who was imbued with Hellenism.

As a matter of fact, the word Logos and the doctrine relative thereto are found in Stoicism and Alexandrine Neoplatonism. The Stoics admitted a Logos immanent in the world as the rational principle of all things, which manifests itself as energy of cohesion and life, as thought and will. This Logos, divine principle and soul of the world, is well fitted in the *pantheistic* conception proper to Stoicism (*q.v.*).

The Neoplatonists, on the other hand, developed the theory of the Logos from the concept of the Demiurge, which Plato placed as intermediate being between the transcendent God and the material world. Thus the Logos of Plato was not God, but something between God and men, a craftsman who molded preexisting matter into imitations of subsisting ideas. Philo adopted and merged together the two antithetic conceptions, formulating a hybrid doctrine of the Logos, which for him became now the divine wisdom, now the image of God, now one of His angels, or again the high priest, or a law and vital force of nature. It is quite difficult to draw a precise concept from the Philonian writings, due in part to the fact that the author frequently makes use of symbolism and rhetoric.

St. John's Logos certainly had nothing whatsoever to do with Philo's, at least for these two obvious reasons: (*a*) while the gospel Logos is a living person, the historical Christ, Creator and Redeemer of the world, the Logos of Philo has no personal features, but is reducible to a vague allegory, variable as the mythological Proteus; (*b*) the gospel Logos is God, truly and properly, while that of Philo is called divine, at times called even God, but in a metaphorical sense, as the author himself declares. For these and other motives, serious criticism no longer speaks of derivation of one doctrine from the other. The true sources of St. John's Logos are the sapiential books of the Old Testament and the Christological doctrines of St. Paul, who applies to Christ the vivid personifications and attributes of the divine Wisdom, which at times is called also Logos in those books of the Old Testament. See *Word.*

BIBLIOGRAPHY

CLARKE, "Sources of St. John's Logos Doctrine," *Irish Eccles. Record* (1922–1923). LEBRETON, *Histoire du dogme de la Trinité,* Vol. 1 (Paris, 1927), "Logos," *CE.* NEWMAN, "Causes of the Rise and Successes of Arianism," *Tracts theological and ecclesiastical* (London, 1902). PETER PARENTE, "Il Verbo," *Simbolo,* Vol. 2 (Assisi, 1942). POHLE-PREUSS, *Dogmatic Theology,* II *The Divine Trinity* (St. Louis, 1946), pp. 88–95. VOSTÉ, *De Prologo Ioanneo et Logo* (Rome, 1925).

Lombard, Peter. See "Outline of the History of Dogmatic Theology" (p. 302).

"lumen gloriae" (light of glory). A supernatural aid bestowed by God on the intellect of the blessed to render it capable of seeing intuitively the divine essence. In Holy Scripture there are only a few minor traces of this light, as in Psalm 35:10: "And in thy light we shall see light"; in Apocalypse 22:4 ff., it is said that the blessed will see the face of God without need of light, because God Himself will illumine them.

The Fathers, commenting on these texts, mention a divine help which makes the human intellect capable of seeing God. Thus Irenaeus, *Adv. Haereses,* l. IV, c. 20; Epiphanius, *Adv. Haereses,* 70, 7.

Toward the end of the thirteenth century the Beghards and the Beguines (see *Beghards*), a pseudo-spiritualistic sect, went around preaching that man with his own powers can attain beatitude, even in this life, without any divine aid. The Council of Vienne (1311–1312) condemned, among other errors attributed to them, the following opinion: "that the soul does not need the light of glory to see God and enjoy beatitude" (*DB,* 475).

The Church *magisterium* thus declares the *existence* of the "light of glory," without entering into the question of its *essence.* The theologians have developed a whole teaching about the *lumen gloriae,* based on those data: all agree, especially after the Council of Vienne, in admitting its existence, but all do not agree on determining its nature.

Some, taking inspiration from nominalism, speak of the beatific vision as of an increated thing actuated by God's power in the blessed soul which remains simply passive: thus the light of glory would be God Himself, inasmuch as He illumines the soul. This theory is antipsychological because it does not take into account that cognition, whether in the natural or the supernatural order, is a *vital* act and, therefore, must spring forth from the powers of the soul and remain in the soul as its own act. St. Thomas, coherent in his analysis of the beatific vision and the principles of human psychology, teaches that, since the created intellect is not proportionate to the immediate intuition of the divine essence, it must be *disposed* and *prepared* for it by an inherent and permanent force or energy. To put it more clearly, he reduces the *lumen gloriae* to a *habitual quality* (similar to a virtue) infused by God in the intellect of the blessed to elevate it *operatively* to the immediate vision of the divine essence. This infused quality forms one sole operative principle with the intellect, so that the vital act of the beatific vision proceeds in its entirety from both, the intellect and the *lumen,* under diverse aspects. This teaching has now become the common one. The *lumen gloriae* (*id sub quo* — that under which the vision proceeds) does not exclude immediacy of the vision, and it is more or less intense according to the degree of sanctifying grace in which the soul is found at the moment of death.

BIBLIOGRAPHY

St. Thomas, *Summa Theol.,* I, q. 12, a. 5; *Summa Contra Gentiles,* l. 3, c. 53–54. Chollet, *La psychologie des élus* (Paris, 1900), Ch. 6. Terrien, *La grâce et la gloire* (Paris, 1897).

Lutheranism. This term can be taken: (1) as a religious sect, one of the many swarming from the so-called Reformation of Martin Luther; (2) as a doctrinal system, created by Luther and propagated by him and by his first disciples in opposition to the Church and to the Catholic doctrine. This second acceptation of Lutheranism is the one that interests the theologian.

Luther (1483–1546) was born at Eisleben, but lived most of his life in Erfurt and Wittenberg in Germany. His childhood was saddened by oppression of stern discipline at home and in school. He was extraordinarily talented, but had exuberant emotions and violent passions, always in conflict with his religious education, which was not devoid of superstition. He became an Augustinian friar, after experiencing a great fright during a thunderstorm. He studied in an environment dominated by the nominalism of Ockham (which played down human *reason*) and Augustinianism (which discounted human *freedom* and activity under the action of God).

In the monastery he showed himself at first scrupulous in the observance of religious life, but gradually began to succumb to the concupiscence of the flesh, whence the violent drama of his spirit frightened by the thought of damnation. As professor of Holy Scripture at Wittenberg in 1515–1516, he expounded St. Paul's Letter to the Romans, which speaks of original sin and the problem of justification. In St. Paul he believed he found the greatest principle of his system; namely, that *faith without works* is sufficient to justify and sanctify man. The moral and intellectual shipwreck of his spirit was already accomplished when, in 1517, the occasion presented itself to make it evident; it was the preaching of the indulgences entrusted to the Dominicans, against which Luther vigorously protested (not without motivation of jealousy), fastening his 95 theses against the doctrine of indulgences (*q.v.*) to the door of the Church of the Castle of Wittenberg. In 1520, Leo X issued against Luther and his errors the bull, *Exsurge Domine*. Thus began the Lutheran rebellion which was to sever so great a part of Europe from the true Church of Christ.

Outline of the Lutheran doctrine: (1) Original justice (*q.v.*) was *connatural* to Adam, like sight to the eyes. (2) Original sin (loss of original justice) has, therefore, corrupted intrinsically human nature in such a way that man is no longer capable of doing any good at all. (3) By original sin human reason has degenerated and *free will* no longer exists. (4) Therefore, man is no longer responsible for his acts, especially since he is tyrannically dominated by *concupiscence,* which is intrinsically sinful even in its instinctive movements. (5) Man, fallen through original sin, is incurable, so deeply that not even God can heal him any more. Therefore the Redemption (*q.v.*) is entirely a work extrinsic to us, a work done by Christ, who substitutes Himself for us in order to pay the penalty of our sins to the divine justice (*penal substitution*). Human justification is done *extrinsically* — in a negative way, i.e., by *covering up* sin (not by removing it), and in a positive way, i.e., by *attributing* (*imputatio*) to us the holiness and the merits of Christ. (6) There is no *habitual grace* in us; actual grace is not a power or a quality of the soul, but is God Himself working in us. (7) The only good act man can do is the act of *fiducial faith* or abandonment of self to God, by which he confides in His mercy and trusts that his sins have been pardoned. (8) Consequently, the *sacraments* have no longer any *raison d'être:* Luther keeps baptism, penance (by which the remission of sins is declared but not effected), and the Supper (which is no longer the Mass). The bread and the wine in the Eucharist remain as they are, but Christ makes Himself present in them (companation), not through the consecration alone, but also by virtue of the faith of the faithful. (9) The *monarchical Church* with its hierarchy is a human institution: there is no intermediary between the individual and God. The only source from which man can and must draw divine truth is the Bible, interpreted individually under the illumination of God (*free thought and inquiry*). Tradition has only a human value. The true Church of Christ is the invisible Church (influence of *Wicliffe* and *Huss*). (10) The denial of indulgences, of purgatory, of the invocation of the saints, of prayers for the dead.

Lutheranism might be characterized as an individualistic *pseudo-supernaturalism.*

BIBLIOGRAPHY

DENIFLE, *Luther et le luthéranisme,* trans. Paquier (1910–1913). MCHUGH, "Lutheranism," *CE.* PAQUIER, "Luther," *DTC.* SCHMID, *Doct. Theol. of Evang. Luth. Church* (Philadelphia, 1889). WOLF, *The Lutherans in America* (New York, 1889).

M

Macedonians. Name derived from Macedonius, bishop of Constantinople (A.D. 360), who, however, does not seem to have professed the erroneous doctrine of the so-called Macedonians. This teaching, already proposed by Arius and Eunomius, consisted in the denial of the *divinity of the Holy Spirit,* who was held to be a *creature* of the Son. Therefore, these heretics are more properly called Pneumatomachists (enemies of the Spirit) or Marathonians, from the name of one of their leaders, Marathonius, bishop of Nicomedia. Informed of this new error, the last one influenced by Arianism, St. Athanasius, from his retreat in the Egyptian desert, wrote three letters to Bishop Serapion to refute it. The heresy was condemned by the I Council of Constantinople (A.D. 381); Pope Damasus ratified its decisions in the Council of Rome in 382.

BIBLIOGRAPHY

CAYRÉ, *Manual of Patrology,* trans. Howitt, Vol. 1 (Paris, Tournai, Rome, 1936), pp. 295, 318. TIXERONT, *History of Dogmas,* trans. H.L.B., Vol. 2 (St. Louis, 1914), pp. 58–66.

"magisterium" of the Church. The power conferred by Christ upon His Church and strengthened with the charism of infallibility, by which the teaching Church (*Ecclesia docens*) is constituted as the unique depositary and authentic interpreter of divine revelation to be proposed authoritatively to men as the object of faith for their eternal salvation. That this teaching power is of divine institution can be perceived clearly from the words with which Christ, on the point of leaving this earth, entrusts to the Apostles the mission of evangelizing the world: "Going therefore, teach ye all nations" (Matt. 28:19); "Go ye into the whole world, and preach the gospel to every creature" (Mark 16:15). The means, therefore, established by Christ for the propagation of His teaching is not writing, but oral preaching, living *magisterium,* to which He assures His personal assistance to the end of the world, saying in the sequence of the text quoted from St. Matthew: "Behold I am with you all days, even to the consummation of the world." These words prove also that the *magisterium* founded by Christ is perpetual and infallible (see *infallibility*). Entrusted to the Apostolic College (Apostles as a body) after the constitution of Peter's primacy, foundation, and supreme pastor of the Church (Matt. 16:18; John 21:15 ff.), this teaching authority resides primarily in Peter and his successors as in its source, and then in the Apostles and their successors, the bishops, subordinately to the Vicar of Jesus Christ.

Tradition, from St. Ignatius to St. Irenaeus and St. Augustine, recognizes this hierarchical constitution, and against doctrinal and moral aberrations makes constant appeal to the teaching of the Roman Church and its bishop, in whom St. Peter lives along with his primacy (see *primacy of St. Peter*). St. Augustine, picking up the voice of Tradition, goes so far as to say that he would not even believe the Gospel if the Church *magisterium* did not propose it to him to believe (*Contra ep. fundam.*, c. 5, *PL*, 42, 176).

According to Catholic doctrine, therefore, Holy Scripture and Tradition are only the *remote rule* of faith, while the *proximate rule* is the living *magisterium* of the Church, which resides in the Roman pontiff and in the bishops, inasmuch as they are subject to and united with him. The Vatican Council (sess. 4, c. 4, *DB*, 1832) has sealed this truth by defining that in the primacy of Peter and his successors is included the supreme power of teaching, which is *veritatis et fidei numquam deficientis charisma* ("the charism of never failing truth and faith"). Luther dared to impugn this truth that had been lived by fifteen centuries of Christianity and, denying the *magisterium* of the Church, proclaimed in its stead Holy Scripture, entrusted to the individual interpretation of the faithful, as the one sole rule of faith. But even to prescind from its open contradiction to revelation, this theory shows itself false by its own fruits matured over a period of four centuries: the innumerable Protestant sects with their characteristic doctrinal confusion and degeneration are an evident proof of the failure of that principle and its falsity (see *Protestantism; articles, fundamental*). Reason itself sees the necessity of an easy and sure guide for the life of faith, considering the difficulty, for a great part of mankind, of the study and interpretation of Holy Scripture.

BIBLIOGRAPHY

BAINVEL, *De magisterio vivo et traditione* (Paris, 1905). BILLOT, *De Ecclesia Christi* (Rome, 1927), p. 356 ff. Various treatises *De Ecclesia.*

Maldonatus. See "Outline of the History of Dogmatic Theology" (p. 303).

man. In the light of Christian doctrine the concept of man reposes on principles which have to do with the natural sciences, philosophy, and theology. Supposing the scientific and philosophical treatment, we set forth the statements of revelation and of the ecclesiastical *magisterium* on the nature, dignity, and end of man.

1. Man is a living being, composed of *matter* and *spirit.* This truth is guaranteed by the account of Genesis and by the whole traditional teaching of the Church, which defends the grandeur and immortality of the soul (IV Lateran Council, Council of Vienne, V Lateran Council, Vatican Council), and with it the dignity of the body (cf. the sacramental liturgy, the matrimonial legislation, the funeral rite, the dogma of the resurrection of the flesh).

2. The soul, superior to the body because of its intelligence and free will (image of God), is not, however, in conflict with it, but is its substantial form (Council of Vienne), so that soul and body constitute one sole being, or individual, or person.

3. Man's personality is sacred: through it we conceive human rights and duties, through it we understand equality and fraternity, above all differences of sex, of race, of social and cultural position. For the Church there are no castes, but only persons,

issued from the hands of the Creator and destined to the same supreme end, the possession of God. Every man has been redeemed by the same divine blood of Jesus Christ.

4. The individual, considered in himself and in his relations with God, ranks first; then the family, society, the State. Civil society and even religious society, like the Church, are for the human person. But this individualistic statement does not involve isolation, because Christian doctrine presents all humanity as one big family, of which God is the Father. Moreover, it teaches that man adheres to Christ through faith, becomes a member of His Mystical Body (*q.v.*), in which are fused and harmonized, without destruction, human personalities in one sole palpitation of supernatural life.

5. Man is a creature of God, naturally limited and dependent; he is, in addition, fallen from his primitive perfection through original sin (*q.v.*). Thus are explained the suffering and anguish of the present life which, after the example of Christ and by virtue of His merits and redeeming grace, is transformed into a conflict in which man must co-operate freely with God in order to win his own salvation.

Philosophical and religious systems have made man either a conglomeration of matter, or a pure spirit, or a disintegrated being with his soul in conflict with his body; now they have debased his dignity, again they have elevated him to the rank of a god; often, they have rejected intelligence, more often free will, or they have absorbed man in the organism of society and of the State. But no one, except the Church, has been able to avoid the many shoals and to present so harmonious a doctrine on man and his destiny as the one we have sketched in this article.

BIBLIOGRAPHY

Aveling, "Man," *CE*. Pohle-Preuss, *Dogmatic Theology*, III *God: Author of Nature and the Supernatural* (St. Louis, 1945), pp. 124–178. *The Teaching of the Catholic Church*, ed. Smith, 2 vols. (New York, 1949), pp. 286–311. Teilard De Chardin, "Homme," *DA*. Zacchi, *L'uomo* (Rome, 1944).

Manichaeism. A religious doctrinal system founded and diffused in the second century by Manes or Manet (*Mana* — spirit of the luminous world), a philosopher of Persian descent, born in the Babylonian region. The childhood of Manes is rich with legend. Many sources are lost and, therefore, it is difficult to reconstruct the history of Manichaeism and its founder. Certainly, the new sect spread with surprising rapidity in Europe, in the Near and even the Far East, despite persecutions and hostility of all kinds. In those times Chaldea was a concentration point for nearly all the religions of the West and the East; thus, it was easy for Manes to elaborate a *syncrisis* of various elements.

From the fragments of Manichaean writings and still more from indirect sources, first of which is St. Augustine, a Manichaean before being converted to Christianity, we can reconstruct in synthesis the doctrine of Manichaeism, which, moreover, had its liturgy and its ascetics. The fundamental principle of Manichaeism is dualism between spirit and matter, light and darkness, good and evil. The principle of good is God, identified with the light; the principle of evil is Hyle (matter), which the people identify with the devil (Satan). The origin of the world and of man is complicated with mythology, which reminds us of Gnosticism (*q.v.*). There is talk of original sin, of the slavery of the soul which Jesus comes to liberate (Redemption). Man, like the world, is a mixture of good and evil; to be saved, he must observe strict mortification in *words* and in *works,* especially in the struggle against sensuality. Fasts, vegetarian diet, abstinence from marriage and from sensual pleasures form the austere moral code, at least of the *Elect* (the real faithful). Greater liberty is granted to the *Auditors.* Manichaean eschatology draws from the Christian teaching and other sources. A Manichaean Church with its hierarchy was founded, which administered two sacraments: baptism and eucharist (bread and water, consecrated).

St. Augustine refuted the various aspects of Manichaeism in a series of works. However, it was not completely disbanded, but continued to exist more or less subreptitiously here and there. It reappeared strong and threatening after the eleventh century with rejuvenated form in the heresy of the Cathars (Albigenses in Southern France), against whom Innocent III had to promote a crusade, such was the audacity and profound corruption of this sect (see *Albigenses*).

The IV Lateran Council (1215) in its definitions aims at the Albigenses together with other religious sects (*DB,* 428 ff.).

BIBLIOGRAPHY

Arendzen, "Manichaeism," *CE.* Bardy, "Manichéisme," *DTC.* Cumont, *Recherches sur le manichéisme* (Bruxelles, 1912). Tondelli, *Mani* (Milan, 1932).

manism. See *animism.*

Marathonians. See *Macedonians.*

Marcionism. A heresy of the second century, headed by Marcion, against whom Tertullian wrote his work *Adversus Marcionem,* which informs us about the man and his doctrine. Marcion had some contacts with the Gnostics (see *Gnosticism*), but was not a Gnostic. He took, on the contrary, an anti-Gnostic position, because he preferred to the proud science (*gnosis*) a rigorous and practical asceticism, proposed as the one means of salvation. In considering the differences between the Old and the New Testaments, Marcion came to the conclusion that the Gospel is the antithesis and the indictment of the Old Testament. The Apostles failed to understand Christ and, what is more, they adulterated His thought. Only St. Paul understood thoroughly the divine Master when He condemned Judaism. In the Old Testament God is the God of justice and severity, sowing sorrows and tribulations in mankind; the God of the New Testament, on the other hand, is the God of goodness and love who manifests Himself in Jesus Christ, *Saving Spirit,* man only in appearance, who dies for us to free us from the tyranny of the Demiurge (God of the Old Testament). We adhere to the Saviour by mortification of the flesh, by abstaining from pleasures and luxury, and by suffering willingly, even martyrdom.

Expelled from the Christian communities, Marcion established an ecclesiastical organization and hierarchy of his own. He attracted many followers, especially by the example of his austere life. His immediate follower, *Apelles,* however introduced some real changes in the master's system. The *Encratites* (*q.v.*), who condemned marriage, hark back to Marcion. It cannot be denied that Marcion was animated by a sincere desire of ascetical perfection for himself and others, but he committed the grave error of repudiating the doctrinal wealth of Christianity and the genuineness of the apostolic Church, the work not only of the other Apostles but of Paul as well, whom

Marcion arbitrarily set against the others. The opinion of some scholars (cf. E. Buonaiuti, *Storia del Cristianesimo,* I), who love to see in Marcion a providential reformer and even a martyr to the official church, is an evident exaggeration and error in the evaluation of historical data. In the bosom of the true Church Marcion would have found satisfaction for his ascetic tendencies, coupled with a providential check on his aberrations.

BIBLIOGRAPHY

AMANN, "Marcion," *DTC.* ARENDZEN, "Marcionites," *CE.* TIXERONT, *History of Dogmas,* trans. Howitt, Vol. 1 (St. Louis, 1910), pp. 183–189.

marks of the Church. The *characteristic signs* which distinguish the Church, as the real and true institution of Christ, from the many religious societies which claim that honor.

According to the common teaching, confirmed in great part by the Vatican Council (*DB,* 1794), the marks (*notae* — notes) of the Church are the four qualities or endowments which the Nicene-Constantinopolitan Symbol attributes to the religious society founded by Jesus Christ: *unity, sanctity, catholicity,* and *apostolicity* (*qq.v.*). It should be noted, however, that these properties constitute the identification and individual marks of the true Church, not in that they have their origin in the supernatural and hidden principle that rules the ecclesiastical organism, but inasmuch as they are manifest *externally* and *visibly* to the eyes of all as the *effect* of that mysterious force. For example, unity is a mark of the Church not because the souls are spiritually united through faith, grace, and the Holy Spirit, to the one Head, Christ, but because from this invisible and real communion of spirits there results, *externally* and *experimentally,* concord in dogma, in liturgy, in hierarchy; the unity of millions of men, professing the same faith, frequenting the same sacraments, obeying the same pastors.

Those who can be classed as Christians are divided into three large groups: *Protestants, Schismatics, Catholics.*

It is clear that Protestantism (*q.v.*), considered in its various sects, lacks *unity,* since each sect is independent; it lacks *sanctity,* because in five centuries of existence it has not produced any masterpiece of grace, like the canonized saints of the Roman Church; it lacks *catholicity,* because none of its sects is present in a really conspicuous way and at one time in all the world; it lacks *apostolicity,* because it has rejected the power of orders (in Protestantism all are priests!) and the power of jurisdiction, by detaching itself from the apostolic stock.

Analogous observations hold for the *Schismatic Churches,* which surely lack *unity,* by constituting independent and national patriarchates (*autocephalous*), and *catholicity,* because they are limited to definite Eastern localities.

The *Roman Church,* on the other hand, appears as clearly individualized by these four marks, which are like four refulgent jewels, attracting upon her the eyes of the infidels and assuring Catholics of her divine mission (cf. Vatican Council, *DB,* 1794). The *unity* of this Church is evident, completely centered in the pope, that very vigilant custodian of dogmatic, liturgical, and disciplinary unity. Virtue visibly flourished in her and the fruits of *sanctity* are seen maturing so conspicuously and in such great numbers as to require, to record them, a society of scholars, the Bollandists. Evident, too, is the fact of the original, simultaneous, progressive *universality* of this Church, which unfolds her tents from one pole to the other. Finally, the *apostolicity* of her origin is proved visibly in the uninterrupted succession of popes in the Apostolic See, to which all the others are united.

BIBLIOGRAPHY

ST. THOMAS, *In Symbolum Apostolorum Expositio*, a. 7–8. *The Teaching of the Catholic Church*, ed. Smith, 2 vols. (New York, 1949), pp. 701–706. THILS, *Les notes de l'Eglise* (Gembloux, 1932). ZAPELENA, *De Ecclesia*, Vol. 1 (Rome, 1941).

martyrdom (Gr. μαρτύριον, from μάρτυς — witness). The testimony one renders to Christ and His doctrine by voluntarily undergoing death or at least sufferings inflicted on him precisely out of hatred toward Christ and His religion.

This concept is already in the Gospel: Jesus Himself prophetically exhorts His disciples to be the witnesses of His life and His words (John 15:27; Luke 24:26). He even predicts in detail their lot: they will be chased from the Synagogue, betrayed by their own relatives, accused and hauled before kings and governors, and put to death for *His name* (Matt. 10:17, 24; Luke 21:12). The Apostles protest before the whole world that they are the *martyrs*, the witnesses of Christ, and serenely go forth to meet death (Acts 2:32; 1 Pet. 5:1).

The martyrdom of the Apostles and of their earliest associates is a bloody seal of the *historical reality* of the Gospel, considered as a fact, and of its truth, considered as the *teaching* of our Saviour. Those martyrs attested with their blood what they had *seen*, had *heard*, and what they *believed*, whereas the martyrdom of the martyrs of the following centuries, who died because they *believed*, has rather a *moral* than a historical value.

Martyrdom, taken as a whole, constitutes an apologetic argument, or motive of credibility, for *the truth of the Christian faith*. The sacred name of martyr belongs only to one who renders testimony to the *divine truth*, which is only in Christ and His Church; this generous testimony of blood, founded on the faith, is such, according to Christian doctrine, that it substitutes for baptism and renders the soul of the martyr worthy of immediate entrance into heaven. The Church prays *to* the martyrs, but has never prayed *for* the martyrs.

Outside the Church there is no true and proper martyrdom: a heretic in *good faith*, who dies for Christ, perhaps may be counted among the martyrs; but a *contumacious* heretic who dies for his sect is not a martyr because he does not testify to the divine truth but to a human teaching.

BIBLIOGRAPHY

ST. THOMAS, *Summa Theol.*, II–II, q. 124. ALLARD, "Martyre," *DA; Ten Lectures on the Martyrs* (New York, 1907). DORONZO, *De Baptismo et Confirmatione* (Milwaukee, 1947), Index Analyticus: "Martyrium." HASSATT, "Martyr," *CE*. HEDDE, "Martyre," *DTC*.

Mary (Hebr. *Miriam*, of doubtful etymology, probably meaning lady). The scarcity of prophetic texts and historical gospel data on the Mother of Jesus embarrasses only a superficial and overcurious reader; actually, we have at our disposal all the essential elements for a complete judgment on the personality, greatness, and mission of Mary. She is in the foreground of the divine plan of salvation as outlined in the Old Testament and realized in the New. In the tragedy of the first sin, in contrast with Eve, the Mother of the Messias takes her stand beside Him in the definitive victory over Satan (see *protoevangelium*). There is a consciousness of her presence in the successive centuries of Messianic expectation. In 734 B.C. the striking announcement of Isaias (7:34; cf. Matt. 1:22) reveals her as Mother-Virgin of the

Emmanuel (see *virginity of Mary*), and the contemporary Micheas (5:1–2) shows her giving birth at Bethlehem. In the sixth century B.C., the prophet of Israel's tragedy sees in her "the new prodigy" and "the woman who protects the hero" (Jer. 31:22).

In the gospel story Mary dominates the accounts of the infancy of Jesus, which, as even non-Catholic critics recognize, go back through Luke to her own testimony. The mention of her name, her descent from David (Luke 1:26–27, 32, 69), her condition of fiancée about to conclude marriage with Joseph, of the House of David, provide us with the framework for the narrative of the annunciation of the divine maternity, which is the key for the perfect understanding of the psychology and personality of Mary. Conscious of the gravity of the angelic proposition, she accepts only after asking explanations on the circumstances of the event (Luke 1:26–38). The tumult of thoughts and feelings that wells up in her heart gushes forth in the *Magnificat,* which shows how very familiar Mary was with the sacred texts and how very much in harmony her Messianic expectation was with the most authentic prophetic tradition (Luke 1:39–56). From then on Mary appears as an instrument of choice graces. At her voice the precursor in Elizabeth's womb becomes aware of the presence of the Lord. The intimate tragedy of Joseph, confronted with the mysterious maternal condition of his wife, is resolved by the revelation of the great mysteries fulfilled in her (Matt. 1:18–24). The account of Jesus' birth gives Mary the leading role (Luke 2:16), while the Magi, first fruits of paganism around the Messias' crib, find Jesus in her arms (Matt. 2:11). The troubles following Bethlehem's joys outline for Mary a path of persecution and sorrow, which is explicitly revealed to her in the prophetic words of old Simeon (Luke 2:22–38); the future awaiting her during the whole life of Jesus. The long interlude of the calm life at Nazareth is broken by the episode of Jesus missing and found in the Temple, which gives us an insight into both Mary's delicacy of heart, anxiously looking for her Child and the silent faith with which she accepts the mysterious remark, made by Him, that His mission is independent of any human bond (Luke 2:41–52). The thirty years Mary lived intimately with her Son, whom she knows is the Son of God, in an altogether normal life and without any extraordinary event to reveal to her eyes or to the people of Nazareth (cf. Matt. 13:55; Mark 6:3) the divine nature and the power of Jesus, constitute the exact measure of the depth of her faith and virtue.

Mary may be considered materially absent during the public ministry of Jesus; however, at Cana of Galilee, the first miracle of Christ is exhibited as an exception made through His mother's intercession. This incident shows how well she knows her Son and how sure she is of His omnipotence. The discretion and the decision of Mary's intervention with her Son are matched with the respect Jesus shows her before men, addressing her with the solemn title, *Mulier* — "Woman" (John 2:1–11; cf. 10:26).

Twice Mary meets her Son in His apostolic journeys (John 2:12; Matt. 12:46, and parallel texts), but her presence is not stressed. Twice Jesus speaks of His Mother (Matt. 12:49–50, and parallel texts; Luke 11:27) and His words, while apparently hard, are nevertheless the best praise of her. Jesus says: "Whosoever shall do the will of my Father that is in heaven, he is my mother"; and, in answer to the woman who had exalted the Master's mother, calling her "blessed," He affirms: "Rather, blessed are they who hear the word of God and keep it." In both cases, far from refusing praise to Mary, He holds her up as a perfect model, for He means that men ought to know that Mary was great not only as the Mother of Jesus, but also because she reacted to that gratuitous privilege with all her capacity of love, obedience, and sacrifice.

Mary reappears during Jesus' passion: sorrowing Mother under her Son's cross, who entrusts her to His beloved apostle (John 19:25–27) as the sign and pledge of a wider maternity.

The historian of the primitive Church shows Mary at the head of the disciples assembled in expectation of the Holy Spirit (Acts 1:14), Mother and Mistress of the Church.

In an absolutely normal, exterior life Mary was able to keep closed up in her heart the most secret mysteries of God. At the time of the annunciation she was about twelve years old. We do not know how old she was at the time of her glorious passage, but we can say that she lived a full life. (See *Assumption of the Blessed Virgin; Co-Redemptrix; Immaculate Conception; maternity, divine; maternity, spiritual; virginity of Mary.*)

BIBLIOGRAPHY

De la Broise, *La Sainte Vierge* (Paris, 1924). Dublanchy, "Marie," *DTC*. Garofalo, *Le parole di Maria* (Turin, 1943). Gibbons, "The Position of the Blessed Virgin in Catholic Theology," *Am. Cath. Quarterly Review*, Vol. 3, n. 12. Landucci, *Maria SS. nel Vangelo* (Roma, 1945). Lesêtre, "Marie," *DBV*. Livius, *The Blessed Virgin in the Fathers of the First Six Centuries* (London, 1893). Maas, "Virgin Mary (The Blessed)," *CE*. O'Shea, *Mary and Joseph* (Milwaukee, 1949). Otten, *A Manual of History of Dogmas*, Vol. 2 (St. Louis, 1915), pp. 397–417. Scheeben, *Mariology*, trans. Geukers, 2 vols. (St. Louis, 1946–1947). Stewart, *The Greater Eve* (London, 1912). *The Teaching of the Catholic Church*, ed. Smith, 2 vols. (New York, 1949), pp. 513–548. Vassall-Phillips, *The Mother of Christ in Tradition, Theology and Devotion* (London, 1922). Vitti, "Maria negli splendori della Theologia biblica," *Civilitá Cattolica* (1942), III, pp. 193–201.

See also under the above-mentioned entries.

Masoretic. The name given to the original Hebrew text of the Old Testament, provided with the phonetic signs and the critical annotations of the Masora (Tradition).

The Masora, which had its beginning in the age of the Scribes (five to four centuries, B.C.), was codified by the Hebrew doctors of the Academy of Tiberias between the sixth to the tenth centuries, A.D. It aims at the best conservation and understanding of the Hebrew text. Currently Old Testament scholars use the Masoretic edition.

BIBLIOGRAPHY

Abbot, *Essays chiefly on the Original Texts of the Old and New Testaments* (London, 1891). Drum, "Massorah," *CE*. Ginsburg, *Introduction to the Massoretico-critical edition of the Hebrew Bible* (1897). Kittel, Kahle, have recently published (Stuttgart, 1937) a critical edition of the Massoretic text. Lesêtre, "Massore," *DBV*. Vandervorst, *Introduction aux textes hebreu et grec de l'Ancien Testament* (Malines, 1935). Zarb, *Il testo biblico* (Rome, 1939).

Mass (Lat. *missio* — dismissal; from the fourth century the whole body of the ceremonies of the Eucharistic Sacrifice received its name from the ceremony of dismissing the catechumens before the Offertory of the Mass). The Mass is the Sacrifice of the New Law. The supreme act of cult could not be lacking to Christianity, which is the perfect religion, and therefore Christ enriched His Church with the unbloody sacrifice so that it might be the perpetual commemoration and perennial application of the merits acquired in the bloody sacrifice of the cross. Indeed, the Mass is the repetition of the Last Supper, according to the Lord's command: "Do this for a commemoration of me." Now, the Last Supper was a true sacrifice because the expressions used by Christ: "This is my Body, which is *given* for you" (Luke 22:19), "This is my blood of the new testament, which shall be *shed* for many unto remission of sins" (Matt. 26:28), according to biblical style, are properly *sacrificial terms* (cf. Gal. 1:4; Eph. 5:2; Lev. 1:5, 15; 1 Pet. 1:19). This conclusion is efficaciously confirmed by the prophecy of Malachias (1:10–11), which predicts a sacrifice whose characteristics of holiness and universality are verified only in the Mass, and by Tradition which, by its liturgical praxis and open testimonies of the Fathers, assures us of the will of Christ to institute a real and proper sacrifice to endure to the end of the world (1 Cor. 11:26). From these data of revelation the Church has an excessive store of reasons to oppose, in the Council of Trent (sess. 22), the Protestants who absolutely ostracize the sacrifice of the altar.

Theologians questioned for a long time how the liturgy of the Mass, which is accomplished in the three great acts of Offertory, Consecration, and Communion, realizes in itself the true essence of sacrifice. In all real sacrifices, offerer, victim, and sacrificial act are to be considered. This act includes two elements: the one material, i.e., oblation, the other formal, i.e., immolation.

All are in agreement, after the declaration of the Council of Trent, in recognizing that Christ is the Priest and the principal Victim that is offered and immolated in the act of the double consecration of bread and wine. But the agreement is sharply split when it comes to explaining in just what the sacrificial aspect of the double consecration essentially consists.

Leaving aside the opinion of Bellarmine, Suarez, and Franzelin, who affirm a physical immolation in the Mass, which seems excessive, as well as that of De la Taille and Lepin, who are satisfied with the oblation alone and, therefore, err on the short side, it would seem best to hold to the traditional teaching that represents the sacrifice of the Mass as a real oblation and immolation of a mystical and sacramental order. This teaching begins, as it were, from the original datum of the double consecration: the body alone being under the species of bread by virtue of the words (*vi verborum*), and only the blood being in the same manner under the species of wine, it follows that the body of Christ, not in itself but only as contained under the appearances of bread, *is separated* from the blood as contained under the distinct appearances of wine; thus we have a true, but mystic, immolation, such as is realizable now, given the impassibility of the glorious body of the Redeemer. This teaching, which is in perfect alignment with the Council of Trent (*DB,* 938, 940), is supported by the most beautiful testimonies of Tradition, from the Nazianzen to St. Augustine, and by the authority of great theologians, from St. Thomas to Billot.

BIBLIOGRAPHY

St. Thomas, *Summa Theol.,* III, q. 83. Billot, *De sacramentis* (Rome, 1932). Boland, *Of Mass* (London, New York, 1923). Clarke, *Handbook of Divine Liturgy. A Brief Study of the Historical Development of the Mass* (London, 1910). Connell, *De sacramentis* (Brugis, 1933), pp. 258–287. Doronzo, *De Eucharistia,* Vol. 2, *De Sacrificio* (Milwaukee, 1948). Fortescue, *The Mass* (London, 1913). Gihr, *The Holy Sacrifice of the Mass,* trans. from the German (St. Louis, 1914). Lebreton, "Eucharistie," *DA,* col. 1563 ff. Lepin, *L'idée du sacrifice de la Messe* (Paris, 1926). Lucas, *Holy Mass* (London, 1914). MacDonald, *The Sacrifice of the Mass* (London, St. Louis, 1924); "The Sacrifice of the New Law," *The Ecclesiastical Review* (Dec., 1905). Mortimer, *Eucharistic Sacrifice* (London, 1901). Pierse, *The Mass in the Infant Church* (Dublin, 1909). Piolanti, *De sacramentis,* Vol. 2 (Rome, 1945). Pohle, "Mass (Sacrifice of the)," *CE.* Pohle-

Preuss, *Dogmatic Theology,* IX *The Sacraments,* Vol. 2, *The Holy Eucharist* (St. Louis, 1946), pp. 272–400, 349–370. Rock, *Hierurgia;* or, *The Holy Sacrifice of the Mass,* revised by Weale, 2 vols. (London, 1907). Roschini, *L'essenza del sacrificio eucaristico* (Rome, 1936). Ruch, Gaudel, Rivière, Michel, Jugie, Cabrol, "Messe," *DTC.* De la Taille, *Esquisse du Mystère de la Foi* (Paris, 1924); *Mysterium Fidei* (Paris, 1931). *The Teaching of the Catholic Church,* ed. Smith, 2 vols. (New York, 1949), pp. 880–918. Vaughan, *The Holy Sacrifice of the Mass* (St. Louis, 1900). Vonier, *A Key to the Doctrine of the Eucharist* (Westminster, 1946), pp. 86–157, 223–269.

Mastrius. See "Outline of the History of Dogmatic Theology" (p. 303).

materialism. See *pantheism.*

maternity, divine (of the Blessed Virgin). The foundation of all the greatness and the privileges of Mary. The title, θεοτόκος (*Dei Genitrix, Deipara:* Mother of God, God-bearing), expressed this truth in the common language of the faithful from the first centuries. Theodore of Mopsuestia and Nestorius (fifth century; see *Nestorianism*) were the first to impugn that title, maintaining coherently with their Christological error that Mary gave birth to the man Jesus of Nazareth, in which the divine Word dwelt. Mary, therefore, according to the Nestorians, is mother of Christ (man), not mother of God; and that is also evident from the fact that the eternal God cannot be born in time. St. Cyril of Alexandria opposed this heresy with the weight of centuries of Tradition as well as the force of theological reasoning based on the mystery of the hypostatic union (*q.v.*). The Council of Ephesus condemned Nestorianism (a. 431), affirming, together with the true divinity of Christ, the divine maternity of Mary; it was called, for this reason, "Mary's Council."

Holy Scripture several times calls Mary Mother of Jesus in the proper sense of the word (Matt. 1:18; John 19:25). Elizabeth even greets her as *mater Domini mei* ("Mother of my Lord"). In order to prove theologically this truth of faith, a simple reasoning will suffice: Christ is the incarnate Word, i.e., a divine Person subsisting in both the divine nature and the assumed human nature. Now Mary gave birth to Christ in His personal integrity, although through the line of human nature; therefore, she is truly mother of the Word, i.e., of God. It would be impertinent to object to the fact that the Word with its divine nature does not derive from Mary, before whom it existed: St. Cyril answered this by saying that our human soul is infused by God and does not derive from our parents; nevertheless none of us hesitates to call himself son of his own mother as to his whole being. We should remember that the Word is the term of an eternal generation from the Father and of a temporal generation from His Mother; two generations, two births, but not two *filiations* (relationships of son). Christ is the Son of God and remains such even when He assumes human nature: no change, no new relationship in the immutable Him. He is also truly the Son of Mary, but the mutual relationship is real (i.e., is a *relatio realis* in the philosophical meaning) only in the direction Mother to Son, not in the direction Son to Mother. Finally, no son is so much his mother's as Jesus is Mary's, since she conceived Him without insemination from man.

BIBLIOGRAPHY

St. Thomas, *Summa Theol.,* III, q. 35. Campana, *Maria nel dogma cattolico* (Turin, 1936). Merkelbach, *Mariologia* (Paris, 1939). Pohle-Preuss, *Dogmatic Theology,* VI *Mariology* (St. Louis, 1946), pp. 4–23. Roschini, *Mariologia,* 4 vols. (Milan, 1940–1949). Scheeben, *Mariology,* trans. Geukers, Vol. 1 (St. Louis, 1946), pp. 132–195. Terrien, *La Mere de Dieu et la Mere des hommes*

(Paris, 1902). *The Teaching of the Catholic Church*, ed. Smith, 2 vols. (New York, 1949), pp. 513–517. VASSALL-PHILLIPS, *The Mother of God* (London, 1920).

maternity, spiritual (of the Blessed Virgin). Mary, true Mother of the Son of God (see *maternity divine*), is the spiritual mother of the whole human race, in whose salvation she co-operated with the Redeemer. This truth is foreshadowed on Calvary when the dying Christ entrusted the Blessed Virgin to John, and John to her: "'Woman, behold thy son!' Then he says to the disciple: 'Behold thy mother'" (John 19:26–27). Origen commented that Christ lives in every perfect Christian, who, therefore, is called son of Mary. The Fathers draw a parallel between Eve, mother of sinners (the dead), and Mary, mother of those vivified by divine grace (cf. Justin, Irenaeus). Besides the testimony of the dying Jesus, there is a profound theological reason touched on by St. Augustine (*De Virginitate*, 5, 6): Mary is the Mother of all men because she is the Mother of Christ, of whom men are mystical members. Pius X: "In the most chaste womb of His Mother, Christ took His flesh and with it a spiritual body, composed of the future faithful.... Therefore, in a spiritual and mystical way we are called sons of Mary and she is the Mother of us all" (encycl., *Ad diem illum*).

BIBLIOGRAPHY

ALBERT THE GREAT, *Mariale*, q. 29, § 3. O'CONNELL, *Our Lady Mediatrix of All Graces* (Baltimore, 1926), pp. 33–60. HOGAN, *Mother of Divine Grace* (London, 1921). MERKELBACH, *Mariologia* (Paris, 1939), p. 296 ff. ROSCHINI, *Mariologia*, Vol. 2 (Milan, 1942), p. 481 ff.

matrimony (Lat. *matris munus*—office of mother). The sacrament which prepares new candidates for the kingdom of God. In the first pages of Holy Scripture (Gen. 2:23 ff.; cf. Matt. 19:4 ff.) the structure of matrimony is sketched as a natural contract (*officium naturae*). Its elements are: (1) It is instituted indirectly in the constitution of the two sexes, which attract each other by natural instinct, and directly by the positive intervention of the Creator, narrated in Genesis. (2) It is constituted, in each instance, by the mutual consent by which a man and a woman unite for the purposes intended by God. (3) It is characterized by two basic qualities, i.e., unity and indissolubility: "two in one flesh." (4) It is ordered to procreation, as its principal end: "increase and multiply" (Gen. 1:27–28); to mutual help, as its secondary end: *adiutorium simile sibi* ("a helper like himself," Gen. 2:18); and to the discipline of the disorderly instinct of the flesh, as an accessory end. (5) It has a sacred character, recognized by all peoples in the religious ceremonies with which it is surrounded, and openly revealed by God in the New Testament when he called matrimony the symbol of the future union of Christ with the Church (Eph. 5:32). From the fall of Adam to the time of the Redemption this primitive unity and indissolubility was not always observed. Not only were the pagans hardened to divorce and polygamy, but even the chosen people, on account of their hardheadedness, wrung, so to speak, a sort of dispensation from God Himself, and very quickly degenerated to that low moral level from which Christ came to free the world.

First of all, Christ restored marriage to its primitive purity, putting back into effect the law of unity (Matt. 19:9; Mark 10:11; Luke 16:18), sanctioning that of indissolubility with the well-known *Quod Deus coniunxit homo non separet* ("Let no man sever what God has joined together," Matt. 19:6). He then elevated the institution of matrimony to the *dignity of a sacrament.* This elevation, foreshadowed in Christ's manner of acting, suggested more clearly by St. Paul (Eph. 5:20–32), and openly taught by Tradition, transferred the *officium naturae* into the supernatural order and put it in the light of the union of Christ with the Church, from which it receives its proper physiognomy. Indeed, as the union of Christ with the Church (1) is born of that generous self-giving, (2) through which Jesus Christ in the effusion of His purest love gives Himself forever (indissolubility) to one Spouse alone (unity), (3) to make her spiritually fruitful, till His Mystical Body is completed: so Christian marriage, (*a*) finds its genesis in mutual self-giving expressed externally in the words of the contract (the sensible rite of the sacrament), (*b*) which produces between the man and woman a bond which is *one,* because exclusive of a third party, and *indissoluble,* because lasting till death, (*c*) for the principal end of fecundity, that is of multiplying citizens in the kingdom of God, to which is added the secondary purpose of mutual help and comfort and the accessory end of moderating the movements of concupiscence.

For the attainment of these ends matrimony asks God for and produces *ex opere operato* sanctifying and sacramental grace, which establishes a particular and constant orientation of the supernatural organism of the husband and the wife, to which is annexed a spirit of uprightness in the procreation of the offspring, of reciprocal justice and charity in bearing the family burdens, and in carrying out the difficult task of raising the children in a Christian way. By reason of its supernatural elevation, matrimony is withdrawn from *civil interference* and put under the vigilance of the Church, which determines the conditions of validity of the marriage contract, establishes the impediments thereto, and judges all matrimonial cases referring to the sacramental bond (cf. Council of Trent, sess. 24). Pius XI issued his splendid encyclical, *Casti Connubii* (1930), on the dignity of Christian marriage and the remedies against modern abuses.

BIBLIOGRAPHY

St. Thomas, *Summa Theol.,* III, *Suppl.,* qq. 41–68. Boyer, *Synopsis praelectionum de Matrimonio* (Rome, 1942). Divine, *The Law of Christian Marriage* (New York, 1908); *The Sacraments Explained* (London, 1905), pp. 431–515. Doronzo, *De sacramentis in genere* (Milwaukee, 1946), Index Analyticus: "Matrimonium." Gannon, *Holy Matrimony* (London, 1928). Gasparri, *Tractatus canonicus de matrimonio* (Vatican City, 1932). Godefroy, Le Bras, Jugie, "Marriage," *DTC.* Lavaud, *Mariage, nature humaine et grâce divine* (Fribourg en Suisse, 1942). Palmieri, *De Matrimonio christiano* (Rome, 1897). Pohle-Preuss, *Dogmatic Theology,* XI *The Sacraments,* Vol. 4, *Extreme Unction, Holy Orders, Matrimony* (St. Louis, 1946), pp. 140-242. Ryan, "Marriage (History of)," *CE.* Scheeben, *The Mysteries of Christianity,* trans. Vollert (St. Louis, 1946), pp. 593–610. Selinger, "Marriage (Moral and Canonical Aspect of)," *CE. The Teaching of the Catholic Church,* ed. Smith, 2 vols. (New York, 1949), pp. 1062–1100.

matter and form (of the sacraments). Whenever Scripture speaks of a sacrament, it represents it as a rite composed of *things* and of *words:* thus baptism is accomplished by a washing with water together with the Trinitarian formula is pronounced (Matt. 28:19; for the other sacraments, cf. Acts 8:15–17; Matt. 26:26–28; James 5:14; Acts 6:6, etc.). But Holy Scripture does not assign greater value to the words than to the things done, nor does it join up the sensible rite with its meaning (cf. Matt. 28:19; Rom. 6:3–11); it shows, finally, only concretely that all the sacraments are composed of things and words. These three indeterminations of Holy Scripture, like small clouds, are dissipated gradually as the Fathers and theologians penetrate further in their analysis of the sacramental composite.

In the twelfth and thirteenth centuries, having exactly determined the *sacramental septenary* (see *sacraments, number of*), the theologians were able to state in the abstract that all the sacraments are composed, in their sensible sign, of things (*res*) and words (*verba*); however, spurred on by a profound spirit for systemization, they were not only content to state the fact, but also endeavored to illustrate the manner in which this is accomplished by adapting to the sacramental world the hylomorphic theory (Gr. ὕλη — matter, and μορφή — form), which, following in the steps of Aristotle, they had very successfully applied to the physical world. The simple reasoning that motivated them is: if in the physical composite the potential and indetermined element is called *matter* and the *determining* and *actual* element is called *form,* in the same way, in the sacramental composite the indetermined element may be called matter and the determining one, form; now, it appears that in the rite of the sacrament, e.g., of baptism, the thing, i.e., the water, being indifferent as to indication of cooling or of purification, is determined to signify purification by the words which clearly express it: "I baptize thee, i.e., I *wash* thee in the name of the Father, etc." It is, therefore, fitting that the water be called matter and the words, form.

Certain non-Catholic writers (Harnack, Turmel) have been scandalized by such doctrine, as if theology had been made the slave of Aristotelian philosophy.

The reason given above shows sufficiently the opportuneness of the hylomorphic terminology applied to the sacraments; it is, indeed, the proper function of the theologian, according to the teaching of the Vatican Council, to illustrate dogma *ex eorum quae naturaliter cognoscit* [*ratio*] *analogia* ("through the analogy of those things that it naturally knows" *DB,* 1796).

Moreover, the Church, to which Christ not only committed the duty of guarding the deposit of revelation but also the power of formulating and adapting it to the capacity of the faithful, has for seven centuries been using such terminology in several documents of her solemn *magisterium* (cf. *DB,* 672, 695, 914, 1963). Therefore, the Catholic theologian has every right to use a formula which, besides being consecrated by many centuries of ecclesiastical use, helps him to clear up many obscure points of sacramental doctrine.

BIBLIOGRAPHY

St. Thomas, *Summa Theol.,* III, q. 60. Doronzo, *De sacramentis in genere* (Milwaukee, 1946), Index Analyticus: "Forma"; "Materia." Michel, "Matière et forme dans les Sacraments," *DTC.* Umberg, *Systema Sacramentarium* (Oeniponte, 1930).

Maximus, Confessor. See "Outline of the History of Dogmatic Theology" (p. 302).

Mazzella. See "Outline of the History of Dogmatic Theology" (p. 303).

mediation. Physically, it is the condition of one who finds himself between two extremes from which he is distinguished, although having something in common with them. Morally, it is the action of one who endeavors to unite and conciliate the extremes between which he finds himself.

It is a truth of faith that Christ is the perfect Mediator between God and men. St. Paul, in 1 Timothy 2:5, says: "For there is one God, and one mediator of God and men, the man Jesus Christ." Thus also the Fathers and the Church *magisterium* (cf. Council of Trent, sess. 51, *DB,* 790).

Reason: Christ, as God-Man, finds Himself in the conditions required for physical mediation between the Divinity and humanity. Also the perfection of moral mediation is to be attributed to Him, because the Word became Incarnate precisely to reconcile mankind with God (see *Incarnation*). The Word, as God, is equal to the Father, and so cannot be mediator: He is mediator, however, as Man, according to His human nature, which made it possible for Him to suffer and die and make reparation for us. His human actions and sufferings have a redemptive value in that they are proper to the Word, who sustains and directs the assumed nature. Christ, therefore, is Mediator according to His human nature, but not independently of the Divinity. St. Augustine (*Sermo XII,* 21): "Behold the Mediator: the Divinity without the humanity is not mediator; the humanity without the Divinity is not mediator; but between the Divinity alone and the humanity alone, the human Divinity and the Divine humanity is mediator" (*RJ,* 1500).

Mary, as Mother of the Word Incarnate, participates subordinately in the mediation of Christ with God, and is also Mediatrix between Christ and men. Her mediation consists principally in praying in order to obtain for us the application of the fruits of the Redemption, but it cannot be restricted to this office, because the Blessed Virgin, associated with Christ, co-operated with Him in the great work of the Redemption, contributing to the acquisition of the fruits of salvation (see *Co-Redemptrix*).

BIBLIOGRAPHY

St. Thomas, *Summa Theol.,* III, q. 26. Bittremieux, *De Mediatione Universali B. M. Virginis quoad gratias* (Brugis, 1926). Humphrey, *The One Mediator* (London). O'Connell, *Our Lady Mediatrix of All Graces* (Baltimore, 1926), pp. 61–100. Roschini, *Mariologia,* Vol. 2 (Milan, 1942), p. 272 ff. Scheeben, *Mariology,* trans. Geukers, Vol. 2 (St. Louis, 1947), pp. 185–273. Wilhelm, "Mediator (Christ as)," *CE.*

Mediatrix. See *Co-Redemptrix; mediation.*

Medina. See "Outline of the History of Dogmatic Theology" (p. 303).

members of the Church. The Church is an organism socially and hierarchically constituted in which circulates supernatural life. As a member can share in the life of the organism in a perfect way, or can be stricken with paralysis or even torn from the organism itself, so men, in their relations with the Church, can find themselves in the following dissimilar conditions:

1. Either they are perfectly united to the organism both through the internal bond of grace and charity, and through the external bond of faith, cult, and hierarchy (see *unity, mark of the Church*): these are the *living members* of the Church, in which divine life is diffused throughout.

2. Or, having broken the internal bond through sin, they still conserve the external bonds by professing the same faith, communicating in the same sacraments, and obeying the same pastors: these are the *dead* or paralyzed members of the Church, in whom the vital sap no longer flows, as in dead branches. But it is profitable to them that they remain materially united to the organism, because it is easier for them to be revived and receive again its beneficial influxes.

3. Or, having once adhered to the Church, by at least external acceptance of all the juridical bonds (included in the reception of baptism), they have afterward repudiated these bonds. Such are: the *heretics,* who tenaciously deny some truth to be believed on divine Catholic faith, or

who nurture doubts on such a truth; the *apostates,* who reject as a whole the truths of the Christian faith; the *schismatics,* who refuse submission to the Roman pontiff and do not have relations (*communio*) with the other members of the Church (*CIC,* Can. 1325, § 2). These are the *members separated* and wrenched from the organism of the Church.

4. The *Catechumens* who accept the Christian faith and are disposed to obey its pastors, although spiritually belonging to the Church, juridically cannot be called members of it, because they have not yet received baptism which is the act by which a man enters the ecclesiastical society as a member (*CIC,* Can. 87). The *infidels* belong to the Church only *in potency.*

BIBLIOGRAPHY

St. Thomas, *Summa Theol.,* III, q. 8, a. 3; *Comment. In 3 Sent.,* dist. 13, q. 2, a. 2. Bellarmine, *De Ecclesia militante,* l. 3, c. 3. Franchi, *De membris Ecclesiae* (Rome, 1938). Mazzella, *De Ecclesia,* n. 590. *The Teaching of the Catholic Church,* ed. Smith, 2 vols. (New York, 1949), pp. 706–710. Vellico, *De Ecclesia Christi* (Rome, 1940), pp. 533–547.

Mennonites. See *Anabaptists.*

merit. The right to a reward due for a morally good action. Merit can be *de condigno* (condign; adequate), if there is an equal proportion between the good act and its reward, and *de congruo* (congruous; of convenience) if, in the lack of such proportion, there intervenes some reason of convenience or of benevolence that moves the rewarder.

Supernatural merit is that which arises from an action performed under the influence of divine grace, and thus in relationship with the supernatural end: the beatific vision. Five *conditions* are required for supernatural merit: (1) *state of mortal life* (*status viatoris* — state of the wayfarer), because death is the end of the test (see *death*); (2) *state of sanctifying grace,* because sin renders relationship impossible with God; (3) *free will,* without which there is no responsibility and, therefore, no reason for reward or punishment; (4) *good work,* since evil deserves punishment; (5) *divine agreement* or consent (accepting and ordering the good work to its reward), because the supernatural order is absolutely gratuitous and no creature can acquire a true and proper right with reference to God, without His own divine disposition in this regard. Man, fulfilling these conditions, can merit, even condignly (*de condigno*), the increase of grace and life eternal, called a "crown of justice" by St. Paul.

Christ, during His mortal life, merited for Himself the glorification of His human body (His soul already enjoyed the beatific vision), and for the whole human race He merited, especially by His passion and death, all supernatural gifts and life eternal. His merit, like His satisfaction, has an *infinite* value, and this value is, more probably, according to the *rigor* of justice (i.e., implies the proper and full concept of justice), because it is the merit of the Word of God Himself, who is the operating subject in His assumed nature. Mary has merited *de congruo* for us all that Jesus merited *de condigno.*

Lutheranism, holding human nature intrinsically corrupted by original sin to the point of the loss of free will, denied all possibility of merit in man. The Council of Trent condemned this error, asserting both free will and, under the influence of grace, merit (*DB,* 809 and 842).

BIBLIOGRAPHY

St. Thomas, *Summa Theol.,* I–II, q. 114. Doronzo, *De Poenitentia,* Vol. 3 (Milwaukee, 1951). Hugon, *Le mystère de la Rédemption* (Paris, 1927), Ch. 7. Joyce, *The Catholic Doctrine of Grace* (New York, 1920), pp. 158 ff., 245 ff. Peter Parente, *De Verbo*

Incarnato (Rome, 1939), p. 331 ff. POHLE, "Merit," *CE.* POHLE-PREUSS, *Dogmatic Theology,* VII *Grace* (*Actual and Habitual*) (St. Louis, 1946), pp. 397–436. RIVIÈRE, "Mérite," *DTC.*

Messias (Hebr. *Maschiach* — Anointed; Gr. Χριστός — Christ). The name is derived from the anointing with which the kings were consecrated in the Jewish theocracy. The title at one time was common to all the kings of the Jews, but afterward was reserved for the supreme King who was to bring eternal salvation to the people.

Messianism is the body of the Old Testament prophecies relative to the person, origin, and qualities of the Messias, and the spiritual kingdom He would come to found.

BIBLIOGRAPHY

CEUPPENS, *De Prophetiis messianicis in A.T.* (Rome, 1935). DENNEFELD, "Messianisme," *DTC.* GEDDES, "Messias," *CE.* LESÊTRE, "Messie," *DBV.* SANDAY, *The Life of Christ in Recent Research* (Oxford, 1907). TOUZARD, "Juif (Peuple)," *DA,* cols. 1614–1654.

metempsychosis (Gr. μετά — between, after, and ψυχή — soul). The theory of the transmigration of the human soul from one body to another (of man or of animal) for the purpose of purification from guilt. Modern spiritists and theosophists prefer the term *reincarnation* (restricted to human bodies only).

Traces of metempsychosis are found among primitive peoples under the influence of animism (*q.v.*). India, however, is the classical home of metempsychosis. It was Buddha who adopted and spread it as an element in the solution of the problem of evil and of suffering. The guilty soul must free itself from the stain of sin by an equal compensation of virtuous actions for the sinful ones: this is the famous law of the *Karma,* which regulates mechanically the expiation of guilt. After a series of transmigrations the soul is finally purified and passes into the *Nirvana,* absolute calm without desires or activity (according to other sects it is an absorption of the individual soul in *Brahma*). Metempsychosis is found also in Egypt and in Greece, where it prevailed in *Orphism* and in the followers of Pythagoras. Plato drew it from these sources (cf. the dialogue Phaedon); Plotinus, too, spoke of metempsychosis. In modern times spiritism (*q.v.*) has rehabilitated metempsychosis.

The theory of metempsychosis is absurd: (*a*) *psychologically,* because it neglects or destroys the unity of the human individual and his personality, based on the substantial union of *this* soul with *this* body; and also because it fails to keep the due proportion between form and matter; (*b*) *morally,* because it perverts the sense of expiation, which demands of the individual recognition of the guilt to be expiated. The soul which passes from body to body, according to that theory, has no memories of its preceding existences. This amnesia, too, is inexplicable. Metempsychosis is not compatible with Catholic doctrine, which teaches the substantial and personal unity of man and, immediately after death, the appearance of the soul before God's tribunal to receive immediately the reward or the penalty merited (see *death; judgment, divine*).

BIBLIOGRAPHY

ALGER, *Doctrine of a Future Life* (New York, 1866). DE LA VALLÉE-POUSSIN, *Bouddhisme* (Paris, 1925). HEDDE, "Métempsycose," *DTC.* LYALL, *Asiatic Studies* (London, 1882). MAHER, "Metempsychosis," *CE.* McDONNELL, "The Ancient Indian Conception of the Soul," *Journal of Theological Studies* (1900). TYLOR, *Primitive Culture* (London, 1871).

Methodists. A Protestant sect widely diffused, which numbers today more than eleven million members. *Methodism* (from *method,* to which much attention is given by this sect) was founded in the eighteenth century by John Wesley, an Anglican priest disgusted with dissipation and spiritual aridity of Anglicanism who, following upon his reading of the *Imitation of Christ,* first dedicated himself to a life of intense piety, and then to a fervent apostolate of preaching and works of charity that took him from one end of the globe to the other. To assure the duration of his revival movement, which found opposition and hostility in the official Anglican Church, he severed connections with that Church and founded his own community, strongly organized with bishops, priests, and deacons, with regulations for life and apostolate, and with particular and general assemblies for the continuous control of the movement.

The Methodist doctrine is substantially Protestant, based on the 39 Anglican articles: but Methodism is characterized by a lively piety, mortification (with systematic fasts), struggle against evil and sin, and zeal for the salvation of souls. Like all Protestant movements, Methodism split into various sects: *Methodist Episcopal Church, Methodist Protestant Church* (which denies the episcopate), etc.

BIBLIOGRAPHY

Buckley, "History of Methodists in the U. S.," *Amer. Church Hist.,* Series V (New York, 1907). Hedde, "Méthodisme," *DTC.* Piette, *La réaction wésléyenne, in L'évolution protestante. Etude d'histoire religieuse* (Bruxelles, 1925). Smith, *History of Wesleyan Methodism* (London, 1857–1862). Stevens, *History of Methodism* (New York, 1858–1861); *History of the Meth. Episc. Church* (New York, 1864). Weber, "Methodism," *CE.*

millenarianism (or chiliasm) (Gr. χιλιάς — a thousand). A theory of Jewish origin developed on the stock of the Messianic traditions. The prophets preached a kingdom of the future Messias as a golden age rich in glory and happiness. Enlarging on this concept, the Rabbis delighted in describing that kingdom in vivid colors, stressing its material character and fixing its duration at 1000 years, after which will come the universal judgment and the end of the world.

St. John, in the Apocalypse (Chap. 20), used the images and the language employed at that time in Jewish circles to express Christian thoughts and mysteries on the future of humanity and of the Church of Christ. Literally, the sacred text speaks of a defeat of Satan, relegated to the abyss, and hence of a triumphal reign in which the souls of the martyrs and the saints, priests of Christ, will rule with Him 1000 years. This glorification of the saints is called the *first resurrection.* After that period, Satan will be freed for a short time and will put up a great fight once more to seduce men, but in the end he will be conquered, together with his minister, the *Antichrist,* and then the end of the world will come with the universal resurrection and judgment.

Some Fathers (St. Irenaeus, St. Justin, Tertullian), interpreting this text literally, admitted *two resurrections* (that of the saints and the universal one) and between them the millenary reign of Christ on earth. Other writers (Cerinthus, Apollinaris) perverted the concept of that reign, representing it as a period of frenzied sexual extravagances. Protests immediately followed (Caius, a Roman priest, and Origen) and finally St. Augustine interpreted the Apocalypse in the symbolic and allegoric senses, eliminating, once and for all, millenarianism from the field of orthodoxy. The millenary kingdom, St. Augustine explains, is but the Christian era in which Satan is relatively defeated under the sanctifying action of the Redeemer and His Church. He will be definitively conquered at the end of the world after a brief struggle. That first resurrection of which St. John speaks is but the glorification of the holy souls who reign in heaven with Christ, and, in a way, even on earth by the light of their example.

The Church has tacitly remained on the line traced by St. Augustine, adopting his teaching and never looking with favor on the opposite opinions. In July, 1944, the Holy Office declared that millenarianism may not be sustained, even in its mild form (*AAS,* 1944, ser. II, Vol. XI, n. 7).

BIBLIOGRAPHY

St. Augustine, *De Civitate Dei,* 20, 7. Bardy, "Millénarisme," *DTC.* Gry, *Le millénarisme dans ses origines et son développement* (Paris, 1904). Kirsch, "Millennium and Millenarianism," *CE.* Pohle-Preuss, *Dogmatic Theology,* XII *Eschatology* (St. Louis, 1946), pp. 155–160. Schneider, *The Other Life* (New York, 1920), p. 298 ff. Tackson, *The Millennial Hope* (Chicago, 1919).

minister (Lat. *minister* — helper, servant, etc.). The person legitimately appointed (see *orders, holy*) to distribute grace by means of the sacraments and to offer the Sacrifice of the New Law. Jesus Christ, having determined the Sacrifice and instituted the sacraments, did not choose to assist, like an ordinary spectator, at the carrying out of His work, but remained at the center of His sacramental and sacrificial economy, invisibly but eternally operating; it is He who offers the sacrificial oblation and sanctifies through the sacred symbols. Therefore, having established a plan of redemption in which the invisible always manifests itself in the visible, consistency and harmony demanded that His activity, veiled under the sacrificial rite and the sacramental symbols, should in some way be rendered perceptible to the senses through a human minister. In fact, Christ did choose among His disciples (cf. Luke 27:19; John 20:21–23; 1 Cor. 1:4; 2 Cor. 5:18–20) visible ministers to whom, in imitation of His Father who really communicates to creatures the dignity of efficient causes, He transmitted a real participation of His sanctifying power. This power, however, is connected with and subordinated to Christ's own action of principal cause, so that the ministers are but an irradiation of His priesthood and an exterior manifestation of His activity of eternal Pontiff, the "long hand," as it were, through which He operates.

In an economy in which the efficacy of the sacraments depends totally on the sanctity and the mysterious action of Christ, it is easily understood that neither *faith* nor *state of grace* is required in the minister for their validity and efficacy.

In the first Christian centuries lively polemics were waged between Catholics (St. Cyprian Martyr against Pope St. Stephen), and later (fifth century) between St. Augustine and the Donatists who obstinately maintained that sacraments administered by heretics and sinners are not valid because *nemo dat quod non habet* ("no one can give what he does not have"). The ability and holiness of the Bishop of Hippo succeeded in weakening the age-old schism and in clarifying the Catholic teaching, according to which, *sacramenta sancta per se, non per homines* ("the sacraments are holy of themselves, not by the virtue of men"), because Christ is the principal Distributor of their graces, while the ministers are only instruments channeling the waters flowing for the enrichment and fruitfulness of the field of souls; it does not matter whether a pipe be of gold or silver, of iron or lead, provided it conveys the water. However, for valid administration, the ministers must have the intention of doing what the Church does (see *intention of the minister of the sacraments*).

The minister, ordinarily, is a *homo viator* (wayfarer or pilgrim, in regard to the beatific vision), and is, generally, one marked with the character of the priesthood (see *orders, holy*). He is distinct from the subject or receiver of the sacrament, except in the Eucharist, when the priest administers communion to himself, and in matrimony, in which man or woman is at once partial minister and subject of the sacrament.

BIBLIOGRAPHY

St. Thomas, *Summa Theol.*, III, q. 64, a. 4–10. Batiffol, *Le catholicisme de St. Augustin* (Paris, 1920), pp. 77–348. Doronzo, *De sacramentis in genere* (Milwaukee, 1946), Ch. 5. Piolanti, *De sacramentis,* Vol. 1 (Rome, 1945). Pohle-Preuss, *Dogmatic Theology,* VIII *The Sacraments,* Vol. 1, *The Sacraments in General, Baptism, Confirmation* (St. Louis, 1945), pp. 162–187. Tixeront, *History of Dogmas,* trans. H.L.B., Vol. 2 (St. Louis, 1914), pp. 393–407.

miracle (Lat. *miror* — I wonder). In a broad sense, it is an *extraordinary* thing which calls attention and excites wonder. St. Augustine, speaking from a *subjective* viewpoint, calls the miracle a difficult and unusual happening, above the power and the expectation of the observer, whose possibility and realization has been prepared by God. St. Thomas rightly adds the *objective* notion of an extraordinary intervention of God, and defines (*Summa Theol.,* I, q. 110, a. 4): "A miracle is that which is done by God outside the order of all created nature." The theologians explain and specify this definition: (*a*) done by God as principal cause — He may use any creature as instrumental cause; (*b*) done in the world; (*c*) outside or above the natural order, i.e., in a way superior to the forces of all nature; (*d*) outside or above, but not against the natural order, because the miracle is not a violation of the laws of nature but an exceptional happening brought about by a special, divine power that intervenes in created things, producing an effect superior to their natural power.

The *possibility* of the miracle rests chiefly on the absolute dominion of God as first and free cause of the universe, whose laws are subordinate to Him and cannot limit either His freedom of action or His power. Only the absurd and the sinful are impossible to God.

A miracle may surpass the power of nature's forces (*a*) as regards the substance of the event, e.g., the resurrection of the flesh; (*b*) as to manner, e.g., certain instantaneous cures. Finally, some miracles are the object of faith and thus are outside the order of sense experience; others are external happenings or facts, tangibly evident, and are intended by God to prove a truth of faith. It is these last that the Vatican Council (sess. III, c. 3, *DB,* 1790) calls: "Most certain signs of divine revelation — signs adapted to the intelligence of everyone."

BIBLIOGRAPHY

St. Thomas, *Summa Theol.,* I, q. 110, a. 4. Callan, "Nature and Possibility of Miracles," *Irish Theol. Quart.* (Oct., 1910). Cotter, *Theologia fundamentalis* (Weston, 1940), pp. 63–79. De Grandmaison, "Jesus Christ," *DA,* cols. 1412–1417. Driscoll, "Miracle," *CE.* Fenton, *We Stand With Christ* (Milwaukee, 1942), pp. 291–318. Garrigou-Lagrange, *De Revelatione* (Paris, 1926). Hay, *The Doctrine of Miracles Explained* (New York, 1873). Hogan, "The Miraculous in Church History," *Amer. Cath. Quart.* (April, 1898). Marsh, *Miracles* (London, 1906). Michel, "Miracle," *DTC.* Newman, *Essays in Miracles* (New York, London, 1890). Wallace, *Miracles and Modern Spiritualism* (London, 1897).

missal. See *liturgy.*

mission, divine (Lat. *mittere* — to send). The procession of one divine Person from another with respect to a particular effect produced in a creature, in which the Person becomes present in a certain new manner.

Divine mission includes two essential characteristics: (*a*) that the Person sent proceed from the Person sending Him; (*b*) that a new effect be produced in the creature. The mission may be *visible* or *invisible*.

1. *Visible mission*. The Son sent by the Father to take on human nature (Incarnation): "When the fulness of the time was come, God sent his Son" (Gal. 4:4). The *Incarnation* of the Word is a new effect, which, as an action *ad extra* (see *operation, divine*), is common to the three Persons, but terminatively (as regards its term) is exclusively of the Word, who alone becomes incarnate. The relationship, however, between the Word and the assumed nature (see *Incarnation*) does not add anything to the Person assuming, who remains unchanged; this relation is a real one (*relatio realis*) on the part of the assumed nature to the Person, but only a relation of the mind (*relatio rationis*) in the direction from the Person to the assumed nature. Another visible mission is that of the Holy Spirit under the form of a *dove* (in the baptism of Jesus in the Jordan) and of *tongues of fire* (in the Cenacle). These figures or forms were signs indicating the presence and the action of the Holy Spirit; as extrinsic effects they are attributed to the three Persons together, but as signs they have reference only to the Holy Spirit. There is evidently a great difference between the visible mission of the Son, who makes a human nature His own, and the mission of the Spirit, who only uses signs to manifest Himself.

2. *Invisible mission*. This is more difficult and complex. It is actuated only in the infusion of sanctifying grace, by which God communicates Himself, gives Himself to the human soul, which becomes His living temple, according to the Gospel: "We will come to him, and will make our abode with him" (John 14:23). Strictly, this invisible mission is of the Son or of the Holy Spirit, to whom grace has reference as light or as love; but in a wider sense this mission is also of the Father, inasmuch as He gives Himself together with the other two Persons.

Some wish to attribute this divine indwelling in the sanctified soul to the Holy Spirit in a very special way (see *indwelling of the Holy Trinity*).

BIBLIOGRAPHY

St. Thomas, *Summa Theol.*, I, q. 43. Hugon, *Le mystère de la très Sainte Trinité* (Paris, 1930), p. 262 ff. Klein, *The Doctrine of the Trinity*, trans. Sullivan (New York, 1940), pp. 211–241. Michel, "Trinité (Missions et Habitation des Personnes de la Trinité)," *DTC*, cols. 1830–1855. Pohle-Preuss, *Dogmatic Theology*, II *The Divine Trinity* (St. Louis, 1946), pp. 248–252. Scheeben, *The Mysteries of Christianity*, trans. Vollert (St. Louis, 1946), pp. 149–180. *The Teaching of the Catholic Church*, ed. Smith, 2 vols. (New York, 1949), pp. 139–142.

missionology (or missiology). The science of Missions for the conversion of the infidels. The missionary problem, always alive in the Catholic Church, has in recent times had an extraordinary development under the impulse given to it, especially by Benedict XV and Pius XI, who, in their respective encyclicals *Maximum illud* (1919) and *Rerum Ecclesiae* (1926), traced the lines of a new missionary program. In order to stress progressively the great importance of the missionary problem and adequately to prepare the souls called by God for this great undertaking, Pius XI decided to establish missionological institutes, of the university type, with an organic program of studies. Missionology (which some prefer to call missiology) includes a *theoretic* section, divided into *doctrinal* (dogma, moral theology, canon law, biblical and patristic theology) and *descriptive* (historical, geographic); and a *technical* section (pastoral, medicine, languages). Many auxiliary studies complete the program.

BIBLIOGRAPHY

BARBERO, *Le Missioni — Compendio di Missionologia doctrinale, descrittiva e operativa* (Rome, 1939). DE MONDRAGONES Y G. ESCALANTE, *Manual de Missionologia* (Vitoria, 1933).

modalism. A complex Trinitarian heresy which arose in the East at the end of the second century and afterward was spread widely in the Western Church. It defends monotheism rigidly up to the point of conceiving the Trinity of the divine Persons as *three modes of being* and of self-manifestation of the one God: The same divine Person, in so far as it creates and generates, is Father; in so far as it is generated and redeems men, is Son (Christ); in so far as it sanctifies, is Holy Spirit. There is, therefore, no real distinction of divine Persons, but only one Principle of everything, i.e., the Father, who has created, has become incarnate, has died, has risen. Hence the names of *monarchianism* (one sole Principle) and *Patripassianism* (passion of the Father) given to the modalistic heresy. Its first author was Noetus, who was condemned by the Presbytery of Smyrna, where he preached his false doctrine; his disciples, Epigon and Cleomenes, came to Rome to spread their master's teaching. Hippolytus wrote against Noetus. A similar doctrine was held at Rome by a certain Praxeas, who was vigorously opposed by Tertullian. Later on, at the beginning of the third century, another Easterner came to Rome, who may be called the architect of the modalistic error, Sabellius (hence the other name, *Sabellianism,* well known in the following centuries). Sabellius refined monarchianism by reducing the divine Persons to simple transitory *modalities:* God is now Father, now Son, now Holy Spirit, according to His mode of acting. Thus the Trinitarian dogma was radically eliminated. Pope Callixtus excommunicated Sabellius. Paul of Samosata professed also Sabellianism, together with adoptionism (*q.v.*). Later Sabellianism underwent considerable development and modification.

BIBLIOGRAPHY

BARDY, "Monarchianisme," *DTC.* CAYRÉ, *Manual of Patrology,* trans. Howitt, Vol. I (Paris, Tournai, Rome, 1936), pp. 173–176. CHAPMAN, "Monarchians," *CE.* TIXERONT, *History of Dogmas,* trans. H.L.B., Vol. I (St. Louis, 1910), pp. 286, 379 ff., 421.

modernism. A heresy, or rather a group of heresies, which have arisen in the very bosom of the Church at the beginning of this century under the influence of modern philosophy and criticism, with the pretense of elevating and saving the Christian religion and the Catholic Church by means of a radical renovation. Leaders of the movement: in France, Le Roy and Loisy; in England, Tyrrel; in Germany, Schell; in Italy, the authors (anonymous) of *The Program of the Modernists,* who have no originality, but repeat the ideas of others; E. Buonaiuti is another obstinate follower and defender of modernism in Italy. Pope Pius X issued two documents against modernism: The Decree of the Holy Office, *Lamentabili* (July 3, 1907, *DB,* 2001 ff.), and the encyclical, *Pascendi* (Sept. 8, 1907). The decree consists of a list of 65 condemned propositions; the encyclical is a lucid and deep analysis of these modern theories in conflict with sound philosophy and the patrimony of the entire Christian doctrine. To get an exact idea of modernism it suffices to read this pontifical document which, despite the protests of the modernists, has, with the passing years, progressively shown itself to be objective and efficacious.

In brief outline, the encyclical declares modernism to be a hybrid amalgamation of verbal Catholicism with real naturalistic rationalism, based on *three philosophical systems:* (1) *agnosticism* (from Kantianism), which combines subjectivism, phenomenalism, and relativism, depreciating rational knowledge; (2) *immanentism,* according to which human consciousness bears in itself, virtually, every truth, even divine, which is developed under the stimulus of the religious sense (from the doctrine of Kant and Schleiermacher); (3) *radical evolutionism,* according to which true reality is not being, but becoming, both within and outside man (from Hegel and, still more, from *Bergson*).

Consequences of a religious character: (*a*) Impossibility of demonstrating the existence of a personal God, distinct from the world. (*b*) Religion and revelation are natural products of our subconsciousness, dogma being its provisional expression, subject to continual evolution. (*c*) The Bible is not a divinely inspired book and, therefore, must be studied critically like any human book, subject to errors. (*d*) Science has nothing to do with faith: the critic, as such, can deny things he admits as a believer. (*e*) The divinity of Christ does not derive from the Gospels, but is the result of Christian consciousness. (*f*) The expiatory and redemptive value of Christ's death is merely the opinion of St. Paul. (*g*) Christ did not institute the Church or the primacy of Peter, passed down later to the Roman pontiffs: the ecclesiastical organization of today is the result of human circumstances and is subject to continual change. (*h*) The sacraments were instituted by the Apostles, who believed they were thus interpreting the instructions of the Master. These sacraments are useful only for keeping alive in men the thought of the ever beneficent presence of the Creator. (*i*) The rigid dogmatism of the Roman Church is irreconcilable with real science, which is bound up with universal evolution and follows its conditions.

Pius X rightly concludes that modernism, by virtue of these deleterious principles, leads to the suppression of all religion and, therefore, to atheism (see *immanentism; pragmatism; sentiment, religious; subconsciousness*).

BIBLIOGRAPHY

FARGES, LEBRETON, "Modernisme," *DA.* GAUDEAU, *Les erreurs du Modernisme* (Paris, 1908). GODRYEZ, *The Doctrine of Modernism and Its Refutation* (Philadelphia, 1908). OTTEN, *Manual of History of Dogmas,* Vol. 2 (St. Louis, 1925), pp. 530–533. RICKABY, *The Modernist* (London, 1908). RIVIERE, *Le Modernisme dans l'Eglise* (Paris, 1929); "Modernisme," *DTC.* ROSA, *L'Enciclica Pascendi ed il Modernismo* (Rome, 1909). VERMEERSCH, "Modernism," *CE.*

Molina. See *Molinism.*

Molinism. A theological system linked with the name of Louis Molina, a Spanish Jesuit and theologian of the sixteenth century. Taking occasion from a dispute which arose in the University of Salamanca since 1582, regarding a thesis of the Jesuit *Prudencio de Montemayor* on the freedom of Christ, Molina endeavored to delve into the question of the relationship between human freedom and divine knowledge, predestination and grace. He published, therefore, a book entitled *Concordia,* in 1588, with the purpose also of fighting Lutheranism and Calvinism which denied man's freedom. The Dominican *Bañez* (see *Bannesianism*) censured several propositions in the book, thus inciting the famous controversy between the Dominicans and the Jesuits, which is still unsettled.

Fundamental principles of Molinism: (*a*) God concurs in the action of every creature, even in the free, human act, with a *general* and indifferent movement, which acts not *on* but *with* the creature (two co-ordinate agents) with reference to the same effect. It is a *simultaneous* concurrence, which our will may use as it pleases. (*b*) There is, in addition, a *special* concurrence for supernatural acts, and this is *prevenient* grace which, together with the free will, constitutes a system of two causes co-ordinated for the same effect, i.e., the salutary act, which from the will draws its *vitality* and from grace its *supernaturality*. (*c*) Actual grace is reduced to the very vital act of the will, in so far as it is supernatural. (*d*) Three knowledges may be distinguished in God: knowledge of *simple intelligence,* whose object is every *possible* thing; knowledge of *vision,* whose object is every *real* thing (including the future); and *middle knowledge* (*scientia media*) whose object is the *hypothetical* or *conditioned future*. The first two sciences are admitted by the Thomists also, while the third is proper to Molinism; by virtue of the middle knowledge, God, even before willing, foresees in His essence what a free man would do *if* he were put in one or other possible order of things. (*e*) With His middle knowledge God explores human free will according to the various possible orders of creation and man's eventual correspondence with grace: in this way He establishes *predestination,* subordinately to His prevision of merits (*post praevisa merita* — "after foreseeing man's merits"). While Bannesianism grants more to the decrees of the divine *will* in the question of prevision of the future and of predestination, Molinism attributes more to the divine *intellect*. Certain modern theologians endeavor to conciliate these two systematic positions by a sound syncretism.

BIBLIOGRAPHY

D'Alès, *Providence et libre arbitre* (Paris, 1927). De Regnon, *Bannésianisme et Molinisme* (Paris, 1890); *Bañez et Molina* (Paris, 1883). Garrigou-Lagrange, *St. Thomas et le Néomolinisme* (Paris, 1917). Gayraud, *Thomisme et Molinisme* (Toulouse, 1889). Michel, "Science," *DTC,* cols. 1610–1619. Pohle, "Molina," *CE;* "Molinism," *CE*. Pohle-Preuss, *Dogmatic Theology,* I *God: Knowability, Essence, Attributes* (St. Louis, 1946), pp. 383–390; VII *Grace* (*Actual and Habitual*) (St. Louis, 1946), pp. 255–266. Vansteenberghe, "Molinisme," *DTC*.

Molinosism. The pseudomystic system formulated in Italy and diffused throughout Europe by the Spanish priest *Michael Molinos* († 1696), who came to Rome in 1664 on the occasion of a beatification cause and, remaining there, wrote the *Spiritual Guide*. The volume is divided into three books: the first treats of the obscurities, aridities, and sensations with which God purifies souls, then of interior recollection and acquired contemplation; the second speaks of the spiritual Father and of internal and external penances; the third discusses the means by which God purifies souls, of infused contemplation, of annihilation of the spirit, and of interior peace.

The *Guide,* confused and emphatic but not lacking warmth of feeling, was published with ecclesiastical approbation and, at first blush, made a good impression, due partly to the author's good reputation of piety and zealous ministry and due also to the protection of Cristina of Sweden, of Cardinal Azzolini, and even of Pope Innocent XI. But some attentive readers quickly discovered the poison in the *Guide;* the first to point it out were the Jesuits, then Archbishop Caracciolo of Naples. The rumor having grown to sizable proportions, Molinos was reported to the Holy Office and put in prison (1685). After careful examination, 68 propositions were extracted from the work and condemned by a Holy Office decree and by the bull, *Coelestis Pastor,* of Innocent XI (1687). The reading of these propositions, recognized as his own by Molinos, affords a measure of the gravity of the false and harmful mysticism, of which the author had become a teacher, followed enthusiastically by not a few souls, including the Oratorian of Iesi, Pier Matteo Petrucci, afterward a cardinal, who defended Molinos and the *Guide* with writings, which were put on the *Index of Forbidden Books.*

The fundamental principles of Molinosism are reducible to the following (cf. the condemned propositions in *DB,* 1221–1288): Man must mortify his faculties and his free will to attain a sort of mystical death, in which the soul merges with its Creator, as into one sole thing. Prayer must be a habitual abandonment to God, without words, without petitions, without works. Immersed in God, the soul must no longer worry about what happens in the body: the devil may work the most obscene actions in the flesh, without the soul's contracting any guilt. What is more, God humiliates souls this way, by subjecting them to gravest sensual disorders by means of the devil, in order to purify them. It is not necessary to repent or to confess these sins, as it is not necessary to do penances and undergo voluntary mortifications. In a word, the mystic soul should be like a corpse, in which only God operates as He pleases. In this monstrous theory it is easy to identify the consequences of genuine Lutheranism, which had denied free will and man's activity in order to affirm the inevitability of sin and the necessity of abandonment to God, who sanctifies not by removing guilt but only by concealing it.

BIBLIOGRAPHY

Bigelow, *Molinos the Quietist* (New York, 1882). Dudon, *Le quiétist espagnol Michel Molinos* (Paris, 1921). Paquier, "Molinos," *DTC.* Perez Goyena, "Molinos," *CE.* Pourrat, "Quiétisme," *DTC,* cols. 1561–1573.

See under *quietism.*

monarchianism. See *modalism.*

monergism (Gr. μόνη — one alone, and ἐνέργεια — activity). An error launched, after the condemnation of Monophysitism at the Council of Chalcedon (451), by some stubborn *Anti-Chalcedonians,* particularly by the clever *Severus of Antioch,* who in his work Philalethè endeavors to prove that — whatever opinion one may have on the two natures in Christ and their union — it is certain that the Man-God is one, sole-operating subject and, consequently, His activity can be only one (*theandric*). This principle of *dynamic unity* in Christ was developed by others and prepared the way for the heresy of *Monotheletism,* logically connected with monergism. The question of theandric operation (*q.v.*) is also a part of the error of Monotheletism.

BIBLIOGRAPHY

Jugie, "Monophysisme," *DTC,* col. 2216. Lebon, *Le monophysisme sévérien* (Louvain, 1909).

monism (Gr. μόνος — sole, unique). A term first used by Wolff to mean a system opposed to *dualism.* Classical dualism distinguishes the world of spirit from that of matter to the point of asserting the eternity of both (Plato); or it is the Aristotelian system of matter and form (hylomorphism), united, however, harmoniously in the so-called *synolus* (the whole, the composite being), while in the Platonic conception the soul is a prisoner of the body by violence. Consequently, we distinguish a spiritualistic monism (all is spirit) and a materialistic monism (all is matter).

An example of *spiritualistic monism* is the substantialism of Baruch Spinoza († 1677), who reduced all reality to one, sole substance (divine), manifested in two *modes* (corresponding to two of the infinite attributes of God): *thought,* which constitutes the world of spirit, and *extension*, which constitutes the world of matter. The one and the other, however, are immanent in the one, divine substance. With this static conception is connected *idealistic-dynamic monism* (see *idealism*), which resolves everything in the *idea* (Hegel) or in the *act of thought* (Gentile): this is the evolutionistic monism of "becoming." Opposed to this is *materialistic monism*, which had a notorious champion in Ernest Haeckel († 1910), who celebrates in his work the triumph of matter to the point of a kind of religious apotheosis. Outstanding scientists, however, have uncovered the impostures of Haeckel, who contaminated science with trickery for propagandistic purposes.

Beside these well-determined forms of monism are others less definite, in which the monistic tendency dominates one sector or another of thought, nature, or human life: such is *humanitarian*, or *sociological*, or *biological* monism. If these partial forms may at times be admitted without encountering difficulties of the moral or religious order, certainly absolute monism, either spiritualistic or materialistic, is irreconcilable with Christian thought and Catholic doctrine because it necessarily implies *pantheism* (*q.v.*), i.e., confusion of God and the world, and the denial of creation. But monism is evidently false also from the philosophical and scientific viewpoint.

BIBLIOGRAPHY

CARUS, *Monism, Its Scope and Import* (Chicago, 1891). KLIMCKE, *Il Monismo e le sue basi filosofiche* (Florence, 1914). MALLEBRANCQ, "Monisme," *DA*. ROYCE, *The World and the Individual* (New York, 1901). TURNER, "Monism," *CE*. VEITCH, *Dualism and Monism* (London, 1895).

Monophysitism (Gr. μόνος — only, and φύσις — nature). Christological heresy of Eutyches, who affirmed that there is only one nature in Christ. See *Eutychianism*.

monotheism (Gr. μόνος — sole, and θεός — God). A religious system which, in opposition to *polytheism* (*q.v.*), admits one sole God. Monotheism par excellence is the Christian religion, which in the Old and New Testament offers the highest concept of the one God possessing a variety of attributes, which do not violate the absolute unity of His infinite essence. New Testament revelation represents God in three Persons: Father, Son, and Holy Ghost; also in this mystery of the Holy Trinity, which the Church *magisterium* expresses with the formula "one nature in three Persons," monotheism remains intact (in an *absolute*, substantial sense), because plurality of persons is affirmed only in the *relative* line. Monotheism, wonderfully preserved in the Jewish tradition which converges into Christianity, was the primitive religion; polytheism is but a degeneration, as most recent studies of the comparative history of religions have demonstrated.

BIBLIOGRAPHY

AIKEN, "Monotheism," *CE*. GWATKIN, *The Knowledge of God and Its Historic Development* (Edinburgh, 1906). IVERACH, *Theism in the Light of Present Science and Philosophy* (New York, 1899). SCHURMANN, *Belief in God, Its Origin, Nature, and Basis* (New York, 1890).

See under *God; polytheism*.

Monotheletism (Gr. μόνος — sole, and θέλω — I will). The last of the great Christological heresies, which puts in Christ only one will (the divine), thus mutilating the human nature assumed by the Word, as *Apollinarianism* and *Monophysitism* had done before (*qq.v.*).

Monotheletism stems from Monophysitism, bridged by the subtle theories of Severus of Antioch on the activity (ἐνέργεια) of Christ (see *monergism*). From the asserted unity of operation it was easy to pass to unity of will; this passage matured slowly from the sixth to the seventh centuries. Political circumstances favored the development of this heresy. Heraclius († 641) wanted religious peace in the Empire, while discord was still alive on account of the numerous Monophysitic sects. Sergius, the Patriarch of Constantinople, courtesan more than Churchman, endeavored to satisfy the Emperor's wish by composing a series of nine anathematisms (633), in which Catholic doctrine was reconciled with Monophysitism through means of a compromise — Monotheletism. Protests from vigilant Catholics were not lacking. Sergius tried to draw Pope Honorius I to his side, writing to him a deceitful letter in which, among other things, he said that to speak of two wills in Christ was scandalous, seeing that the faithful immediately concluded that the two wills are discordant. Pope Honorius, while remaining on the orthodox terrain of the two wills, acquiesced good-naturedly to Sergius' viewpoint, admitting the *moral unity* of Christ's wills. Sergius used the Pope's reply abusively in order to propagandize his error. Two champions of the faith rose up against him: St. Maximus Confessor and St. Sophronius, Patriarch of Jerusalem, who in various letters and writings uncovered the Monotheletic error.

Martin I, in a Council at Rome (649) in which St. Maximus took part, condemned the heresy and, with it, the "Type" with which Constans II tried to impose silence on the controversial issue. The Pope and St. Maximus were mistreated and exiled. Only under Constantine IV Pogonatus, Agaton being pope, could the VI Ecumenical Council (the 3rd of Constantinople) be assembled (680–681), which repeated and developed the decisions of the Roman Council of 649, defining that the will is a property of the nature, and that since in Christ there are two natures, there are also two wills, always in agreement, because directed by one sole agent, the Person of the Word. Thus was reinforced and perfected definitively the doctrine of the Council of Chalcedon on the integrity of Christ's two natures and their respective, distinct properties, wills, and activities. The Council deplored also the action of Honorius I, in that he had imprudently favored Sergius' error (*DB*, 262 ff., 289 ff.).

BIBLIOGRAPHY

AMANN, "Honorius I," *DTC*. CAYRÉ, *Manual of Patrology*, trans. Howitt, Vol. 2 (Paris, Tournai, Rome, 1940), pp. 297–306. CHAPMAN, "Monotheletism and Monothelites," *CE*. CHILLET, *Le monothélisme exposé et critiqué* (Brignais, 1911). JUGIE, "Monothélisme," *DTC*.

Montanism. A heresy of an ascetic nature dating from about A.D. 170. In Phrygia (Asia Minor) a certain Montanus (whence Montanism), converted to Christianity, began to have ecstasies and other strange phenomena, as if he were inspired. Two ladies, Priscilla and Maximilla, followed him, and had like experiences. Quickly a movement jelled, following the Prophet, who, among other things, preached that *the end of the world* is approaching, and, with it, the second descent of Christ on earth.

Montanism, unlike Gnosticism, is an *ascetic praxis,* a rigoristic discipline or mode of life, rather than a doctrine. Montanus claimed he was inspired and moved by the Paraclete, who had descended upon him and inspired him to start a more rigid Christianity (prohibition of second marriages, prolonged fasts, austere mortifications, etc.). From the East the Montanist heresy spread widely and reached Rome; even Tertullian succumbed to it, later dying as a heretic outside the Catholic Church. Several bishops took measures against Montanism, which was finally condemned by Pope Zephyrinus.

BIBLIOGRAPHY

Chapman, "Montanists," *CE.* Cunningham, *The Churches of Asia* (London, 1880). De Soyres, *Montanism and the Primitive Church* (London, 1878). Tixeront, *History of Dogmas,* trans. H.L.B., Vol. 1 (St. Louis, 1910), pp. 192–199.

Mopsuestenus (Theodore of Mopsuestia). See *Nestorianism.*

motion, divine. See *concourse, divine.*

mystery (Gr. *μυστήριον,* from *μύειν* — to close; cf. Lat. *mutus*). A hidden or secret thing, particularly of a sacred character (cf. the Eleusinian mysteries of Cybele, of Isis, etc.). In Holy Scripture the word *mystery* means, in addition to secret thing in general, the divine things of the kingdom of heaven (Matt. 13:11), and in St. Paul, the revelation of the salvation of the world through Christ the Redeemer (Eph. 3:9; Col. 1:26; etc.). In the past century, the Church *magisterium* has fixed definitively the meaning of the term (Gregory XVI, Pius IX, Leo XIII). The Vatican Council (sess. 3, c. 4, *DB,* 1795 ff.) gives the definition: "The divine mysteries of their very nature so transcend the created intellect that, even when revealed and believed, they still remain veiled and obscure during this mortal life."

In the strict sense, therefore, a mystery is a truth, whose existence can be known by human reason only by way of revelation, while its essence cannot be properly and fully understood, even after revelation. Thus, e.g., the mystery of the Holy Trinity. In a broad sense we call it also a truth known only through revelation but comprehensible by reason once it has been revealed, e.g., the creation of the world in time. Human reason cannot *demonstrate* a mystery taken in the strict sense, but can illustrate it and defend it from objections. The contradiction between a mystery of faith and the principles of reason can be no more than apparent, since supernatural and natural truth both derive from the same source, God, who is substantial Truth.

BIBLIOGRAPHY

Garrigou-Lagrange, *De Revelatione* (Paris, 1926). McHugh, "Mystery," *CE.* Michel, "Mystère," *DTC.* Newman, *Critic. Essays,* I (London, 1888). Penido, *Le rôle de l'analogie en théologie dogmatique* (Paris, 1931). Scheeben, *The Mysteries of Christianity,* trans. Vollert (St. Louis, 1946), pp. 3–21.

Mystical Body. The expression goes back at least to the ninth century (cf. Ratramnus and Paschasius Radbertus); in the Fathers (cf. Ambrose) we find the term *"mystical Head"* referred to Christ; some ecclesiastical writers speak of "mystical members of Christ, of the Church" (cf. Bede).

In the Gospel of St. John, Christ likens Himself to the vine, of which men are the branches or tendrils (Ch. 15), and in the prayer at the Last Supper He insists on the concept of unity and mutual immanence of Himself in men and of men in Him (Ch. 17). But it is St. Paul who develops extensively this theme and represents Jesus Christ as an immense organism, a body, of which He is the Head and men the various members (cf. Epistles to the Corinthians, Colossians, Ephesians, and Romans). Here is a synthesis of the teaching of St. Paul: Christ, incarnate Word, is the new Adam, Head of humanity which is redeemed in Him, and He constitutes with it a Body, which is the mystical Christ. This Body in a large sense embraces all mankind, because Christ died for the salvation of all; but in a strict sense it is the Church, which man enters through baptism, to be ingrafted onto Christ and thus to participate in the supernatural life, which flows from the Head into the members by the action of the Holy Spirit, who is the soul of the Mystical Body. The unity of this organism is so real and deep that St. Paul does not hesitate to say (Gal. 3:28): "You are all one [εἷς] in Christ," i.e., as St. Thomas translates, you are with Christ one sole *mystical person*. Here "mystical" is not opposed to real, but stands for a supernatural reality, although not of the physical type. "Christ in us" is for St. Paul the great mystery that God reveals in the Gospel: through it we live in Christ, who continues in us His passion, death, and resurrection (*solidarity*). On this mystery, as on their base, rest the Redemption and the Church (*qq.v.*).

The Fathers develop the thought of St. Paul either in a rather strict *ecclesiological* sense (Ignatius, Cyprian) or in a wider *soteriological* sense (Irenaeus, Athanasius, Cyril of Alexandria, Chrysostom). St. Augustine harmonizes the two tendencies. The recent encyclical, *"Mystici Corporis"* of Pius XII, is a profound and erudite doctrinal commentary of this truth of faith. In the light of the Mystical Body it considers first the relations between Christ and His Church, of which He is Head, Supporter, and Saviour; then the relations and bonds of union between the faithful and Jesus Christ, condemning the exaggerations of false mysticism, which tends to absorb man and his personality in Christ to the point of fusing and identifying them in one physical person.

BIBLIOGRAPHY

St. Thomas, *Summa Theol.*, III, q. 8. Ceriani, *La vita del Corpo Mistico* (Como, 1943). Mersch, *The Whole Christ,* trans. Kelly (Milwaukee, 1938). Mura, *Le corps mystique du Christ* (Paris, 1936). Pius XII, encyclical, *Mystici Corporis Christi, AAS,* July 20, 1943. See S. Tromp's commentary in *Textus et Documenta* (n. 26) of the Gregorian University. Prat, *The Theology of St. Paul,* trans. Stoddard, 2 vols. (Westminster, 1927). *The Teaching of the Catholic Church,* ed. Smith, 2 vols. (New York, 1949), pp. 65–69, 659–690. Tromp, *De Ecclesia quod est corpus mysticum Christi* (Rome, 1937). Tyrrell, "The Mystical Body," *Hard Sayings* (New York, 1902).

mystics — mysticism (Gr. μύω — I close the mouth). Mystics in a *practical* sense is a mode or condition of intense supernatural life, implying a spiritual and quasi-experimental knowledge of God, accompanied often by extraordinary psychic phenomena (ecstasies, stigmata, etc.). In the *theoretical* sense, mystics is the science that studies this elevated spirituality either from a *theological* viewpoint (mystical theology) or from a *psychological* viewpoint (psychology of mystics). The essential part of mystics is that savory experimental knowledge of God, which goes also under the name of contemplation (*q.v.*); it has its roots in grace and the infused virtues, especially in faith and charity, and also in the gifts of the Holy Spirit. Begun in the human spirit with man's co-operation, it reaches its apex when it is actuated unexpectedly by divine influence, without human co-operation, determining both internal and external phenomena which can hardly be analyzed or explained. St. Teresa reduces the degrees of mystical contemplation to four: (1) *quiet,* in which the spirit reposes quietly without freeing itself entirely from every distraction; (2) *full union,* in which the sense of God's presence is lively and every distraction is conquered; (3) *ecstasy* (*q.v.*), in which the use of the senses ceases, as does every bodily motion; (4) *transforming union* or *spiritual nuptials,* in which the soul relishes the presence of God and feels itself sharing His divine life.

There are various opinions and systems of classification about the phases and phenomena of the mystical life. According to the common opinion, the mystical life consists essentially in an act of the highest knowledge of God, which must be classified between faith and the beatific vision which is immediate, and in an act of love which accompanies that knowledge. The psychic phenomena are a repercussion, as it were, of those two essential acts.

Mysticism is a mystical tendency or system. It is found outside of Christianity in the mystery religions (e.g., *Orphism*) and in philosophical teachings like that of Plotinus. In Christianity, outside of the orthodox mysticism lived and professed by great souls like St. Bernard, St. Francis of Assisi, St. Catherine of Siena, St. John of the Cross, St. Teresa, and St. Paul of the Cross, there have been sporadic uprisings of degenerated mysticism, which the vigilant Church immediately condemned, e.g., Molinosism (*q.v.*). There is, moreover, in many psychologists and physiologists a superficial prejudice against mysticism. They would like to reduce all forms of mysticism to morbid manifestations (hysteria, neurasthenia, etc.), but they fail to consider that, according to Catholic teaching, mysticism is primarily an intense, supernatural life and, secondarily, a manifestation of extraordinary psychic phenomena, which must be in harmony with the holiness and the moral equilibrium of the mystic.

BIBLIOGRAPHY

Butler, *Western Mysticism* (London, 1922). Delacroix, *Etude d'histoire, et de psychologie du mysticisme* (Paris, 1908). Divine, *A Manual of Mystical Theology* (London, 1903). Farges, *Mystical Phenomena* (London, 1925). Fenton, *The Theology of Prayer* (Milwaukee, 1939). Gardeil, *La structure de l'âme et l'expérience mystique* (Paris, 1927). Garrigou-Lagrange, *Christian Perfection and Contemplation,* trans. Doyle (St. Louis, 1937). Goodier, *Ascetical and Mystical Theology* (London, 1938). Hodgson, *English Mystics* (London, 1922). Pascal Parente, *The Mystical Life* (St. Louis, 1946), pp. 3–28; *The Ascetical Life* (St. Louis, 1947), pp. 231–236; *Quaestiones de mystica terminologia* (Washington, D. C., 1941). Poulain, "Theology (Mystical)," *CE.* Saudreau, *L'état mystique* (1921). Sauvage, "Mysticism," *CE.* Sharpe, *Mysticism* (St. Louis, 1910). Stolz, *The Doctrine of Spiritual Perfection,* trans. Williams (St. Louis, 1938). Tanquerey, *The Spiritual Life,* trans. Branderis (Tournai, 1932). Watkin, *The Philosophy of Mysticism* (London, 1920). Williamson, *Supernatural Mysticism* (London, 1921).

N

naturalism. See *rationalism.*

nature (Gr. φύσις; Lat. *nasci, nascitura* — about to be born). It meant, first of all, the *generation* of living beings; then the principle of this generation; finally the *intrinsic principle* of motion and action (Aristotle).

The nature of a thing coincides with its essence; but while essence refers to *being,* which realizes the thing, nature refers to *acting,* which expands it. Nature is usually termed *principium quo remotum operationis* ("remote principle of operation"), while the faculties are *principium quo proximum,* and the *suppositum* (subsisting individual) or *person* (*q.v.*), is *principium quod,* i.e., the acting subject.

Nature is distinguished from *suppositum* or person as a part from its whole. Nature with its constitutive elements and its laws constitutes the *natural order,* limited in being and in operation, in its passive and active potency. The *supernatural* (*q.v.*) order is that which transcends the natural order.

God can elevate, as He actually did,

human nature to the supernatural order by grace. Human nature, however, with respect to this supernatural order, has neither exigency nor *active* capacity, but merely a *passive* capacity, called obediential potency (*q.v.*).

BIBLIOGRAPHY

St. Thomas, *Summa Theol.*, III, q. 2, a. 1; *Opusculum De Ente et Essentia.* Dubray, "Nature," *CE.* Peter Parente, *De Deo Trino* (Rome, 1938), p. 73 ff.

neophyte (Gr. νεόφυτος — new plant). Used by St. Paul (1 Tim. 3:6) to indicate figuratively a new convert. Moreover, the Apostle in another place (1 Cor. 3:6–8) compares the work of the gospel worker to that of a farmer. The word *neophyte* has passed into ecclesiastical language to designate the newly baptized. In the passage just mentioned St. Paul recommends to Timothy not to ordain a neophyte as bishop. The old canon law, adopted afterward by the Decretales, established the *defectus fidei confirmatae* ("the lack of confirmed faith"), proper to those who were baptized after becoming converted to the true faith in advanced age, as an irregularity or impediment to ordination. The new Code of Canon Law has suppressed this irregularity, but puts the neophytes in the category of those who are *simpliciter impediti* until, in the judgment of their ordinary, they have been sufficiently tested (*CIC,* Can. 987, § 6).

BIBLIOGRAPHY

Amann, "Néophyte," *DTC.* Cappello, *De sacra ordinatione* (Rome, 1935), n. 524. Leclercq, "Néophyte," *DACL.*

Nestorianism: One of the great Christological heresies of the fifth century, which broke the personal unity of Christ by positing in Him two subjects, one divine and one human. The principal author of this heresy is Nestorius, Bishop of Constantinople, and former disciple of Theodore of Mopsuestia in the Antiochian School. A realism with naturalistic tendencies was dominant in that school: they considered the two elements in Christ, the divine and the human, as real entities, concrete, standing by themselves, united only *morally*.

Faithful to his master, Nestorius developed his teaching in these fundamental points: (*a*) Christ is a perfect Man like one of us; His human nature has, therefore, its own subsistence, its own autonomy and, therefore, its own personality. (*b*) In Christ the Man, however, is present the Word, Son of God, who dwells in the assumed humanity as in a temple. (*c*) Christ Man and the Word are in themselves two distinct subjects, but form morally one sole thing (*prosopon unionis*), like a king and his legate. (*d*) Since the union between the two subjects is only accidental, it is not allowable to attribute to the one the properties of the other. (*e*) The Virgin Mary is not properly the Mother of God (θεοτόκος), but the Mother of Christ Man (see *maternity, divine*). (*f*) Only Christ Man is Redeemer, Priest, and Victim, not the Word who is in Him.

Moreover, Nestorius shows himself at least favorable to Pelagianism (*q.v.*). He is obscure and reticent on the *intrinsic* character of justification (*q.v.*), and, coherently with his Christology, he denies transubstantiation (*q.v.*), although admitting the real presence of the Word in the consecrated bread (impanation). Cyril of Alexandria fought against Nestorius; the ardor of the struggle was increased also by the imprecision of the terminology, especially of the words οὐσία, φύσις, ὑπόστασις (essence, nature, hypostasis or person). But the fight was more than a discussion of terminology: Cyril knew and demonstrated that he was defending the *real unity* of Christ against the deleterious *dualism* of Nestorius. The heresy was condemned in the Council of Ephesus (431), which defined the divine maternity of Mary and the real, true, substantial *unity* of the divine element and the human element of Christ in the one person of the Word (see *hypostatic union*).

BIBLIOGRAPHY

D'ALÈS, *Le dogme d'Ephèse* (Paris, 1931). AMANN, TISSERANT, "Nestorius," *DTC.* BETHUNE, BAKER, *Nestorius and His Teaching* (London, 1908). CHAPMAN, "Nestorius and Nestorianism," *CE.* JUGIE, *Nestorius et la controverse nestorienne* (Paris, 1912).

New Testament. See *Testament, New.*

noematics. See *senses of Scripture.*

nominalism. A philosophical current with wide repercussions in theology, inaugurated systematically by Roscelin (eleventh century), continued by Abelard, and developed in the fourteenth century by Ockham and Biel. Nominalism is one of the solutions given to the problem of the *universals,* to which the Scholastics devoted themselves energetically from the beginning. Supposing that *sensation* or *phantasm* (with its individual, particular character) is distinct from *concept* or *idea* (with its universal character, e.g., Socrates as man), the question arises as to what is in general the value of universal concepts, e.g., humanity. Against the *exaggerated realism* of Platonic origin, which made of those concepts so many real and subsisting forms, the nominalists hold that they are pure *words* or *names* which we use to indicate individuals resembling one another. The universal concept has no reality outside of the mind: the only extramental reality is the singular thing, the individual (this flower, Peter, Paul, etc.).

With Abelard, nominalism became *conceptualism* (the universal is not only a word, a name, but also a true concept). Ockham inquired further into the relationship between concept and reality, concluding that the concept has its *subjective* reality in the soul (*ideal objectivity*), but in no wise outside the soul (prelude to Kantianism). Nominalism in this last form reduces a great part of metaphysics to logic and depreciates the capacity of human reason, preparing the way for later skepticism. In theology, the denial of the real distinction between nature and person compromises the Trinitarian and Christological doctrine; the negation of *habits* upsets the doctrine of grace, and approaches Lutheranism (*q.v.*). St. Thomas solved the problem of universals by teaching a *moderate realism:* the universal exists *formally* in the intellect, but has a *real foundation* in things outside.

BIBLIOGRAPHY

GIACON, *Guglielmo di Occam: Saggio storico-critico sulla formazione e sulla decadenza della Scolastica* (Milan, 1941). DE WULFF, *Histoire de la Philosophie médiévale,* (Louvain, 1942), Vol. 1, p. 93 ff.; Vol. 2, p. 157 ff.; "Nominalism, Realism, Conceptualism," *CE.* TURNER, *History of Philosophy* (Boston, 1903). VIGNAUX, "Nominalisme," *DTC.*

notions, divine. Distinctive marks by which the individual divine Persons are recognized. There are five of such marks: *innascibility* (impossibility of being generated); *paternity,* proper to the *Father* (*q.v.*); *filiation,* proper to the *Son* (*q.v.*); *active spiration,* proper to the Father and the Son together; *passive spiration* or simple *procession,* proper to the Holy Ghost. To the notions correspond the *notional acts,* which are two: generation and spiration (considered actively and passively, according to the terms). The two notional acts coincide with the two processions, which are, precisely, the generation of the Word and the breathing or spiration of the Holy Spirit, the first procession being by way of knowledge and the second by way of love.

The nine proper names — Father, Principle, Unbegotten, Son, Word, Image, Holy Spirit, Love, Gift — are usually called notional.

BIBLIOGRAPHY

St. Thomas, *Summa Theol.,* I, q. 41. Peter Parente, *De Deo Trino* (Rome, 1938), p. 185 ff. Pohle-Preuss, *Dogmatic Theology,* II *The Divine Trinity* (St. Louis, 1946), pp. 236–243.

O

obediential potency. The capacity of a creature to be elevated by God to a state and action above its nature and its natural potency. According to the Thomists (who claim to express faithfully St. Thomas' mind), it is reducible to a sort of nonimpossibility (*nonrepugnantia*). According to the Scotists and the Suaresians, it includes also a disposition and a tendency, although such tendency cannot reach its object without an intervention of God. The question is quite delicate, because on its solution depends the gratuitous nature of the *supernatural* order (see *supernatural*). If the Scotistic opinion is pushed too far, the supernatural order becomes the term of a natural tendency and hence is no longer *undue,* as Catholic doctrine teaches it to be. If the Thomists' position is stressed, the supernatural may appear too *extraneous* to nature, and one does not easily understand how it can be inserted in nature and bring nature to its perfection.

Blondel's philosophy harks back to the Scotistic position, putting in human nature a *call* to the supernatural. Baianism and modernism are a degeneration of that same immanentistic tendency (see *immanentism; Baianism; desire of God*).

BIBLIOGRAPHY

St. Thomas, *Quaest. Disp. De Veritate,* q. 29, a. 3. Bainvel, *Naturel et surnaturel* (Paris, 1931). De Broglie, "La place du surnaturel dans la philosophie de saint Thomas," *Recherches de science religieuse* (1924). Pirotta, "Disputatio de potentia oboedientiali," *Divus Thomas* (Piacenza, 1930).

obex (obstacle to grace) (Lat. *obex* — obstacle, impediment). A moral indisposition which renders the infusion of grace impossible. It is distinguished from what we may call *obex of the sacrament,* which is the lack of a requisite, on account of which the sacrament is invalid, e.g., feminine sex which is an impediment to the validity of orders.

The *obex of grace* in the sacraments instituted to confer justification to man in mortal sin (baptism and penance, called for that reason *sacraments of the dead*) consists in the lack of imperfect contrition or attrition (see *contrition*), which is a minimum requirement. In the sacraments instituted to increase grace (confirmation, Eucharist, extreme unction, orders, and matrimony, called for that reason *sacraments of the living*), the obex consists in the lack of sanctifying grace (or of attrition in the case of one who is unconsciously in mortal sin). In both cases a certain attachment to sin is present.

The receiver of a sacrament may be conscious or not of his moral indisposition. If he is conscious of it, the obex is termed *formal* and, since it implies an actual affection to grave sin, it makes reception of the sacrament not only fruitless but also sacrilegious. If, on the other hand, the subject is unconscious of his indisposition, the obex is called *material,* and is constituted by habitual adherence to a past serious sin, which renders reception of the sacrament fruitless, but not sacrilegious, since good faith excuses from sin.

BIBLIOGRAPHY

ST. THOMAS, *Summa Theol.*, III, q. 69, a. 9–10. CONNELL, *De sacramentis* (Brugis, 1933). DORONZO, *De sacramentis in genere* (Milwaukee, 1946), Index Analyticus: "Obex." JANOT, *Les sept fontaines* (Paris, 1939).

oblation. See *sacrifice.*

Oecolampadius. See *Presence, Real, Eucharistic (fact).*

oils, holy. See *extreme unction.*

Old Testament. See *Testament, Old.*

omnipotence. Potency in the *passive* sense is capacity to receive the action of others; in an *active* sense, it is the power to act and produce. Passive potency is contradictory in God (see *Act, Pure*), but *active potency* or *power* is rightly predicable of Him, provided it be purified of all imperfection.

It is a truth of faith that God not only is potent, but omnipotent (cf. Apostles' Creed, Vatican Council, *DB,* 1782). The sources of revelation are rich in testimonies (Gen. 17:1; Tob. 13:4; Apoc. 4:8; the Fathers). St. Thomas affirms that the divine potency or power is founded in His being, for a being is potent inasmuch as it is in act, and a higher being is more in act, and therefore is more potent. Now God is being of His very essence, i.e., infinite; therefore, He has infinite power of acting. Omnipotence is the power of doing anything, except what is impossible or "not-do-able" in itself, i.e., what is opposed to the very nature and formal reason of being, like sin and evil, which are rather non-beings (see *evil*). Thus, also, God cannot do what is metaphysically absurd, e.g., that what is passed has not been (a contradiction). The omnipotence of God considered in itself is termed *absolute* power; considered in reference to the other attributes and to the present order in creation it is called *ordered* power. God could, e.g., destroy the immortal soul (absolute power), but He does not do it on account of His wisdom, and, in this sense, actually cannot do it (ordered power).

Leibnitz held that God could not create a better world than ours (optimism). Catholic doctrine recognizes the relative goodness of this created world, but teaches that the divine omnipotence could do more and better, according to divine freedom (see *freedom*).

BIBLIOGRAPHY

ST. THOMAS, *Summa Theol.*, I, q. 25. McHUGH, "Omnipotence," *CE.* SERTILLANGES, *St. Thomas d'Aquin,* Vol. 1 (Paris, 1925), p. 268 ff. *The Teaching of the Catholic Church,* ed. Smith, 2 vols. (New York, 1949), pp. 93–95.

Only-Begotten ("Unigenitus"). Said of the Word (*q.v.*) because He is the only term of the divine *generation* by way of intellection. The Holy Spirit does not proceed by generation but by *spiration* and, therefore, is not called Son. The word *Only-Begotten* (*Unigenitus*) is read in St. John (Ch. 1: μονογενής), who considers the Word in Himself; St. Paul, on the contrary, considers Him with respect to creatures and calls Him Firstborn (Col. 1:15; *Primogenitus:* πρωτότοκος). The Arians abused this expression (see *Arianism*) to make the Word the first of all the creatures. But St. Paul, like St. John, excludes absolutely this sense in the passage mentioned and elsewhere, because he asserts energetically that through the Word all things have been created and that the Word was prior to them, subsisting in the divine nature (Phil. 2:6). For St. Paul *Firstborn* means generated before creatures, which have not been generated by God, but made and created. The Synoptics use the expression υἱὸς ἀγαπητός (loved son), which, according to sure documents in the Greek dialect of the time, meant *only-son* (only-begotten).

The profound reason why there is only one Son in God stems from the nature of His procession, which takes place according to divine intellection; the act of divine intellection is only one, being identical with the unique essence of God and, therefore, cannot have more than one term. In the generated Word is all the divine nature, as thought in an infinite way, which does not admit of plurality.

BIBLIOGRAPHY

St. Thomas, *Summa Theol.*, I, q. 27. Lebreton, *Histoire du dogme de la Trinité,* Vol. 1 (Paris, 1927), pp. 268 *n.*, 398–399, 508 ff.

ontologism (Gr. ὄν — being, and λόγος — discourse, science). A philosophical system sketched by the French Oratorian Malebranche († 1715) and developed organically in Italy by Vincent Gioberti and his disciples, who gave to it its name.

Malebranche (cf. especially *Recherche de la vérité*) maintained as the fundamental point of philosophy that we have the innate idea of the infinite Being (God) and that we contemplate intuitively in it the object of all our ideas. Gioberti taught (cf. *Introduzione allo studio della filosofia*) that the primary object of philosophy is the Idea, which is the first reality and the first absolute and eternal truth (*first ontologicum* and *first logicum*). This absolute Idea (God) is the object of a first intuition of our intellect, from which all our knowledge develops. Such intuition, vague and confused initially, determines itself into a judgment: "The Being is necessarily," and from this judgment into the ideal form: "The Being creates the existing." From this formula Gioberti developed all his philosophy, linking it to the best Italian tradition, which is said to go back to St. Bonaventure and St. Augustine. But this genealogy is arbitrary. St. Augustine speaks of God as the Light, the Sun of the soul, not in the sense that the soul sees the divine essence intuitively, but in the sense that God has impressed in the soul a luminous image of Himself, on account of which the intellect knows truth (cf. *De Trinitate,* l. 14, c. 15, and l. 12, c. 15, n. 24).

Likewise, St. Bonaventure (*Itinerarium mentis in Deum, Breviloquium*) describes the various ascendant grades of human knowledge and arrives at the highest peak, which is not the intuitive vision of God (reserved for the other life), but the ideal contemplation of Being as Pure Act, in the light of which all our knowledge is clarified. Neither St. Augustine, therefore, nor St. Bonaventure ever affirmed an intuitive vision of God in this life as the natural beginning of human knowledge as Gioberti maintained. Although Gioberti denied that Antony Rosmini is an ontologist (*Introd.,* t. I, p. 357, and t. II, p. 64), it cannot be denied that the obscure Rosminian system shows itself vulnerable to the accusation of ontologism when it asserts that the human intellect perceives immediately and intuitively the indetermined being, which the Father abstracts from the Word and which is only logically distinct from the Word (*Theosophy,* v. II, p. 445).

The Church has explicitly condemned ontologism, which is summed up in seven propositions (Decr. of the Holy Office, 1861, *DB,* 1659 ff.); likewise, in forty propositions (Decr.

of the Holy Office, 1887, *DB,* 1891 ff.) it has rejected the concept of Rosmini, whose ontologistic character is evident from the first seven propositions. Theologically, ontologism is erroneous because it eliminates the supernatural character of the intuitive vision of God, making it a natural heritage of our present life. Philosophically, ontologism, by confusing being in general with God, leads toward pantheism; moreover, it is not justified but is contradicted by psychological experience, in which there is no trace of intuition of God.

BIBLIOGRAPHY

FONCK, "Ontologisme," *DTC.* GENTILE, *Rosmini e Gioberti* (Pisa, 1898). MICHEL, "Rosmini," *DTC.* SAUVAGE, "Ontologism," *CE.* WEHRLÉ, "Malebranche," *DTC.* ZIGLIARA, *Della luce intellectuale e dell'ontologismo* (Rome, 1874).

operation, divine. As being or existence is distinguished from essence in creatures, so operation is distinguished from nature or substance and is reducible to an accident (*actio*). But God, who is essentially being (see *essence, divine*), is also essentially action: in Him operation is identified with substance, which, therefore, is essentially dynamic. On account of His highest simplicity, is it impossible to distinguish really in God several operations by *specific* or *numerical* distribution: one sole, most simple act is all His activity (knowing, willing, acting).

A *distinctio rationis ratiocinatae* (distinction not wholly of our reason but based on the object reasoned on), however, is legitimate (see *attributes of God*) between the various operations, which are customarily attributed to God and from which spring the divine relations, constitutive of the Persons (see *Trinity*). Especially important is the distinction between *operatio ad intra* and *operatio ad extra.* The first is *immanent* in the absolute sense (i.e., formally and virtually); the second is immanent formally, but is virtually *transient.* In fact, every action in God, being identical with His essence, has to be immanent: but it is called transient in a certain way in that its power places a real effect outside of God; such is, for instance, the creative act. The principle of the *ad extra* operation is the Triune God, the whole Trinity, which necessarily acts as one, with the same omnipotent will; on the other hand, the *ad intra* operations can be exclusive to this or that divine Person, e.g., generation and spiration (see *notions, divine*).

BIBLIOGRAPHY

ST. THOMAS, *Summa Theol.,* I, q. 27, a. 1; q. 45, a. 6–7.

operation, theandric. See *theandric operation.*

orders, Anglican. See *Anglican orders.*

orders, holy (Lat. *ordo* — order, rank). The sacrament by which priests of the New Alliance are appointed. Christ, by right of nature and by divine vocation, is the High Priest of the New Testament. But, because He was to withdraw His visible presence and wanted to render visible and perpetual (as human nature requires) the application of His saving work, from the first days of His public life Jesus selected disciples whom He lovingly trained at His school. To crown, as it were, this divine training, He instituted the sacrifice of the Mass and, as by a supernatural investiture expressed in the words: "Do this for a commemoration of me" (Luke 22:19; 1 Cor. 11:24), He transmitted to the Apostles the priestly power of renewing the unbloody offering in perpetual commemoration of the bloody immolation of Calvary, thereby constituting them representatives of men to God (ascendant mediation). On the day of the Resurrection, and on that of the Ascension, He conferred on them the power of remitting sins (John 20:21–23) and the threefold power of teaching, ministry, and government (Matt. 28:19–20), thus establishing them representatives of God with men (descendant mediation).

Number of orders. Just as He constituted a hierarchy of jurisdiction by conferring on Peter (John 21:15–18) primacy over the other Apostles, Jesus, in the days He passed with them after His Resurrection *loquens de regno Dei* ("speaking about God's kingdom"), must have given opportune instructions for a parallel hierarchy of orders (see *hierarchy*), for, immediately after Pentecost we find this hierarchy constituted in three grades: the episcopate, the priesthood, and the diaconate (orders of divine institution; Council of Trent, sess. 23, Can. 6). Only later (fourth and fifth centuries) did the Church add lower grades to the hierarchy: subdiaconate, acolythate, exorcistate, lectorate, and ostiariate (orders of ecclesiastical origin).

The *conferring of orders* of divine origin was always reserved to the bishop, while the collation of the other orders (except subdiaconate, in the Latin rite) may be done by a simple priest (cardinal, abbot, vicar apostolic), in accordance with the holy canons. According to a distinction, which in past centuries entered into ecclesiastical language, the episcopate, priesthood, diaconate, and subdiaconate are termed *major orders* and the one receiving them is said to be *in sacris,* while the orders of acolyte, exorcist, lector, and porter (ostiary) are called *minor orders* by the Latins. The Easterners, on the other hand, consider as minor orders the subdiaconate together with the lectorate (the only orders of ecclesiastical origin admitted by the Eastern Church).

The *rite of ordination.* In conferring orders on the Apostles Christ did not use any sign, but right after the Ascension we see the action appear which remains the essential rite in the collation of major orders: the laying on of hands together with a prayer (cf. Acts 6:6; 13:13; 2 Tim. 1:6). The tradition or consignment of the sacred instruments and all the other rites are venerable and suggestive ceremonies of a complementary kind, and were introduced gradually in the practice of various churches and finally incorporated into the *Roman Pontifical.*

The *effects* are the character and grace. The *character* of orders is: (1) The *most perfect participation of the priesthood of Christ,* because it confers immediate power over the body of Christ in the act of making it present through the words of transubstantiation and of offering it in acceptable sacrifice to the Father (ascendant mediation). He who can act on the Head has also the right to exercise influence over the body, and hence the priest who consecrates the physical body of Christ acquires a direct power over the Mystical Body, which he teaches, sanctifies, and governs. (2) The *greatest right to grace,* for in transmitting the most perfect participation of the priestly office it demands a correspondingly more intense reproduction of the feeling of victim in the priest's soul, according to the *priest-victim* equation of the New Economy (*sacerdos suae hostiae et hostia sui sacerdotii* — "priest of his own victim and victim of his own priesthood"). Then again, since the character makes the priest the living ciborium of the Divinity, it demands that he be adorned with the most precious jewels of the rarest virtues. (3) The conferring of a pre-eminent position in the ecclesiastical society, because it makes of the priest the leader, the father, and the teacher of the people.

The *sanctifying grace,* which this sacrament increases *ex opere operato,* is like the final touch that assimilates the soul to Christ. To it is added the sacramental grace which involves an increase of all those virtues and gifts which we may call professional: the gift of piety and the virtue of religion, for the worthy offering of the sacrifice; the gift of wisdom to instruct; and the virtue of prudence to govern.

The Council of Trent defends this doctrine against the denials of the reformers (sess. 23, *DB,* 938–968). Three great documents on the dignity of the priesthood were promulgated: *Exhortatio ad clerum catholicum* (1908), by Pius X, and the encyclicals, *Ad catholici sacerdotii* (1935), by Pius XI, and *Menti nostrae,* by Pius XII.

BIBLIOGRAPHY

St. Thomas, *Summa Theol.,* III, *Suppl.,* qq. 34–40. Ahaus, "Orders (Holy)," *CE.* Michel, "Ordre. Ordination," *DTC.* Perinelle, *Le sacerdoce* (Paris, 1936). Pohle-Preuss, *Dogmatic Theology,* XI *The Sacraments,* Vol. 4, *Extreme Unction, Holy Orders, Matrimony* (St. Louis, 1946), pp. 52–139. *The Teaching of the Catholic Church,* ed. Smith, 2 vols. (New York, 1949), pp. 1022–1061. Tixeront, *Holy Orders and Ordinations,* trans. Raemers (St. Louis). Van Rossum, *De essentia sacramenti Ordinis* (Rome, 1931). Wordsworth, *The Ministry of Grace* (London, 1901); *Ordination Problems* (London, 1909).

Oriental Church (Congregation of the). See *Holy See.*

Origen. See "Outline of the History of Dogmatic Theology" (p. 301); *Origenism.*

Origenism. A collection of errors attributed to Origen, but not always with sufficient reason. In his vast works, Origen endeavored to give scientific expression to the truths of faith, putting to use the flower of Hellenic culture. More than any other writer he felt the influence of *Platonism* and, therefore, while holding firm to the basic principles of faith, he let himself be led into erroneous or very disputable interpretations, phrases, and opinions. His disciples (some of them at least) attached more attention to the dross of his teaching than to its substance, and so they developed a number of errors on the divine processions, the angels, the soul, and especially *eschatology* (*q.v.*). This is the so-called *Origenism* which was condemned as a whole by the II Council of Constantinople (A.D. 553) under Pope Vigilius.

BIBLIOGRAPHY

Bardy, "Origène," *DTC.* Bigg, *The Christian Platonists of Alexandria* (Oxford, 1886). Cayré, *Manual of Patrology,* trans. Howitt, Vol. 1 (Paris, Tournai, Rome, 1936), pp. 213, 217–220, 296, 396–397, 468–469. Fairweather, *Origen and Greek Patristic Theology* (Edinburgh, 1901). Fritz, "Origénisme," *DTC.* Prat, "Origen and Origenism," *CE.*

original justice. See *innocence* (*state of*).

original sin. See *sin, original.*

orthodox (Gr. ὀρθός — right, and δόξα — opinion, statement). In the theological field it means that which corresponds perfectly with the doctrine of faith (antonym, heterodox). But the term has a historical importance due to its abusive employment, by way of usurpation on the part of the Byzantine Church, after the schism attempted by Photius (ninth century) and consummated in the eleventh century by Michael Cerularius. The so-called "Orthodox" Church applied this name to itself, as if it were the custodian of the true faith.

If we prescind from the primacy of

the pope, the so-called "Orthodox" Church does not present real dogmatic divergencies from the Roman Catholic Church, especially in the beginning. In the course of centuries, however, certain doctrinal or liturgical disagreements have been stressed, or even created, by reaction against the definitions of the popes or of the ecumenical councils. But the true and fundamental reason of the Eastern Schism and, therefore, its principal error is the negation of the primacy of jurisdiction of the Roman pontiff, as successor of St. Peter.

BIBLIOGRAPHY

CALLAN, "Orthodoxy," *CE*. FORTESCUE, "Orthodox Church," *CE; The Orthodox Eastern Church* (London, 1929). JANIN, *Les Eglises séparées d'Orient* (Paris, 1930). JUGIE, "Grecque (Eglise)," *DA; Theologia Dogmatica Christianorum Orientalium*, Vol. 1 (Paris, 1931). PERRIN, *Les Eglises Orientales* (Rome, 1929). ZANKOV, *The Eastern Orthodox Church*, trans. Lourie (London, 1929).

ostiariate (Lat. *ostiarius* — porter). The lowest of the four minor orders (see *orders, holy*). The office of the porter or *ostiarius* is indicated in the exhortation of the ordination: "He is to ring the bells, open the doors of the church and the sacristy, prepare the book for the preacher" (*Roman Pontifical*).

Its origin is explained by the ancient practice of putting some person in charge of guarding the sacred edifices. The Church adopted this practice from the earliest days of the persecutions, because, occupying buildings dedicated to worship, it felt the need of guarding them and of anticipating, inasmuch as possible, enemy attack. The first mention of this order goes back to the third century.

BIBLIOGRAPHY

ST. THOMAS, *Summa Theol.*, III, *Suppl.*, q. 37, a. 2. KIRSCH, "Porter," *CE*. KURTSCHEID, *Historia Iuris Canonici*, Vol. I (Rome, 1941). TIXERONT, *Holy Orders and Ordinations*, trans. Raemers (St. Louis).

P

pagans. See *infidels.*

pain. See *penalty; suffering.*

Palamites. See *vision, beatific.*

Palmieri. See "Outline of the History of Dogmatic Theology" (p. 303).

pantheism (Gr. πᾶν — all, and θεός — God). A doctrine which consists essentially in drawing together the world and God up to the point of identifying them. There is a *crude* form of pantheism which holds the cosmic elements or brute matter to be the Divinity; hence *idolatry, fetishism* (*qq.v.*). But there also is a *scientific* pantheism, deserving closer attention, which offers an organic and scientific conception of all reality, the world and God together. In other words, this systematic pantheism presents itself as an absolute monism (unitarian concept of reality), and monism is either *materialistic,* like Haeckel's († 1910), or *spiritualistic,* like that of Spinoza or of Gentile.

Materialistic monism, which denies spirit and spiritual values, thus reducing everything to matter, closely approaches crude pantheism. It is contradictory in itself and deserves little consideration. Spiritualistic monism is at once more elegant and insidious, reducing all reality, even material, to spirit and its activity. It first came to life with Spinoza as a *substantialism* (reality is one, sole substance manifesting itself in two *modes:* extension and thought, hence as matter and as spirit, which is God and world at once); then it took the form of idealism, i.e., of an *idea* in perennial becoming (Hegel), or of an *absolute ego* (Fichte), or of a *thinking act* (Gentile). *Immanentism* (*q.v.*) is also a form of pantheism of the intellectualistic or sentimentalistic type.

Every variety of pantheism has latent in it an irremediable contradiction, which falls into the absurd, namely: the identification of the Infinite with the finite. God, absolute Being, is necessarily infinite and, therefore, one, eternal, immutable. The world, on the contrary, is obviously multiple and, therefore, participated, finite, changeable, temporal, i.e., constrained to be actuated successively. It is absurd to try to identify these two beings. The Christian concept of *creation* solves fully the relationship between God and world, between Infinite and finite.

BIBLIOGRAPHY

FLINT, *Anti-Theistic Theories* (Edinburgh, 1894). GERARD, *The Old Riddle and the Newest Answer* (London, 1904). PACE, "Pantheism," *CE*. PLUMTRE, *General Sketch of the History of Pantheism* (London, 1881). SCHALCK, "Panthéisme," *DTC*. SERTILLANGES, *Les sources de la croyance en Dieu* (Paris, 1928), Ch. 18. VALENSIN, *Panthéisme* (Paris, 1922); "Panthéisme," *DA*.

paradise. A word of Persian origin, *pairidaeza* (analogous to the Hebr. *pardes* — park), whence the Gr. παράδεισος, which the Septuagint used to translate the Hebrew גַּן — *gan* (garden, park). In the Vulgate we read *paradisum voluptatis,* in accord with the original Hebrew גַּן בְּעֵדֶן *gan be'eden; eden* in Hebrew, etymologically, means, pleasure, delight, and has been taken in the Vulgate with this meaning. But the Septuagint took the word *eden* as the proper name of a region and translated παράδεισος ἐν Ἐδέμ (park in Eden). This interpretation is more probable. But the Hebraic etymology of *Eden* and the memory of the felicity of our First Parents have made of Eden the place and symbol of enjoyment and perfect delight. The word *paradise* has come to be used in the same way. In the Old Testament, paradise was restricted to mean the place in which God put Adam and Eve and from which He expelled them after their sin. In the New Testament and in Christian literature the *earthly paradise,* in the ancient sense of the word, is distinguished from the *heavenly paradise,* in the sense of a place where the blessed enjoy the vision of God. Thus understood, paradise, also called *heaven,* is, foremost, a *state* or condition of beatitude (*q.v.*), in which the vision and fruition of God are the source of eternal happiness.

But paradise is also a *place,* as is demanded by the presence there of the humanity of Jesus Christ, of the Blessed Virgin, assumed into heaven corporally, and of all the glorious bodies after the general resurrection (*q.v.*). Nothing can be said about the location of paradise.

BIBLIOGRAPHY

DRISCOLL, "Terrestrial Paradise," *CE*. GIETMAN, "Nimbus," *CE*. HETZENAUER, *Theologia biblica* (Freiburg i.-Br., 1908), p. 24. HONTHEIM, "Heaven," *CE*. PESCH, *De Deo creante et elevante* (Freiburg i.-Br., 1925), n. 217 f. POHLE-PREUSS, *Dogmatic Theology,* XII *Eschatology* (St. Louis, 1946), pp. 28–44. SCHNEIDER, *The Other Life* (New York, 1920). *The Teaching of the Catholic Church,* ed. Smith, 2 vols. (New York, 1949), pp. 1248–1282. VAUGHAN, *Life Everlasting* (London, 1922).

Parousia (Gr. παρουσία — presence, coming, return). It means the return of Christ, as Judge of the living and the dead, at the end of the world. Christ spoke in His great eschatological discourse of this second and glorious coming; the Apostles, especially Paul, mention it frequently in their epistles.

The chief difficulty of the New Testament texts, relative to the Parousia, comes from the impression they seem to give that Jesus and the Apostles held the triumphant apparition to be imminent. If this were so, neither Jesus nor the Apostles would have thought of founding and organizing a Church which would last only for a very short time. And such has been the conclusion of a large sector of non-Catholic scholars, of which Loisy is the best-known representative. The Church has intervened with official documents condemning the eschatological theory in general, defended by the modernists (*DB,* 2033), as well as their interpretation of the texts of the apostolic Epistles (Decr. of the Biblical Comm., June 18, 1913).

Since Jesus is the Son of God, and the Apostles, as hagiographers, are inspired by the Holy Spirit, it is obvious that they could not have been mistaken about the time of the end of the world. Nor can we think that the Apostles expressed only their personal views with respect to the imminence of the Parousia, without thereby compromising biblical inspiration, since in the Bible it is not possible to introduce a distinction between ideas and words of man and ideas and words of God (see *inspiration*). Jesus refused to reveal the time of His Second Coming and the end of the world (Mark 13:22 ff.), while He commanded the Apostles to spread the Gospel and the Church to all the world, promising to assist them with His presence and power "up to the consummation of the world" (Matt. 28:20). Paul puts the Thessalonians at ease, who were worrying about the proximate return of Jesus Christ, by telling them that before that time a great apostasy will have to take place, and the Antichrist will have to show himself (2 Thess. 2:3–4); there is no sign of apocalyptic phrenitis in St. Paul, who is busy founding churches, organizing them, giving regulations to his successors for the development and propagation of Christ's message.

Since it was a question of future events, both Jesus and the Apostles, in speaking of the Parousia, employed the prophetic style, characteristic of which is the lack of tense distinction and the presentation of far-removed events as close and united to one another.

Each man's death is followed by his meeting with Christ his Judge; when, therefore, the Apostles exhort to vigilance in anticipation of the coming of Christ, they are referring to this private judgment. Moreover, they had lived with Christ not much longer than two years and had only fully understood Him after He had risen and returned to heaven. The intense desire of Him, of seeing Him again, had its influence on the Apostles who reverted to the thought of the glorious return of that Christ whom they had seen Victim of the hatred of men.

BIBLIOGRAPHY

ALLO, *L'Apocalypse* (Paris, 1933), pp. CXIX–CXLIII. BILLOT, *La Parousie* (Paris, 1920). CAVALLA, "Il tempo della Parusia nel pensiero di San Paolo," *Scuola Cattolica,* 65 (1937), pp. 443–480. PRAT, *The Theology of St. Paul,* trans. Stoddard, 2 vols. (Westminster, 1926–1927). See Analytical Summary: "The Last Ends," at the end of Vol. 2, p. 503.

participation. See *analogy*.

Pasch (or Passover). One of the three great liturgical solemnities, together with Pentecost and the Feast of the Tents (or Tabernacles), by which the Jewish people commemorated the benefits received from God whether in the order of nature or of grace in the course of its unsettled history. The Hebrew name for Easter is *Pesach;* in Aramaic, *Paschàh,* whence the Latin *Pascha* and the English *Pasch*. The verb root *Psch* (*Pàsach*) means "to hop over," "pass beyond" (hence the English name *Passover*), the festival having been instituted in memory of the survival of the firstborn of the Hebrews during the tenth plague in Egypt, when the exterminating angel "passed over," i.e., spared the Hebrew houses marked with the blood of the lamb (Exod. 12:13, 23, 27).

The Feast lasted from the fourteenth to the twenty-first of the month of *Nisan* (March–April), during which time special sacrifices were offered in the Temple. The first and last days were full holydays with rest from work (Exod. 12; Lev. 23:1–14). On the fourteenth each head of a family brought a lamb or kid to the Temple, bled it, and sprinkled its blood on the altar, burning the fat; upon his return home he roasted the animal on a cruciform spit formed by two pieces of wood, in order not to break the bones. After sunset there followed the great Paschal supper, during which the lamb was eaten with unleavened bread and bitter herbs, to the accompaniment of prayers and instructions. The partakers were obliged to be in the required condition of legal purity. Every fragment of meat remaining was religiously burned. During the Paschal week only azymes (unleavened bread) was used — hence the name of "Feast of the Azymes" used in the Gospels.

In later times the Feast was very much elaborated. The Paschal Lamb became a real, true sacrifice and represented the immolation of Christ (1 Cor. 5:7, where *Pascha* indicates metonymically the "Lamb"; 1 Pet. 1:19; cf. John 19:33–36). The Paschal banquet in which Israel renewed its pact with God was a figure of the Eucharistic banquet (1 Cor. 10:17). Jesus Christ instituted the Eucharist precisely at the end of the last Paschal supper of His life.

BIBLIOGRAPHY

Aherne, "Pasch or Passover," *CE*. Dembitz, *Jewish Services in Synagogue and Home* (Philadelphia, 1898). Esterley, Box, *Religion and Worship of the Synagogue* (London, 1907). Kortleitner, *Archaeologia biblica* (Oeniponte, 1927), pp. 256–267. Lesêtre, "Pâque," *DBV*.

passibility of Christ. See *Docetism; propassions.*

passion of Christ. The pains and sufferings, taken as a whole, sustained by Christ in His soul and body, especially in the last days of His life, which terminated in the tragedy of the cross.

Errors: Docetism, from the first century, which denied the physical reality of Christ's body by reducing it to an appearance. Aphthartodocetism (in the fifth century) of Monophysitic origin (*qq.v.*), which predicated of Christ an *incorruptible* body. Based on these theories, many thought that the passion and the physical pain of Jesus were a miracle. The Theopaschites went to the opposite excess by attributing passibility to the Divinity Itself. The Church, condemning all these errors, has always taught, on the basis of revelation that the Redeemer's humanity is altogether like our own, sin excepted, as St. Paul says (Heb. 2:17; Phil. 2:6 ff.), and therefore: (*a*) like us, He had sensible passions, except for any disorder in them (see *propassions*); (*b*) He felt real and proper pain and sufferings of the flesh, i.e., had a perfect *passibility;* (*c*) although the passion of the humanity is proper to the Word, it does not at all affect the Divinity, which remains absolutely impassible.

To prove the truth and reality of the pain and of all the passion of Christ, it suffices to read the Gospel which speaks in realistic language of His weariness (John 4:6), His hunger and thirst (Matt. 4:2; John 19:29), His mortal sadness to the point of sweating blood. In the Old Testament, the Messias was prophesied as the "Man of sufferings or sorrows." St. Thomas demonstrates that the suffering of Jesus Christ, proportionately to His infinite love, was maximum both extensively and intensively; nevertheless, His soul, even during the passion, continued to enjoy the beatific vision in the intellective faculty, like a mountaintop that basks in the sun while the roaring tempest batters its flanks.

BIBLIOGRAPHY

St. Thomas, *Summa Theol.*, III, q. 46. Jugie, *Julien d'Halicarnasse et Sevère d'Antioche* (Paris, 1925). *The Teaching of the Catholic Church,* ed. Smith, 2 vols. (New York, 1949), pp. 440–476.

Patripassianism. See *modalism; monarchianism.*

Pelagianism. A great heresy of the fifth century, diffused chiefly in the Western Churches by the Breton monk, Pelagius, who came to Rome about 400, where he met Rufinus, a disciple of Theodore of Mopsuestia (see *Nestorianism*) and a disclaimer of the transmission of original sin (*q.v.*). Quickly Pelagius followed this trend, helped in the propagation of his ideas by his loquacious disciple Celestius.

The Pelagian heresy can be reduced to a *naturalistic* system on the anthropological level, to the prejudice of the supernatural: it has also a Stoic tint in its exaltation of man's moral strength against evil. Its basic principles are: (*a*) The sin committed by Adam injured or harmed him alone and in no wise is it transmitted to his descendants by generation. (*b*) Babies are born in the identically same condition in which Adam was before his sin: hence they are innocent and friends of God. (*c*) Babies, even nonbaptized, reach eternal life. (*d*) Man, with his natural forces and his free will, can avoid all sin and win the beatific vision. (*e*) Grace, as an entity intrinsic to man, does not exist, nor is it necessary; grace is Christ's example, the law, and free will itself. (*f*) The Redemption is not a regeneration of man in his soul vivified by grace, but is rather the call for a higher life to be won by one's own efforts.

Pelagianism is bent on destroying the whole supernatural order. St. Augustine immediately saw the gravity of the danger and joined battle without truce for the defense of the Christian truth, first against Pelagius and Celestius, who had gone to Africa, and then against Julian, Bishop of Eclana, who had systematized the Pelagian error. Through the work of St. Augustine the heresy was condemned in 418 in a great Council at Carthage, approved by Pope Zozimus, who briefed its definitions in an *"epistula tractoria,"* which was sent to all the churches. Julian of Eclana, together with seventeen other Italian bishops, refused to endorse the pontifical letter, and went in exile into the East, to join Theodore of Mopsuestia. Pelagianism was condemned also in the Council of Ephesus, together with Nestorianism (431), and in the II Council of Orange (529, *DB,* 101 ff., 126 ff., 174 ff.).

BIBLIOGRAPHY

Cayré, *Manual of Patrology,* trans. Howitt, Vol. 1 (Paris, Tournai, Rome, 1936), pp. 391–394. De Plinval, *Pélage* (Lausanne, 1943). Gaudel, "Péché originel," *DTC.* Hedde, Amann, "Pélagianisme," *DTC.* Pohle, "Pelagians and Pelagianism," *CE.* Pohle-Preuss, *Dogmatic Theology,* VII *Grace* (*Actual and Habitual*) (St. Louis, 1946), pp. 82–96. Warfield, *Two Studies in the History of Doctrine: Augustine and the Pelagian Controversy; The Development of the Doctrine of Infant Salvation* (New York, 1897).

See under *Semi-Pelagianism.*

penalty (Gr. ποινή). The privation of a good which the rational creature undergoes involuntarily on account of its own guilt. Penalty is therefore an evil (*malum poenae*), which stems from another evil (*malum culpae*). Although evil (*q.v.*), being a privation or lack of good, follows naturally the lot of every finite good, yet we know from revelation that God had created man in such a state that, had he not sinned, he would not have suffered evil.

As a consequence of original sin, evil has invaded the world under the form of sin and of punishment. Punishment is divided into *concomitant* and *inflicted:* the former stems naturally from guilt and accompanies it, e.g., remorse or loss of honor; the second is imposed by the judge (God or man) in relationship to guilt. Moreover, the punishment inflicted may be *medicinal* or *vindictive*, according as the judge threatens to inflict it (*poena comminata*) to keep man away from guilt, or actually inflicts it to re-establish the violated order. In theology, the punishment inflicted by God on him who dies obstinate in grave guilt is subdivided into *poena damni* (pain of loss: loss of God) and *poena sensus* (pain of sense: positive suffering inflicted by God) (see *hell; damned*). Justice forbids that punishment be inflicted for guilt that is not voluntary on the part of the individual's own will: therefore babies who die unbaptized are deprived of the beatific vision (*poena damni*), but will not be punished positively like the demons and the damned (*poena sensus*).

Juridically, the penalty is in proportion to *crime,* which the *CIC* (Can. 2195) defines as: "an external violation, morally imputable, of a law provided with a canonical sanction, at least undetermined." The penal sanction belongs to the coercive power of a perfect society such as is the Church. The penalties established by the Church are multiple and all aim principally at the good of the delinquent and at the common good of the Christian family. In the old discipline there were corporal penalties also. Nowadays the spiritual penalty prevails. There are three categories of ecclesiastical penalties:

1. *Medicinal* penalties or *censures* are inflicted especially on the contumacious for the purpose of bringing about their repentance. They are: (*a*) *excommunication,* by which one who is guilty of an external crime is separated from the communion of the faithful; (*b*) *interdict,* which is inflicted on persons and things and which involves privation of some sacraments, or in general of some sacred thing; (*c*) *suspension,* which is inflicted on clerics only and involves privation of an office or benefice.

2. *Vindictive* penalties are inflicted for the purpose of *expiation,* e.g., privation of Christian burial, deposition or degradation of a priest.

3. *Penal remedies and penances,* like warning, surveillance, the recitation of certain prayers, spiritual exercises.

BIBLIOGRAPHY

St. Thomas, *Summa Theol.,* I–II, q. 87. Billot, *De personali et originali peccato* (Rome, 1924), p. 77 ff. *Code of Canon Law,* Book 5. Gans, "Censures (Ecclesiastical)," *CE.* Ortolan, "Censures Ecclesiastiques," *DTC.* Roberti, *De delictis et poenis* (Rome, 1929).

penance (Lat. *poenitere* — to repent). The sacrament in which the priest, the representative of God, remits sins committed after baptism. Jesus Christ instituted it on the day of the Resurrection when, breathing on His Apostles, He said: "Receive ye the Holy Ghost. Whose sins you shall forgive, they are forgiven them; and whose sins you shall retain, they are retained" (John 20:22–23). The expression "forgive sins" signifies a total pardon of sin, in so far as sin is an offense against God. By virtue of these words of universal character, the Church has defined that the power conferred by Christ is not only all inclusive, i.e., having no limitations of any kind either with respect to the number or to the gravity of the sins (against the Montanists of the second century, and the Novatians of the third century), but is also unsusceptible of being twisted in any way from its natural meaning or contorted to signify the power of preaching and baptizing (against Luther), or of *declaring* sins remitted (against Calvin), or of attenuating their punishment (against the Anglicans. Cf. Council of Trent, sess. 14, *DB,* 894, 912, 913, 919, 920).

From the same words it is deduced also that the power conferred on the Apostles and their successors is of a *judicial nature.* Since, in fact, this power can be applied in two positive and opposite acts (the act of remitting or the act of retaining), it involves knowledge of the cause of the delinquent and a *judgment* on the subject, whereby that power may be, in a concrete case, determined to the one or the other of the two acts, to which it is of itself indifferent. Hence, this judicial power can be exercised only by the pronouncement of a sentence after an objective evaluation of the penitent's cause and in accord with divine law, which establishes that pardon be granted to the sincerely repentant sinner who confesses his sin and agrees to make condign satisfaction for it. Therefore, the elements constitutive of the sacramental rite of penance are the sentence of the judge or absolution (form) and the three acts of the sinner: contrition, confession, satisfaction (matter) (*qq.v.*).

The absolution, which determines sacramentally the three acts of the penitent, restores sanctifying grace to him. In other words, the sinner recovers in this sacrament adoptive sonship, the benevolence of the Father, who, having put on him again the "first robe" of justification, readmits the new prodigal son into His house, restoring his lost rights to him. However, the measure of this restitution of primitive rights, i.e., the reviviscence of merits (*iura ad premium gloriae*), corresponds to the fervor with which the penitent rises from his fall, according to the axiom "God gives Himself in proportion to the fervor He finds in us." Connected with the restoration of the supernatural organism is the new orientation which the *sacramental grace* impresses on it: an increase of the virtue of penance and of the helps of actual grace, through which the penitent's soul finds itself under the constant impetus of an inclination (the spirit of penance) which, if supported by his docility, is able to make him ascend to the highest peaks of sanctity. The ascent toward the reconquest of spiritual integrity is rendered easier by the readmission of the healed member to the participation of the goods of the Communion of Saints. Furthermore, the Church, like the mother who is more merciful according to the greater need of her child, showers more abundantly the treasures of the merits of Christ, the Virgin, and the saints, on the spiritually more needy member, especially, by the granting of indulgences (*q.v.*).

BIBLIOGRAPHY

St. Thomas, *Summa Theol.,* III, qq. 84–90; *Suppl.,* qq. 1–28. D'Alès, *De sacramento Paenitentiae* (Paris, 1926). Boyer, *De Paenitentia et Extrema Unctione* (Rome, 1942). Doronzo, *De Poenitentia,* 4 vols. (Milwaukee, 1949–). The first volume treats directly of penance as a sacrament and as a virtue. Galtier, *De Paenitentia* (Paris, 1931); *Le péché et la pénitence* (Paris, 1929); *L'Eglise et la rémission des péchés* (Paris, 1932); "Pénitence," *DTC.* Hanna, "Penance," *CE.* Jenkins, *The Doctrine and the Practice of Auricular Confession* (London, 1783). O'Donnell, *Penance in the Early Church* (Dublin, 1907). Palmieri, *De Poenitentia* (Prati, 1896). Piolanti, *De sacramentis,* Vol. 1 (Rome, 1945). Pohle-Preuss, *Dogmatic Theology,* X *The Sacraments,* Vol. 3, *Penance* (St. Louis, 1946). *The Teaching of the Catholic Church,* ed. Smith, 2 vols. (New York, 1949), pp. 955–989. Wiseman, *Lectures on the Principal Doctrines and Practices of the Catholic Church* (London, 1844). The teaching of the Catholic

Church on the sacrament of penance was particularly attacked by H. Ch. Lea, *A History of Auricular Confession and Indulgences in the Latin Church,* 3 vols. (Philadelphia, 1896).

perfection. Etymologically, perfect stems from the Latin *perficere* (finish, do through to the end), and means "completely done." But, if we prescind from action, which renders a thing perfect, perfection may be considered simply as full possession of act, i.e., as actuality in opposition to the potential or the virtual state. In this sense God is infinitely perfect, because He is Pure Act, Being subsisting by essence, who does not admit of any limitation or any evolution to further acquisition.

Every perfection is a mode of being: where there is subsisting being, all perfections are in act. Since goodness is that to which beings tend as to their proper perfection, the most perfect Being, God, is the highest Good, Goodness Itself, source and end of all finite good. St. Thomas (*Summa Theol.,* I, q. 4, a. 4) writes: "All things are said to be good with the divine goodness, because it is the exemplary, effective, and final principle of all goodness." Plato asserted the primacy of *goodness,* hence the dialectics of love (cf., e.g., the *Symposium*).

BIBLIOGRAPHY

St. Thomas, *Summa Theol.,* I, q. 4. Garrigou-Lagrange, *God: His Existence and His Nature,* trans. Rose (St. Louis, 1947–1948); *The One God,* trans. Rose (St. Louis, 1943), pp. 229–235. Peter Parente, *De Deo Uno* (Rome, 1938), p. 193 ff. Pohle-Preuss, *Dogmatic Theology,* I *God: Knowability, Essence, Attributes* (St. Louis, 1946), pp. 180–190, 241–264. *The Teaching of the Catholic Church,* ed. Smith, 2 vols. (New York, 1949), pp. 85–88.

Perrone. See "Outline of the History of Dogmatic Theology" (p. 303).

perseverance, final. A great gift of God by which man, at the moment of death, is in the state of sanctifying grace and, therefore, is saved. Actually, perseverance refers primarily to the process of living under the influx of God's grace. Man, clad with sanctifying grace, given the weakness of his nature marred by original sin and the devil's attacks, is always in danger of losing God's friendship by succumbing to temptation, notwithstanding his resolution to the contrary. There is not in this life a fixed state of the soul in grace that, as in the case of the blessed, makes relapse into sin impossible. With fine psychological sense, St. Thomas (*Summa Theol.,* I–II, q. 109, a. 8, 9) presents the explanation: As sanctifying grace heals the mind but does not nullify concupiscence, there arise in man sudden and unexpected movements of the passions, which the mind — not always vigilant and alert — is not always successful in dominating for a continuous tension is psychologically impossible. Hence guilt, which returns from time to time; we resist for a time, but soon grow weary of watching and fighting and finally capitulate deliberately.

The Council of Trent expounds (sess. 6, c. 22) that man, already adorned with sanctifying grace, cannot persevere in holiness without a *special help* from God. Even more — according to the same Council (c. 16), sanctified man needs a particular, divine help for final perseverance, which is the *magnum donum* (great gift) veiled by the mystery of predestination (*q.v.*).

The gift of final perseverance is complex, since it supposes the state of sanctifying grace and requires, in addition, a continuous influx of efficacious, actual grace for the whole life, and especially at the hour of death, bristling with psychological difficulties and temptations. Besides, that gift includes timely dispositions of divine providence, joining the state of grace with the exact instant of death, on which depends man's eternal status. Surely man must collaborate with God by co-operating freely with His grace, in order to merit eternal salvation; but it is also certain that such a decisive moment, on which converge so many diverse elements, must lie in His hands. Man cannot be sure of final perseverance. Neither can he merit it in the true sense of the word (see *merit*); but he can, according to a happy expression of the Fathers, merit it by prayer (*suppliciter merere*).

BIBLIOGRAPHY

St. Thomas, *Summa Theol.*, II–II, q. 137; I–II, q. 109, a. 9–10; q. 114, a. 9. St. Augustine, *De dono perseverantiae* (*PL*, 44). Michel, "Persévérance," *DTC*. Newman, "Perseverance in Grace," *Discourses to Mixed Congregations* (London, New York, 1906). Sollier, "Perseverance (Final)," *CE*.

person. Boethius defines it as the "individual substance of a rational nature"; St. Thomas, more concisely and exactly, as the "distinct being, subsisting in an intellectual nature."

The best pagan philosophy (e.g., Aristotle) never explored fully the problem of person. The concept of "person" is almost exclusively Christian, for it developed in the light of the mysteries of the Trinity and the Incarnation. These mysteries suggested the distinction between nature and person, which was the first conquest of Christian thought. The Scholastics, following in the steps of the Fathers, elaborated a rich doctrine with varied positions. The person is a whole, of which the *nature* is the basic part; in addition to the nature, it includes "individuating principles" which stem from matter, *accidents*, and *individual existence*, putting the individuated nature outside of its causes and in the world of reality. If this individuated and distinctly subsisting nature is rational, it is called a person; if irrational or even inanimate, it is termed a *suppositum*. Which of these elements, however, is formally and definitively constitutive of person as such? This problem has been given various solutions: *subsistence* has been called the formal characteristic of person, but the schools differ as to the *negative* or *positive* mode of interpreting this subsistence.

1. *Negative:* Scotus maintains that subsistence or personality is *incommunication* (a nature in that it does not communicate with another); Tiphanius, taking up again this opinion, tries to give it a positive content by saying that subsistence is the *totality*, or state of *completeness*, of a nature in itself.

2. *Positive:* Some theologians (Cajetan, Suarez) reduce subsistence to a *substantial mode*, which would terminate the nature; others (Capreolus, many moderns) reduce it to the *actual existence*, i.e., to the very act of existing, proper to a substance. This last opinion is preferable on account of its simplicity and greater adherence to the definitions of the Church *magisterium*. For example, in the Incarnation the human nature of Christ is not a person, because it does not have its own existence or act of existing, but subsists by virtue of the divine act of existence of the Word, thus participating in the Word's divine personality. Modern philosophy tends to hold that person is constituted by self-consciousness; against this opinion there are both philosophical and theological difficulties. Consciousness of the *ego* presupposes existence of the *ego;* consequently it reveals the *ego,* but does not constitute it.

BIBLIOGRAPHY

St. Thomas, *Summa Theol.*, I, q. 29, a. 1–2. Geddes, "Person," *CE*. Peter Parente, *La genesi cristiana della personalitá* (Rome, 1933); *De Verbo Incarnato* (Rome, 1938). Pohle-Preuss, *Dogmatic Theology,* II *The Divine Trinity* (St. Louis, 1946), pp. 220–228; IV *Christology* (St. Louis, 1946), pp. 129–132.

TERRIEN, *S. Thomae Aq. doctrina sincera de unione hypostatica* (Paris, 1894).

Petavius. See "Outline of the History of Dogmatic Theology" (p. 303); *indwelling of the Holy Trinity.*

Phantasiasts. See *Docetism.*

Pietism. A religious current founded in Germany, toward the end of the seventeenth century, by Jacob Spener († 1705), following on the lead given by Jacob Böhme, a shoemaker († 1624). Spener proposed to awaken dormant Protestantism with a blaze of lived piety (hence the name *Pietists*) through the intense exercise of prayer. Thus less stress was placed upon the importance of doctrinal formulas of faith, and the Lutheran theory of extrinsic justification, as an imputation of Christ's sanctity, gave way to the concept and the practice of a progressive, laborious conformity to Christ, the Model of perfection. Pietism was a partial repudiation of Lutheranism and a yearning for Catholicism, kindled spontaneously in those *collegia pietatis* instituted by Spener, like our houses of retreat and spiritual exercises. In this fervor of piety, priority was naturally given to the heart and to the emotions.

Spener's ideas were embraced and elaborated fully by August Franke († 1727), who used that leaven for the rehabilitation of pedagogy and the school system, to which he devoted his entire life at Halle, the foyer of Pietism. But in time this movement degenerated into strange forms either of the apocalyptic type, like the millenaristic sect (*q.v.*) of Eva Buttlar and of the Swiss Brügler (both blemished by immorality); or of the pseudohedonistic type, like the Labadists; or of the symbolistic type with a rationalistic slant, like the "New Jerusalem" sect of Emmanuel Swedenborg in Scandinavia. These and other degenerations have their roots in the *sentimentalist subjectivism* of Pietism, antidogmatic and antihierarchical. However, Pietism had efficacious influence on the various sectors of intellectual and civil life: two great musicians Bach and Handel draw artistic inspiration from it in their musical compositions. In the eighteenth century Pietism was revived in the Confraternities of *Herrnhut* of Nic. Lud. Zinzendorf, with Lutheran base.

BIBLIOGRAPHY

CRISTIANI, "Réforme (Evolution du Luthéranisme)," *DA,* cols. 620–622. FRIES, *Die Stiftung A. H. Franke* (1913). HÜBENER, *Der Pietismus* (1901). LAUCHERT, "Pietism," *CE.*

piety. See *gifts of the Holy Ghost.*

Pneumatomachists. See *Macedonians.*

Polycarp. See "Outline of the History of Dogmatic Theology" (p. 301).

polytheism (Gr. πολύς — many, and θεός — god). A religious system which admits more than one divinity. It is the antithesis of monotheism (*q.v.*).

Many controversies have flared up among students of the history of religions, especially in modern times, about the origin of polytheism. The work of Max Müller, who is considered the founder of the scientific study of religions, is noteworthy. In the first phase of his research he thought he could tie up the origin of polytheism with a linguistic phenomenon, *polionymia,* i.e., plurality of names, of genders, of endings, which would have favored personification of various divinities. Later he connected the origin of polytheism with three sources: (1) the *physical* source (natural things, like stones, rivers, trees, stars, etc.); (2) the *anthropological* source (domestic and social relations); (3) the *psychological* source (consciousness of the *ego* in relationship to the infinite). To these overspeculative theories are added those of fetishism and of animism (*qq.v.*), as well as astral mythology, totemism (relation between tribes and animals), Magism, etc. All these theories are in general agreement in asserting that the primitive religion was polytheistic and mythological; with the progress of civilization monotheism is said to have developed gradually.

But a direct and accurate study of the facts has led to the discovery of a worship of a supreme being, which is found more or less in all primitive peoples. The supreme being or great god is represented as creator of all, even of inferior spirits or divinities, as omnipotent, immense, just. This fact, quite constant and uniform in the most ancient peoples, shows that monotheism is prior to polytheism, and that the latter is a degeneration of the former.

This truth is also contained in Holy Scripture (cf. Wisdom, Romans), which describes the guilty aberration of man, who, although knowing the Supreme Being, dared to turn his mind and heart from Him and form for himself absurd divinities, personifying objects, plants, and animals.

BIBLIOGRAPHY

Chantepie de la Saussaye, *Manuel d'histoire des religions* (Paris, 1909). Magnin, "Religion," *DTC*. Pinard de la Boullaye, *L'étude comparée des religions*, 3 vols. (Paris, 1929), Vol. 1, Ch. 1. Pohle-Preuss, *Dogmatic Theology*, I *God: Knowability, Essence, Attributes* (St. Louis, 1946), pp. 217–223.

See under *God; monotheism.*

pontiff, Roman. See *Roman pontiff.*

"Pontifical, Roman." See *liturgy.*

pope (Gr. πάπας — father). The name Tradition has reserved for the Bishop of Rome, who, as successor of St. Peter, is the heir of the primacy over the entire Church (see *primacy of St. Peter; Roman pontiff*). By virtue of this prerogative, for twenty centuries the pope has been the greatest reality at the center not only of Roman but of world history (*Urbis et Orbis*). "After Constantine turned the Roman eagle around and made him fly counter to heaven's course" (as Dante expresses it in the *Divina Commedia, Paradiso,* 6, 1–2), transferring to the Bosphorus his glorious nest, Rome, having become the coveted objective of so many barbarians, adventurers, and conquerors, would quite soon have become a rubble heap of proud ruins, had not her Bishop made himself her defender. From St. Leo the Great to the present Holy Father, the pope, by spontaneous and universal recognition of the nations, has been greeted *defensor Urbis* (defender of the City).

The world (*orbis*), in its turn, consciously or unconsciously gravitates around the Vicar of Christ. The Christian world is constituted, strengthened, and defended by the papacy. From Rome, as from a luminous focus, beam forth the rays which disperse the darkness of paganism and barbarism and extend the zone of divine influences. Ireland (truly the first-born of the Church), the Franks, the Germans, the Scandinavian countries, the Slavs enter the luminous orbit of the cross because the pope entrusted to Patrick, to Boniface, to Ansgar and Willibrord, to Cyril and Methodius, the *missio canonica* which made them authentic heralds of the Gospel. Having made Europe Christian, the pope unified and stabilized it by creating the Holy Roman Empire, which even in its degeneration served to assure the sense of unity and universality to the world of the Middle Ages. When the Moslem threat, the arrogance of rebel princes, and the seething heresies fixed the wedge to split the great block of Christianity, the pope declared Crusades, fulminated excommunications, assembled councils. After the fever of nationalism and the rebellion of Martin Luther (real paralysis of Christianity) threw Christian Europe into confusion and disorder; after Jansenism and Gallicanism did their best to split the inner structure of the Church, the papacy, in addition to its strong condemnations of the seventeenth and eighteenth centuries, convoked the Vatican Council for the purpose of neutralizing once and for all the last germs dissolvent of ecclesiastical unity. Thus, entirely centered in its visible head, the Church, having given all she could to the Christian world, now as never before turns her maternal eyes toward the world of paganism, confidently hoping for an abundant compensation for the defection of so many among her children.

BIBLIOGRAPHY

Batiffol, *Cathedra Petri* (Paris, 1928). Cotter, *Theologia Fundamentalis* (Weston, 1940), pp. 383–407. Hergenröther, *Catholic Church and Christian State* (London, 1876). Joyce, "Pope," *CE*. Martin, "Pape," *DTC*. Mourret, *La Papauté* (Paris, 1929). Pucci, *Il Vescovo di Roma nella vita della Chiesa* (Turin, 1943). Rivington, *The Primitive Church and the See of Peter* (London, 1894). *The Teaching of the Catholic Church,* ed. Smith, 2 vols. (New York, 1949), pp. 716–721.

See under *Roman pontiff*.

porter's office. See *ostiariate*.

positivism. Rather than a system it is a tendency of thought, which developed in the past century as a reaction to the currents of idealism. Against the subjectivistic constructions of idealism and sentimentalistic dreams of romanticism, its ally, there arose toward the end of the nineteenth century a positive current of thought which preferred experience to theory, sensation to abstract concept, and fact to principle. It was a strong summons to minds to come down from lofty speculations to the concrete reality of nature and human life, under the impulse of the practical sciences, which had an extensive development in that epoch. Positivism has its remote roots in English empiricism of the seventeenth century (Locke) and in the French sensism of Condillac; but its proximate roots are found in Kantian criticism, which had depreciated knowledge in the metaphysical zone (noumenon) to the advantage of the empirical or phenomenical zone. Confining themselves to the fact and the world of senses, the positivists draw close to materialism, but detach themselves from it by admitting the possibility of a supersense reality, e.g., God. The materialist denies it; the positivist is an *agnostic* in that he says he is ignorant as long as he is not able to demonstrate it empirically.

The founder of positivism in France was Auguste Comte († 1857), a man of genius but lacking balance, who pivoted his system on the theory of the three stages: the *theological,* the *metaphysical,* and the *positive,* which mark the steps in the progress of humanity from naïve imagination, to abstract reasoning, to the direct knowledge of nature, in which dominate the phenomenon with its laws — object of experience. Human life itself is reduced to a complex of phenomena and of social and individual physical laws. There is no God above nature, but only humanity, the great being, to which worship should be given.

In England, positivism takes on a more scientific and practical cast with Herbert Spencer († 1903), who adopts the evolutionistic theory and applies it to cosmology, anthropology, sociology, and ethics. According to Spencer, there is in the universe an *unknowable* which science and religion must respect, contenting themselves with knowing the facts and leaving the mysteries aside. The positivistic current in England manifests itself also in the utilitarianism of G. Bentham († 1832) and of Stuart Mill († 1873); in France, in the empirical sociology of E. Durkheim († 1917), which reduces psychology, ethics, and religion to social facts and products. Finally, positivism took root in Italy also, especially through the work of Roberto Ardigo († 1920), but in a bland form, neither very philosophical nor very scientific, adapted to men of mediocre stature, little solicitous about the great problems that transcend daily life. The disagreement between positivism and Christian philosophy and theology is evident.

BIBLIOGRAPHY

ALLIEVO, *Del Positivismo* (Turin, 1883). DE BROGLIE, *Le Positivisme et la science expérimentale* (Paris, 1881). ROURE, "Positivisme," *DA*. SAUVAGE, "Positivism," *CE*. TURNER, *History of Philosophy* (Boston, 1903).

power of Christ. Three powers are distinguished in the incarnate Word: (1) the divine power (omnipotence) which belongs to Him as God; (2) the power proper to every human nature, which belongs to Him as perfect Man; (3) an *instrumental* power of divine origin, which is exercised, however, with the concourse of the human nature, according to the exigencies of the redeeming mission of the Saviour. It is evident that omnipotence cannot be communicated to the humanity of Christ, because it belongs properly and exclusively to an infinite Being. But it is theologically certain that humanity has concurred and still does concur in certain communicable divine actions, like working miracles, producing and infusing grace in souls.

The gospel descriptions leave no doubt in this matter: "And all the multitude sought to touch him, for virtue went out from him, and healed all" (Luke 6:19). Jesus healed the deaf-mute by touching his ears with His fingers and his tongue with saliva (Mark 7:32). Such gestures would be a comedy unworthy of Jesus if His humanity did not contribute really to the miraculous cure. The Fathers are unanimous in the same teaching: the fruits of the Redemption pass through the flesh of the Word, which Cyril of Alexandria calls *vivifying* (*DB*, 123).

According to the common teaching, the sacraments themselves are subordinated to the sanctifying power of the humanity of Christ. But there is discussion on the nature of this instrumental function of both the humanity of Christ and the sacraments; some theologians prefer *physical* instrumentality (more consonant with Tradition); others, a simply *moral* instrumentality. St. Thomas stands for the physical.

BIBLIOGRAPHY

ST. THOMAS, *Summa Theol.*, III, qq. 8 and 48. HUGON, *La causalité instrumentale dans l'ordre surnaturel* (Paris, 1924), Ch. 3. PETER PARENTE, *De Verbo Incarnato* (Rome, 1939), p. 221 ff.

power of jurisdiction. See *hierarchy*.

power of orders. See *hierarchy*.

pragmatism (Gr. πράγμα — action, deed). A philosophico-religious system which began in America toward the end of the nineteenth century, mainly through the works of Charles Sanders Peirce and especially of William James, who is considered the true founder and popularizer of the new theory. Begun as a *method,* pragmatism developed into a doctrine and a system which can be defined in general as a tendency to consider everything from the practical viewpoint, i.e., in terms of *action,* seeking in action itself the reason of truth and certainty, of life and religion. The starting point of pragmatism is the devaluation of the theoretical world of ideas; ideas have no value of themselves, but are considered only in function of action. In order to act and accomplish, man needs a conviction, a *belief;* the ideas must, therefore, converge toward a belief which is to become the principle of action. If in the course of action it is seen that an idea helps, then it will be said that it is *true.* The truth of an idea depends on its practical verification. This is the so-called scientific method of the pragmatists in opposition to the intellectualistic methods in the search of truth. Thus it appears clear that for the pragmatists there exists no immutable or eternal truth: truth, on the contrary, develops itself and is in continual flux of becoming, like action itself, which is the purpose of life.

In the religious field pragmatism rejects all external revelation of truth and all conceptual systems, limiting itself to the consideration of individual religious feeling and consciousness, called by the technical term of *religious experience.* Through this experience the individual feels the divine and elevates himself to God by an act of faith, which is pure will to believe (not adhesion of the intellect to revealed truths) and tendency to verify the utility and advantage of believing. This act of faith may appropriate to itself even a previously formed religion such as Christianity, but only provisionally and in so far as such religion proves itself useful and efficacious in practice. Theoretic discussions of principles are useless in the field of religion just as they are useless in philosophy. Pragmatism is an anti-metaphysical system because it is anti-intellectualistic (basically it is sensism, which goes back to the English empiricism of Locke and Hume). Viewed as a critique of knowledge, it falls into *disastrous relativism* by denying the first logical principles and the stability of truth with correspondingly disastrous repercussions in the moral field. Goodness and truth become something subjective, subordinated to convictions of the individual and his experimental tests.

From a religious viewpoint pragmatism is a radical denial of all revealed religion and makes God's very existence conditioned by psychological experience, which is an exaltation of the will against reason. Pragmatism stems especially in the matter of religion, from the Lutheran principle of *fiducial faith* (see *Lutheranism*).

BIBLIOGRAPHY

Blanche, "Pragmatisme," *DA.* Leclère, *Pragmatisme, Modernisme, Protestantisme* (Paris, 1909). Papini, *Sul Pragmatismo. Saggi e ricerche* (Milan, 1913). Pratt, *What Is Pragmatism* (New York, 1909). Schinz, *Anti-Pragmatism* (New York, 1909). Turner, "Pragmatism," *CE.* Walker, *Theories of Knowledge* (New York, 1910).

prayer. Commonly defined as an elevation of the soul to God in order to express to Him our feelings and our petitions. Psychologically, prayer is an act of the *intellect,* whereas devotion is an act of the *will,* which gives itself readily to God's service; both appertain to the virtue of *religion,* which inclines man to render due reverence and honor to God (St. Thomas). In a broad sense, any movement toward God or work done for Him can be called prayer. But, strictly speaking, prayer is elevation of the mind to God (subjective aspect), and request or petition (objective aspect).

A divine model of prayer is the *Pater Noster,* dictated by Jesus, who has given an example of the continuous use of prayer and who has exhorted us to pray always.

Prayer, as an act of religion, is a duty; but it is also a need of the soul, which feels its own infirmities and indigence and turns in humility and confidence to the One who can help it. Prayer can be *mental* (silent) or *oral* (vocal). The sound of the word does not serve to communicate with God, who knows all things, but to excite our own affections. Those who admit universal fatalism or determinism deny the value of prayer, rejecting the concept of a provident God. But, even when divine providence is admitted, a vexatious question can arise: prayer, if effective, would seem to change God's plan (which is immutable). St. Thomas maintains that *ab aeterno* divine providence has disposed that certain effects should be conditioned by prayer and subordinate to it, and so prayer enters together with the other elements in the design of God.

The terminus proper of our prayer is God alone, the Triune God: but we pray also to the Blessed Virgin and to the saints that they may intercede for us. The efficacy of prayer depends on the divine mercy, but ordinarily it is proportionate also to the dignity of the one praying. Mary's power of intercession is significantly called by the Fathers *omnipotentia supplex.* Jesus Christ as Man prayed on earth and, according to St. Paul, He continues to intercede for us in heaven. Even the sinner can and should pray the best he can; God hears his prayer not in justice but in mercy.

The entire Christian liturgy bears witness to the usefulness, beauty, and necessity of prayer (see *contemplation; mystics*).

BIBLIOGRAPHY

St. Thomas, *Summa Theol.*, II–II, q. 83. D'Alès, "Prière," *DA.* Faber, *Growth in Holiness* (London, 1854). Fenton, *The Theology of Prayer* (Milwaukee, 1939). Fisher, *A Treatise on Prayer* (London, 1885). Fonck, "Prière," *DTC.* Pascal Parente, *The Mystical Life* (St. Louis, 1946), Index: "Prayer"; *The Ascetical Life* (St. Louis, 1947), Index: "Prayer." Poulain, *The Grace of Interior Prayer,* trans. Smith (London, 1928). Wynne, "Prayer," *CE.*

predestinarianism. A doctrine derived from a misunderstanding of some expressions of St. Augustine concerning the gratuity of grace and the weakness of our free will as a consequence of original sin (*q.v.*). The first predestinarian was the French priest Lucidus (fifth century), who, fighting the Semi-Pelagians (*q.v.*), fell into rigorism as regards the doctrine of predestination. His error was repeated in the ninth century by the monk Gottschalk, and later by Wicliffe and Huss.

Luther, Calvin, and Jansenius (see *Calvinism; Jansenism*) accentuated the pessimistic tone of this heresy, which may be summarized as follows: (*a*) through original sin, man has lost his liberty, becoming a slave of concupiscence; (*b*) God does not will the salvation of all men, but only of some who are gratuitously predestined to glory and are not, therefore, obliged to co-operate with grace; (*c*) the actions of the predestined are necessarily good, while the actions of those who are not predestined are necessarily infected with sin; (*d*) the divine decree, which determines the eternal fate of men, precedes all consideration of merits or demerits, because God creates some men for heaven and others for hell (Calvin, *Inst. relig. christ.*, 1, 3, 21); (*e*) Christ did not die in behalf of all men (Jansenius). The Church has condemned such errors on several occasions (cf. *DB,* 316, 320 ff., 816, 827).

BIBLIOGRAPHY

Amann, "Prédestinatianisme," *DTC.* Lavaud, "Prédestination (IV. La controverse au IX siècle)," *DTC.* Pohle, "Predestinarianism," *CE.*

See under *predestination.*

predestination. The general meaning is to prearrange in view of an end. In a theological sense, predestination is the order or plan conceived by God to bring the rational creature to its supernatural end, which is life eternal (St. Thomas).

1. *Holy Scripture:* St. Paul speaks of it most insistently (Rom. 8; Eph. 1), employing the term *προορίζω* to indicate a plan of God, which envisages as a whole the Christian salvation of mankind (cf. Lagrange, *Comm. on the Epistle to the Romans*), to be effected through grace and the heavenly gifts, human co-operation, however, not being excluded.

2. *Tradition* culminates in St. Augustine, who, against the Pelagians, developed amply the thought of St. Paul, conceiving the idea of a category of men, whom God, according to His will and choice, helps in such a way as to assure their salvation. To other men God grants some help, but not as efficacious as to the predestined; in fact, these are not saved. The intimate nature of predestination is a mystery, but none can accuse God of injustice, since original sin has made humanity a "mass of damnation," and God, out of His sheer goodness, selects in it a group of souls predestined infallibly to eternal life. Moreover, no one is damned without his own guilt (cf. *De praedestinatione sanctorum; De gratia et libero arbitrio*).

3. *The Church* has defined gratuitousness of predestination to grace and glory, but has condemned the predestinationism of Gottschalk, Huss, Wicliffe, Luther, and Calvin, who put those predestined to paradise and those predestined to hell on the same footing, independently of merit or demerit.

4. *The theologians:* St. Thomas adopts substantially the teaching of St. Augustine, but smoothens some of its rough angles and tempers the question, taking into account all its elements.

In the sixteenth century a violent controversy concerning the divine concourse and knowledge flared up between Dominicans (*Bannesians*) and Jesuits (*Molinists*), which was brought before the pope, but without definitive results (*Congregatio de Auxiliis*). Naturally the question invested, later on, the problem of predestination, especially on the following point: in predestining to eternal life does God, in His mind, take account of the meritorious co-operation of man? The Bannesians say "No" (*predestination ante praevisa merita*); some Molinists say "Yes" (*predestination post praevisa merita*), whereas still other Molinists (the Suarezians), stand rather for the "no" of the followers of Bañez. This point, however, is not the only one contested. In any system the mystery remains and perhaps consists in the complex multiplicity of the elements (grace, divine knowledge, free will, etc.). Christian doctrine, however, insists on two things: (*a*) to be saved we must co-operate with grace; (*b*) no one is damned unless it be through his own fault (cf. II C. of Orange, C. of Kiersy, C. of Trent: *DB,* 198 ff., 316 ff., 826–827, 850).

BIBLIOGRAPHY

St. Thomas, *Summa Theol.,* I, q. 23. D'Alès, "Prédestination," *DA.* Friethoff, *Die Predestinationslehre bei Thomas von Aq. und Calvin* (Freiburg, Helv., 1926). Garrigou-Lagrange, *Predestination,* trans. Rose (St. Louis); *The One God,* trans. Rose (St. Louis, 1943), pp. 653–717. Lemonnyer, Simonin, Garrigou-Lagrange, Lavaud, "Prédestination," *DTC.* Peter Parente, *De Deo Uno* (Rome, 1938), pp. 291–329. Pohle, "Predestination," *CE.* Pohle-Preuss, *Dogmatic Theology,* VII *Grace* (*Actual and Habitual*) (St. Louis, 1946), pp. 187–221. Scheeben, *The Mysteries of Christianity,* trans. Vollert (St. Louis, 1946), pp. 697–730.

predetermination. See *concourse, divine; grace, efficacious; Bannesianism.*

premotion, divine. See *concourse, divine.*

presbyter (Gr. πρεσβύτερος — ancient). After the institution of the deacons (*q.v.*), the Acts of the Apostles mention on repeated occasions the "presbyters" who, in the Church of Jerusalem, are invested with administrative functions and with a spiritual ministry. In the Council of Jerusalem they appear as making the decisions together with the Apostles (Acts 11:30; 15:2, 4, 6, 22, 23; 20:28). St. James (5:4) says they anoint the sick (see *extreme unction*). Paul institutes presbyters in all the churches with powers and duties of pastors and teachers (Acts 14:23; 20:28–31) so that they may be the continuers of his apostolic mission. In some texts (Acts 20:28 with 20:17; cf. 1 Pet. 5:1–5) the equivalence between "presbyters" and "bishops" is clearly stated (see *bishops*), whose designation is made by Paul's delegates, Titus and Timothy, who transmit the necessary powers by the laying on of hands (1 Tim. 4:14; 2 Tim. 1:6).

Probably the presbyters were simple priests who, in the churches founded by St. Paul, had care of God's flock under the high authority of the Apostle and Founder, who was the only bishop. At Paul's side, his delegates, Titus and Timothy, have episcopal powers (ordination of deacons and presbyters).

From the beginning of the second century, the name "presbyters" is reserved — with some few exceptions — to ecclesiastical persons, inferior to bishops. Even today presbyters are commonly called priests.

BIBLIOGRAPHY

AUFFROY, "Sacerdoce catholique," *DA*. BOUDINHON, "Priest," *CE*. MANNING, *The Eternal Priesthood* (London, 1883). MICHEL, "Prêtre," *DTC;* "Prêtresse," *DTC*. MOBERLEY, *Ministerial Priesthood* (London, 1897). POHLE, "Priesthood," *CE*. POHLE-PREUSS, *Dogmatic Theology,* XI *The Sacraments,* Vol. 4, *Extreme Unction, Holy Orders, Matrimony* (St. Louis, 1946), pp. 94–98. RUFFINI, *La gerarchia della Chiesa negli Atti degli Apostoli e nelle lettere di S. Paolo* (Rome, 1921), pp. 67–90. SANDAY, *Conception of Priesthood* (London, 1898). *The Teaching of the Catholic Church,* ed. Smith, 2 vols. (New York, 1949), pp. 1022–1061.

See under *hierarchy; orders, holy; priesthood of Christ.*

prescience (foreknowledge). The knowledge of future things attributed to God. *Future* is that which is contained virtually in its own cause with a relationship or tendency to be realized by it. This relationship to real existence is not found in the concept of "possible." The "future" is: (*a*) *necessary,* if it depends on a cause determined by fixed natural law, e.g., an eclipse; (*b*) *contingent,* if it depends on a cause not determined necessarily, as is the free, future act, proper to the human will; (*c*) *absolute* or *conditioned,* according as it is independent or dependent on a condition. If the condition is such that it will never happen — though possibly it could — the future is called *hypothetical* or *futurible;* e.g., if Christ returned to earth to preach again before the judgment, the whole world would be converted.

A famous controversy flared up in the sixteenth century between the Dominicans and the Jesuits on the divine foreknowledge. We must distinguish the *fact* from the *manner.* (1) First of all, it is a definite theological principle that the creatures are not the cause of God's knowledge, but rather the divine knowledge is the cause of the creatures — taken, however, in co-operation with the divine will. (2) It is an article of faith that God knows all things, including any kind of future events whatever (Vatican Council, sess. 3). St. Augustine, in *De Civitate Dei,* 5, 9, affirms: "Who does not know in anticipation all future things surely is not God." (3) The mode or manner according to which God knows the future is mysterious and draws its particular difficulty from the general difficulty of the relationship between the Infinite and finite, eternity and time.

The greatest difficulty lies in conciliating divine prescience with human free will. Thomism (see *Bannesianism*) starts from God and defends His dominion even over human acts, which He foresees inasmuch as He determines them with His omnipotent will, physically moving the human will to do what He wills. Thus, the mystery vanishes as far as God is concerned, but it grows on the human side (see *concourse, divine*). Molinism (*q.v.*) starts with man and defends free will in regard to the influence of grace and divine prescience, adopting the so-called *middle knowledge* (*scientia media*) in which God would know, before His will comes into play, what a man would do in this or that creatable order of things. The mystery vanishes in man, but grows in God.

The Church permits discussion in the matter. Perhaps the truth is partially on both sides. The mystery lies in the complexity of the elements in play: free act, which involves intellect and will, divine knowledge (exemplary cause), divine will (efficient cause), presentiality (see *eternity*).

BIBLIOGRAPHY

St. Thomas, *Summa Theol.,* I, q. 14, a. 13. D'Alès, *Providence et libre arbitre* (Paris, 1927). Garrigou-Lagrange, *God: His Existence and His Nature,* trans. Rose (St. Louis, 1947–1948); *Providence,* trans. Rose (St. Louis, 1947).

presence of God. It may be considered with reference to *place* or to *time*. In regard to place, God is present contemporaneously everywhere because of His infinity and immensity (see *infinity*). But, as St. Thomas remarks (*Summa C. Gent.,* IV, 68), God is everywhere not in the way a body extends itself into the space, i.e., having one part here and one part there, but by reason of His simplicity He is in the entire universe and entirely in each part of it. The base or reason of this omnipresence is His action: God is present in every creature inasmuch as He acts (conserving its being, moving it in its operation). And since the action and the essence of God are identical, where He acts, there He is, wholly and essentially. With reference to time, God is actually present to all its moments (past, present, future) because He is eternal (see *eternity*), and as such He transcends and dominates all time. This is His natural omnipresence, expressed by the Scholastics in three formulas: *per potentiam,* in so far as He operates in all things; *per praesentiam,* in so far as He is eternal and sees all things, according to the words of Holy Scripture *omnia nuda et aperta sunt oculis eius* (Heb. 4:13); *per essentiam,* because in Him action and essence are identical.

In addition to this presence which is called *subjective,* God is present *objectively* in every intellect which knows Him and in every will which loves Him. Finally, God makes Himself present in a special way in the human soul sanctified by grace (*supernatural* presence), which becomes, therefore, the temple of God (St. Paul). But even here the basic reason of His presence is a divine action in the creature. It is, however, undeniable that God makes Himself present in the sanctified soul also as the object of supernatural faith and love, pending and in preparation for the beatific vision, of which the life of grace is a prelude (see *mission, divine; indwelling of the Holy Trinity*).

BIBLIOGRAPHY

St. Thomas, *Summa Theol.,* I, q. 8; q. 43, a. 3 and 6. Devine, "Presence of God," *CE.* Garrigou-Lagrange, *The One God,* trans.

Rose (St. Louis, 1943), pp. 253–267. SERTILLANGES, *St. Thomas d'Aquin* (Paris, 1925), Vol. 1, p. 195 ff. TYRRELL, *Hard Sayings* (London, 1898).

See under *indwelling of the Holy Trinity.*

Presence, Real, Eucharistic (fact). A dogma of Catholic faith that under the species of bread and wine, once consecration has been performed, the body, blood, soul, and divinity of our Lord Jesus Christ are really present. This truth, being above the powers of reason and foreign to experience, can be admitted only on the basis of divine revelation.

God has revealed this mystery to us in three facts narrated in the New Testament which are forged together like the rings in a chain: the promise, the institution, and the celebration of the Eucharist in the nascent Church. The *promise* is related by St. John. Jesus, climaxes, as it were, the three miracles He had just wrought (the multiplication of the loaves, the walking on the waves, and the preternatural landing of the boat), by elevating the thoughts of His audience to a spiritual bread, which is identical with His own flesh, not subject to nature's law, and which, when eaten, has the effect of bringing souls to the portals of eternal life. The most salient words are: "Amen, amen, I say unto you: except you eat the flesh of the Son of man, and drink his blood, you shall not have life in you. He that eateth my flesh, and drinketh my blood, hath everlasting life: and I will raise him up in the last day. For my flesh is meat indeed: and my blood is drink indeed" (6:54–56). Jesus spoke so clearly that the disciples declared they could not accept the content of His words, whereas St. Peter, as spokesman for the Apostles and expressing, in its germ as it were, the faith of the whole Church, cried out: "We have believed and have known that thou art the Christ, the Son of God" (John 6:70).

Engraved upon the souls of the Twelve, the words of the promise are the natural background against which the scene of the Last Supper (the institution) is set. When Christ took the bread and said: "This is my Body," and, holding the chalice of wine in His hands, added, "This is my Blood" (Matt. 26:26–28; Mark 14:22–23; Luke 22:19–20; 1 Cor. 11:24–25), the Apostles in the actions and words of their Master immediately recognized the fulfillment of the promise made at Capharnaum. Obedient to His command "Do this for a commemoration of me," the Apostles immediately after Pentecost began the celebration of the Eucharist at Jerusalem (Acts 2:42), at Troas (Acts 20:7–11), at Corinth; it was precisely in this last city that those disorders came about which provoked St. Paul's letter, in which the faith of the nascent Church is, as it were, photographed in the act of its normal exercise (cf. 1 Cor. 10:14–21; 11:17–34).

Tradition walks firmly in the path traced by the Apostolic faith: the first Christian generations adhered to the Real Presence as to the fundamental cell of dogma and piety. The Doctors of the fourth and fifth centuries made it the subject of their catecheses, homilies, and discussions, and used it as a foundation and sure premise in settling Trinitarian, Christological, and ecclesiological controversies, which were then stirring in the bosom of Christianity. From the sixth to the tenth centuries the Church transmitted to the new peoples regenerated unto Christ the torch of eucharistic faith, which was taken up with such sincere enthusiasm that when, in the eleventh century, Berengarius († 1088) impugned, for the first time in history, the Real Presence, the faithful rose in a body up against the heretic and constrained him to abjure his error. But while

Berengarius' denial provoked a strengthening in Eucharistic faith and increased the gravitational pull of medieval civilization around the central mystery of the Eucharist, the heresy of the Protestant sacramentarians (Zwingli, Carlstadt, Oecolampadius), who reduced the Eucharist to an empty symbol of the body of Christ, and the heresy of Calvin and the Anglicans, imagining the sacrament of the altar as a bread permeated with a mysterious force emanating from the body of Jesus present in heaven only, turned many from the profession of this dogma. Against these errors the Council of Trent (sess. 13) defined that in the Eucharist "is contained truly, really, and substantially the body, the blood, the soul, and the divinity of our Lord Jesus Christ," and condemned those who asserted Him "as present in sign or figure or only virtually" (*DB,* 883).

As regards the *way, mode,* and *condition* of the Real Presence, see *transubstantiation; presence, real, eucharistic (mode); eucharistic accidents.*

BIBLIOGRAPHY

St. Thomas, *Summa Theol.,* III, q. 65, a. 1. Batiffol, *Etudes d'histoire et de théologie positive (Eucharistie)* (Paris, 1903). Connell, *De sacramentis* (Brugis, 1933), pp. 176–192. Doronzo, *De Eucharistia,* Vol. 1 (Milwaukee, 1948), pp. 173–224. Goossens, *Les origines de l'Eucharistie* (Gembloux, 1931). Lebreton, "Eucharistie," *DA.* Piolanti, *De sacramentis,* Vol. 2 (Rome, 1945). Pohle, "Eucharist," *CE.* Pohle-Preuss, *Dogmatic Theology,* IX *The Sacraments,* Vol. 2, *The Holy Eucharist* (St. Louis, 1946), pp. 10–87. Rauschen, *Eucharist and Penance,* trans. from the second German edition (St. Louis, 1913). Ruch, Bareille, Bour, Vernet, De Ghellinck, Mangenot, Godefroy, "Eucharistie," *DTC. The Teaching of the Catholic Church,* ed. Smith, 2 vols. (New York, 1949), pp. 863–872. Wiseman, *Lectures on the Real Presence* (London, 1842).

presence, real, eucharistic (mode). The mode or manner of the eucharistic presence of the body of Christ, considered in itself (*absolute* mode) and in its relationship to the sensible species (*relative* mode), is essentially bound up with transubstantiation. This action, since it is effected between two substances to the absolute exclusion of the accidents which remain unvaried, has, as its proper term and objective, the substance of the body and blood of Christ; therefore, *directly,* i.e., by virtue and force of the words of consecration (*vi verborum*), only the substance of the body of Christ is present under the species of bread, and only the substance of His blood, under the species of wine. But since in Christ, after His resurrection, body, blood, soul, and divinity are inseparably united by virtue and force of natural concomitance or co-existence (*vi naturalis concomitantiae*), the whole of Christ is present under each species, as the Council of Trent defines (*DB,* 885), with all its *quantity* as befits a body that enjoys the fullness of sensitive life. But, since directly and *per se,* only the substance of the body and of the blood is present, quantity, which is present by consequence and *per accidens,* is bound to exist and to be present after the manner of substance (*per modum substantiae*). If, in fact, quantity were present in its proper and natural way, it would exert the pressure of its weight, extending beyond the dimensions of the host, etc., all of which is contradicted by experience, which thus confirms the conclusion logically derived from the dogma of transubstantiation.

Although this mode of presence is mysterious, the human intellect cannot demonstrate it to be contradictory or repugnant, since it is entirely ignorant of the intimate nature of the two extremes on which this marvel hangs: the divine omnipotence, which is inexhaustible, and the nature of corporeal substance, which baffles the acumen of the philosopher and escapes the eye of the scientist, as is clearly evidenced by the multiple conjectures formulated on the essence of bodies. Moreover, the human mind can be helped to glimpse the possibility of this mystery. The Gospel tells us that Christ's glorious body appeared wrenched loose, as it were, from gravity and impenetrability, when He walked on the waves and penetrated into the cenacle through closed doors. Again, since Christ's body with its quantity is present in the Eucharist after the manner of substance (which, like the soul is in the entire body and entirely in each single part of it), it follows that Christ's body is present, whole and entire, in the whole host and in all its individual parts, both before and after the breaking or fraction of the host (as the Council of Trent defines, *DB,* 885). However, we cannot say that before the fraction it is present infinite times, because number depends on quantitative division and, so long as quantity remains undivided, the substance of a thing is present one time only, under its dimensions.

The substance of Christ's body, too, is present in a special *manner,* which excludes all modes of presence that may be found in nature. It is not present through *quantitative contact,* because, although it has all its dimensions, it is not referred to the species of bread through them; nor is it present through *informative or virtual contact,* as the soul in its body or, respectively, an angel in a place, since Christ's body does not act on the species as a formal or efficient cause; nor is it present by *ubiquity,* such as is proper to God, because the intrinsic power of the Lord's body is limited and, therefore, cannot embrace all beings containing them in its power. But it is present *by the simple and mysterious relationship of contained to container,* the species acquiring the relationship of container with respect to the body of Christ by virtue of *transubstantiation,* and hence as this relationship is multiplied, the presence is multiplied. This mode of presence, mysterious and glorious at once and reserved to the body of Christ, is given a technical term sanctioned in the Council of Trent (*DB,* 874): "sacramental."

BIBLIOGRAPHY

St. Thomas, *Summa Theol.,* III, q. 66. Billot, *De sacramentis,* Vol. 1 (Rome), pp. 457–508. Connell, *De sacramentis* (Brugis, 1933), pp. 211–227. Doronzo, *De Eucharistia,* Vol. 1 (Milwaukee, 1948), pp. 384–447. Piolanti, *De sacramentis,* Vol. 2 (Rome, 1945). Pohle-Preuss, *Dogmatic Theology,* IX *The Sacraments,* Vol. 2, *The Holy Eucharist* (St. Louis, 1946), pp. 88–101, 129–135, 158–184. Van Hove, *De SS. Eucharistia* (Mechliniae, 1941), pp. 47–68. Vonier, *A Key to the Doctrine of the Eucharist* (Westminster, 1946), pp. 206–222.

preternatural. That which surpasses nature, its laws and its active and passive potency or capacity. According to the Catholic doctrine, we distinguish between a natural and a *supernatural* order (*q.v.*). The supernatural has various grades: the *absolute supernatural,* which transcends all created nature, and is, in the line of substance, God Himself; in the line of accidents, e.g., grace (*q.v.*); the *relative supernatural,* which transcends only one sector of created nature, as, e.g., infused knowledge which transcends human nature but is natural in the angels; and finally, the *preternatural,* which, although surpassing the natural conditions of a being, is only an extraordinary perfectioning of it, as, e.g., immortality of the body, which does not transcend absolutely human nature since it is but the extraordinary prolongation of the life already existing in the body.

In the state of original innocence (*q.v.*) sanctifying grace and the infused virtues (*supernatural gifts*) must be distinguished from an aggregate of *preternatural* gifts, which constitute the *integrity* (*q.v.*) of human nature (bodily immortality, infused knowledge, and immunity from concupiscence).

A miracle (*q.v.*) belongs to the supernatural world when the happening is miraculous in its *substance,* and to the preternatural world when it is miraculous only in the *mode* or *manner* in which it is performed.

Finally, *preternatural* is customarily termed that which cannot be explained by the commonly known laws of nature, e.g., certain hypothetically diabolic phenomena, among them, according to some authors, spiritistic phenomena (see *spiritism*).

BIBLIOGRAPHY

Bainvel, *Nature et Surnaturel* (Paris, 1920). Peter Parente, *De creatione universali* (Rome, 1943), p. 173 f. Verriele, *Le surnaturel en nous et le péché originel* (Paris, 1932).

priest. See *presbyter*.

priesthood of Christ. The Latin word for priest is *sacerdos* (*sacra dans* — giving holy things) and his state or office is called *sacerdotium*. The priest or *sacerdos* in the proper sense of the word is a mediator, divinely constituted, who offers to God a true sacrifice in recognition of His supreme dominion and in expiation of human guilt, thus procuring for men the appeasement and friendship of God. "Priest" and "sacrifice" are correlative and are found in every religion.

It is a truth of faith that Jesus Christ is a perfect Priest (Council of Ephesus and Council of Trent, sess. 23, *DB,* 122). Revelation is clear: "The Lord hath sworn, and he will not repent: Thou art a priest for ever according to the order of Melchisedech" (Ps. 109:4). St. Paul in his commentary on this text (Epistle to the Hebrews) develops amply the doctrine of the priesthood of Christ, showing its excellence in comparison with the priesthood of the Old Testament, which is surpassed and abrogated. Christ is the holy and immaculate Pontiff who, by offering the sacrifice of Himself on the cross one time only, has wrought for all time the redemption of humanity from sin.

Theological reason also proves that Christ is truly a Priest, because He is a perfect Mediator (see *mediation*) and has offered a real *sacrifice* (*q.v.*). The theologians discuss the formal constitutive reason of Christ's priesthood. The most probable opinion is that Christ is Priest because of the hypostatic union, which makes Him a true Mediator. We may consider, as integrative elements of the same priesthood, sanctifying grace, which is in Christ as individual Man and as Head of the Mystical Body of the Church, as well as the designation or vocation of Christ by the Father (Heb. 5). The Catholic priesthood is a participation of the priesthood of Christ, the one true Priest, living and operating in each of His ministers.

BIBLIOGRAPHY

St. Thomas, *Summa Theol.,* III, q. 22. Grimal, *The Priesthood and Sacrifice of Our Lord Jesus Christ,* trans. Keyes (Philadelphia, 1915). Pius XI, Encyclical *Ad Catholici Sacerdotii* (1935). Pohle-Preuss, *Dogmatic Theology,* V *Soteriology* (St. Louis, 1945), pp. 127–139. *The Teaching of the Catholic Church,* ed. Smith, 2 vols. (New York, 1949), pp. 477–489. Thouvenin, "Jésus Christ," *DTC,* cols. 1335–1342. Vosté, *Studia Paulina* (Rome, 1928), Ch. 6.
See under *presbyter*.

priesthood, participated. See *orders, holy*.

primacy of St. Peter. The power of jurisdiction (see *hierarchy*) — not of simple directive authority or of excellence or of honor — conferred by Jesus Christ on the Prince of the Apostles, by force of which he became supreme head and ruler of the whole Church.

The Vatican Council, defining this

point of doctrine (*DB*, 1832), merely interpreted authentically the words of Christ, whose historicity is admitted even by the rationalists.

The primacy of Peter, indeed, is *insinuated* in the changing of his name, *promised* in the colloquy at Cesarea of Philippi, *conferred* after the resurrection on the banks of the Lake of Tiberias, and *exercised* in the nascent Church.

Jesus imposed on Simon the name *Peter* (Matt. 10:2; Mark 3:16; Luke 6:14; John 1:42). According to biblical customs, change of name had great significance: when God wished to establish the patriarchate, He chose Abram to be head and center of that institution and changed his name to *Abraham;* when He instituted the Synagogue He chose as its head another great patriarch, Jacob, and changed his name to Israel. The mysterious meaning of the new name was revealed by the Master in the memorable scene that took place at the foot of Mt. Hermon: "Jesus saith to them [Apostles]: But who do you say that I am? Simon Peter answered and said: Thou are Christ, the Son of the living God. And Jesus answering said to him: Blessed art thou, Simon Bar-Jona: because flesh and blood hath not revealed it to thee, but my Father who is in heaven. And I say to thee: That thou are Peter, and upon this rock I will build my church, and the gates of hell shall not prevail against it. And I will give to thee the keys of the kingdom of heaven. And whatsoever thou shalt bind upon earth, it shall be bound also in heaven: and whatsoever thou shalt loose on earth, it shall be loosed also in heaven" (Matt. 16:15–19).

In these words the Saviour spoke to Peter in terms of the future: it is the promise! The conferring of that power comes after the resurrection near the Lake of Tiberias; Jesus now speaks in the present: "Simon, son of John, lovest thou me more than these? He saith to him: Yea, Lord, thou knowest that I love thee. He saith to him: Feed my lambs. He saith to him again: Simon, son of John, lovest thou me? He saith to him: Yea, Lord, thou knowest that I love thee. He saith to him: Feed my lambs. He said to him the third time: Simon, son of John, lovest thou me? Peter was grieved, because he had said to him the third time: Lovest thou me? And he said to him: Lord, thou knowest all things: thou knowest that I love thee. He said to him: Feed my sheep" (John 21:15–17).

Representing His Church with the image of an edifice, of a kingdom, of a flock, Jesus makes Peter the foundation, the key bearer, the shepherd. "In the first comparison, that of the building, stability of doctrine is more particularly brought out, in the second the power of governing is more stressed, and in the third especially envisaged is pastoral care and affection; but in each comparison the primacy of St. Peter is abundantly and perfectly portrayed" (Card. Capecelatro). The history of the infant Church shows the son of Jona had full consciousness of being "pastor" (shepherd) not only of the lambs but also of the sheep — of all Christ's flock; in fact, immediately after the Ascension, Peter acted as the supreme head of the Church. It was Peter who proposed in the Cenacle that a substitute be named to take the place of Judas Iscariot in the Apostolic College; it was Peter who was the first to preach on Pentecost; it was Peter who received the first pagans into the bosom of the Church at Cornelius' home, although Paul is par excellence the missionary of the Gentiles; it was Peter who questioned and reproved the couple guilty of lying; it was Peter who, like a president, was the first to speak at the Council of Jerusalem.

BIBLIOGRAPHY

St. Thomas, *Summa Contra Gentiles,* l. 4, c. 76. Florit, *Il primato di S. Pietro negli Atti degli Apostoli* (Rome, 1942). Glez, "Primauté du Pape," *DTC.* Ruffini, *La Gerarchia della Chiesa negli Atti degli Apostoli* (Rome, 1921).

See under *Church; pope; Roman pontiff.*

Priscillianism. An assortment of errors attributed to Priscillian (fourth century). Sulpicius Severus, in his *Historia Sacra* (beginning of the fifth century), speaks of the life and the errors of this man of Spanish descent, of his quick genius, austere habits, and strong inclination to asceticism. Priscillian soon became the head of a religious sect in which women were the predominant element. Bishop Idacius of Emerita condemned the errors of Priscillian in the Synod of Saragoza (380). Priscillian, however, was not discouraged. On the contrary, he had himself ordained a priest and later consecrated Bishop of Ávila. Finding Spain too hostile, he and his fellow bishops attempted to seek refuge in Rome under Pope Damasus, but the Pope refused to receive them, and so did St. Ambrose in Milan. Finally he was accused before Emperor Maximus at Treves and condemned to death. His followers, however, continued to spread their errors with fanatic zeal, until the Council of Braga (563) formulated 17 anathematisms against Priscillianism.

The Priscillians, according to these anathematisms, taught the following errors: (*a*) *Sabellianism* (*q.v.*) by denying the real distinction of the three divine Persons. (*b*) *Arianism* (*q.v.*) by denying the existence of Christ before His birth by Mary. (*c*) *Docetism* (*q.v.*) because they attributed to Jesus an apparent body. (*d*) *Pantheism* by asserting that the angels and souls are emanations of the divine substance. (*e*) The demon, derived from dark chaos, is essentially bad. (*f*) Matrimony and bearing of offspring are diabolical works. (*g*) Corruption of the holy text of Sacred Scripture.

Modern critics, after accurate study, hesitate to attribute all the above-named errors to Priscillian. Up to what point he taught or paved the way to so many errors, in part already condemned by the Church, cannot as yet be determined. It is certain, however, from the fragments of his works, that Priscillian had a predilection for the Apocrypha (*q.v.*) and used ambiguous expressions about the Trinity; at times he leans to Gnosticism or Manichaeism, at least in his expression. It may be that his disciples misunderstood and exaggerated his doctrine.

BIBLIOGRAPHY

Babut, *Priscillien et le Priscillianisme* (Paris, 1909). Bardy, "Priscillien," *DTC.* Healy, "Priscillianism," *CE.* Schepps, *Priscilliani quae supersunt* (Vienna, 1889). Tixeront, *History of Dogmas,* trans. H.L.B., Vol. 2 (St. Louis, 1914), pp. 229–241.

privilege. See *law.*

procession, divine. Materially, *procession* means motion from one point to another; such motion is repugnant to the divine nature. Only immanent processions are attributed to God, i.e., the mere origin of one term from another. There are, in fact, in God two immanent operations proper to spirit: intellection and volition. Although these operations are identified with the divine nature, by analogy with what happens in us we are not able to conceive them except as relations between two terms (*operating — operated*). But reason would never have succeeded in forming any idea of the divine processions, unless revelation had explicitly manifested them: "For from God I proceeded. . . . The Spirit . . . who proceedeth from the Father" (John 8:42; 15:26).

The Church has defined as a truth of faith that the Son proceeds from the Father (*Deum de Deo*) and the Holy Spirit from the Father and the Son (*Qui ex Patre Filioque procedit*).

First Procession: The eternal generation of the Son from the Father. Holy Scripture calls the term which proceeds Son, Only-Begotten, Firstborn; but calls Him also Word (Λόγος; *q.v.*). From this we conclude that the Son proceeds by way of intellection and, therefore, of spiritual generation. In fact, our intellection consists in conceiving and, as it were, generating an idea, which is the spiritual reproduction of the thing known.

Second Procession: Actuated by way of volition and, therefore, of love. God, knowing Himself in the Word, contemplates and loves Himself by an adhesion of Self to Self. The doctrine of faith teaches that only the first procession is generation which gives origin to but one Son (Only-Begotten). The Holy Spirit is not a Son, but simply the term of love-procession, and He proceeds from the Father and the Son as from one, sole principle (Council of Florence, *DB,* 691).

The Schismatic Greeks do not admit the origin and derivation of the Holy Spirit from the Son (see *"Filioque"*).

BIBLIOGRAPHY

St. Thomas, *Summa Theol.,* I, q. 27. Hugon, *Le mystère de la très Sainte Trinité* (Paris, 1930). Joyce, "Trinity," *CE.* Michel, "Processions divines," *DTC.* Peter Parente, *De Deo Trino* (Rome, 1938), p. 101 ff.; "Il mistero della SS. Trinità," *Il Simbolo,* Vol. 1 (Assisi, 1941). *The Teaching of the Catholic Church,* ed. Smith, 2 vols. (New York, 1949), pp. 123–133.

Propaganda Fide (**Congregation of**). See *Holy See.*

propassions. The name for the sensitive passions of Christ's humanity: love, desire, hope, fear, sadness, etc. Of themselves these passions are an integral part of human nature, as functions proper to *concupiscible* and *irascible* appetite. When subject to reason, they are lively forces for good: but, as a result of original sin, the passions become rebellious to the point of beclouding reason and weakening free will. This rebellion, however, is not such as to eliminate free will and responsibility for one's own actions, as Luther pretends. The Church has defined (Council of Trent, sess. 5, *DB,* 792) that concupiscence comes from sin and excites to sin, but is not a sin *per se* (in itself) nor can it be harmful to one who resists with the grace of God.

As there was a real *passibility* in the body of Christ, so also there were true passions in His soul. Moreover, the Gospel itself attests their existence: "With desire I have desired to eat this pasch with you" (Luke 22:15); "My soul is sorrowful even unto death" (Matt. 26:38), etc. But the passions of Christ were devoid of all disorderliness and absolutely subject to reason, because in Him there was no original sin, even no possibility of sinning (see *impeccability*). This is the reason why theologians call the passions of Christ *propassions,* in so far as they are irreprehensible (St. John Damascene). St. Thomas explains: the passions of Christ differ from ours because they could not incite to evil or influence His reason or will in any way.

BIBLIOGRAPHY

St. Thomas, *Summa Theol.,* III, q. 15. Chollet, *La psychologie du Christ,* Vol. 2. Hugon, *Le mystère de l'Incarnation* (Paris, 1931), Ch. 4. Peter Parente, *De Verbo Incarnato* (Rome, 1939), p. 230 ff.

prophecy (Gr. προφάναι — speak for another, in the name of another). In general, it means "interpretation." In a narrower sense, it is the manifestation of things hidden from men, and is, more specifically, "the certain and determined prediction of a future event not knowable from natural causes."

Being a miracle of the intellectual order, prophecy, together with the true and proper miracle, is an external criterion for the knowledge and recognition of revelation.

BIBLIOGRAPHY

ST. THOMAS, *Summa Theol.,* II–II, qq. 171–174; *Quaest. Disp. De Veritate,* q. 12. DEVINE, "Prophecy," *CE.* FENTON, *We Stand With Christ* (Milwaukee, 1942), pp. 357–403. MANGENOT, "Prophétie," *DTC.*

See under *prophet.*

prophet (Gr. προφήτης, derived from the verb προφάναι — speak in another's name). In Old Testament history the prophets appear as the supreme and authentic teachers sent by God, who speak in His name, are zealous for His honor, communicate to men His will with respect to the conservation, explanation, and realization of the Pact made with the people through Moses, and to the preparation of the New Pact, which Christ was to seal with His blood.

Called directly by God, without class distinction and without preparation, prophets are thrown into the tumult of social and political life to extend to all, both kings and subjects, their activity and authority.

God communicates with them by means of visions or, more rarely, of dreams. In the visions the object could be represented to the external senses or to the internal senses under the form of images or symbols, or God could impress directly on the prophet's intellect intelligible species and elevate it by supernatural light in order to render it capable of seeing into the mysteries of divine providence. It is certain that the prophets were conscious of the divine communications, but they did not necessarily understand all they saw or said, since their minds, being an *instrumentum deficiens* (deficient medium), could not attain an exhaustive knowledge of God's full intentions in His communications (St. Thomas, *Summa Theol.,* II–II, q. 173, a. 4).

Prevision of the future by the Old Testament prophets could be exercised either on facts contained within the limits of their time or on Messianic events, relative to the future salvation of Israel and of the world (see *Messias*). In this second case the prophecies are of highest value and interest and give the measure of the divine origin and eternal actuality of the Old Testament.

BIBLIOGRAPHY

CALÈS, "Prophecy, Prophet and Prophetess," *CE.* RICCIOTTI, *Storia d'Israele,* Vol. 1 (Turin, 1934), p. 381 ff. TOBAC, COPPENS, *Les prophètes d'Israel* (Malines, 1932). VAN DEN OUDENRIJN, *De prophetiae charismate in populo israelitico* (Rome, 1924).

Protestantism. A word originated in the second diet of Spires (1529) which defended the freedom of practice of the Catholic cult in the countries ravaged by Lutheranism, especially with respect to the celebration of the Mass. Five princes and fourteen cities, adhering to the Lutheran heresy, presented a *protest* (*Protestants*) against these claims.

Today Protestantism signifies all the religious sects, Churches, and doctrines stemming from the current of the so-called *Reformation* started by Luther, Zwingli, Calvin, and Henry VIII. The number of these sects is so vast (more than 300) that it is not easy to make a synthesis of them. Disintegration, begun right under Luther's eyes, is the fatal law proper to and characteristic of Protestantism. There are *three principal trunks,* from which new ramifications are constantly sprouting forth:

1. *Lutheranism.* Up to the end of the eighteenth century, it gave birth to various doctrinal evolutions more or less bound up with the principles of Luther; it experienced the radical transformations of Lessing († 1781), as well as of skeptical or pantheistic philosophies (Spinoza) and, more recently, of rationalistic criticism (Schleiermacher, Ritschl, Von Harnack). Gradually the *conservative* tendency opposed these innovations, especially in the ascetico-liturgical field.

2. *Calvinism* (Franco-Swiss Protestantism). Harassed since its beginning by the Socinian schism, it was revived in the past century as Unitarianism (*q.v.*), and then by the Arminian schism in the Netherlands. In France, great conflicts developed in the nineteenth century between the *conservative* current and the *liberal* current, which is becoming bolder and increasingly radical.

3. *English Protestantism.* This is the most prolific in sects (numbering more than 200): Presbyterians (divided into various sections), Congregationalists, Baptists, Quakers, Methodists (founded by John Wesley), Irvingians (by Ed. Irving, † 1834), Darbysts (by N. Darby, who expects an early return of Christ), etc. Anglicanism, the most predominant form of English Protestantism, is today divided into: (*a*) High Church, conservative right-wing party (closest to Catholicism); (*b*) Low Church, moderate left-wing party, democratic, basically truly Protestant and, therefore, anti-Roman; (*c*) Broad Church, radical, left-wing party, open to modernism and to all the new currents to a point of compromising the most basic truths of faith. Various efforts have been made to recapture that unity which, on the other hand, is the force and life of the Catholic Church.

See *Anglicanism; Adventists; Methodists; pietism; Puritanism; Quakers; quietism.*

BIBLIOGRAPHY

BAUDRILLART, *The Catholic Church, the Renaissance and Protestantism,* trans. Gibbs (London, 1908). BELLOC, *How the Reformation Happened* (London, 1928). CRISTIANI, TRÉSAL, GOYAU, DE GEUSER, D'ALÈS, JOURNET, ALBERS, BOUVIER, etc., "Réforme," *DA.* CRIVELLI, *I Protestanti in Italia, Isola del Liri* (1936–1939). DEDIEU, "Protestantisme," *DTC.* DÖLLINGER, *Die Reformation,* 3 vols. (Ratisbon, 1843–1851). MARITAIN, *The Three Reformers* (London, 1929). OTTEN, *A Manual of History of Dogmas,* Vol. 2 (St. Louis, 1925), pp. 438–447. SHAUGHNESSY, "Protestantism," *CE,* Supplement, I. WILHELM, "Protestantism," *CE.* WYNNE, "Réforme (XIV Le Protestantisme aux Etats Unis d'Amérique)," *DA,* cols. 782–792.

protocanonical. See *Canon of the Bible.*

protoevangelium. The first announcement of the Redemption, contained in Genesis 3:15, is designated by this term. After the sin of our first parents, God judged and condemned them and, having turned to the tempting serpent, said: "I will put enmities between thee and the woman, and thy seed and her seed: she shall crush thy head, and thou shalt lie in wait for her heel." "The woman" is not Eve personally, because she has already been defeated by Satan; it could be Eve inasmuch as she represents the whole feminine sex of which she is the first parent and unique exemplar. The "seed" signifies the descendants; but the prophecy of victory is fulfilled only in Christ (who, in so far as He is man, is of the descendants of Eve), because all other men are unable, except through the grace merited by Him, to triumph over the enemy. Consequently "the woman" — in Hebrew the definite article is used — is Mary, who, being the only creature conceived without original sin, is the only woman who can say that she never yielded in the struggle with the serpent. Since "the seed" of Satan indicates also the wicked ones dominated and instigated by him (John 8:41–44), we can see in the progeny of the woman the faithful partakers in Christ's victory. The "enmity" is concluded on Satan's part by an ineffective attack and on the part of Christ by a definitive triumph.

The Vulgate (*q.v.*) translation "she shall crush thy head" puts "the woman" in the foreground, whereas the original text of the prophecy stresses the victory of the "seed of the woman," i.e., of Christ. The older Latin versions had the masculine "he," and the author of the Vulgate, St. Jerome, knows that this is the exact translation, but out of deference for the traditional interpretation which saw the Blessed Virgin in "the woman," St. Jerome gave preference to the feminine "she." The biblical argument for the Immaculate Conception of the Blessed Virgin (*q.v.*) is not taken from the expression "she shall crush thy head," but from the implacable "enmity" between the woman and Satan.

BIBLIOGRAPHY

Ceuppens, *De Protoevangelio* (Rome, 1922). Scheeben, *Mariology,* trans. Geukers, Vol. 1 (St. Louis, 1946), pp. 241–244.

providence, divine (Lat. *providere* or *praevidere* — to see in advance). The plan conceived in the mind of God, according to which He directs all creatures to their proper end. It is a part of *prudence* and refers mainly to the means to be chosen with reference to the end; it resides in the *intellect,* but presupposes the willing of the end; it precedes the *government* of things, which is the practical execution of providence.

Against the materialists, fatalists, pessimists, and deists of the eighteenth century, the Church defends divine providence (Vatican Council, *DB,* 1784), which shines out in the pages of Holy Scripture (cf. Wisd. 14, Matt. 6), and in the writings of the Fathers (cf. *RJ,* Index, "Providentia").

Reasons: (*a*) There is in the world an order and a tendency to the end; but this order, like all cosmic reality, must pre-exist intentionally in the mind of the First Cause. (*b*) God is not only the Efficient Cause, but also the Final Cause of all things, and as such must have conceived the means of directing back to Himself, as to their supreme End, all created things.

No creature escapes this providential order, since providence is bound up with divine causality and, like it, is universal. Therefore, free will also is subordinate to divine providence (Matt. 6:30), which does not disturb the order of nature, but conserves and directs it, using necessary causes to produce necessary effects, and contingent causes, as human wills are, to obtain contingent and free effects. Physical and moral evil, which we see in the world, is not opposed to divine providence, if we consider: (1) that it is permitted, not caused directly by God; (2) that it depends on the deficiency of finite being; (3) that it is to be examined not in an isolated and particular way but in the framework of the universal order, which may demand the sacrifice of this or that particular being (see *evil*).

BIBLIOGRAPHY

St. Thomas, *Summa Theol.,* I, q. 22. D'Alès, "Providence," *DA.* Bruce, *The Moral Order of the World* (London, 1899); *The Providential Orders of the World* (London, 1897). Garrigou-Lagrange, *God,* trans. Rose (St. Louis, 1947–1948); *The One God,* trans. Rose (St. Louis, 1943), pp. 625–652; *Providence,* trans. Rose (St. Louis, 1947); "Providence," *DTC.* Maccosh, *The Method of Divine Government* (Edinburgh, 1850). Peter Parente, "Il male secondo la dottrina di S. Tommaso," *Acta Pont. Acad. Rom. S. Thomae Aq.* (1940). Pohle-Preuss, *Dogmatic Theology,* III *God, Author of Nature and the Supernatural* (St. Louis, 1945), pp. 79–85. Sertillanges, *St. Thomas d'Aquin,* Vol. 1 (Paris, 1925), p. 312 ff. *The Teaching of the Catholic Church,* ed. Smith, 2 vols. (New

York, 1949), pp. 214–247. WALKER, "Providence (Divine)," *CE.*

prudence. See *virtue.*

punishment. See *penalty.*

purgatory. Place and state in which the souls of the just who died in venial sin and with the debt of temporal punishment for grave sins remitted, are subjected to purifying sufferings until, having paid their debt, they are worthy of paradise. The existence of purgatory is a truth of faith defined by the Council of Trent (sess. 25, *DB,* 983).

Holy Scripture: "It is . . . a holy and wholesome thought to pray for the dead, that they may be loosed from sin" (2 Mach. 12:46). St. Paul (1 Cor. 3:11 ff.) speaks of those who, having some remnants of sin mixed with good works, will be saved in the next life *quasi per ignem* (through fire).

Tradition: In the first centuries there was no explicit doctrine on purgatory, but they had the liturgical usage of prayers for the dead, reflected also in the epigraphy of the Catacombs. From the time of St. Augustine the doctrine of purgatory was developed, which continues substantially unchanged in the East and the West. The Scholastics treat of purgatory as of something belonging to the doctrine of faith. Luther and Calvin were wrong, therefore, in rejecting purgatory as a diabolic invention.

The Church, while defending the existence of purgatory, has not defined explicitly what its pains are: incidental mention is made of fire in the I Council of Lyon, in a Letter of Clement VI (*DB,* 456 and 570 ff.). Certainly there is in purgatory a temporary pain of loss (*poena damni* — privation of the vision and possession of God), mitigated by the sure hope of entering paradise after due expiation. A pain of sense (*poena sensus*) commonly is admitted by the Fathers and theologians, fire not excluded. Purgatory will last only to the day of judgment.

BIBLIOGRAPHY

ST. THOMAS, *Summa Theol.,* III, *Suppl.* and Appendix. BERNARD, "Purgatoire," *DA.* BILLOT, *De novissimis* (Rome, 1921). CANTY, *Purgatory: Dogmatic and Scholastic* (Dublin, 1886). COLERIDGE, *The Prisoners of the King* (London, 1836). HANNA, "Purgatory," *CE.* JUGIE, *Le Purgatoire* (Paris, 1942). MICHEL, "Purgatoire," *DTC.* OXENHAM, *Catholic Eschatology* (London, 1878). POHLE-PREUSS, *Dogmatic Theology,* XII *Eschatology* (St. Louis, 1946), pp. 75–101. SADLIER, *Purgatory: Doctrinal, Historical, Practical* (New York, 1886). SUTCLIFFE, *The Old Testament and the Future Life* (Westminster, 1947), pp. 121–125. *The Teaching of the Catholic Church,* ed. Smith, 2 vols. (New York, 1949), pp. 1141–1175. VAUGHAN, *Thoughts for All Times* (Springfield, Mass., 1916), pp. 156–171. WISEMAN, *Lectures on the Principal Doctrines and Practices of the Catholic Church* (London, 1836).
See under *eschatology.*

Puritanism. Rather than a sect, it is a rigoristic tendency of Protestantism, similar to Jansenistic rigorism. *Puritanism* is rooted especially in Calvinism and is based on two fundamental principles: faithful and exclusive attachment to the Bible as the only rule of faith, and the consciousness of being in the number of the predestined. Hence a proud piety, joined with contempt of life's pleasures and sense satisfactions, which reminds us of the attitude and the style of the Pharisees. This tendency is generally encountered wherever Calvinism is dominant, but is developed especially in England from the start of Anglicanism down to our times. The term *puritan* appears for the first time in 1564, under Elizabeth, to indicate those Episcopalian Anglicans who wanted to purge the common book of prayers (*Prayer Book*) from its residues of Catholicism. The Queen, with the help of

Archbishop Whitgift, unleashed a fierce persecution against the Puritans, who sided with the democratic Presbyterians in opposition to the Episcopalians. James I stated two famous principles: the *divine right of kings,* and the *divine right of bishops.* The Puritans lined up against both, with the result of a civil war.

Politically, Puritanism favored parliamentarism, which prepared the way for modern democracy. On religious grounds, it accentuated the aversion to Roman papism, infiltrating the Low Church. Psychologically, it has made the individual a self-idolater, a presumptuous builder of his virtue and his fortune.

BIBLIOGRAPHY

BARCLAY, *Inner Life of the Religious Societies of the Commonwealth* (1876). BURTON, "Puritans," *CE.* BYINGTON, *The Puritan in England and New England* (London, 1896). CAMPBELL, *Puritanism in Holland, England and America* (London, 1892). CRISTIANI, "Puritanisme," *DTC.* NEAL, *History of the Puritans* (1732–1738). RUST, *The First of the Puritans and Their Books of Common Prayer* (Milwaukee, 1949). TRÉSAL, "Réforme (VI La Réforme en Angleterre)," *DA,* cols. 664–673.

Q

Quakers (Eng., to quake). A Protestant sect founded in England in the seventeenth century by George Fox, a poor shoemaker and visionary, who spent his life between imprisonments and persecutions. In one of the trials he stood, Fox threatened the judge, exhorting him to *quake* for the wrath of God; then the judge called him ironically the "Quaker": hence the name of the sect.

Quakerism carries the *religious individualism* of Protestantism to the extreme. Luther offered the Bible as source and rule of faith: Fox and his followers recognize no law of religious life except *internal divine illumination.* No teaching authority, no worship, no sacraments — but prayer and meditation to feel the divine in oneself, to taste and savor the light of Christ in the inmost soul. This *quietistic* teaching was overcome by the Quaker, Elizabeth Fry, heroine of evangelical charity toward the poor, the imprisoned, the outcasts of fortune. Today the Quakers number about 150,000, most of them in the United States. They are characterized by their aversion to war, which they consider the fruit of wickedness exclusively.

BIBLIOGRAPHY

CLARKSON, *Portraiture of Quakerism* (London, 1806). CRISTIANI, "Quakers," *DTC.* LOUGHLIN, "Friends, Society of (Quakers)," *CE.* JANNEY, *History of the Religious Society of Friends From the Rise to the Year 1828* (Philadelphia, 1837–1850).

quietism: A pseudohedonistic tendency developed within the Church which places spiritual perfection in prayer and contemplation, conceived passively as abandonment to God. The soul, in giving itself completely to God, renounces its free activity and the control of the flesh and passions to the point of conciliating the basest sensuality with mystical adhesion to God. This attitude of the spirit implies the scorn of *ascetics* understood as a laborious co-operation with grace for the conquest of perfection, and of all the other traditional means suggested by divine revelation and the experience of the saints.

Quietism spread in several countries under various forms. In Spain we find the sect of the *Alumbrados* (Enlightened) since the sixteenth century. In France, there was a double quietist current: the one moderate, restricted to the method of contemplative prayer and abandonment to God, described in the writings of Boudon, Surin, Epiphane, and especially of Fénelon (attacked by Bossuet); the other bolder and more compromising, headed by Madame Guyon, a fanatic who joined sensual mysticism to contemplative mysticism by the theory of the passivity of the soul in temptations and in sins of lust. In her shady venture, the Barnabite Fr. La Combe was involved, perhaps in good faith. Morbid quietism raged in Italy more than in any other place, chiefly through the work of Miguel Molinos, a famous pseudomystic (see *Molinosism*). To have an idea of moderate quietism it suffices to read the propositions extracted from a work of Fénelon (*Explication des maximes des Saints sur la vie intérieure*), condemned by Innocent XII in 1699 (*DB*, 1327–1349). But no one developed the quietistic theory to its extreme consequences as Molinos did in his famous *Spiritual Guide,* which contains the 68 propositions condemned by Innocent XI in 1687 (*DB,* 1221 ff.).

BIBLIOGRAPHY

Dudon, "Quiétisme au XVII siècle," *DA.* Huvelin, *Bossuet, Fénelon, le Quiétisme,* 2 vols. (Paris, 1912). Menendez y Pelayo, *Heterodoxos españoles* (classical work, recently republished by M. A. Bonilla, at Madrid). Pace, "Quietism," *CE.* Pascal Parente, *The Ascetical Life* (St. Louis, 1947), pp. 236–244. Pourrat, "Quiétisme," *DTC.* Vaughan, *Hours With the Mystics* (New York, 1893).

See under *Molinosism.*

R

rationalism. In general it is the tendency to appreciate the value of human reason, applying it preferentially for the solution of all life's problems, not excluding religion. In this sense, rationalism is intellectualism, and is opposed to voluntarism, mystical sentimentalism, agnosticism, skepticism, pragmatism, and all *irrational* or *extrarational* currents. This healthy and dignified rationalism does not conflict with faith; on the contrary, it is in perfect harmony with it. St. Thomas, together with the better-known Scholastics, is a luminous example of this kind of rationalism, in which faith and reason join their lights and help each other (*fides quaerens intellectum, intellectus quaerens fidem*), the principle being fully respected of the subordination of reason to faith, and of philosophy to theology.

But rationalism, in the strict sense, is a system that claims the supreme and absolute dominion of human reason in all fields, subjecting to its control every phenomenon and every truth, the supernatural world and God's authority not excluded. This system tends to *humanize* the divine, when it does not eliminate it entirely, and to *naturalize* the supernatural, when it does not reject it. Such tendency to overevaluate reason even in the field of faith reveals itself here and there since the first centuries of Christianity: e.g., in the latter part of the fourth century in the heresies of the Anomoeans, Nestorians, Pelagians (*qq.v.*), connected with the Antiochian School (naturalistic in tendency). But really heterodox rationalism began with Humanism, when the study of the classics awakened and accentuated in man a proud *individualism,* a fever for knowledge, for investigation, for scientific research, for autonomy in the theoretical and practical field, and an immoderate attachment of the mind to itself and to nature. Rationalism developed rapidly into a sinuous current of systems, from the naturalism of Telesio, Bruno, and Campanella, to the subjective construction of Cartesianism, to empiric scientism, to Luther's free interpretation of the Bible, then to Encyclopedism and eighteenth-century Illuminism, down to Kant, with his cult of autonomous and autochthonous reason, arbiter of theoretical and practical truth. With

Kant rationalism reached its critical systemization; in the eighteenth-century it resumed its development to the most antithetical consequences, such as absolute idealism and materialistic monism.

With regard to the religious problem, rationalism runs the gamut from a vague deism to pantheism and, finally, to atheism (*qq.v.*). The Catholic religion has withstood the attack of rationalism throughout the centuries, contending every inch of ground and barring its passage. The phases of this struggle are pointed out in the *Syllabus* of Pius IX and in the definitions of the Vatican Council (cf. *DB,* 1700 ff., and 1781 ff.).

BIBLIOGRAPHY

AVELING, "Rationalism," *CE*. BENN, *History of Rationalism in Nineteenth Century* (London, 1906). CONSTANTIN, "Rationalisme," *DTC*. FILLION, *Les étapes du Rationalisme* (Paris, 1911). HURST, *History of Rationalism* (New York, 1882). PETER PARENTE, "Il piú tragico divorzio," *L'Enciclica "Summi Pontificatus," Commento* (Rome, 1940).

Real Presence. See *Presence, Real, Eucharistic* (*fact* and *mode*).

Rebaptizers. See *Donatism*.

Redemption (Lat. *redimere* — buy back, redeem). In ancient literature redemption signified ransom, i.e., liberation of slaves or goods in bond through payment. In the religious field redemption is understood with reference to sin, which is an *offense* against God and a *moral slavery,* i.e., it has an *objective* and a *subjective* aspect; therefore, redemption involves at once a reparation or expiation or satisfaction (*objectively*) and a ransom or liberation or reintegration (*subjectively*). These two meanings are well expressed in the German *Erlösung* (ransom) and *Versöhnung* (expiation). The term "redemption" is enriched by Christian religion, which is essentially a message of salvation, a soteriology centered in Jesus, whose name, according to the Hebraic *etymon,* means precisely *Saviour.*

An outline showing approximately the rich content of the Catholic concept of Redemption could be expressed in the following terms: Man by sinning has offended God and made himself a slave of sin and of the devil who suggested it to him. Since man is incapable of repairing so great a destruction, the Word of God becomes incarnate, binding humanity to Himself (the *Mystical Body*), expiates and makes reparation to the offended God in the place of sinful man (*vicarious satisfaction*) by meriting for all reconciliation with God and liberation from slavery to Satan and sin. Lutheranism has exaggerated the *objective* aspect, reducing Redemption to a *penal substitution* of Christ in the place of man, who, on his own part, has to do nothing (*extrinsicism*). The Socinians, Liberal Protestants, and modernists on the other extreme, reduce Redemption to an *individual* work of man himself, to which Jesus Christ contributes by the moral influence of His example (*subjective moralism*). But Catholic doctrine, based on divine revelation, avoids excesses and harmoniously tempers the various elements and aspects in an organic system: Christ the Redeemer substitutes Himself for us in expiation, but we are in Him by the solidarity and dependence proper to the Mystical Body; He redeems us by His whole life on earth, and particularly by His death, which is an expiatory sacrifice, having physico-moral efficacy. But man, in order to actuate in himself the salvation wrought by Christ, must adhere freely to Him by faith and charity and by the use of the sacraments. These concepts are drawn from:

Isaias, Ch. 53 (the soteriological poem of the "Servant of Jahweh"); *Synoptics* (Matt. 20:28; 29:28; Mark 10:45; 14:24; Luke 19:10; 22:20); *John* (1:29; 10:15; Apoc. 5:8; 1 John 2:2); *Peter* (1 Pet. 1:18; 2:21); and especially from *St. Paul,* who stresses particularly the redemptive value of Christ's death (cf. Rom. 3:24; Eph. 1:7; 5:2; 1 Tim. 2:6; Gal. 3:13; Heb., *passim,* etc.). Even the rationalists recognize that all of St. Paul's teaching is a lively realistic and complex soteriology, animated by the concept of the Mystical Body, through which Christ's passion, death, and resurrection become our own, as Adam's sin became ours.

All the constitutive elements of the Redemption are found more or less developed in the Fathers, according to the various periods or schools. Some, the Westerners especially, stress Pauline *realism;* others (Easterns), Joannine *mysticism* (redemption: deification of man through the incarnate Word, Light-Life). At times they have recourse to vivid metaphors and allegories to illustrate more effectively this mystery to the people, as, e.g., Christ "disburses" His blood to Satan in order to free man from his tyranny; God fools the devil, who vents his ferocity on the innocent Christ, in the belief He was really a sinner, and by this fatal mistake Satan loses his right to torment men any longer. The rationalists were wrong in trying to represent these oratorical expedients of the Fathers as a real Christian *mythology.* The Council of Trent set down explicitly and carefully the chief points of the Catholic doctrine of Redemption against the Lutheran errors (sess. 5 and 6, *DB,* 787 ff.).

BIBLIOGRAPHY

St. Thomas, *Summa Theol.,* III, qq. 48–49. D'Alès, "Rédemption," *DTC.* Hugon, *Le mystère de la Rédemption* (Paris, 1927). Pohle-Preuss, *Dogmatic Theology,* V *Soteriology* (St. Louis, 1945), pp. 13–75. Richard, *Le dogme de la Rédemption* (Paris, 1932). Rivière, *The Doctrine of the Atonement,* trans. from the French, 2 vols. (London, 1909); "Rédemption," *DTC.* Scheeben, *The Mysteries of Christianity,* trans. Vollert (St. Louis, 1946), pp. 405–465. Sollier, "Redemption," *CE.* *The Teaching of the Catholic Church,* ed. Smith, 2 vols. (New York, 1949), pp. 52–65, 477–512.

relation, divine. According to Aristotle and St. Thomas, relation is one of the nine accidents, and its formal definition is "Order of one thing to another" (*ad aliquid* — *πρός τι*). It involves a *subject* (e.g., father), a *terminus* (son), a *foundation* or reason on account of which the subject has reference to the terminus (generation, between father and son). Differently from the other accidents, relation, more than a perfection *in* the subject, is a reference *to* the terminus, and its essential characteristic lies precisely in that reference (*esse ad*), while its inherence in the subject (*esse in*) is secondary, and may be *real* or only *logical.* Thus paternity lies wholly in the relationship of one individual to another by virtue of generation; thus also the intelligible object implies a real relation to the knowing intellect, but such relation does not add anything to that object.

It is a truth of faith that in God there are real relations, because in revelation we find correlative terms, such as Father and Son. This doctrine stems also from the divine processions (*q.v.*): a divine procession is inconceivable without a terminus *a quo* and a terminus *ad quem* in relationship between themselves. Since the processions are two, the terminuses are four and the relations between these are four, as may be illustrated in the following diagram:

paternity
F ⟶ S
1st procession
filiation
F ⟵ S

active spiration
F,S ⟶ HS
2nd procession
passive spiration
F,S ⟵ HS

These relations are distinct from the divine nature only by a *distinctio rationis ratiocinatae* (a distinction of reason with foundation in the thing itself; see *attributes of God*), but are *really* distinct between themselves, since they are in opposition (paternity-filiation) in an irreducible way and, therefore, require distinct subjects of attribution (paternity in the Father and filiation in the Son). Only active spiration is not in opposition to paternity and to filiation, and so it has as subject both Father and Son; but it is in opposition to *passive spiration,* which, therefore, demands a distinct terminus (the Holy Spirit).

Of the four real relations in God, three are numerically distinct and, thus, constitute the three divine Persons: the Father, who is subsisting Paternity, the Son, who is subsisting Filiation, the Holy Spirit, who is subsisting Spiration of Love. According to the *esse in,* the Persons subsist by force of the one divine being with which They are really and absolutely identical; according to the *esse ad,* They are distinct *ratione ratiocinata* (by a distinction of reason with foundation in the thing itself) from the essence, but really distinct among Themselves. This real mutual distinction, being purely *relative,* does not violate the absolute unity of God.

BIBLIOGRAPHY

St. Thomas, *Summa Theol.,* I, q. 28. Joyce, "Trinity," *CE.* Peter Parente, "Il Mistero della SS. Trinità," *Il Simbolo,* Vol. 1 (Assisi, 1941). Pohle-Preuss, *Dogmatic Theology,* II *The Divine Trinity* (St. Louis, 1946), pp. 228–235. *The Teaching of the Catholic Church,* ed. Smith, 2 vols. (New York, 1949), pp. 134–139.

religion (Lat. *relegere* — read over, think over [divine things]; or *religare* — bind [to God]; or *reeligere* — choose again [God lost by sin]). Generally speaking, it is a bond, a moral union between God and men, as is evident from the history of religions and from the consideration of the natural relationship of the rational creature to the Creator. *Subjectively,* religion is a voluntary disposition of the soul to recognize God as the supreme Being and Lord of the universe, and to pay Him due worship. *Objectively,* it is the whole of truths and principles, by which our life is ordered and directed to God, supreme End.

In both senses religion invests the whole man: intellect, will, practical activity. Religion is not, therefore, the cult of duty immanent in autonomous reason (Kant); or the consciousness of the divine immanent in us, followed and surpassed by philosophical synthesis (idealists); or an instinct of the subconscious (modernists); or a provisional substitute of the science of natural phenomena (positivists). Religion accompanies the human race constantly in every phase of its intellectual, moral, and civil evolution: therefore, it fills real needs of human nature.

Religion is *natural* if it flourishes spontaneously in the soul from the thought of a God, Creator and Lord, and implies a tendency to the natural end, proportionate to the human intellect and will. It is *supernatural* if it is based on a positive *revelation* of God, which involves speculative truths to be believed and rules of conduct to be followed with reference to the attainment of an end transcending the proper powers and exigencies of human nature. Such is the Christian religion, wholly orientated toward the beatific vision, an absolutely supernatural end. Given the existence of a personal God, man cannot rightly refuse to render Him external and internal worship; and since various religions claim to be revealed, man has the obligation of seeking the true revelation by means of *external* criteria (miracles and prophecies) and *internal* criteria (loftiness and nobility of doctrine and precepts in harmony with the purest aspirations of the human heart).

See *revelation; cult.*

BIBLIOGRAPHY

St. Thomas, *Summa Theol.,* II–II, q. 81. Aiken, "Religion," *CE.* Bowne, *The Essence of Religion* (Boston, 1910). Brinton, *The Religious Sentiment* (New York, 1876). Cotter, *Theologia Fundamentalis* (Weston, 1940); cf. Index, "Religion." Garrigou-Lagrange, *De Revelatione* (Paris, 1914). Hettinger, *Natural Religion* (New York, 1893). Kellogg, *The Genesis and Growth of Religion* (New York, 1892). Lang, *The Making of Religion* (New York, 1898). Lilly, *The Great Enigma* (New York, 1892). Tanquerey, *De vera religione,* etc. (Rome, 1931). *The Teaching of the Catholic Church,* ed. Smith, 2 vols. (New York, 1949), pp. 2–10.

Religious (Congregation of). See *Holy See.*

resurrection, general. A truth of faith defined by the IV Lateran Council (1215, *DB,* 429): "Both the reprobate and the elect will rise with the bodies, which they now have, to receive according to their bad or good actions . . . etc." The resurrection is one of the articles of the Creed. This truth is explicitly revealed in both Old and New Testaments: Job 19–23; Isaias 26:19; Ezechiel 1:14; Daniel 12:2; 2 Machabees 7:1–13; 12:39–46. In the New Testament we find many clear and definite texts, especially in St. Paul (1 Cor. 16; 1 Thess. 4, etc.), who puts our resurrection in close relationship to that of our Lord (cf. also John 5:28). *Tradition* is unanimous in upholding this doctrine (from Didache to Tertullian, who wrote *De Resurrectione Carnis,* and to St. Augustine, who insisted on the *identity* of the mortal and the risen body). Reason cannot demonstrate, but can see the convenience of this supernatural truth. St. Thomas maintains that the perfection of man is the soul and its own proper body: as the body has been associated with the soul in mortal life, so it is just and right that it be united to the soul in eternal life and share with it the joy or the punishment merited.

The resurrection is *universal* for all men and it implies the individual identity of each risen person. To have this identity it suffices that the soul take on again at least one part of the matter with which it was substantially united before death. This principle eliminates many difficulties. St. Thomas answers with sobriety several curious questions on the conditions of the risen body (cf. *Summa contr. Gent.,* IV, 80–85, and *Summa Theol., Suppl.,* qq. 75–86). St. Paul (1 Cor. 15) describes the qualities of the glorious body, which the theologians reduce to four: impassibility, subtility, agility, and splendor. The body will thus feel and reflect the beauty and virtues proper to the blessed soul.

BIBLIOGRAPHY

St. Thomas, *Summa Theol.,* III, *Suppl.,* qq. 75–86; *Summa Contra Gentiles,* 1, 4, qq. 79–80. D'Alès, "Résurrection de la chair," *DA.* Darragh (Anglican), *The Resurrection of the Flesh* (London, 1921). Maas, "Resurrection," *CE.* Michel, "Résurrection des morts," *DTC.* Pohle-Preuss, *Dogmatic Theology,* XII *Eschatology* (St. Louis, 1946), pp. 121–148. *The Teaching of the Catholic Church,* ed. Smith, 2 vols. (New York, 1949), pp. 1211–1247. Vonier, *The Life of the World to Come* (London, 1926), pp. 132–168.

See under *eschatology.*

Resurrection of Christ. That Jesus Christ rose from the dead to new life is a truth, historically attested by all the Evangelists and by St. Paul, which from the first days of Christianity formed not only a part of the gospel message, but its very basis and soul, as well as the central element of the doctrine and liturgy of the nascent Church.

Modern criticism has utilized all possible means to destroy the historic reality of this fact: fraud of the Apostles, theory of hallucination or of merely apparent death of Jesus, etc. But up to the present time none of these contradictory attempts has succeeded in seriously solving the problem. Catholic exegetes, against all the assaults of criticism, old or new, from Reimarus to Loisy, set down these firm points: (1) The real death of Christ and His burial is narrated by the Evangelists with wealth of detail and decisive circumstances. (2) Christ's return to life in all His physical reality, testified to by unimpeachable persons, like Peter and Paul, in public, in presence of the Jews, who would have contradicted them if at all possible. (3) Before the Evangelist's account, we have the energetic testimony of St. Paul (between A.D. 53–55), who saw Christ on the way to Damascus and went to Jerusalem, where he conversed with Peter and James, from whom he could get detailed information on Christ's Resurrection, which for him was the *raison d'être* of the faith and of the apostolate. And St. Paul attests it in a quasi-ritual language that re-echoes the original catechesis of the first Christian community the day after the Ascension of Jesus. (4) The psychological phenomenon of hallucination was impossible in unsettled and bewildered minds, as the Apostles' were; so true is this that at the first apparition of the risen Christ they were afraid and Jesus had to persuade them of the reality of His body by eating and drinking and having them touch Him. (5) The time between Jesus' death and the first testimony of His Resurrection is so brief as to be absolutely insufficient for the formation of a legend. (6) If the Evangelists had wished to invent a legend and deceive others, they would have gotten together on their narratives, which, on the contrary, present a variety of detail and richness of individual style that prove precisely the truth and objectivity of their testimony. (7) Reducing to fraud or hallucination the change wrought by the Resurrection in the Apostles, so timid and cowardly before, as well as St. Paul's conversion and work, is altogether absurd.

The Resurrection is not only the supreme proof of Christ's divinity but also the reason for the blazing of faith, apostolate, and martyrdom, which characterized the earliest days of Christianity.

BIBLIOGRAPHY

St. Thomas, *Summa Theol.,* III, q. 53. Cotter, *Theologia fundamentalis* (Weston, 1940), Index: "Resurrectio Jesu." Cox, *The Resurrection* (London, 1890). De Grandmaison, *Jesus Christ,* 3 vols. (New York, 1930–1934), Vol. 2, Ch. 4. Fenton, *We Stand With Christ* (Milwaukee, 1940), Index: "Resurrection of Christ." Lepin, *Christologie* (Paris, 1908), p. 77 ff. Maas, "Resurrection," *CE.* Marsh, *The Resurrection of Christ, Is It a Fact?* (London, 1905). Milligan, *The Resurrection of Our Lord* (London, 1884). Ricciotti, *The Life of Christ,* trans. Zizzamia (Milwaukee, 1947). Simpson, *The Resurrection and Modern Thought* (London, 1911). Sutcliffe, *The Old Testament and the Future Life* (Westminster, 1947), Ch. 12. Williams, *Our Lord's Resurrection* (London, 1882).

revelation (Lat. *revelare* — remove the veil; equivalent to manifesting an obscure thing). Theologically, revelation is the act by which God manifests Himself primarily in the creation of the universe, which reflects analogically the divine attributes invisible of themselves (cf. Rom. 1:19): this is *natural revelation.* But God has manifested Himself in a particular way by means of the prophets and of Jesus Christ: and this is *supernatural revelation,* which transcends the natural order, either by reason of the *object* of revelation (mystery) or only on account of the mode or manner in which a truth, natural in itself, is manifested (e.g., immortality of the soul). Formally, supernatural revelation is a gratuitous, oral teaching given by God to men with reference to salvation and eternal life.

Possibility: Revelation is possible *on the part of God,* because He is the Source of all truths and, therefore, can teach His creature, limited in being, in intelligence and in knowledge. It is possible *on the part of man,* for if man can learn from other men, *a fortiori* he can learn from God. Revelation is, therefore, both possible and fitting, even in the case of mysteries, the imperfect knowledge of which in the ideal order is none the less fruitful in the practical order.

Necessity: Divine revelation is *absolutely* necessary in order to know truths transcending the power of human reason, as is evident; it is *morally* necessary for the human race in its actual state to know easily, with firm certitude and without admixture of error, the sum total of natural religious truths necessary for the right orientation of our life (Vatican Council, sess. 3, c. 2, *DB,* 1786).

Rationalism and modernism either pervert the meaning of revelation, deny it in the name of the autonomy of reason, or reduce it to a progressive consciousness of the divine. Naturalistic systems, like Pelagianism, do not recognize any necessity of revelation. See *sentiment, religious; subconsciousness.*

BIBLIOGRAPHY

BAINVEL, *De vera religione et apologetica* (Paris, 1914). COTTER, *Theologia fundamentalis* (Weston, 1940), pp. 35–79. FENTON, *We Stand With Christ* (Milwaukee, 1942), pp. 10–92. GARRIGOU-LAGRANGE, *De Revelatione* (Paris, 1926). JUNG, "Révélation," *DTC.* PASCAL PARENTE, *The Mystical Life* (St. Louis, 1946), pp. 221–237. TANQUEREY, *De vera religione, De Ecclesia, De fontibus revelationis* (Rome, 1941).

reviviscence of merits. Human works, with reference to eternal life, are termed: *dead* if performed while in the state of mortal sin, *live* if performed while in the state of grace, *mortified* if performed while in the state of grace but presently deprived of their efficacy of leading to their reward on account of a subsequent fall into mortal sin.

What happens to mortified works at the moment of justification? Scripture and the Fathers explicitly assert that, in restoring His friendship to the sinner, God readmits him to the enjoyment of the spiritual goods acquired before his straying from the paternal home. It is therefore an incontestable fact that the merits reacquire their efficacy with reference to the attainment of the eternal reward. But in what measure? Opinions disagree on this point. Suarez maintains integral restitution, while St. Thomas teaches that merits are given back to the penitent in proportion to the fervor of his conversion, according to the principle that God "gives Himself to the extent of the ardor He finds" (Dante, *Purg.,* 15, 70). The first opinion exalts God's mercy, while the second — very severe at first blush — is more consonant with theological principles and more capable of exciting fervor in penitents. Regarding other nuances in the teaching of St. Thomas, pointed out by his disciples, cf. Boyer, *De Poenitentia* (Rome, 1942), pp. 275–277.

BIBLIOGRAPHY

ST. THOMAS, *Summa Theol.,* III, q. 89, a. 2. BILLOT, *De sacramentis,* Vol. 2 (Rome, 1930), p. 115 f. DORONZO, *De Poenitentia,* Vol. 4. MICHEL, "Reviviscence (Reviviscence des merites)," *DTC,* cols. 2634–2644. MARINO, "La reviviscenza dei meriti secondo la dottrina del Dottore Angelico," *Gregorianum* (1932), pp. 75–108. SUAREZ, Opusculum 5: "Relatio de reviviscentia meritorum," *Opera Omnia* (Parisiis, 1858), pp. 436–513.

reviviscence of the sacraments. If a sacrament, validly received but unproductive of grace on account of an impediment or *obex* (*q.v.*), is later rectified by removing the *obex,* it is said to revive, producing grace by virtue of the rite formerly applied.

From this description it appears that reviviscence requires certain conditions: (1) On the part of the subject, the removal of the impediment is necessary. (2) On the part of the sacrament, the requirements are: (*a*) that it be valid but *without fruit* or inform (without the supernatural form of grace), because if the sacrament is invalid it does not exist, and if it does not exist it cannot act; (*b*) that the *external rite be past,* because if it still exists we cannot speak of revival but of normal conferring of grace; (*c*) that the external right *leave in the recipient some effect,* because reviviscence involves a causal influence on the part of the external rite, which would be inconceivable did it not leave a real imprint of its passage. (3) On the part of God, finally, the requirement is the will of conferring the sacramental grace even in this extraordinary way.

Those sacraments effectively revive in which the foregoing conditions are met. Three of these conditions are met in all the sacraments, except penance: the removal of the impediment, the sacrament valid but inform, the passing away of the external rite. It remains only to inquire if the other two conditions are fulfilled: the permanence of some sort of effect and God's will to bestow grace extraordinarily.

The permanence of a real effect, i.e., of the character, is found in baptism, confirmation, and orders; also, the positive will of God is deduced from the fact that otherwise original sin could never be removed in one who receives baptism unworthily, and that the faithful who received confirmation and orders unworthily would be forever deprived of the corresponding sacramental graces which are so extremely necessary for the fulfillment of the duties to which they are deputized. Also as regards extreme unction and matrimony, while, on the one hand, we find permanence of an *interior unctio* and of a *vinculum* (bond), on the other, we deduce the divine will from the fact that here, too, the faithful would remain deprived of the sacramental helps so efficacious in overcoming the final temptation of the death agony and in facing successfully the difficulties of married life.

Only penance and the Eucharist do not revive, the former because it cannot be at the same time valid and inform, according to the doctrine of many theologians, and the latter because it would be counter to the principles of divine action. In fact, in the hypothesis of reviviscence of the Eucharist, one who all his life made daily sacrilegious Communions would only have to make a simple act of contrition in the sacrament of penance to receive as many increases of grace as the sacrileges he has committed. It is truly repugnant to think that God may wish to put such a reward on sin.

BIBLIOGRAPHY

St. Thomas, *Summa Theol.,* III, q. 69, a. 10 (with the commentaries of John of St. Thomas, Gonet, Billuart). Doronzo, *De sacramentis in genere* (Milwaukee, 1946), Index Analyticus: "Reviviscentia." Marin Sola, "Proponitur nova solutio ad conciliandam causalitatem physicam sacramentorum cum eorum reviviscentia," *Divus Thomas* (Freiburg, 1925), pp. 49–63. Michel, "Reviviscence (Reviviscence des Sacraments)," *DTC,* cols. 2618–2628.

Richard of St. Victor. See "Outline of the History of Dogmatic Theology" (p. 302).

rite (Lat. *ritus* — religious observance). In ecclesiastical usage it is the total amount of ceremonies (bows, benedictions, signs of the cross, imposition of hands, anointments, etc.) and formulas (prayers, hymns, antiphons, verses, etc.), of which the liturgical acts are composed.

Of these rites, some are *essential,* i.e., constitute the very essence of the sacrifice or of the sacraments (*matter* and *form; q.v.*), have a divine origin, and remained unchanged throughout all the vicissitudes and transformations of the liturgy in its two thousand years of development. Others are *accidental,* i.e., they compose the frame into which are fitted, developed, and illustrated the essential rites; these are of ecclesiastical origin and are enlarged, changed, and at times disappear under the influence of historical incidents and according to the diversity of temperaments and religious environments. This variety of accidental rites, within the basic unity of the Christian cult, has given rise to the different liturgical families, which have been flourishing in the Church since the fourth and fifth centuries:

The Antiochian rite, embracing the Greco-Jerusalem, the Syro-Maronite, the Chaldean, and the Byzantine liturgies (this last, called of St. John Chrysostom, is the most widely diffused, being used in Turkey, Greece, Bulgaria, Romania, Serbia, and Russia).

The Alexandrian rite, from which stem the Greek liturgy of St. Mark, the Coptic, and the Ethiopian liturgies.

The Gallican rite, which included the Ambrosian, the Mozarabic, the Celtic, and the Gallican liturgies.

The Ancient Roman rite (to which the African was kindred). In the Carolingian Age a kind of liturgical osmosis between the Roman and the Gallican rites took place, giving origin (at least in its basic physiognomy) to the present Latin liturgy, which is predominant in the Catholic world.

BIBLIOGRAPHY

ATTWATER, *Christian Churches of the East,* Vol. 1, 3 ed. (Milwaukee, 1947). BRIGHTMAN, *Eastern Liturgies* (Oxford, 1896). CALLEWAERT, *De S. Liturgià universim* (Brugis, 1925). DUCHESNE, *Christian Worship, Its Origin and Evolution,* trans. McClure (London, 1903). FORTESCUE, "Rites," *CE.* HAMMOND, *Liturgies, Eastern and Western* (Oxford, 1878). SHIPMAN, "Rites in the United States," *CE.*

See under *cult; liturgy.*

Rites (Congregation of). See *Holy See.*

"Ritual, Roman." See *liturgy.*

Roman pontiff. The successor of St. Peter, i.e., the heir of his primacy over the entire Church (see *primacy of St. Peter*).

The supremacy conferred on the son of Jona was not a personal privilege, since the Church, being an edifice, a kingdom, a sheepfold destined to last unto the consummation of the world, always has need of its foundation, its key bearer, its pastor; the primacy, therefore, had to be perpetuated through the centuries, and St. Peter had to live in his successor, the Roman pontiff (cf. *DB,* 1825).

But why in the bishop of Rome and not in another? Why in the bishop of Rome and not rather in that of Jerusalem where Jesus died? Because the Redeemer, who had prearranged all human history for the end of salvation, selected Rome, the great metropolis, as center of His Church. He chose it by inspiring the Prince of the Apostles to locate definitively his seat in that city, so that the bishops who succeeded him in that see would inherit *ipso facto* the privileges of the primacy.

Clear testimonies and indisputable facts in the nascent Church demonstrate that from the beginning both the bishop of Rome and the faithful of the world have full consciousness of the high pre-eminence of the

Roman Church. In the beginning of the second century, St. Ignatius of Antioch greets the Church of Rome as προκαθημένη τῆς ἀγάπης (Rom., *Prologue*). The most natural meaning of this expression, as Duchesne observes, is that the Roman Church presides over all the churches taken as one body. As the bishop of a particular church presides over the works of charity in that church, so the Roman Church presides over those same works in all Christianity. At the end of the same century, St. Irenaeus of Lyons writes these famous words: "It is necessary that every church be in agreement with it [the Roman Church], on account of its more powerful principality [*propter potiorem principalitatem*]; this means that all the faithful scattered throughout the world must be in agreement with it, because in it has been always conserved intact the tradition which had its origin from the Apostles" (*Adv. haereses,* III, 3, 27). In the middle of the third century St. Cyprian exalts Rome as the "Principal Church whence priestly unity has had its origin" (*Ep.,* 12, 4). There is much factual evidence to accompany these documents, proving the practical recognition of the Roman primacy. The first century had not yet ended when Pope Clement in imperative tones recalled to obedience the rebellious Christians of Corinth (*Ep.,* 44, 3, 45; 40, 12). In the second and third centuries the bishop of Rome appears as arbiter of ecclesiastical controversies, which he settles authoritatively, especially those concerning the faith; even the heretics have recourse to all sorts of intrigues to gain the confidence of the Holy See and procure for themselves the favor of the Chair of Peter.

The primacy, according to the Vatican Council definition (*DB,* 1831), involves an *ordinary, immediate, universal, supreme, full, jurisdictional* authority over the flock of Christ, in matters of both faith and discipline.

The sixteenth-century reformers did their utmost to defame the texts on Peter's primacy, his coming to Rome, his heritage transmitted to his successors (the three truths forming one block). Modern Protestants explain everything through evolution: a unique center of Christianity, they say, is the last thing to be formed; such a center is not at the base but at the vertex of the pyramid. At first the Christian communities are amorphous, later they organize in small oligarchies (collective government by priests); afterward comes the monarchical episcopate. But many years will have to pass before the bishops scattered throughout the world recognize the bishop of Rome as their head. This easy theory is freely contradicted by the texts quoted above and by many others that could be adduced.

BIBLIOGRAPHY

St. Thomas, *Summa Contra Gentiles,* l. 4, c. 76. Ballerini, *De vi ac ratione primatus Romanorum Pontificum et de ipsorum infallibilitate in definiendis controversiis fidei* (Veronae, 1766). Batiffol, *Cathedra Petri* (Paris, 1938); *L'Eglise naissante* (Paris, 1927); *La paix constantinienne* (Paris, 1929); *Le Siège Apostolique* (Paris, 1924). Bellarmine, *De Romano Pontifice.* Glez, "Pouvoir du Pape dans l'ordre temporel," *DTC.* Palmieri, *De Romano Pontifice* (Rome, 1931).

See under *pope.*

S

Sabellianism. See *modalism.*

sacramentals. In a broad sense, they are all those rites and ceremonies which accompany the observance of the divine cult and the administration of the sacraments; in a narrow sense, they are "certain rites, actions, or particular things which the Church customarily uses, in imitation of the sacraments, in order to obtain, through her intercession, certain effects, especially of spiritual character" (*CIC,* Can. 1144).

Their *origin* goes back to the nascent Church, since the ancient ecclesiastical writers speak of them as common practice among the faithful. They are instituted by the Church and produce their effects not *ex opere operato,* but *ex opere operantis Ecclesiae,* in as much as the Church, because of her dignity and in virtue of her powerful intercession, obtains from God, although not infallibly and for those who worthily receive the sacramental, the spiritual effect for which it was instituted.

The sacramentals are divided into two classes: exorcisms and blessings or benedictions.

Exorcisms consist in the imposition of hands and the recitation of certain prayers for the purpose of expelling the devil from the soul and body of the believer. They are applied to irrational creatures also, so that the devil may not use them abusively to harm man.

Benedictions are divided into constitutive and invocative. The constitutive benedictions are applied to men and to irrational creatures to consecrate them to God (e.g., blessing of the virgins, consecration of chalices). The invocative are imparted to man for the purpose of obtaining some divine benefit (e.g., the blessing of St. Blaise), and to irrational creatures that their use may be beneficial to man's soul and body (e.g., blessing of the table).

BIBLIOGRAPHY

Arendt, *De sacramentalibus* (Rome, 1900). Doronzo, *De sacramentis in genere* (Milwaukee, 1946), pp. 540–560. Gasquet, *Sacramentals* (London, 1928). Lambing, *Sacramentals of the Holy Catholic Church* (New York, 1892). Leclercq, "Sacramentals," *CE.* Michel, "Sacramentaux," *DTC.* Paschang, *The Sacramentals According to the C.J.C.* (Washington, D. C., 1925). Pohle-Preuss, *Dogmatic Theology,* VIII *The Sacraments,* Vol. 1, *The Sacraments in General, Baptism, Confirmation* (St. Louis, 1945), pp. 111–120. Stolz, *De sacramentis* (Freiburg i.-Br., 1942), Appendix. Van Noort, *De sacramentis,* Vol. 1, nn. 152–158. Vermeersch-Creusen, *Epitome Iuris Canonici,* Vol. 2, nn. 461–469.

Sacramentarians. See *Presence, Real, Eucharistic (fact).*

Sacraments (Congregation of the). See *Holy See.*

sacraments, institution of. To institute a sacrament (see *sacraments, nature of*) means to attach to a sensible rite the efficacy of producing the signified grace.

Christ who, as God, had the absolute and independent power (*potestas auctoritatis*) of uniting to poor material elements the power of causing grace, as Man also, obtained from the Father so great a dominion over grace, in view of the merits acquired in His passion, that He was constituted the dispenser of all supernatural goods. Armed with this power (*potestas excellentiae*), the Redeemer was free to transmit grace either immediately or through means of sensible rites. Revelation assures us that He, while retaining the power of influencing souls in extraordinary ways corresponding to His infinite wisdom (*non enim alligavit gratiam suam sacramentis*), chose the second way. Indeed, Scripture and Tradition describe the direct intervention of Jesus Christ in determining for His Church the use of the various rites communicative of grace: baptism (John 3:5; Matt. 28:19); confirmation (Acts 8:14; 19:6); Eucharist (John 6:1–72; Matt. 26:26–29; Mark 14:22–25; Luke 22:15–20; 1 Cor. 11:23–25); penance (John 20:21–23); extreme unction (James 5:13–15); orders (Luke 22:19; 1 Cor. 11:26); matrimony (Matt. 19:4–9; Eph. 5:20–32).

These critically verified testimonies, strengthened by statements of the most ancient ecclesiastical writers, not only show that the repudiation of five sacraments by the reformers of the sixteenth century is unjustified, but also lay bare the prejudice of those liberal Protestants who subscribed to the following statements of Harnack: "For us there is no sadder spectacle than these transformations of the Christian religion, which from what originally was, namely, the adoration of God in spirit and truth, becomes the *cult of symbols*. It was to destroy this form of religion that Jesus Christ suffered crucifixion, but here it comes back to life under the mantle of His name and His authority."

The Gospel, on the contrary, assures us that Christ, far from having the iconoclast spirit of destroying religious rites and symbols, freely underwent death to transform them from *infirma et egena elementa* ("weak and needy elements") to means of resurrection and life.

Based on the New Testament documents and the Fathers, the Church, although allowing freedom of discussion on the *mode* of institution, has solemnly defined in the Council of Trent *the fact* itself, i.e., that Jesus Christ has instituted all the sacraments actually in use (*DB,* 844).

BIBLIOGRAPHY

ST. THOMAS, *Summa Theol.,* III, q. 4. DORONZO, *De sacramentis in genere* (Milwaukee, 1946), pp. 383–419. FRANZELIN, *De sacramentis* (Rome, 1911). KENNEDY, "Sacraments," *CE.* MICHEL, "Sacrements," *DTC.*

sacraments, nature of (Lat. *sacramentum* — sacred oath, military oath, etc.; Gr. *μυστήριον* — hidden thing). A sacrament is a sensible sign, productive of grace. In other words, the sacrament in its external rite is a symbol; namely, an exterior representation of a reality not attainable by the senses; e.g., in baptism, the exterior sign, constituted by the water and the words pronounced by the minister, symbolizes and represents an interior and invisible reality, namely, the renewal and purification of the soul. The sacrament, therefore, is not only the symbol of a superior reality, but produces by virtue of the latent action of God that same reality which it signifies. It is, therefore, a sign that really contains what it represents, realizing and producing it as a true cause.

The elements that concur in the intrinsic constitution of a sacrament are, therefore, two: symbolism and causality, the concept of sign (see *matter and form*) and the concept of cause (see *causality of the sacraments*), closely bound up in reciprocal relationship.

The existence, the constitution of the sensible rite and the efficacy of the individual sacraments, is dependent on their *institution* by Jesus Christ (see *sacraments, institution of*); indeed, only He, who is God, could attach to poor and material elements, like water, oil, bread, etc., the power of producing spiritual and supernatural effects, like sanctifying grace (*q.v.*), sacramental grace (*q.v.*), and the character (*q.v.*).

The peaceful possession of this doctrine by the Church, fruit of many centuries of reflexion on the data of revelation (cf. Rom. 6:3–11), was disturbed by the sixteenth-century reformers, who denied that the sacraments of the New Law have the dignity of being causes of grace and considered them to be mere symbols exciting to faith (Luther), or pledges of divine benevolence (Calvin), or identification cards of Church membership (Zwingli), or mere insignia distinguishing the faithful from infidels (Carlostadt and Socinians).

The Council of Trent asserted, against such impoverishment of dogma, the causal efficacy of the sacraments and condemned one after another the errors of Protestantism, in the 13 canons of the seventh session (*DB,* 844–856).

Likewise the modernists, who repeated in substance Luther's error, were condemned by Pius X, in 1907 (*DB,* 2089).

BIBLIOGRAPHY

St. Thomas, *Summa Theol.,* III, qq. 60–65 (with the commentaries of Cajetan, John of St. Thomas, Gonet, Billuart, Pègues, etc.). Bellarmine, *De sacramentis.* Connell, *De sacramentis* (Brugis, 1933), pp. 1–94. Divine, *The Sacraments Explained* (London, 1905). Doronzo, *De sacramentis in genere* (Milwaukee, 1946), pp. 1–113. Franzelin, *De sacramentis in genere* (Rome, 1911). Janot, *Les sept fontaines* (Paris, 1939). Kennedy, "Sacraments," *CE.* Martindale, *The Sacramental System* (New York, 1928). Meagher, *Six Sacraments,* ed. Lattey (London, 1930). Piolanti, *De sacramentis* (Rome, 1945). Pohle-Preuss, *Dogmatic Theology,* VIII *The Sacraments,* Vol. 1, *The Sacraments in General, Baptism, Confirmation* (St. Louis, 1945), pp. 3–31. Pourrat, *The Theology of the Sacraments* (London, 1924); "Sacrement," *DA.* Scheeben, *The Mysteries of Christianity,* trans. Vollert (St. Louis, 1946), pp. 558–582. *The Teaching of the Catholic Church,* ed. Smith, 2 vols. (New York, 1949), pp. 733–766. Vonier, *A Key to the Doctrine of the Eucharist* (Westminster, 1946), pp. 10–52.

sacraments, number of. The Council of Trent defined (*DB,* 844) that seven sacraments, neither more nor less, were instituted by Jesus Christ, namely: baptism, confirmation, the Eucharist, penance, extreme unction, holy orders, and matrimony.

Actually, Holy Scripture and the Fathers speak of seven rites, in which are verified the distinctive elements of a sacrament; therefore, the sacraments instituted by Christ are seven. We grant that neither the Bible nor Tradition enunciates in an abstract and exclusive way the septenary number, and that it is only in the twelfth century that we are able to find such formal enumeration of the seven sacraments. But that does not mean that the ancient writers did not know the fact; it merely indicates that, although they admitted and used the seven rites, they had neither the occasion nor the means to list them as seven. They did not have the *occasion* both on account of the lack of errors in this matter with the corresponding lack of stimulus to profound doctrinal analysis and abstract expression, and on account of the practical nature of these institutions which was conducive rather to stressing their right use than to constructing their theoretical synthesis. They did not have the *means;* they knew, indeed, that baptism, confirmation, etc., consist of a symbolic rite with the power of producing that which they signify, but their knowledge did not extend beyond the mere fact. Even when Origen and St. Augustine began the process of abstraction, following the Neoplatonic philosophy which was wont to stop at symbolism rather than to sound the mysteries of causality, they found it easy to apply the notion of sign to our rites, but had no incentive to developing in their respect the idea of cause. Thus appeared the abstract concept of sacrament as a sacred sign, a concept so vague and indetermined as to allow placing in the same category all the symbols with which the liturgy overflowed. Only when the Scholastics of the twelfth and thirteenth centuries, favored by the Aristotelian philosophy, added to the idea of sign a differentiating characteristic, that of cause, did it become easy to reserve the name "sacrament" to those sacred signs which at once were cause of what they symbolized, and to group under one heading and label the seven rites productive of grace.

On the other hand, the fact that the list of the seven sacraments, once formally determined, was unanimously accepted by the theologians and immediately accepted throughout the Catholic world tends to prove that the list was merely an expression of what the Church had been always practicing and explicitly teaching. Such practice and doctrine are efficaciously supported by the ancient heretical sects (Nestorians, Monophysites, Jacobites, etc.) who, though separated from the Catholic Church from the fifth and sixth centuries, professed the sacramental septenary. Therefore, even in those remote times, the tradition of the seven sacraments was deep rooted, for, had there been any doubt about the Apostolic origin of such doctrine, the heretics would have capitalized on such doubt by abandoning the sacramental septenary in order to create a deeper moat between them and Rome.

BIBLIOGRAPHY

St. Thomas, *Summa Theol.,* III, q. 65. Bittner, *De Numero Sacramentorum Septenario* (Breslau, 1859). Doronzo, *De sacramentis in genere* (Milwaukee, 1946), pp. 496–538. Franzelin, *De sacramentis in genere* (Rome, 1911). Kennedy, "Sacraments," *CE.* Michel, "Sacrements," *DTC.* Pohle-Preuss, *Dogmatic Theology,* VIII *The Sacraments,* Vol. 1 *The Sacraments in General, Baptism, Confirmation* (St. Louis, 1945), pp. 32–57. Pourrat, *The Theology of the Sacraments* (London, 1924).

Sacrifice, Eucharistic. See *Mass.*

sacrifice of Christ. A sacrifice, in general, is the offering and the real or equivalent destruction of a material thing, performed by a legitimate minister and directed to God for the purpose of recognizing His Lordship and expiating human guilt.

There is no religion without sacrifice, which is the most solemn act of worship. Sacrifice stems from the feeling of one's dependence on the Creator, to whom man owes all, even his very life. In order to express recognition of this subjection, man offers to God things necessary to life, if not life itself, as happened more than once. To the feeling of subjection is added the consciousness of guilt and the desire of expiation in order to regain God's friendship. It is a truth of faith that Christ's death was a real and proper sacrifice (Council of Ephesus and Council of Trent, *DB,* 122, 938, 950). Indeed, in the Gospel Christ's death is often referred to in technical, sacrificial terminology: *hostia* (*θυσία*), *victima propitiatoria* (*ἱλαστήριον*), etc. Christ is called the Lamb that takes away the sins of the world, the Lamb slaughtered (Apoc. 5:6). St. Paul, especially, develops this doctrine, in his *Letter to the Hebrews.*

With the sacrifice of the cross is intimately connected the sacrifice of the Mass, which draws its value from it (see *Mass*). Christ is Priest and Victim in both.

BIBLIOGRAPHY

St. Thomas, *Summa Theol.,* III, q. 48, a. 3. Doronzo, *De Eucharistia,* Vol. 2 (Milwaukee, 1948), Index Analyticus: "Sacrificium coeleste"; "Sacrificium Coenae"; "Sacrificium Crucis." Gardeil, "Sacrifice," *DTC.* Grimal, *The Priesthood and Sacrifice of Our Lord Jesus Christ,* trans. Keyes (Philadelphia, 1915). Pohle-Preuss, *Dogmatic Theology,* V *Soteriology* (St. Louis, 1945), pp. 111–126. Vosté, *De passione et morte Jesu Christi* (Rome, 1937), p. 331 ff.

Salmeron. See "Outline of the History of Dogmatic Theology" (p. 303).

sanctification. The transforming action which makes man holy. Sanctification, therefore, implies essential reference to the concept of sanctity or holiness. Holy (Hebr. קָדוֹשׁ *qôdês,* from קָדַשׁ *qâdás* — to separate) means that which is separated from profane things and consecrated to God. Sanctity, in fact, has a negative aspect (withdrawal from sin) and a positive aspect (friendly union with the Divinity). In the Old Testament, despite its motives of interior holiness, there gradually prevailed a kind of extrinsic and legal sanctity, which reached its apex in Pharisaism. Christ kindled the flame of true sanctity, representing it as a regeneration, a new life, nourished principally by love to the degree of a mysterious participation in the very life of God. Its negative aspect (purification and liberation from sin) is developed particularly by St. Paul, while its positive aspect (vital communication and mutual immanence between God and man), more particularly by SS. John and Peter, who speak of a participation of the divine nature in redeemed man (see *"consortium," divine*). These precious elements of written revelation, elaborated by the Fathers and the theologians, concur to form the theology of sanctification, sealed by the *magisterium* of the Church.

Sanctification has three phases: *genetic, static,* and *dynamic*. Genetically, sanctification in the present order is the passage from a state of sin to friendship with God through grace. (As regards such passage, see *justification*.) Statically, sanctification is the condition of man elevated by sanctifying grace and its annexed gifts. It may be called sanctity in its being or essence. Dynamically, sanctification is the supernatural activity of the sanctified man, who tends to win an increasingly intense life of union with God by practicing virtue and by assiduously struggling against the passion and temptation.

History records two opposite errors with respect to sanctification: Pelagianism (*q.v.*), which rejects original sin and the necessity of grace, attributing to nature the work of sanctification (naturalism); and Lutheranism (*q.v.*), which, at the other extreme, exaggerates original sin, denies the possibility of man's regeneration and collaboration with God, reducing our sanctification to an external imputation of the divine sanctity. The Church has condemned both errors, teaching, in harmony with revelation, that sanctification is the work of God, who infuses grace but requires man's free co-operation both at the time of the acquiring of grace and afterward in the keeping and the increasing of God's gift. Sanctified man must struggle and work continuously to progress in holiness, especially under the impulse and by the exercise of charity (*q.v.*), which is the measure of true sanctity.

BIBLIOGRAPHY

St. Thomas, *Summa Theol.*, II–II, q. 184. Karrer, *Le sentiment religieux dans l'humanité et le christianisme,* trans. from the German (Paris, 1937). Michel, "Sainteté," *DTC*.

sanctity (mark of the Church). Sanctity or holiness is the second characteristic endowment or distinguishing mark which the Nicene-Constantinopolitan Creed attributes to the Church and which stems from its intimate nature. If, indeed, the Church is "the union, in social form, of Christ with man," it must be holy, like all that is in contact with God.

The Bible represents sanctity as a characteristic attribute of the Church: "Christ also loved the Church, and delivered himself up for it: That he might sanctify it . . . [and] present it to himself a glorious church, not having spot or wrinkle, or any such thing; . . . [that] it should be holy, and without blemish. . . . He chose us in him before the foundation of the world, that we should be holy and unspotted in his sight" (Eph. 5:25–27; 1:4); "Who gave himself for us, that he might redeem us from all iniquity, and might cleanse to himself a people acceptable, pursuer of good works" (Tit. 2:14).

The holiness of the Church is threefold: sanctity of principles, of members, and of gifts. Sanctity of principles consists in the fact that the Church is endowed with means which are suited to produce sanctity in men (*active sanctity*). Truly, the dogmatic and moral doctrine of the Church (*magisterium*) is the leaven that raises the human mass from the darkness of earth to the splendor of heaven, its sacraments (*ministerium*) are the channels which transmit sanctifying grace, and its authority (*imperium*) is directed solely to guiding the faithful along the way of perfection.

Sanctity of members (*passive sanctity*) is obvious in the continuous spectacle, that has been going on since the beginning of Christian history, of the very many faithful living according to the commands of the Gospel (*common sanctity*) and especially of the many others who, by following the evangelical counsels, have reached the arduous heights of heroism (*perfect sanctity*), which is usually approved and certified by canonization. The entire history of Christian peoples, from St. Paul to St. Benedict, from St. Francis of Assisi to St. Teresa of Jesus, from St. Vincent de Paul to St. John Bosco, is crisscrossed by luminous wakes of heroic sanctity.

The holiness of *gifts* (*signs of sanctity*) emerges from the gift of miracles, through which the Holy Spirit is accustomed to manifest His presence in the whole Mystical Body (miracles are, indeed, *gratiae gratis datae,* i.e., graces gratuitously given for the edification of the Church), as well as in certain singularly virtuous members of the Church, since, ordinarily, God employs the souls dearest to Him for the working of His marvels.

BIBLIOGRAPHY

St. Thomas, *In Symbolum Apostolorum expositio,* a. 7–8. Cotter, *Theologia fundamentalis* (Weston, 1940), pp. 411, 465–476. De Poulpiquet, *L'Eglise* (Paris, 1927). Joyce, "Sanctity (Mark of the Church)," *CE.*

sanctity of Christ. Generally speaking, holiness signifies association with the Divinity. In a concrete and Christian sense, it involves a certain participation in the divine nature by means of grace, an adoptive filiation or sonship, and immunity from guilt.

The humanity of Christ is most holy by reason of the hypostatic union and of the boundless grace with which it was enriched. (*a*) On account of the hypostatic union the assumed humanity subsists by the very being of the Word. Thus no closer union with God is conceivable, nor can anything belong to God more properly than that humanity. By that same union Christ-Man is not an adopted Son but the natural Son of God, and, therefore, is impeccable (see *impeccability*). (*b*) In addition to this sanctity of a *substantial* character, the humanity of Christ has a sanctity of an *accidental order* by virtue of grace and the supernatural gifts. By the hypostatic union Christ's humanity *is* holy; through grace and the gifts it *acts* in a holy way, i.e., in a godly way. The grace in Christ is so full that, as St. John says, "of His fullness we all have received." Thus the humanity of the Saviour is the inexhaustible source of all sanctity; the splendors of the one and holy Church are an irradiation of that most holy humanity.

The Gospel speaks of a progress of Jesus in wisdom and grace (Luke 2:52). He was, nevertheless, full of all wisdom and grace from the first instant of the incarnation. That progress, as the Fathers suggest, must be understood not in a *real* sense, but in the sense of progressive manifestation.

Sanctity of Mary. Conceived without stain of sin (see *Immaculate Conception*), she was immune to all sin and its concupiscence, even venial sin (Council of Trent); she was thus full of a perfect grace, superior to that of the saints and the angels, and infinite in some way, i.e., not in an absolute sense, but proportionately to her sublime dignity as Mother of God.

BIBLIOGRAPHY

CHOLLET, *La psychologie du Christ* (Paris, 1909). HUGON, *Le mystère de l'Incarnation* (Paris, 1931), p. 208 ff. MERKELBACH, *Mariologia* (Paris, 1939), p. 157 ff. POHLE-PREUSS, *Dogmatic Theology,* IV *Christology* (St. Louis, 1946), pp. 207–247. *The Teaching of the Catholic Church,* ed. Smith, 2 vols. (New York, 1949), pp. 389–392. THOUVENIN, "Jésus Christ," *DTC,* cols. 1274–1295.

satisfaction of Christ (Lat. *satisfactio*). In Roman law satisfaction meant the compensation for a debt to be paid or for an offense to be expiated (the *Wergeld* of Germanic medieval law). Tertullian used this juridical term to signify the penitential works enjoined in the penitential discipline. Consequently the term passed into the liturgy (first the Mozarabic) to signify the works and intercessions of the saints in behalf of sinners.

St. Anselm applied satisfaction to Christ the Redeemer, developing a whole doctrine which was later incorporated in the framework of scholasticism. In his work, *Cur Deus Homo* ("Why the God-Man?"), he insisted on the concept of satisfaction as an *objective* reparation for the natural order disturbed by guilt, so as to establish a juridical proportion between guilt and satisfaction. St. Thomas integrated this concept with the *moral* element of Christ's passion (love, obedience) and with the principle of the *solidarity* between Christ, the Head, and men, the members of His Mystical Body. An adjective was later added to the term, and *vicarious satisfaction* was used to indicate the substitution of Christ for men in satisfying the divine justice and in liberating them from the slavery to the devil and sin. This satisfaction offered by Christ, especially through His passion and death, has an infinite value, because it is proper to the Word (see *theandric operation*). According to St. Thomas, three elements concur in its constitution: *love, justice, pain.* The first is the formal and most important element; the second is the guiding or directing reason; the third is the material element (see *Redemption*).

BIBLIOGRAPHY

ST. THOMAS, *Summa Theol.,* III, q. 48, a. 2. ST. ANSELM, *Cur Deus Homo.* DORONZO, *De Poenitentia,* Vol. 3. RICARD, *De satisfactione Christi in Tract. S. Anselmi "Cur Deus Homo"* (Louvain, 1914). SOLLIER, "Redemption," *CE.*

See under *Redemption.*

satisfaction, sacramental. The voluntary acceptance of works requiring sacrifice (prayer, alms, mortification) in order to expiate the temporal punishment or penalty which remains after the remission of sin. Holy Scripture teaches us (Wisd. 10:2; Gen. 3:17; cf. Num. 20:1; 2 Kings 12:13–14) that God does not always remit, together with the guilt and the eternal penalties, all the temporal punishment. The priest, therefore, when giving absolution imposes works of satisfaction (penance), which the penitent must accept. The effects of satisfaction are: compensation, according to the rules of justice, for the outrage of God's honor caused by sin, the healing of the forces of wounded human nature, and the reparation of the scandal of sins committed in the presence of the brethren.

The Protestants objected, claiming that satisfaction is proper only when there is equality of nature between the guilty and the offended person, whereas the distance between God and man is infinite. What could a creature ever do that might satisfy his debt toward God? The Council of Trent reiterated: "Satisfaction is not so much our own, but of Christ and through Him, in whom we live and move and satisfy, and do worthy and fruitful penitential works, which have their value from Him, are offered to

God by Him, and are accepted by the Father through Him" (sess. 14, c. 8; *DB,* 904). Therefore, all our works, through their sacramental application made by the priest, bear the imprint of the blood of Christ. Man, as a living member of the Mystical Body, receives the influence of the Head, lives of His life, His works, His merits, His satisfaction; the current of the divine life of Jesus propels, as it were, the tiny boat of human life toward the banks of eternity.

BIBLIOGRAPHY

ST. THOMAS, *Summa Theol.,* III, *Supplementum,* qq. 12–15. CAPELLA, *De satisfactione Jesu Christi et satisfactione nostra* (Ferrariae, 1551). DORONZO, *De Poenitentia,* Vol. 3, Ch. 6. GALTIER, "Satisfaction," *DTC.* HANNA, "Penance," *CE.* POHLE-PREUSS, *Dogmatic Theology,* X *The Sacraments,* Vol. 3, *Penance* (St. Louis, 1946), pp. 217–231.

schism (Gr. σχίσμα — separation, division). The crime of one who separates himself from the Catholic Church to form another sect under the pretext that the Catholic Church errs or approves disorders and abuses. Schism is distinct formally from heresy, because heresy breaks the *dogmatic bond* by professing error, while schism breaks the *social bond* by the refusal of obedience to the legitimate pastors. However, in the long run, schism falls fatally into heresy, because it eventually denies the authority and the infallibility of the Church.

The history of Christianity is marred by flighty and proud minds that rebelled against the legitimate authorities and became autonomous, forming dissident sects. The chief schisms were those of the Novatians in the third century and of the Donatists in the fourth and fifth centuries. The saddest one, however, is the Greek Schism, started by Photius (ninth century), which keeps apart from the bosom of the true Church so many Christian peoples who at one time counted among their number outstanding saints and doctors.

Schismatics are members wrenched from the body of the Church, dried up branches, as it were. If they are in bad faith they cannot be saved, because, as St. Augustine says, *foris ab Ecclesia constitutus et separatus a compage unitatis et vinculo caritatis, aeterno supplicio punieris, etiamsi pro Christi nomine vivus incendiaris* ("Constituted outside of the Church and separated from the sinews of unity and bond of charity, you will be punished with eternal torture, even should you be burned alive for Christ's name," *Ep.,* 173, *ad Donatum*).

BIBLIOGRAPHY

ST. THOMAS, *Summa Theol.,* II–II, q. 39. ATTWATER, *Christian Churches of the East,* Vol. II, rev. ed. (Milwaukee, 1948). BATIFFOL, *Le catholicisme de saint Augustin* (Paris, 1929). CONGAR and JUGIE, "Schisme," *DTC.* FORGET, "Schism," *CE.* FORTESCUE, "Schism (Eastern)," *CE; The Orthodox Eastern Church* (London, 1907). JUGIE, *Theologia Dogmatica Christianorum Orientalium,* Vol. I (Paris, 1927); *Le Schisme Byzantin* (Paris, 1942). SALEMBIER, "Schisme d'Occident," *DA.*

Schools of Alexandria and Antioch. See "Outline of the History of Dogmatic Theology" (p. 301); *allegorism; Arianism; Monophysitism; Nestorianism.*

science, divine. Science is the knowledge of things not only in themselves but also in their proper causes. It is a perfect intellectual knowledge, and in this sense science is properly predicated of God.

Divine revelation exalts the wisdom of God. St. Paul gathers its most ancient testimonies in the exclamation "O the depth of the riches of the wisdom and of the knowledge of God!" (Rom. 11:33.) The Church defines (Vatican Council, sess. 3, c. 1; *DB,* 1782) that God is endowed with an infinite intellect. The concept of divine *omniscience* is familiar to all Tradition for these reasons: (*a*) Intellectuality is the highest perfection of the human and angelic creature: but created perfections must be in God in an eminent way (see *analogy*). (*b*) The order and finality of the cosmos reveal an intelligent Cause. (*c*) Intellectuality and, therefore, knowledge are connatural properties of all spiritual beings; to know means to receive "intentionally" in oneself the *forms* of external things without altering or losing one's own form; this is possible only to spirit, which, while remaining identical with itself, is able to become all things by knowing them. Since God is spiritual in the highest sense, He is supremely intelligent; what is more, by reason of His simplicity (*q.v.*), His intellect and knowledge are identical with His essence and, therefore, His knowledge is most perfect and infinite, as is His essence. God knows, above all, Himself (*primary object*), then all creatures present, past, and future, and all possible things. The Scholastics distinguish: *scientia visionis,* for real things, and *scientia simplicis intelligentiae,* for possible things. The Molinists add the *scientia media* (see *Molinism; prescience*).

There is discussion among theologians on the *mode* of God's knowledge of creatures; the best opinion is that which holds *mediate* knowledge: God, by knowing perfectly His essence, knows in it also all things real and possible, for all things are actual or potential imitations of the divine essence. If God knew things directly, i.e., outside of Himself, they would in a certain way actuate and modify the divine intellect, which is repugnant. Knowing all things by a most simple act, which is identical with His essence, God does not reason, like we do, by passing from one known object to another, but grasps intuitively and exhausts with one single act all the intelligibility of His own nature and of all created or creatable beings.

BIBLIOGRAPHY

St. Thomas, *Summa Theol.,* I, q. 14. Garrigou-Lagrange, *God,* trans. Rose (St. Louis, 1947–1948); *The One God,* trans. Rose (St. Louis, 1943), pp. 416–479. Michel, "Science (II Science de Dieu)," *DTC,* cols. 1598–1620. Pohle-Preuss, *Dogmatic Theology,* I *God: Knowability, Essence, Attributes* (St. Louis, 1946), pp. 327–422. Sertillanges, *St. Thomas d'Aquin,* Vol. 1 (Paris, 1925), p. 210 ff. Toner, "God," *CE.*

science of Christ. The total knowledge which Christ has both as God and as Man. As God, the Word has in common with the Father and the Holy Spirit that act of divine intellection which is identical with the divine essence and through which the Triune God knows Himself and all things possible and real (past, present, and future). This truth is based on the true divinity and consubstantiality of the incarnate Word (Council of Nicaea) and on the integrity of His divine nature (Council of Chalcedon). It is rejected by Monophysitism, Agnoetism, and the theory of kenosis (*qq.v.*).

This divine knowledge of the Word, being infinite, could not be communicated formally to the assumed soul of Christ, which, instead, had to have those kinds of knowledge that are possible to the intellectual creature, namely: the beatific vision, infused knowledge, and acquired knowledge. (*a*) The *beatific vision* is proper to the blessed; it could not, therefore, be lacking to Christ, even during His life on earth, on account of the hypostatic union, which is a much greater perfection than the beatific vision. (*b*) *Infused knowledge* is a gift of God, consisting in the infusion of intelligible species in the intellect which is thus enabled to understand things without the concourse of the senses; this knowledge accompanies the beatific vision in the blessed and the angels and, therefore, was also in Christ, Head of the angels and King of the blessed. (*c*) *Acquired knowledge* is that which the human mind obtains by means of *abstraction* of species or ideas from the phantasms of sense cognition; Christ, as perfect Man, must naturally have this knowledge, in which only He could make progress, according to the Gospel (Luke 2:52). These three kinds of knowledge, being of different character, can exist together in the same soul, and Christ uses now one, now another. Nor are they superfluous, since they have different gradations of luminousness.

Divine knowledge, as well as the threefold human knowledge of Christ, exclude from Him any ignorance whatever; if Jesus says (Mark 13:32) that He does not know the day of the final judgment, this expression must be understood in the sense that He cannot *manifest* it (thus the Fathers). Cf. Decree of the Holy Office, 1918, *DB,* 2183–2185.

BIBLIOGRAPHY

St. Thomas, *Summa Theol.,* III, qq. 9–12. Hugon, *Le mystère de l'Incarnation* (Paris, 1931), p. 243; "Le décret du Saint-Office touchant la science de l'âme du Christ," *Revue Thomiste,* 1918. Maas, "Knowledge of Jesus Christ," *CE.* Michel, "Science" (IV. Science de Jésus-Christ), *DTC,* cols. 1628–1665. Parente, *De Verbo Incarnato* (Rome, 1939), p. 194 ff. Pohle-Preuss, *Dogmatic Theology,* IV *Christology* (St. Louis, 1946), pp. 247–277. *The Teaching of the Catholic Church,* ed. Smith, 2 vols. (New York, 1949), pp. 392–397. Thouvenin, "Jésus-Christ," *DTC,* col. 1273 f.

Scotus. See "Outline of the History of Dogmatic Theology" (p. 303); *analogy; person.*

Scripture, Holy. See *Bible.*

seal of confession. The most grave obligation of keeping secret all that has been revealed by the penitent with reference to absolution in the sacrament of penance, and whose revelation would render that sacrament onerous and odious. The *primary subject* of such obligation is the confessor; the *secondary subject,* all those who, either by accident or design, legitimately or illegitimately, have heard something pertaining to confession. Obviously the penitent is not held to secrecy. The object of the secret is: (1) all mortal sins, generally or specifically, and all venial sins confessed specifically; (2) all that might constitute damage or hardship on the penitent, if it were revealed. Hence, virtues, supernatural gifts, etc., do not come within the object of this secret. Even when the confessor denies absolution he is held to the secret, for as the IV Lateran Council teaches, *Radix unde sigillum enascitur non est absolutio sed penitentiale iudicium* ("The root whence the seal arises is not absolution but penitential judgment," i.e., the fact of submitting one's sins to the confessor's judgment in the sacrament).

This obligation is founded on: (*a*) *Natural law,* because the penitent manifests his sins on condition of secrecy; a quasi-contract is stipulated between penitent and confessor. (*b*) *Positive divine law;* in fact, since Jesus Christ instituted the sacrament of penance in the form of a judgment, which requires the revelation of sins, He implicitly imposed the sacramental seal. Indeed, if it were not included in the penitential judgment, confession would become odious, harmful, scandalous: things our Saviour, infinite Justice, Sanctity, and Mercy, absolutely could not permit. (*c*) *Ecclesiastical law,* as is obvious from the severe canonical legislation. It is apparent, therefore, that this secret is so strict that it cannot be revealed, except by the penitent's permission, even when the confessor's life or the public good is at stake. Historically, it is a fact that there exists a special action of divine providence insuring the keeping of this secret. With few exceptions, the ministers of God have always merited the confidence reposed in them by the faithful, at times even sealing it with their blood.

BIBLIOGRAPHY

ST. THOMAS, *Comment. In 4 Sent.*, dist. 2, q. 3, a. 4. DOLHABARAY, "Confession (X Science acquise en)," *DTC,* cols. 960–974. DORONZO, *De Poenitentia,* Vol. 2 (Milwaukee, 1951). HONORÉ, *Le secret de la confession* (Brugis, 1924). KURTSCHEID, *A History of the Seal of Confession,* trans. Marks (St. Louis, 1927). NOLAN, "Seal of Confession," *CE.* PRÜMMER, *Manuale Theologiae Moralis,* Vol. 3, n. 443–448.

Semi-Arians. Originating from Arianism (*q.v.*), the Semi-Arians attempted through insidious subtleties to sabotage the Nicene definition concerning the ὁμοούσιος (consubstantial, said of the Word with respect to the Father). The chief Semi-Arian sects are:

1. The *Anomoeans* (Gr. ἀνόμοιος — dissimilar), founded by Aëtius and Eunomius, the closest to Arianism. Insisting on the concept of ἀγέννητος (unborn) as proper to God, they denied the divinity of the Word and His consubstantiality with the Father, for the reason that the Word is generated, the only-begotten Son. St. Basil and St. Gregory of Nyssa fought them vigorously (see *Anomoeanism*).

2. The *Omoeans* (Gr. ὅμοιος — similar), also called *Acacians* (from Acacius of Caesarea, † 366). The Word, according to them, is not consubstantial with the Father, but only similar to Him (see *Acacians*).

3. The *Homoiousians* (ὁμοιούσιος— of like substance), the largest among the Semi-Arian sects, called also *Basilians* (from Basil of Ancira, † 366). They reject the ὁμοούσιος of Nicaea and hold that the Word is not of the same substance of the Father, but of a substance *similar* to that of the Father. St. Athanasius and the Cappadocians (St. Basil, St. Gregory of Nyssa, and St. Gregory Nazianzus) tried, as best they could, to follow a conciliatory course in the midst of so many aberrations, which consisted not in sacrificing the substance of the Nicene definition, but in abstaining from stressing the disputed expressions, even the word ὁμοούσιος. This was a prudential measure and not a retractation of the doctrine they had defended, as some modern critics have unjustly insinuated, speaking of them as *Neo-Nicenists.*

BIBLIOGRAPHY

D'ALÈS, *Le dogme de Nicée* (Paris, 1926), p. 126 ff. CHAPMAN, "Semiarians and Semiarianism," *CE.* TIXERONT, *History of Dogmas,* trans. H.L.B., Vol. 2 (St. Louis, 1914), p. 50 f.

Seminaries (Congregation of). See *Holy See.*

Semi-Pelagianism. A mitigated form of Pelagianism (*q.v.*) sprung up on the occasion of certain expressions of St. Augustine (before he became bishop) on the beginning of faith and good will (cf. *De libero arbitrio; De Diversis Quaestionibus,* 85, especially question 86). The chief authors of the movement were John Cassian, of St. Victor, near Marseilles, Gennadius of Marseilles (from whom the Semi-Pelagians are called also *Marsilians*), Faustus, Bishop of Riez, and Vincent of Lerins, who wrote the famous *Commonitorium,* in which he evidently opposes St. Augustine, without naming him. St. Augustine, close to death, was informed of the new heresy by two good laymen, Prosper Aquitanus and Hilary, and wrote two works against it. Later Prosper composed a poem *De Ingratis* (i.e., on those who do away with grace) against the Semi-Pelagians. Another defender of St. Augustine was St. Fulgentius, who attacked Faustus especially.

The chief points of the heresy are: (*a*) Grace is not required to *begin* faith and sanctification, but only to complete them. (*b*) God grants grace according to our merits and our positive dispositions to receive it. (*c*) Final perseverance is the fruit of our own merits.

Through the work of St. Caesarius of Arles a council was assembled at Orange in 529 (Conc. Arausicanum II), which reinforced the condemnation of Pelagianism (already issued in the Council of Carthage of 418, and in that of Ephesus in 431), and rejected the new error of Semi-Pelagianism, defining (according to the teaching of St. Augustine) that: (*a*) Grace is always necessary for every good act in supernatural life, even for the initial one. (*b*) Grace is absolutely gratuitous and God distributes it freely. (*c*) Without grace it is not possible to persevere in good to the end and so win eternal life. The definitions of this Council were approved by Pope Boniface II (cf. *DB,* 174 ff.).

BIBLIOGRAPHY

Cayré, *Manual of Patrology,* trans. Howitt, Vol. 1 (Paris, Tournai, Rome, 1936), pp. 601–603, 635–637. Pohle, "Semipelagianism," *CE.* Pohle-Preuss, *Dogmatic Theology,* VII *Grace* (*Actual and Habitual*) (St. Louis, 1946), pp. 96–110. Tixeront, *History of Dogmas,* trans. H.L.B., Vol. 3 (St. Louis, 1916), pp. 264–301.

senses of Scripture. Since all authors write to communicate ideas, every text carries its own particular meaning. An exclusive property of the biblical texts is that they often have, in addition to their literal sense — which springs up directly from the words — a sense which is called *typical.* Such is the case when the words or the things expressed, or the persons described, have not only a literal, historical meaning, complete in itself, but are also pointed to signify other things, events, or persons. The *type* or figure is the thing or fact or person intended to signify another, called the *antitype.* For example, Adam was the type of Christ, Christ is the antitype of Adam (Rom. 5:14). Between type and antitype there must be a relationship of resemblance, e.g., the priesthood of Melchisedech, who offers as sacrifice to the Most High bread and wine, is a type of the priesthood of Christ, who offers under the species of bread and wine His own flesh and blood (Heb. 7:3).

It is obvious that God alone could direct words and events toward future doctrines and realities, and, therefore, the typical sense of the biblical texts can be established only on the testimony of the Bible itself or of Tradition, namely: on the sources of revelation.

We distinguish *Messianic, moral,* and *anagogical* (which aims upward or on high) types, according as their content is Messianic or moral or respective of life eternal. Jerusalem, e.g., is, in the literal sense, the capital of the Kingdom of Judea, in the typical Messianic sense it is the figure of the Church, in the typical moral sense it is the figure of the soul of the faithful, and in the anagogical sense it is eternal beatitude. The typical sense, in all its forms, is proper to the Old Testament; in the New Testament only anagogical types are to be found. Since the typical sense derives from divine revelation, it has a probative value in dogma; but it should be noted that nothing is found expressed in the Bible in the typical sense which is not enunciated as well in the literal sense.

BIBLIOGRAPHY

Cotter, *Theologia fundamentalis* (Weston, 1940), pp. 677–686. Höpfl, Gut, *Introductio generalis in S. Scripturam* (Rome, 1940), pp. 453–468. Steinmueller, *A Companion to Scripture Studies,* Vol. 1 (New York, 1941), pp. 226–245.

See under *hermeneutics.*

sentiment, religious. Skilled psychologists, both ancient and modern, discuss the nature of sentiment without being able to define it. Some hold that sentiment derives from an *affective* or *emotive* faculty, distinct from both the volitive (*motive*) and the *perceptive-intellective* faculties. Some reduce sentiment to *psychological* phenomena, while others consider it as a *representative* or *intellective* function.

The Scholastic theory, formulated by St. Thomas, who followed Aristotle, presents the surest guarantees of truth, despite its age. According to this teaching, there are in man only two kinds of psychic faculties: the *cognitive* and the *appetitive,* each being distinguished in *sensible* and *supersensible* or *spiritual.* We have, therefore, the zone of the senses with the corporal organs, the sensations and the passions which belong at once to the body and to the soul that informs the body. From this inferior zone we pass to the spiritual zone, in which function the immaterial faculties of intellect and will. *Sensation,* proper to the sense faculties, is originated from a passive impression of the external world on the senses, which becomes a *perception* of the object and its representation (phantasm-image); hence follows in the appetitive faculty a *movement* toward the object perceived, namely, an impulse, accompanied by physical emotion, which is usually called *passion* (love, hate, joy, sadness, etc.).

As the sense appetite has its passions subordinate to sense representations, so the rational appetite, i.e., the will, has its *affections* subordinate to intellective representations (concept-ideas). Sentiment is placed among these affections of the will, which, residing in a spiritual faculty, has repercussions in the sense zone and, like sensation, has both an *active* and a *passive* character, inasmuch as it may be termed an impression directed to an action. The gamut of the sentiments is indefinite, but love is its fundamental note.

The religious sentiment is born from the knowledge of God the Creator, which inspires man with humble subjection, adoration, or fear. According to Catholic doctrine, religious sentiment does not precede but accompanies and follows the knowledge of God, and it is a precious energy for the development of piety and spiritual perfection. But from the rise of Lutheranism, sentiment has become for many the unique or the chief source of religion, which is reduced to a mere *psychological experience* (see *experience, religious*). This is also true of Schleiermacher, the founder of sentimental theology, and of the Pragmatists (see *Pragmatism*), who furnish modernism (*q.v.*) with its theories. Psychological sentimentalism, consisting in an exaggeration of sentiment, becomes in religious matters anarchy and confusion which lead unconsciously to pantheism and atheism.

BIBLIOGRAPHY

See under *experience, religious.*

septenary, sacramental. See *sacraments, number of.*

"sigillum sacramentale." See *seal of confession.*

sign. An intermediary between the thing known and the cognitive faculty. A sign manifests something distinct from itself either because it is the perfect image of that thing (e.g., a photograph, a *species expressa*), in which case it is called *formal sign,* or because it is so intimately connected with the thing signified as to recall it spontaneously, in which case it is called *instrumental sign.* The bond between the thing signified and the instrumental sign may have its foundation either in nature, e.g., smoke with respect to fire (*natural sign*), or in the human will, e.g., a flag with respect to the country (*conventional sign*), or, finally, in both, e.g., the eagle by the daring of his flight has a special aptitude to signify acuteness of intellect, but that, in a concrete case, the eagle signifies St. John the Evangelist depends on the will of the Church, which has chosen this symbol (*mixed sign*), following a prophetic vision of Ezechiel. All our life with its multiple social relations is based on signs and symbols; words, which are the most important factor in human fellowship, are purely conventional signs. Consequently, the Founder of the perfect religion, which is an elevation and orientation of our life to God, could not neglect this element. In fact, our Lord instituted seven sacramental signs, which not only recall to mind the most wonderful realities of the supernatural order (grace, the character, etc.), but ingraft them with divine efficacy on the soul of the believer (see *sacraments, nature of*).

The Church, faithful imitator of her divine Founder, has surrounded the seven sacraments with many other holy symbols (the *sacramentals*) and has ornamented the ecclesiastical liturgy with multiple rites which help the Christian to understand and, as it were, to experience the realities sealed up in the invisible world of grace.

BIBLIOGRAPHY

St. Thomas, *Summa Theol.*, III, q. 60. Doronzo, *De sacramentis in genere* (Milwaukee, 1946), Index Analyticus: "Signum." Gredt, *Elementa Philosophiae Aristotelico-Thomisticae,* Vol. 1 (Freiburg i.-Br., 1931), n. 9. Maritain, *Les degrés du savior* (Paris, 1932), p. 769; *L'esprit dans sa condition charnelle* (Paris, 1939), pp. 80–89.

simplicity of God. Simple, antonym of composite, excludes all composition (physical, metaphysical, substantial, accidental, logical). There is a *negative* simplicity, like that of the mathematical point, which involves rather poverty and imperfection, and there is also a *positive* simplicity, which means perfection, like that of a spirit.

The IV Lateran Council and the Vatican Council define that the divine essence is *absolutely simple* (*DB,* 428, 1782), coherently with revelation which represents God as purest Spirit and as Being Itself (see *essence, divine*).

The Scholastics demonstrate scientifically the absolute simplicity of God by an argumentation *ab absurdo:* Every composite is posterior to and dependent on its parts; it is necessarily caused, because its parts would not unite into the whole without the influence of an extrinsic cause; it is finite, because its various parts limit each other reciprocally in order to be distinct. Now to be dependent, caused, finite is obviously repugnant to the nature of the supreme Being. Therefore God is altogether simple, namely: (1) In God there can be no distinction between essence and existence, otherwise existence would be extrinsic to His essence and, therefore, caused, and His essence would be a potency, as it were, with respect to the existential act (which is inconsistent with God, Pure Act); God Himself would then be a Being by participation and not the very self-subsisting Being. (2) Likewise, in God there can be no real distinction, and thus no composition between nature and person, otherwise His nature would be a formal part of His person, i.e., would be finite, no longer divine. (3) Nor can there be accidental composition in God, for no further determination can be made to the infinite and most perfect substance of God. Every accident is perfective of the subject in which it inheres. Therefore, God is simple in the most absolute way; however, in His most simple Being and Pure Act all perfections are implicitly contained.

Simplicity belongs, in some degree, to all spiritual beings, like the human soul (*q.v.*).

BIBLIOGRAPHY

St. Thomas, *Summa Theol.*, I, q. 3. Garrigou-Lagrange, *God*, trans. Rose (St. Louis), pp. 1047–1948. Parente, *De Deo Uno* (Rome, 1938), p. 177 ff. Pohle-Preuss, *Dogmatic Theology*, I *God: Knowability, Essence, Attributes* (St. Louis, 1946), pp. 202–212. Sertillanges, *St. Thomas d'Aquin*, Vol. 2 (Paris, 1925), p. 166.

sin, original. The sin committed by our first parents, as is narrated in Holy Scripture (Gen. 2 f.). God enriched Adam and Eve with gifts (see *innocence; integrity*) and placed them in the earthly paradise, full of every material good. He wanted from His creatures a very simple proof of fidelity, a test very easy to pass: He forbade them to eat of the fruit of the "tree of knowledge of good and evil," threatening most severe punishment if they disobeyed. Satan, under the form of a serpent, tempted Eve who, enticed by his words, picked the fruit and tasted of it. She, in turn, handed it to her husband who, to please her, did not hesitate to eat of it, despite the divine prohibition. Immediately guilt darkened their minds and upset the harmony of their whole being. They felt their senses rebel and became ashamed of their nakedness, trying to flee from God by hiding behind the trees. God, as He had warned, exacted the penalties of the first sin and expelled the guilty from paradise, who inaugurate for themselves and all humanity after them the unending journey of suffering, miseries, and tribulations.

Holy Scripture often recalls this tragic event: "From the woman came the beginning of sin, and by her we all die" (Ecclus. 25:33); "By the offense of one, many died. . . . By the disobedience of one man, many were made sinners" (Rom. 5:15, 19). St. John recalls the role of the devil: "He was a murderer from the beginning" (John 8:44). Tradition is unanimous on this doctrine. Some traces of the event are found in the religious mythologies of the pagan world, which, however, appear as deformations in comparison with the dignity and the dramatic sobriety of the biblical narrative.

The rationalists deny the historicity of the sacred narrative, alleging incongruities or absurdities of detail (an apple the cause of such ruin, a serpent speaking to the woman, etc.). Our exegetes have answered these objections adequately: (*a*) God, after so great generosity, had a right to impose a test; (*b*) in His infinite goodness, He is satisfied with a very light one; (*c*) He manifests clearly His precept and its sanctions; (*d*) the sin of our first parents *materially* was the eaten fruit, but *formally* was pride and rebellion against God, for the devil suggests to Eve that if they eat of the fruit they will not die but will become similar to God; Adam prefers his wife to God, and both Eve and he disobey through their proud desire of becoming gods. Their sin thus became grave, so much more so because they were rich in spiritual light and strength, thus having no excuse, no pretext to adduce in attenuation of their guilt, which was pure malice. Besides, if divine justice struck, and rightly so, divine mercy and goodness intervened immediately with the promise of the Redeemer who will crush the evil serpent.

Consequences of original sin in the first parents themselves are: (*a*) privation of both *supernatural* gifts (*grace* and the *infused virtues*) and of *preternatural* gifts (*integrity*); (*b*) state of sin with accompanying guilt and stain (see *sin, personal*); (*c*) debt of eternal punishment; (*d*) wounding of nature, on account of which the passions rise in rebellion against reason, hamper the free exercise of the will, and make good difficult.

The Church has defined (Council of Trent, sess. 5, *DB*, 788) that Adam's whole being through sin was *in deterius commutatum* ("changed for the worse"); but she condemned Lutheranism (*q.v.*), which maintains the intrinsic corruption and incurability of nature after original sin (*DB*, 792 and 815 ff.). See *transmission of original sin.*

BIBLIOGRAPHY

St. Thomas, *Summa Theol.*, II–II, qq. 164–165. Ceuppens, *De historia primaeva* (Rome, 1934). Gaudel, "Péché originel," *DTC*. Harent, "Original Sin," *CE*. Hetzenauer, *Theologia biblica* (Freiburg i.-Br., 1908). Pohle-Preuss, *Dogmatic Theology*, III *God: Author of Nature and the Supernatural* (St. Louis, 1946), pp. 232–307. Scheeben, *The Mysteries of Christianity*, trans. Vollert (St. Louis, 1946), pp. 237–310. *The Teaching of the Catholic Church*, ed. Smith, 2 vols. (New York, 1949), pp. 320–359. Verrièle, *Le surnaturel en nous et le péché originel* (Paris, 1932).

sin, personal. A willful transgression of God's law. More technically it may be defined: Aversion from God, the last End, by a voluntary adhesion to a finite good. Aversion (i.e., turning away) from God is the *formal* element of sin, while the disorderly adhesion to the created good (in which such aversion is implicit) is the *material* element.

Certain moralists contrived a distinction between *theological* and *philosophical* sin: the former would include the knowledge of God and His law and, therefore, the consciousness of offending the Creator; the latter would be an act morally evil in itself, but not offensive to God, in the case that the sinner does not know God and His law. The Church has condemned this opinion (*DB*, 1290); he who sins, indeed, feels that he acts against a law which re-echoes from the depths of his inner being, independently of any human influence, and in such law there is always an implicit knowledge of a supreme Legislator, who is God Himself. The infraction of the law is, therefore, a conscious offense against God, and sin is necessarily theological.

Sin is *personal*, if it is committed voluntarily by the individual; it is *original*, if it belongs to the human race, and therefore, is called also *sin of nature* (see *sin, original*). Moreover, the *act* of sin is distinguished from the *state* of sin that follows as its consequence, and which is usually called *habitual* sin. In this last, two aspects are considered: the *reatus culpae* (guiltiness) and the *macula peccati* (stain of sin). The *reatus culpae* is the state of aversion from God caused by the sinful act; the *macula peccati* is the privation of sanctifying grace, light and beauty of the soul. In the present order, aversion from God always coincides with privation of grace, and so, *in concreto*, the *reatus* and the *macula* are one and the same thing.

Willfulness is an essential element of sin: it must be present in the sinful act. The sinful state, on the contrary, is voluntary on account of the willfulness of the act from which it stems. Finally, it should be noted that the real sin is the *mortal* sin, which kills the soul by severing it from God; *venial* sin is called sin by *analogy*, because it does not imply aversion from the ultimate end, but only a slackening in its pursuit.

BIBLIOGRAPHY

St. Thomas, *Summa Theol.*, I–II, qq. 71–89. Billot, *De personali et originali peccato* (Rome, 1925). Manning, *Sin and Its Consequences* (New York, 1904). O'Neil, "Sin," *CE*. Sharpe, *Evil, Its Nature and Cause* (London, 1906). Scheeben, *The Mysteries of Christianity*, trans. Vollert (St. Louis, 1946), pp. 243–272. *The Teaching of the Catholic Church*, ed. Smith, 2 vols. (New York, 1949), pp. 925–952.

skepticism (Gr. σκέπτομαι — I look, I consider). A doctrine and a tendency which subjects to discussion and rejects partially or entirely the objective value of human knowledge and, therefore, its certainty. Skepticism had its origin with the Sophists, who for oratorical and political reasons taught how to demonstrate, by specious argumentation, the truth of a thesis, and at once, by the same device, the truth of its antithesis. Socrates fought energetically against these disturbers of the mind by stressing the value of universal concepts, which are a solid basis of truth and certainty. But the founder of skepticism as a system of universal doubt was Pyrrho of Elis († 275 B.C.): from him skepticism took the name *Pyrrhonism* in opposition to Stoic dogmatism. The Platonists, who depreciated experimental knowledge, reducing it to the rank of mere opinion, underwent skeptic influence of the middle and the new academies (Arcesilaus, † 241 B.C., and Carneades, † 126 B.C.). But systematic skepticism had forceful disciples in two philosophers, Enesidemus of Crete († A.D. 130) and Sextus Empiricus (second half of the second century A.D.), who wrote the famous *Hypothiposes* in defense of the Pyrrhonian principles.

Skepticism crops out here and there with its corrosive doubt throughout the centuries, as in the teaching of Descartes (*methodical doubt*), in the phenomenalistic system, and also in Kantianism (*q.v.*), which compromised the objective value of knowledge, denying to reason the capacity of reaching the *noumenon,* i.e., the thing in itself. All anti-intellectualistic systems are tainted with skepticism: thus the fideism of Jacobi, the pessimistic voluntarism of Schopenhauer, the pragmatism of James.

Skepticism has a sort of original sin which vitiates its entire structure: it doubts the capacity of reason to attain truth and certainty and rejects the value of knowledge. The logical result of this is that no truth or theory is certain and sure, even that of the skeptics! The human intellect, made naturally for truth as the eye is made for light, can be mistaken sometimes, *per accidens,* but not always, *per se,* otherwise nature would be an absurdity. Modern philosophy which, from Descartes to Kant, has attacked the dignity of nature and the natural capacities of the human mind, has fallen into a skeptic maze, which idealism unsuccessfully has tried to overcome. The one remedy is the moderate realism of Christian philosophy which, together with the best Greek philosophy, constructs science and metaphysics on the postulate of a natural relationship or equation between being and thought, nature and mind.

BIBLIOGRAPHY

Brochard, *Les sceptiques grecs* (Paris, 1923). Maccoll, *Greek Sceptics from Pyrro to Sextus* (London-Cambridge, 1869). Mercier, *Critériologie générale* (Louvain, 1926). Mivart, *On Truth* (London, 1889). Owen, *Evening With the Skeptics,* 4 vols. (London, 1881); *The Skeptics of the French Renaissance* (London, 1893); *The Skeptics of the Italian Renaissance* (London, 1893). Walker, "Scepticism," *CE.*

solidarity. See *Mystical Body; satisfaction of Christ.*

Son. The proper name of the Second Person of the Holy Trinity, derived from the very nature of the first procession (*q.v.*), which is a true spiritual generation (see *Only-Begotten*).

Also the name *Word* (*q.v.*) belongs properly to the Son, because He is the term of the divine intellection. It should be noted that intellection, as well as volition, is common to the three Persons, who know by virtue of the one and unique intellective act which is identical with the divine essence. But only the Father, by understanding, says the Word (cf. St. Thomas, *Summa Theol.,* I, q. 34, a. 1, ad 3).

In addition, the Son is called *Image,* according to the testimony of St. Paul: "Who is the image of the invisible God" (Col. 1:15). The reason for this title lies in the peculiar character of the mental word, term of intellection; in fact, the word is the faithful image of what the intellect has conceived in itself and assimilated. In the Word, the Father contemplates, as in a living likeness, Himself, the whole divine nature and through it all created and creatible nature. Jesus Christ calls Himself Son of God, in the proper sense, and also Son of Man, a Messianic expression which harks back to Daniel.

BIBLIOGRAPHY

St. Thomas, *Summa Theol.,* I, qq. 34–35. Hugon, *Le mystère de la très Sainte Trinité* (Paris, 1930), p. 192 ff. Joyce, "Trinity," *CE.* Pohle-Preuss, *Dogmatic Theology,* II *The Divine Trinity* (St. Louis, 1946), pp. 49–96. Scheeben, *The Mysteries of Christianity,* trans. Vollert (St. Louis, 1946), pp. 87–95.

See under *Logos; Word.*

Sophronius. See "Outline of the History of Dogmatic Theology" (p. 302); *Monothelitism.*

soteriology (Gr. σωτηρία — salvation, redemption). The doctrine of the spiritual salvation of man. The history of religions and of religious philosophies brings out two psychological elements, which are more or less dominant in all systems: the consciousness of *sin* and the yearning for *liberation.* From the brokenhearted accents of the most ancient penitential hymns of *Babylon* to the pessimistic meditations of *Buddha* on the evils of human life and the necessity of averting them; from the suggestive pages of Plato (cf. the *Phaedon*) on the emancipative character of death to the spiritual drama of the initiated in the *Mysteries* of Dionysia, Isis, and Mithra, paganism is pervaded by the consciousness of sin and the desire to be healed from it. Hence the expiatory character of the sacrifices (see *expiation*). These sentiments are more vivid and pure in the books of the Old Testament, especially in the prophecy of *Isaias,* which speaks of a mysterious Servant of Jahweh, who by his sufferings and his immolation will free men from the slavery of sin (Ch. 53).

These obscure aspirations, disseminated in the consciousness of the peoples, are a providential preparation for Christianity, which is essentially a message of salvation, a soteriology in act. This soteriology is centered in Christ; the very name of Jesus in Hebrew means *Saviour,* and the Gospel explains the reason why this name was given to Him by the angel: "Thou shalt call his name Jesus. For he shall save his people from their sins" (Matt. 1:21). The Precursor of Jesus prepared the way by preaching *penance* (Matt. 3:2). Jesus Himself declared He had come into the world to give His life as the price of redemption for men (Matt. 20:28; Mark 10:45); and in the Last Supper He celebrated the Eucharistic Sacrifice of His body and of His blood poured forth unto the remission of sins. These motifs of the Synoptics return with greater vividness in St. John, who calls Jesus the "propitiation" for the sins of the whole world (1 John 2:2).

St. Paul, especially, developed this soteriological doctrine. The rationalists, with evident exaggeration, say that he is the creator of it. Certainly St. Paul, who had experienced in himself the dramatic change from the death of sin to the life of grace, speaks with incomparable expressions of the interior torment of man, slave of guilt and of the passions of corrupt nature, and then of the one way of liberation and salvation which is in Christ the Redeemer by His bloody immolation. It is necessary to die and rise with Him in order to live the new life in Him and to win back the freedom of sons of God (cf. Rom. 6:4; 7:15 ff.; 8:34 ff.; Gal. 2:19 ff.; Col. 1:20; Eph. 5:2; Heb. 9:12 ff., etc.).

Genuine Christian soteriology has been deformed and mutilated by the Protestants, the rationalists, and the modernists (see *Redemption*). The soteriological problem comes to the surface of modern life in that sense of unrest and anguish which dominates in many sectors of tired and confused modern thought.

BIBLIOGRAPHY

HUBY, *Christus* (Paris, 1912). OTTEN, *A Manual of History of Dogmas,* Vol. 2 (St. Louis, 1915), pp. 196–213. POHLE-PREUSS, *Dogmatic Theology,* V *Soteriology* (St. Louis, 1945). PRAT, *The Theology of St. Paul,* trans. Stoddard, Vol. 2 (Westminster, 1927). See on p. 503 Analytical Summary: "The Work of Redemption."

See under *Redemption; satisfaction of Christ.*

Soto. See "Outline of the History of Dogmatic Theology" (p. 303).

soul. A spiritual substance which, together with the body, constitutes man. Sound philosophical systems have always admitted the existence, the spirituality and the immortality of the human soul, endowed with the faculties of intelligence and will, and their proper spiritual operations which are the noblest among human acts and which manifest the specific nature of man. This philosophical doctrine is amply confirmed and enriched by the combined lights of revelation and theology.

1. *Holy Scripture.* (*a*) The soul is *created* by God and was directly infused in the body of Adam: "And the Lord God formed man of the slime of the earth: and breathed into his face the breath of life, and man became a living soul" (Gen. 2:7). (*b*) In his soul man resembles God and reflects His image in a particular manner (Gen. 1:6, 26); such affirmation implies that the soul is not something material (cf. Eccles. 12:7). (*c*) The soul is *immortal;* the Gospel gives ample testimony to this truth (cf. Matt. 10:28); as regards the Old Testament, see particularly Wisdom 2:23; 3:1, 4, 10; Psalms 48:15–16, etc. (*d*) From these texts is also proved that the soul is the formal element of man, the vital and rational principle on account of which man is man, i.e., a living animal specifically distinct from the brutes.

2. *Tradition* generally repeats and develops the written revelation concerning the nature and properties of the soul. However, Tertullian proposes the strange theory of a *corporeal traducianism* (*q.v.*), teaching that the soul of the child is generated through the seed of its parents. Later St. Augustine, although rejecting Tertullian's opinion, seemed to lean toward a *spiritual traducianism* (the soul of the child generated by the soul of its parents, as light from light), in order to expound more efficaciously against the Pelagians (see *Pelagianism*) the transmission of original sin. However, the holy Doctor did not exclude *creationism,* i.e., the creation and immediate infusion of the individual souls into their bodies.

Scholastic theologians discussed more subtle questions, for example: in what moment does God infuse the soul (modern theologians commonly answer: in the very first moment of fecundation). More important is the question of the unity of the soul and of its nature as the substantial form of the body. Plato denied the substantial union of the soul with the body and divided the soul itself into three elements (trichotomy). Some rare traces of such theory is found also among Scholastic doctors. The Franciscan, Peter John Olivi, distinguishing in the soul the essence and its three elements or grades (the rational, the sensitive, and the vegetative), maintained that only the last two (the sensitive and the vegetative) inform the body: the soul, in so far as it is rational, is united substantially with the body (composing with it one sole individual), but not formally. The Council of Vienne condemned this opinion and defined that the rational soul is the immediate substantial form of the body (*DB*, 481).

The Scotists still maintain that, besides the principal substantial form which is the soul itself, the body has a secondary corporeal form (*forma corporeitatis*). The Thomists, on the contrary, in full concordance with the doctrine of the Church, teach that the rational soul is the only substantial form which constitutes man, as man, as animal, as living being, as body, as substance, and as being (see *immortality*).

BIBLIOGRAPHY

St. Thomas, *Summa Theol.*, I, qq. 75–77; *Quaestiones de Anima*. Boyer, *De Deo Creante et Elevante* (Rome, 1940), p. 122 ff. Driscoll, *Christian Philosophy, The Soul* (New York, 1898). Maher, Boland, "Soul," *CE*. Mercier, *Psychologie*, Vol. 2 (Louvain, 1928), p. 347 ff.

Spirit, Holy. See *Holy Ghost.*

spiritism. A doctrinal and practical system which claims to put living men in communication with the spirits of the other world. The evocation of the dead and of the spirits of the other world was in practice among the ancients, but in the past century as a consequence of a strange episode that happened in the Fox family at Hydesville in the United States (1847), evocation of, and communication with, spirits became a spreading fashion and was systemized under the specious name of spiritism to the point of becoming a new religion. Today spiritism is a very complex and garbled affair by reason of the confused superimposition of numerous elements added to the simple experiences of the Fox sisters. No longer merely the moving tables with typtology (tap language), but mysterious writings, luminous phenomena, levitation, formation of images and their materialization, divination, etc., together with the various theories of magnetism, hypnotism, somnambulism, telepathy, perispirit, od, reincarnation, etc., have been added in an effort to give a scientific character to phenomena which on account of their very extravagance provoke suspicion and distrust. The principal actor in spiritism is the *medium,* connecting link between the spirits and the mortals. Famous mediums were Florence Cook, who worked with the scientist Crookes, and Eusapia Palladino. It is proved that fraud and imposture have played a great role in spiritistic phenomena; to the fraud of the mediums should be added the credulity and suggestibility of the public. There remains, however, a nucleus of real facts, which can be explained by natural forces (magnetism, muscular vibration, telepathy).

From a moral viewpoint, spiritism often presents censurable aspects, not to mention the disorientation of conscience and the loss of mental balance determined by its frequent practice. From a theological viewpoint, the alleged communication with the dead and the spirits, not to mention the frauds of spiritism, cannot be sustained. In the Bible and in Christian hagiography we come across cases of deceased persons, of angels, and of demons appearing to the living to warn, help, tempt, or punish them. Such communications, however, always take place in a sober atmosphere, in which rules the will of God who arranges or permits them. In spiritism, on the contrary, we find a spectacle of exhibitionism, often grotesque, which is repugnant to the sanctity of God and to the dignity of the angels and the disincarnate spirits. There remains only the *possibility* of diabolical intervention for those phenomena which could not be given a natural explanation.

From this we easily understand why the Church, abstaining from any statements on the nature of the various phenomena, allows, within the limits of prudence, the use of magnetism and hypnotism, while it opposes any participation whatsoever in spiritistic performances on account of their superstitious character and the dangers to which the faithful may be exposed as regards faith and morals. (Cf. Decree of the Holy Office, April 24, 1917, *AAS,* 1917, June 1, p. 268.)

BIBLIOGRAPHY

CAPRON, *Modern Spiritualism* (Boston, 1855). CARRINGTON, *The Physical Phenomena of Spiritualism* (Boston, 1907). DE HEREDIA, *Spiritism and Common Sense* (New York, 1922). GEARON, *Lo spiritismo et il suo fallimento* (Turin, 1934). PACE, "Spiritism," *CE.* RAUPERT, *Modern Spiritism* (London, 1904). ROURE, *Le Spiritisme d'aujourd'hui et d'hier* (Paris, 1923); "Spiritisme," *DTC;* "Spiritisme," *DA.* WALLACE, *Miracles and Modern Spiritualism* (London, 1877).

State and Church. The concept of State is complex and, therefore, the term is not always used in the same sense: some understand by it rather the authority, the power, the government; others, rather the social organism, the nation. We may say that the State consists of the authority, as the *formal* element, and of the multitude, as the *material* element. From this we can form an approximate definition of the State as being a stable union of families and of individuals in a determined territory, under the same authority, for the purpose of procuring the common good. The concept of *nation* includes unity of race and history, which is not a necessary element of the politically constituted State. Varied and contradictory are the opinions about the origin of the State as a civil society and about the nature of the State as a supreme authority.

1. *Contractualism* (Hobbes, Rousseau): Civil society originates from a contract or convention of primitive men who, motivated by the desire of eliminating individual strife and disorders, have renounced the fullness of their private liberty by subjecting themselves to a "general will" personified in the sovereign State. This conception is phantastic and without historical foundation.

2. *Absolutism:* The State is all, and the individual is for the State. This concept is dominant in paganism, and in various forms was adhered to by Plato and Aristotle. But absolutism has gained strength in modern times through the idealistic theories of Hegel and his followers, who consider the State as something divine, as a religion, as an absolute will, which absorbs the life and liberty of the human person: such is State worship with a pantheistic background, which has been used in support of totalitarian, despotic regimes of our time. Theories of this kind, which represent a retrogression to abandoned pagan conceptions, are refuted, if not otherwise, by their evil consequences.

3. *Liberalism* (*q.v.*): In harmony with the principles of the French Revolution, liberalism affirms the sovereignty of the *people* and the perfect equality of citizens in the exercise of their proper rights. The State (the authority) is a delegate of the people, with the function of maintaining public order and of regulating by legislation the harmony and the equilibrium of the individual freedoms. This is the theory of the *"gendarme state,"* to which Kant also contributed, by separating ethics and law, leaving the former to the autonomy of individual reason, and the latter to the protection, rather *negative* than *posi-*

tive, of the State. The liberal State is agnostic not only politically and economically, but also with reference to the problem of religion and to the Church.

4. *Positivism* (*q.v.*): Basing itself on evolutionistic theories, positivism explains the origin and the nature of the State after the fashion of the natural development of an organism, without the influence of immutable principles or of free will, but according to a deterministic law.

These and other theories, although having some true points, sin by way of exaggeration: they concede too much either to nature, or to the human will, or to the authority of the State, or to the individual. But their gravest fault is absolutism, which makes of the State an idol to which the sacred personality of man must be immolated. It seems strange that democratic trends, such as socialism, are inspired also by this same concept, attributing to the State direct and immediate interference in the interest and in the private life of the individuals.

With respect to the problem of religion, all these theories are either deficient or erroneous, because they suggest either the *disinterestedness* of the State (liberalism), or the absorption of religion in the very life of the State declared to be divine, ethical, religious (idealistic absolutism), or the open persecution and elimination of every positive religion, of the Catholic Church especially (atheistic communism and socialism). Against such doctrines, which bear poisonous fruits in the politico-social field, stands the Christian doctrine with its classical traditions, with its human and divine principles, drawn from reason and revelation. Recently, this doctrine has been summarized, illustrated, and proclaimed by Leo XIII, especially in the encyclicals *Immortale Dei, Libertas,* and *Rerum Novarum;* by Pius XI in his *Quadragesimo Anno;* and by Pius XII in various allocutions. From these and other documents of the ecclesiastical *magisterium* we can draw the following fundamental outline of Christian doctrine with respect to civil society, the State, and the relations of the State with the Church:

1. Society, like the family unit, has a natural origin, because man is social by nature (Aristotle) and insufficient unto himself. He needs the organized help of his fellows to be able to develop his aptitudes and to attain his end. Since it is natural, society has God Himself as its Author.

2. The end of society and of the State is the *common good* of the temporal order, distinct from and superior to the private good. The pursuit of this end requires *juridical protection,* which defends rights and assures justice in the relations of subjects among themselves, and *positive assistance* or help to all kinds of private initiative: economic, industrial, cultural, etc. In pursuing the common good, the State cannot impede, but must, on the contrary, facilitate for citizens the attainment of the *supernatural* end itself (proper to religious society), to which all men are destined.

3. The authority of the State comes from God; the people by their will, explicit or implicit, have only the function of designating the person or the subject of the authority.

4. In view of the objective subordination of the temporal end of man to his supernatural end, it is evident that the Church, as a religious society instituted by God precisely for the supernatural end, cannot be dependent on the State. The State, on the contrary, must be *indirectly* subordinate to the Church, by avoiding interference in spiritual things concerning the Church and also by avoiding such legislation and action in temporal matters which would im-

pede in any way the exercise of religious authority over the faithful, respecting in the faithful the right of religious freedom.

5. The State has the duty of recognizing and professing religion, because the State, like the family and the individual, derives from and depends on God. Consequently, the State, in strict logic and in strict justice, has the obligation of defending the Catholic Church and of prohibiting other religious cults. Only as a prudential measure may it tolerate them.

6. In order to avoid harmful conflicts with a State which does not follow these principles, the Church negotiates a *concordat,* which is a bilateral agreement on rights and duties, reservation always being made of the principle of the superiority of the Church.

BIBLIOGRAPHY

ANTOINE, "Etat," *DA.* BILLOT, *De Ecclesia Christi,* Vol. 2, "De habitudine Ecclesiae ad civilem potestatem" (Rome, 1927). DAUSON, *Religion and the Modern State* (New York, 1938). LATTEY, "Etat (Culte d')," *DA.* MACKSEY, "State and Church," *CE.* ODDONE, *La costituzione sociale della Chiesa e le sue relazioni con lo Stato* (Milan, 1932). STURZO, *L'Eglise et l'Etat* (Paris, 1937). *The Teaching of the Catholic Church,* ed. Smith, 2 vols. (New York, 1949), pp. 726–730. VALTON, "Etat," *DTC.*

See under *vicar of Christ.*

Suarez. See "Outline of the History of Dogmatic Theology" (p. 303).

subconsciousness. A term brought into current use in the second half of the past century, especially by Myers, who believed he discovered (1886) outside the periphery of human consciousness a psychological substratum, vague and obscure in itself, but rich in perceptive and emotive resources, which he called precisely subconsciousness. W. James adopted the theory and applied it to religious experience (*q.v.*). According to these authors, a "conscious ego" exists in us, clear and normal, which is our ordinary personality; but in the depths of our mind there is hidden a *"subconscious* ego," called also *subliminal,* in which are elaborated intuitions and vague sentiments unknown to us, but which gradually group themselves, merge, and suddenly erupt into the zone of the "conscious ego," where they determine new aspirations, new directive ideas, a new life. In the obscure, subliminal consciousness is elaborated especially the sentiment of the divine, which is the root and source of religion. The real revelation is not in the Sacred Books, does not come from the outside, but springs up from the depths of the subconscious self. The *magisterium* of the Church takes up such religious sentiments of the collective consciousness and formulates them into dogmas, which are not immutable truths but provisional expressions, of a practical-symbolic nature, of religious experience (see *dogma; symbolism; pragmatism*).

This theory of James, through Le Roy, has passed into modernism (*q.v.*), upsetting the concept of revelation, of the Church, and of the whole Christian religion.

In Protestant circles, more precisely in the Anglican theology, the theory of the subconscious has been applied to Christology, to explain the personality of the Man-God. According to one of the foremost representatives of that theology, W. Sanday (*Christology, Ancient and Modern,* 1910; *Personality in Christ and in Ourselves,* 1911), Christ was a perfect man in whose subliminal conscience, however, there developed a sentiment of union with the Word of God, which gradually passed into His clear consciousness, where it determined the persuasion of a personal fusion between Christ the Man and the Son of God. Christian consciousness has translated this experience and sentiment of Jesus into the dogma of the hypostatic union (*q.v.*).

All this theory of the subconscious, founded on an exaggeration and arbitrary interpretation of obscure sentiments (which can be given a much simpler explanation), is in conflict with sound psychology, which asserts a hierarchy and gradation in the faculties of the spirit (intellect, will, sensibility); it is also unacceptable from a religious standpoint, because it perverts the sense of revelation and dogma by eliminating the historical value of Christianity, and because, in Christology, it tends to a Nestorian solution of the personality of Christ (see *Nestorianism*).

BIBLIOGRAPHY

Bois, *La valeur de l'expérience religieuse* (Paris, 1908). Dehove, "Subconscient et Inconscient," *DA*. Johnson, *Anglicanism in Transition* (London, 1938). Michelet, "Religion," *DA*, col. 899 ff. Myers, *Human Personality* (1905).

subdiaconate (Gr. ὑποδιάκονος — under-servant). The lowest of the major orders (see *orders, holy*). The subdeacon, as his name indicates, is essentially the servant of the deacon, whom he helps in his multiple duties, which at present are reduced to pouring the water in the chalice, singing the epistle, assisting at the altar by presenting the chalice and paten, washing the corporal and the other sacred linens.

The most ancient documents which speak of this order are the epistolary of St. Cyprian and the letter of Pope Cornelius to Fabius of Antioch (A.D. 261).

At Rome there were seven subdeacons, as there were seven deacons. Afterward, there is mention of the obligations of chastity and of the recital of the *Breviary* as annexed to this office, which only at the end of the twelfth century was placed among the major orders in the Western Church. In the Eastern Churches it is still considered as a minor order.

BIBLIOGRAPHY

St. Thomas, *Summa Theol.*, III, *Suppl.*, q. 37, a. 2. Fanning, "Subdeacon," *CE*. Kurtscheid, *Historia Iuris Canonici*, Vol. 1 (Rome, 1941). Taunton, *The Law of the Church* (London, 1906). Tixeront, *Holy Orders and Ordinations*, trans. Raemers (St. Louis).

See under *orders, holy*.

subjectivism. The tendency to exaggerate the value of the knowing subject to the point of absorbing objective reality in him. Subjectivism has been characteristic of modern philosophy since the time of Descartes. Descartes, by his famous *Cogito, ergo sum* ("I think, therefore I am"), began to subordinate being to thought, inverting the order followed by the Aristotelian-Thomistic philosophy which defines truth as an adequation of the intellect to the thing, and subordinates thought to being. Even in the zone of sense knowledge Descartes began to deny the objectivity of certain sensations. English empiricism pushed similar denials (Locke) to the point of eliminating the reality of matter (Berkeley) and of reducing all reality to a flux of subjective sensations (phenomenalism of Hume). Kant (see *Kantianism*) was able to save only a phenomenal reality, sacrificing the objective reality of the substance of things (the *noumenon*). Idealism (*q.v.*) did the rest, rejecting all reality outside of the thinking subject (Fichte, Schelling) and of the idea (Hegel) or the act of thinking (Gentile).

Thus was finally affirmed the absolute immanence of the object in the subject, denying all transcendence, i.e., all reality extraneous to thought and outside of it. Nowadays a reaction has begun against this subjective immanentism by a return to that moderate realism, which is proper to the Christian philosophy.

BIBLIOGRAPHY

See under *idealism; immanentism.*

subordinationists. Heretics of the second and third centuries who prepared the way for Arianism (*q.v.*) by teaching that the Word is not God in the proper sense, but rather a most excellent creature intermediate between God and the world (cf. Demiurge of the Platonists and the Aeons of the Gnostics). The Word is, therefore, subordinate to the true God. The consequence of subordinationism is the denial of the divinity of Jesus Christ, held to be not the natural but only the *adoptive* Son of God (see *adoptionism*). At the end of the second century Theodotus the Elder at Rome, and Paul of Samosata, at Antioch in the third century, spread subordinationism and adoptionism. Both were condemned by the Church. Subordinationism passed to Arius through Lucian of Antioch.

In the first-century apologists (Justin, Athenagoras, Tatian, Origen, and especially Tertullian), there are some phrases which suggest subordinationism (Word — God in the second place, *minister* of God in creation, etc.). But, after thorough study of the texts and their context, the apparent difficulty vanishes: these writers were the first to attempt to illustrate with human language the relationships of the divine Persons, and they hazarded various phrases, somewhat unlucky and ambiguous, in attempting to express the procession of the Word from the Father. The defect is only in the words, which may be interpreted benignly, in view of the general doctrine of these apologists, which is sound and affirms substantially the equality of the three Persons.

BIBLIOGRAPHY

CAYRÉ, *Manual of Patrology,* trans. Howitt, Vol. 1 (Paris, Tournai, Rome, 1936) (cf. on p. 729, "Doctrinal Index," n. 45). PARENTE, *De Deo Trino* (Rome, 1938), pp. 36 ff., 69. TIXERONT, *History of Dogmas,* trans. H.L.B., Vol. 1 (St. Louis, 1910) (cf. Index: "Subordinationism").

subsistence. See *hypostatic union.*

substance (Lat. *substantia,* Gr. ὑπόστασις — that which is underneath, a quasi-substratum). In the scholastic language it is defined: that which of its nature can exist in itself and does not require a subject of inhesion in order to exist. It is opposed to accident, which cannot naturally exist unless in a subject that sustains it, like the color on the wall. Substance, thus understood, and accident are the supreme categories or predicaments that divide real being: everything that exists is either substance or accident. It is necessary to distinguish created substance, which is that defined above, from the uncreated substance (God), which exists not only *in se* (in itself) and *per se* (by itself), but also *a se* (from itself, as it were, not from another). Substance is not the object of the senses, as are accidents, but of the intellect, nor by this fact is it less real than accidents. Sensism, which is the basis of empiricism (*q.v.*) and of phenomenalism, has induced the negation of the substance of things (Locke, Hume). Along with this current go the positivists (*q.v.*) and the so-called actualists, who reduce substance either to the series of events or phenomena or to the very activity of things (Taine, Ribot, Paulsen, Huxley). Against such negation it suffices to appeal to the testimony of consciousness, which attests the permanence of one same subject, of one same "ego," notwithstanding the continuous succession of mutations and phenomena. Catholic doctrine stands for the reality of substance, really distinct from its accidents, on which basis it illustrates the mystery of *transubstantiation* (*q.v.*), by which the substances of bread and of wine are converted into the body and the blood of our Lord, while the accidents or species of the one and the other consecrated element remain intact. Substance may be taken also in the sense of essence of the thing (that by which the thing is constituted in its species), being then divided into *first* and *second.* First substance (Aristotle: οὐσία πρώτη) is that which is individuated and subsisting in its physical reality, e.g., John; second substance (οὐσία δευτέρα) is the specific abstract essence of the individual subject, which is attributed to all the individuals of the same species, e.g., humanity, common to all men.

First substance coincides, in rational beings, with person (*q.v*). In man there are two substances, one material (the body), the other spiritual (the soul), completing each other and forming together one composite substance or essence, to which the unique act of being gives a profound unity. In God there is only one and most simple substance, in which, however, subsist three Persons, constituted by three distinct relations (see *Trinity*).

BIBLIOGRAPHY

Boyer, *Cursus Philosophiae,* Vol. 1 (Paris, 1936), p. 346 ff. Jolivet, *La notion de substance* (Paris, 1929). De Munnynck, "Substance," *CE.* Walker, *Theories of Knowledge* (New York, 1910).

suffering. Like all things that are most simple and well known, it is difficult to adequately define suffering. It may, however, be described by opposing it to joy and pleasure. St. Thomas proposes a profound concept of pleasure, deriving it from the *perfect activity* of being as from its proper cause. Suffering, therefore, depends on a disorder of activity (impediment, deficiency, or excess of action). Like pleasure, suffering is *sensible* or *spiritual:* the former, called also *physical,* affects animal life and has only reference to present happenings, like sensation on which it depends; the latter is called *moral,* is proper to man, and saddens the spirit without limitation of time or space. In man, sense suffering is greater than in animals because of the presence of intellectual knowledge. Suffering dominates human life so as to constitute one of the most difficult enigmas. The problem of suffering is bound up with the problem of evil (*q.v.*), from which it stems like a sad flowering. The solutions attempted for these two problems are, therefore, analogous.

The chief extra-Christian solutions are:

1. *Mazdaism* (theologico-religious solution): the religion of the Persians, reformed by Zarathustra (sixth century B.C.), who admits a Principle of good (*Ahura Mazda*) and a Principle of evil (*Ahura Mainyu*). The suffering of life lies in the conflict between these two Principles, and is reflected in man in the conflict between soul and body.

This *dualism,* which *Manichaeism* (*q.v.*) adopted and spread, is metaphysically absurd and morally deleterious, as is witnessed also by history (see *Albigenses*).

2. *Buddhism* (ascetico-moral solution): Buddha (sixth century B.C.) starts with a pessimistic concept of life, detecting evil and suffering in every part of it. Since the root of suffering lies in desire, he proposes, as a remedy against it, the extinction of every desire and every passion and the renunciation of activity and life, so as to find refuge in a sort of egoistic contemplation.

This is a negative solution, antipsychological (the passions cannot be destroyed, but disciplined) and antisocial (the desertion of life).

3. *Greek philosophy:* Several systems attempted a solution to the prob-

lem of suffering: the Socratic-Aristotelian solution of ethical rationalism (knowledge — good, happiness); the hedonistic solution of the Epicureans, the Stoic doctrine of virtue, consisting in indifference and imperturbability (*ataraxia*). All these solutions are unilateral and, therefore, defective.

4. *Modern philosophy* returns to the old motifs of the exaggerated optimism (Leibnitz idealism) or of the excessive pessimism (Schopenhauer, Hartmann).

Christianity, coherently with its teaching on evil, sees in suffering a natural condition of the human being, aggravated by original sin. One should not attempt to escape suffering, but should face it; it is licit to fight it and eliminate it, inasmuch as possible, but it is better to endure it and make of it a powerful lever of the spirit. In Christ's school the faithful learn not only to endure but to love suffering as a means of purification. The problem of individual and social suffering, as well as the problem of evil, cannot be solved except in the consideration of eternal life, as end and goal of our present existence.

BIBLIOGRAPHY

COLONNA, *Il dolore cristiano* (Naples, 1914). ZACCHI, *Il problema del dolore* (Rome, 1928). See under *expiation*.

supernatural. That which surpasses and transcends, in being or in operation, all created nature. Nature (*q.v.*), being created, is finite and limited in its essential constitution, in its grade of being, and, consequently, in its capacity of acting and of receiving. An element is called supernatural: (*a*) when it is outside of and above the constitution of a created nature; (*b*) when it cannot be the term proportionate to the active potency of that nature; (*c*) when it is not due to that nature, either physically or morally. Such is *divine grace,* a gift gratuitously infused by God in the rational creature, which, therefore, becomes similar to God (*deiform*) in being and operation. The supernatural is a generous communication of God to His creature either by way of intuitive intellection, like the beatific vision (*q.v.*), or by way of an *accidental modification* of nature, like grace. Created nature with respect to the supernatural has no exigency or tendency of its own, but a mere passive capacity to receive the action of God, which elevates it to a superior order. This capacity is called *obediential potency,* through which nature is obedient to the special influence of God. It represents the point of insertion of the supernatural in our nature.

In addition to the *absolute* supernatural (grace, miracle) there is the *relative* supernatural, which does not transcend all created being, but only one or another particular nature (e.g., infused knowledge, natural to the angel, supernatural in man), and the *preternatural* which, while surpassing created nature, does not transcend it, but perfects it in its own order (e.g., immortality of the body).

Thomism maintains a sharp line of distinction between created nature and the supernatural; Scotism, on the other hand, tends to bind, without discontinuity, one and the other (see *desire of God*).

BIBLIOGRAPHY

BAINVEL, *Nature et surnaturel* (Paris, 1931). CAPÉRAN, *La question du surnaturel* (Paris, 1938). MICHEL, "Surnaturel," *DTC*. POHLE-PREUSS, *Dogmatic Theology,* III *God: Author of Nature and the Supernatural* (St. Louis, 1945), pp. 179–231. VERRIÈLE, *Le surnaturel en nous et le péché originel* (Paris, 1932). SOLLIER, "Supernatural Order," *CE*.

superstition. The act or practice of paying a divine worship to one to whom it should not be paid (that is, to creatures), or in worshiping God in an undue manner. He honors God in an undue manner who renders to

Him a *false* worship (e.g., by performing Jewish ceremonies which are definitively abrogated in the New Testament) or a *superfluous* worship (e.g., lighting a certain number of candles, holding a particular position, etc.). He, on the other hand, pays a divine worship to creatures (particularly to the devil), who abandons himself to acts of idolatry or indulges in divinations, in vain observation, or in magic.

Idolatry (*q.v.*), as the word indicates, is the adoration of idols. The idol is the material image of a false god, like Jupiter, Mercury, the moon, the sun. Whether the cult is paid to the image or to the thing or person represented by it, idolatry, no matter how elevated its object, always amounts to the adoration of a *creature,* animate or inanimate. There is nothing more contrary to reason and to faith.

Divination is the art of predicting the future or of knowing occult things by means not established by God, which always implies the invocation of diabolical intervention. St. Thomas distinguishes nine species of divination, in which the devil is directly called upon: prestidigitation, oneiromancy, necromancy, pythonism, geomancy, hydromancy, acromancy, pyromancy, haruspicy. We read in the *Summa Theologica* (II–II, q. 95, a. 3) the explanation of these names. Theologians add six other species of divination, in which the devil is implicitly invoked: astrology, the observation of signs (*augurium*), presagement (*omen*), chiromancy, physiognomy, sortilege.

Vain observation is the use of means disproportionate for obtaining a determined effect, e.g., pretending to know all the knowable by pronouncing mysterious words, to heal all illnesses by using inefficacious medicines, to determine what will be the course of the day from some banal circumstances, e.g., meeting an old woman or a hunchback, etc. *Magic* is a kind of vain observation, being the art of working astounding effects by means of mysterious or disproportionate causes.

BIBLIOGRAPHY

St. Thomas, *Summa Theol.*, II–II, qq. 92–96. Brand, *Observations on Popular Antiquities* (London, 1888). Gardette, "Magie," *DTC.* Graham, "Divination," *CE.* Ortolan, "Divination," *DTC.* Prümmer, *Manuale Theologiae Moralis,* Vol. 2, nn. 501–519. Roure, "Superstition," *DA.* Séjourné, "Superstition," *DTC.* William, "Superstition," *CE.*

suppositum. See *person.*

"Syllabus" (Gr. συν λαμβάνω — I take together). An authentic collection of errors condemned by Pius IX. This collection is composed of 80 propositions taken from the many and diversified documents of the same Pontiff (allocutions, letters, encyclicals). The *Syllabus* was promulgated in 1864, together with the encyclical, *Quanta cura.*

The 80 propositions are divided into ten paragraphs: (1) pantheism, naturalism, and absolute rationalism; (2) moderate rationalism; (3) indifferentism, latitudinarianism; (4) socialism, communism, secret societies, etc.; (5) errors on the Church and its rights; (6) errors on civil society, both in itself and its relations to the Church; (7) errors on natural and Christian ethics; (8) errors on Christian matrimony; (9) errors on the civil power of the Roman pontiff; (10) modern liberalism.

Theologians disagree on the dogmatic value and the character of this pontifical document. Some (Franzelin among them) favor the opinion that both the *Syllabus* and the accompanying encyclical are documents of the infallible *magisterium* of the Pope. Others (e.g., Dupanloup) although recognizing the importance and the doctrinal value of the *Sylla-*

bus, do not attribute to it the character of infallibility. Still others attribute to it only the value of its sources.

All three opinions have an amount of probability; but, although the first is not most certain, the *Syllabus* is without doubt a very important document of the papal *magisterium,* and has become the object of the *magisterium* of the bishops who have accepted it. Therefore, its doctrine must be received at least with great respect and obedience as the voice of the Church, if not with the assent given to matters of divine faith. Nevertheless, several propositions in the *Syllabus* require acceptance as matters of divine faith, not by force of the *Syllabus* itself, but of the previous documents from which they are derived.

BIBLIOGRAPHY

BAINVEL, *De magisterio vivo et traditione* (Paris, 1905), p. 104. BRIGNÉ, "Syllabus," *DTC.* CHOUPIN, *Valeur des décisions doctrinales et disciplinaires du Saint-Siège* (Paris, 1913); "Syllabus," *DA.* HAAG, "Syllabus," *CE.*

Symbol (Gr. συμβάλλω — I put together, I compare). Etymologically and according to the most common usage, even in classic works, it is equivalent to sign, countersign, mark of identification. In ecclesiastical language the same term was in early use to signify an official *formula of faith,* which was like the distinctive badge of the Christian. The most ancient and most important of all is the *Symbol of the Apostles,* which recently has given rise to animated discussions among critics from every sector.

The question presents many difficulties of detail, but substantially is resolved as follows. In the West, from the first half of the second century there had been in use a brief formula, called *regula fidei,* which served for the administration of baptism and for catechesis (cf. St. Justin and St. Irenaeus, later Tertullian). This formula, proper to the Roman Church, is found in Greek in the letter of Marcellus of Ancyra to Pope Julius (337), and in Latin in Nicetas of Remesiana (fifth century) and Rufinus of Aquilea (*c.* 400), who made a commentary on it, mentioning an ancient tradition according to which that formula was composed at the order of Jesus Christ by the Apostles as they were on the point of dispersing for the evangelization of the world. As regards the East, the matter is not clear, but it is certain that the Easterners had no fixed formula up to the fourth century, when the Council of Nicaea promulgated its *Symbol,* which is an enlarged version of the Roman formula.

Based on these and other data, some critics hold that the first *Symbol of Faith* was born at Rome, probably through the work of St. Peter and St. Paul, in a concise form, expressing only the mysteries of the Trinity, the Incarnation, and the Passion and death of our Lord. From Rome the Symbol spread throughout the world, undergoing various changes and additions, as can be seen in the accurate collections made by Denzinger (*DB,* 1 ff.). Today we have two versions of the *Symbol* in use in the Church: the *Roman-Gallican* (for catechetics and private recital) and the *Nicene-Constantinopolitan* (for the Mass), which was composed following the great Trinitarian heresy of Arius. Besides these two principal forms there are other less solemn ones, among them the so-called *Athanasian Symbol* (which is not of St. Athanasius), a limpid synthesis of Trinitarian and Christological doctrine, which the Church has inserted in the Breviary.

BIBLIOGRAPHY

BATIFFOL, "Apôtres (Symbole des)," *DTC.* CAYRÉ, *Manual of Patrology,* trans. Howitt, Vol. 1 (Paris, Tournai, Rome, 1936), pp.

37–42. DUNLOP, *Account of All the Ends and Uses of Creeds and Confessions of Faith* (London, 1724). JENNER, "Creed (Liturgical Use of)," *CE.* LUCAS, "Creed," *CE.* McDONALD, *The Symbol* (New York, 1903). MICHEL, "Symboles," *DTC.* SCHAFF, *A History of the Creeds of Christendom* (London, 1878). TIXERONT, *History of Dogmas,* trans. H.L.B., Vol. 1 (St. Louis, 1910), pp. 142–148. VACANDARD, "Apôtres (Symbole des)," *DA.*

symbolism (from Gr. σύμβολον — sign, mark, badge). A representation, through a sign or formula, of some truth which transcends the sensible world or even the common intellectual world. Symbolism has always been in use both in civil custom (e.g., flag, symbol of the fatherland) and, even more abundantly, in religious practices. Perhaps the Egyptian is the most symbolic of religions; also the mystery religions (Eleusis, Isis, Mithra, etc.), flourishing shortly before and after the beginning of the Christian era, have a remarkable symbolism in their rites. Christianity adopted and developed, especially in its liturgy, the symbolic character already current in the Synagogue under the influence of the ancient revelation, and did not disdain to use even pagan symbolic ceremonies, purifying them from any shadow of superstition. Actually, symbolism is dominant in all the sacramentary life of the Church.

But with the modernists, symbolism became an abused and equivocal word and concept (see *modernism*), when they applied it to dogma (*q.v.*). According to them, a dogma or dogmatic formula, defined by the ecclesiastical *magisterium,* has not a *theoretical value,* i.e., a value adequate to the object which is signified, but only a symbolical and *practical value,* i.e., it is meant to be only the symbolic interpretation of a religious sentiment or fact, which becomes a rule of action. For example, when the Church defines the paternity of God, this expression does not have the value of a theoretical truth, because we cannot know what God is in Himself, but represents symbolically God as a Father, in order that we may behave toward Him like sons. Thus modernism tried to depreciate and eliminate the entire doctrine of faith, determined by the Church in its dogmatic formulas.

It is true that dogmatic language, being merely human and finite, can express divine things, not *adequately,* but only *analogically* (see *analogy*); it is, however, a miscomprehension and error to confuse the analogical with the equivocal, and thus fall into agnosticism (*q.v.*). When we say in the Creed that the glorious Christ sits at the right hand of the Father, the expression is to be understood in a figurative, symbolic sense, but by way of figure and symbol it encloses a sure and certain truth, namely: Christ, as incarnate Son of God, has in common with the Father regal glory, dignity, and power, in which also His humanity shares. Therefore, every dogma expresses primarily a *truth to be believed,* and, as a consequence, a *rule of action;* and its practical aspect is efficacious in direct proportion to the sureness and the firmness of its theoretical character. The Church, therefore, conformed to her principles in condemning the pragmatic symbolism of modernism with respect to dogma. Cf. the Decree of the Holy Office (*Lamentabili*), *DB,* 2022 and 2026. See *dogma.*

BIBLIOGRAPHY

CHOSSAT, "Modernisme," *DA.* DORONZO, *De sacramentis in genere* (Milwaukee, 1946), Index Analyticus: "Symbolismus." GARDEIL, *Le donné révélé et la Théologie* (Juvisy, 1932). GARRIGOU-LAGRANGE, *Le sens commun, La philosophie de l'être et les formules dogmatiques* (Paris, 1922), p. 299 f. JENNER, *Christian Symbolism* (London, 1910). THURSTON, "Symbolism," *CE.*

synod. See *council.*

T

Taborites. See *vision, beatific.*

teaching Church. See *"Ecclesia discens."*

temperance. See *virtue.*

temptation. An experiment made on a person to test his capacity, virtue, inclinations (*St. Thomas*). Temptation can have a good or an evil purpose. In Holy Scripture we read oftentimes that God tempts men; e.g., He induces Abraham to immolate his son in order to test his fidelity. Man also can tempt his fellow for good or for evil. But, strictly speaking, in Catholic doctrine temptation is proper to the devil, who, as St. Ambrose says, *semper invidet ad meliora tendentibus* ("always envies those striving for higher things"). It is a truth of divine faith that the devil tempts men to evil: Jesus Himself in the "Our Father" has us pray for this purpose, among other things, that God may not lead us into temptation. St. Peter describes vividly the threats of the tempter: "Be sober and watch: because your adversary the devil, as a roaring lion, goeth about seeking whom he may devour" (1 Pet. 5:8). The most disastrous temptation was that of Satan in the form of a serpent which brought about the fall of our first parents and of all humanity (Gen. 3).

After considering the *fact* of temptation, theology goes on to a study of its *mode*. St. Thomas makes a fine and profound analysis of the influence of the angelic spirit on the human being. An angel can influence another angel *intellectually* by strengthening the intellective power of the other, and thus manifesting a truth which he, as a superior angel, knows more perfectly. With respect to the will, an angel can influence another less decisively, because its influence is restricted to presentation of the appetible object which, unless it is the supreme good, does not determine infallibly the will. Besides, God alone can move interiorly the angel's will, because God alone is Maker of the will and of its natural inclination.

Based on these principles, St. Thomas proves that the devil can influence the human intellect, not by directly producing or arousing its thoughts, but by exciting the imagination and, therefore, the phantasms, on which the intellect works. The devil can also exercise his influence on the will in two indirect ways, namely, either by way of *persuasion,* presenting to the will through the imagination and the intellect an appetible object, or by exciting the *passions* which solicit and disorientate the will. All this, however, is only an external influence, because internally it is God alone who always moves. Under any kind of diabolic influence the will does not lose its freedom and, therefore, tempted man is always responsible for his sin. He can and must resist, with the help of divine grace, as the Church teaches against the false doctrines of Molinos (*DB,* 1237, 1257, 1261 ff.). See *Molinosism.*

Original sin makes human nature more susceptible to temptations, especially more serious ones; but God bestows on the man of good will grace proportionate to his needs and does not permit that he be tempted above his powers, as St. Paul attests (1 Cor. 10:13). Christ, too, was tempted by the devil; but His temptation was merely *exterior* and could not affect even the sensitive life of His soul, because His senses and passions were altogether subject to reason (see *propassions*).

BIBLIOGRAPHY

St. Thomas, *Summa Theol.*, I, q. 3; III, q. 41. Boyer, *De Deo creante et elevante* (Rome, 1940), p. 417 ff. Brouillard, "Tentation," *DTC.* Pesch, *De Deo creante et elevante* (Freiburg i.-Br., 1925), n. 480 ff.

Tertullian. See "Outline of the History of Dogmatic Theology" (p. 301); *traducianism.*

Testament, New (see *Bible*). The body of 27 books relative to the history of Christ and His revelation and to the early years of the Church. By analogy with the books of the Old Testament (*q.v.*) they are divided into three categories:

Historical Books:
1. Gospel according to St. Matthew (28 chs.)
2. Gospel according to St. Mark (16 chs.)
3. Gospel according to St. Luke (24 chs.)
4. Gospel according to St. John (21 chs.)
5. Acts of the Apostles (28 chs.)

Didactic Books:

a) Epistles of St. Paul
6. To the Romans (16 chs.)
7. 1 to the Corinthians (16 chs.)
8. 2 to the Corinthians (13 chs.)
9. To the Galatians (6 chs.)
10. To the Ephesians (6 chs.)
11. To the Philippians (4 chs.)
12. To the Colossians (4 chs.)
13. 1 to the Thessalonians (5 chs.)
14. 2 to the Thessalonians (3 chs.)
15. 1 to Timothy (6 chs.)
16. 2 to Timothy (4 chs.)
17. To Titus (3 chs.)
18. To Philemon (1 ch.)
19. To the Hebrews (13 chs.)

b) Epistles of the other Apostles, or Catholics
20. Of St. James (5 chs.)
21. 1 of St. Peter (5 chs.)
22. 2 of St. Peter (3 chs.)
23. 1 of St. John (5 chs.)
24. 2 of St. John (1 ch.)
25. 3 of St. John (1 ch.)
26. Of St. Jude (1 ch.)

Prophetic Book:
27. The Apocalypse (22 chs.)

All the books are occasional writings, but have a unique theme: the story of human redemption in its realization and in its immediate and future developments. As regards the Gospels, see that entry. The Acts, written by the author of the third Gospel, offer in their lines and principal features the history of the foundation and spread of the Church, first in the Jewish circles and later in the field of paganism, focusing the narrative around the two great figures of Peter and Paul. The greater part of the apostolic epistolary is due to Paul, the most versatile, profound, and powerful writer of the New Testament. Thirteen of his letters bear, according to Greco-Roman usage, the name of the writer in the initial greeting, and the fourteenth (Epistle to the Hebrews) is attributed to him by Tradition. Their character is multifarious (from a theological treatise down to a simple letter of recommendation) and, despite their origin from particular circumstances regarding a community or an individual, they are permeated with such a wave of divine eloquence, such fullness of truths and of moral teachings, that they become for us a source of spiritual *enlightenment,* full of life and actuality. The epistles of the other Apostles are called catholic (i.e. universal) because they have a more general destination; they bear, however, the same character of occasional writings and of theological richness.

The Apocalypse of St. John is the only prophetic book of the New Testament. It opens with seven messages to the seven churches of Asia Minor and goes on to present, under the form of complicated and phantasmagorical visions proper to the apocalyptic literary style, the vicissitudes of the struggle between paganism and ultimately victorious Christian truth.

All the books of the New Testament were written and preserved in the Greek language, except Matthew's Gospel, which was originally composed in Aramaic, the language spoken by the Jews in Palestine; it was, however, soon translated into Greek. All traces have been lost of the Aramaic original.

To date, more than 4000 codices of the Greek text of the New Testament are known. Their most ancient fragments, written on papyrus, are traced to the first decades of the second century. Parchment came into use in the fourth century for the transcription of the holy text, and paper from the tenth century. The current division of the New Testament into chapters (as well as of the Old Testament) dates from 1214, while the division into verses dates from 1555 and is the work of Robert Stephanus.

BIBLIOGRAPHY

DURAND, "Testament (The New)," *CE.* GIGOT, *Outlines of the N. T. Hist.* (New York, 1898). HÖPFL, GUT, *Introductio specialis in N. T.* (Rome, 1938). JACQUIER, *Histoire des livres du N. T.*, 4 vols. (Paris, 1924–1928). LATTEY, *The New Testament* (Cambridge, 1937). SEISENBERGER, *Practical Handbook for the Study of the Bible* (New York, 1933). SIMON, *Scripture Manual,* Vol. 2 (New York, 1943), General and Special Introduction to the N. T. STEINMULLER, *A Companion to Scripture Studies,* Vol. 3 (New York, 1943), cf. bibliography on pp. 1–12.
See under *Bible*.

Testament, Old (see *Bible*). The body of 46 books which constitute the first part of the Bible and contain the history of the ancient revelation and of the preparation of men, through the people of Israel, for the coming of the Messias. The following is a list of the books and their order, as designated by the Council of Trent in 1546 (see *Canon of the Bible*).

Historical Books:

1. Genesis (50 chs.)	Books of Moses, called *Pentateuch* (five parts), and by the Hebrews, *The Law*.
2. Exodus (40 chs.)	
3. Leviticus (37 chs.)	
4. Numbers (36 chs.)	
5. Deuteronomy (34 chs.)	

6. Josue (24 chs.)
7. Judges (21 chs.)
8. Ruth (4 chs.)
9. 1 of Samuel or 1 of Kings (31 chs.)
10. 2 of Samuel or 2 of Kings (24 chs.)
11. 1 of Kings or 3 of Kings (22 chs.)
12. 2 of Kings or 4 of Kings (25 chs.)
13. 1 of Paralipomenon or Chronicles (29 chs.)
14. 2 of Paralipomenon or Chronicles (36 chs.)
15. 1 of Esdras (10 chs.)
16. 2 of Esdras or Nehemias (13 chs.)
17. Tobias (14 chs.)
18. Judith (16 chs.)
19. Esther (16 chs.)

Didactical or Sapiential or Poetic Books:

20. Job (42 chs.)
21. Psaltery or Psalms (150 psalms)
22. Proverbs (31 chs.)
23. Ecclesiastes (12 chs.)
24. Canticle of Canticles (8 chs.)
25. Wisdom (19 chs.)
26. Ecclesiasticus (51 chs.)

Prophetic Books:

a) Greater Prophets

27. Isaias (66 chs.)
28. Jeremias (52 chs.)
29. Lamentations (5 chs.)
30. Baruch (6 chs.)
31. Ezechiel (48 chs.)
32. Daniel (14 chs.)

b) *Lesser Prophets*

33. Osee (14 chs.)
34. Joel (3 chs.)
35. Amos (9 chs.)
36. Abdias (1 ch.)
37. Jonas (4 chs.)
38. Micheas (7 chs.)
39. Nahum (3 chs.)
40. Habacuc (3 chs.)
41. Sophonias (3 chs.)
42. Aggeus (3 chs.)
43. Zacharias (14 chs.)
44. Malachias (4 chs.)

Continuation of the Historical Books:

45. 1 Machabees (16 chs.)
46. 2 Machabees (15 chs.)

The Old Testament is a harmonious collection of books of various authors and epochs, staggered over a period of time running from the sixteenth to the second centuries B.C.

The *historical books* begin their narrative from the origins of the universe and of man, centering on events relative to the people of Israel from its origins as a nation down to its catastrophe and its attempts at Restoration (175–135 B.C.). The account is neither continuous nor homogeneous and presents notable gaps.

The next group of books is called *didactical,* because their purpose is the instruction of the reader, or *sapiential,* because their principal theme is wisdom conceived as perfect knowledge and faithful religious practice, or *poetic,* because of their literary form.

The *prophetic books* collect biographical episodes and résumés of discourses of the prophets which God sent between the eighth and the fifth centuries B.C. to preserve Israel in the faith and to rekindle the Messianic hopes (see *prophet; Messias*).

The books of the Old Testament are nearly all written and preserved in the Hebrew language; some passages of Daniel and of Esdras and some sporadic verses of other books are written in Aramaic. Some books were written originally in Greek (Wisdom and 2 Machabees), while of others the originals have been lost and have come down to us in the Greek translation (1 Machabees, Baruch, Judith, Tobias, Ecclesiasticus, of which two thirds of the original text was found in the last years of the past century).

The books of the Old Testament were written on papyrus or, to obtain greater durability, on parchment cut in the form of strips wound around sticks. At the present time about 3000 manuscripts of the Hebrew text are known, of which the most ancient dates from the ninth century A.D. The text we read today received its definite form in the first century B.C. and corresponds satisfactorily to the original (see *Masoretic*).

The current division into chapters dates from A.D. 1214 and is due to Stephen Langton; the division into verses dates from 1528 and is the work of Sante Pagnino.

The Old Testament forms an inseparable unity with the New, of which it was "the figure" (1 Cor. 10:6–11). It was the "pedagogue" which led Israel to Christ (Gal. 3:24), who was the end of the Old Testament (Rom. 10:4). Containing the multiple and fragmentary communications of the ancient, divine revelation, it necessarily postulates the New Testament which illumines and completes it with the full revelation brought by the Son of God (Heb. 1:1–2). St. Augustine says: "In the Old Testament is hidden the New and in the New the Old is manifested" (*Quaest. in Hept.*, 2, 73).

BIBLIOGRAPHY

Amann, "Testament (ancien et nouveau)," *DTC.* Coppens, *The Old Testament and the Critics* (Paterson, 1942). Dennefeld, *Histoire des livres de l'A.T.* (Paris, 1929). Gigot, *General Introduction to the Studies of the Holy Scripture* (New York, 1905). Merk, "Testament (The Old)," *CE.* Newton, *Notes on the Covenant* (Cleveland, 1934). Ricciotti, *Dalla Bibbia* (Bologna, 1921); *Storia d'Israele,* 2 vols. (Turin, 1932–1934). Steinmueller, *Some Problems of the Old Testament* (Milwaukee, 1936); *A Companion to Scripture Studies,* Vol. 2 (New York, 1942), cf. bibliography on pp. 1–4.

See under *Bible.*

Tetragrammaton (Gr. τετραγράμματον — of four letters). It indicates the name by which God is commonly designated in the Hebrew Bible (about 6823 times). It consists of four letters: J H W H and is read *Jahweh.* While other names signify the nature of God (e.g., *'el, 'elohim*), this one designates His very person and is the most holy and incommunicable name. After the exile (fifth century B.C.) the Hebrews, out of reverence, avoided pronouncing it; at the time of Christ it was licit for the high priest alone to mention it during the solemn annual ceremony of the expiation.

After the destruction of the Temple of Jerusalem (A.D. 70), the sacred name was substituted in the Bible by *Adonai* (My Lord) and *Elohim* (God). The four original letters were preserved, but there were added to them the vowels of the other two names which were pronounced by the reader, substituting the consonants: in the Bible *Jehovah* or *Jehowih* were written, but one read *Adonai* and *Elohim.* By ignorance of such substitution the erroneous reading *Jehovah* entered into use in the fourteenth century.

The Tetragrammaton was revealed by God to Moses as a new name, when He entrusted to him the task of freeing the people from the slavery of Egypt (Exod. 3:13–16; 6:3–8). Its meaning is given by Exodus 3:14: "God said to Moses: I AM WHO AM. He said: Thus shalt thou say to the children of Israel: HE WHO IS, hath sent me to you." The name, in fact, derives from the Hebrew root HJH (*hajah*) or HWH (*hawah*) and is the first person singular of the imperfect tense, improperly so called, and which would better be called preformative on account of its morphological property of being formed from the root by means of a preforming letter *J*. From the verbal sentence "I am who am," spontaneous passage was made to the name represented by the third person: JaHWeH — "he who is," which signifies: He who truly is, He whose essential property is to be (see *essence, divine*). Some authors derive the name from the causal form of the verbal root, obtaining the meaning: "He who gives being," i.e., "the Creator."

In all the vast domain of the Semitic languages, to which the Hebrew belongs, no other divine name is formed from a verb, especially from a preformative tense; all the other names are of noun formation, for the most part substantive. This shows that the Tetragrammaton is not a spontaneous product of the popular religion or an invention of men; it is, as the Bible says, directly revealed by God.

BIBLIOGRAPHY

CEUPPENS, *Theologia biblica,* Vol. 1 (Rome, 1938), pp. 19–32. MAAS, "Jehovah," *CE.* POHLE-PREUSS, *Dogmatic Theology,* I *God: His Knowability, Essence, Attributes* (St. Louis, 1946), pp. 134–143. VACCARI, "Iahve e i nomi divini nelle religioni semitiche," *Biblica,* 17 (1936), pp. 1–10.

theandric operation (from the Gr. θεός — God, and ἀνήρ, ἀνδρός — man, hence, human-divine, godly-manly). The expression θεανδρικὴ is found for the first time in a letter of Pseudo-Dionysius (end of the fifth and beginning of the sixth centuries), to a monk, called Cajus, and signifies the complex activity of Christ, God and man at once. It naturally led the mind to a *monophysitic* interpretation (see *Monophysitism*), suggesting the idea of a mixed and hybrid action, confusedly human and divine. Since Monophysitism had been condemned by the Council of Chalcedon (451), the ambiguous formula "theandric operation" was rejected by Catholic writers (St. Maximus Confessor), and by the Lateran Council of 649 (*DB,* 268).

St. John Damascene later on adopted and defended theandric operation as an orthodox expression. In reality that formula, rightly understood, has a correct dogmatic sense: Since there are two distinct natures in Christ, there are also two series of operations, the one divine (to create, to conserve the being of creatures), the other human (to speak, to move around). But the human nature, subsisting in the person of the Word, is sustained by it in being and operation. Therefore, every human operation of Christ can be called also divine as proper to the Word, which is the acting principle not only of the divine activity, but also of the human. Moreover, the Word used and still uses His humanity, as an instrument, for certain divine actions, e.g., in working miracles; therefore, also these actions are rightly called theandric.

BIBLIOGRAPHY

ST. THOMAS, *Summa Theol.,* III, q. 19, a. 1. BILLOT, *De Verbo Incarnato* (Rome, 1922), p. 323 ff. MARIC, *Pseudo-Dionysii Areopagitae formula christologica celeberrima de Christi activitate theandrica* (Zagreb, 1932). MICHEL, "Théandrique (Opération)," *DTC.* POHLE-

PREUSS, *Dogmatic Theology,* IV *Christology* (St. Louis, 1946), pp. 161–165.

theodicy (Gr. θεός — God, and δίκη — justice). This term was used for the first time by Leibnitz in his work *Essai de Theodicée sur la bonté de Dieu, la liberté de l'homme et l' origine du mal* (Amsterdam, 1710). He chose this term, restricted to the divine attribute of justice, in view of the character and scope of his essay; but later it was used as the equivalent of the other truly classical term: natural theology. In this sense, theodicy is the science of God and of divine things, acquired through the natural light of reason. It is distinct from true and proper theology (*q.v.*) because it prescinds from divine revelation and faith.

Through the study of the external world and of man, theodicy demonstrates rationally not only the existence of God, but also many of His properties and attributes which are reflected in created things. Therefore, theodicy is the apex of philosophy as well as a part of apologetics (*q.v.*).

BIBLIOGRAPHY

AVELING, *The God of Philosophy* (London, 1906). BROSNAN, *God Infinite and Reason* (New York, 1928). HETTINGER, *Natural Religion* (New York, 1890). HONTHEIM, *Theodicea* (Freiburg, 1926). JOYCE, *Principles of Natural Theology* (London, 1923). KEMPF, "Theodicy," *CE.* PALUMBO, *Theodicea* (Rome, 1940).

theology (Gr. θεός — God, and λόγος — discourse). The science which, through the combined lights of reason and divine revelation, treats of God and creatures in relationship to God. This is supernatural theology, which involves revelation on the part of God and faith on the part of man. It considers everything in the light of the Divinity, which is its *formal object* and its soul. As such it is distinguished from theodicy, a purely rational science of God.

Theology begins with fundamental principles taken without discussion from the sources of revelation (Holy Scripture and Tradition, interpreted by the living *magisterium* of the Church) and, analyzing and comparing them with the principles of reason, develops all their richness into a body of derived truths, which are called *theological conclusions.* Theology, therefore, has the character of a true science, which derives from the science of God Himself, as a finite radiation of it.

Divisions: (*a*) *Positive* theology, which studies the data of revelation with a critico-historical method. (*b*) *Speculative* theology, which plumbs those data with the light of reason illumined by faith, revealing in explicit concepts their virtual content. According to the unitary conception of the Middle Ages, all ecclesiastical knowledge is substantially theology, burgeoning forth from the *sacred page,* i.e., on the revealed word of God. A wonderful example of this unity is the *Summa Theologica* of St. Thomas Aquinas, which embraces everything from exegesis to law. Later, especially from the sixteenth century, the various disciplines (exegesis, patristics, history, archaeology, liturgy, law), began to be separated from the main block of theological science, which is constituted by the doctrine of faith (*dogmatic theology*) and the doctrine of morals (*moral theology*); finally moral theology, too, was distinguished from dogmatic theology (seventeenth century).

BIBLIOGRAPHY

ST. THOMAS, *Summa Theol.,* I, q. 1. BROUILLARD, "Théologie Morale," *DA.* CONGAR, "Théologie," *DTC.* FENTON, *The Concept of Sacred Theology* (Milwaukee, 1941), pp. 1–180. GARDEIL, *Le donné révélé et la Théologie* (Juvisy, 1932). GARRIGOU-LAGRANGE, *De Revelatione* (Paris, 1926); *The One God,* trans. Rose (St. Louis, 1943), pp. 39–92. HALL, *Introduction to Dogmatic Theology* (New York, 1907). POHLE, "Theology (I Dogmatic)," *CE.* POHLE-PREUSS, *Dogmatic Theology, I God: His Knowability, Essence, and Attributes* (St. Louis, 1911), pp. 1–14. RABEAU, *Introduction à l'étude de la Théologie* (Paris, 1926). SCHEEBEN, *The Mysteries of Christianity,* trans. Vollert (St. Louis, 1946), pp. 733–796. *The Teaching of the Catholic Church,* ed. Smith, 2 vols. (New York, 1949), pp. 35–37.

Theopaschism (Gr. θεός — God, and πάσχω — I suffer). It is an error of Monophysitic origin begun in the fifth century through the work of the monk Peter Fullo, who added the words *Qui crucifixus es pro nobis* ("Who wast crucified for us") to the formula *Sanctus Deus, Sanctus Fortis, Sanctus Immortalis.* The words can be understood in an orthodox sense, because truly the Word (God) was crucified, according to the human nature. But in that epoch the addition was an expression of the heresy of Eutyches, who taught the absorption of the human nature in the divine, which therefore was the only one remaining to suffer and die.

BIBLIOGRAPHY

See under *Eutychianism.*

Theotocos. See *maternity, divine.*

Thomas Aquinas. See "Outline of the History of Dogmatic Theology" (p. 302); *Thomism.*

Thomism. In the proper sense it is the doctrinal system of St. Thomas; in a broad sense it includes the interpretation of his thought in the philosophical and theological fields. Since it is not possible to give here, even briefly, an adequate, synthetic view of Thomism, we will mention only some of its fundamental characters:

1. *Moderate realism,* proper to Greek philosophy through the work of Aristotle; primacy of the absolute and subsisting being in God, analogically participated in varying degrees in creatures, in which it is really distinct from essence.

2. *Sane dualism:* God really distinct from the world, but also immanent in it by His presence and by His power which conserves the being of created nature and moves it to action. The created being is a synthesis of *act* and *potency* which tends to become actuated more and more under the influence of natural causes. The material world is composed of *matter* and *form* (hylomorphism); man, of soul and body, which, however, are substantially united in one sole being. Such composition is attributed also in the supernatural order to the sacraments, instrumental causes of grace. Likewise, *nature* is really distinct from *person,* which is constituted by its own substantial act (fruitful application to the mysteries of the Trinity and of the hypostatic union). Finally, a real distinction between *substance* and *accidents* (application to the mystery of the Eucharist).

3. *Intellectualism:* primacy of the intellect over the will and sentiment; frequent use of natural reason in theology, subordinate, however, to revelation and faith. Rational view of the world and its laws: harmony between the laws of being and the laws of thought. Objectivity of our knowledge in the light of being.

4. Sharp distinction between the *natural* and the *supernatural orders;* the one is elevated to the other by way of *obediential potency* (pantheism and false mysticism are eliminated).

BIBLIOGRAPHY

D'ALÈS, "Thomisme," *DA.* GARRIGOU-LAGRANGE, "Thomisme," *DTC; The One God,* trans. Rose (St. Louis, 1943), pp. 1–37. On the importance and significance of the *Theological Summa* of St. Thomas and his methods. GILSON, *Thomisme* (Paris, 1927). HORVATH, *La sintesi scientifica di S. Tommaso* (Turin, 1932). KENNEDY, "Thomism," *CE.*

Pohle-Preuss, *Dogmatic Theology,* VII *Grace (Actual and Habitual)* (St. Louis, 1946), pp. 231–248. Villeneuve, "Ite ad Thomam," *Angelicum,* 13 (1936), pp. 3–23; "Le Thomisme avant et après l'encyclique 'Aeterni Patris,'" *Rev. Domin.,* 26 (1929), pp. 273–282, 339–354, 478–496.

Toletus. See "Outline of the History of Dogmatic Theology" (p. 303).

tonsure (Lat. *tonsura,* from *tondere* — to cut, to shave, to clip). A sacred ceremony, consisting in cutting the hair of the head, by which the Church intends to segregate the aspirant from the world, dedicate him to the divine cult, and render him capable of jurisdiction and of ecclesiastical benefices.

It is not an order, but a kind of preparation for receiving holy orders; as man is prepared for baptism by means of exorcisms and for matrimony by means of sacred engagements, so it is convenient that he be prepared for the service of God and holy orders by means of tonsure (cf. *DB,* 958).

Through this ceremony, the candidate becomes a cleric and enjoys the privileges of the *ecclesiastical forum* and of the *canon.* The privilege of the forum exempts the cleric from subjection to lay courts and puts him under the ecclesiastical court; the privilege of the canon prohibits violence against the cleric and punishes with excommunication any one who dares to strike him *suadente diabolo,* namely, unjustly or with malice.

The origin of tonsure can be traced definitely to the fourth or fifth century, when the Church was no longer hampered in the free exercise of divine cult, and hence was able to give it a determined organization and to distinguish with particular signs the persons regularly deputized to it.

BIBLIOGRAPHY

St. Thomas, *Summa Theol.,* III, *Supplementum,* q. 40, a. 1, ad 3. Gasparri, *De Sacra Ordinatione* (Paris, 1893). Kurtscheid, *Historia Iuris Canonici,* Vol. 1 (Rome, 1941). Taunton, *The Law of the Church* (London, 1906). Tixeront, *Holy Orders and Ordinations,* trans. Raemers (St. Louis).

Tradition (Gr. παράδοσις — transmission, precept, oral doctrine). In the theological sense, it is the word of God concerning faith and morals, not written but transmitted orally from Christ to the Apostles and from them to their successors down to us.

Tradition is said to be *not written;* not in the sense that it cannot be contained in any writing, but in that it was not written under divine inspiration (*q.v.*). For example, that infants are validly baptized is Tradition, namely: word of God, nonwritten revelation, because it is not contained in any inspired written work, although it is recorded in the works of nearly all ancient ecclesiastical writers.

Tradition is called *divine* if it was taught directly by Jesus Christ; it is called *divine-apostolic* if the Apostles did not learn it from the lips of the Lord, but received it through inspiration of the Holy Spirit according to the promise of Christ: "The Paraclete, the Holy Ghost . . . will teach you all things, and bring all things to your mind, whatsoever I shall have said to you" (John 14:26; cf. *DB,* 782).

Having established, as their fundamental principle, that the Holy Scripture contains all divine revelation, the Protestants logically denied the existence of Tradition and restricted themselves to the Bible as the sole rule of faith. The Council of Trent, on the contrary, defined that doctrine regarding faith and morals "is contained both in the written books and in nonwritten tradition" (sess. 4; *DB,* 783), and at the same time declared that one must accept *pari pietatis affectu et reverentia* ("with like pious affection and reverence") (*DB,* 783) the two sources of revelation (cf. Vatican Council; *DB,* 1787).

The economy established by Jesus Christ for the propagation of the Gospel shows efficaciously the existence of Tradition. Indeed, after having preached and not written His doctrine, Jesus entrusted to His Apostles the mission not of writing, but of propagating orally (Matt. 28:18; Mark 16:15; Acts 1:8) all that they had heard from His lips or would learn from the inspirations of the Holy Spirit (John 14:36).

All Christian antiquity considers the apostolic Tradition conserved in the various Churches, particularly in the Roman Church, as the transmitting channel of the revealed word, equal to Holy Scripture. (Cf. especially St. Irenaeus, *Adv. Haereses,* l. 3, c. 4, No. 1, and the entire classical work of Tertullian, *De Praescriptione Haereticorum.*)

The principal *instruments* by means of which divine Tradition has been conserved are the professions of faith, the sacred liturgy, the writings of the Fathers, the practice of the Church, the acts of the martyrs, and archaeological monuments. Its *organ* is the living *magisterium* of the Church (the Roman pontiff and the bishops united with and subordinate to him).

BIBLIOGRAPHY

St. Thomas, *Summa Theol.,* III, q. 64, a. 2, ad 2. Bainvel, "Tradition," *CE.* Franzelin, *De Divina Traditione* (Rome, 1887). Michel, "Tradition," *DTC.* Newman, *Essay on the Development of Christian Doctrine* (London, 1894). Pérennes, "Tradition Chrétienne dans l'histoire," *DA.* Van Den Eynde, *Les normes de l'enseignement chrétien dans la littérature patristique des trois premiers siècles* (Paris, 1933).

traditionalism. A philosophico-religious system which depreciates human reason and establishes the tradition of mankind, which is bound up with the genesis of language, as the criterion of truth and certainty. The principal traditionalists are: De Bonald (†1840), Lamennais (†1854), Bautain (†1867), and Bonnety (†1879). According to a first, *rigid form* of traditionalism, man would not have been able to know any truth without the divine revelation made to Adam and transmitted down to us. In a *mitigated form* the traditionalists deny to human reason only the capacity of arriving at the truths of the ethico-religious order.

The Church has condemned this error; Lamennais did not submit, but degenerated more and more in his teachings and died impenitent. Bautain and Bonnety retracted their error (cf. *DB,* 1613 ff., 1622 ff., 1649 ff.). Traditionalism, by minimizing the power and dignity of human reason, leads logically to fideism (*q.v.*).

BIBLIOGRAPHY

Garrigou-Lagrange, *De Revelatione* (Parisiis, 1926), p. 217 ff. Michel, "Traditionalisme," *DTC.* Palumbo, *Theodicea* (Rome, 1942). Rickaby, *First Principles of Knowledge* (London, 1901). Sauvage, "Traditionalism," *CE.*

traducianism (Lat. *tradux* — vine branch bent and buried so that it becomes a plant). A theory which explains the origin of individual human souls through derivation, either material or spiritual, from parents to their offspring. Traducianism is, therefore, either *corporeal* or *spiritual.*

Tertullian was the author of corporeal traducianism. He speaks of it in an interesting book *De anima* (Chs. 25–27), the most ancient Christian treatise on psychology; it should be noted, however, that this book was written by Tertullian after his adherence to Montanism. The interpretation of this book is not easy, because the author was forced to coin Latin terms to express Christian concepts which up to that time had been expressed in Greek. Some writers do not find clearly formulated in Tertullian's work the concept of the *true spirituality* of the soul, and in this deficiency they see the seed of the theory of traducianism, which involves the materiality of the soul. Others, more lenient, excuse the inaccuracy of language, clearing the thought of the great Apologist of any materialistic intention and explaining his traducianistic doctrine by his preoccupation of rendering more intelligible the transmission of original sin (*vitium originis*). However, the judgment of St. Augustine, a more authoritative interpreter than anyone else, is very severe: "Those who hold that individual souls derive from the first soul, given by God to the first man, and say that they are drawn from the parents, *if they follow the opinion of Tertullian,* certainly mean to say that the souls are not spirits, but bodies: and this is most false" (*Epist.,* 109, No. 14). *Corporeal traducianism,* as proposed by Tertullian, is truly contrary to the spirituality of the soul, which cannot be multiplied and transmitted, as the body is, through the human seed, without losing its essential character of spirit, by which it is independent of matter in its being and in its operation.

The Church has condemned this traducianism as heretical (cf. Anastasius II, *Epist. ad Gallos; DB,* 170). Under the same preoccupation as Tertullian (i.e., in order to give an easier explanation of original sin), St. Augustine admits a *spiritual traducianism,* namely: a derivation of the soul of the child from the souls of its parents; however, the holy Doctor himself acknowledges that his opinion is difficult and obscure (*Epist.,* 190).

Notwithstanding the authority of St. Augustine, traducianism, even merely spiritual, was gradually abandoned after the fifth century, and all writers conformed to the opinion held by the Church, which is decisively favorable to creationism (*q.v.*), as appears in several documents (cf. *DB,* 20, 348, 527, 533, etc.). Spiritual traducianism is absurd, for a spiritual substance, like the soul, being simple, cannot be divided or in any way transmuted into another.

BIBLIOGRAPHY

St. Thomas, *Summa Theol.,* I, qq. 90 and 117. Bainvel, Parisot, Lamy, "Ame," *DTC.* Boyer, *De Deo creante et elevante* (Rome, 1940), p. 123 ff. Dubray, "Traducianism," *CE.* Michel, "Traducianisme," *DTC.*
See under *creationism.*

transmission of original sin. St. Paul writes: "By one man sin entered into this world, and by sin death; so also death passed upon all men, in whom all have sinned" (Rom. 5:12).

This text, which re-echoes other Holy Scripture passages, reveals to us the mystery of the transmission of Adam's sin to all his descendants. Tradition enjoyed peaceful possession of this revealed truth until the fifth century, when Pelagius (see *Pelagianism*) began to deny it. The Church rose up against him, and St. Augustine gave many years of his life in attacking and refuting the new heresy.

The transmission of original sin is a truth of *defined faith* (cf. the Council of Carthage, approved by Pope Zosimus; the II Council of Orange, approved by Pope Boniface II; the Council of Trent, sess. 5; *DB,* 101, 174 ff., 787 ff.). But from the rise of Scholasticism (eleventh century), discussion began about the character and essence of original sin in Adam's descendants. At the time of Luther and of the Council of Trent, the discussion became even more intense, because Luther was teaching that the essence of original sin lay in *concupiscence* (*q.v.*), which he claimed is intrinsically sinful and invincible to the point of extinguishing the use of reason and free will.

The Council of Trent condemned Luther's errors, affirming that in fallen man there still remain reason, free will, the substantial integrity of nature, and its possibility of being healed through the grace of Christ. Likewise, it determined the character of the transmitted sin, teaching, among other things, that by propagation "Adam's sin is inherent in each of us as his *own* sin." The theologians, commenting on this text, have proposed various opinions on the essence of original sin, as transmitted; e.g., God made a pact with Adam, as the moral head of the human race, that he might be able to transmit the supernatural gifts to his descendants, or lose them, both for himself and his children, or the will of his descendants was transferred, as it were, in Adam at the moment of sinning, etc.

St. Thomas' explanation, as illustrated by Billot, is still the best: (*a*) Adam is the head and source, not moral but ontological, of mankind; in him was all our nature. (*b*) Original justice (see *innocence*) was in him as an accidental perfection of the human species, which united mankind to God. (*c*) Adam broke this bond voluntarily and deprived the nature that was in him of such accidental perfection. (*d*) The nature, thus deprived and destitute, i.e., loaded with the guilt and stain of sin (see *sin, personal*), is passed down to his descendants, who thus find themselves in a state of *voluntary* sin, not through their own will but through that of the sinful act committed by Adam. (*e*) The sin of the descendants consists *formally* in the privation of grace, *materially* in the privation of integrity (*q.v.*) and, therefore, in concupiscence. (*f*) By baptism the stain of sin is taken away through the infusion of grace (formal element), while concupiscence (the material element) remains.

Original sin is propagated by carnal generation, the term of which is the whole man, both as to his soul and to his body which is a part of the nature infected with guilt (destitute of sanctifying grace). Through original sin our nature is wounded, but not intrinsically corrupted (Lutheranism, Baianism, Jansenism). St. Thomas explains this wounded condition of our nature in the sense that the nature, infected by sin but remaining substantially whole, is sick in its faculties of action, which are weak and disorientated with respect to their proper object (truth and goodness). Since in the descendants original sin is not voluntary by their own will, but by the will of Adam, those who die with only original sin will suffer the pain of loss (*poena damni*), which stems from the sin itself (privation of the beatific vision), but cannot be subjected to the punishment of the senses (*poena sensus*), which is a positive pain inflicted by God, and cannot be conceived but as an effect of a voluntary sinful act of the sinner himself. St. Augustine maintained a punishment of the senses, although very light, but neither the Church nor the theologians agree with him in this contention.

BIBLIOGRAPHY

St. Thomas, *Summa Theol.*, I–II, qq. 81–83. Billot, *De personali et originali peccato* (Rome, 1924). Harent, "Original Sin," *CE.*

transubstantiation (fact) (Lat. *trans* — beyond, over, across; *substantia* — substance; therefore, passage from one substance into another). The manner in which the body of Christ is made present under the Eucharistic species. This word, which appeared for the first time in theological literature during the Berengarian controversy (eleventh to the twelfth centuries), was immediately adopted by the Church *magisterium* and became the identification card of orthodoxy, like the Homoousian of Nicaea and the Theotocos of Ephesus. Its real content was proposed explicitly by the Council of Trent, in the following definition: transubstantiation is "a singular and wondrous conversion of the total substance of bread into the body and of the total substance of wine into the blood of Christ, the external appearances only remaining unchanged" (*DB,* 884). Conversion is the passing of one thing into another; transubstantiation is a *singular* conversion, i.e., unique in the whole order of nature; in fact, all conversions that take place in the created world either stop at the quantitative or qualitative change of things, or at most go as far as to change their substantial form, as in the change of wine into vinegar. But in nature we find no conversion that goes so far as to change *matter* itself, the common substratum on which is imprinted all the variety of the corporeal world. Now this is precisely what happens through the divine omnipotence in the Eucharist: the total passing of both, the matter and the form of bread, into the body of Christ, only the accidents remaining intact and unchanged.

The characteristic of transubstantiation is the *total* passing of the one substance into the other; from this, as from their ultimate source, flow all the differences between natural conversions and the Eucharistic conversion. In fact: (1) Whereas in natural conversions matter remains unchanged, in the fashion of a bridge on which the different substantial forms relieve one another, in the Eucharistic conversion even the matter is changed and passes entirely, together with its form, into the substance of Christ's body. (2) Consequently, while in natural conversions there is a mere succession of forms which, as it were, plunge into and out of the potentiality of matter, in the Eucharistic conversion we have not only a succession of forms but a real mutation of one form into another. (3) From which it follows, finally, that, whereas in natural conversions, by reason of the succession of forms, both the term *a quo* (starting point) and the term *ad quem* (finishing point) undergo alterations (corruption and generation, respectively), in the Eucharistic conversion — since the matter does not remain — any succession of forms is excluded, and, therefore, while the conversive action affects the whole substance of bread which is instantly transmuted into the substance of the body of Christ, it does not reach in any way or affect the body of the Lord, which remains intact, unaffected, and impassible. For these reasons transubstantiation is a *singular* conversion, altogether outside the orbit of experience. For the same reason it is *wondrous,* i.e., mysterious, because it is foreign to experience from which the intellect ascends naturally to its ideas or concepts; we cannot conceive it adequately, but must satisfy ourselves with pallid images and analogies.

This doctrine stems logically from an attentive analysis of the words of institution: "This is My body," and from the teaching of Tradition, which created a new terminology in an effort to express this truth more adequately: "transmutation," "trans-elementation," "transformation," which was the prelude to the happy term "transubstantiation," proposed by the Council of Trent as the "most suitable and apt" expression of the Catholic dogma (*DB,* 884).

Luther rejected transubstantiation, admitting only *companation,* i.e., coexistence of the substance of bread and of the body of Christ. Rupert of Deutz, John of Paris, and Bayma erred on the nature of transubstantiation, imagining a kind of hypostatic union of the bread with the body of the Lord (*impanation*); Durand, Descartes, and Rosmini, erroneously likened the Eucharistic conversion to *physiological assimilation.*

BIBLIOGRAPHY

St. Thomas, *Summa Theol.,* III, q. 65 (with the commentaries of Cajetan, Lépicier, Billot, etc.). Cachia, *De natura transubstantiationis* (Rome, 1929). Doronzo, *De Eucharistia,* Vol. 1 (Milwaukee, 1948), pp. 224–261. Mattiussi, *De Eucharistia* (Rome, 1925). Michel, "Transubstantiation," *DTC.* Pohle, "Impanation," *CE.* Pohle-Preuss, *Dogmatic Theology,* IX *The Sacraments,* Vol. 2, *The Holy Eucharist* (St. Louis, 1946), pp. 102–123, 198–217. Simons, *Indagatio critica in opinionem S. Thomae Aquinatis de natura intima transubstantiationis* (Indore, 1939). De la Taille, *Mysterium Fidei* (Paris, 1931), Elucidatio 50. *The Teaching of the Catholic Church,* ed. Smith, 2 vols. (New York, 1949), pp. 857–863.

transubstantiation (mode). Certain theologians of the sixteenth and seventeenth centuries, having accepted as a point of faith the total conversion of the substance of bread and of wine into the body and blood of Jesus Christ, thought they could keep the formal concept of transubstantiation by understanding it in an improper or *equivalent* sense. They said that the substance of bread is *annihilated* directly or indirectly to make room for the body of Christ, which would be made present under the species of bread by a kind of *reproduction* (Suarez and Lessius) or by *adduction* from heaven, without Christ leaving that blessed place or passing through the intermediate space (Bellarmine and Lugo).

These opinions, however, do not seem to run true with the Tridentine definitions. The Council teaches that transubstantiation is a singular and wondrous conversion, by which the glorious and impassible body of Christ is made present (*DB,* 884). But, given the annihilation of the bread and the reproduction or the adduction of the body of Christ, it is impossible to speak of a *real conversion,* which implies, in its formal concept, the passing of one thing into another, and not the falling of one thing into nothingness in order to make place for another, whether produced or adduced. Moreover, how could the glorious and impassible body of Christ be adduced under the Eucharistic species without undergoing a change, at least extrinsic, without leaving Its previous place in heaven, without traversing intermediary space? How, finally, could the same body of Christ be reproduced as many times as there are consecrations in the world and still remain the one and identical body which was born of the Virgin, died on the cross, and sits at the right hand of the Father?

For these reasons we must discard such theories and follow the doctrine of St. Thomas, which is the common opinion and the only one in perfect harmony with the definitions of the Church. According to the Angelic Doctor, in the Eucharist the substance of bread is not annihilated, and the body of Christ is made present not by reproduction or by adduction, but simply by the total conversion of the substance of bread into the pre-existing body of Christ, glorious and immutable (see the preceding entry).

BIBLIOGRAPHY

St. Thomas, *Summa Theol.,* III, q. 75, a. 1–4 (with the commentaries of Cajetan, Billot, Mattiussi, De la Taille). D'Alès, *De Eucharistia* (Paris, 1929), pp. 91–94; *Eucharistie* (Paris, 1929). Doronzo, *De Eucharistia,* Vol. 1 (Milwaukee, 1948), pp. 261–315. Michel, "Transubstantiation," *DTC.* Pohle-Preuss, *Dogmatic Theology,* IX *The Sacraments,* Vol. 2, *The Holy Eucharist* (St. Louis, 1946), pp. 123–127. Vonier, *A Key to the Doctrine of the Eucharist* (Westminster, 1946), pp. 176–205.

Trinity. The most sublime Christian mystery, revealing to us the intimate being and the innermost life of God. It can be expressed formally in these terms: God *absolutely* one in nature or essence, and *relatively* three in persons (Father, Son, and Holy Ghost), who are really distinct from each other, as opposite relative terms of the divine intellection and will, but are *consubstantial,* i.e., identical with the divine substance. Hence, the three Persons are equal, and to each belongs all the divine attributes. The only thing that is proper and exclusive to the Persons are the *opposite relations* (*Paternity, Filiation, Active Spiration,* and *Passive Spiration*), which stem from the two immanent *processions,* that, namely, of the Son from the Father by way of intellection (which has the character of *spiritual generation*) and that of the Holy Spirit from the Father and the Son by way of volition and love.

By force of the relations, each of the three Persons has a distinct mode of possessing the divine essence, as happens in a triangle,

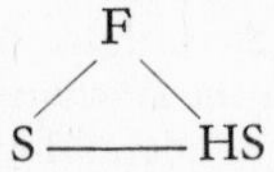

in which every angle closes the same surface, but in its own proper direction (S, F, HS; F, S, HS; S, HS, F).

This mystery, only dimly foreshadowed in the Old Testament, is fully revealed in the New, especially in St. Paul and St. John. The baptismal formula, enjoined by Christ Himself, is the compendium of the Trinitarian mystery, which seals the rebirth of man. Arius (see *Arianism*), the first to disturb the Trinitarian faith in the Church, was condemned by the Council of Nicaea (325).

The extreme errors concerning this mystery and constantly condemned by the Church are Modalism and tritheism (*qq.v.*). The Christian Trinity does not brook comparison with the Babylonian, or the Persian, or the Egyptian *triad* (polytheistic groupings), or with the Indian *Trimurti* (Brahma, Visnu, Siva), a belated cosmogonic elaboration of popular myths, built up on a polytheistic theme. Not even the *Saccidananda* (being, knowing, happiness) of the Hindu theology can be compared to our Trinity, because the clear concept of person is lacking in it.

BIBLIOGRAPHY

St. Thomas, *Summa Theol.,* I, q. 27, a. 1. Bardy, Michel, "Trinité," *DTC.* Billot, *De Deo Trino.* Hugon, *Le mystère de la très Sainte Trinité* (Paris, 1930). Joyce, "Trinity," *CE.* Lebreton, "Trinité," *DA.* Peter Parente, "Il mistero della SS. Trinità," *Il Simbolo,* Vol. 1 (Assisi, 1941). Pohle-Preuss, *Dogmatic Theology,* II *The Divine Trinity* (St. Louis, 1946). Scheeben, *The Mysteries of Christianity,* trans. Vollert (St. Louis, 1946), pp. 25–190. *The Teaching of the Catholic Church,* ed. Smith, 2 vols. (New York, 1949), pp. 38–41, 111–179.

tritheism (Gr. τρεῖς — three, and θεός — God). A Trinitarian error, sprung up, it seems, in the sixth century in the East through the work of the Alexandrian John Philoponus. Adhering to the principles of the Antiochian School, he thought that, as there cannot be a real nature that is not hypostasized (i.e., in the case of a rational nature, subsisting as a person), so it is not possible to imagine a real person that does not have its own distinct nature; since there are in God three Persons really distinct, there must be also three distinct natures (i.e., three Gods — tritheism).

In the eleventh century the nominalist, Roscelin, in a different manner arrived at the same conclusion, as St. Anselm, who refuted him with stringent dialectic in his *Epistola de Incarnatione Verbi,* informs us Roscelin was condemned by the Council of Soissons (1092). The Abbot Joachim of Flora also professed a kind of tritheism (in opposition to Peter Lombard, the famous master of sentences), by denying a common nature to the three divine Persons, according to the principles of nominalism. His work, *Libellus de unitate seu de essentia Trinitatis,* has been lost, but his error is known to us through the second chapter of the IV Lateran Council (1215, *DB,* 431–433).

BIBLIOGRAPHY

AMANN, "Trithéisme," *DTC*. BARDY, "Jean Philopon," *DTC*. CHAPMAN, "Tritheists (Tritheites)," *CE*. GORGE, "Roscelin," *DTC*. JORDAN, "Joachin de Flore," *DTC*. TIXERONT, *History of Dogmas,* trans. H.L.B., Vol. 3 (St. Louis, 1916), pp. 188–194.

truth. Consists in the conformity of the intellect and the intelligible. The object of the intelligence is being, and, therefore, every being is true inasmuch as it has a reference to the intellect that knows it. This order or relationship can be *logical* or *ontological*. The first is had when the intelligible object does not depend in its being on the intellect that knows it; this is proper to the human intellect, which must become conformed to things. The relationship is ontological when the intelligible object depends in its being on the intellect that knows it and causes it; this is proper to only the divine intellect, which, says St. Thomas, creates by thinking (see *science, divine*). There is thus in man *logical truth,* which is conformity of the intellect to the thing, and *ontological truth,* which is conformity of the thing to the divine intellect. Our intellect is measured by things. In any case truth is *formally* in the intellect and *fundamentally* in things, inasmuch as they have relationship to an intellect that either only knows them, or causes and knows them.

Idealism, in its conception of being and truth, has erroneously applied to man what is proper to God. In God there is perfect truth. He is the very subsisting Truth, because there is a perfect conformity, even complete identity, between His intellect and His essence (object), in which are also virtually found all things possible and real. And since intellection is the life of the spirit, there is in God, in addition to truth, life: what is more, He is Life.

BIBLIOGRAPHY

ST. THOMAS, *Summa Theol.,* I, qq. 16 and 18; *Quaest. Disp. De Veritate*. HOBHOUSE, *The Theory of Knowledge* (London, 1906). MICHEL, "Vérité, véracité," *DTC*. POHLE-PREUSS, *Dogmatic Theology,* I *God: His Knowability, Essence, Attributes* (St. Louis, 1946), pp. 225–239. SERTILLANGES, *St. Thomas d'Aquin,* Vol. I (Paris, 1925), pp. 216 ff., 238 ff. WALKER, "Truth," *CE; Theories of Knowledge* (London, 1911).

type. See *senses of Scripture.*

U

Ubiquitarianism (Ubiquitism). See *kenosis.*

ubiquity. See *infinity; presence of God.*

"Unigenitus." See *Only-Begotten.*

union, hypostatic. See *hypostatic union.*

Unitarianism. A Trinitarian error of the sixteenth century. The principal author of this error is Faustus Socinus († 1604), whence the sect of *Socinians*. By interpreting the Holy Scripture arbitrarily, according to the Lutheran principle (liberty of thought), the Socinians believed they could demonstrate that the mystery of the Trinity is foreign to the Gospel, which, they claimed, teaches only the doctrine of a unique God (*Unitarianism*). The error was spread in England and in America. Unitarianism is reductively a kind of *modalism* (*q.v.*).

BIBLIOGRAPHY

ALLEN, *A History of the Unitarians in the United States,* Vol. 10 of "American Church Historical Series" (New York, 1894). COOKE, *Unitarianism in America* (Boston, 1902). CRISTIANI, "Unitariens," *DTC*. DRUMMOND-UPTON, *The Life and Letters of James*

Martineau, and a Survey of His Philosophical Works, 2 vols. (New York, 1902). EMERTON, *Unitarian Thought* (New York, 1911). KOHLMANN, *Unitarianism Theologically and Philosophically Considered* (Washington, 1821). WEBER, "Unitarians," *CE.*

unity (mark of the Church). The first endowment or property which the Nicene-Constantinopolitan Symbol attributes to the Church, and which arises spontaneously from its nature and end. Since, indeed, the Church is "the union of man with Christ in a social form," it cannot help being one, as Christ is one, and as also the human race is one, which Christ the Redeemer drew into the orbit of His divine influence.

The truth of this conclusion is confirmed by Holy Scripture in the images employed to represent the Church (all of which put in bold relief the unity of the Church): architectonic ("an edifice," Matt. 16:18), social ("a kingdom," Matt. 16:19), anthropological ("a body," Rom. 12:4–6; 1 Cor. 12:12–27; Eph. 4:4), sacramental ("a spouse," Eph. 5:24–32), pastoral ("a sheep fold," John 10:16). Christ Himself, in His sacerdotal prayer, by asking the Father *ut unum sint* ("that they may be one," John 17:20–22), points to the natural unity of the three Persons of the Holy Trinity, as to the prototype of the mystical unity which must reign among the members of the Church.

This unity implies profession of the same faith (*symbolico-dogmatic bond*), participation in the same means of salvation (*liturgico-sacramental bond*), submission to the same pastors, especially to the Roman pontiff, the hinge, the center, and the acme of ecclesiastical unity (*hierarchico-social bond*). To the unity of faith is opposed *heresy* (*q.v.*); to the unity of grace caused by the sacraments is opposed *sin* (which does not separate from the Church, but only paralyzes the member who is affected by it); to the unity of government is opposed *schism* (*q.v.*).

Unity does not suppress variety, does not level different human values, but rather enhances them by promoting those liberties which make the Church the spouse of Christ, adorned with a multifarious garment. Indeed, in dogmatic unity there reigns the theological freedom of the schools, in which the highest intellects are tempered; the variety of rites which nourish the piety of the faithful shines forth in the unity of worship; in the unity of government thrive very many national and regional particularities, in which the hierarchy, imitating God who *disponit nos cum magna reverentia* respects the characteristics of the individual peoples.

Two splendid encyclicals were issued on the unity of the Church: *Satis cognitum* (1896), by Leo XIII, and *Mortalium animos* (1928), by Pius XI.

BIBLIOGRAPHY

ST. THOMAS, *In Symbolum Apostolorum expositio,* a. 7–8. CALLAN, "Unity (Mark of the Church)," *CE.* CONGAR, *Chrétiens désunis. Principes d'un "Oecuménisme" catholique* (Paris, 1937). COTTER, *Theologia fundamentalis* (Weston, 1940), cf. Index: "Unitas Ecclesiae." HURTEVENT, *L'unité de l'Eglise du Christ* (Paris, 1930). MICHEL, "Unité de l'Eglise," *DTC.* NEWMAN, *Diff. of Anglicans,* I, lect. 10. SCHRADER, *De unitate romana* (Freiburg i.-Br., 1862). SPALDING, *Evidences of Catholicity* (Louisville, 1870).

unity of God. Unity, in the *transcendental* sense, is the absence of division; all that is undivided is one, and in this sense every being is one, i.e., undivided (even if it is divisible, i.e., composed, like man). In the *predicamental* sense, unity is a quantitative, numerical element.

Faith teaches that God is absolutely *one* in all senses of the word (pure monotheism). Reasons: (*a*) *God is one* in the transcendental sense, because He is absolutely *simple* and excludes from Himself all composition, all division, all divisibility. (*b*) *God is one and unique* numerically, because He is subsisting Being Itself, therefore infinite; now it is absurd to admit more than one Infinite.

Let us make the supposition of two Infinites, *A* and *X*, with their possible relationships:

(1) $A = X$; (2) $A < X$; (3) $A > X$.

In the first case, *A* and *X* being equal would not be infinite because inferior to their sum total; in the second case, *A* less than *X* would be finite; in the third case, *X* less than *A* would be finite. All this proves mathematically — not to mention metaphysics — the absurdity of all forms of polytheism, as well as of pantheism which, by identifying God with the world, collection of many beings, falls back necessarily into a form of polytheism.

The Trinity does not destroy the unity of God, because unity is in the order of the *absolute,* while the Trinity is in the order of the *relative* (see *Trinity*).

BIBLIOGRAPHY

St. Thomas, *Summa Theol.,* I, q. 2. Sertillanges, *St. Thomas d'Aquin* (Paris, 1925), p. 208; *Les sources de la croyance en Dieu* (Paris, 1928), Chs. 1–3. Garrigou-Lagrange, *The One God,* trans. Rose (St. Louis, 1943), pp. 293–305. *The Teaching of the Catholic Church,* ed. Smith, 2 vols. (New York, 1949), pp. 79–82, 91–93.

V

vain observation. See *superstition.*

Vasquez. See "Outline of the History of Dogmatic Theology" (p. 303).

Vega. See "Outline of the History of Dogmatic Theology" (p. 303).

vicar of Christ. The title used since the thirteenth century by which the pope has been commonly designated. The expression is, however, more ancient: used in the *Roman Synod* of 495 (*Vicarium Christi te videmus*), it was taken up by St. Peter Damian at the time of the investiture struggle in opposition to the imperial polemicists, who attributed to the emperor the title *Vicarius Dei.* St. Bernard finally used the expression with particular insistence and applied it to the pope both in his celebrated work *De Consideratione,* dedicated to his former disciple Pope Eugene III, and in his letters. The authority of St. Bernard influenced not only authors like John of Salisbury, St. Thomas of Canterbury, Gerhoh of Reichersberg, and Queen Eleanor of England, but also Innocent III, the first pontiff who used to a great extent that magnificent title whose dogmatic rightness and value is evident from all that is contained under the entry, *Roman pontiff.*

BIBLIOGRAPHY

Maccarone, *Chiesa e Stato nella dottrina di Innocenzo III* (Rome, 1940), pp. 34–47. Rivière, *Le problème de l'Eglise et de l'état au temps de Philippe Le Bel* (Louvain, Paris, 1926), pp. 435–440.

See under *pope; Roman pontiff.*

Victoria (de). See "Outline of the History of Dogmatic Theology" (p. 303).

virginity of Mary. Virginity, in the proper sense, is the physical integrity of the organs of generation. On several occasions the virginity of Mary was the target of heretics: first the Jews spread evil tales on the conception and birth of Jesus; they were followed by Cerinthus and Celsus, and later in the fourth century by other heretics, such as the Antidicomarians (*q.v.*), refuted by Epiphanius; Jovinianists, condemned in the Roman Synod of 390; Bonosus, reproved by Pope Siricius; Helvidius, impugned by St. Jerome. The Lutherans and the Socinians re-echo the ancient errors, while the modern rationalists hold the virginity of Mary to be a myth.

It is a truth of Catholic faith that our Lady maintained her state of perfect virginity at all times: before the birth, in the birth, and after the birth of Christ. The Apostles' Creed says: "Born of the Virgin Mary"; in the most ancient liturgies the title Mary ἀειπαρθένος (always-virgin) is frequent. In the Roman Council of 649 (under Martin I) Mary is defined immaculate, always a virgin, who conceived without man's seed and remained intact even after childbirth (*DB*, 256). "Behold a virgin shall conceive, and bear a son, and his name shall be called Emmanuel" (Isa. 7:14). This text is certainly Messianic, and hence the Virgin is Mary; in Hebrew the reading is *alma* or הָעַלְמָה (*ha'halmah*), which the rationalists say should be translated young woman, and not virgin, which would be expressed in Hebrew by *bethulla* or *betullah*. But biblical usage justifies the meaning "virgin" for *alma,* as is evident from the versions (the Seventy translate ἡ παρθένος — virgin). The context also requires that sense, for a prodigious event is prophesied. The Gospel quotes this prophecy (Matt. 1:18–23) and relates with precise details the virginal conception of Jesus by virtue of the Holy Spirit. Christ *putabatur* (was thought or reputed to be) the son of Joseph (Luke 3:23). Luke, with delicate shading of language, suggests that the childbirth of Mary did not violate her virginity (2:7).

The Fathers see the virginity of Mary after childbirth in the prophecy of Ezechiel: "This gate shall be shut, it shall not be opened, and no man shall pass through it: because the Lord the God of Israel hath entered in by it" (44:2). Tradition is unanimous in defending the perpetual virginity of Mary: St. Augustine affirms (*Sermo,* 186): "a virgin conceiving, a virgin bearing, a virgin pregnant, a virgin with child, a virgin forever."

The theological reason is in the divinity of the Word and in the divine maternity of Mary, to which any corruption was repugnant.

Nor does the title *first-born* given to Jesus create any difficulty; it is evident from documents that this word signified the *first born,* even when there were no other children. The brothers of Jesus, of which the Gospel speaks (Matt. 12:46; Luke 8:18), are only His relatives, according to the Hebrew use of the word.

BIBLIOGRAPHY

St. Thomas, *Summa Theol.,* III, q. 28. Conway, *The Virgin Birth* (New York, 1924). Merkelbach, *Mariologia* (Paris, 1939), pp. 216–263. Pohle-Preuss, *Dogmatic Theology,* VI *Mariology* (St. Louis, 1946), pp. 83–104. Scheeben, *Mariology,* trans. Geukers, Vol. 1 (St. Louis, 1940), pp. 61–131. *The Teaching of the Catholic Church,* ed. Smith, 2 vols. (New York, 1949), pp. 517–523. Vosté, *De conceptione virginali Jesu Christi* (Rome, 1933).

virtue. An operative habit which St. Thomas, following Aristotle, defines: "A good quality of the mind, by which we live rightly and which no one can use for evil." To virtue is opposed the bad habit, which is called vice.

The *natural virtues* are acquired by the constant repetition of good acts, and are distinguished into *intellectual* virtues (*dianoetic*) and *moral* virtues (ethic). The fundamental virtues, called also *cardinal* (*cardo* — hinge), are four: (1) *Prudence:* "right reason of actions to be done" (*recta ratio agibilium*), or the choice and order of means with respect to the end. It is the queen of the cardinal virtues and resides in the intellect. (2) *Jus-*

tice: "the constant and perpetual will of rendering to everyone his right." A habit which inclines the will to do what it ought, according to reason. It is a social virtue (i.e., having reference to others). (3) *Temperance:* moderates the *concupiscible* appetite (passion of sense pleasure). (4) *Fortitude:* moderates and strengthens the *irascible* appetite against difficulties.

The *supernatural virtues* are habits infused by God in the faculties, together with sanctifying grace which is, however, infused in the very *essence* of the soul.

According to the common doctrine, the *moral* virtues listed above are to be placed also among the supernatural virtues; they are ordained to perfect and elevate the corresponding natural virtues. However, the principal infused virtues are the *theological* virtues, so called because they have God as their *formal object* (while the moral virtues have a finite good for their object). The theological virtues are three: (1) *Faith,* which inclines the *intellect* (and the will) to adhere firmly to the revealed word of God (see *faith*). (2) *Hope,* which inclines the will to trust in the good and omnipotent God for the obtaining of eternal life and the graces to merit it. (3) *Charity,* which inclines the will to love God for Himself, as well as ourselves and our neighbors for God's sake. It is the queen of the theological virtues, for it unites us to *God, as God* and as present. Since its proper and most formal object is God, as supreme end, charity may be considered, with St. Thomas, as the form, mother, root, and motor of all the other virtues — a thought amply developed by St. Paul (1 Cor. 13; see *charity*).

Charity is intimately connected with sanctifying grace and, therefore, they are infused together and, through sin, are lost together. Faith and hope, on the contrary, can remain in the sinner without grace and charity; in such case they are called *inform* faith and hope (i.e., without the form of charity), while they are called *formed* when they are united with charity.

At the moment of the infusion of grace all the virtues and gifts of the Holy Spirit are also infused (see *gifts of the Holy Ghost*). Cf. Council of Vienne (*DB,* 483) and Council of Trent (*DB,* 800).

BIBLIOGRAPHY

St. Thomas, *Summa Theol.,* I–II, qq. 61–62. Billot, *De virtutibus infusis* (Rome, 1928). Bonomelli, Martindale, *A Doctrine of Hope* (London, 1921). Michel, "Vertu," *DTC.* Otten, *A Manual of History of Dogmas,* Vol. 2 (St. Louis, 1915), pp. 253–271. *The Teaching of the Catholic Church,* ed. Smith, 2 vols. (New York, 1949), pp. 622–654. Ullathorne, *Groundwork of the Christian Virtues* (London, 1888). Waldron, "Virtue," *CE.*

vision, beatific. The supernatural end to which God has willed to destine man gratuitously, elevating him by grace to an activity proportionate to that end. The beatific vision consists in the *immediate* and *intuitive* contemplation of the divine essence, of which the human intellect is made capable by the *light of glory,* which is a supernatural power infused in the blessed by God, proportionately to the degree of sanctifying grace possessed by each one of them at the moment of death. This vision, supreme term of the whole supernatural economy, is clearly enunciated in Holy Scripture: "We see now through a glass in a dark manner; but then face to face. Now I know in part; but then I shall know even as I am known" (1 Cor. 13:12). From this last sentence it is evident that the beatific vision is a participation of the knowledge of God. St. John, also: "We shall see him as he is" (1 John 3:2).

Although impossible in the natural order, the beatific vision is not absurd in the supernatural order, because the adequate object of our cognition is being, and God as being, however transcendent, is not extraneous to that object; therefore the human intellect can be elevated through divine power to the point of reaching the essence of God, although, on account of its natural limitation, it cannot exhaust all the intelligibility of that essence. The theologians say that the blessed see God *totum sed non totaliter* ("whole but not wholly") and, moreover, they see Him in diverse degrees of intensity, according to the power of the light of glory proportionate to grace. Nevertheless, they are all equally happy, because each one sees as much as he is able to see.

The primary object of the intuitive vision is God in His unity and trinity and in His attributes; created things are the secondary object, seen in the divine essence, being an effect and an imitation of it. The Palamites (from Gregory Palamas, † 1359, schismatic archbishop of Thessalonica) distinguished in God *essence* and *power*, maintaining that the blessed see only a divine power, which is the uncreated splendor that shone on Christ on Mount Thabor (whence the name of *Taborites*). The doctrine of the Church on the beatific vision is defined in the Constitution *Benedictus Deus* of Benedict XII (*DB,* 530), and in the Councils of Vienne and Florence (*DB,* 475, 693) (see *beatitude*).

BIBLIOGRAPHY

St. Thomas, *Summa Theol.,* I, q. 12. Michel, "Gloire," *DTC;* "Intuitive (vision)," *DTC.* Sartori, *La visione beatifica* (Turin, 1927). Scheeben, *The Mysteries of Christianity,* trans. Vollert (St. Louis, 1946), pp. 651–694. Terrien, *Le grâce et la gloire* (Paris, 1897).

voluntarism. A system or a philosophical tendency which overrates the function of the will. It is generally opposed to intellectualism. Plato, notwithstanding his exaltation of his noetic world, assigns the primacy to the subsisting idea of good and creates the dialectics *of love* for the conquest of good and truth. Through the works of Plotinus he influences the thought of St. Augustine, who, although an intellectualist, accentuates the activity and the importance of the appetitive and affective faculty. St. Bonaventure and the Franciscan School, influenced by St. Augustine, assert the primacy of the will in this life and in the other, subordinating the intellect to the will. Under the influence of Aristotle the intellectualistic current, headed by St. Thomas, stands for the primacy of the intellect, placing beatitude essentially in an act of intuitive knowledge and contemplation, while Scotus assigns it to an act of love. The intellectualism and voluntarism of the Scholastics are not exactly two opposite systems, mutually exclusive, but two positions, two trends in the investigation of the same truth and in the construction of doctrinal systems. St. Thomas has written wonderful pages on the will and love, as Scotus has done on the intellect and truth.

In modern times, on the contrary, exclusivistic trends have developed in the lines of intellectualism and voluntarism. Kant (see *Kantianism*) opens the way for this conflict when he seeks, in his *Critique of Practical Reason,* to rebuild by way of the will, of sentiment, and of faith what he had nullified in his *Critique of Pure Reason.* From Kantian practical reason stems the fideism of Herder and Jacobi, and the sentimentalism of Schleiermacher. Arthur Schopenhauer († 1860) builds his philosophy on the concept of a will as a blind appetite, unintelligent and unintelligible, which in man manifests itself as the will to live, always unsatisfied (pessimism); analogous is the philosophy of E. Hartmann († 1906), who assigns an *unconscious will,* always avid of unattainable felicity, as principle of the life of the universe. Against these two pessimists, Nietzsche († 1900) affirms his optimistic voluntarism with the theory of the *superman,* who must struggle and triumph over the weak and inept. G. Wundt, too († 1920), a celebrated psychologist, reduces the life of man and of the universe to a universal will, in perpetual evolution and transformation of its reality. In religion, the voluntaristic tendency manifests itself in pragmatism (*q.v.*) and also in the philosophy of action of Blondel.

Exaggerated voluntarism, as a negation of the dignity and function of the intellect, is not reconcilable with Catholic doctrine.

BIBLIOGRAPHY

GEMELLI, "La volontá nel pensiero del Ven. Duns Scoto," *Scuola Cattolica* (1906). LADD, *A Theory of Reality* (New York, 1899). ROUSSELOT, "Pour l'histoire du problème de l'amour au moyen âge," *Beitr. zur Gesch. der Philos. des Mittelalter,* VI, 6 (Münster, 1908). WALKER, "Voluntarism," *CE.*

Vulgate (common). The Latin translation of the Bible, which the Church uses and prescribes officially in teaching, in preaching, and in the liturgy. Its name is derived from the wide circulation it had throughout the West since the seventh century. Its author is St. Jerome († 420), the greatest doctor in interpreting Holy Scripture. Not all the work, however, in the Vulgate is his: some books are still reproduced according to the older Latin translation, which was made, for the Old Testament, from the Greek translation (Wisdom, Ecclesiasticus, Baruch, 1 and 2 Machabees); others are revised from the Greek (New Testament and Psalms); the rest is a direct translation from the originals and the personal work of the great Doctor.

In 1546 the Council of Trent defined the Vulgate to be *authentic,* i.e., immune from all error in matters of faith and morals, a genuine source of revelation, and a faithful expression of the written word of God. The Council did not intend to prejudice, with this decree, the authority of the original text of the Bible or of the ancient translations. The decree was provoked by the uncertainties induced in the religious controversies of the sixteenth century, when some scholars, with the flourishing of linguistic studies, wanted to substitute the ancient ecclesiastical translation with other translations, which were the fruit of private effort and often expressed the thought and trends proper to their various authors. At the same time the Council ordered the preparation of a corrected edition of the Vulgate, which was published after 50 years of work under Sixtus V in 1590, and again, after a successive revision, in 1592 under Clement XIII; for this reason the actual edition of the Vulgate is called Sixtine-Clementine Vulgate.

In 1907 Pius X entrusted to the Benedictine Fathers the task of preparing a critical edition of the Vulgate with the aim of eliminating the imperfections which accumulated in it in the course of long centuries of continuous transcriptions. Up to 1944, ten books of the Bible have been published in 5 tomes.

BIBLIOGRAPHY

CHAPMAN, *Notes on the Early Hist. of the Vulgate Gospels* (Oxford, 1908). DURAND, "Vulgate latine et S. Jérome," *DA.* GASQUET, "Vulgate," *CE.* PIUS XII, Encyclical, *Divino Afflante Spiritu.* QUENTIN, *La Vulgate à travers les siècles* (Rome, 1926). SALMON, *La révision de la Vulgate* (Rome, 1937). STEINMUELLER, *A Companion to Scripture Studies,* Vol. 1 (New York, 1941), pp. 175–196; cf. bibliography on pp. 169–171. VOSTÉ, *De latina bibliorum versione quae dicitur "Vulgata"* (Rome, 1927).

W

Waldenses (or Waldensians). A religious sect founded by a merchant of Lyons, Peter Waldo (Lat. *Valdus*). Deeply impressed by the sudden death of a friend, in 1176, this rich merchant abandoned the world, distributed his wealth to the poor, and dedicated himself to the evangelical life, preaching Christ and poverty. First the bishops, then the Holy See became concerned about this movement which was accompanied by rebellion against the official Church.

In 1184 the Waldenses were excommunicated, but this did not hinder them, and they continued to spread even in Italy, especially in Piedmont and Lombardy. Quickly their doctrine revealed its opposition to the hierarchy, the sacraments, and Catholic worship; the Holy Scripture was the subject of their particular study. Upon the advent of the Lutheran Reformation, the Waldenses adhered to the new heresy, and thus exposed themselves to bitter persecution during the Counter-Reformation, especially in the mountainous regions of Piedmont. Nowadays the Waldenses in large part follow Calvinism (*q.v.*).

BIBLIOGRAPHY

CHABRAND, *Vaudois et Protestants des Alpes* (Grenoble, 1886). CRISTIANI, "Vaudois," *DTC*. CURTIS, *A History of Creeds and Confessions of Faith* (Edinburgh, 1911). GIBSON, *The Waldenses, Their Home and History* (Edinburgh, 1903). MELIA, *The Origins, Persecutions and Doctrines of the Waldenses* (London, 1870). OTTONELLO, *La Chiesa Valdese* (Pinerolo, 1935). SCHAFF, *Creeds of Christendom* (New York, 1877). WEBER, "Waldenses," *CE*.

will, divine. The will is the rational appetite, namely: the faculty of tending to good, known as such by the intellect. Where there is intelligence there is will, the one being inseparably related to the other: we know in order to love and we love in order to integrate the perfection of our own nature. The object of the will is good, i.e., being inasmuch as it is perfective of the subject that tends to it.

It is an article of faith that in God there is a will, and consequently a will as infinite as the divine nature, with which it is identical (Vatican Council, sess. 3, Ch. 1). Written and oral revelation exalts, together with the wisdom of God, His omnipotent will which nothing can resist (cf. Esth. 13:9). Reason dictates that whatever is in the effect, as such, must also be in the cause; moreover, the proof of the divine intellectuality carries implicitly the demonstration of the divine will. As the divine intellect, so the will, has for its *primary object* God Himself, His essence, in that it is infinite Goodness; its *secondary object* are all the creatures. As God does not know creatures, except by knowing His essence, so He does not will them except by willing Himself, with one sole most simple act, identical with His nature. *Deus est suum intelligere et suum velle* ("God is His act of understanding and of willing"), says St. Thomas.

Freedom of God was denied by the Stoics, and partially by Abelard, Arnold of Brescia, Eckart, Wycliffe, Luther, and Calvin. The optimists (Malebranche, Leibnitz), and somewhat also Gunther, Hermes, and Rosmini, have assigned a limit to it. The Church, basing her teaching on revelation, has always defended the divine liberty with respect to the world (Vatican Council, *DB,* 1783 and 1805). Truly God cannot help willing Himself, supreme Good, but He is free to will or not will creatures, since He is infinite and sufficient to Himself. Creation can be only a free effusion of love.

The divine will is the efficient, realizing cause of all things: it is fulfilled infallibly when it is *absolute* or *consequent,* not when it is only *conditioned* or *antecedent.*

Since in God there is infinite volition, there is also infinite love, rather, God is Love (St. John); He loves Himself infinitely, and in Himself and through Himself He loves all creatures.

BIBLIOGRAPHY

St. Thomas, *Summa Theol.,* I, qq. 19–20. Garrigou-Lagrange, *God,* trans. Rose (St. Louis, 1947–1948); *The One God,* trans. Rose (St. Louis, 1943), pp. 487–605. Hall, *The Being and Attributes of God* (London, 1909). Pohle-Preuss, *Dogmatic Theology,* I *God: His Knowability, Essence, Attributes* (St. Louis, 1946), pp. 421–453. Sertillanges, *St. Thomas d'Aquin,* Vol. 1 (Paris, 1925), p. 241 ff. *The Teaching of the Catholic Church,* ed. Smith, 2 vols. (New York, 1949), pp. 105–109. Toner, "God," *CE.*

will of Christ. The will is the appetite proper to the rational creature, namely: the faculty that tends to good, known through the intellect. The adequate object of the will is absolute good, to which the will adheres naturally without possibility of hesitation, just as the intellect adheres to certain and evident truth. On account of this quasi-infinite potentiality, the will in the presence of limited particular goods is not dominated, but dominates and chooses, according to the practical judgment of reason. In this consists freedom of the will.

In Christ, in addition to the *divine will,* common to the three Persons of the Holy Trinity, there was the human will, which is an integrating part of human nature. *Monothelitism* (*q.v.*), by denying this truth, mutilates the humanity of Christ, which the Council of Chalcedon defined as perfect and integral. But there was no conflict between the two wills of Christ, because the human was subordinate to the divine. In Gethsemani He prays the Father that He remove the chalice of the passion: it is the human will that speaks as a natural tendency to its proper good, considered *in se* and *per se.* To this will, called by the philosophers *voluntas ut natura* (θέλησις), the passion was repugnant, because it was not a good in itself. But from the standpoint of reason, the passion was a means necessary for a great good, the Redemption, as is a surgical operation for health; and in this sense Christ accepted it in harmony with the divine will, putting into action the human will, called *ratio* (βούλησις), which adheres to what is good not in itself, but for an extrinsic motive (the passion on account of the Redemption).

The subordination of the human will to the divine does not violate the freedom of Christ-Man. It was a precept of the Father that He should die on the cross: His perfect sanctity, rich in the light of the beatific vision, did not allow in Him the slightest hesitation with respect to that kind of death. Nonetheless, He faced it *freely,* with full consciousness, spontaneity, and loving adhesion, as a son carries out the categorical command of his father. And because the death of Christ was free, it was also meritorious.

BIBLIOGRAPHY

St. Thomas, *Summa Theol.,* III, qq. 18–19. Hugon, *Le mystère de l'Incarnation* (Paris, 1931), p. 285 ff. Parente, *De Verbo Incarnato* (Rome, 1939), p. 208 ff. Pohle-Preuss, *Dogmatic Theology,* IV *Christology* (St. Louis, 1946), pp. 154–161. Van Noort, *De Deo Redemptore* (Hilversum, 1925).

wisdom. See *gifts of the Holy Ghost.*

Word (Gr. λόγος). *Psychologically,* it is the term of intellective cognition (idea, concept, word of the mind); *theologically,* it is the Second Person of the Holy Trinity, who proceeds from the Father by way of intellection and of true, spiritual generation. God, knowing Himself (Father), generates *ab aeterno* the idea of Himself (Word-Son), His substance or divine nature remaining immutably identical. Therefore, the Word is really distinct from the Father, not in an absolute sense, but only in the order of *relation,* i.e., as term of filiation opposed to paternity. Absolutely speaking, the Word is *consubstantial* (ὁμοούσιος) to the Father, i.e., of the same substance or nature of the Father and, therefore, in everything equal to Him: the Father is God as thinking, the Son is the same God as thought.

The doctrine of the Word, vaguely foreshadowed in the Old Testament, is clearly revealed in the New, especially in the Prologue of the Gospel of St. John, who makes these statements about Him: (*a*) *eternity:* "In the beginning was the Word"; (*b*) *personality:* "And the Word was with God"; (*c*) *divine nature:* "And the Word was God"; (*d*) *creative power:* "All things were made by Him"; (*e*) *the Incarnation:* "And the Word was made flesh."

St. Paul, although not using the expression "Word," teaches the same truth, attributing the same divine prerogative to Christ, whom he calls *Firstborn Son* of the Father, substantial *Image* of Him, *Creator,* together with the Father, of the universe (Phil. 2:6; Col. 1:16; Heb. 1:2 ff.).

Arius, who taught that the Word is a creature, was condemned by the Council of Nicaea (325). As regards the origin of the doctrine of St. John, see *Logos.* Cf. also *Trinity, Son, Only-Begotten, Arianism.*

BIBLIOGRAPHY

Klein, *The Doctrine of the Trinity,* trans. Sullivan (New York, 1940), pp. 131–150. Lebreton, *Histoire du dogme de la Trinité,* Vol. 1 (Paris, 1927). Michel, "Verbe," *DTC.* Vosté, *De prologo joanneo et Logo* (Rome, 1925).

See under *Logos; Trinity.*

worship. See *cult.*

Y

Yahweh. See *Tetragrammaton.*

OUTLINE OF THE HISTORY OF DOGMATIC THEOLOGY

Theology[1] is at once a human and a divine science, because it is an elaboration of the data of divine revelation, made by reason in the light of faith. The truths revealed by God are immutable and, therefore, are not subject to intrinsic evolution; the understanding of those truths by the human intellect, however, is not immediate or adequate from the beginning, and must therefore follow the natural laws of our knowledge, developing and progressing.

Consequently, theology has a history which marks the stages of the immense effort made by reason throughout the centuries in its study of the word of God, so as to understand it better and better and bring out explicitly its hidden riches.

According to the intensity and nature of such continuous study, the history of theology is usually divided in three epochs: the *patristic,* the *scholastic,* and the *modern.*

1. *Patristic Epoch* (period of *fermentation*). During this era the revealed truths were first condensed into concrete formulas, with simple *expository* style (*Apostolic Fathers:* Clement of Rome, Ignatius Martyr, Polycarp, Pseudo Barnabas, etc.); then they were put into contact with religious, political, and philosophical paganism in a *polemic* style (*apologists:* Justin, Athenagoras, Aristides, Irenaeus, Tertullian, etc.); finally, they were elaborated rationally with a *scientific* method under the influence of Hellenistic, philosophical trends. This brings us to the beginning of the third century, when, after the apologetico-polemic test had been victoriously met, the Fathers gave themselves to studying more deeply the truths of faith and presenting them in a scientific manner, corresponding to the requirements of the culture of that time. Their minds polarized around two centers, which became the foundries of great theological works: the *Alexandrian School,* in Egypt, inspired by Neoplatonism and hence given to mysticism and symbolism; the *Antiochian School,* in Syria, adhering to Aristotelian thinking and, therefore, tending to concreteness and realism, even in matters of faith.

From these two schools came the geniuses of Christian orthodox thought, as well as the most famous heretics. A large part of patristic theology, especially Eastern, is connected with the vicissitudes of these two schools.

Alexandrian School: Clement († 211), Origen († 255), powerful genius who attempted the first vast synthesis of Christian thought with Greek, especially Platonic, thought, Athanasius († 373) and Cyril († 444), who fought vigorously against the two great heresies (of Antiochian origin), *Arianism* and *Nestorianism.* With the Alexandrian School are connected the three Cappadocian Fathers: Basil, Gregory of Nyssa, and Gregory of Nazianzus (second half of the fourth century). From the same school, *Apollinarism, Monophysitism,* and *Monothelitism,* great Christological heresies, originated.

Antiochian School: Lucian and his disciples, among them Arius the heresiarch, Eusebius of Nicomedia, later Diodorus of Tarsus, Theodore of Mopsuestia, an acute writer with naturalistic tendencies who sowed the seeds of two great heresies of Antiochian origin: *Nestorianism* and *Pelagianism* (this last developed es-

[1] Up to about the seventeenth century theology included all the ecclesiastical disciplines; in that epoch a distinction began to be made between dogmatic, moral, etc. (see *theology*).

pecially in the Western Churches). The school of Theodore formed the heretic Nestorius and the great John Chrysostom, Father of the Church.

In the East, through the crucible of the great Trinitarian and Christological heresies, the science of God matured in its entirety, i.e., as a *theology,* in its most proper and highest sense, which the Fathers restricted to the study of the divine life in itself (*Trinity*), and as the science of the Incarnation, to which the ancients gave the beautiful Greek name of *Economy*.

In the West, by the side of some repercussions of these eastern currents, we find the development of a less speculative and more practical theology according to the traditions and the spirit of Rome. Hilary († 366) re-echoes the Trinitarian doctrine of Athanasius, Ambrose († 397), the thought of Basil and of other easterners; St. Jerome († 419), the Father of biblical exegesis, is outstanding for his passionate study of Holy Scripture.

But the greatest of all the Fathers was Augustine († 430), who, converted to Christianity, brought into it the treasure of a vast culture and the power of an incomparable genius. With these resources he was able to spread his wings over the whole patrimony of Christian doctrine, assimilate its soul, and, by means of the positive criterion of the Westerners, reduce to a grandiose and organic synthesis four centuries of doctrinal elaboration, matured especially in the eastern schools. He added of his own, in the dramatic struggle against Pelagian naturalism, a rich doctrine about original sin and grace, which can be called a vast and luminous supernatural anthropology. Augustine is the creator of systematic theology, which is the point of confluence of all patristics and the point of departure of Scholasticism.

The last faint glimmers of patristics appear in the West with Leo the Great († 461) and Gregory the Great († 604), in the East with Leontius Byzantinus († 543), Maximus Confessor († 662), Sophronius († 638), and finally with John Damascene († 749), who aptly summarizes the doctrine of the Greek Fathers.

2. *Scholastic Epoch* (*systematic synthesis*). This era begins in the eleventh century with St. Anselm, called the Father of Scholasticism, who opened the way for a fruitful speculation on dogmas by stressing the use of reason in the sphere of faith. Following in the footsteps of St. Augustine, he was inspired by the motto, *fides quaerens intellectum,* i.e., holding firmly to the divine truth by lively and unconditioned faith, he sought to penetrate its content by exercising all the power and all the resources of natural intelligence. The work of St. Anselm has two aspects: one, *supernatural* (mystical adhesion to truth), the other *human* (dialectical elaboration of the faith). Hence, the two trends that dominate in turn all Scholasticism: the *mystic* current of Augustinian inspiration, which, through St. Bernard and the French school of St. Victor (Hugh and Richard), passes in the twelfth century into the Franciscan Order and culminates in the teaching of St. Bonaventure; the *dialectic* current, which threatens to degenerate in *Abelard* (the strongest philosopher of the twelfth century), but is happily tempered by Peter Lombard, the author of four books of *Sentences,* in which is gathered and winnowed the choicest growth of patristic doctrine (this work is the basic text on which the later *Summae Theologicae* are modeled). Thus moderated by the force of the authority of the Fathers, the dialectical trend grows increasingly stronger and more decided under the impulse of Aristotelianism incorporated into Scholasticism through Arabic philosophy (Avicenna, Averroes), and triumphs first with Albert the Great, and then with the greatest of the Scholastics, St. Thomas Aquinas.

With St. Thomas we reach the thirteenth century, when Italy was a veritable springtime of life, thought, and art. It is the age of St. Francis of Assisi, of Giotto, and of Dante, when the most beautiful of cathedrals flourish under blue Italian skies. The marvelous *Summa Theologica* of St. Thomas Aquinas is in the field of philosophy and theology what the *Divine Comedy* is in the field of art and literature: it can be said that Dante translates into poetry the robust thought of St. Thomas.

With the Englishman Duns Scotus, called the Subtle Doctor on account of his acumen, dialecticism touches its zenith and quickly afterward degenerates into formalism that marks a period of decadence in Scholasticism (fourteenth to the sixteenth centuries). Humanism and the Lutheran Reformation threw discredit on Scholasticism, which, however, did not die out, but, on the contrary, girded itself for a rebirth through John Capreolus († 1444), called the Prince of Thomists because of his lively defense of the thought of St. Thomas. This upsurge received still greater impetus through the influence exercised by two classical commentaries on the two *Summae* of St. Thomas, made by the powerful genius of Tommaso de Vio (Cajetan) († 1534), who wrote the commentary on the *Summa Theologica,* and of Francesco de Silvestris (Ferrariensis) († 1526), who produced the commentary on the *Summa Contra Gentiles.*

3. *Modern Epoch* (*analyticism*). After the Council of Trent Scholasticism, and especially Thomistic doctrine, resumed its upward movement, thanks to great theologians, most of them Spanish: Francisco de Victoria, Melchior Cano, Dominic Soto, Dominic Bañez, Diego Alvarez, Bart. Medina, John of St. Thomas, all of the Dominican Order; Francisco Toledo, Luis Molina, Gregorio de Valencia, Gabriel Vasquez, Francisco Suarez, of the Society of Jesus; A. Vega, Fr. Herrera, Bart. Mastrius, Fr. da Mazzara, of the Franciscan Order.

But Lutheranism obliged the theologians to defend the correct interpretation of Holy Scripture and the doctrinal patrimony of the Fathers; hence the large development of exegesis and of the historical element of theology, as well as of its polemic character. In this triple field the Jesuit theologians deserve the greatest credit: it suffices to mention the great controversialist, Card. Bellarmine († 1612), the exegetes Salmeron and Maldonatus, and D. Petavius († 1652), who collected methodically the dogmatic thought of the Fathers in four volumes. In the eighteenth century there was another period of decadence, from which Scholastic theology rose after the French Revolution, at the beginning of the past century. This revival was characterized by a renovation of Scholasticism upon contact with modern philosophy and by a flourishing of positive theology in harmony with progress in historico-biblical studies. The restoration began in Germany with Kleutgen and Liebermann, and gained strength in Italy with the Jesuits, John Perrone († 1876), Dom. Palmieri, and Camillo Mazzella, professors at that same "Collegio Romano" which has been made illustrious more recently by the teaching of Franzelin and Billot, the former outstanding in positive theology, the latter, in speculative.

Neo-Thomism and Neo-Scholasticism have gained ground in all the Catholic universities; inculcating the grandeur of the classical, speculative theology, they call back to saner traditions philosophical thinking, lost in the labyrinths of the conflicting trends of the nineteenth century.

On the other hand, our positive theology has gained decided strength against rationalistic criticism. It integrates and illuminates with new light profound, medieval speculation, through serious exegetical, patristic, and historical study and research.

Conclusion. Theology born with patristics has its first milestone in the work of St. Augustine; with Scholasticism it attains the highest peaks of acute and serene speculation, in full harmony of reason with faith (St. Thomas). It is shaken profoundly by Humanism and the Lutheran Reformation and rises with a polemic and positive historical character (sixteenth and seventeenth centuries); then it loses its compact unity, due to the apologetic exigencies of the eighteenth century and the beginning of the nineteenth century. On contact with philosophical, historical, and biblical rationalism, it resumes its march on new roads, in an endeavor to put its precious and classical content in harmony with the requirements and forms of modern thought.

The reform of ecclesiastical studies, urged by Pius XI in his constitution, *Deus Scientiarum Dominus,* has stepped up the rhythm of ecclesiastical studies which are marching with efficacious methods toward new progress in the understanding and illustration of the immutable divine truth.

BIBLIOGRAPHY

Allievo, *Disegno di storia della Teologia* (Turin, 1939). Bellamy, *La Théologie catholique au XIX siècle* (Paris, 1904). Cayré, *Manual of Patrology,* trans. Howitt, Vol. 2 (Paris, Tournai, Rome, 1940), Book IV. Fenton, *The Concept of Sacred Theology* (Milwaukee, 1941), pp. 181–264. Grabmann, *Die Geschichte der scholatischen Methode,* 2 vols. (Freiburg i.-Br., 1909–1911). Otten, *A Manual of History of Dogmas,* Vol. 2 (St. Louis, 1925), pp. 1–27. Pohle, "Theology (I Dogmatic)," *CE.* Zybura, *Present-Day Thinkers and the New Scholasticism* (St. Louis).

INDEX OF ENTRIES